The Experiences of Black Women Diversity Practitioners in Historically White Institutions

Tristen Brenaé Johnson
Moffitt Cancer Center, USA

A volume in the Advances in Human Resources Management and Organizational Development (AHRMOD) Book Series

IGI Global
PUBLISHER of TIMELY KNOWLEDGE

Published in the United States of America by
IGI Global
Information Science Reference (an imprint of IGI Global)
701 E. Chocolate Avenue
Hershey PA, USA 17033
Tel: 717-533-8845
Fax: 717-533-8661
E-mail: cust@igi-global.com
Web site: http://www.igi-global.com

Library of Congress Cataloging-in-Publication Data

Names: Johnson, Tristen, 1989- editor.
Title: The experiences of Black women diversity practitioners in historically white institutions / Tristen Johnson, editor.
Description: Hershey PA : Information Science Reference, [2022] | Includes bibliographical references and index. | Summary: "The book will center Black women's experiences before, during, and after the dual pandemics at historically white higher education, corporate America, and healthcare institutions and how these experiences affected their ability to perform their jobs"-- Provided by publisher.
Identifiers: LCCN 2022007828 (print) | LCCN 2022007829 (ebook) | ISBN 9781668435649 (hardcover) | ISBN 9781668435656 (paperback) | ISBN 9781668435663 (ebook)
Subjects: LCSH: Diversity in the workplace--United States. | African American women--Employment. | African American women employees--Social conditions. | African American women employees--Attitudes. | Leadership in minority women--United States. | Employees--Training of--United States. | Industrial sociology--United States.
Classification: LCC HF5549.5.M5 E96 2022 (print) | LCC HF5549.5.M5 (ebook) | DDC 658.30089--dc23/eng/20220505
LC record available at https://lccn.loc.gov/2022007828
LC ebook record available at https://lccn.loc.gov/2022007829

This book is published in the IGI Global book series Advances in Human Resources Management and Organizational Development (AHRMOD) (ISSN: 2327-3372; eISSN: 2327-3380)

British Cataloguing in Publication Data
A Cataloguing in Publication record for this book is available from the British Library.

Advances in Human Resources Management and Organizational Development (AHRMOD) Book Series

Patricia Ordóñez de Pablos
Universidad de Oviedo, Spain

ISSN:2327-3372
EISSN:2327-3380

Mission

A solid foundation is essential to the development and success of any organization and can be accomplished through the effective and careful management of an organization's human capital. Research in human resources management and organizational development is necessary in providing business leaders with the tools and methodologies which will assist in the development and maintenance of their organizational structure.

The **Advances in Human Resources Management and Organizational Development (AHRMOD) Book Series** aims to publish the latest research on all aspects of human resources as well as the latest methodologies, tools, and theories regarding organizational development and sustainability. The **AHRMOD Book Series** intends to provide business professionals, managers, researchers, and students with the necessary resources to effectively develop and implement organizational strategies.

Coverage

- Strategic HRM
- Employee Evaluation
- Workplace Culture
- Personnel Retention
- Human Relations Movement
- Employee Communications
- Succession Planning
- Performance Improvement
- Work-Life Balance
- Change Management

IGI Global is currently accepting manuscripts for publication within this series. To submit a proposal for a volume in this series, please contact our Acquisition Editors at Acquisitions@igi-global.com or visit: http://www.igi-global.com/publish/.

The Advances in Human Resources Management and Organizational Development (AHRMOD) Book Series (ISSN 2327-3372) is published by IGI Global, 701 E. Chocolate Avenue, Hershey, PA 17033-1240, USA, www.igi-global.com. This series is composed of titles available for purchase individually; each title is edited to be contextually exclusive from any other title within the series. For pricing and ordering information please visit http://www.igi-global.com/book-series/advances-human-resources-management-organizational/73670. Postmaster: Send all address changes to above address.

Titles in this Series

For a list of additional titles in this series, please visit: http://www.igi-global.com/book-series/advances-human-resources-management-organizational/73670

Socio-Economic Disparities, Vulnerable Communities, and the Future of Work and Entrepreneurship
JoAnn Denise Rolle (Medgar Evers College, City University of New York, USA) and Micah Crump (Medgar Evers College, City University of New York, USA)
Business Science Reference • © 2023 • 335pp • H/C (ISBN: 9781668469903) • US $240.00

Handbook of Research on Promoting an Inclusive Organizational Culture for Entrepreneurial Sustainability
Rafael Ignacio Perez-Uribe (Santo Tomas University, Colombia) David Ocampo-Guzman (Santo Tomas University, Colombia & EAN University, Colombia) and Nelson Moreno-Monsalve (EAN University, Colombia)
Business Science Reference • © 2023 • 395pp • H/C (ISBN: 9781668452165) • US $295.00

Global Perspectives on Maintaining Gender, Age, and Religious Diversity in the Workplace
Kakul Agha (Skyline University College, UAE) and Mireia Las Heras Maestro (IESE Business School, Spain)
Business Science Reference • © 2022 • 407pp • H/C (ISBN: 9781668451519) • US $215.00

Promoting Inclusivity and Diversity Through Internet of Things in Organizational Settings
Gurinder Singh (Amity University, Noida, India) Vikas Garg (Amity University, Noida, India) and Richa Goel (Amity University, Noida, India)
Business Science Reference • © 2022 • 320pp • H/C (ISBN: 9781668455753) • US $240.00

Leadership Strategies for the Hybrid Workforce Best Practices for Fostering Employee Safety and Significance
Matthew Ohlson (University of North Florida, USA) and Lakshmi Goel (University of North Florida, USA)
Business Science Reference • © 2022 • 253pp • H/C (ISBN: 9781668434536) • US $250.00

Handbook of Research on the Complexities and Strategies of Occupational Stress
Adnan ul Haque (Yorkville University, Canada)
Business Science Reference • © 2022 • 611pp • H/C (ISBN: 9781668439371) • US $295.00

Sustainability and the Future of Work and Entrepreneurship for the Underserved
JoAnn Denise Rolle (Medgar Evers College, City University of New York, USA) and Micah Crump (Medgar Evers College, City University of New York, USA)
Business Science Reference • © 2022 • 452pp • H/C (ISBN: 9781668443224) • US $250.00

IGI Global
PUBLISHER of TIMELY KNOWLEDGE

701 East Chocolate Avenue, Hershey, PA 17033, USA
Tel: 717-533-8845 x100 • Fax: 717-533-8661
E-Mail: cust@igi-global.com • www.igi-global.com

Table of Contents

Foreword xii

Preface xiv

Acknowledgment xviii

Chapter 1
An Ode to My Daughter: Navigating PWIs in the 21st Century 1
Andriette Jordan Fields, University of Denver, USA
Alana D. Fields, University of Pittsburgh, USA

Chapter 2
Lifting as We Climb 21
Vernese E. Edghill-Walden, Northern Illinois University, USA
Raja Staggers-Hakim, Springfield Technical Community College, USA
Anne M. Edwards, Purdue University, USA

Chapter 3
Leading Transformative Change as the "First": An Examination of the Institutionalization of a Southern PWI's DEI Strategic Plan 40
Atiya Kai Stokes-Brown, Coastal Carolina University, USA

Chapter 4
The Fierce Urgency of No: Moving From Aspirational to Operational 57
Kerri-Ann M. Smith, Queensborough Community College, USA
Timothy G. Lynch, College of Staten Island, USA

Chapter 5
Masks Off: Portraits of Black Female Diversity Practitioners During a Double Pandemic 79
Tracie Denise Jones, School of Humanities, Arts, and Social Sciences, MIT, USA

Chapter 6
Of Protest and Paradox: Leading DEI in Minnesota 99
Lauren L. Jones, University of Minnesota, USA

Chapter 7
Training in Diversity, Inclusion, and Equitable Mindfulness 121
Tiara A. Cash, Crowned Vitta LLC, USA
Tristen Brenaé Johnson, The Tristen Johnson, LLC, USA

Chapter 8
Black Women, Emotional Intelligence, and Organizational Opportunities for Growth 145
Adela E. Jiménez, Independent Researcher, USA
Charnise Virgil Moore, Independent Researcher, USA

Chapter 9
Deconstructing Standards of Whiteness to Establish the Power of Black Women............ 167
Norka Blackman-Richards, Queens College, USA
Jilma V. Jiménez, Independent Researcher, USA
Eleonor Pusey-Reid, MGH Institute of Health Professions, USA

Chapter 10
Black, White, and Everything in Between: Trials of a Black DEI Professional in PWIs............ 192
Stephanie Reed, Aspire2Higher Personal and Professional Development, Inc., USA

Chapter 11
Intersectionality in Leadership: Spotlighting the Experiences of Black Women DEI Leaders in Historically White Academic Institutions............ 213
Natasha N. Johnson, Georgia State University, USA

Chapter 12
Footsteps: Wisdom and Insight Into Navigational Capital for New Black Women Diversity Officers............ 239
Toby S. Jenkins, University of South Carolina, USA
Coretta Jenerette, University of South Carolina, USA
Michelle L. Bryan, University of South Carolina, USA
Shirley S. Carter, University of South Carolina, USA

Chapter 13
The DEI Industrial Complex: Undermining Black Woman Leadership............ 261
Aysa Gray, Queens College, USA
Norka Blackman-Richards, Queens College, USA
Selena T. Rodgers, York College, USA

Compilation of References 281

About the Contributors 320

Index............ 328

Detailed Table of Contents

Foreword ... xii

Preface ... xiv

Acknowledgment ... xviii

Chapter 1
An Ode to My Daughter: Navigating PWIs in the 21st Century ... 1
Andriette Jordan Fields, University of Denver, USA
Alana D. Fields, University of Pittsburgh, USA

The goal of this chapter is to elucidate on how socio-cultural practices and systems within private and public institutions of higher learning influence and regulate Black women's attitudes, behaviors, and agency utilizing a womanist/feminist lens. Historically, Black women's bodies have been a topic of discussions relating to body images. These bodies have been undermined, disrespected, and shamed, portrayed in the media as angry, ugly, hypersexualized. Theses tropes and more have a bearing on how Black women are received or deemed invisible daily in various spaces i.e., PWI. A Black woman's positionality, femininity, hair, and identity politics, coupled with other unique identities, affect the social and political context impacting how systems are navigated at PWIs. The ability or inability to endure assumptions, stereotypes, and aggressions can confuse those that cross the line thinking that behaviors of disrespect are acceptable. Suggestions/advice are offered for success and keys for thriving, not simply surviving, at PWIs.

Chapter 2
Lifting as We Climb ... 21
Vernese E. Edghill-Walden, Northern Illinois University, USA
Raja Staggers-Hakim, Springfield Technical Community College, USA
Anne M. Edwards, Purdue University, USA

This chapter will chart Black women's historical and continued commitment to education and racial uplift by examining 21st century Black women directors of Black cultural centers (BCCs). Their contributions to the education of Black college students on predominantly white campuses as a form of liberation and racial uplift echo the race work undertaken by Black women throughout history. While historical and 21st century Black women educators share a spirit of persistence, resilience, passion, and commitment for racial uplift in the Black community, despite the compounding racism and sexism they face while helping to educate and uplift the next generation of Black students and leaders, 21st century Black women educators are seeking to advance their personal and professional lives as well.

Chapter 3
Leading Transformative Change as the "First": An Examination of the Institutionalization of a Southern PWI's DEI Strategic Plan 40
Atiya Kai Stokes-Brown, Coastal Carolina University, USA

Although extant literature on chief diversity officers in higher education has provided insight into their roles, priorities, and standards of practice, few studies have exclusively explored the perspectives and experiences of Black women CDOs. This qualitative study draws on theories of organizational change, critical race theory, and critical race feminism to make meaning of and interpret the experience as an inaugural Black woman chief diversity officer at a public regional institution in the South, with a focus on the author's experience leading the strategic planning process. This study advances the research on Black women in higher education, spotlighting the distinctive, layered, and intersectional journey of one Black woman CDO working in a predominately White institution in the South.

Chapter 4
The Fierce Urgency of No: Moving From Aspirational to Operational 57
Kerri-Ann M. Smith, Queensborough Community College, USA
Timothy G. Lynch, College of Staten Island, USA

The discussion in this chapter affirms the intentional and collaborative partnership built between the Inaugural Faculty Fellow for Diversity, Equity, and Inclusivity (FFDEI), a Black, middle-aged, immigrant woman, who is a tenured member of the faculty, and a senior executive, a White, middle-aged man at a community college. The chapter engages reflection as analysis, situating the experience of a Black woman in a quasi-administrative DEI role and that of a White male senior executive in the context of historical and contemporary allyship and accompliceship. Coupled with historical references to emphasize the significance of transformational leadership, the partnership leads to the development of a values-centered model for DEI work at an urban community college in one of the country's largest university systems.

Chapter 5
Masks Off: Portraits of Black Female Diversity Practitioners During a Double Pandemic 79
Tracie Denise Jones, School of Humanities, Arts, and Social Sciences, MIT, USA

The purpose of this chapter is to explore the perceptions and experiences of Black female diversity practitioners during the dual pandemics of COVID-19 and the racial reckoning of 2020. Using portraiture as a methodology and Black feminist thought (BFT) as a framework, this chapter gives voice to two Black women who worked at Ivy League institutions as diversity practitioners from March 2020 through June 2021. This chapter places the portraits of Black female diversity practitioners at Ivy League institutions within the larger discourse about the impact that the dual pandemics of COVID-19 and the racial reckoning of 2020 had on higher education administrators.

Chapter 6
Of Protest and Paradox: Leading DEI in Minnesota ... 99
Lauren L. Jones, University of Minnesota, USA

This chapter glances into the experience of leading diversity, equity, and inclusion (DEI) work while living in Minneapolis before, during, and after the murder of George Floyd, the subsequent uprisings, and racial reckoning of 2020. Ironically, the progressive state of Minnesota has been the site of multiple state-involved murders while also consistently voting Democrats into the White House and U.S. congress. This Minnesota paradox creates a unique place for DEI work. The author explores theories of white guilt and white saviorism, provides context about the racial and social environment of Minnesota, and provides recommendations for Black women DEI practitioners and those that employ them.

Chapter 7
Training in Diversity, Inclusion, and Equitable Mindfulness ... 121
Tiara A. Cash, Crowned Vitta LLC, USA
Tristen Brenaé Johnson, The Tristen Johnson, LLC, USA

This chapter explores how two Black women working as diversity, equity, and inclusion (DEI) independent consultants teamed up to create the Training in Diversity, Inclusion, and Equitable Mindfulness (TDIEM) workshop series. TDIEM workshops are interactive educational sessions that teach DEI concepts through the lens of Equitable Mindfulness. Equitable Mindfulness utilizes the application of mindfulness (present moment experience) for everyone– removing personal and systematic barriers that work against inclusivity and transformative change within themselves and within the communities they work within (Cash et al., 2021). Here the authors discuss Black women's positions as DEI workers as well as the history of mindfulness, outline the TDIEM workshop series, present challenges to collaborating and facilitating this curriculum in White spaces, and offer recommendations for practice for other Black women DEI practitioners to use for future work in White spaces.

Chapter 8
Black Women, Emotional Intelligence, and Organizational Opportunities for Growth ... 145
Adela E. Jiménez, Independent Researcher, USA
Charnise Virgil Moore, Independent Researcher, USA

Since the end of 2019, the world has been trying to identify ways to deal with the dual pandemics of COVID-19 and the racial reckoning that arose during the summer of 2020. Organizations have scrambled to re-energize diversity, equity, and inclusion (DEI) initiatives. The questions to be asked are why are organizations focusing their efforts on DEI initiatives, and how can they be successful? This chapter introduces and examines emotional intelligence as a vehicle leveraged by both authors and many other Black women, including Black diversity, equity, and inclusion (DEI) practitioners, as a means for advancement within their organizations. The authors further offer that in order for organizations to achieve equity and inclusion, emotional intelligence is a required baseline, and the support of DEI practitioners in this arena will create an array of positive effects, such as a harmonious work environment, self-actualized individuals including Black women, and thus personal, community, and organizational success.

Chapter 9
Deconstructing Standards of Whiteness to Establish the Power of Black Women............................. 167
Norka Blackman-Richards, Queens College, USA
Jilma V. Jiménez, Independent Researcher, USA
Eleonor Pusey-Reid, MGH Institute of Health Professions, USA

This chapter will examine standards of whiteness that are embedded in current organizational cultures and how these standards impact Black women (BW) in the workplace; particularly after the dual pandemics of COVID-19 and the racial reckoning of 2020. The authors widen the perspective beyond the confines of diversity, equity, and inclusion (DEI) as a role, to discuss cultural issues that universally diminish the power of BW, and that DEI practitioners should inherently be charged to recognize, name, and be empowered to eradicate. The work introduces microdevaluation as a construct encompassing an array of racial aggressions often experienced by BW in public settings. The authors further examine the effects on innovation caused by the lack of inclusion of the voice of the BW within organizations. The chapter ends by providing recommendations that organizations and institutions must adapt in order to transform and achieve equity for BW and reap the benefits afforded by diversity and inclusion.

Chapter 10
Black, White, and Everything in Between: Trials of a Black DEI Professional in PWIs.................. 192
Stephanie Reed, Aspire2Higher Personal and Professional Development, Inc., USA

With this chapter, the author sheds light on the experiences of a Black woman hired to create, administer, and manage the day-to-day needs of diversity offices at two small, white private liberal arts universities. The chapter will include insights on the very racism and implicit bias the author experienced, reported, and helped diminish. The chapter also describes the seemingly impossible task of managing change and transformation on private institutions rooted in white supremacist traditions and built upon a history of exclusion. To do this, the author shares personal narratives from colleagues collected via online surveys. The author describes the personal angst experienced while collecting, reporting, and managing the many micro-aggressions, experiences with racism, transphobia, and other reported biases. The author considers the mental gymnastics necessary to serve the needs of the institution and attempt to protect personal integrity and sanity.

Chapter 11
Intersectionality in Leadership: Spotlighting the Experiences of Black Women DEI Leaders in Historically White Academic Institutions.. 213
Natasha N. Johnson, Georgia State University, USA

Due to their multiple identities, Black women navigate gendered and racialized pathways to leadership in the US education industry. The journey for Black women in and en route to positions of academic leadership is even more nuanced and multiplicative. Little, though, is known about the effects of their intersecting identities and the structural barriers they encounter in this sphere. To deepen our communal understanding of this phenomenon, this chapter highlights the existing theories and research on the race-gender dyad in the context of academic leadership. Examining the individual and layered effects of race and gender on the professional realities of Black women leaders in higher education, the author spotlights the unique experiences of Black women DEI practitioners and leaders in historically White academic institutions. Given the numerous components at play when Black women lead in predominantly White institutions and settings, this chapter concludes by discussing opportunities to advance relevant research and practice in this arena.

Chapter 12
Footsteps: Wisdom and Insight Into Navigational Capital for New Black Women Diversity Officers 239
Toby S. Jenkins, University of South Carolina, USA
Coretta Jenerette, University of South Carolina, USA
Michelle L. Bryan, University of South Carolina, USA
Shirley S. Carter, University of South Carolina, USA

This chapter is a collaboration between four Black women (Toby, Coretta, Michelle, and Shirley) who currently serve as diversity officers in higher education. Each author has worked in higher education for over 20 years. The authors reflect on and critically assess this lived experience for essential strategies, perspectives, and practices that might be valuable to professionals who are new to the work. The purpose of this chapter is to curate a collection of reflective insights and wisdom derived from the field-from the authors' professional experiences as Black women diversity officers at predominantly White institutions. The chapter serves as a strategic map to help new Black women diversity officers navigate the challenging landscape of diversity, equity, and inclusion (DEI) work in higher education. Each author shares a personal story along with key lessons learned. A list of suggested professional resources is also provided.

Chapter 13
The DEI Industrial Complex: Undermining Black Woman Leadership 261
Aysa Gray, Queens College, USA
Norka Blackman-Richards, Queens College, USA
Selena T. Rodgers, York College, USA

The DEI initiative is a multi-year project to support campuses in shifting power to create an anti-racist and equity-based space through liberatory practices, grassroots organizing, and equity-centered education. In this paper, the authors reflect on their communal work to disrupt injustice through an intersectional framework. To frame this paper, the authors first outline the historical and present impact of DEI work within academia, highlighting anti-blackness and misogynoir. Next, the authors introduce the term DEI industrial complex and provide an overview of the framework. After providing this analytic framework, the authors further explore how incidents of undermining Black leadership manifest within the academy. Asserting agency over the DEI complex, the concluding section offers essential survival tools.

Compilation of References 281

About the Contributors 320

Index 328

Foreword

When I was asked by my dear friend, Dr. Tristen Johnson, to write the forward to this book, I was immediately honored and excited to be a part of this much-needed conversation. My next thought was, *"Black women gotta go through so much,"* which my sister friend, Dr. Christa Platt, coined and now has me saying whenever White supremacy slithers its way into our personal and professional space. As two Black women working within DEI, we have found ways to laugh our way through. Every time we look at one another and say, *"Black women gotta go through so much,"* we get out a good belly laugh, regroup, and get back to work.

Although we laugh, smile, and do this hard work gracefully, like many Black women practitioners, we constantly stand in front of burning buildings flailing our arms, trying to get people to notice the fire. As we stand between the burning building and minoritized people, we are left with third-degree burns that we clean and redress, ignoring how deep the wounds are. We stay and continue to fight for others while slowly being poisoned by disrespect, disregard, dishonor, and being uninvited to the very tables we helped to build. We still find ways to keep going and doing the necessary work while fighting systems that are reluctant and resistant to change. *"Black women gotta go through so much."*

This book is powerful because of the space it provides for Black women's voices, the autonomy they have to speak in their chosen dialect, the ways it highlights the fact that Black women have always been leaders of change, and the gap this literature helps to fill. The Black women who have authored these chapters are allowing you into vulnerable and intimate spaces—undressing their wounds to share their traumatic experiences of racism, sexism, classism, and discrimination. Most honorably, they also provide tools, techniques, and advice on moving beyond low-hanging fruit and creating sustainable change.

If you are a Black woman reading this, prepare to be affirmed, empowered, and equipped with more armor to help you navigate the DEI work you are officially and unofficially doing within your institutions. I saw myself within the pages of each chapter and reflected on the last fourteen years I have spent working at a historically White institution. As a DEI consultant, I connected to shared challenges and was reminded that I am not out here doing this work alone.

If you are not a Black woman, be prepared to listen, learn, and believe what is written in each chapter. Understand and respect that these women are experts in their fields and have spent their careers supporting, protecting, and helping everyone with little reward beyond knowing that they are changing environments for others. Study each chapter, use the information to challenge your institutions, and ask the hard questions. Assess how your institution supports Black women practitioners. Equip yourself with the knowledge and experience needed to be considered an ally.

Institutional leaders, I urge you to assign this book to your staff and use it as a resource as you build your DEI strategic plans and goals. Use these chapters to reassess how you treat, pay, and include Black women at your institutions. Let it inspire you to address the practices, policies, and behaviors hindering necessary change. Make sure that Black women are filling multiple seats at the table and being treated as consultants, not simply there to meet a diverse committee quota. Remember that when Black women fight, they fight for change that will improve the lives of everyone. Let this book be the charge you need to always fight for them.

Angell Howard
Illinois State University, USA

Preface

Diversity, equity, and inclusion (DEI) in the workplace are not new concepts. Organizations across the United States that have some type of DEI components or DEI programming efforts correlate them with advanced innovation and better business practices. While the importance of increasing DEI continues to grow within various sectors (e.g. higher education, corporate institutions) there are still persistent concerns about systemic racism and ongoing discriminatory practices at these organizations, specifically historically White institutions (HWIs). Many Black women at these institutions whose main job responsibilities are centered on educating, increasing, and sustaining DEI programming efforts are and have been on the frontlines of this work. These Black women are and will continue to be dedicated champions of DEI.

However, in the wake of the dual pandemics of 2020, COVID-19 and the on-going systemic and institutionalized racial injustice, many organizations heightened their responses and initiatives surrounding diversity, equity, and inclusion and Black women DEI practitioners were again, on the frontlines. As DEI efforts continue to expand in various organizations across multiple sectors, scholarly attention should be paid to the career experiences of Black women in diversity practitioner roles before, during, and after the transformative stresses of the dual pandemics of 2020 and how these intersecting factors affected their ability to be successful in their DEI roles. Recognizing their professional experiences is important to our discipline's acknowledgement that while many institutions publicly (re-)pledged their commitment to DEI efforts in 2020, Black women diversity workers and other members of these institutions continued to face various forms of discrimination, similar to the discrimination they experienced prior to institutional celebrations of cultural and policy changes.

A THEORETICAL PERSPECTIVE

In the preface of her groundbreaking book, *Black Feminist Thought (BFT)*, Black Feminist scholar, Patricia Hill Collins (2000) said, "I remain less preoccupied with coming to voice because I know how quickly voice can be taken away. My concern now lies in finding effective ways to use the voice that I have claimed while I have it" (p. xiii). This statement is reflected in each woman who contributed to this book. They tell their stories uniquely and use their voices as tools to advocate for themselves, DEI work, and also to push back on the everyday oppression they and others face within the pervasive socially constructed environments of HWIs. This book dedicates a collective voice to ground and root Black Feminist Thought as a theoretical perspective within DEI dialogue and scholar-practitioner research.

BFT centers Black women as intellectuals and curators of their own knowledge, especially when their voices have been suppressed under the confines of White dominance. Black women DEI workers, like the women Collins (2000) highlights in her book, "use their voices to raise important issues that affect Black African women" (p. 3) and issues that affect other members of various social identity groups in their workspaces. Black women have been at the forefront of marginalization and subjugation throughout history in various institutions like politics, corporate America, and education. It is in these arenas where they have been silenced and often ignored.

In terms of academia or academic literature, this powerful social arena has previously been dominated by White, primarily male, scholarship. The academic scholarship of Johnson (2021) built on the premise of Evans-Winters' (2019) research of how "Black feminism has been overlooked and devalued by White scholars" (p. 45). In the context of this collaborative book, Black women were asked to express their experiences within the current boundaries of long established Eurocentric views of what "scholarship" or "scholarly writing" is supposed to look like. These restrictions limit the creativity and unique voices of competent Black women. Collins (2000) identifies this as part of a "larger system of oppression [that] works to suppress the ideas of Black women intellectuals and protect White male interests and world-views" (p. 5). To present an oppositional gaze (hooks, 1992) back at the strict rules of this academic system, each author was encouraged to write from her own positionality as a Black woman diversity practitioner. They write in their own dialect to give their chapter a personal touch, "recognizing Black Feminist perspectives are essential to telling the stories of Black women...in diversity roles" (Johnson, 2021) and by doing so, help to establish foundation and precedent for those that follow.

IMPORTANCE OF TOPIC AND TARGET AUDIENCE

The relative absence of existing literature about Black women in these particular professional roles shows the fertile need for more ongoing research about best practices for DEI practitioners and organizations, and strategies to support and uplift Black women in these roles. Providing insights and commentary on often overlooked tensions of their intersectional identities at odds with the actual lived experiences of their positions as DEI practitioners is a central and significant aim of this work. The authors of this book provide practical strategies, evidence-based and experiential-based approaches to DEI, and tangible tips for HWIs and other institutions to look inward at the culture and practices of their organizations that indirectly contradict their DEI values in ways that directly affect Black women diversity practitioners. Finally, this book is an intentionally structured and first of its kind resource for higher education staff and administration, Black women diversity practitioners, administration, leaders in business, hospital administration, libraries, students and educators of higher education, researchers, and academicians.

ORGANIZATION OF THE BOOK

This book is comprised of 13 chapters authored and/co-authored by Black women DEI leaders in higher education, corporate America, or working as independent consultants. They discuss research and experience-based best practices for Black women in the DEI field; personal and lived experiences with racism, sexism, and classism in various HWIs as DEI practitioners; and successful ways they implemented DEI strategies in their organizations before, during, or after COVID-19 and the heighted racial injustice of 2020.

Chapter 1 is a foundational chapter that sets the tone about various experiences with racism, sexism, and classism that Black women face in White institutions in general. It is a mock conversation from a mother to her daughter with strategies on how to overcome these controlling images in historically oppressive spaces. The authors also offer advice on how to thrive at predominately White institutions.

In Chapter 2, the authors begin with a historical lens on the racial uplift of the Black community by highlighting the work of "race" women and their connections to Black cultural centers. They then examine the racial uplift of 21st century Black women or "race" women who serve as directors of Black cultural centers at HWIs. They explore ways in which these directors advance their careers while experiencing discrimination and while working to help educate the next generation of Black students.

The third chapter explores DEI work through the lens of the first Black woman Chief Diversity Officer (CDO) at a southern predominately White Institution. Using critical race theory and critical race feminism as theoretical frameworks, the author posits the ways in which she made meaning of her experiences while leading a strategic planning process in the south. The author then provides significant practical recommendations to support Black women CDOs.

Chapter 4 takes a different approach by exploring the collaboration between a Black woman Inaugural Fellow for Diversity, Equity, and Inclusivity and a White male senior executive. They explore how allyship plays a key role in transformative change at a community college. The Black woman provides information on the challenges she faced in this new administrative role and the White man discusses how he had to recognize his privilege and shift his mindset to transformational change to serve historically minoritized communities on campus. They used this partnership to advance the college's DEI agenda and provide recommendations for practice on how to move from aspirational to operational.

In Chapter 5, the author introduces portraiture, a methodology of inquiry that captures various aspects of the human experience. In this case, the author uses this method to explain the experiences of two Black women DEI practitioners during the dual pandemics of COVID-19 and the pervasive environment of systemic racism brought into national crisis in 2020 after the murder for George Floyd. These stories offer recommendations for Black women DEI practitioners to center self-care in the face of adversity during times of crisis.

Chapter 6's author reports from the United States' epicenter of the racial reckoning of 2020, Minneapolis, Minnesota. This chapter visits the concept of "White urgency." White urgency is the idea of addressing DEI crisis quickly instead of with intention. The author discusses her experience working at a HWI in the aftermath of the murder of George Floyd and in disrupting White urgency at the institution.

Training in Diversity, Inclusion, and Equitable Mindfulness (TDIEM) is the topic of Chapter 7. The authors outline the ways in which they combined their skills in DEI and Equitable Mindfulness into a research-based training curriculum for institutions as independent consultants. This partnership developed to teach organizations how to incorporate mindfulness practices within DEI applications to assist in removing personal and systemic barriers. The chapter concludes with recommendations for practice for Black women DEI practitioners who aspire to use these tools for future trainings.

In Chapter 8, the authors outline how organizations can use emotional intelligence (EI). EI is leveraged as a key skill for institutions if they desire to have successful DEI initiatives. The chapter concludes with recommendations on how to use EI to build better relationships with Black women DEI practitioners.

Chapter 9 encourages Black women and institutions to deconstruct traditional standards of Whiteness in organizations. The authors examine how Black women have historically had to conform to Eurocentric ideas of professionalism and behaviors that are detrimental to Black women. The chapter suggests that standards of Whiteness must be dismantled to support Black women and for institutions to truly thrive in inclusion.

The tenth chapter highlights the trials of racism, sexism, and implicit bias faced by a Black woman DEI practitioner at two predominantly White private universities. While experiencing discrimination, the author simultaneously worked to demolish discrimination in her role. She brings in the voices of other Black women DEI workers who share similar stories at their institutions. The chapter concludes with suggestions on how White universities can improve their DEI efforts on their campuses beginning with support for Black women DEI practitioners.

Chapter 11 is an extensive literature review on theories surrounding the intersection of race and gender for Black women as they navigate the path to leadership roles. The experiences of Black women DEI practitioners through this intersectional lens are presented. The author provides future research directions to propel the research in this area.

In Chapter 12, the authors leverage their 20 years of experience in the DEI field to offer strategies to Black women who aspire to work in the field. They provide experienced-based suggestions and tools to be successful in the roles. The chapter concludes with the authors providing personal resources to share with new DEI officers.

Chapter 13 introduces the DEI Industrial Complex. This complex suggests that HWIs only address the "low-hanging fruit" within the diversity, equity, and inclusion issues at their institutions and ignore the need for organizational change to address issues of systemic oppression. Black women DEI professionals experience the negative effects of this mindset. The chapter ends with best practices to end the DEI Industrial Complex in institutions.

Tristen Brenaé Johnson
Moffitt Cancer Center, USA

REFERENCES

Collins, P. H. (2000). *Black feminist thought: Knowledge, consciousness, and the politics of empowerment,* (2nd ed.). Routledge.

Evans-Winters, V. E. (2019). *Black feminism in qualitative inquiry: Mosaic for writing our daughter's body*. Routledge. doi:10.4324/9781351046077

hooks, b. (1992). *Black looks: Race and representation.* Routledge.

Johnson, T. B. (2021a). *The experiences of Black women in diversity roles at 4-year predominantly White institutions* (Order No. 28150595) [Doctoral Dissertation]. Illinois State University.

Acknowledgment

I would like to thank every author who contributed to this book. The long hours you dedicate every day to serving as diversity practitioners do not go unacknowledged and unnoticed. This book is dedicated to you.

For her guidance and encouragement to pursue this book opportunity, to advance my professional and academic career, and to stand up for what I believe in, I'd like to thank Dr. Saran Donahoo.

My career in diversity, equity, and inclusion has been advanced by my mentor and friend, Angell Howard. She is one of the people who provided me advice and resources to develop in this field. She is the epitome of a true DEI champion.

Chapter 1
An Ode to My Daughter: Navigating PWIs in the 21st Century

Andriette Jordan Fields
University of Denver, USA

Alana D. Fields
University of Pittsburgh, USA

ABSTRACT

The goal of this chapter is to elucidate on how socio-cultural practices and systems within private and public institutions of higher learning influence and regulate Black women's attitudes, behaviors, and agency utilizing a womanist/feminist lens. Historically, Black women's bodies have been a topic of discussions relating to body images. These bodies have been undermined, disrespected, and shamed, portrayed in the media as angry, ugly, hypersexualized. Theses tropes and more have a bearing on how Black women are received or deemed invisible daily in various spaces i.e., PWI. A Black woman's positionality, femininity, hair, and identity politics, coupled with other unique identities, affect the social and political context impacting how systems are navigated at PWIs. The ability or inability to endure assumptions, stereotypes, and aggressions can confuse those that cross the line thinking that behaviors of disrespect are acceptable. Suggestions/advice are offered for success and keys for thriving, not simply surviving, at PWIs.

INTRODUCTION

In December 1922 *Crisis* magazine, Langston Hughes published *'Mother to Son'*, a poem conveying a mother's warning to her son utilizing the analogy about the stairs one's forced to climb called life. This analogy speaks to the determination necessary to make it up the proverbial stairs of life. The imagery of stairs is the mother's attempt to explain how arduous life will be. She admonishes her son about how the journey will be difficult with obstacles, but for him not to give up.

Hughes, a product of the Harlem Renaissance, wrote comprehensively on racism and oppression that Black Americans endured. Understanding his background, the poem depicts the struggles a young

DOI: 10.4018/978-1-6684-3564-9.ch001

Black man will encounter as he grows up. The extended metaphor of the staircase represents the adversities of life, and the mention of it not being a "crystal" referencing that the stairs would not be smooth, but dangerous, torn up, filled with "tacks" and "splinters." Hughes' twenty-line free verse inspired the conversation with my daughter who is working as a postdoctoral researcher at a Predominately White Institution (PWI). She had constant questions on how to navigate the institution and processes, and these inquiries prompted a conversation about how Black women survive these spaces, without losing their integrity and their minds. This chapter focuses on lessons learned from one Sistah to another, in this case from mother to a daughter, utilizing Hughes' poem as a guide for providing advice. We will briefly examine the historical positioning of African American/Black women and discuss three pertinent concepts: femininity, hair politics, and identity politics. Utilizing a Womanist/Feminist approach, we will elucidate on a Womanist social justice perspective, transitioning into a conversation with Black women at PWIs and briefly analyzing their experiences while cultivating strategies to thrive and not simply survive.

Mother to Daughter

Well daughter, Here's the word
Life at a PWI Ain't been no Ivory tower
It's had microaggressions,
And microinsults,
And mircroassaults.
And places where no one looks like you are present, Lonely!
But, every day,
We keep going back,
We keep trying, standing, believing
And sometimes that Imposter Syndrome sneaks in,
We doubt ourselves, and second guess our thoughts.
So, girl don't you question, don't you doubt, that Black girl magic.
You are strong, intelligent, and powerful
Cause if you weren't, they wouldn't be working
So hard to keep you feeling unwanted
out of place, and down and out!
And, when you find it kind of hard,
don't forget we've been here before,
So, girl don't you question, don't you doubt, that Black girl magic!

BACKGROUND

Historically, Black women's bodies have been the topic of negative discussion, whether relating to body images or reproductive issues. These bodies have been undermined, shamed, and portrayed in film and media platforms as distracting, ugly, fat, big-boned, and/or hypersexualized. Cooper (2018) summarizes the negative discussions with "We are told we are irrational, crazy, out of touch, entitled, disrupted, and not a team player" (p.2). Black women are often slated as the "angry Black women" when they are passionate or simply defending their point of view or perspective. These tropes have a bearing on how Black women are received or not received on a daily basis, in various spaces (i.e., boardrooms, classrooms, churches, and PWIs).

Black women's intersecting identities play differently from other bodies. Black women, historically, have graciously moved through society from hush harbors to the big house, to cleaning houses, to the board room, the Ivory Towers, and most recently the White House. These women have made profound contributions despite the violent and oppressive conditions surrounding them. They have remained standing strong regardless of the disparaging language used against them, the stereotypes affixed to their character, and the physical harm frequently levied on their Black bodies. Black woman must know, and remember, whose shoulders they are standing on - that they are descendants of powerful, resilient, and resourceful women. Black women come from women who have made a way out of no way, women who have stood against the odds and beat them, women who have endured identity labels placed on them promulgating stereotypes.

A Black woman's positionality - in addition to other unique identities - affect the context impacting how she navigates the social and political systems at PWIs. Whether she's Democratic, Republican, Atheist, Christian, Muslim, or Jew, gay or straight, her political, social, or religious standing in the community does not and should not dictate who she is and how she's received and perceived by various communities. Her ability and inability to withstand the assumptions, stereotypes, and aggressions can confuse others who cross the line in thinking that behaviors of disrespect are acceptable. In Beyond Respectability, Cooper reminded us that we must take seriously, acknowledge, appreciate, and trust Black women. The environments in which we work are not always life-giving. Cooper (2017) also revisits respectability politics which was a tool of survival and thriving in harsh conditions. Black women had to survive and find ways to endure through those labels placed on them. These Black women were doing diversity work as race women, working to uplift their race. Ironically, this notion of surviving and thriving still exists today in the twenty-first century. As a Black woman working at a private PWI I find that it is taboo to question inequities in white spaces out loud for my survival and thriving, regardless of how apparent it is those inequities must be addressed to properly execute my responsibilities as diversity worker.

Spillers (2000), offered timeless words which provide a sampling of the various identities constructed for African American women:

I am a marked woman, but not everybody knows my name, "Peaches" and "Brown Sugar," "Sapphire" and "Earth Mother," "Aunty," "Granny," "God's Holy Foot," a "Miss Ebony First," or "Black Woman at the Podium": I have described a locus of confounded identities, a meeting ground of investments and privations in the national treasury of rhetorical wealth. My country needs me, and if I were not here, they would have to invent me. (p. 257)

These stereotyped notions of identity challenge the identity of African American/Black women. These identities force upon us, often fall into three basic categories: the help (mammy), the vixen (jezebel) or the gladiator (strong Black Woman) and have proven complicated (Yancy, 2008).

The historical assumptions about Black bodies are what Butler (2006) might call racist phantasmatic productions that are projections from the white imaginary. When one thinks of the "the help" (mammy) it evokes the vision of her domesticity, whose sole purpose appears to be to serve whiteness. In fact, in "Black Women's Identity: Stereotypes, Respectability, and Passionlessness (1890-1930)" Mgadmi (2022) discussed the pervasive conversations about how Black women are depicted in society and how their femininity was juxtaposed against white womanhood. Mgadmi (2022) provided insight on the tropes that have followed Black women for centuries:

(t)he old slave mammy or "Aunt Jemima" figure pervaded a body of work about Black womanhood. She was generally dark-skinned, strong-bodied, thick-lipped, obese, and ugly, often being the favorite servant, skilled cook, and the most devoted housekeeper, she incarnated the perfect mother in the house capable of nurturing White children and at the same time looking after her children and sustaining her family. She was "the all-mother figure" and "mother earth," a "superwoman" stronger than her man and less feminine than other women. (p. 41)

Any observation, be it verbal or visual messaging, shared about African American/Black women by popular culture, requires a critical eye and ear. The ideas of knowing and staying in your place, being subservient, and other concepts for Black women have been recognized by several authors/scholars. hooks (1981) addressed these and similar issues in *Ain't I a Woman?: Black Women and Feminism.* Beauboeuf-Lafontant (2009) argued that the idea of strength undermines its real function: to defend and maintain a stratified social order obscuring Black women's experiences of suffering, acts of desperation, and anger. Beauboeuf-Lafontant traced the historical and social influences of prescriptive Black femininity, looking at how concepts of self-image and strength generate an interruption from broader forces of discrimination and power. Jordan-Zachery (2009) provided insight into the gendering process of policy making, explaining how relations of power and forms of inequality are circuitously constructed impacting the lives of Black women.

The socio-cultural practices within private and public institutions of higher learning influence and regulate Black women's attitudes, behaviors, and agency... similarly to how white dominated spaces influenced them throughout history. Delpit (2006), stated:

We do not really see through our eyes or hear through our ears, but through our beliefs. To put our beliefs on hold is to cease to exist as ourselves for a moment - and that is not easy. It is painful as well, because it means turning yourself inside out, giving up your own sense of who you are, and being willing to see yourself in the unflattering light of another's angry gaze. (pg. 47)

Delpit's poignant statement speaks to the how stereotypical labels become the truths by which people govern themselves - creating their philosophies, and modes of operation - which can be found in homes, places of worship and the workplace. As a Black woman in the academy, there are two places and/or personality types we find ourselves designated/labeled as, either the mammy or the bitch. One is known for being the mothering figured, always attempting to accommodate and take care of the needs of others, sometimes to the detriment of oneself. Conversely, the latter is any Black women that's confident, outspoken, who speaks truth to power; she is seen as confrontational and lacks the ability to be a team player. This binary dichotomy proves stifling and restrictive, limiting the talents, skills, and potential of Black women.

The Triple Threats to Black Women's in PWIs

This chapter has as its aim the enlightenment of those on the journey of Black women on the margins, and how they historically have navigated hair and identity politics and the questioning of their femininity.

It is an effort to engage justice work as it relates to ethnic, racial, and gender inequities. Black women's hair, identity, and femininity have come into question for centuries becoming the triple threat to her positionality in the world and especially in PWIs. These three factors have been utilized as strategies of containment, which are concerted efforts of keeping them out of spaces of leadership, power, and the denial of respect. Through the lens of Womanist ethics, the African American woman's predicament will be examined. Black women's race, gender, and hair place them in marginalized and often disenfranchised positions. Sitting at these intersections of systems of power, which greatly influence their access to happiness, and the resources to maintain their pursuit of happiness, wholeness, and radical acceptance in these institutions (Crenshaw, 1990; Hill Collins, 2008; William, 2015). The labels have been applied in explicit and surreptitious manners, often rendering the recipient of the labels powerless.

According to Floyd-Thomas (2019):

A womanist is radical because she claims her agency and has a subjective view of the world where she is not a victim of circumstances, but rather responsible, serious, and in-charge. Therefore, the intergenerational lesson of radical subjectivity is to recover one's sense of identity, out of the hold of hegemonic normativity. (p. 33)

Here we will critically observe and examine the verbal and visual messages that are continually shared about African American women. Utilizing the media as a window to view African American women in order to understand the forced constructed identities established for them, it is essential to analyze three salient concepts: *hair politics, femininity, and identity politics*. It is believed that hair politics have been constructed in such a way that this concept provides a window into femininity, which in turn constructs identity politics. Prince (2009) elucidated challenges of forced identities placed on African American women in mass media, and within institutions of higher learning, are often portrayed and received in various manners. Within this analysis, we are reminded of three, salient tropes - Mammy, Jezebel, and the Strong Black Woman - examining racial and gendered stereotypes and the ramifications of being labelled. By examining how Black women are depicted in the media - and how their social identities are constructed without their input - we can see how vital it is to speak truth to power, reconstruct history, and expose the myths and socially constructed concepts surrounding femininity, hair politics, and identity politics, which in turn often dictate our feminine status within society. These concepts dictate the positionality of Black women and encompass areas from the court room to the classroom, to church (the pulpit to the pews), to the "Ivory towers - PWIs". Work within the DEI arena requires one to have thick skin and the ability to navigate white fragility and the institutional complicity of these inequities with grace and candor. Unfortunately, a Black woman with such keen abilities as myself will find themselves dealing with leadership that is either threatened or fearful of presence and concerned that you are rocking the boat of collusion and comfort with systems of white supremacy.

The Spaces We Live In (Femininity, Hair Politics, and Identity Politics)

Femininity

Femininity is defined as having qualities traditionally ascribed to women, such as sensitivity, softness, weakness, or gentleness. This is a problematic definition on many levels. Black feminists are a unique group, distingué because of subordination within intersecting oppressions such as race, class, gender, sexuality, socioeconomic status; regrettably, effects of institutionalized racism in the twenty-first century remain visible and palpable. We encounter racism in everyday workplaces such as PWIs, stores, secondary school, housing, and daily social interactions.

Black women have had their femininity called into question for centuries – from Sojourner Truth to Serena Williams. These limiting and often disempowering gender labels will be utilized as model examples of the experiences of Black/African American women in contemporary contexts, as we explore hair and identity politics.

Hair Politics

Dr. Althea Prince, writer and sociologist, deals with Black cultural life by sensitively charting Black women's journeys with their hair: how it is perceived, judged, and graded on the yardstick of mainstream society's standards of beauty. Prince (2009) posited: "hair is at the heart of many Black women's senses of who they are in the wider world that they navigate daily" (p.16). Prince provided enlightenment on the misreading of a person's hair as a signifier, and how the misreading can have repercussions that could be trivial in a social situation, or far-reaching in the worst-case scenario, leading many to be judged with a social or political interpretation of who they are, solely based on their hairstyle. Prior to the Crown Act of 2019, hair politics have been operationalized to both prohibit and judge African American women from excelling in professional settings due to what was often deemed as "unprofessional" hair.

Historically, the conversation about the texture of hair follows Black people, specifically those of African descent, from century to century. This conversation has been the topic of discussion as it relates to beauty and acceptability and continues to determine Black women's standing. These discriminatory and intersecting forms of oppression directed at Black women influences how they look, live, work, interact with other and even view their bodies and identities (Donahoo, 2021). Donahoo (2021) provides insight into the interconnections of identity politics, hair politics and femininity, through her article "Why We Need a National CROWN Act", where she elucidates on how black hair has been and remains one of the foci of discrimination and repression, establishing white beauty as the norm. The CROWN Act SB-188 2019 (Creating a Respectful and Open World for Natural Hair) provides legislative intervention and was written to protect Black women and men from discrimination at work, school, and as they go about their daily lives.

As of January 2022, twelve states have passed the CROWN Act: California, New York, New Jersey, Virginia, Colorado, Washington, Maryland, Connecticut, New Mexico, Delaware, Nebraska, and Illinois. Two other states have passed a similar bill. The passing of this bill is vital to protect individuals from the act of weaponizing Black hair, which spans from early childhood to the workplace. These discriminatory standards for Black hair that Black women continue to encounter when embracing their natural hair must be challenged until we have a national CROWN Act.

Additionally, Higginbotham (1993) stated,

… that race serves, as a "global sign," a "metalanguage," since it speaks about and lends meaning to a host of terms and expressions, to myriad aspects of life that would otherwise fall outside the referential domain of race. Race impregnates the simplest meanings we take for granted. It makes hair "good" or "bad," speech patterns "correct" or "incorrect." It is, in fact, the apparent overdeterminancy of race in Western culture, and particularly in the United States, that has permitted it to function as a metalanguage in its discursive representation and construction of social relations. (p. 6)

Most African American women have some personal story as it relates to their hair, often a determinant of one's standing in society. As a Black woman with natural hair working in DEI at a PWI, there have been occasions where complimentary comments about my hair are given, along with my professional apparel. My grandmother instilled in me the fact that "you don't dress for where you are but for where you aspire to be." These unsolicited compliments/conversations and obsession about Black women hair in the workplace are also portrayed in the media and have prevented qualified Black women from moving up at their respective institutions and cost others their jobs.

Spike Lee's 1988 musical comedy-drama *School Daze* was a portrayal about undergraduates in fraternity/sorority life clashing with classmates at an HBCU during homecoming weekend. The movie addresses colorism, elitism, classism, political activism, hazing, self-esteem, social mobility, and hair texture bias within the African American community. This satirical film provides examples, and sheds light on the relational conflict constructed because of hair (color, length, and texture) which creates a fracture between women of the same race, socio economic status; women who have bigger issues to fight, like the oppression of misogynoir they are experiencing. Moya Bailey coined the term "misogynoir" as the ways anti-Black and misogynistic representation shape broader ideas about Black women, particularly in visual culture and digital spaces. In short, Bailey (2021) posits, where racism and sexism meet—an understanding of anti-Black misogyny.

In 2006, R&B singer India Arie wrote the song *I Am Not My Hair* - the refrain is: "Hey (hey) I am not my hair, I am not this skin, I am not your expectations, no (hey) I am not my hair, I am not this skin, I am the soul that lives within." Then she asks a couple of questions: "Does the way I wear my hair make me a better person? Does the way I wear my hair make me a better friend? Does the way I wear my hair determine my integrity? I am expressing my creativity." As Arie so gracefully shared, your hair does not and should not determine your standing in society, in the board room, or the ivory tower. We must shed these oppressive, socially constructed constraints if we want to thrive in PWIs, preventing identity politics from having a strong hold on our lives.

Identity Politics

Identity politics is a heavy-laden phrase and has come to signify a wide range of political activities and theorizing founded by the shared experiences of injustice of members of particular social groups. The Combahee River Collective (CRC) Black feminist statement is a key document confirming Black women and identity politics. Our identities are part of every political element of this country. CRCs statement of politics was actively committed to struggling against racial, sexual, heterosexual, and class oppression, and see (Taylor, 2017). Particularly, Black women assert or reclaim ways of understanding their distinctiveness that challenge dominant oppressive characterizations, with the goal of greater self-determination (Heyes, 2014). Martin (1993) wrote:

The heart of Black women's identity politics points toward the necessary cultural and political activity, in and for African American women's moral agency – an agency that is marked by both critical deconstruction of difference as domination and, the critical action of difference as creative power. (p. 43)

The concepts of identity politics, hair politics, and femininity - and their interconnectedness - have significant influences on how the forms of embodiment of African American women are represented, understood, and approached in society as we know it.

Negative messages are frequently heard by African American/Black women and faced on PWI campuses daily. While racism experienced at PWIs are behaviors that are offensive and harmful; interestingly, routinely microaggressions (both conscious and unconscious acts) are also experienced daily by Black people and continue to be problematic, harmful, and offensive. Microaggressions are akin to constant razor cuts on one's body, mind, and soul. There are three forms of microaggression: microinsults, microinvalidations and mircroassaults. Dr. Sue reminded us in his article that racial microaggressions are brief commonplace, daily verbal, behavioral, and/or environmental indignities, intentional or unintentional, that communicate hostile, derogatory, or negative racial slights and insults toward people of color, and are unfortunately normalized (Sue et al, 2007, p. 271).

The racial inequities experienced by African American women are so deeply ingrained in the fabric of American society that they are nearly unobtrusive. This type of racism is disguised and covert, it is a more ambiguous and nebulous practice, often difficult to identify and acknowledge. Practices supporting ongoing racial inequities, lack of inclusion, and other acts of disrespect and oppression are the ethos of many PWIs in their inability to welcome and accept those of other cultures, especially African American women who are faculty, staff, or students (Sue et al, 2007, p. 271). African American women have struggled for their full humanity to be recognized since the time of enslavement and if we are honest, they remain in a space of bondage even in the 21st century. Feminist activist Pearl Cleage affirmed: "the belief that women are full human beings capable of participation and leadership in the full range of human activities – intellectually, politically, socially, sexually, spiritually and economically" (Collins, 2000, p. 28), and this gives us reason to pause and realize and recognize Black women's humanity.

Attending and working at a PWI affords me the opportunity to have first-hand experience of navigating these spaces. As a PhD student, I remember participating in a library orientation where one of the head librarians opening statements were, "this orientation is only for PhD students" while she looked in my direction. She repeated the statement again looking eye to eye at me. Now I was the only Black person in that session, it was clear that this message was directed to me. This message of, are you in the right place, or do you belong here are subtle messages sent and received around PWI campus. These pervasive aggressions must be addressed and confronted; how I navigated this space not only affect me but those following me. I decided that working at the institution in DEI was where I hopefully might make a difference. As a Womanist ethicist the lens which I view my work provides insight from experiences which allows one to glean these microaggressions that other students, faculty, and staff with whom I identify may also be experiencing such slights.

A Womanist/Feminist Approach

This chapter utilizes a Womanist/feminist perspective. Womanism is a social justice perspective rooted in Black women's and other women of color's daily experiences and daily methods of problem solving in everyday spaces, extended to the problems of:

1. ending all forms of oppression for all people,
2. restoring the balance between people and the environment/nature, and
3. reconciling human life with the spiritual dimension.

Floyd-Thomas (2019) suggested that a womanist sociologist ethical analysis enables the womanist ethicist to interpret and transform the world of Black people. Black feminists and womanist researchers use a mixed methodologies approach to excavate the experiences of being a Black woman, like gaining insight into their experiences at PWIs. A womanist sociologist analysis and womanist ethicist approach are applied here to mine the stories of Black women's lived experiences, with suggestions of how to develop strategies of resistance which will empower women to aspire for leadership rolls, fight against imposter syndrome, and replace the systemic structures originally devised for cisgender white males.

Womanist sociological ethical analysis is an approach that seeks to empower and liberate Black women through examining their lived experiences using both quantitative and qualitative analysis to understand how interlocking systems of oppression create inequalities and social stratifications. From those experiences, the womanist ethicist and researcher can then formulate the social tasks needed to dismantle those oppressions for Black women to realize liberation. Using a multi-disciplinary approach of ethical analysis and sociology, the womanist ethicist can see the social world through the eyes of Black women to gain a full understanding of the material realities that must be examined to achieve justice and liberation for Black women, their families, and the communities where they live.

Within this section we will examine strategies of containment utilized to keep Black women out of higher leadership roles.

Despite the pain and trauma often experienced, Black women's ongoing commitment to PWIs is a manifestation of the utopian imagination of a world where Black people are treated justly and humanely and where generation Z–Alpha and the unchurch (those who have no interest or interaction with formalized religion) lead the way towards the liberation of all Black people from patriarchy and white supremacy.

Using a womanist analysis enables us the ability to provide a copious description of how PWIs have used respectability norms to police and control Black women's behaviors and their reactions to microaggressions, microinsults and mircroassaults through labelling "good' and "bad" Black woman. One can make the case for why the PWIs need to recognize Black women's lives and spirituality as coetaneous experiences that must not be separated. The use of narratives from Black women working at two PWIs will provide a depiction of how Black women arrive at and make decisions, determine meaning, and examine the ethical values they use to determine their actions in spaces where they are often the only Black woman.

Finally, the womanist sociological analysis is used to examine the pain and trauma Black women experience as a starting point to explore creative possibilities for dismantling the outsider/within culture that shames and excludes Black women because of their ability to withstand trauma while making it look easy and painless. As a Black woman, it is impossible to listen to the herstories of other women and remain unaffected by those stories. Moreover, ethical positionality has been and continues to be contested terrain; the Black church, family, intimate partners, and lawmakers all seek control over Black women's bodies. How do we make sure that Black women are empowered to navigate PWIs, while keeping their righteous mind intact? What is at stake if we choose to leave or stay in these spaces? The reclamation of agency is the Black Girl Magic (Jones, 2019) required to remain sane in these often-volatile spaces, known as PWIs.

Collins (2000), stated "Publicly articulating RAGE typically constitutes less a revelation about OPPRESSION than a discovery of VOICE" (p.50). Egbuonu (2021) featured Hill-Collins' revised statement on Rage as defining the power of finding your voice to express the full spectrum of emotions as a Black woman. Hill-Collins stated, "speaking your own truth, claiming your own truth, and claiming all parts of yourself, including your rage. Claiming the full range of voice is claiming the full range of self." Collins asked,

(W)hy would we reject anger when there is so much to be angry about? That affects us, that affects our children, that affect our communities, that affects our loved ones. Why would we want to tamp that down to become a good girl?" (Egbuonu, 2021)

Unfortunately, Black women find themselves in a quandary: if we assert ourselves, or we stand in our own truth, we are considered aggressive, angry, violent, and out of control. The trope of "angry Black woman" is over-utilized when Black women request/demand simply to be treated with respect.

Cooper (2017) had two cardinal commitments: seeing the Black female body as a form of possibility and not a burden and centering the Black female body as a means to cathect Black social thought. However, in the 21st century, the politics of respectability no longer works. Millennials lead the way in lacking interest in the insistence on proper behavior and comportment. For years Black women have applied the politics of respectability as an approach to navigating hostile public spheres, and to avoid other forms of bodily harm customarily imposed on Black women. Black women perfected the art of performing the politics of respectability in an effort of protection, given the attempts to make Black women's bodies as inconspicuous and sexually innocuous as possible due to the constant surveillance of Black bodies.

The concept of the politics of respectability is connected to a history of subjugation and stigmatization, and the notion among many members of the community that consequences for "bad" behavior were not simply inflicted on individual Black people but had implications for the entire community. Conversely, Higginbotham introduced the concept of the politics of respectability. Higginbotham (1993) described the role Black women played in the struggle for racial equality, as a strategy employed to challenge the subordinate position Blacks occupied throughout much of the United States. In the Black Baptist women's movement, Higginbotham (1993) noted that "the politics of respectability emphasized reform of individual behavior and attitudes both as a goal in and of itself and as strategy for reform of the entire structural system of American race relations" (p. 187). Interestingly, those who followed the politics of respectability thought it important for group members "to counter racist images and structures" by adhering to "dominant society's norms of manners and morals" according to Higginbotham (Higginbotham, 1993, p. 187), believing that if group members behaved better, they would be treated better by society. The politics of respectability, Higginbotham argued, did not eschew, or ignore political aims, nor did it give in to a system of racial inequality and White supremacy. To the contrary, the politics of respectability was inherently political, providing supporters with what they believed to be a reliable opportunity to upend the racial order of the day. This ideological positioning of the politics of respectability centered the problem of racial inequality, not simply in the hearts, minds, and systems of white Americans, but also in the predilections and behaviors of Black folks.

BLACK WOMEN'S SURVIVAL IN PWIs

Navigating the challenges associated with working at a PWI requires deliberate communication, strength, tenacity, and resoluteness. Regardless of one's tenure status - be it one year, ten years, or twenty years - the experiences and the stories of Black women in PWIs are the same; whether staff or students, mid-level administration, or a part of senior leadership, Black women are managing campus politics, multiple service responsibilities (such as being a faculty member, advisor, and director of a programming all while working toward tenure), the stories are all the same. We are often undervalued, underpaid, and underestimated. Breeden (2021) concurs with this assessment of the experiences of Black women at

PWIs. Breeden verifies specific strategies used and barriers faced when navigating racism and sexism for Black women in senior - level administrative positions in student affairs is fraught are fraught with micro/macro and blatant racialized aggressions. Breeden's qualitative analysis utilizes a Black feminist thought theoretical framework and narrative inquiry to amplify the voices and experiences of Black women in senior-level positions in student affairs at PWIs.

Higher education institutions advertise equal opportunities and advancement for all and these statements are often tied to their avowed commitment to their Diversity, Equity, and Inclusion plans and/or departments. However, Black women fight against the harmful tropes such as the Help (Mammy), Vixen (Jezebel) or the Gladiator (Strong Black Woman) within institutions of higher education. These reductive depictions of Black women rooted in the slave trade live on today and unfortunately even in the academy. These harmful tropes deliberately situate Black women in a place of subordination, often rendering them powerless despite their skill, ability, and knowledge levels. Black women are given the largest and most difficult task to accomplish with little or no support, be it staff or resources and expected to make miracles happen. Barriers for Black women at work and in society cannot be broken until institutions sanction structural changes and address the prevalent systems of oppression: racism, sexism, and other isms.

Joy James (1997) examined African American intellectual responses to racism and the role of elitism, sexism, and anti-radicalism in Black leadership and politics throughout history. James's analysis found:

whether as a depraved or an elevated mulatto, a mammy or a Jezebel, a bondswoman or a free woman, the image of the Black woman was conditioned by Whites' patriarchal values. More strikingly, while trying to display the dehumanizing legacy of slavery and to mitigate the blemishes of Blacks in order to advance their own people, many Black scholars (such as Edward Franklin Frazier, Booker T. Washington, members of The American Negro Academy or "The Talented Tenth", DuBois, Alexander Crummcil, Bess Beatty, William Wells Brown, Alexander Crummell, and George Washington Williams) too often enhanced negative stereotypes about Black women. (p. 40)

James and others established a historical foundation that identifies the sources for the negative tropes and conversations about Black women as licentious Jezebels, mammies, etc. as tropes rooted in environmental and cultural differences between whites, Africans, and bonded by enslavement conditions. Unfortunately, these socially constructed concepts are embedded in the American ethos. For centuries, Black women have fought against the generational memory of disrespect and degradation, only to find themselves in similar - if not the same - situations of their ancestors, whether they are in the classroom or the boardroom. The ultimate goal of the Black woman is to move from surviving to thriving. Thriving in every place, space, and circumstances they find themselves.

SOLUTIONS AND RECOMMENDATIONS

How We Got Over

It is important to note that Black women are not a monolith, yet there are shared collective perspectives that can inform polices, and practices. Black women don't worship the same, don't talk or dress the same nor do they share the same idiosyncrasy. These institutional roadblocks of questioning competences, integrity, intellectual and emotional capabilities, temperament and if all else fails their "fit" for the organization are the hallmark of PWIs; however, as the tides change, institutions must contemplate on several practices: recruitment, promotion, and retention of Black women in significant areas and positions of power. Black women should also be honored and rewarded for the contributions they bring to their various institutions of higher learning. Black women must be celebrated via university wide efforts not only in diversity and equity spaces, and also with financial rewards and promotions. The Cornell University Diversity, Equity, and Inclusion certificate program suggests that scholars have begun to deliberate about inclusion as encompassing two sets of experiences or states. The first is experiencing a sense of belonging, where the work environments are spaces where people feel they are a valued member in the work group. The second important factor is the feeling that one's uniqueness or difference is valued and integrated. These are the first steps toward fostering an inclusive climate and community

Before we attempt to tackle the situation in PWIs in the 21st Century, Black women might want to consider visiting or revisiting the sage wisdom from our progenitors such as Anna Julia Cooper, Maya Angelou, Patricia Hill-Collins, Toni Morrison, Maxine Waters, Stacey Abrams, and many others, that have navigated tumultuous terrain/spaces and have opened doors that we have the privilege of walking through. Giddings (1984) developed a thoughtful testimonial to the profound influences of African American women on race and women's movements throughout American history, sharing how Black women have transcended racist and sexist attitudes by confronting white feminists and Black male leaders alike and initiating social and political transformations. Anna Julia Cooper (1988) posited, "Only the Black woman can say "when and where I enter in the quiet, undisputed dignity of my womanhood, without violence and without suing or special patronage, then and there the whole race enters with me (p.13)." For centuries Black women have traversed unfriendly terrain, navigating the intersection of racism, sexism, classism, and heterosexism.

While we as Black women stand on the principles of justice and equality, we often fail to seek and demand justice for ourselves. We are guilty of selling ourselves short and overworking because we are and have always been expected to endure. We must have a mindset not of surviving but of thriving. Morrison (1971) poignantly stated "she had nothing to fall back on; no maleness, not whiteness, not ladyhood, not anything. And out of the profound desolation of her reality she may have well invented herself (para. 9)." Shakur (2001) firmly advises Black women: "It our duty to fight for our freedom. It is our duty to win. We must love each other and support each other. We have nothing to lose but our chains (p. 52)."

As an African American woman working in the office of Diversity, Equity, and Inclusion at a PWI, I must first remember that many have paved the way for us and as we enter these spaces of higher learning. I found that specifically at PWIs, the subliminal messages of "this is not your place," and "you don't belong" are pervasive, often making people want to run or leave. Maybe I am wired differently because these messages reminded me of our ancestors who fought for us to be in these very spaces. These messages fueled my determination to stand in the mist of adversity and disrespect, refusing to relinquish my space and I am keenly aware that I am not only standing for myself but for my children and my children's children.

I find it important to speak up and remind those in leadership that representation is not equitable. When we are having conversations about students, staff, and or faculty, I notice that people of color, specifically Black people, are not considered in the conversation. Working in the Office of Diversity, Equity, and Inclusion at a PWI, where wealth and privilege run rampant, it is so easy for meetings to happen and without considering or centering those who do not fit into the image of "wealth" and "privilege". Having the ability and stamina to withstand adverse and blatant disregard and disrespect proves exhausting, yet we must remember that the struggle and battle is paving the way for those coming behind us. This work is not for the faint of heart.

Over the last 400 years, Black women have battled sexism, racism, and classism, to achieve significant gains in higher education. While women, specifically white women have made progress, Black women repeatedly experience of neglect regarding advancement, professional development, salary, and mentorship opportunities, especially in senior-level positions. Despite years of systemic oppression, Black women excel in various capacities as authors, athletes, teachers, professors, lawyers, deans, staff, and students and other careers; unfortunately, these experiences are taking a toll on Black women's mental, physical, and spiritual health.

Black women are no longer tolerating disrespect and neglect. They are choosing to speak up and demand their place at the table, they are vocal about inequities, and they are learning the importance of self-care. I've decided that I have lived on this earth too long to tolerate certain behaviors, so I constantly look for ways to resist and still be heard.

Breeden's (2021) article Our Presence is Resistance: Stories of Black Women in Senior - Level Student Affairs Positions at Predominately White Institutions, discovered three emerging themes:

1. "We are better than they are because we have to be": Tales of Black women as chronic overachievers.
2. "You don't need a mentor; you need an advisory board": Find multiple streams of support.
3. "What do I do next?" (p.31)

Breeden (2021) posited that even when these Black women navigated the intersections of racism and sexism, gained years of experience, degrees and certifications which made them more qualified for their roles, they still carried the additional labor (both physical and emotional) of advocating for all students, especially students of color. This notion of "being better" emerged in two ways: the personification of the "superwoman syndrome," which results in workplace burnout and the notion of "killing ourselves" by taking care of everything for everyone. The superwoman syndrome manifests itself when a Black woman plays the roles – of mom, grandma, auntie, counselor, and teacher - while believing they must attend all events and need to know all the names of the students of color. The idea that the Black woman must take care of everything is outdated and overwhelming. Unfortunately, all the overextending of time, money, and self, along with the lack of acknowledgement of services provided, often leads to burnout and eventually quitting the field completely. Self-care is priority. I have found if I don't manage taking care of myself no one else will, in fact, if allowed, additional work will be given without extra compensation or consideration.

I manage to persist in this often-hostile environment by first understanding and studying the barriers encountered. One must become familiar with the structures, systems, and policies that are embedded in the cultural and ethos of your various institutions. Second, I had to develop the skill of speaking my truth, with the understanding that there is a strong possibility that there might be discipline or consequences for speaking my truth. However, I speak my truth anyway. You must show up. Do not allow or participate in your silence. Third, I believe in authenticity. I know that when I show up, as a Black woman, I will shift the atmosphere. Therefore, it is vital that I am relentless in my walk and speech, understanding that after everything is said and done, I must look at myself in the mirror and my children in their face knowing that I attempted to make this world a better place for them and their children.

CONVERSATIONS WITH BLACK WOMEN

Conversations with Black women in PWIs can be cathartic for all associated, affording them an opportunity to release pressures mentally, physically, and spiritually. We surveyed eight Black women that were our colleagues and friends. The eight Black women's educational degree levels included Master's degrees (n=4) and PhDs (n=4). All are currently employed at PWIs. An anonymous survey link was sent out to five colleagues of the co-authors. Additional recruitment was completed through snowball sampling, where research participants invite other participants to participate in the study. Six respondents have worked at their PWI for five years or less, one has worked at their institution between six and ten years, on one has worked at their institution between ten and twenty years. We asked these women three open-ended questions to allow respondents free-form responses regarding their experiences at PWIs.

We asked these eight women what their most rewarding experience at their institution had been. Interestingly, one respondent shared that quarantining during this pandemic has allowed them to work remotely. She shared, "The limited small talk and in-person activities have greatly reduced the amount of microaggressions and discriminatory experiences" (Respondent response). A common response about a rewarding experience was connecting with other Black, Indigenous, People of Color (BIPOC) researchers, colleagues, and students and "...the ability to teach students the true narrative about the systems of oppressions that exist and impact it has on the work they do..." (Respondent response). The opportunity to connect with other people of similar identity politics and speak openly and honestly about those shared lived experiences is and always has been a source of refuge for Black women, from convening in the kitchen to the secret Black girl meetings in the office for venting about microaggressions. When navigating a PWI as Black women, we must often find sanctuary in communing with one another and supporting our Black students along the way. We asked these women about their most rewarding experiences first because we must next acknowledge the challenges they've experienced.

When asked what daily challenges and barriers they have experienced at their PWIs, the responses were enraging and, unfortunately, expected. Respondents commonly experienced microaggressions, disrespect along with feeling overworked, being underpaid, and feeling underappreciated. One respondent shared frustration with the "assumption that passion equals anger," and was constantly "being referred to as overly critical/intimidating" (Respondent response). Another respondent shared that the lack of diversity in the field of international education results in bias towards Black women in the field. Several respondents who referred to disrespect as a consistent challenge shared experiences of disrespect from both colleagues and students. This is a constant experience which has caused one respondent to, "always have to second guess people's intentions and meaning." These are frustrating experiences that some would consider paranoia, however Black women in academia have found a critique is considered aggression, passion equals anger, and they are presumed uneducated or undereducated. This is simply righteous pessimism.

So how do we overcome these daily challenges and cultivate more rewarding experiences for Black women in academia? The consistent otherizing of Black women in America must stop. There is a great need to reclaim and dismantle the false opinions of the present-day realities and misperceptions of Black women's personas. We must transform the perception of Black women and commence the celebration of the extraordinary heritage of exceptional Black women that exist, while igniting hope for the next generation.

We asked the women, what are the best practices to navigate PWIs and create a nurturing environment for Black women in academia? The overwhelming response was finding community with other

Black women (and women of color) in your institution because, "...they can relate to what I'm going through and give great advice and support" (Respondent response). Creating relationships with other Black women provides, "a safe space to share concerns, use as a sounding board and not feel isolated" (Respondent response). The resounding sentiment was the desire for a safe space within the institution to share their stories and strategize tactics to navigate these supremely white spaces. One respondent suggested they only found solace in leaving PWIs all together and contracting work from the institution so as not to be beholden to them for basic salary – therefore allowing them to "...speak my truth with discernment." It is notable that none of the respondents ventured to offer institutional or systemic fixes necessary. This fact is solely due to their stated belief that these institutions must do the work for themselves – institutions have the capability to research and organize institutional resources to make appropriate changes if they are committed to changing/transforming their environments. It's been said that the "the burden of the brutalized is not to comfort the bystander". Although they are aware those are the very mechanisms through which the challenges and barriers of microaggressions, microinsults, and mircroassaults are made possible. Rather, these Black women chose to focus on what emboldens and empowers them, the creation of safe spaces to hold each other in tenderness and understanding. And that is Black Girl Magic.

These women experiences range from those that work directly in DEI spaces, to those that are affected by their institutional policies, processes, or the lack thereof. Their faces have various levels of melanin; however, their stories are similar, if not the same as they shared their journeys at a PWIs. We must share these stories to support and protect those presently in these spaces and to prepare those stepping into these treacherous places, assisting them as they navigate the PWI halls. A salient example of the experiences of Black women is the confirmation process for Judge Ketanji Brown Jackson, which created visceral reactions in many Black women around the world, many unable to watch the confirmation proceedings, including myself. This hearing was a public display of disrespect despite the achievements, skills, capabilities, and credentials of Judge Ketanji Brown Jackson. Similarly, in PWIs these spaces are not safe for Black women to bring their authentic selves, they cannot express themselves, sharing passion, joy, disappointments, and more. These spaces often underestimate Black women's power and resiliency. My strength and ability to stand in the face of adversity and questioning is always on display. Black women that have strong, stern demeanors often find their positionality located in two places: the angry black woman or the strong black woman to be feared. I find this prevalent when I failed to smile or make my white colleagues feel comfortable during uncomfortable conversations or situations. My responses, demeanor and attention to details appear to be suspect, when questioning motives and processes that are exclusive continuing to leave many on the margins.

FUTURE RESEARCH DIRECTIONS

Black women have made incredible progress in the world and in higher education. They have held positions such as presidents of colleges and universities, lawyers, attorney generals, doctors, and surgeon generals, and we have a growing number of PhDs. However, despite these accomplishments, there is very little research on Black women's experiences in senior- level positions in the academy in general and student affairs specifically at PWIs. Additionally, there is a need for more research on Black women in senior leadership positions at PWIs, along with a burgeoning issue of how Black women are navigating the dual medical and humanitarian pandemic. Future research possibilities to enhance the understanding of the experiences Black women in PWIs after the COVID-19 surge: 1) Exploring the experiences of Black Women who report to Black male supervisors, 2) understanding the dynamics and accommodations provided after remote working is proven viable 3) exploring the approaches for training opportunities post COVID-19 constraints 4) finally gain an understanding of the mental health support and accommodations.

CONCLUSION

Black women must learn how not to internalize the white gaze, the destructive norms, values, and the symbolism of whiteness which can wreak havoc on the Black mind, body, and soul. Therefore, there is the need for something supernatural like Black Girl Magic.

Black Girl Magic is a movement that was popularized by CaShawn Thompson in 2013 (Olayinka, 2021). The concept was born as a way to "celebrate the beauty, power and resilience of Black women," and to congratulate Black women on their accomplishments. In her final speech as First Lady, Michelle Obama provided a powerful statement that can be a mantra for all Black women:

"When you are struggling and you start thinking about giving up, remember the power of hope. The belief that something better is always possible, if you're willing to work for it and fight for it. Our hope is if we work hard enough and believe in ourselves; then we can be whatever we dream, regardless of the limitation that others may place on us. The hope that when people see us for who we truly are; maybe, just maybe they too will be inspired to rise to their best possibilities." (Reilly, 2017)

Obama's encouragement to believe in oneself, understanding that if you work and fight for that which you are working towards despite limitations and obstacles, dreams and goals can be achieved and therein lies the magic. Black Girl Magic is more than a hashtag, it is a movement, it is a term that is connected to deeply rooted pain and unspoken historical events of oppression, discrimination, and dehumanization (Workneh, 2016). Black women must remember that this ancestorial gift is within us, not in some of us, but within each and every one of us.

One suggestion for healing from the experiences in the academy is to tap into that Black Girl magic. This is a must for Black women to move beyond those things that limit them. The priority of Black Girl Magic is to consider and practice self-care like deep breathing or another activity that promotes rest, recovery, and reflection.

In order to achieve longevity, a second important factor is required: one must walk, talk, and live into one's authentic self. She must be cognizant of herself appreciating every curve, curl, perfection, and imperfection, knowing that she is one of a kind.

ACKNOWLEDGMENT

This research received no specific grant from any funding agency in the public, commercial, or not-for-profit sectors.

REFERENCES

Arie, I. (2006). I am not my hair. [Song]. On Testimony: Vol. 1, Life & Relationship [Album]. Motown Records.

Bailey, M. (2021). *Misogynoir transformed: Black women's digital resistance*. NYU Press. doi:10.18574/nyu/9781479803392.001.0001

Beauboeuf-Lafontant, T. (2009). *Behind the mask of the strong black woman: Voice and the embodiment of a costly performance*. Temple University Press.

Breeden, R. (2021). Our presence is resistance: Stories of black women in senior-level student affairs positions at predominantly white institutions. *Journal of Women and Gender in Higher Education*, *14*(2), 166–186. doi:10.1080/26379112.2021.1948860

Butler, J. (2006). *Precarious life: The powers of mourning and violence*. Verso.

Collins, P. (2000). *Black feminist thought: Knowledge, consciousness, and the politics of empowerment*. Routledge.

Cooper, A. (1988). *A voice from the South*. Oxford University Press.

Cooper, B. (2017). *Beyond respectability: The intellectual thought of race women*. University of Illinois Press. doi:10.5406/illinois/9780252040993.001.0001

Delpit, L. (1995). *Other people's children: Cultural conflict in the classroom*. The New Press.

Donahoo, S. (2021). Why we need a National CROWN Act. *Laws*, *10*(2), 26. https://www.mdpi.com/2075-471X/10/2/26. doi:10.3390/laws10020026

Egbuonu, O. (Director). (2021). *(In)Visible portraits* [Film]. OWN Spotlight.

Floyd-Thomas, S.M. (2019). Katie's Canon: Enfleshing womanism, mentoring, and the soul of the black community. *Journal of Feminist Studies in Religion, 35*(1), 101 104. doi:10.2979/jfemistudreli.35.1.12

Giddings, P. (1984). *When and where I enter: The impact of black women on race and sex in America*. Morrow.

Heyes, C. (2012, February 7). *Identity politics*. The Stanford Encyclopedia of Philosophy. https://plato.stanford.edu/archives/win2014/entries/identity-politics/

Higginbotham, E. (1993). Righteous discontent: The women's movement in the Black Baptist Church, 1880-1920. Cambridge.

Hooks, b. (1981). *Ain't I a woman? Black women and feminism*. South End Press.

Hughes, L. (1922). Mother to son. *Crisis Magazine.*, *25*(2), 48.

James, J. (1997). *Transcending the talented tenth*. Routledge.

Jones, F. (2019, February 8). For CaShawn Thompson Black Girl Magic was always the truth. *Beacon Broadside*. https://www.beaconbroadside.com/broadside/2019/02/for-cashawn-thompson-black-girl-magic-was-always-the-truth.html

Jordan-Zachery, J. (2009). *Black women, cultural images, and social policy*. Routledge. doi:10.4324/9780203883167

Lee, S. (Director). (1988). *School Daze* [Film]. Columbia Pictures.

Martin, J. (1993). The notion of difference for emerging womanist ethics: The writings of Audre Lorde and bell hooks. *Journal of Feminist Studies in Religion*, *9*(1-2), 39–51.

Mgadmi, M. (2022). Black women's identity: Stereotypes, respectability and passionlessness (1890-1930*). Revue LISA/LISA e-journal, 7*(1), 40-55. doi:10.4000/lisa.806

Morrison, T. (1971, August 22). What the black woman thinks about Women's Lib. *The New York Times*, SM14.

Olayinka, J. T., Gohara, M. A., & Ruffin, Q. K. (2021). #BlackGirlMagic: Impact of the social media movement on Black women's self-esteem. *International Journal of Women's Dermatology*, *7*(2), 171–173. doi:10.1016/j.ijwd.2021.01.006 PMID:33937485

Prince, A. (2009). *The politics of black women's hair*. Insomniac Press.

Reilly, K. (2017, January 6). *Read what Michelle Obama said in her final remarks as First Lady*. Time. https://time.com/4626283/michelle-obama-final-remarks transcript/

Shakur, A. (2001). *ASSATA: An autobiography*. Lawrence Hill.

Spillers, H. (2000). Mama's baby, Papa's maybe: An American grammar book. In J. James & T. D. Sharpley-Whiting (Eds.), *The black feminist reader,* (pp. 257–279). Blackwell Publishers.

Sue, D. W., Capodilupo, C. M., Torino, G. C., Bucceri, J. M., Holder, A. M., Nadal, K. L., & Esquilin, M. E. (2007). Racial microaggressions in everyday life: Implications for clinical practice. *The American Psychologist*, *62*(4), 271–286. doi:10.1037/0003-066X.62.4.271 PMID:17516773

Taylor, K. (2017). *How we get free: Black Feminism and the Combahee Collective*. Haymarket Books.

Workneh, L. (2016, June 26). *Jesse Williams: 'Just because we're magic, does not mean we're not real'*. HuffPost. https://www.huffpost.com/entry/jesse-williams-bet-awards-humanitarian-award_n_57708ceb e4b017b379f65077

Yancy, G. (2008). *Black bodies, white gazes: The continuing significance of race*. Rowman & Littlefield Pub.

ADDITIONAL READING

Brown, N. E., & Young, L. (2015). Ratchet Politics: Moving Beyond Black Women's Bodies to Indict Institutions and Structures. *National Political Science Review*, *17*(2), 45–56.

Byrd, A. (2004). Claiming Jezebel: Black female subjectivity and sexual expression in Hip-Hop. *The Fire this time: Young activists and the new feminism*, 3-18.

Carr, N. R. (2016). *Misreading Mammy: Towards a sexual revolution of contemporary/third wave Black Feminisms*. University of Miami. https://scholarship.miami.edu/esploro/outputs/doctoral/Misreading-Mammy-Towards a-Sexual-Revolution-of—Contemporary Third-Wave-Black Feminisms/991031447572002976

Collins, P. H. (2004). *Black sexual politics: African Americans, gender, and the New Racism*. Routledge. doi:10.4324/9780203309506

Crenshaw, K., Ritchie, A. J., Anspach, R., Gilmer, R., & Harris, L. (2015). Say her name: Resisting police brutality against Black Women. New York.

Donovan, R. A., & West, L. M. (2015). Stress and mental health: Moderating role of the strong Black woman stereotype. *The Journal of Black Psychology*, *41*(4), 384–396. doi:10.1177/0095798414543014

James, S. M., & Abena, P. A. Busia. (1993). Theorizing Black Feminisms: The visionary pragmatism of Black Women. Taylor & Francis.

Joseph, R. L. (2016). Strategically ambiguous Shonda Rhimes: Respectability politics of a black woman showrunner. *Souls*, *18*(2-4), 302–320. doi:10.1080/10999949.2016.1230825

Lewis, J. A., Mendenhall, R., Harwood, S. A., & Browne Huntt, M. (2013). Coping with gendered racial microaggressions among Black women college students. *Journal of African American Studies*, *17*(1), 51–73. doi:10.100712111-012-9219-0

Tyree, T. (2011). African American stereotypes in reality television. *The Howard Journal of Communications*, *22*(4), 394–413. doi:10.1080/10646175.2011.617217

KEY TERMS AND DEFINITIONS

Black Woman: A woman with African diasporic ancestry, with historical connections to the enslaved people brought across the Atlantic; known to have strong will and tenacious attitudes for survival, pertaining deep spiritual beliefs.

Femininity: A socially constructed understanding of qualities/attributes of being, associated with women.

Hair Politics: An identifier utilized to associate one with a particular group or utilized to discriminate against a group of people based on texture, length, style, and social group association. A way of subverting the system to reject patriarchal objectification and conformity to standards of beauty.

Herstories: A term applied to history written by women, providing a woman's opinion, acknowledging her story, from her perspective.

Identity Politics: A political approach where groups of specific gender, sexuality, race, religion, and social backgrounds approach their political motives - often to attain justice and equality.

Intersectionality: A lens through which you can see where power comes and collides, where it interlocks and intersects. It is a lens, a prism, for seeing the way in which various forms of inequality often operate together and exacerbate each other. -Kimberle Crenshaw

Mircroassaults: The use of overtly derogatory expressions to shame, disrespect, and put down people of color.

Microinsults: Those acts of rudeness, intentional and unintentional, that are insensitive and humiliating to a person's culture, race, heritage and/or identity.

Microinvalidations: Conscious and unconscious verbal statements or actions utilized to ignore, negate, and/or dismiss people of color in an effort to deem them invisible or insignificant.

Womanist: The acknowledgement of Black women's and women of color's views, beliefs, and contributions to society all from the lens of a Black women's perspective. A type of feminism on a deeper and richer level, i.e., Alice Walker's definition of womanist, "...Womanist to feminist as purple is to lavender"

Chapter 2
Lifting as We Climb

Vernese E. Edghill-Walden
Northern Illinois University, USA

Raja Staggers-Hakim
Springfield Technical Community College, USA

Anne M. Edwards
Purdue University, USA

ABSTRACT

This chapter will chart Black women's historical and continued commitment to education and racial uplift by examining 21st century Black women directors of Black cultural centers (BCCs). Their contributions to the education of Black college students on predominantly white campuses as a form of liberation and racial uplift echo the race work undertaken by Black women throughout history. While historical and 21st century Black women educators share a spirit of persistence, resilience, passion, and commitment for racial uplift in the Black community, despite the compounding racism and sexism they face while helping to educate and uplift the next generation of Black students and leaders, 21st century Black women educators are seeking to advance their personal and professional lives as well.

INTRODUCTION

This chapter researches the historical and contemporary perspectives of Black women's professional careers in cultural centers at predominantly White institutions (PWIs). While the chapter provides historical context for Black women in cultural centers and their contributions to higher education, it also incorporates the authors' lived experiences in these roles, and how they came to this research. Dr. Vernese Edghill-Walden, lead author, and Dr. Raja Staggers-Hakim are both former directors of cultural centers at predominately White institutions. Below they share their accounts of their experiences in those roles. Dr. Anne Edwards is currently the director of a Black Cultural Center. She shares her current experience under the section "Black Women and Race-Specific Positions: Transforming the Next Generation" and discusses the implications for next generation cultural center leaders.

DOI: 10.4018/978-1-6684-3564-9.ch002

Dr. Vernese Edghill-Walden's Reflection

I started working in higher education in the late 1980s. I was eager to begin my professional career in, what was called at that time, Minority Affairs or Multicultural Affairs. I fell in love with this work as an undergraduate student and knew that my career in higher education would focus on supporting Black students. As a young professional, I was a Black Cultural Center director for twelve years. It was one of the most rewarding professional experiences while also being one of the most complex and challenging. I loved nurturing, advising, and mentoring young Black student leaders. To see their transformation from freshman year to senior year was and still is priceless. However, this transformational work required advocacy, a commitment to uplift the Black community, and a skilled interpreter between the institution and the students. These responsibilities did not come with resources or equitable salary and the position was often marginalized and undervalued. Often this work challenged my work-life balance. Despite the feelings of marginalization, lack of resources and salary inequity, it did not stop my fervent commitment to support and help Black students succeed in these White spaces. Often negotiating from the margins, this role required my knowledge, relationships and understanding of the predominantly White college or university's political landscape. These skills assisted my students in finding their voices of resistance, power and resilience while navigating predominately White spaces. As director, I felt the sense of obligation to nurture and teach my students their own history, identity, culture and to impart a sense of responsibility for giving back to the Black community. This work often felt more like my life's work and passion than a job to me.

After twelve years, I left higher education and pursued other career and educational opportunities and educational advancement. It was at that time I began to reflect on my experience as director. I began to read more about historical Black women race workers and their role in advancing the Black community and promotion of racial uplift and education. Their narratives were powerful and resonated with my own experiences. It became apparent that the parallels of their lived experiences and that of 21st century Black women race workers in Black cultural centers (BCCs) was a generational trend of race work that should not remain at the margins of research. The historical and present day understanding of race work and racial uplift in this chapter provides a window into generations of brilliant Black women who share a common passion for racial uplift throughout history to present day.

This research was birthed out of my own personal experience as a Black Cultural Center Director. The chapter affirms the importance of Black women's professional voices, experiences, and advocacy as Black Cultural Center Directors. Our lived experiences are complex, grounded in historical experience, and remain relevant and vitally important in today's predominantly White spaces. It is clear this common thread was not a coincidence, but rather part of a strong legacy that must be researched and studied. The voices you hear in this chapter honor this legacy.

Dr. Raja Staggers-Hakim's Reflection

My interest in the health and well-being of black women in higher education—of cultural center directors particularly—began over 14 years ago. Then, I became the first permanent director of the women's center at a small public university in Connecticut. I was one of few women of color in the state in that role at the time, and while I was proud of the position I held and excited about the potential of the role, I was limited by administration and the broader campus community. I found that I was constantly required to perform in the capacity of caretaker, a role that I understood was consistent with western notions and comforts of how Black women were expected to show-up and work in professional situations, as servants, domestics, caretakers of others, etc. My closest colleague ran the multicultural center next door. We were overqualified for the roles we had. She had earned her doctorate years prior, and I was finishing my dissertation and was expected to pass my defense that coming spring.

We respectively had a plethora of knowledge and capacity within our centers and across campus. We relished the work because it was important and gratifying and the minoritized students on the predominantly White college campus sought us out. As such, we were tasked with developing and facilitating conversation spaces that acknowledged the needs and concerns of both students and faculty. The issue became, however, that we had to frame the conversations in a way that was palatable to the administration. We were constantly assessing if a topic was too controversial or if White fragility would show up and threaten our jobs, cause us to have to defend ourselves, or worse, use our already earmarked energies to restore the status quo and nurture a White person back to a certain level of comfort to the detriment of a legitimate concern of a student or staff of color.

The greatest contradiction that I acknowledged in the role of women center director, is that while being tasked to advocate for the most vulnerable populations on campus, students of color, women, LGBTQ students, I was simultaneously targeted for speaking up for and standing with the groups I was hired to support. I was cognizant that I was attacked because of my race and gender. Many felt that I should not have been seated in the position and they watched for the slightest mistake to prove why a more appropriate candidate, code for White, would be more fitting to lead the center. I was often attacked for not being responsive enough to individualized needs of everyone, on campus, in the greater community, etc., who wanted access to me. What stood out to me most during my time as women center director was the specific role black women were expected to fulfill on predominantly White college campuses. Black women at PWIs were often expected to present and to serve in "traditional" maternal roles which limited their capacity to nurturers, servants, and domestics.

Like the mammy archetype, Black women were expected to caretake for the campus. While it appeared that we were to look after the students of color, the administrative expectation was that we serve all students. This was not required of my male and White colleagues. As a new professional completing my doctoral studies in social inequality and medical sociology, I rejected the idea that I was to be available to serve anyone and everyone except myself. That year, I recall talking to my doctor, also a Black woman who resided in the town where I worked and lived. The stress of the workload and the resulting inability to engage in self-care while caretaking for the campus led me to gain 35-pounds in under a year. When I tried to engage in self-care, taking a break, eating lunch with the door closed, not responding to emails after 5 p.m. or on weekends, I was "called out" for not being responsive enough. I was labeled unapproachable, distant, or unavailable.

The role of Cultural Center directors, for the Black women who occupied them, was distinct and different from that of White women or male counterparts who were allowed to be creative and innovative due to more time flexibility, less demands, and no expectation of caretaking for the campus. Years later, when I began teaching full-time, my work as the women center director led me to consider the range of health implications of Black women on college campuses in all capacities and to consider the toll of our silent labor on our health.

This chapter is an endeavor to address the racism and sexism experienced by Black women in higher education. It describes the invisible labor that we perform and the impact of this labor on our well-being. The work is satisfying, and yet the impact it has on supporting and advocating for the most marginalized students is taxing and often underappreciated by administration and the campus community overall. It is our hope that this shines a light on the invisible labor of Black women in higher education and creates a precedent for accurately reviewing the job description, the expectations, and the total labor involved in the work as a cultural center director. In doing so, we can ensure that staff, regardless of race and gender, are provided with adequate support, accommodations, and equitable compensation that demonstrates that our time, labor, and love for our communities are truly valued.

HISTORICAL CONTEXT

The accomplishments and lived experiences of Black women cultural center directors may be understood as advocacy for racial uplift – especially on predominantly White college campuses. Racial uplift can be described as "a group struggle for freedom and social advancement" (Gaines, 1996, p. 1). According to Gaines (1996), the history of racial uplift, "suggests that African Americans have, with an almost religious fervor, regarded education as a key to liberation" (p. 1). Historical links, from Black women post-slavery to contemporary Black women, provide important contextualization for their continued commitment to professions in Black cultural centers. The distinguishing characteristic of historical racial uplift continues to be a significant part of 21st century Black women's rationale for pursuing long and meaningful careers in Black cultural centers.

As advocates for racial uplift, Black women have been architects and organizers, calling for equality and social justice on behalf of the larger Black community, even while they are frequent targets of the same institutional and structural discrimination that they are fighting against. This persistent and impassioned commitment to the Black community provides the first parallel between historical Black women educators and the important work of Black women in Black cultural centers today: their unique and fervent dedication to race work and racial uplift. Their avid commitment to racial uplift and liberation is not a new phenomenon; it is rooted in a long tradition of strong Black women who have dedicated their lives to racial uplift, social justice and Black liberation.

Theoretical Framework

Black women's historical commitment to race work must be examined from the unique intersection of racial and gender discrimination experienced by Black women educators in the past and present. Developed by Patricia Hill Collins, "Black Feminist Thought acknowledges African-American women as women, as people of color, and as a group that has been marginalized economically, socially, and politically" (Staggers-Hakim, 2009, p. 56). Moreover, "Black Feminist Thought is an activist response to race, class, and gender oppression experienced by African-American women," applying a 'matrix of domination' to their experiences and orienting them "relative to power structures" (Staggers-Hakim, 2009, p. 55).

Black Feminist Thought argues that "as a historically oppressed group, U.S. Black women have produced social thought designed to oppose oppression" (P. Collins, 2000, p. 9). This chapter is oriented in Kimberlé Crenshaw's Intersectionality lens, daughter to Black Feminist Thought, which can illuminate the factors that influence Black women's' professional experiences through an exploration of the social, political, and economic conditions of Black women. Inherent to the Intersectionality framework is an examination of the specific experiences deriving from the oppression created from the intersections of race, class, and gender, knowledge imparted by Black Feminist Thought (Staggers-Hakim, 2009, p. 56). This framework provides an understanding of the intersection of race and gender created by structural oppression within the roles played by Black women committed to racial uplift and liberation of the Black community.

Black Women in HBCUs in Late 1890s

In 1896, legalized segregation was confronted when the Plessy vs. Ferguson case was successfully presented to the Supreme Court. This case set the precedent for "separate but equal" and laid the ground- work for Blacks to be entitled to segregated, but equal accommodations. This victory in the courts, additionally, created an essential shift in the strategies Blacks used to move toward equality in the United States. As a result, many more Blacks, under The Plessy vs. Ferguson ruling, took advantage of this new access to education and enrollment in HBCUs in the South increased. However, Blacks remained keenly aware of how inherently unequal legalized "separate but equal" policies were. Consequently, after 1896, Blacks continued to fight for access to equal and equitable facilities and accommodations (i.e. public facilities and schools). Because of the access to HBCUs undergraduate education, much of the legal litigation against segregation focused on the demand for Blacks to be admitted to White graduate and professional schools. However, to avoid integration, many White institutions fought to maintain stringent segregation laws by sustaining the Plessy vs. Ferguson ruling. Despite the outcomes, Blacks continued their struggle with limited success. To illustrate this point, Blacks challenged the University of Kentucky's segregation policies. This case was decided on the basis of The Plessy vs. Ferguson ruling and as a result, the state was required to build a separate School of Engineering at Kentucky State University, the state's first Black institution.

The continual establishment of HBCUs provided Blacks with institutions that could broaden their intellect and continue to help them to defy odds in unprecedented ways. By 1900, career choices for Black males had expanded, and more Black men were able to pursue careers in religion, medicine, teaching, journalism, law and government. However, as reported by Collier-Thomas (1982), according to the 1900 United States Census, the number of Black women outgrew the number of Black men in the field of primary and secondary education. By 1910, under the ruling of "separate but equal", Black women were teaching primarily in schools for Blacks exclusively. Due to the White philanthropic interest, coupled with the Morrill Act and the need for Blacks to educate other Blacks for the workforce, by 1912, there were, according to Amott & Matthaei, (1996), approximately 14 Black women's colleges. Many of the graduates taught in schools that did not go beyond the seventh grade and poor resources. Also many of the Black women teachers viewed their work as a form of social activism. As a result, some opened their own schools or became principals of Black private schools, including Fannie Jackson Coppin, Nannie Helen Burroughs, Lucy Laney, Mary McLeod-Bethune, Charlotte Hawkins Brown, and Fannie Barrier Williams.

The growth in the teaching profession, for Black women, was not insulated from racism and sexism. As late as 1920, individual states created racist and sexist policies which legally restricted married women (Black and White) from teaching. These policies impacted Black and White women's employment in education. Moreover, a high proportion of Black institutions of higher education had White presidents and faculty alike which also influenced sexist hiring practices. These policies further impacted Black women's employment in these institutions as well. Black women were not given teaching jobs in large urban schools. In fact, if they were able to teach on the college level they were employed in rural schools and paid less than White and Black male teachers. More importantly, even though there were more Black women in the labor market, they were paid lower than White women. This would indicate how much race and gender, simultaneously, were used to exploit and divide Black women in the labor market. Therefore, Black women's productive labor, even in the field of education was routinely devalued and viewed as the cheapest form of labor. As the cheapest form of labor, it was used to educate Blacks whose labor would also further be exploited.

Education and Racial Uplift: A Historical Framework

Historically, Black women and men have been the co-architects in establishing the foundation and mission of social justice as well as carrying out its work (P. Collins, 2000). According to Rufus Clement (1966), "...during the long period of American Negro slavery (1619-1865) little or no efforts were made to educate Negroes, even to the simple extent of teaching them to read or write" (p. 299). White prohibition of Blacks' access to formal education, during and post slavery, did not stop Black women from pursuing formal education and community organizing for racial uplift and advancement. These women believed that the pursuit of education would bring freedom and social justice for themselves, their families and their communities. Historically, Black women's struggle for freedom, social advancement, and justice through education for themselves and the larger Black community was preserved as a form of racial uplift.

In the post-slavery south, states resisted the creation of schools for Blacks, thus continuing to prohibit or build barriers to Blacks' access to formal education. In fact, only three southern states allocated funding for the establishment of land-grant institutions specifically for Blacks: South Carolina, Virginia, and Kentucky. Though many small schools were established by Blacks throughout the South, twenty years would pass before there was a further consideration of provisions for formalized Black education after the abolition of slavery by the U.S. government. In 1887 the federal Hatch Act passed, making funding available for the establishment of state agricultural experimental stations at colleges and universities. This legislation was intended to allocate funds equally between Black and White institutions, unless state legislatures said otherwise. Three years later in 1890, the Second Morrill Act was passed, which specifically guaranteed funds for Black educational institutions. The Second Morrill Act provided a more reliable source of funding for Black institutions and set in motion the establishment of many Historically Black Colleges and Universities (HBCUs). These Black institutions developed as state normal or training schools in agricultural and mechanical fields designed to provide necessary training for Negroes. They were supposed to assist in providing Blacks the skills needed for the new economic growth in agricultural industries. By unintended consequence, they legitimized segregated educational institutions (Preer, 1982).

While capitalist Whites saw Black education and training as a way of creating a useful labor pool, Blacks saw this access to education as a source of advancement and freedom from the dehumanizing and exploitative systems of oppression carried over after slavery. However, access to education was not transformed until the 1890 Second Morrill Act. Though the economy demanded trained Black men and women for skilled labor and domestic work, Blacks maintained a relentless determination to pursue education for freedom and liberation from the racist and exploitative American capitalist system. Many college-educated Blacks pursued teaching as a path to their own liberation within this capitalist system as well as a path for the liberation of the larger Black community.

The establishment of Black college initiatives in the south allowed Blacks, especially Black women, to pursue higher education despite racial segregation and the need for productive labor. By 1890, 30 Black women had earned college degrees and "more than 300 Black men" (Perkins, 1993, p. 272). More importantly, Black daughters were encouraged to pursue teaching because it was a respectable and service-oriented profession. Black families perceived teaching jobs as good preparation for self-sufficiency and a path to higher social status and class (Wolfman, 1997).

Despite de facto segregation in the north, free Black men and women were able to pursue higher education. In 1862, in the face of this de facto segregation, and the same year the first Morrill Act was passed, a Black woman by the name of Mary Patterson graduated from Oberlin College in Ohio. Patterson's determination for education was not unique. Many Blacks in both the north and south were committed to this same objective. According to Wolfman (1997), "Many of the formerly enslaved teachers were joined by educated Northern free Black women who went south to teach the newly freed men and women there" (p. 158). This sense of obligation spurred many Black women to teach foundational academic skills by opening and operating Black private schools or seeking employment at Black co-educational institutions.

The actual number of Black female founders of institutions is not well documented, and their efforts have gone largely unrecognized. "Historical records indicate, however, that Haines Normal School in Atlanta (founded 1866), Bethune-Cookman College in Daytona Beach (founded 1904), and Frelinghuysen University in Washington D.C. (1906) were founded by Black women" (Wolfman, 1997, p. 159). Lucy Laney, Mary McLeod-Bethune, and Anna Julia Cooper/Rossetta Lawson founded these schools respectively, and they were created, according to Audrey McClusky (1991), because the women shared a "historical framework and sense of mission to their race and gender" (p. 403).

All the women, except for Laney, were born in the post-reconstruction south. They shared similar views on racial uplift and believed their schools would advance the Black community and Black women's leadership. These women created schools at the margins of society because of their commitment to empowering the Black community and Black women's leadership and struggled to keep them functional during a period of violent attacks against Blacks when Black women were doubly impacted by gender discrimination received from Black and White men and racism from White men and women.

As a result, Laney, McLeod-Bethune, Cooper and Lawson emerged as a group dubbed by historian Evelyn Brooks Higginbotham as "the female talented tenth" in fulfillment of the rallying call by W.E.B. DuBois (McClusky, 1997, p. 404). Lucy Laney firmly believed that Black women must "accept the burden of uplifting the Black masses," and "that schools should provide service to their communities beyond academic training" (McClusky, 1997, p. 406). Despite facing immense racial and gender discrimination, these educators and activists continued to maintain Black educational institutions that contributed to the community and helped to educate and uplift the race from the margins.

In 1925, according to Pero G. Dagbovie (2004), 66-year-old Anna Julia Cooper was the first Black woman to earn a doctoral degree in History from the University of Paris (p. 241). In 1940, Marion Thompson Wright became the first African American to earn a Ph.D. in History from Columbia University – choosing to write her dissertation on "The Education of Negroes in New Jersey" (Dagbovie, 2004, p. 252). Similar patterns of commitment to education, freedom and racial uplift from the margins are evident in the roles of 21st century Black women who serve as Black cultural center directors.

Like the historical Black women educators, Black women leaders of BCCs in the 21st century share a passion for racial uplift despite gender and racial discrimination. The groundbreaking 1954 Brown vs. The Board of Education of Topeka, Kansas decision and the following 1964 Civil Rights Act strengthened desegregation by opening access to all educational institutions regardless of race, class and gender. Both pieces of legislation provided a chance for White institutions to change their discriminatory policies and practices. Consequently, Blacks sought to gain access to White formal education centers as well as employment in White institutions. Anderson suggests that "White colleges and universities began to adopt and display such slogans and clichés as 'equal educational opportunity' and 'equal opportunity employer'" (1968, p. 262). But legal mandates, new admissions policies, and employment practices alone did not provide adequate access to equal employment opportunities. Despite the social and political policies that supposedly granted access, Black people, women in particular, were still met with resistance when seeking formal education and employment at predominantly White institutions.

The History of Black Cultural Centers

In the 1960s, a complex duality of both opportunities for access and exclusionary practices manifested itself repeatedly when White institutions of higher learning enrolled Black students while still sustaining discriminatory practices of not hiring Black faculty and administrators. However, this form of institutional racism was the impetus for the newly enrolled Black students to lead protests against repressive campus climates, thus challenging these institutions to act in order to reduce the level of hostility on campuses. Students demanded social and cultural programming, Black studies programs, Black cultural centers, and a visible presence of Black administrators and faculty on White campuses (Anderson, 1968, p. 265). These movements and subsequent policy changes allowed Blacks to enter the White higher education labor market but typically only offered race-specific, marginalized positions – including Black cultural center directors.

The push for race-specific positions assisted colleges and universities in the recruitment and retention of Black students, staff, and faculty. More specifically, according to Gamson and Arce (1978), Blacks recruited as administrators were, often, sought to fill supportive programs for Black students or for positions with a broad range of responsibilities concerning the affairs of minorities. Over time, the responsibilities of professionals in race-specific positions increased to include not just social and cultural support to students but also to offer additional support that gauged and measured the well-being of students (Gamson et. al., 1980). While a case for inclusion could be made by predominantly White institutions, Drummond (1995) argued that these were junior-level positions with limited resources and limited institutional authority.

Furthermore, researchers (Moore & Wagstaff, 1974; Poussaint, 1974) found that 1970s equal opportunity affirmative action laws forced White colleges and universities to create and staff, "assistant and associate positions," giving only the perception of inclusionary practices of Blacks in administrative hierarchies. Minority affairs offices that were intended to provide support for students of color continued to be junior level race-specific positions with little or no opportunity for advancement toward a higher level of administrative authority. Despite the ancillary position of the opportunities created and earmarked for Blacks and the sacrifices inherent in race-based work, Black men and women fervently pursued educational efforts as a form of racial uplift.

Transforming the Next Generation: Dr. Anne Edwards' Reflection

I first worked in a cultural center as a graduate student, and while I enjoyed my experience, academically I was on a different career trajectory. I had accepted a position to work in the hospitality industry post-graduation and even went so far as to say in my earlier career that I did not want to work in diversity-focused spaces. In 2010 I began working in higher education and by 2012, I was working in career development. Six years later, I was propositioned to be an acting director of a Black cultural center. I realized quickly that this position was a natural calling. I reflected on my earlier career predictions and laughed because not only was I doing the work, but I felt passionate about the work. This section will include my thoughts on generational leadership, the learning and tools required to be successful, and what is necessary to keep future generations interested and equipped to continue the work.

To fully connect the work of historical Black women pursuing education and racial uplift to the work of 21st century Black women in BCCs, an examination of the social, political, and professional evolution of race-based work is needed. There has been a changing of the guard or a shift in race-based leadership focus between the generations of Black women leaders. Currently, several generations are represented in cultural center leadership: Baby Boomers, those born between 1946-1964; Generation X those born between 1965-1979; and Millennials or Generation Y born between 1980-2001 (Berkup, 2014). Those leaders who are Baby Boomers retired or are close to retirement. Millennials are becoming the new directors on the front lines. They are quickly accepting responsibilities for Black cultural center spaces, facilities, staff, and students. They are also facilitating the establishment of new Black cultural center spaces that were born out of modern-day movements such as Black Lives Matter.

Today, the next generations of Black women cultural center leadership will require a comprehensive understanding of the work of previous generations to begin contemplating how to forge ahead. Black women leaders today in cultural center spaces at the forefront of developing support for the intersectional identities of Black people now also desire to pursue personal and professional development for themselves as well. In order for Black women who are in cultural center leadership to truly be successful, they must look for ways not only to lift as they climb, but they must also look for ways to climb as they lift. Historical Black women leaders often made sacrifices in their lives to elevate the needs of the larger Black community.

Historically, the task of educating newly freed Blacks was in large part facilitated by Black women due to society's intimidation by Black maleness (Cooper, 1892). Post-slavery, the focus for newly freed Black people became the construction of a new life, which included education and other societal rights such as voting (Woodson, 1933). At the same time, during the early 19th century, the concept of "true womanhood" emphasized innocence, modesty, piety, purity, submissiveness, and domesticity. Black women were ironically expected to present these characteristics while societally not being perceived as women in the same sense as their White counterparts (Perkins, 1983). Black women directed efforts within their civic, educational, and religious organizations in the Northern United States to emphasize the fact that they encompassed the same attributes often attached only to White women.

Over time, while Blacks espoused education as a means of racial uplift, there was an intra-race conflict on the role of the Black woman. Black women were seen more as nurturers rather than rigorous academicians. In essence, Black women were neither accepted in spaces that advocated for womanhood centered on White women nor was it acceptable that they elevate the interests of themselves above the interests of their race (Cooper, 1982). The idea of racial uplift had been ingrained in Black women since slavery. The issues of the race far outweighed the issues of even gender. This is in addition to the fact that the voices of Black women were left out of mainstream women's suffrage movements. Black women's values have historically been more closely aligned with race (Perkins, 1983).

Contemporarily, my peer colleagues and I represent the next generation of cultural center leadership. Our backgrounds and knowledge bases are varied and represent a variety of work fields-from business, to education on all levels, sociology, Black studies, ethnic studies, and American studies. How we got to this work is varied, but one connecting link is our desire to see uplift in the Black community especially in predominant and historical White spaces. Our career lives might be different from our predecessors. We desire our version of work-life balance which includes a more than decent income, autonomy, and the ability to see our impact. It is often said that millennials don't value loyalty to an institution and that is in many ways true. We instead value a commitment to the work, and there is work to be done in various spaces. Our individual values often guide the roles that we accept, and how we feel the institution supports our values is the reason we stay or leave.

The next generation of cultural center leaders need an understanding of the historical underpinnings of these spaces to keep them grounded and present in race work. Millennials and Gen Z leadership must remember to be receptive to learning and create a balance between their own visions of what they want to accomplish and the perspectives and trajectories of the leaders who came before. As such, it is important that transition takes place before a leadership change to ensure that there is a transfer of information and lessons from the previous generation that are invaluable. Knowing what allies and challenges exist in the institution will assist in the continuation of the work. Likewise, Baby Boomers must fully pass the baton and trust the next generations to continue the work.

Additionally, current and future Millennial and Gen Z leaders must understand that many Black cultural center spaces were developed without solid strategic planning, complete institutional support, and in some cases without a basic understanding of the purpose of the space. These spaces were historically developed with multi-functional purposes in mind. Some universities, for example, have interwoven admissions and enrollment components into their Black cultural center spaces. Black women directors of Black cultural centers are then inherently expected to forgo personal goals and aspirations and sacrifice for the greater good. The question that emerges as this generational shift occurs is what skills, competencies, and foci will current and future cultural center directors need to be successful both professionally and personally while still doing the work of racial uplift?

The answer is to elevate research on how to support Black women leaders in Black cultural center spaces. This is critical for the progression of 21st century Black women leaders who are often charged with preparing the next generation of educators, activists, community organizers, and leaders with the unspoken pre-text that the work must come before them. These discussions are becoming as much of an increasing necessity as the conversation needed about how to preserve as well as advance historical race work in current and future Black cultural center environments. Proof of this shift in thinking is evident in a series of interviews with Black women BCC directors located at large, predominantly White four-year universities in the Midwest and Mid-Atlantic Region of the United States.

A STUDY ON BLACK WOMEN IN BLACK CULTURAL CENTERS

A 2016 series of interviews gauging the effect of race-based work on Black Women directors of Black cultural centers revealed that dedicating a consistent and continued level of commitment can be as rewarding as it is devastating. Previous studies have captured Black women's contributions to higher education and the effect of racism and sexism on their professional advancement. This study extended the existing body of research to explore how Black women in racialized positions negotiated and advocated on behalf of Black students and staff as well as themselves while experiencing oppression based on their own racial and gender identities. The study sought to shed light on Black women's continued desire to contribute to the uplift of Black students from marginalized administrative positions with limited autonomy or support. In-depth interviews were used to capture the unique lived experiences of Black women employed in race-specific positions and allowed them to express their experiences in their own words.

Race-specific positions are defined here as professionals whose main responsibility is to lead Black/African American Cultural Centers in predominantly White academic institutions. Participants interviewed for this study were three Black women directors of Black cultural centers. On average, the participants had 15-26 years of experience in this field. One participant was married, one was divorced, and one woman never married but was in a relationship. Two of the three participants had children between the ages of 10-40 years old.

Directors were interviewed about their roles as directors of BCCs as well as their perceived commitment to the historical mission of BCC's and asked to comment on their institutions' support of their positions and/or centers. Topics explored during the interviews included demographics, institutional and personal support, job responsibilities and expectations, personal effects, race and gender discrimination, and career mobility. These questions explored their perceptions of the racial and gender climate on campus and how the quality of their personal and professional lives might be affected by this work. Their responses spoke to their personal and professional support systems as well as their plans for career advancement.

Black Women and Race-Specific Positions: We Are Lifting

Like the historical Black women activists and educators who believed in lifting as they climbed, Black women BCC directors provide leadership training and serve as advisors to Black students and Black student organizations. They remain committed to racial uplift through teaching and leadership training of collective work and responsibility in complement to their students' academic training. The Black female cultural center directors interviewed for the study were also responsible for planning campus-wide cultural programs to promote African and African American history and culture. They each serve on several committees and task forces that promote cultural diversity on campus and in the surrounding community, allocate resources, plan institutional programming for Black Alumni, fundraise and grant scholarships, and play a major role in faculty, staff and student recruitment and retention efforts.

In addition, these professionals manage facilities, budgets, and resources while supervising center professionals, clerical staff, and graduate/undergraduate staff assistants. In the past 15-25 years, each center in the Midwest and Mid-Atlantic region has undergone facility renovations without an increase in facility budgets or resources. Like the early Black women educators who maintained their institutions on limited resources, these 21st century BCC women leaders are expected to, as one respondent explains, "do more with less." Despite the limited resources, directors acknowledge that, historically, their centers have been sustained and have larger budgets than the women's, Latino, Asian or Native American centers on their campuses.

These 21st century directors became interested in pursuing careers in cultural centers early in their academic life. As undergraduate students, they were either engaged in a cultural center, an active student leader, or worked in residence life. When respondents were asked about what keeps them in this type of work, they said that they see it as "their life's work" and "that they have always wanted to help Black students and the larger Black community to move forward and to achieve their goals." Each director had a long-standing interest in helping the Black community and has always been involved in community work. They saw themselves as advocates, "community activists" and "moving the Black community forward" or having a "passion for students, and "giv[ing] back to the community [by impacting] the educational experience of Black students."

An emerging theme linking the early Black women committed to race work and 21st century Black women leaders was the tremendous personal and professional sacrifices that were made to carry out their laudable work. Twenty-first century Black women BCC leaders, when asked if their work affects their personal lives and health, responded "Yes, Yes, Yes," "Definitely," and "It is hard for it not to."

Directors indicated that their work, often entailing 60–70-hour weeks, negatively affected their overall health and resulted in weight gain and other stress-related illnesses. They were keenly aware of the need to create boundaries between work and home, but they found it difficult, especially early on in their careers. They viewed the extremely long hours and impact on their health as a necessary price of their work in "moving the community forward."

These BCC directors took pride in their work; they wanted to both excel in their professional careers and continue fighting for the community, and so "some things suffer" and "it wears on" them. During interviews, respondents said that their work is a contributing factor in challenges facing their love relationships as well as their health. Each director had missed major family events due to their role or responsibilities as director and admitted that many family members and friends did not understand the work they did or the long hours they spent at work. One respondent suggested that this position, especially when held by a woman, required a very supportive spouse/partner who was willing to take on more of the child-rearing responsibilities to achieve a family/work balance in a home with children.

Recounting her life as a single parent, one respondent described her children's early years as spending long hours and weekends on campus at programs; her "children were raised in the cultural center." She would bring her children to events, and college students would help them with their homework. At the time, she thought that her children were lucky to have opportunities to meet prestigious people and attend cultural programs. However, in retrospect, she feels that she sacrificed quality time with her family because of her responsibilities as a director. The historical accounts of early Black women educators reflected similar sacrifices in their personal lives for the greater good of the Black community and racial uplift. These women held lives of service, in part, to demonstrate the capabilities of Black women (McClusky, 1997, p. 406).

During the interviews, each director confirmed that major professional sacrifices were required in their professionals well. One such sacrifice involved turning down more lucrative job offers and opportunities. When asked why they did not leave, each director expressed concern with the difficulty of recreating the imperative familial support structure in a new place, without which, they could not meet the exacting workload required of their position. Each director discussed their commitment to the maintenance and/or expansion of its important historical legacy. The directors also acknowledged concerns about leaving the institution – questioning the universities' commitment to maintaining the cultural centers' programs and services for Black students. They were unsettled by the idea that, after many years of developing quality programs and services, the institution might change or eliminate cultural center resources, programming, and services. Two of the three directors interviewed were concerned that the program and center would fail and be eliminated entirely if they were to leave the institution. These women's commitment to their work went beyond their professional work-ethic. It echoed the lives and tenacious dedication of the early Black women educators and activists. The early women school founders were respected in their communities, and the institutions they led were considered centers of social transformation; bearing a parallel with the roles Black women play in Black Cultural Centers on predominantly White college campuses in the 21st century.

Race and Gender Discrimination

Black women leading these transformational centers and institutions experienced significant racial and gender discrimination and intolerance. The post-slavery experiences of racism and sexism were demoralizing, and these Black women were met repeatedly with challenges that impacted their visibility as scholars and leaders in society and, at times, in their own communities. In the 21st century, women directors experienced similar racism and discrimination as, according to one director, the "great racial divide" remained on university campuses. Two of the three respondents said that the recruitment and retention of students, faculty, and staff of color was still a major concern. The participants indicated that their help was often commissioned when their institutions faced racial issues. Each 21st century director had a wealth of personal stories at their institution regarding the racial and gender discrimination that they faced. Each discussed how they had to cope with unrealistic job expectations, insulting comments about their race from White colleagues and students as well as degrading remarks about their gender from Black and White male faculty, staff, and students. Each recounted stories about how their competency was challenged and/or misinterpreted. One respondent shared that she was perceived as confrontational and adversarial when she advocated for Black students and the center, and that she was viewed as a "nag" or "whiner."

Black Women and Race-Specific Positions: Are We Climbing?

Black women cultural center directors are committed to racial uplift in their current positions despite the challenges, but they also express an interest in career mobility, job satisfaction, and their ultimate career goals. The 21st century directors interviewed stated their jobs brought them fulfillment because they have an opportunity to be catalysts for change and to help Black students achieve their goals. However, when asked about their next professional steps, none of the respondents saw viable career ladders in their positions. In fact, they mentioned that their positions were unlike other positions in their institutions such as residence life, admissions, or student activities. Those positions had clear career ladders and offered career mobility. Instead, all three directors said that their positions pigeon-holed them; they did not feel that their campuses offered opportunities for career mobility from their current positions.

They believed that their administrative leadership skills were transferable to other positions, but that it was apparent that their administration does not agree. The institutions' limited views of their skills hindered these women's abilities to seek promotions and immobilized their careers. Earlier Black women leaders experienced similar struggles because of the traditional racialized and gendered roles White society reinforced for Black women such as domestics, uneducated laborers, and lower-level teachers in under-resourced rural schools (Cortez, 2009, p. 2; McClusky, 1991, p. 1907). Black women in higher education, past and present, experience limited career mobility due to the political and social policies and practices that perpetuate Black women as less competent than their White and/or male counterparts.

Directors interviewed for this research saw the BCC Director position as leading only to two other positions: Director or Vice President of Multicultural Programs. When asked about their ultimate goals, each respondent acknowledged that they would need to leave their positions if they remained in higher education. Moreover, all the respondents expressed some reluctance for remaining in higher education. While these 21st century BCC women directors have more equitable access to diverse career choices due to polices that limit overt discrimination, each respondent recognized their earning potential and subsequent career options are limited without a Ph.D. Like earlier leaders, these 21st century women have remained committed to uplifting the black community. They each see themselves, even after leaving these positions in the future, working in the community, leading community-based organizations, and empowering Black people. Their passion for empowering and uplifting Black students and the Black community overall has kept them engaged in their work, regardless of the challenges they have faced.

RECOMMENDATIONS

The study of Black women in race-specific positions in higher education must continue to document their experiences further and to describe the significance of their work to both students and college campuses. This study suggests that their contributions are valuable to Black students, faculty, and staff and their sense of belonging on college campuses, especially on PWIs. Additionally, Black women's relentless work, prior to and after the murder of George Floyd advanced diversity, equity, and inclusion efforts on campuses. This labor should be acknowledged, valued, and appropriately compensated provided the significant impact it holds for American educational institutions.

Black women cultural center directors serve as advocates, interpreters, and administrative bridges that support Black student recruitment, retention, and graduation. These positions play a pivotal role in the education and socio-emotional development of Black students in and out of the classroom. Despite their significance, the labor of Black women cultural center directors continues to be devalued, marginalized, and misunderstood. Many institutions still fail to understand the vast and complex amount of service, advocacy, mentoring, counseling, and cultural education these roles provide. These roles work across all divisions and academic units to support and advocate for Black students and to address barriers to their success. Not only is the labor of Black women cultural center director's invisibilized, the extent of responsibilities this position entails are not adequately acknowledged or quantified in standard job descriptions. Hence, the compensation is not equitable to the invisible labor performed. To account for this inequity, we recommend that colleges and universities commission a *higher education compensation and classification study* to address position level or grade, including for cultural center directors, and a salary equity audit by position, gender, and race. These positions should not be aggregated with other director-level positions.

The second recommendation is to create a *Black Cultural Center Leadership and Legacy Institute.* The next generation of center directors must understand the legacy and historical tradition of this work. As a result, there is a need to pass down the social, political, and economic conditions by which these critical roles were established. The institute would provide historical context for the work, explain the importance of social movements, and describe the importance of these roles in advancing institutional support for Black students. New professionals would not only learn the history but develop a network for the next generation of cultural center leaders. *Black Cultural Center Leadership and Legacy Institute* would serve as a think tank for leaders to develop and share new and innovative strategies that add to the body of knowledge and research on the history of cultural centers and the Black women professionals who lead them. Additionally, the institute would provide participants with an understanding of budget, finance, and strategic management, critical elements to cultural center leadership. The space will allow for the converging of generations, with both their knowledge and experience.

CONCLUSION

It is evident that: 1). Past and present Black women leaders in racial uplift share a fervent commitment to education as a tool of liberation and advancement of the Black community 2). Black women experience the duality and intersection of structural oppression based on racial and gender discrimination. This intersectional experience can limit their professional success, but their inherent perseverance and determination helps them to overcome and achieve from the margins of society and the margins of predominantly White institutions, 3). The complex circumstances of both early and present women leaders place them in the position of what Nana Helen Burroughs, founder of the National Training School for Women and Girls in Washington DC, coined as "specializing in the wholly impossible" (McClusky, 1997, pp. 423-424) past and present black women leaders are advocates for and educators in the Black community fighting against the same racism and sexism that they cannot always protect themselves against, and 5). the uniquely complex race and gender discrimination locates their work for racial uplift at the margins and impacts their professional career mobility, health, and lifestyle. In the 21st century, female BCC directors continue to have limited potential for career advancement, salary, or position titles when working at predominately White institutions; these women acknowledged discrimination as a real factor associated with the ceiling placed on the advancement of women in these positions.

The 21st century Black women BCC directors understand they may not advance professionally in academia if they maintain their positions while these posts are not valued at their institutions. Given this limited career mobility, these women continue to develop strategies that strive to support their own career ladders and promote their career mobility. These strategies generally require changing careers or leaving higher education which indicates the lack of a structured career ladder for racialized and gendered positions like BCC directors.

BCC Black women leaders remain committed to the work of racial uplift and the development of Black students motivates them to continue fighting for the center's resources, programs, and services. These women are routinely asked to provide rationale for the centers' existence and to justify its value; this has prompted the participants to question the institutions' support of their center and their work. Despite this complex relationship to the institution, cultural center directors are committed to ensuring the success of the centers and were considered transformational influences on the Black students they serve.

These unique experiences require Black women to acquire and maintain effective coping strategies and networks of support. Keenly aware of the impact of these positions on their lives and health, these women remain committed to this work while experiencing significant role strain related to the demands of the work and family. Women spoke of having social support systems outside of work, although they felt that many people do not understand the demands of their work. Some women rely on "sister friends;" others rely on supportive husbands, and faith, religion, and spirituality play an important role in each of these women's lives. For historical Black women leaders, they found strength and support from other Black women leaders and as a result formed national Black women organizations to provide national support for their efforts in racial uplift and social service work.

According to Edghill (2007), Black women have historically pursued education to address issues of social justice and racial uplift for themselves and the larger Black community. Based on this comparative analysis of historical Black women's leadership in education and the 21st Century Black women BCC directors, Black women share a continued passion for racial uplift and strive for the continued advancement of the Black community and Black youth. Even from the fringes of colleges and communities, the efforts of 21st Century Black women BCC directors reflect a long legacy of Black women committed to racial uplift; despite the challenges of gender and racial discrimination in the 21st century, these women strive to find ways of climbing career ladder while they are educating the next generation of Black student leaders and to advance the Black community. These Black women carry the legacy of the earlier pioneers of racial uplift and share with them the same commitment to freedom and liberation. Continuing to assist and facilitate the education and leadership development of Black college students, these women make great sacrifices to improve and empower the Black community. These contemporary

Black women must find ways, according to Nana Helen Burroughs, to see themselves as "competent women who claim authority over our own lives and destinies" (McClusky, 1997, p. 423).

ACKNOWLEDGMENT

This research received no specific grant from any funding agency in the public, commercial, or not-for-profit sectors.

REFERENCES

Amott, T. J. M. (1996). *Race, Gender and Work: A Multi-cultural Economic History of Women in the United States*. South End Press.

Anderson, T. (1988). Black encounter of racism and elitism in white academe: A critique of the system. *Journal of Black Studies, 18*(3), 259–272. doi:10.1177/002193478801800301

Berkup, S. B. (2014). Working with generations x and y in generation z period: Management Of different generations in business life. *Mediterranean Journal of Social Sciences, 5(19)*, p. 218. Blackhurst, A. E. (2000). Career satisfaction and perceptions of sex discrimination among women student affairs professionals. *NASAP Journal, 37*(2), 7–78.

Bonner, F. B. (2001). Addressing gender issues in historically Black college and university community: A challenge and call to action. *The Journal of Negro Education: Black Women in The Academy: Challenges and Opportunities, 70*(3), 176–191. doi:10.2307/3211209

Clement, R. E. (1966). The historical development of higher education for negro Americans. *The Journal o f Negro Education, 35*(4), 299-305.

Collier-Thomas, B. (1982). Guest editorial: The impact of Black women in education: An historical overview. *Journal of Education, 51*(3), 173–180.

Collins, P. H. (2000). *Black feminist thought: Knowledge, consciousness, and the politics of empowerment*. Routledge.

Collins, S. M. (1997). *Black corporate executives: The making and breaking of a Black middle class.* Temple University Press.

Cooper, A. J. (1988). *A Voice from the South*. Oxford University Press.

Cortez, C. O. (2006). *Crusaders for social justice: Black female educator-activists in social welfare reform in Los Angeles during the golden age of the Black Power movement, 1966--1975*. [Doctoral Dissertation]. USC, USA.

Dagbovie, P. G. (2004). Black women historians from the late 19th century to the dawning of the civil rights movement. *Journal of African American History, 89*(3), 241–261. doi:10.2307/4134077

Drummond, M. E. (1995). Minorities in higher education leadership positions: A report of eight years of disappointment, 1986-1993. *Black Issues in Higher Education*, *23*, 43–47.

Edghill, V. (2007). Black women in race-specific positions on predominantly white campuses: A historical materialist [Doctoral Dissertation]. Howard University, USA.

Gaines, K. K. (1996). *Uplifting the Race: Black Leadership, Politics, and Culture in the Twentieth Century*. University of North Carolina Press. doi:10.5149/uncp/9780807845431

Gamson, Z., & Carlos, A. H. (1978). Implications of the social context for higher education. In M. W. Peterson (Ed.), *Black Students on White Campuses: The Impact of Increased Black Enrollments,* (pp. 23–42). University of Michigan, Survey Research Center.

Gamson, Z., Peterson, M. W., & Blackburn, R. T. (1980). Stages in the response of white colleges and universities to Black students. *The Journal of Higher Education*, *51*(3), 255–267. doi:10.2307/1981008

Gamson, Z., Peterson, M. W., & Blackburn, R. T. (1980). Stages in the response of white colleges and universities to Black students. *The Journal of Higher Education*, *51*(3), 255–267. doi:10.2307/1981008

Hobson-Smith, C. (1984). Black female achievers in academe. *The Journal of Negro Education*, *51*(3), 318–341. doi:10.2307/2294699

Holmes, S. L. (2003). Black female administrators speak out: Narratives on race and gender in higher education. *NASAP Journal*, *6*(1), 45–62.

Hooks, B., & West, C. (1991). *Breaking bread: Insurgent Black intellectual life.* South End Press.

Hu-DeHart, E. (2002). The diversity project: Institutionalizing multiculturalism or managing differences?" *Academe: Diversity on Campus. 86*(5), 38-42. American Association of University Professors .

Hypolite, L. I. (2020). People, place, and connections: Black cultural center staff as facilitators of social capital. *Journal of Black Studies*, *51*(1), 37–59.

Marshall, C., & Rossman, G. B. (1989). Designing qualitative research. *Sage (Atlanta, Ga.).*

McClusky, A. T. (1991). *Mary McLeod Bethune and the education of Black girls in the South, 1904-1923.* [Doctoral Dissertation]. Indiana University, USA.

McClusky, A. T. (1997). We specialize in the wholly impossible: Black women school founders and their mission. *Signs (Chicago, Ill.)*, *22*(2), 403–426.

Moore, W. Jr, & Wagstaff, L. H. (1974). *Black educators in white colleges.* Jossey-Bass Publishers.

Perkins, L. M. (1983). The impact of the "cult of true womanhood" on the education of Black women. *The Journal of Social Issues*, *39*(3), 17–28.

Perkins, L. M. (1993). The role of education in the development of Black feminist thought, 1860-1920. History of Education, 22(2), 265–275.

Poussaint, A. (1974). The Black administrator in the white university. *Black Scholar: The Journal of Black Studies and Research, 6*(1), 8-14.

Poussaint, A. (1974). The Black administrator in the white university. *Black Scholar: The Journal of Black Studies and Research*, *6*(1), 8–14.

Preer, J. L. (1982). *Lawyers v. educators: Black colleges and desegregation in public higher education*. Greenwood Press.

Reason, R. D. (2003). Gender-based salary differences in African-American senior student affairs officers. *NASAP Journal, 6*(1), 67-78.

Rousseau, N. (2009). *Black woman's burden: Commodifying Black reproduction*. Palgrave and MacMillan.

Rusher, A. W. (1996). *African American women administrators*. University Press of America.

Staggers-Hakim, R. (2009). *The moderating effect of discrimination and the intersection of race, class, and gender on obesity*. [Doctoral Dissertation]. Howard University, USA.

Wolfman, B. R. (1997). Light as from a beacon: African American women administrators in the academy L. Benjamin (Ed.), Black Women in the Academy: Promises and Perils (pp. 158–167). University of Florida Press.

ADDITIONAL READING

Cooper, B. (2018). *Eloquent rage: A Black feminist discovers her superpower*. St. Martin's Press.

Edghill-Walden, V., Dixon, K.M., Edwards, A.M., Lewis, J.C., & Thompson, V.J. (2019, June 21). Blk womyn voices: Networking and self care [Audio podcast]. https://soundcloud.com/blkwomynvoices/career-success

Edghill-Walden, V., Boston, T., & Palmer, A. (2018). We speak their names: Counter narratives of Black women liberators. *Black History Bulletin, 81*(1).

Edghill-Walden, V., Pickett, C. W.; Ortiz. E. F., Felton III, J. A., Garcia, D. H., Gooden, A., Outing, D. A., Truong, K. A., Young, P. N., Stevenson, T. N., & Dexter, M. R. (2021). A framework for advancing anti-racism strategy on campus. *A National Association for Diversity Officers in Higher Education Publication*.

Giddings, P. (2006). *When and where I enter*. Bantam Doubleday Dell Publishing Group Incorporated.

Hord, F. L. (Ed.). (2005). *Black culture centers: Politics of survival and identity*. Third World Press.

Johnson, M., Simon, S., Stone, B., & York, K., Dixon, K.M., Edwards, A. M., Lewis, J.C., & Thompson, V.J.. (2020, August 14). Blk womyn voices: Black cultural centers led by Black womyn [Audio podcast]. https://soundcloud.com/blkwomynvoices/black-cultural-centers-led-by-black-womyn

Patton, L. D. (2010). *Culture centers in higher education: Perspectives on identity, Theory, and Practice*. Stylus Publishing.

Staggers-Hakim, R. (2022). *Profiled life: A systems approach to understanding the foundations and persistence of racism in America*. Kendall Hunt.

White, D. G. (1999). *Too heavy a load: Black women in defense of themselves, 1894-1994*. W.W. Norton.

KEY TERMS AND DEFINITIONS

Black Cultural Center: Spaces primarily focused on the preservation of Black culture and in supporting various communities of practice in learning and understanding histories and cultures of the African diaspora.

Black Feminist Thought: A theoretical lens that first seeks to situate Black women as 1). women, 2). people of color, and 3). a group that has been marginalized economically, socially, and politically and further functions as an activist response to compounding oppression relative to power structures.

Generational Leadership: A network within a company, organization or institution where an awareness of generational differences exist and the respective roles and contributions of intergenerational leaders are clearly defined and mutually respected.

Hatch Act: A federal mandate passed in 1887 created to ensure state Black and white land-grant colleges received equal amounts of earmarked funds in order to create a series of agricultural experiment stations.

Intersectionality Theory: A theoretical lens developed by Kimberle Crenshaw that focuses on the political, social, cultural, and gender intersections of marginalized individuals within the context of larger power structures.

Matrix of Domination: Prior to the introduction of intersectionality as a way to define compounding oppression, this term, developed by Black feminist scholar Patricia Hill Collins, was used to refer to interlocking system of race, class, and gender oppression.

Millennials: Born between the 1980s and early 2000s, Millennials, now in their 30 and 40s, are transitioning into advanced positions of leadership in companies and institutions as Generation X and Baby Boomers retire.

Race-Specific Positions: Employment opportunities created specifically to increase the visibility, inclusion, development, and advancement of a race in one or more personal, social, educational, or professional areas.

Racial Uplift: Racial uplift is a term referring to Black people's ability to develop a Black consciousness in uplifting the entire race.

Second Morrill Act: Meant to correct the racially discriminatory inadequacies and inconsistencies of the 1862 Morrill Act, this federal mandate targeted former Confederate states, requiring them to establish separate land-grant institutions for Black students and/or demonstrate that admission to already established public universities was not racially based.

Chapter 3
Leading Transformative Change as the "First": An Examination of the Institutionalization of a Southern PWI's DEI Strategic Plan

Atiya Kai Stokes-Brown
Coastal Carolina University, USA

ABSTRACT

Although extant literature on chief diversity officers in higher education has provided insight into their roles, priorities, and standards of practice, few studies have exclusively explored the perspectives and experiences of Black women CDOs. This qualitative study draws on theories of organizational change, critical race theory, and critical race feminism to make meaning of and interpret the experience as an inaugural Black woman chief diversity officer at a public regional institution in the South, with a focus on the author's experience leading the strategic planning process. This study advances the research on Black women in higher education, spotlighting the distinctive, layered, and intersectional journey of one Black woman CDO working in a predominately White institution in the South.

INTRODUCTION

As institutions of higher learning grapple with social, economic, and political issues of the twenty-first century, a key challenge has been to elevate, integrate, and centralize diversity, equity, and inclusion (DEI) functions in colleges and universities (Williams & Wade-Golden, 2013). Microcosms of the larger systemic inequalities reflected in society; institutions of higher education often reproduce social inequities (Worthington 2020). Institutions established Chief Diversity Officer (CDO) positions to centralize DEI work, with a focus on improving inclusion and integrating this work more fully around the entire campus (Williams & Wade-Golden, 2013). When institutions are sincere in improving the diversity climate and advancing their focus on DEI practices within the institution, CDOs can serve as change agents within the institution, developing sustainable diversity-focused initiatives, addressing systemic inequities, and

DOI: 10.4018/978-1-6684-3564-9.ch003

guide efforts to engage in proactive, inclusive approaches that support cultural and institutional change (Williams & Wade-Golden, 2013; Worthington et al., 2014).

The extant literature on CDOs has provided insight into the roles, priorities, and standards of practice for CDOs. Decades of research highlight the challenges and barriers CDOs face when engaging in the work of shifting culture and building infrastructure that integrates diversity at the core of the educational experience. Recent studies sought to better understand the experiences of women of color CDOs and how their social identities influence how they enact their professional responsibilities. In her 2016 study about the experiences of women of color (Black and Latina) serving as college and university CDOs, Nixon found that "social identities affected how they experienced their lived reality as extreme tokens, and they had to manage their own expectations, in addition to the impressions of others regarding behavior, competency and status, in order to fulfill their functional and symbolic roles" (314). While motivated to advance the institution beyond a focus on compositional diversity and serve as role models for others, her study highlights shared feelings of pain, isolation, doubt, and frustration. In her 2016 dissertation exploring the experienced women of color (Black, Latina and Asian) CDOs, Maraña found similar results, highlighting a shared sense of responsibility and pride in serving in their role and feelings of isolation and discrimination.

Fewer studies have exclusively explored the perspectives and experiences of Black women CDOs. Johnson (2021) explored the experiences of Black women in diversity roles (including the CDO position) at four year predominately White institutions and identified several themes including the belief that Black women in these positions have to "bend" and "shift" (Harris-Perry, 2011) to navigate their predominantly White environments and often have to explore coping mechanisms to navigate their professional environments. Even less is known about the experiences of Black women who serve as the institution's inaugural CDO. In their study of one institution's approach to prepare, hire and support an inaugural CDO, Arnold and Kowalski-Braun (2012) highlight the importance of politics, structures and culture in the planning and implementation process. Yet, there is little to no discussion of how the CDOs social identities influenced the institution's decisions and actions, particularly at historically White institutions. Acknowledging these gaps in the literature, this study seeks to answer the following research questions: How do inaugural Black women CDOs at historically White institutions experience their identities as women and people of color? How do their experiences influence efforts to develop and implement the institution's first diversity, equity, and inclusion strategic plan? To investigate these research questions, I engaged in an autoethnographic study, making meaning of and interpret my own experience as an inaugural Black woman chief diversity officer at a public regional institution in the South, with a focus on my experience leading the strategic planning process. In following sections, I offer a review of the literature on Black women CDOs and use theories of organizational change, critical race theory, and critical race feminism to focus the inquiry and guide this research. A discussion of the methodology is then followed by a discussion of the dominant themes that emerged from the study. This study advances the research on Black women in higher education, spotlighting the distinctive, layered, and intersectional journey of one Black woman CDO working in predominately White institution in the South.

BACKGROUND

Black Women CDO Experiences in Higher Education

The emergence of the CDO position in higher education positions colleges and universities to advance their diversity, equity, and inclusion capacity focus on curriculum, climate and policy making (Stuart, 2010). As senior-level leaders, CDOs responsibilities broadly include leadership of strategic diversity planning and building institutional diversity infrastructure (Stuart, 2010; Williams & Wade-Golden, 2007). The majority of CDOs are people of color and women (Jaschik, 2008; Williams & Wade-Golden 2013). While all CDOs potentially face some form of marginalization to the degree that their role is viewed as a tokenized specialist peripheral to the institution's core functions (Nixon, 2017), extant research suggests that women of color in higher education also experience marginalization based on the intersection of their race and gender (Nixon 2017; Turner, 2002; Turner et. al., 2011). As both racial and gender minorities, women of color CDOs are likely to be "extreme tokens" (Turner et al., 2011, p. 9; Williams & Wade-Golden, 2008), thus influencing "capacity with which CDOs can affect transformational diversity change in their institutions" (Nixon, 2017, p. 303).

CONCEPTUAL FRAMEWORK

Critical Race Theory and Critical Race Feminism

An analysis of the experiences of Black women CDOs in predominately White institutions requires a conceptual framework that reflects potential conditions of marginalization, tokenism and isolation and the intersections of race and gender. Critical Race Theory (CRT) and Critical Race Feminism (CRF) provide avenues to explore nuances between and the intersectional nature of racialized and gendered experiences, offering a roadmap to better understand the challenges faced by women of color leaders in higher education. CRT examines the legacy and lasting impact of race and racism in American society. Developed to address the nation's slow progress and new subtle forms of racism following the Civil Rights Movement (Delgado & Stefanic, 2017; Yosso, 2005), CRT rests on the premise that race is socially constructed and racism is constant and normalized in U.S. society (Creswell, 2007). CRT provides scholars a critical avenue to centralize the voice of marginalized, non-dominant racial identity groups, creating opportunities to explore how lived experiences of racism and sexism might affect women of color (Nixon, 2017; Tate, 1997).

Critical Race Feminism (CRF) further highlights the interconnectedness of race and gender, centering the intersectional identity and experiences of women of color (Howard-Hamilton, 2003; Ngwainmbi, 2004; Wing, 1997). Stories and storytelling are elevated as valued measure of making meaning of and communicating experiences (Vaught, 2008). These theories rest firmly on Crenshaw's (1991) foundational research on intersectionality which highlighted how multiple forms of oppression are experiences when various social identities intersect. These frameworks have been particularly useful when examining the underrepresentation, isolation, and marginalization of Black women in academia (Collins, 2000; 1986; Lloyd-Jones, 2009) as they assume executive-level positions in predominately White institutions.

The efforts of CDOs to effectively address equity, diversity, and social justice issues and facilitate the development and implementation of a strategic diversity, equity, and inclusion plan are greatly influenced by the organizational culture and overall climate at the institution. Transformative leaders like CDOs "work within their organizational cultures following existing rules, procedures and norms" (Bass & Avolio, 1993, p. 112) to create a strong institution-wide coordination of diversity, equity, and inclusion efforts and subsequently more consistent and sustained DEI engagement (Milem et al., 2005). This level of transformation reflects a desire to see institutions of higher learning as enlightened spaces that actively seek to disrupt the reproduction of the broader culture's stratifications rather than replicate and reinforce. Organizational change efforts are influenced by a myriad of factors including institutional history and campus climate; the community; local, state, and national issues; and key institutional stakeholders (students, staff, faculty, alumni, and board members). CDOs often face resistance as "they attempt to modify change-resistant institutional cultures" (Harvey, 2014, p. 92) and their efforts met with fear, protection of current practices, and conflict (Kezar & Eckel, 2000; Kotter, 1995; Stanley, 2016; Tierney, 1997).

These theories collectively contributed to the research questions by highlighting intersections between race, gender, and the challenges of organizational change around DEI. Thus, they serve as an important lens to center and make meaning of my experience as an inaugural Black woman chief diversity officer at a public regional institution in the South guiding organizational change efforts.

METHOD

Autoethnography is the methodology used to explore my experiences shaping the development and implementation of the university's first diversity, equity, and inclusion strategic plan. Autoethnography is an approach to research and writing that seeks to describe and systematically analyze personal experience in order to understand cultural experience (Ellis et al., 2010). Combining autobiography and ethnography, this methodological approach affords the research the opportunity to connect self-exploration and self-awareness with cultural description with the goal of better understanding themselves and others (Bhattacharya, 2017; Ellis & Bochner, 2000; McGowan, 2022). This form of academic writing is commonly used to explore racialized and gender experiences within higher education (Espino et al., 2010; Hernandez et al., 2015; McGowan, 2022; Reddick & Sáenz, 2012). Ellis et al. (2010) state that:

When researchers write autoethnographies, they seek to produce aesthetic and evocative thick descriptions of personal and interpersonal experience. They accomplish this by first discerning patterns of cultural experience evidenced by field notes, interviews, and/or artifacts, and then describing these patterns using facets of storytelling (e.g., character and plot development), showing and telling, and alterations of authorial voice. Thus, the autoethnographer not only tries to make personal experience meaningful and cultural experience engaging, but also, by producing accessible texts, she or he may be able to reach wider and more diverse mass audiences that traditional research usually disregards, a move that can make personal and social change possible for more people (Bochner, 1997; Ellis, 1995; Goodall, 2006; hooks, 1994).

Observations, documents, conversations with key institutional stakeholders serve as the primary sources of data in this study.

INSTITUTIONAL CONTEXT

CDOs work within a university culture is born from the institution's history and values and these characteristics impact the experiences of Black women faculty and administrators at predominately White institutions (Evans & Chun, 2007). This study took place over a two-year period (Fall 2018 – Fall 2020) at a southern midsize public liberal arts university founded in 1954 as a junior college and become independent in 1993. The institution enrolls nearly 11,000 students, offering 100 undergraduate and over 30 graduate-level (doctoral educational specialist, masters) major fields of study including specialized concentrations across six academic colleges. The demographic profile is such that a predominately White faculty and staff serve a predominately White student population.

As institutions of higher learning increasingly establish CDO positions (Nixon, 2017; Williams & Wade-Golden, 2013;), each institution tends to have a unique journey that leads toward the creation of that position (Arnold & Kowalski-Braun, 2012). In alignment with the university's strategic plan adopted in 2015, the university set out to hire an inaugural CDO "and develop a Diversity Council that advances a campus-wide diversity, equity and inclusion plan to assess visible and invisible barriers and establish a system to enable the University to operate as an inclusive institution by December 2017" (2016-2021 CCU Strategic Plan). The university initially launched a search for a Vice President for Diversity and Inclusion in December 2016. According to the Fiscal Year 2016-17 Accountability Report, re-alignment of roles at the University resulted in the search being aborted. The position was revised and a search for an Assistant Vice President (AVP) for Diversity and Inclusion was launched in July 2017. I began my tenure as AVP for Diversity and Inclusion and Chief Diversity Officer in August 2018, reporting directing the Vice President for Executive Initiatives/Chief of Staff. In this role I served on Executive Council, a group of functional administrators representing all areas of the university. Serving in an advisory capacity and meeting bi-monthly, the mission of the Executive Council is to regularly review the operations of the University, review policies that filter up through various departments throughout the University to be presented for final approval from the President and Board of Trustees, and advise the President's Cabinet on matters affecting the University at large. For approximately one year during the time period examined in this study, I was one of two Black women on this council. The remaining time I was the only Black woman on this council.

In July 2019, as part of a re-alignment of roles at the institution, the CDO position was elevated to Vice President for Diversity, Equity, and Inclusion, with the Vice President for Diversity, Equity, and Inclusion reporting directly to the University President and serving on Executive Council and President's Cabinet. President's Cabinet is comprised of senior-level administrators representing all areas university who serve as executive-level support to the University president. For the year I served on President's Cabinet examined in this study, I was one of two women on this cabinet – one Black and one White. This realignment also established a Division of Diversity, Equity, and Inclusion, with the Office of Diversity and Inclusion, Intercultural and Inclusion Student Services, and Accessibility and Disability Services as part of the newly created division. Accessibility and Disability Services had previously been housed in Student Affairs.

As outlined in the university's five-year strategic plan, developing a diversity council that advances a campus-wide diversity, equity, and inclusion plan was a key deliverable for institutional stakeholders. In Fall 2018, an existing council was renamed and its charge was expanded. The Access, Inclusion, and Diversity Council (AIDC) was created to be an advisory and leadership team responsible for developing, overseeing, and monitoring University-wide efforts to achieve itss commitment to diversity and inclusion as central to the vision, mission, and values. A broad group of institutional members were invited to participate in order to ensure a campus-wide grassroots approach to identifying tactics and strategies. Co-chaired by the CDO and Director of Accessibility and Disability Services, a White woman, this Council had the power to create a strategic plan; oversee the implementation of the diversity, equity, and inclusion strategic plan; assess, monitor, and report on progress toward achieving strategic diversity goals; and review and revise (as needed) the university's diversity, equity, and inclusion goals and strategies. The purpose of the strategic plan was to create structural and institution wide commitment (Williams & Wade-Golden, 2007).

In January 2019, students, staff, and faculty were invited to participate in the first All-Campus Climate Survey to help the university better understand student, staff, and faculty perspectives and experiences related to their work and study. Four main themes emerged from various diversity, equity, and inclusion efforts including the Climate Report (released January 2020), from which goals and objectives and strategies were developed: 1. Representation, Equity, and Access; 2. Campus Climate; 3. Inclusive Teaching and Professional Development; and 4. Institutional Leadership and Accountability. These themes were used to develop an initial draft of the diversity, equity, and inclusion strategic plan.

Subsequently, in February 2020 all members of the campus community were invited to participate in strategic engagement sessions to discuss the report's findings, identify key areas of strength, solicit community input about specific actions needed to address areas of opportunity, engage in conversations about the initial draft of the plan, and provide comment and feedback. The sessions were held over a two-week period and were available via Live Stream for those unable to attend in person. After a designated comment period and meetings with numerous constituent groups, the CDO incorporated the majority of recommended changes and submitted the final plan to student, staff, and faculty governance committees for approval. The final plan was formally approved by all three committees in November 2020.

DATA ANALYSIS, TRUSTWORTHINESS, AND POSITIONALITY

Data Analysis

The themes that emerge from the data analysis were generated and analyzed over a two-year period (Fall 2018 – Fall 2020). The entire process involved gathering great deal of data from multiple sources, including feedback from the strategic engagement sessions, notes from formal and informal conversations with institutional stakeholders, notes from regular debriefing conversations with Division of Diversity, Equity, and Inclusion staff and members of the Access, Inclusion, and Diversity Council, and personal narratives about my experience leading this institutional effort. After several initial readings of data, themes were identified using a deductive coding process to identify codes in each data source. The codes were organized into two high-level themes.

Trustworthiness

To ensure trustworthiness and credibility, I communicated regularly with peer debriefers, current and former CDOs at other institutions, and faculty/staff diversity allies to clarify and make meaning of my unique experience as the first chief diversity officer and first Black woman chief diversity officer to lead at the institution. These conversations informed the coding processes and the development of the themes.

Positionality

As a Black woman who has worked at multiple predominately White institutions in the northern and southern regions of the country, I recognize that my identities were essential to the conceptualization of this study, as well as the analysis. Furthermore, being a first-generation college graduate, a tenured full professor, and being a Northerner hired from outside of the institution with no previous affiliation (i.e. graduate or parent/relative of a graduate) afforded me a unique perspective.

FINDINGS

The objective of this study is to illuminate the experiences of an inaugural Black woman chief diversity officer at a public regional institution in the South, with a focus on my experience leading the strategic planning process. Two themes were identified from a deductive analysis of the data: "Can You Be Trusted? You Aren't One of Us," and "Is This Your Job? You Aren't My Boss?" Each theme is presented below.

Can You Be Trusted? You Aren't One of Us

Identifying potential challenges to success and learning about the history of the diversity, equity, and inclusion work at a given institution is critical for CDOs as they begin to develop a strategic plan (Arnold & Kowalski-Braun 2012). During formal and information conversations and meetings with various offices and departments, I came to understand quickly that the campus culture, particularly for faculty and staff, was characterized by a lack of trust in the leadership. Known for low levels of attrition, many stakeholders had been at the institution long enough to experience the relatively fast growth of the institution; worked through numerous reorganizations; and expressed a belief that with this growth came a growing lack of transparency about the inner working of the institution and decision-making processes. As a result, many faculty and staff were predisposed to meet new initiatives or strategic directions from a representative of the administration, particularly 'another new administrator' with skepticism and suspicion.

In an effort to build support for the campus climate survey (which would serve as the foundation for the strategic plan), I spent a significant portion of my first few months in the position meeting with as many people and groups as possible, speaking specifically about the ways in which my CDO position (as a change agent), my faculty roots and sensibilities, and the intentionally collaborative process being used to develop the strategic plan (starting with the survey) could help usher in a new era of transparency with the goal of building trust (Bolman & Deal, 2003). The climate survey instrument was developed in consultation with faculty, staff, and students. Subject matter experts from the campus community, the university's institutional research office, and survey research experts from external consulting firms also collaborated on the development of the survey. In addition, the survey was anonymous, meaning that the project did not collect identifying information of individual subjects (e.g., names, address, email, etc.) to ensure that individual responses would not be linked with participants' identities. Working with the Access, Inclusion, and Diversity Council, I also assured students, staff, and faculty that the results of the survey would be made available to the campus, as there was a strong fear that the results be locked away for no one to see again, particularly if the results were not positive. CDOs can serve as change agents but they are most effective when their positions operate within an organizational structure that ensures and promotes among many things, effective communication, honesty, trustworthiness, and openness to change (Stanley, 2016). The preexisting climate and organizational culture undoubtedly affected my experience leading the strategic planning process.

The idea of trust, specifically trust in my ability to do my job effectively, was also rooted in assumptions about race, gender and the nature of diversity work. In her study of the experiences of five women of color serving as college and university CDOs, Nixon (2017) found

If a CDO's social identities aligned with the those of groups for whom she advocated, she risked allegations that she was acting in her own self-interest...The assumption is that women and people of color care about diversity in some sort of knee-jerk capacity and that they raise alarm bells even when concerns are not warranted. (p. 312)

In three distinct journal entries, I reflected on conversations with campus stakeholders where my objectivity and motives for engaging in this work were explicitly questioned. Talking specifically about aspects of the strategic plan framed around inclusive teaching and diversity, equity, and inclusion professional development, a White male staff member wrote in an email to a White female staff member that he would never support any diversity, equity, and inclusion efforts on campus because as a Black woman, I was clearly biased. The White female staff member, a staff diversity ally, shared the email with me and was one of two people I debriefed with about the message. Debriefing with this colleague was useful but somewhat unusual, as I took to heart the advice that women of color "should be careful about whom they trust and what information they share" (Mitchell & Miller, 2011, p. 203).

Perceived lack of trust can fuel feelings of marginalization and the sense of being the perpetual outsider. Speaking with one CDO, Nixon (2017, p. 306) highlights a similar experience, noting that one of the participants in her study expressed her belief that "CDO-ing is seen as a 'colored thing,' resulting in 'double-triple marginalization, by gender, by ethnicity, and by virtue of one's work." Similarly, Niemann (2012) further point out that diversity work further isolates women of color CDOs because of the implicit assumption that diversity work is feminine work and best performed by those with marginalized identities. Women in male dominated environments find it harder to gain credibility and facing misperceptions about their identity (Kanter, 1977; Turner et al. 2011). This is especially true for women of color, when maleness and Whiteness are the invisible unquestioned standards of unbiased expertise (Turner et al., 2011).

Finally, I also recognized that for some campus stakeholders, trust was also rooted in assumptions about my connection to the institution. In her study of women of color CDOs, Nixon (2017) notes that several participants felt they were insiders by virtue of their positions in the organization and seat at the leadership table, yet outsiders as women of color, often times the only women of color in senior leadership at their institutions. While I too experienced this sense of marginalization because of my race, gender, and leadership status, my journal entries also highlighted a sense of isolation and marginalization because I was a Northerner (or Yankee) hired from outside of the institution with no previous affiliation (i.e. a graduate or parent/relative of a graduate). Interestingly, while I was hired as the first CDO, the work of diversity, equity, and inclusion had rested primarily on the shoulders of a Black woman, native South Carolinian, who had been part of the institution for almost 40 years, first as a student then a staff member and educator. One of her last roles was the director of Intercultural and Inclusion Student Services. In some interactions with key stakeholders during the strategic planning process, I recall feeling there was an unspoken expectation that I would resemble, in attributes and approach, the former director. A similar desire to clone is often identified as cognitive shortcut that leads to bias in hiring (Moody, 2015).

In one feedback meeting focused on progress metrics to assess our ability to retain a diverse faculty and staff (theme - Representation, Equity and Access), it was suggested by a White female faculty member that by supporting and promoting the creation of faculty and staff affinity/employee resource groups, I was bringing a 'Northern sensibility' to this work rather than promoting a best practice, despite the growing body of literature highlighting the importance of these groups to create inclusive environments and minimize turnover (Onyeador et al., 2021). As we moved through the strategic planning process, I intentionally spent time communicating my (distant) family ties to the South and my appreciation for the contributions of my predecessor in an effort to build relationship and trust.

"Is This Your Job? You Aren't My Boss"

From my first day in the CDO role, much of my time was spent meeting as many campus stakeholders as possible to build relationships, establish credibility, and promote guiding principles to assign with aligning institution-wide DEI efforts (Arnold & Kowalski-Braun, 2012). This included sharing an institutional model of DEI where the responsibility for this specific work falls on everyone within the community as opposed to one unit, department, or office and openly talking about CDO duties and responsibilities which include leading, implementing, and making changes to DEI initiatives, programming, and education in an effort to recruit and retain a diverse campus community and cultivate an inclusive environment (Williams & Wade-Golden, 2013). As the campus moved deeper into the strategic planning process and discussed issues like institutional accountability and holding collaborators responsible for making progress, questions would occasionally arise about the role of the CDO and the CDO's authority to create a strategic plan that would impact all aspects of campus.

Extant research suggests that as CDOs advocate and guide efforts designed to transform existing policies, processes, and practices, questioning the authority of the CDO as a form of resistance is common. Executive positioning is presumed to aid against this (Williams & Wade-Golden, 2007). During the time period of this study, the reporting structure for the CDO position changed and by the time we began strategic engagement sessions on campus, my title changed from Assistant Vice President (reporting to a Vice President) to Vice President (reporting directly to the President). The reorganization also gave me responsibility for multiple reporting units and the ability to hire a program manager to lead faculty and staff DEI education and training programs I created and led in my role as CDO. This structure, called the portfolio divisional model, is the most comprehensive and integrated model for implementing DEI goals (Williams & Wade-Golden, 2007). The CDO title suggests the power and authority to enforce the policies created to guide the institution toward its DEI goals. Yet, having the CDO positioned at the executive level during the later portion of the strategic planning process gave me direct access to the President and the ability over time to establish relationships with other Vice Presidents in a way that I had not experienced when I was reporting to a Vice President and served on the Executive Council only. The ability to forge relationships with other senior-level leaders, promote shared responsibility and encourage them to validate the collective work of diversity, equity, and inclusion with their staffs and team members was the biggest long-term benefit of this structural change – but it was a benefit that I did not immediately receive when the restructuring occurred. Thus, the change in positioning was not an immediate source of influence (Williams & Wade-Golden 2007) and did not create greater visibility and legitimacy given link to president (Gravley-Stack et al., 2016; Williams et al., 2005) during the strategic planning process.

Despite title change, I also understood that, for some stakeholders, the perception (and reality) that the CDO lacked the power to ultimately hold campus partners accountable for diversity, equity, and inclusion efforts embedded in the strategic plan influenced their willingness to commit themselves and their units to this work. As noted above, moving toward to the portfolio divisional model would eventually afford me the opportunity to build deeper relationships with senior-level administrators. As these relationships solidified, the idea that the CDO (as a senior-level colleague) would provide leadership consistent with the functioning of other high-ranking, senior level administrators was taken more seriously (Williams & Wade-Golden, 2007), opening the door for deeper and at times difficult dialogues about shared responsibility and a culture of accountability.

As evidenced in the strategic engagement sessions, the lack of authority and perceived credibility mattered for some stakeholders. One participant expressed concern that some of the proposed objectives and progress metrics should be designed exclusively by their office/department and "the diversity folks should stay in their lane." Others were open to working toward various diversity, equity, and inclusion goals but only if their supervisor told them to or if it was part of their formal job description. Coincidently, this comment was made around the time that, in partnership with Human Resources, I worked to integrate performance characteristic specific to diversity, equity and inclusion in the Employee Performance Management process. The changes were implemented in Fall 2020, around the time that the strategic plan was approved by the governance bodies.

Changing an institution's diversity culture is a collective undertaking that requires among other things, accountability (Stanley, 2016). Without the ability to penalize or reward individuals and units based on their degree of progress with the diversity, equity, and inclusion strategic plan, some stakeholders made it clear that even if the strategic plan were approved, they were unwilling to abide by and comply with initiatives generated out the strategic planning process.

RECOMMENDATIONS FOR PRACTICE

While each institution will take a unique path for successfully creating and implementing a CDO position and developing a strategic plan, I believe that my experience highlights the critical importance of committing to the development of the inaugural CDO position utilizing the portfolio divisional model. CDOs have an incredibly difficult role, one that is often misunderstood by other institutional actors or viewed as non-essential. Given the marginalization women of color often experience in academia based on the intersection of their race and gender and the reality that women and people of color mostly take on these roles, taking the time to develop the position using the most comprehensive and integrated design for implementing DEI goals can help set a CDO up for success. Simply put, being a CDO is a difficult job where challenge and resistance is to be expected, but doing this work as a Black woman at a predominately White institution in the South makes the work even more challenging. To support inaugural Black women CDOs, institutions should not underestimate the significance of positional power and create a structure that enhances the development and integration of strategic DEI plans. I acknowledge that having this organizational model in place at the beginning of my tenure would not made some of the issues regarding trust mentioned earlier simply disappear, but I strongly believe that it would have created a solid foundation for me, as an inaugural CDO, to build upon; signaled a stronger institutional commitment to DEI; and highlighted the significance of the CDO position and the work.

A key component of the portfolio divisional model is the creation of a team within the division to guarantee that the responsibility for advancing DEI as critical components of the organization's culture is broadly shared and model the core value that responsibility for DEI falls on everyone within the community as opposed to one unit, department, or office. Prior to the reorganization that occurred in the second year of this study, I worked alone in the newly created Office of Diversity and Inclusion with minimal administrative support from a colleague in another division. While the strategic plan was eventually adopted and implemented, accomplishing this task with no central administrative support and operations staff was extremely challenging and minimized my ability to meet as often as I desired with students, staff and faculty members. To support inaugural Black women CDOs, institutions should provide the resources and staff necessary to make the work of the CDO possible.

RECOMMENDATIONS FOR BLACK WOMEN CDOs

My experience leading the strategic planning process as the inaugural CDO was generally positive, yet, in hindsight, I now recognize some choices I made (good and not so good) that impacted me greatly and wish to share them with other Black women pursuing CDO positions at predominately White institutions in the South.

First, I ultimately chose not to use my voice and advocate for what I knew was needed to successfully implement a CDO position at the university. I accepted this position knowing that the job would be challenging given the organizational structure. Yet, once in the position, fully experiencing the weight of the work and existing climate, I could have sat down with the leadership to advocate for additional resources and explicitly renegotiate the timeline to create and implement the climate survey and strategic plan. In an environment where trust was an issue and I clearly lacked authority, taking more time to develop relationships and build alliances with stakeholders (including faculty, staff, students, board members, and community members) that exert influence over the strategic direction of the institution would have been beneficial. As the newly minted CDO, I was charged with developing and implementing a campus climate survey in my first 6 months in the role. The climate survey report would then serve as the foundation for the strategic planning process. There simply was not enough time to dive into frequent conversations with the community and through conversations, identify and pursue smaller but symbolically important wins that could have strengthen ties between the CDO and various constituency groups. Coincidently, I too like the inaugural CDO at GVSU, believed it useful and important to address in my first year in the role crippling issues impacting the LGBTQIA+ community (Arnold & Kowalski-Braun, 2011). However, it was quickly apparent that without real support, delivering what was identified as the key deliverables (the climate survey and report, the development of the council, the strategic plan, and the creation of a DEI training program) would leave less time to have those conversation and make those connections.

As for why I did not use my voice, I can honestly share that I was afraid to say anything and resigned myself to push through with the available resources because the CDO position was subject to state regulations which included a 12- month probationary period. In that window of time, the University reserved the right to terminate my employment at any time without cause, and with or without notice. Also, in accepting the position, I learned that I would have to wait 12 months before going up for tenure. Simply knowing that I could lose the position and employment for any reason with no tenured professorship to go back to, I made the decision to put my head down and do my best. As I continued to engage in this process, I also found myself increasingly concerned that any failure on my part, with or without the necessary resources, would somehow confirm and validate the lack of trust I felt from some stakeholders.

It was also during this time that I realized that the only way I was going to successfully navigate this challenge was to take time to care for myself emotionally, spiritually, and physically. Even the best CDO position is challenging and requires practitioners to take time to engage in restorative practices that bring balance and joy. I took some time to seriously consider what I needed to feel healthy and strong. Fortunately, my family quickly found a church home, so it did not take long for us to start building community in the church and develop supportive relationships through bible study and life groups. I connected with a therapist who helped me process work and life challenges. I also found it essential to move my body and made it a habit to use my lunch time to do some form of exercise. Together, these activities kept me grounded, positive in spirit, and efficacious while leading the strategic planning process. Thus, my experience very closely aligns with previous research which found that Black women in diversity roles often explore coping mechanisms to navigate their professional environment (Johnson 2021).

CONCLUSION

The hiring of a chief diversity officer in universities and colleges across the nation signals a greater commitment to addressing -isms and -phobias and doing the challenging yet critically important work of diversity, equity, and inclusion. Drawing on theories of organizational change, critical race theory, and critical race feminism to make meaning of and interpret my experience as an inaugural Black woman chief diversity officer at a public regional institution in the South, this chapter highlights the ways in which identity, specifically race and gender, directly impacts one's social reality (Wing, 1997; Wing, 2003) and relate deeply to the subjective experience.

Findings from this study illustrate that institutional culture and identity shaped perceptions about the CDO as an outsider not to be trusted, despite my efforts to be as transparent and communicative as possible. The findings also highlight the critical importance of organizational structure, including the positioning of the CDO, to support the success of the CDO in the strategic planning process. The limited scope of this study narrows the generalizability of these findings. Future studies should move beyond this single institution to explore the experiences of numerous inaugural Black women CDOs in the South, as well as other regions. Despite these limitations, this study advances the research on Black women in higher education, spotlighting the distinctive, layered and intersectional journey of one Black woman CDO working in predominately White institution in the South.

ACKNOWLEDGMENT

This research received no specific grant from any funding agency in the public, commercial, or not-for-profit sectors.

REFERENCES

Arnold, J., & Kowalski-Braun, M. (2011). The journey to an inaugural chief diversity officer: Preparation, implementation and beyond. *Innovative Higher Education, 37*(1), 27–36. doi:10.100710755-011-9185-9

Bass, B. M., & Avolio, B. J. (1993). Transforming leadership and organizational culture. *Public Administration Quarterly, 17*, 112–121.

Bell, D. A. (2000). *Race, racism, and American law*. Palmer Press.

Bhattacharya, K. (2017). *Fundamentals of qualitative research: A practical guide*. Routledge. doi:10.4324/9781315231747

Bochner, A. P. (1997). It's about time: Narrative and the divided self. *Qualitative Inquiry, 3*(4), 418–438. doi:10.1177/107780049700300404

Bolman, L., & Deal, T. (2003). *Reframing organizations: Artistry, choice and leadership*. Jossey-Bass and Sons, Inc.

Collins, P. H. (1986). Learning from the outsider within: The sociological significance of Black feminist thought. *Social Problems, 33*(6), S14–S32. doi:10.2307/800672

Collins, P. H. (2000). *Black feminist thought: Knowledge, consciousness, and the politics of empowerment,* (2nd ed.). Unwin Hyman.

Crenshaw, K. W. (1991). Mapping the margins: Intersectionality, identity politics, and violence against women of color. *Stanford Law Review, 43*(6), 1241–1299. doi:10.2307/1229039

Creswell, J. W. (2007). *Qualitative inquiry and research design: Choosing among five approaches,* (2nd ed.). Sage.

Delgado, R., & Stefanic, J. (2017). *Critical race theory: An introduction*. NYU Press.

Ellis, C. (1995). *Final negotiations: A story of love, loss, and chronic illness*. Temple University Press.

Ellis, C., Adams, T. E., & Bochner, A. P. (2000). Autoethnography, personal narrative, reflexivity. In N. K. Denzin & Y. S. Lincoln (Eds.), *Handbook of qualitative researchm* (2nd ed., pp. 733–768). Sage.

Ellis, C., Adams, T. E., & Bochner, A. P. (2010). Autoethnography: An overview. *Forum Qualitative Sozialforschung / Forum: Qualitative. Social Research, 12*(1).

Espino, M. M., Muñoz, S. M., & Kiyama, J. M. (2010). Transitioning from doctoral study to the academy: Theorizing trenzas of identity for Latina sister scholars. *Qualitative Inquiry, 16*(10), 804–818. doi:10.1177/1077800410383123

Evans, A., & Chun, E. B. (2007). Are the walls really down? Behavioral and organizational barriers to faculty and staff diversity. *ASHE Higher Education Report, 33*(1), 1–139.

Goodall, B. H. L. (2006). *A need to know: The clandestine history of a CIA family*. Left Coast Press.

Gravley-Stack, K., Ray, C. M., & Peterson, C. M. (2016). Understanding the subjective experiences of the Chief Diversity officer: A q method study. *Journal of Diversity in Higher Education*, *9*(2), 95–112. doi:10.1037/dhe0000012

Harris-Perry, M. V. (2011). *Sister citizen: Shame, stereotypes, and Black women in America*. Yale University Press.

Harvey, W. B. (2014). Chief diversity officers and the wonderful world of academe. *Journal of Diversity in Higher Education*, *7*(2), 92–100. doi:10.1037/a0036721

Hernandez, K. A. C., Ngunjiri, F. W., & Chang, H. (2015). Exploiting the margins in higher education: A collaborative autoethnography of three foreign-born female faculty of color. *International Journal of Qualitative Studies in Education: QSE*, *28*(5), 533–551. doi:10.1080/09518398.2014.933910

Hooks, B. (1994). *Teaching to transgress: Education as the practice of freedom*. New York, NY, Routledge.

Howard-Hamilton, M. F. (2003). *Meeting the needs of African American women*. Jossey-Bass.

Johnson, T. B. (2021). The experiences of Black women in diversity roles at 4-Year predominantly White institutions. [Theses and Dissertations]. Illinois State University, USA. 1378. https://ir.library.illinoisstate.edu/etd/1378/

Kanter, R. (1977). *Men and women of the corporation*. Basic Books.

Kezar, A., & Eckel, P. (2000). *The effect of institutional culture on change strategies in higher education: Universal principles or culturally responsive concepts?* ERIC Clearinghouse on Higher Education.

Kotter, J. P. (1995). Leading change: Why transformation efforts fail. *Harvard Business Review*, *73*, 59–67.

Lloyd, J. B. (2009). Implications of race and gender in higher education administration: An African American women's perspective. *Advances in Developing Human Resources*, *11*(5), 606–618. doi:10.1177/1523422309351820

Marana, J. A. J. (2016). *The lived experiences of women of color chief diversity officers* . [Doctoral dissertation]. The Claremont Graduate University, USA.

McGowan, B. L. (2022). Teaching diversity, equity, and inclusion outside of the classroom: An autoethnographic account of a Black male faculty in residence. *Journal of Diversity in Higher Education*, *15*(3), 354–364. doi:10.1037/dhe0000289

Milem, J. F., Chang, M. J., & Antonio, A. L. (2005). *Making diversity work on campus: A research-bases perspective*. Association of American Colleges and Universities.

Mitchell, N. A., & Miller, J. J. (2011). The unwritten rules of the academy: A balancing act for women of color. In G. Jean-Marie & B. Lloyd-Jones (Eds.), *Women of color in higher education: Changing directors and new perspectives,* (pp. 193–218). Emerald Group. doi:10.1108/S1479-3644(2011)0000010013

Moody, J. (2015). *Rising above cognitive errors: Improving searches, evaluations, and decision-making*. CreateSpace Independent Publishing Platform.

Ngwainmbi, J. M. (2004). Feminism, feminist scholarship, and social integration of women: The struggle for African-American women. *Journal of International Women's Studies*, *5*(5), 93–104.

Niemann, Y. F. (2012). Lessons from the experiences of women of color working in academia. In G. Gutiérrez y Muhs, Y. F. Niemann, C. G. González, & A. P. Harris (Eds.), *Presumed incompetent: The intersections of race and class for women in academia,* (pp. 446–499). University Press of Colorado. doi:10.2307/j.ctt4cgr3k.40

Nixon, M. L. (2017). Experiences of women of color university chief diversity officers. *Journal of Diversity in Higher Education*, *10*(4), 301–317. doi:10.1037/dhe0000043

Onyeador, I. N., Hudson, S. T. J., & Lewis, N. A. Jr. (2021). Moving beyond implicit bias training: Policy insights for increasing organizational diversity. *Policy Insights from the Behavioral and Brain Sciences*, *8*(1), 19–26. doi:10.1177/2372732220983840

Reddick, R., & Sáenz, V. (2012). Coming home: Hermanos académicos reflect on past and present realities as professors at their alma mater. *Harvard Educational Review*, *82*(3), 353–380. doi:10.17763/haer.82.3.g311m72q432062uq

Smith, W. A. (2008). Higher education: Racial battle fatigue. In R. T. Schaefer (Ed.), *Encyclopedia of race, ethnicity, and society,* (pp. 615–618). SAGE Publications.

Stanley, C. A. (2016). Reflections on changing a university's diversity culture. *Insight Into Diversity*. www.insightinto diversity.com.

Stanley, W., Watson, K. L., Reyes, J. M., & Varela, K. S. (2019). Organizational change and the chief diversity officer: A case study of institutionalizing a diversity plan. *Journal of Diversity in Higher Education, 12*(3), 255–265. doi:10.1037/dhe0000099

Stuart, R. (2010). Diversity to the next level. *Diverse Issues in Higher Education*, *27*(8), 12–14. http://diverseeducation.com/

Tate, W. F. IV. (1997). Chapter 4: Critical race theory and education: History, theory, and implications. *Review of Research in Education*, *22*(1), 195–247. doi:10.3102/0091732X022001195

Tierney, W. G. (1997). Organizational socialization in higher education. *The Journal of Higher Education, 68*(1), 1–16. doi:10.2307/2959934

Turner, C. S. V. (2002). Women of color in academe: Living with multiple marginality. *The Journal of Higher Education*, *73*(1), 74–93. doi:10.1080/00221546.2002.11777131

Turner, C. S. V., González, J. C., & Wong, K. (2011). Faculty women of color: The critical nexus of race and gender. *Journal of Diversity in Higher Education*, *4*(4), 199–211. doi:10.1037/a0024630

Vaught, S. E. (2008). Writing against racism: Telling white lies and reclaiming culture. *Qualitative Inquiry*, *14*(4), 566–589.

Williams, D. A., Berger, J. B., & McClendon, S. A. (2005). *Toward a model of inclusive excellence and change in postsecondary institutions*. Association of American Colleges and Universities.

Williams, D. A., & Wade-Golden, K. C. (2007). *The chief diversity officer: A primer for college and university presidents*. American Council on Education.

Williams, D. A., & Wade-Golden, K. C. (2013). The chief diversity officer. Sterling, VA. Stylus Publishing, LLC.

Wing, A. K. (Ed.). (1997). *Critical race feminism: A reader*. NYU Press.

Wing, A. K. (Ed.). (2003). *Critical race feminism: A reader,* (2nd ed.). NYU Press.

Worthington, R. (2020). Antiracism as an institutional imperative: A primer and review. file:///C:/Users/Gigi%20Secuban/Downloads/Antiracism%20and%20Self-Study%20Slides.pdf.

Worthington, R. L., Stanley, C. A., & Lewis, W. T. Sr. (2014). National Association of Diversity Officers in Higher Education standards of professional practice for chief diversity officers. *Journal of Diversity in Higher Education*, *7*(4), 227–234. doi:10.1037/a0038391

Yosso, T.J. (2005). Whose culture has capital? A critical race theory discussion of community cultural wealth. Race, Ethnicity and Education, 8(1), 69–91.

ADDITIONAL READING

Collins, P. H. (1989). The social construction of Black feminist thought. *Signs (Chicago, Ill.)*, *14*(4), 745–773. doi:10.1086/494543

James, R. J. (2022). *Higher calling: A qualitative study of the lived experiences of Black women presidents of 4-year colleges and universities.* [Doctoral dissertation]. USC, USA. https://scholarcommons.sc.edu/etd/6576

Myers, L. W. (2002). *A broken silence: Voices of African American women in the academy*. Bergin & Garvey.

Olow, S. (2021). A qualitative study of lived experiences of Black women in leadership positions in K-12 educational settings. *Educational and Organizational Learning and Leadership Dissertations, 9.* https://scholarworks.seattleu.edu/eoll-dissertations/9

Stone, P. M. (2018). *How Have Female African American Chief Diversity Officers (CDO) Made Meaning of the Role Political Skill Plays at Predominately White Research Institutions?* (Order No. 10744139). ProQuest Dissertations & Theses Global. (2011012566).

West, N. M. (2022). Embodying Black feminist epistemology to make green grass grow: The transition from administrator to academic for a Black woman in student affairs. *Journal of Diversity in Higher Education*, *15*(5), 630–642. doi:10.1037/dhe0000375

KEY TERMS AND DEFINITIONS

Black: A term used to describe members of the African diaspora, regardless of national origin.

Chief Diversity Officer: A senior leader who develops and implements DEI initiatives within an organization and advances DEI as core values and critical components of the organization's culture.

Diversity: Identity in its various forms and expressions, including, but not limited to, race, ethnicity, gender identity, gender expression, sexual orientation, sex, socioeconomic status, language, national origin, religion, age, (dis)ability status and political perspective.

Equity: Promoting justice within procedures and processes and the removal of barriers that prevent full participation, as well as the provision of information and resources that empower individuals to fully engage in all aspects of community life.

Inclusion: The involvement and empowerment of all people to create a climate where differences are welcomed and all supported, respected, valued, and heard.

Strategic Planning: A process in which an organization's leaders define their vision for the future and identify their organization's goals and objectives.

Chapter 4
The Fierce Urgency of No: Moving From Aspirational to Operational

Kerri-Ann M. Smith
https://orcid.org/0000-0002-8184-3709
Queensborough Community College, USA

Timothy G. Lynch
College of Staten Island, USA

ABSTRACT

The discussion in this chapter affirms the intentional and collaborative partnership built between the Inaugural Faculty Fellow for Diversity, Equity, and Inclusivity (FFDEI), a Black, middle-aged, immigrant woman, who is a tenured member of the faculty, and a senior executive, a White, middle-aged man at a community college. The chapter engages reflection as analysis, situating the experience of a Black woman in a quasi-administrative DEI role and that of a White male senior executive in the context of historical and contemporary allyship and accompliceship. Coupled with historical references to emphasize the significance of transformational leadership, the partnership leads to the development of a values-centered model for DEI work at an urban community college in one of the country's largest university systems.

INTRODUCTION

The authors work at a community college located in the most diverse county in the United States. While the institution is designated as a Hispanice Serving Institution (HSI), its faculty and senior leadership are primarily White people. Community colleges are sites for innovation and transformation in all aspects of the academy. Pedagogy and leadership have the potential to blossom and bloom and, in the case of the institution discussed in this chapter, create outcomes that can shift and change conversations around diversity, equity, and inclusivity (DEI) when done intentionally.

The discussion in this chapter delineates the intentional and collaborative partnership built between the Inaugural Faculty Fellow for Diversity, Equity, and Inclusivity (FFDEI), a Black, middle-aged, immigrant woman, who is a tenured member of the faculty, and the former interim president and now

DOI: 10.4018/978-1-6684-3564-9.ch004

provost and senior vice president of the college, a White, middle-aged man. Central to the discussion are the perspectives, observations, and reflections of the Black woman, sharing the challenges and benefits of approaching a quasi-administrative role from a Black feminist perspective. The conversation includes the reflections of a White male senior administrator who was challenged to shift his lens from transactional to transformational to better serve the minoritized members of the campus community. At the intersection of their multiple identities and experiences, they find a collaborative synergy that situates their work in a context to advance the college's academic diversity, equity, and inclusivity agenda from aspirational to operational. Their reflections, coupled with historical references to allyship and accompliceship, emphasize the significance of transformational leadership, through a Values-Centered model for DEI work at an urban community college.

BACKGROUND

Black women have led revolutions in the quest for liberation for Black people for centuries. History accounts for the arduous, intellectual, emotional, and physical labor undertaken by Black women. Leaders such as Nanny of the Maroons, the Ghanaian-Jamaican matriarch, who famously led the First Maroon War against the British (McLean, 2017; Tuelon, 1973) moved the dial toward liberation for Black people. Later on, journalists Ida B. Wells, who cofounded the National Association for the Advancement of Colored People (NAACP), and Claudia Jones, the radical feminist whose work centered Black people across the globe (Boyce-Davies, 2016) challenged patriarchy and racism simulatenously. In later years, Anna Julia Cooper and Mary Church Terrell, Black women intellectuals who were instrumental to the suffrage movement and to Black liberation (Guy-Sheftall, 2009) and Black Panthers, Elaine Brown, Assata Shakur, Angela Davis, and Kathleen Neal Cleaver, joined in the collective action against oppression in the struggle for Black liberation (Cleaver, 1999). Contemporary women such as Tarana Burke, who founded the 2006 #MeToo movement in fierce defense of women's rights, and the founding of Black Lives Matter by Alicia Garza, Opal Tometi, and Patrisse Cullors, in 2013, have championed the current movement toward the liberation of Blacks in the United States of America and across the globe (BBC).

The aforementioned are members of a small corpus of myriad Black women who sacrificed comfort and convenience for the sake of radical liberation with the understanding that "the master's tools will never dismantle the master's house" (Lorde, 1984). Indubitably, these women had concerns and fears that were transmuted by their courage and determination to affect change, thus they persisted despite adversity to advance the work of justice. The same is true for Black women in higher education, particularly at institutions where White leadership predominates. At its inception, higher education in the United States was designed to cater to the needs of White men (Oluo, 2020). When Mary Jane Patterson, earned her bachelors degree in 1862, she became the first known Black American woman to achieve this goal (Journal of Blacks in Higher Education). It wasn't until 1921 that Georgianna Simpson became the first Black woman to earn a Ph.D. in the United States (Witynsky, 2021). Today, the complexity of being both woman and Black in higher education spaces continues to simultaneously render Black women invisible yet hypervisible and tokenized (Smith, Alves, Weathersby and Yi, 2019). Existing research shows that Black women are least represented at the highest rank of professor (Davis and Brown, 2017) and in senior administrative ranks in academic affairs. Invariably, underrepresentation leads to cultural taxation, disproportionate emotional labor, abject isolation, and an overbearing and inequitable service demands (Ahmed, 2012; Matthew, 2016; Padilla, 1994).

Allies and Accomplices

Although Black women have led and supported many movements to address oppression in the United States, there have been White allies who have contributed to these efforts through their service. Abolitionists such as John Brown and Benjamin Lay in the early 19th century, Cynthia Dunn and Herbert Kohl during the Civil Rights Movement (Brown, 2002), and contemporary antiracist scholars such as Tim Wise have joined arms with Black people to organize against White supremacy. These allies and accomplices acknowledge and leverage what Peggy McIntosh (1988) names their "White privilege" in support of Black liberation. McIntosh specifically highlights the qualities of both White and male privilege, stating that men rarely "go beyond acknowledging that women are disadvantaged to acknowledging that men have an unearned advantage" (p. 2) and goes on to name 46 ways in which White privilege presents in everyday life.

Oluo (2020) calls for a rejection of White male privilege as the status quo and advises that "those of us with privilege of race or status divorce ourselves from the lure of proximity to White male power," a path that has been deleterious for Black people throughout history (p. 276). Oluo illuminates what McIntosh's work failed to acknowledge—that there is an underlying assumption that the term "male" is based on Whiteness and proximity thereto, and the examples of male privilege noted in McIntosh's work may not be congruous with the historical positioning of Black men, who are not automatically assigned the same "unearned" privileges as White men. McIntosh (2010) posits, however, that acknowledging White or male privilege requires reflection and a commitment to using "unearned privilege" to enact change or to "weaken systems of unearned advantage" to dismantle systemic oppression (p. 7).

Concerning allyship, Erskine and Bilimoria (2019) suggest the use of "allyship" as a "verb that involves an active, lifelong, and consistent practice of unlearning beliefs and actions" (p. 321) and actively building relationships that leverage the power of the more dominant group in support of people of color, particularly Afro-diasporic women. Like McIntosh, Erskine and Bilimoria suggest that reflection and action, particularly around covert and overt power and privilege are tantamount to antiracist White allyship. They propose a few approaches for supporting Black women, in particular, such as "engaging in prosocial behaviors," "providing sponsorship, mentorship, and protection from adverse organizational dynamics," and "engaging in positive deviance and demonstrating the courage to interrupt the status quo" (p. 325-326) and affirm the positive outcomes of allyship for Black women in work spaces. The researchers also present a 2018 study conducted by LeanIn.Org and a subsequent Pew Research Center survey, acknowledging the complexity of gender-specific dynamics between White men/women and Black women, noting that White men face and fear critiques such as performative allyship, virtue signaling, opportunistic alignment, and might hesitate to mentor junior-level women because of #metoo considerations. According to the study, these concerns might deter White men in senior leadership positions from serving as allies to Black women, for fear of offending others or making themselves vulnerable to criticism from the outside.

Some scholars have registered opposition to the term 'ally,' stating that it functions more as a noun rather than a verb as allyship often lacks advocacy (Jackson et al., 2020; Powell & Kelly, 2017; Suyemoto et al., 2021). This opposition influenced their use of "accomplice" as a more apposite term for partnership dismantling systemic oppression. According to these scholars, White accomplices can effectively promote liberation for Black people by advocating for and even creating access to resources and power, particularly in spaces rooted in the White supremacy culture of exclusion, particularly when in leadership roles. The dimensions of transformational leadership theory provide a lens through which allyship and accompliceship can be analyzed in predominantly White higher educational spaces.

Transformational Leadership Theory

Transforming (Burns,1978) or *transformational* leadership (Bass,1985) theory is characterized by a leader's ability to strategically motivate, elevate, and empower to achieve organizational goals. Transformational leadership influences morality, values, and culture (Korejan & Shahbazi, 2016; Stewart, 2006). Conversely, *transactional leadership* is a form of management in which a leader enters an agreement with employees, and "the two parties (in principle) engage in a respectful exchange of valuables…so that the organization receives the benefits of the labor" (Reid & Dold, 2018, p. 94). In *transformational leadership,* morals and values influence outcomes based on the humanity of those involved in the organization, while in *transactional leadership,* valuables are central to performance measures and outcomes.

According to Burns (1978), the *transformational* leader is one whose vision awakens the consciousness of employees and who recognizes that "change occurs when the mutual interests are realized by action" (cited in Reid & Dold, 2018, p.94). Bass, on the other hand, asserts that change occurs when a leader facilitates the convergence of the fundamental goals, needs, beliefs, and values of people with a collective purpose that results in effective change. Stewart (2006) explains that Bass' research led to the belief that leaders are made and that an "optimal leader" (p.13) will engage the following dimenstions of transformational leadership:

1. *idealized influence*, characterized by modeling high ethical behaviors to earn respect and trust,
2. *inspirational motivation*, articulating a clear vision that inspires high standards and optimism,
3. *intellectual stimulation*, a community approach to planning while developing leaders who think independently to foster innovation,
4. *personal consideration*, which is characterized by mentorship and guidance that is intentionally designed to celebrate and build future leaders.

The dimensions of transformational leadership, coupled with accompliceship through shared power and access, can buttress the efforts of DEI practitioners, especially in today's dynamic, diverse, and rapidly evolving world. This chapter will explore how a DEI practitioner and a provost engage in practices associated with transformational leadership to achieve their goals.

MAIN FOCUS OF THE CHAPTER

When Trayvon Martin was murdered in 2012, the world met Rachel Jeantel, Martin's friend whose testimony became crucial to the case against his murdered, George Zimmerman. When Michael Brown was murdered by police officer Darren Wilson two years later, the world saw an image of an intrepid Ieshia Evans facing police officers in riot gear in the middle of a Baton Rouge, LA street at a #BlackLivesMatter protest. Two years following Brown's death, the world met Philando Castile's girlfriend, Diamond Reynolds, who bravely broadcast Castile's brutal murder at the hands of a police officer Jeronimo Yanez via Facebook Live, for the entire world to see. Black women have been key influencers in contemporary revolutionary change, at the risk of their own comfort. These contemporary changemakers echo the intrepid spirits of ancestors such as Mamie Till, the mother of Emmitt Till who insisted on an open casket at her son's funeral to display the brutality he suffered at the hands of White racists, and of revolutionary women such as Nanny of the Maroons and Harriet Tubman.

On May 25, 2020, in a deliberate act of courage, 17-year-old Darnella Frazier recorded the murder of George Floyd by police officer Derek Chauvin. Her 9:29 recording changed the way the United States and many of its institutions viewed police violence and advanced the ongoing fight for justice surrounding the deaths of Philando Castile, Jordan Davis, Michael Brown, Trayvon Martin, Walter Scott, Tamir Rice, Breonna Taylor, Attatiana Jefferson, Sandra Bland, and countless others towards accountability and justice. Frazier recorded with a purpose and with the understanding that her testimony would not be enough–that she needed evidence to show the world how injustice was heaped as a bag of hot coals on the neck of George Floyd. In a moment of violence and abject racism, Frazier knew she had a duty and obligation to Floyd and to our justice system (Frazier, 2021). Her video single-handedly ignited the quest toward justice for George Floyd in the form of a guilty conviction for his murderer, Derek Chauvin.

Frazier chose in a split second to be the help Floyd needed, even in death. At 17 years old, she knew that her voice was not enough–that she had to hold in her hand both the memory and the evidence to stare justice in the face and win as a Black woman. That decision changed the course of her life, and of history in the U.S., and of that experience, Frazier (2021) notes in an Instagram post, "even though this was a traumatic life-changing experience for me, I am proud of myself. If it weren't for my video, the world wouldn't have known the truth. I own that." Frazier's decision was both sacrificial and revolutionary. She was the catalyst for a global movement at the expense of her mental health, peace, safety, and comfort without knowing whether it would be worth the cause.

When the proliferation of Frazier's video catapulted the United States of America into an urgent state of radical racial reckoning, businesses, colleges, and universities everywhere were compelled to openly acknowledge and confront race and racism on a global scale and within their walls. A 2021 NASPA report notes that college presidents and marketing departments expediently drafted solidarity statements and convened task forces and committees to do fact-finding on the state of race and racism on their campuses. Faculty and staff of color began to reject feelings of isolation, tokenization, and rejection, subsequently challenging the status quo and holding institutions accountable. At the institution at which both authors of this article work, this incident became a catalyst for change that had been long overdue (NASPA, 2021).

Two Sides of the Story: Personal Narratives

Dr. Kerri-Ann M. Smith

At the time of George Floyd's murder, I was serving as a member of the president's advisory council for DEI and had spent almost seven years offering advice, suggestions, and resources to help move the college's diversity agenda forward. Our then interim president, a White man, requested that the Chief Diversity Officer (CDO), a White woman, send our committee (with high priority) an invitation to participate in a town hall for our college. Prior to the request, there had been a charged email exchange on our campus' community dialogue amongst White faculty members that was both unnerving and triggering. Faculty were sharing opinions with racially-charged undertones, all while remaining silent about the possible feelings of their Black and Brown colleagues during a season of racial unrest. At the same time, we were now being asked to help draft a statement to the campus, as other campuses had done, that would demonstrate that the college somehow cared about the Black members of our community–quintessential virtue signaling and transactional leadership.

The email request made me angry and resentful. Over the course of my then eight years at this institution, our campus leadership created what McNair et al (2020) call equity obstacles, as there was a strong and deliberate avoidance of race and racialized consequences (p. 25), and the leadership had seemingly committed to "the pervasiveness of White Privilege and Institutionalized Racism" (p. 34), along with a strong proclivity for "evasive reactions to racist incidents" (p. 37) on our campus. I was angry that the CDO had not reached out to the committee to share empathy or support prior to this moment but was now hastily invoking our intellectual labor without acknowledging our humanity. I was angry with the interim president for not having a relationship with what should have been *his* advisory committee and for conveniently soliciting support for what seemed like a vapid, disingenuous display of entitlement, privilege, and virtue signaling at the committee's expense. I did not know the interim president and had only interacted with him once in his entire time at the college. I did not know his position on DEI, but his intentions felt contrived, considering he had never shown interest in us as a group prior to this incident.

The dual agony of enduring a pandemic where Black people were dying at alarming rates, the despondency of watching a police officer take yet another Black life, and the gloom of feeling ignored as colleagues sent harmful emails all surfaced in anger as I stared at a request for labor during my summer vacation. To make matters worse, the request started with an excuse, not an apology, for not having reached out to us before. In the next sentence of the CDO's email, we were patronized with thanks for all of the things we [I] had said and been saying for years that had gone undone. The request for our labor, during our annual leave, and as we processed the pain of Floyd's death felt like anvils on my head, especially since neither the interim president nor his designee had attempted to intervene when racially-charged debates ensued on the virtual campus listserv, for the preservation of the mental health of our Black community members.

My response was to reply-all to the email, fiercely declaring that I would do no such duty and that if the president wanted my labor, he would need a different approach. I had just earned tenure a few months prior and was aware that my dossier for promotion to Associate Professor would have been on Dr. Lynch's desk within days or moments after my response, but I felt compelled to reject this audacious request and intrusion on my time and intelligence with what felt like zero concern for what my heart was enduring/grappling with, in the midst of the COVID-19 pandemic. It felt like tokenization and an assault on my time, brain, and energy, and I came out defensively swinging. Again, I interpreted this as emotional bludgeoning, rejection, and invisibility all at the same time, and we knew that given the momentum of the protests surrounding the death of George Floyd, this time had to be different.

Dr. Timothy G. Lynch

I was appointed Interim President of the college in late summer 2018, just 18 months following my appointment as provost, and served in that capacity for 23 months. During my time in office, the campus weathered the usual storms associated with reaccreditation, crumbling infrastructure, contract negotiations, and budgetary, fiscal, and enrollment challenges. We were also beset by a global pandemic, national and international racial unrest, and a deeply divided campus community.

Following the murder of George Floyd and subsequent protests which occurred in the waning days of my presidency, the cabinet felt that a heartfelt message of sympathy and support was warranted. Other campuses had done so, and it was only right that ours—located in the most racially diverse county in the

United States and with a heterogeneous student population that was more than a quarter each of Black, Latinx, and Asian—did the same. Many of our sister colleges within the network issued poignant statements, with the most profound coming from a Black woman president of a College of Criminal Justice. I was struck by the juxtaposition of how this leader could reconcile her feelings as a Black woman, alongside her position as president of a "cop college." On the other hand, I struggled with what to say and how to say it. As a straight, White, middle-aged, able-bodied, American-born, English-speaking, Christian male, I internalized fear (Erskine & Bilimoria, 2019; McIntosh,1988) and wondered if any words of support or sympathy to the Black members of our campus community would seem inauthentic or hollow.

In an effort to have a meaningful statement, I thought it pertinent and impactful to engage select faculty governance leaders (Department Chairpersons, members of the Senate Steering Committee, Faculty Executive Committee, and the Faculty Diversity Strategic Plan Committee) in the drafting process. My effort to include diverse voices in a matter of concern to the entire community was sincere and rooted in the best of intentions, but it was perceived as a request to absolve myself of responsibility by burdening Black, Indigenous, and People of Color (BIPOC) colleagues with my responsibilities.

What came next was revelatory: An extended exchange of candid emails that triggered frustration, embitterment, and above all else, fatigue on the part of my colleagues. I heard that they were tired of being asked to do more and of being expected to answer for the crimes of White people with assertions that "it's alright, we know not all of you are like this" and with stories of countless hostile interactions with law enforcement officers, ignorant colleagues, and passive, indifferent administrators. It was eye-opening and, frankly, embarrassing to learn that such a situation existed on a 21st-century campus, and while unaware, I –as interim president—was both culpable and complicit. The buck stopped with me, and I was passing fake currency in this transaction.

It was clear that the time for vapid town halls, open forums, and the like had passed: what was needed was to move from talk to task and from aspirational to operational. Although I felt that the status of interim meant I should "do no harm" by not committing my successor to anything controversial (or expensive), I also recognized that no meaningful change would occur without, well, transformational change. The incident led me to a deep exploration of materials that would allow insight into the feelings my colleagues were expressing. My actions toward the colleagues on the DEI team were transactional, but what my campus deserved from me was a leader who was *transformational.* I committed to learning, growing, listening intently, and advocating for change using my power and positionality and by equipping my team with a person whose expertise could move the agenda forward with my support. Thus, I created the inaugural position of Faculty Fellow for Diversity, Equity, and Inclusivity (FFDEI).

Pivoting From Aspirational to Operational

Dr. Timothy G. Lynch

There is an axiom in the corporate world that "you change the person, or you change the person," meaning that you get folks to agree with your way of thinking, or you find others that do, and I knew that no reasonable person would look at a plan for achieving racial and social justice and think "no, that's too costly and controversial." In the first meeting of the Division of Academic Affairs with our newly appointed FFDEI, in January 2021, I affirmed our commitment to transform the college's diversity efforts from aspirational to operational.

Korejan and Shahbazi (2016) affirm that a transformational leader "constantly looks for potential motives in followers and aims to draw followers' attention to superior needs and conversion of individual interests into collective interests" (p. 454). I acknowledge that in the case of DEI and as a White male leader, the concept of interest convergence, an idea in Critical Race Theory (Bell, 1992) that suggests that Black people only achieve racial justice when their interests also benefit White people, could be used as a critique of my decision to pivot from transactional to transformational around these issues. The institution for which I worked, desperately needed to emerge from a culture of silence and marginalization to cater to our Black and Brown colleagues. I was compelled to discard the fake currency and move our college from aspirational to operational. My Black colleagues had shared their thoughts and feelings around isolation and marginalization and I considered those my marching orders to effect change that would create a more welcoming environment for them. I also shared these thoughts and ideas with the incoming president, who had just been appointed, and we forged forward to ensure that their ideas did not go unaddressed.

Dr. Kerri-Ann M. Smith

In his National Public Radio (NPR) article, David Shih (2017) notes that "interest convergence is the most sobering and viable approach for the contentious issues around diversity, equity, and inclusion" (para. 20) and that weak diversity policies "trade binding commitment for symbolism and good intentions" (para.16). Perhaps using my expertise in this role was the pivot the college needed to move from good intentions (aspirational) to binding commitment (operational) but I was not sure of how doing this work would be beneficial to me or my career.

The faculty fellow position was designed to be temporary and would count as service to the college, an area that would not necessarily serve me professionally, as I have rendered more than enough service to the college in my ten years there. There was no additional financial compensation with the position (but a full course release with a 9-5 schedule, which is less flexible than my faculty schedule), no measurable power or influence to make final decisions, and would last a short 18 months. Newkirk (2019) refers to these limited and limiting practices in DEI work as "ephemeral," and "finite," (p.215). I consider them the exploitative three horsemen (uncompensated service, no power, and temporary) of DEI work, and Black women are often at the helm of justice and change, shouldering the burden at their own risk (Collins, 2000). As Bleweis et al (2021) report, Black women are already at the margins of income inequality, despite their high participation in the labor force, earning a mere 64 cents to every $1 compared to White non-Hispanic males in 2020. A 2017 report by the American Council on Education (ACE) shows that men, on average, outearn women in higher education by $13,874 at public institutions and $18,201 and that income, promotion and tenure, and leadership gaps are all exacerbated for women of color.

Nixon (2017) cites a 2008 national study by Jaschik indicating that Black women represent 12.3% of Executive Vice Presidents in higher education but 59% of all Chief Diversity Officers. This would suggest then, that Black women are more responsible for managing diversity programming, compliance, research, and planning than their peers from other races. The critical agency (Baez, 2000) and cultural capital (Yosso, 2005) that Black women accord to higher education results in advocacy for people of color (and often themselves) and serves to effect systemic change, often at their own expense. Yet, a recent survey (Eddy et al, 2022) of over 700 community college leaders across the United States indicates that women of color are less likely to find safe spaces for authentic dialogue around race and racism at their institutions. The concurrent struggle to convince predominately white institutions to acknowledge the impacts of sytemic racism, while advocating for immediate change to retain a diverse faculty and staff can prove daunting. Among survey respondents, women held the majority of lower and mid-level ranks such as Director (66%) and Dean (64%), but are dismally represented at the more senior levels such as Vice President (55%) and President (38%). Overall, the respondents of color account for 41% of those at the position of director, while only 24% at the position of president (Eddy et al, 2022), indicating that people of color are less represented among the respondents in the positions of power, where budget and policy decisions are made.

Understanding that DEI work is often under or unfunded, powerless, and temporary, and while firmly believing that we needed the academic component to the DEI work we do at our institution, the reality of sitting in such a liminal space seemed performative and contrary to good sense, for me as I considered my professional goals. The fear of being silenced resided in the depths of my soul but the fear of not having a say was far more palpable, so I applied and was appointed the Inaugural FFDEI.

Operationalizing Diversity, Equity, And Inclusivity

Dr. Kerri-Ann M. Smith

I began serving as the FFDEI January 2021, and the provost ensured the position was not only supported theoretically but was assigned a budget for programming, professional development, and research. This unprecedented fellowship was designed to improve curriculum and pedagogy. It also provided more opportunities for mentoring junior faculty of color and support for campus-wide DEI programming. Additionally, the position provided access to a wealth of resources allowing me to learn critical administrative skills that are not normally part of faculty duties.

Before the fellowship was announced, I had joined forces with colleagues from around the college, similar to other colleges mentioned in a 2021 NASPA report, to form the first Black Faculty and Staff Association (BFSA) for the college. For me, the fellowship would be both a conduit to decision-making processes and an obstacle to organizing and developing new accountability measures for the administration. My role in the BFSA caused me much consternation around respectability (Cooper, 2017) since joining the administration would mean functioning under the exigencies of tone-policing, body awareness (a skill I have yet to perfect because my facial muscles are averse to foolishness), and secrecy guised as confidentiality, at the expense of others. This involvement was my concept of the obscurity of upper-level leadership, where everyone maintained silence and operated in secrecy for the good of the institution.

I accepted the role as the Inaugural FFDEI, despite my apprehensions, with the awareness that historically, diversity roles function as "paradoxes of simultaneous visibility and invisibility, high rank and low resources, and recognition and tokenism" (Nixon, 2017, p. 302), and I was hesitant to bear the cost. Newkirk (2019) acknowledges that functioning in a space as the only person of color (for me, Black and woman) can feel isolating and alienating. I had only been to the fifth floor, where our senior administrators sit, a handful of times and had never seen my reflection in anyone there. I was also viscerally aware of being tokenized as "the diversity person," as I had been labeled early in my career at this institution. I anticipated becoming emotionally drained, physically tired, and overwhelmed by an expectation for making monumental shifts for which I had no responsibility in the first place (Lomax, 2021). I also must admit that the idea of devoting eight hours a day to sitting in front of a computer screen was contrary to why I joined the academy. It was contrary to my family values of spending as much time raising my Black daughters and building them up to face the world, and contrary to my idea of existing outside of the exploitative superwoman trope often assigned to Black women who society unfairly expects to simultaneously exhibit strength and vulnerability. This was not "soft life," as Tálábí (2022) describes in her Instagram poem of the same title. In my first discussion with the provost about my new role, I was honest about my apprehensions. The college was moving into unchartered territory, and I was stepping in, unarmored but ready to take up space.

The provost shared his own apprehensions, which were similar to those Erskine and Bilimora (2019) notes for White men in leadership roles. This partnership, however, allowed him to offer reassurance that as an accomplice and ally, he would do the necessary work to immerse himself in learning and engaging in anti-racist practices to support the process of interrupting bias (Davis, 2018; Naulty, 2016; Oluo, 2020; Prutzman & Johnson,1997). One key strategy the provost utilized was to strategically make me his direct report, thus removing barriers to leadership that might have otherwise impeded the immediate implementation of the vision I outlined for the position, as FFDEI.

We both participated, along with other colleagues, in two training programs: the NYU Metropolitan Center for Research on Equity and the Transformation of Schools Center for Strategic Solutions and the USC Equity Institute. We also had frequent (and sometimes uncomfortable) conversations about race and racism. The provost advocated for a budget for my work--an unprecedented shift in DEI operations at our institution. The funding supported a summer stipend, allowing for the work to be continuous during faculty annual leave and access to resources for program planning and professional development. Additionally, the Dean of Academic Initiatives, a member of the Office of Academic Affairs leadership team, designated a portion of his budget to support my work on curriculum design, thus extending the reach beyond what my assigned budget could accommodate. The additional funding allowed me access to a wider range of faculty members and students, who could be paid for their contributions and time as they helped restructure the college's curriculum. The idea to move from aspirational to operational became more than just talk; the college was, indeed, walking the walkthrough allyship and transformational leadership practices.

In the fall of 2020, a newly appointed president declared that the college's central focus would be on advancing equity and building a culture of care. She appointed a cabinet-level Executive Advisor for Equity, whose focus was to analyze data to identify equity gaps and make recommendations for solutions. The Executive Advisor, along with the Chief Diversity Officer, and I, the FFDEI, created an alliance that addressed DEI as a team rather than in silos.

RECOMMENDATIONS FOR PRACTICE

Transformational leadership requires action that is intentional and engaging. As a new administrator, I required mentorship, training, and support. The senior vice president worked as an accomplice for the DEI projects and plans I implemented, and I have been able to thrive and enact impactful change within the division of academic affairs partly due to his deliberate use of transformational leadership methods. Following are examples of how Bass' dimensions of transformational leadership theory have been employed to create a symbiotic relationship in support of my work and the overall DEI mission of the college:

1. **Honoring Time:** A major component of my fellowship is the full release from my academic duties. This release allows me to focus on the projects and research associated with my role. This time also allows me to stay up-to-date with research and to attend and participate in relevant conferences and

seminars for professional development and intellectual growth. By honoring time, there is a model of *idealized influence*, which allows room for me to cultivate a sense of pride in supporting others while equipping myself with the necessary tools to succeed in making a difference in our division.

2. **A Joint Commitment to Integrity**: Central to my work and our partnership was an unwavering commitment on both Dr. Lynch and my part to uphold the integrity and to persist beyond aspirational plans to operationalize DEI efforts in the Office of Academic Affairs. The commitment involved participating in training programs (NYU Metropolitan Center for Research on Equity and the Transformation of Schools Center for Strategic Solutions training and the USC Equity Institute), establishing bi-weekly check-ins, and engaging in spirited and courageous conversations where we grappled with issues, ideas, and implementation plans. We were charting new territory by using terms such as "anti-racist" and "culturally responsive pedagogy" and demanding that our campus moves from "talk to task" to ensure belonging for all members of our community. This joint commitment to integrity through courageous inquiry is an example of how *intellectual stimulation* can support the work of a Black woman DEI practitioner.
3. **Mutual Trust**: Dr. Lynch's expertise with administrative functions and mine with DEI and social justice allowed for effective and impactful partnership in enhancing the infrastructure for DEI work in the Office of Academic Affairs. An important component of our work was the establishing of implicit trust based on mutual respect. Implicit trust removes a barrier where the partner needs to first work to "prove" themselves worthy in order to gain the trust of the other. Offering implicit trust eradicates a function of white supremacy that often permeates higher education, in which information is withheld and only disseminated on a need-to-know basis until someone joins the proverbial 'inner circle.' Dedication to operationalizing diversity, equity, and inclusivity requires implicit mutual trust and a commitment to information-sharing.

In our reciprocal partnership, Dr. Lynch apprised me of details that would help to support my work, and I kept him aware of DEI 'mines' or potentially negative experiences our faculty and staff could be experiencing. Our commitment to mutual respect and trust also included an understanding that mistakes were inevitable and welcomed. This was my first administrative role, so there was much to learn about processes, systems, and operational planning. This required support from the provost and other experienced colleagues, which indubitably added to their workload. The establishment of mutual trust is an example of both *idealized influence* and *inspirational motivation* because it was the trust that allowed me to take bold chances and think creatively without the fear of judgment from senior leadership.

4. **Mentorship:** Without the support of committed administrators, DEI work becomes ornamental. There must be an unwavering commitment to both teaching and learning, which both require time. In order for me to thrive in my role, I needed mentorship and guidance from experienced administrators such as my boss and other colleagues in the division. The provost opened his virtual doors to unlimited questions and anticipate roadblocks and assuaged any

Inclusion in processes and conversations with senior leadership is also paramount to the role of a DEI professional. In some cases, the DEI representative might only be tapped for problem-solving, and their experiences as lone advocates (in my case, the only Black woman on the entire executive floor in this role) can sometimes go overlooked. Therefore, the working model we adopted was for the provost to include me, the FFDEI, in conversations, provide me with mentorship and guidance in administrative processes, and develop my professional standing. In 1:1 meetings, he encouraged me to articulate my accomplishments on my curriculum vita and résumé, and supported me with contextualizing and delivering presentations from an administrative perspective, and with analyzing data to help the administration make key decisions on faculty recruitment and retention. This form of support and guidance exemplifies *individualized consideration*, where the motivation becomes intrinsic and beneficial to a Black woman DEI practitioner.

Honoring Sacrifice

As the Inaugural FFDEI, participating in the process of culture-shifting has been challenging but most rewarding because of the collaborative nature of the work and the impact of the transformational leadership model. Great things can be accomplished when leaders understand the positionality of power, function as accomplices, and intentionally provide access to innovation and creativity that might not fit the status quo. That is, essentially, a key aspect of diversity is that excellence requires diversity. Direct access to the senior vice president/provost and a shared understanding of our values and commitment to DEI has made working in a temporary inaugural role less procedurally challenging. It is, however, emotionally taxing and mentally strenuous yet rewarding work. However, having allies and accomplices has been instrumental to my success in the role.

Furthermore, the role requires sacrifice, and there is no comfort and convenience in uprooting years of underlying and untouched White supremacist practices. There are days that feel burdensome, but most of the days, I understand the gravity of my work and honor and lean on the sacrifices of Nanny of the Maroons, Ida B. Wells, Anna Julia Cooper, Dorothy Irene Height, my mentors, my mother, and my intrepid ancestors who never "winced or cried aloud" (Henley, 1888, line 6).

Outcomes

While the initial appointment for FFDEI was 18-months, it remains a priority of the Office of Academic Affairs to implement further changes. Thus, the term has been extended to 2 years, to allow for operationalizing and implementation of plans, particularly around curriculum development and training. In one and a half year, that was compounded by the COVID-19 pandemic and a primarily virtual modality, I have supported the implementation of a few key changes at the college:

1. **Promulgation of Tenure and Promotion Guidelines**--Diversity work often assumes that there is a magical antidote for the poison of systemic racism that has pervaded academe since its inception (Bell, 1992; Oluo, 2020; Stein, 2018). That assumption tends to derail meaningful, operational change that can be made possible when more structural changes are implemented, and the college's operational plan incorporates diversity efforts in all divisions, thus making diversity part of the college's imperative rather than just the job of one person or division. In order to operationalize anti-racist practices in the scope of my position as the FFDEI, we set out to promulgate tenure and promotion guidelines, by which faculty have long regarded as obscure and nebulous. The provost requested that departmental chairs collaborate with their constituents to create detailed guidelines for tenure and promotion within their departments. These guidelines were then submitted to the college's Publications Committee and will now be posted publicly for all to access. Demistifying the tenure and promotion process allows faculty to have access to the guidelines that individual

departments use for personnel and budget committee decisions, thus providing a department-created rubric for how they operate, even in the absence of a faculty mentor.

2. **Targeted Mentoring Program**: Mentoring for junior faculty is a dynamic process that requires deep commitment and training for both mentors and mentees. Our college often hires entry-level professors on the tenure track and, in most cases, new graduates from doctoral programs or post-doctoral fellowships. For most who graduate doctoral programs, there are few courses in that focus specifically on "how to be a professor." Graduate students often focus on their coursework and research and, if given an opportunity, the course they have been assigned to teach or the research assistantships they've been offered. Thus, walking into the academy as a first-timer or even at a new institution having worked elsewhere can become daunting. My position helps to allay fears and build bridges for such members of our faculty and I created an opt-in email list-serv for junor faculty of color who are interested in mentoring.

In my role as FFDEI, I have found that faculty members of color with whom I work are affirmed and reassured by the presence of an advocate in the Office of Academic Affairs, so I have devoted specific office hours to accommodate their need for conversation and connection. I created and distribute a monthly newsletter for the group, that features tips for tenure and promotion, kudos and recognition for faculty achievements, and professional development opportunities available to faculty. In addition to mentoring, the provost and I along with two other colleagues secured funding to make our college the first community college with membership in the National Center for Faculty Development and Diversity, a robust resource of webinars, and activities focusing on faculty development. I also designed a series of informal discussions called FaculTEA (Tenure Enrichment Activities) where junior faculty gather to learn about publishing or other topics related to tenure and promotion.

3. **Relevant Programming:** My first effort in supporting the campus as FFDEI was to implement a lecture series that deliberately focused on relevant issues for faculty of color as they work toward tenure and for staff of color seeking professional development and support. With encouragement and support from Dr. Lynch, I designed and implemented a six-part lecture series primarily featuring nationally-recognized faculty and administrators of color. Topics for the lecture series included work/life balance, finding grant funding, balancing service obligations with research requirements, overcoming imposter syndrome, navigating racism in the academy, and moving from academic to the executive in the academy. A major feature of our lecture series was a targeted "backstage" component where junior faculty of color met with our speakers in a more intimate setting to ask questions that they might not have felt comfortable asking in a large group and to grow their network. An initial analysis of the exit surveys from the attendees indicate that they felt a strong sense of belonging and a strong connection to the experiences articulated by the presenters.
4. **Curriculum Guidelines:** To help develop guidelines for curriculum revision, I convened the Taskforce for Anti-Racist Curriculum (TARC). Members of TARC created discipline-specific guidelines that support anti-racist practices and center critical pedagogy. The main component of this task force was the presence of students as equal stakeholders in the process. The task force defined and delineated terms that would guide the college's curricular plan. I participated in processes to train and equip the task force with tools to center antiracism and build curricular guidelines that would center antiracism and culturally responsive methodology in the curriculum. Members of TARC

will serve as discipline-specific liaisons for college's operational plan for advancing antii-racism in the college's curriculum.

Looking Ahead

As I develop my agenda to continue as FFDEI, particularly as it relates to curriculum and development, I am using what I have learned so far to develop and test a Values-Centered Praxis for DEI work. The Values-Centered Praxis approach situates the DEI goals in the context of a well-defined common language, using existing theoretical frameworks and practice or praxis. To move from aspirational to operational, our goals and values must be inextricably linked to measurable outcomes, vis-a-vis shared values and expectations. In other words, the Office of Academic Affairs, as the academic leadership body of the college, must define its core values using an equitable, inclusive, socially just framework that is understood by all its members. The Values-Centered Praxis is predicated on five influential concentric domains, with the core values at the center:

1. **Core Values:** A shared understanding and clear definition of 1) who the organization/group is, 2) who they want to be, and 3) how they will get to that goal.
2. **Institutional Culture:** The core values drive all the work, conversations, and practices of the institution. The environment is designed and shaped to fit its core values, and all members and all output and input espouse these values. Goals and practices are clear, and all members have a clear understanding of how they can participate in the culture.
3. **Faculty Satisfaction/Investment:** The institution has engaged faculty members who use the core values to drive their research, pedagogy, and service. They engage in values-based practices such as high-impact practices, culturally relevant pedagogy, engaging and impactful research, etc. Ample mentoring and support systems are in place, and retention practices are equitable. There are opportunities for collaboration and community-building, and affinity spaces are part of the college's culture.
4. **Academic and Social Practices:** Student-centered curricula focus on meeting students through an asset-based lens with the expectation that students are given a chance at optimal achievement. With this approach, students are active and equal partners in all aspects of their experience. Affinity spaces are intentional and targeted to ensure student satisfaction. Students have ownership of the shared values and are partners in their development. They invest in their own experience and feel the college is also mutually invested in their growth, as indicated through culturally relevant practices, policies, and programming.
5. **Leadership/Stakeholders Values**: Encircling the inner core are those who lead the institution and make final decisions regarding budgets and mission. Leaders and stakeholders are investing in the inner circles, and the inner circles are driving their investment decisions through critical reflection and feedback. The arrows denote the symbiotic relationship between the inner circles and the outer, all-encompassing sphere of leadership. The institution's leadership pours resources (financial and human) into each concentric circle, thus allowing the institution to function at its highest potential. They engage in critical reflection practices to see how systems can be shifted, changed, or adapted to fit the needs of the inner circle.

The principles are demonstrated in Figure 1, where there is a symbiotic relationship between the various aspects of the institution, with the core values at the center. The model holds institutional divisions and leaders responsible for defining and shaping culture and makes room for student partnership and participation in the process. Figure 2 exemplifies the way the model can be used in a specific context.

CONCLUSION

When merged with the deliberate efforts of transformational leaders in the academy, effective planning, and engagement strategies such as a values-centered praxis can save professionals, particularly Black women, in DEI positions from emotional and physical fatigue that results in "setting themselves on fire to keep the academy warm" (Smith, Alves, Weathersby & Yi, 2020, p. 134).

Much like the Darnella Fraziers, Rachel Jeantels, Diamond Reynoldses, and Ieshia Evanses of the world who have taken a stand, Black women in DEI roles in higher education know that there is much on the line when they dare to occupy them, particularly in academic spaces that are fraught with contention over the true meaning of Critical Race Theory.

Sometimes, the impetus behind true organizational transformation lies in the unwillingness of Black women to continue struggling without meaningful outcomes (Collins, 2000). Sometimes, the fierce 'no' creates an urgency that the administration cannot ignore. In this case, it made room for intentional change in a system that had, for too long, silenced and marginalized Black people at our institution. Sometimes the urgency of the 'no' opens the door to lasting change through allyship and accompliceship. It is worth noting that just shy of a year into my appointment, the provost was selected to serve as interim president at another institution on short notice. This sudden shift in support created challenges, particularly because of the partnership we had established with the work, but I have persevered with the initiatives, with the support of the president and interim provost.

Like Frazier, Black women in diversity roles persist and persevere with the hope that our contributions to the field will someday lead to liberation for ourselves and our colleagues at our respective institutions. To lighten the load, carefully curated transformational leadership models that are operational and not simply aspirational can affirm and support these 'women on fire,' who represent more than half of diversity officers in higher education and who can lead institutions through these pivotal, crucial, and transformational periods of racial, social, and cultural growth and critical development.

ACKNOWLEDGMENT

This research received no specific grant from any funding agency in the public, commercial, or not-for-profit sectors.

REFERENCES

Ahmed, S. (2012). *On being included*. Duke University Press.

American Council on Education. (2017). Pipelines, pathways, and institutional leadership. *American Council on Education Higher Ed Spotlight*. https://www.acenet.edu/Documents/HES-Pipelines-Pathways-and-Institutional-Leadership-2017.pdf

Baez, B. (2000). Race-related service and faculty of color: Conceptualizing critical agency in academe. *Higher Education*, *39*(3), 363–391. doi:10.1023/A:1003972214943

Bass, B. M. (1985). *Leadership and performance*. Free Press.

BBC.com. (2020). Black lives matter founders: We fought to change history and we won. *BBC News*. https://www.bbc.com/news/world-us-canada-55106268

Bell, D. (1992). *Faces at the bottom of the well*. Basic Books.

Boyce-Davies, C. (2016). *Left of Karl Marx*. Duke University Press.

Brown, C. (2002). *Refusing racism: White allies and the struggle for civil rights*. Teachers College Press.

Burns, J. M. (1978). *Leadership*. Harper and Row.

Cleaver, K. (2007). Women, power, and revolution. *New Political Science*, *21*(2), 231–236. doi:10.1080/07393149908429865

Collins, P. H. (2000). *Black Feminist Thought*. Routledge.

Cooper, B. (2017). *Beyond respectability:The intellectual thought of race women*. University of Illinois Press. doi:10.5406/illinois/9780252040993.001.0001

Davis, C. U. (2018). Laying new ground: Uprooting white privilege and planting seeds of equity and inclusivity. *Journal of Distance Education*, *18*(3), 120–125. doi:10.1080/15290824.2018.1481965

Davis, S. & Brown, K. (2017). Automatically discounted: Using Black feminist theory to critically analyze the experiences of Black female faculty. *NCPEA International Journal of Educational Leadership Preparation*, *12*(1).

Eddy, P., VanDerLinden, K., & Hartman, C. (2022). Leadership for social justice in community colleges: A national survey.

Erskine, S. E., & Bilimoria, D. (2019). White allyship of Afro-diasporic women in the workplace: A transformative strategy for organizational change. *Journal of Leadership & Organizational Studies*, *26*(3), 319–338. doi:10.1177/1548051819848993

Frazier, D. (2021, May 25). *This is my truth. 1 Year Anniversary. Rest in peace to George Floyd* [Photograph]. Instagram. https://www.instagram.com/p/CPT5_oIBlie/?utm_medium=copy_link

Guy-Sheftall, B. (2009). Black feminist studies: The case of anna julia cooper. *African American Review*, *43*(1), 11–15. doi:10.1353/afa.0.0019

Henley, W. E. (1888). *Invictus*. https://www.poetryfoundation.org/poems/51642/invictus

Jackson, R. G., Huskins, K., Skelton, S., & Thorius, K. (2020). Ally and accomplice: Two sides of the same coin. *Equity Dispatch, 4*(3). https://greatlakesequity.org/sites/default/files/202003022136_newsletter.pdf.

Korejan, M. M., & Shahbazi, H. (2016). An analysis of the transformational leadership theory. *Journal of Fundamental and Applied Science*, *8*(3), 452–461. doi:10.4314/jfas.v8i3s.192

Lomax, T. (2021). DEI dreaming: Confusing inclusion and tokenism. *The Feministwire*. https://thefeministwire.com/2021/11/dei-dreaming-confusing-inclusion-and-tokenism/?fbclid=IwAR3JLd2_TP2pe-rxJwBXoW14FOCd5q7PHIcTLHqaGfcgBef5V4aecwaY7Yo

Lorde, A. (1984). The master's tools will never dismantle the master's house. In A. Lorde (Ed.), *Sister outsider essays and speeches,* (pp. 110–114). Crossing Press Feminist Series.

Matthew, P. (2016). *Written/unwritten:Diversity and the hidden truths of tenure*. University of North Carolina Press. doi:10.5149/northcarolina/9781469627717.001.0001

McIntosh, P. (1988). *White privilege and male privilege: A personal account of coming to see correspondences through work in women's studies*. (Working Paper No. #189). https://nationalseedproject.org/images/documents/White_Privilege_and_Male_Privilege_Personal_Account-Peggy_McIntosh.pdf

McIntosh, P. (2010). *Some notes for facilitators*. Wellesley Centers for Women. https://nationalseedproject.org/images/documents/White_Privilege_and_Male_Privilege_Personal_Account-Peggy_McIntosh.pdf

McLean, M. (2017). From Nanny of the maroons to Portia Simpson. In E. Brown & G. Gong (Eds.), *Global perspectives on gender and sexuality in education: Raising awareness, fostering equity, advancing justice*. Information Age Publishing.

McNair, T., Bensimon, E., & Malcom-Piquex, L. (2020). *From equity talk to equity walk*. Jossey-Bass. doi:10.1002/9781119428725

NASPA. (2021). *Moving from words to action: The influence of racial justice statements on campus equity efforts*. https://naspa.org/report/moving-from-words-to-action-the-influence-of-racial-justice-statements-on-campus-equity-efforts

Naulty, K. (2016). Strategies for confronting unconscious bias. *Colorado Lawyer*, *45*, 45–52.

Newkirk, P. (2019). *Diversity, Inc*. Boldtype Books.

Nixon, M. (2017). Experiences of women of color university chief diversity officers. *Journal of Diversity in Higher Education*, *10*(4), 301–317. doi:10.1037/dhe0000043

Oluo, I. (2020). *Mediocre:The dangerous legacy of white male America*. Seal Press.

Padilla, A. (1994). Ethnic minority scholars, research, and mentoring: Current and future issues. *Educational Researcher*, *23*(4), 24–27. doi:10.2307/1176259

Powell, J. S., & Kelly, A. (2017). Accomplices in the academy in the age of Black Lives Matter. *Journal of Critical Thought and Praxis*, *6*(2), 42–65. doi:10.31274/jctp-180810-73

Prutzman, P., & Johnson, J. (1997). Bias awareness and multiple perspectives: Essential aspects of conflict resolution. *Theory into Practice*, *36*(1), 26–31. https://eric.ed.gov/?id=EJ546687. doi:10.1080/00405849709543741

Reid, W. M., & Dold, C. J. (2018). Burns, Senge, and the study of leadership. *Tampa Library. Faculty and Staff Publications.* https://digitalcommons.usf.edu/cgi/viewcontent.cgi?article=1008&context=tlib_facpub

Shih, D. (2017). A theory to better understand diversity and who really benefits. *NPR,* https://www.npr.org/sections/codeswitch/2017/04/19/523563345/a-theory-to-better-understand-diversity-and-who-really-benefits

Smith, K. M., Alves, K., Weathersby, I., & Yi, J. (2020). Invictus: Race and emotional labor of faculty of color at the urban community college. *Journal of the Assembly for Expanded Perspectives on Learning*, *25*, 119–135.

Stein, S. (2018). Confronting the racial-colonial foundations of US higher education. *Journal for the Study of Postsecondary and Tertiary Education*, *3*, 77–98. doi:10.28945/4105

Stewart, J. (2006). Transformational Leadership: An evolving concept examined through the works of Burns, Bass, Avolio, and Leithwood. *Canadian Journal of Educational Administration and Policy*, *54*, 1–29. https://eric.ed.gov/?id=EJ843441

Suyemoto, K., Hochman, A., Donovan, R., & Roemar, L. (2021). Becoming and fostering allies and accomplices through authentic relationships: Choosing justice over comfort. *Research in Human Development*, *18*(1), 1–28. doi:10.1080/15427609.2020.1825905

Tàlàbí, A. (3 April, 2022). Kpoem: soft life. [Video]. Instagram. https://www.instagram.com/p/Cb5V-V53Im2i/

Titcomb, C., & JBHE (2022). *Key Events in Black Higher Education.* Journal of Blacks in Higher Education. https://www.jbhe.com/chronology/

Tuelon, A. (1973). Nanny, maroon chieftainess. *Caribbean Quarterly*, *19*(4), 20–27. doi:10.1080/00086495.1973.11829168

Witynski, M. (2021). 100 years ago Georgiana Simpson made history as the first black woman to graduate with a PhD. *UchicagoNews.* https://news.uchicago.edu/story/100-years-ago-georgiana-simpson-made-history-first-black-woman-graduate-phd

Yosso, T. J. (2005). Whose culture has capital? A critical race theory discussion of community cultural wealth. *Race, Ethnicity and Education*, *8*(1), 69–91. doi:10.1080/1361332052000341006

ADDITIONAL READING

Brown, A. C. (2018). *I'm still here: Black dignity in a world made for whiteness*. Convergent Books.

Collins, P. H. (1998). *Fighting words: Black women and the search for justice*. University of Minnesota Press.

Cooper, B. (2018). *Eloquent rage*. St. Martin's Publishing Group.

DeCuir-Gunby, J. T., & Gunby, N. Jr. (2016). Racial microaggressions in the workplace: A critical experience of African-American educators. *Urban Education, 51*(4), 390–414. doi:10.1177/0042085916628610

Douglas, T. M., Shockley, K. G., & Toldson, I. (2020). *Campus uprisings: How student activists and collegiate leaders resist racism and create hope*. Teachers College Press.

Gurin, P., Dey, E., Hurtado, S., & Gurin, G. (2002). Diversity and higher education: Theory and impact on educational outcomes. *Harvard Educational Review, 72*(3), 330–366. doi:10.17763/haer.72.3.01151786u134n051

Harris-Perry, M. (2011). *Sister citizen: Shame, stereotypes, and black women in America*. Yale University Press.

Patton, L. D. (2015). Disrupting postsecondary prose: Toward a critical race theory of higher education. *Urban Education, 51*(3), 315–342. doi:10.1177/0042085915602542

KEY TERMS AND DEFINITIONS

Allyship: volunteering support on behalf of the values and experiences of marginalized groups through words and deeds that show a clear understanding of their needs.

Black Liberation: the quest for freedom of Black people from White supremacist cultural norms and systems.

Equity: The deliberate practice of creating conditions that meet the needs of all constituents in order to promote success and achievement for all.

Faculty Fellow: an opportunity for members of the faculty to assume a leadership role in the administrative ranks to learn and study leadership in specific areas. Fellows often work on specific topics or projects for a set amount of time, while conducting research and developing programs specific to their expertise and leadership commitments.

Marginalization: forcably pushing specific racial or ethnic groups into sub-standard systems or second-class citizenship because of systemic racism.

Service: community hours and leadership provided by faculty members at higher educational institutions as part of their commitment to the greater good of the institution. This may include committee work, curriculum development, faculty governance work, and affinity group leadership.

Tokenization: the use of marginalized persons for the benefit of the majority at an institution, without adequate consideration for the needs of the individuals involved. Tokenization removes individuality and exists on the premise that one person's thoughts, behaviors, actions, and desires may represent an entire racial or ethnic group.

White Privilege: a societal phenomenon that renders Whitness as the standard, thus putting those who are of any White ethnic group at an advantage over others. This deleterious system of thought limits the success of Black, Asian/Pacific Islander, and Hispanic people and ingratiates White people into power, simply based on the color of their skin.

APPENDIX 1

Figure 1. Values-Centered Praxis for Institutions

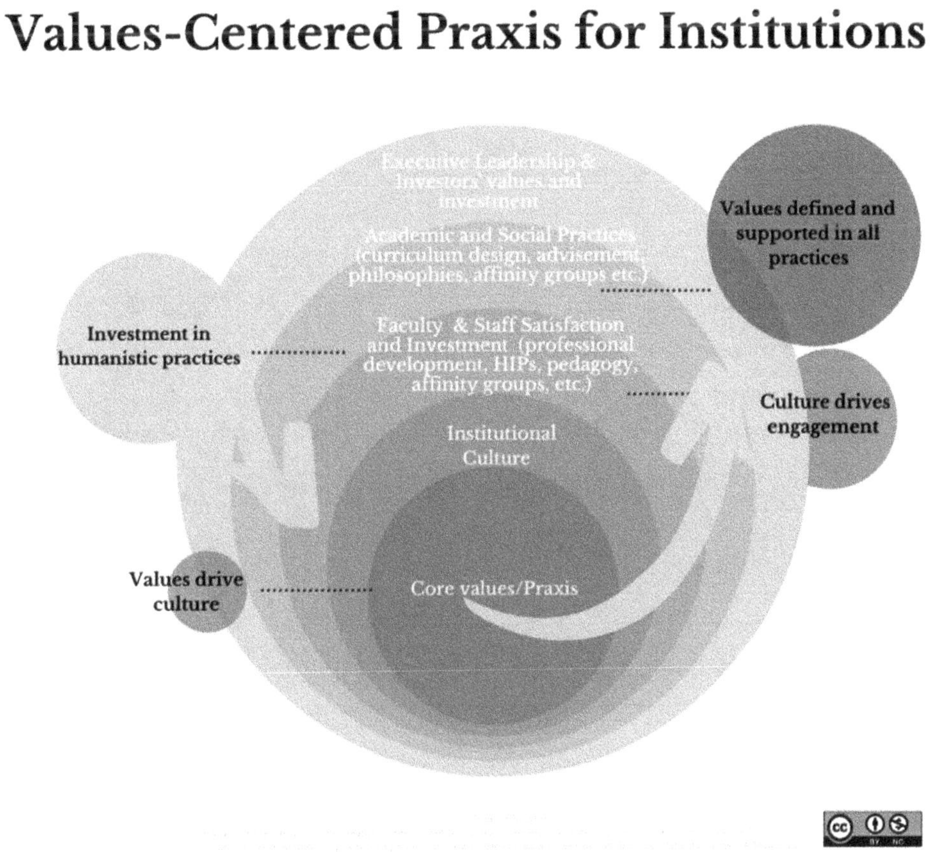

APPENDIX 2

Figure 2. Values-Centered Praxis for DEI Curriculum Design

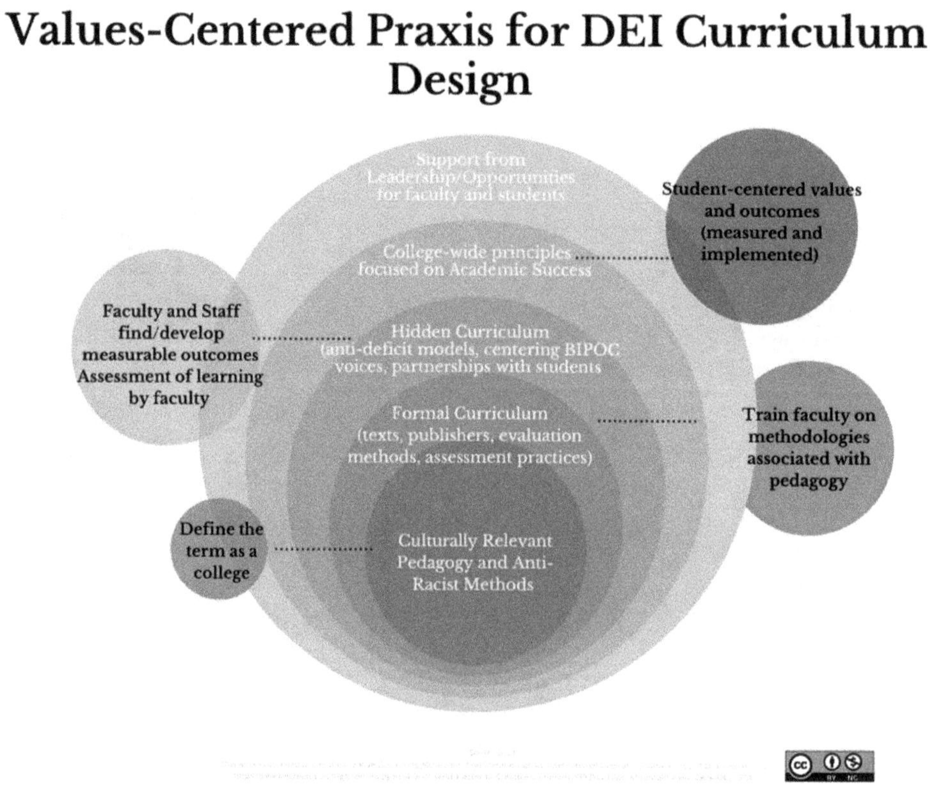

Chapter 5
Masks Off:
Portraits of Black Female Diversity Practitioners During a Double Pandemic

Tracie Denise Jones
School of Humanities, Arts, and Social Sciences, MIT, USA

ABSTRACT

The purpose of this chapter is to explore the perceptions and experiences of Black female diversity practitioners during the dual pandemics of COVID-19 and the racial reckoning of 2020. Using portraiture as a methodology and Black feminist thought (BFT) as a framework, this chapter gives voice to two Black women who worked at Ivy League institutions as diversity practitioners from March 2020 through June 2021. This chapter places the portraits of Black female diversity practitioners at Ivy League institutions within the larger discourse about the impact that the dual pandemics of COVID-19 and the racial reckoning of 2020 had on higher education administrators.

INTRODUCTION

This chapter provides Black women a place and space where they can tell their stories, which contain the truth of their human experience. The portraits in this chapter can be used as a vehicle for reimagining the best practices organizations can use to support, retain, and improve work environments and cultures. In addition, these stories can provide guidance and tools of the trade to new practitioners in the field. Delgado (1989) stated, "stories can provide a way of uprooting unjustified exclusion, allowing individuals to rethink and reconstruct institutions" (pg. 24). Stories challenge our assumptions and can shift our core beliefs. Personal narratives have shaped the ways in which Black women have found solace and community.

Several studies that center the experiences of Black women in predominately white institutions reveal that they often spend much of their time and energy planning for and responding to the expectations others project upon them (Collins, 2001; Wallace et al., 2012; Whitaker, 2018). The intersections of race, gender, and class are always present as they navigate the academy. The multiplicity of identities that

DOI: 10.4018/978-1-6684-3564-9.ch005

they hold contribute to the multiplicity of oppression that can and do impact their emotional, physical, psychological, and social well-being (Willis, 2019).

This chapter is situated in the framework of Black feminist thought (BFT), which is an authentic form of liberation (Collins, 2001). BFT allows Black women to be the producers of knowledge; it provides them the opportunity to tell their stories on their own terms. These stories are written in the form of portraits. Portraiture, a methodology developed by Sarah Lawrence-Lightfoot, is a form of writing that allows the investigator's voice to be purposefully woven into the portrait, which is created as a result of the writer's interactions with the actors in the story (Hackmann, 2002).

Portraiture captures the complexity, dynamics, and subtlety of the human experience. Portraitists seek to record and interpret the perspectives and experiences of the people they are documenting by illuminating their voices; their visions; and their authority, knowledge, and wisdom (Lawrence-Lightfoot & Hoffman-Davis, 1997). The portraits in this chapter can be used as a vehicle for reimagining best practices for supporting and retaining Black female diversity practitioners and improving their work environments. In addition, these stories can provide guidance to Black women who are new to the field.

REFLECTIONS ON THE DOUBLE PANDEMIC

I have a duty to speak the truth as I see it and share not just my triumphs, not just the things that felt good, but the pain, the intense, often unmitigated pain. It is important to share how I know survival is survival and not just a walk through the rain. —Audre Lorde, The Master's Tools Will Never Dismantle the Master's House

A Portrait of Zora

It was a Friday, and as usual I had back-to-back meetings with no break in between. I purposely scheduled Zora as my last meeting of the day so I wouldn't have to rush our conversation. I was grateful that she agreed to be interviewed, considering that she was a senior administrator who had a highly visible role at her institution. I wanted few or no distractions, so I could be respectful of her time and fully engaged in our conversation.

As I signed into Zoom, I tried to gather my composure, fix the loose strands of curls that had been going rogue all day, and skim through my notes. As I popped into Zoom, I could see Zora was patiently waiting for me. Her smile gave me permission to relax. I felt my shoulders droop and took a deep breath. It was the first time today that I'd taken the time to just breathe. I felt the tension melt away from my body, and I smiled back and said, "Sorry, I'm late. It's just been one of those days."

"No need to apologize," she said. "It's good to see you!" Once again, Zora had centered and humanized me. I felt a sense of calm rush over me. I put my screen on speaker view, and her image came into focus. Her almond-colored skin glistened as if it had just been kissed by the sun, and her locks loosely framed her face and cascaded down her back. She was fully present.

We started the conversation by checking in and sharing stories about our week. Ten minutes in, I realized we hadn't even discussed why we were meeting. Pivoting the conversation, I asked her for permission to record. The red recording light showed up in the corner of my screen, and that was my signal to begin: "I'm looking to explore the perceptions and experience of Black women who are diversity practitioners at an Ivy League institution during the dual pandemic of COVID-19 and the racial reckoning of 2020 and 2021."

After I spoke, I realized how stiff and robotic I sounded. I relaxed my shoulders, leaned back in my chair, and reminded myself this was a conversation with one of my sisters. The voice in my head said, "I've got this!" And suddenly, I did. "To get us started," I said, "could you share how would you describe the dual pandemic?" Zora leaned back as she processed my question. I could tell that she was giving it serious consideration. Then she said:

The reason why I'm pausing is because I used to describe it as a dual pandemic up until last summer, when my best friend introduced me to this scholar...this sister, Subini Ancy Annamma, who goes by Septima Snark on Twitter. She challenged people around that framing of dual pandemic. She challenged us to stop calling the racial reckoning the dual pandemic. Because the pandemic is something that we can't control. Racism is something that we can. I no longer refer to this as a racial reckoning, the pandemic, dual pandemic. I think like everyone has understood that COVID has just highlighted what we're experiencing which is racial challenges. Racism in the pandemic is something that has ultimately tried to call us to our better selves, our higher selves, because it's awakened so many of us to the things that either we never saw or didn't want to see.

The question sparked something inside of Zora. As she continued to speak, I felt her energy shift, and that awakened something inside of me. All the emotions that I had been suppressing began to well up, and for the first time I just let myself go, mentally and physically. No false pretense, no mask: I just listened. My movements were subtle. I'm not sure Zora even noticed. I could tell she was pulling from her well of remembrance as she continued:

For those of us who saw, and knew, and talked specifically about systems of oppression. The other aspects of our lives, like we were talking about before we started down this path, our well-being, our mental health, our quality of life, really prioritizing our humanity. When you are forced to be in shelter, locked in place with your family, just not be able to move about freely, all the things that you take for granted. You quiet yourself and you reexamine what you thought were things that you needed to have, what you thought were priorities that you have now gone without, and you realize "I don't need all those things to be happy."

The pandemic has really just amplified my awareness, what's important: my family, my relationship to God, my friends, my relationship to myself, joy. It's being intentional about practices of care and love and the connection to human relationships and all those things that we take for granted. But it's been powerful to see, particularly at the height of it, how it impacted people's perspectives and intentions around addressing racism and oppression. That was really, really powerful. I say that because I think we all knew that was a moment.... The heightened awareness around this moment that wasn't...it just wasn't going to last long.

I think I just sustained elements of that, but we're also seeing a shifting back into the norms. But it was really powerful to see how people globally responded to the murder of George Floyd and the murder of Breonna Taylor and the murders of all the people during that particular time. Just what the world was seeing or saying was really, really powerful.

She paused for a moment, and I could tell she was deep in thought processing what she had just said. Taking advantage of the silence, I asked her, "How did the death of George Floyd and the number of people that you named and the protest impact your life personally and professionally?" Slowly lifting her gaze, she focused on me. She took her time before responding:

I think when you're steeped in the work already, you're already managing the level of stress and trauma that comes with this awareness and with the engagement. The awareness and the engagement and the work of trying to dismantle these systems of oppression, racism so forth.

Her voice trailed off for a minute, but she came right back. I could tell she was tying the threads of her thoughts together as the melodious sound of her voice picked up:

Because my work is so directly tied to it, I rarely get a break from it. Then you add George Floyd's murder, and it's another layer added on to the existing trauma. I think what was different, adding that to the experience of COVID and being confined and not having access to the same types of supports, seeing people and being in community in the same ways, things that helped nourish me, not having these things made it even more challenging to be able to move through.

I nodded my head in agreement, realizing that I had also not been able to take a break from the trauma. I was still swimming in the cesspool of stress, trauma, and all the emotions that I'd buried. It was affirming to know that I wasn't alone in my feelings. While I was in my head, Zora continued:

Those spheres of trauma. The challenges living in a predominantly White environment, and then particularly during that time, seeing the emergence of the Black Lives Matter signs on the lawns, in the windows of folks' homes.... It really was harder to quite frankly be around people who are not people of color because it was just painful to have to try to either hold back your pain or try to talk about your pain or try to help other people who are not people of color to process your pain. Because it was in the context of the pandemic, and I'm dealing with all the stress around that, I had less of a tolerance for the capacity for engagement in the world, even with friends who were close in a way.

It was like, I don't have time. I can't do that. I can't do it. It was something that was.... It was a period that was even more difficult than normal because of the harshness of...the enormity of the tragedy and then coupled with the elements of the pandemic. I had less of an ability to exist.... Grief, anger...all of that.

The feelings that we negotiate every day, but aren't as heightened and amplified every day, they were all brought to bear during this period. I had less of the ability to manage and to resist. I had to just do what I had to do to take care of myself and just stay close to family and people I didn't have to explain myself to, and people who could relate in the same way.

Her words resonated with me. I wanted to know more, so I asked, "How did that impact you professionally then? With all that you were dealing with, was there an expectation?" Zora replied:

Professionally, one of the first things I expressed early on when I started my work was something I've actually realized a long time ago, which is the importance of being vulnerable and transparent in this work. It became even more of a priority during that time. By that, I mean.... because I'm committed to my own feeling and feelings, I try not to push away things as they come up. As I am feeling things, I may tear up. I may get emotional. When we're in certain environments, our society does not encourage people to feel. Doesn't encourage people to show emotions. For me, that's a major...showing emotions and being authentic is a major antiracist principle.

I was committed to just being transparent of the fact that I might tear up in a meeting. I might get emotional. There were moments...there were times when I did get emotional. That was probably the biggest thing: To just really feel...allow myself to feel the feelings particularly during that period, because the stress was so heavy with all that happening in the world. From George Floyd's murder and all the other murders and then the trial and then January 6th. I mean, it was nonstop pressure. Just allowing myself to be human and feel my emotions and display emotions and not worry about holding back was a huge impact on me professionally.

A comfortable silence fell between us. I was processing her words and reflecting on my own practices. Was I humanizing myself, did I allow for vulnerability? Zora's words triggered something inside of me, yet I continued with my script:

As a higher educator administrator, doing diversity work, how did these two situations, like you said, ongoing racism and COVID, impact the way in which you did your work and what people expected you to do because of your work?

Zora replied:

I think it connects with what I was just saying. I came to the work even more deeply rooted in a commitment to heal and to be authentic and to help other people understand the importance of connecting to their feelings and being human and connecting to each other as human beings and prioritizing our humanity. That commitment was amplified even more. It's more than just reading books about racism, oppression, and taking workshops.... It's really understanding what is happening here as a result of our disconnection from ourselves and each other. I'm fortunate to be [in] an environment where people appreciate that understanding of the work.

I'm fortunate that I didn't feel burdened by unrealistic expectations. I didn't feel I was coming into a work where people were expecting me to walk on water and do back flips. People were really realistic.... Not that they had the answers and I didn't have all the answers, but they knew that one person can't solve this problem. It's work that...has to be spread out.

I followed up: "I'm going to...ask you about being at an Ivy League institution. Do you think that being a part of an Ivy League helped or hindered your work?" Zora replied:

I think immediately, I mean, you understand the level of privilege that comes along with being in an Ivy League. You connect that to an increased capacity to do more and to have a broader reach, and to harness the resources that the institution has to have an impact.

You know that no institution is perfect, and that there are challenges with every institution, and there's so much that you don't know. But the motivation, one of the motivations is how can you work within an institution and try to help the institution commit to a cultural change and shift and so forth, and then utilize resources to do that work, and then to hopefully have impact that's beyond the institution. I think with Ivy Leagues in particular, there's a responsibility because of the status and resources that come along with it to think not just about just the institution and the insular work, but then how can we benefit the broader world.

I began to steer our conversation in a different direction:

I'm going to shift a little because this chapter is about Black women who are diversity practitioners. You know there's research that says there are subtle and not-so-subtle ways that race and gender stereotypes can combine to create double obstacles for Black women in higher education. This can lead to enormous stress. Even before the pandemic and this exacerbation of racial trauma, did you experience any of that during this timeframe?

Zora replied:

Absolutely. Because I mean, like you said, if the pandemic weren't at play, COVID 19, when you come to the work as a Black woman who's awake, and aware, and actively engaged in the work of dismantling racism, oppression, like I said earlier, it's a lot. It's always in you, and you're always working at it one shape or form or another. That stress that you experience, there's no compartmentalizing it and there's no real separation from it. I didn't experience any direct overt racism in my work experience.

But the simple fact that I am a Black person, a Black woman, and all that comes along with holding the position in that space, and what I have to manage and navigate as a result of my positionality, and being the minority in the spaces that I'm holding, it's hugely stressful...hugely stressful.

You're assigned to be engaged with groups, and you're in the minority and.... So, you're talking to predominantly White people about racism, oppression, and diversity, and trying to grapple with these really hard themes with the majority of people who don't look like you.... That's hard. That's some hard maneuvering. That's some hard stuff. And then you add to that being at an Ivy League.... All the stress that goes along with just being...at an institution and then being in an academic environment, and then you add...being an Ivy League, this stress is built into it.

Every situation, every meeting, every gathering, whatever, I'm always like, "We can do this." Take my deep breaths and doing all the work that I have to do to prepare myself mentally, spiritually, physically before entering the room, every room. Hugely stressful.

While she was speaking, I remembered a picture I had seen of Michelle Obama, taken right before she was entering a room. I envisioned Michelle experiencing what Zora had just said. I asked her:

If you were talking to a larger group of senior administrators who hire people to do this work, what would you want them to understand about your positionality and the way in which you do this work?

And what would you want them to know about what support systems might look like to help Black women in these roles?

Without hesitation, Zora said:

I want them to know about Black women and the history of Black women in this country. I'd want them to have a deep understanding of the historical origins of this nation, the role of Black women…literally going way back to the plantation. I mean, really have a consciousness around who we are, and who we have been and how we have been.... What our role has been in helping to really develop this nation. The challenges we have experienced, the challenges that have impacted the way we see ourselves and the way others in the world see us, and have a deep appreciation for that.

Go beyond the stereotypes, go beyond what you see on the news, the commercials, the sound bites, and really do a deep dive and get an understanding of what we have experienced. How all of that, we carry with us and bring into the room, bring into these roles. It's in our cellular memories, it's in the bodies, it's been passed down. All of that, at some level we are resisting to open our mouths. To have a sensitivity and appreciation for the extra layer of work that goes along with this work that we do. That's number one. A deep understanding and awareness of the experience of the Black woman in this nation.

In terms of supports, always keeping that at the helm, always being mindful of that, and making sure that woman is not an island, on her own. Making sure that woman has support, has administrative support, has resources, and is able to connect and build relationships, is set up well to be able to do that. Whatever institutionally can be provided to make sure that the work is supported, and that she knows that she is not alone.

I was deeply feeling what she was saying, but I realized I wanted to discuss her professional background. So, I said:

I'm going to ask another question that I should have asked first. You did not do a traditional student affairs pathway. In fact, your doctorate is not in higher ed or student affairs. Can you share how you came to this work, and why you chose to do it?

Zora replied:

I come to this work rooted in the consciousness that is committed to managing racism and oppression through a healing framework, and I have a multidisciplinary background. I didn't set out to become a diversity practitioner, but my journey led me to this role. I accept this assignment because of this capacity to have an impact on the work of dismantling racism in the world and healing and liberation. And I think the work...the root of diversity is...I think…I know the root of diversity and getting us into a place where we are living into the fullness of our diversity, which is a place of wholeness, there isn't just one path, there isn't just one way. It's really helpful to have a variety of experiences to help you understand the multiple dimensions of humanity and systems of oppression.

My background is in law, my background is in the social sciences, and I'm rooted in spirituality and faith. Ultimately, this work is an expression of my ministry and my commitment to, number one, being a better human myself and supporting the work of building humanity and others and spaces that I inhabit. That's my approach to the work. That's what led me to this role.

"Awesome." I couldn't believe that was my response. I was in my head. I had to remind myself, "She's in this conversation with you. Stop judging yourself." With that self-affirmation out of the way, I gave myself permission to continue:

One last question. For Black women who are thinking about entering this field, especially those who are early in their career, considering everything that's happened over the past 2 years, what advice would you give them before stepping into one of these roles?

Zora took some time before responding and slowly but confidently said:

Know that there is not one way. Only step into the role if you feel called to step into the role. You will know if you're called. Because there's so much interest now in this work. We're being called from all corners of the universe to be diversity officers. Well, there are requirements. I'm not just talking about whatever someone might carve out as a traditional path. There's a certain level of sustainability that is required. To do the work right and well, you have to be called and committed. You have to know how to take care of yourself as you do the work so that you can remain rooted and grounded. If you're a person of faith, I would suggest that you rely on your faith and really engage in practices that help you to stay connected to God.

If you don't claim a faith, I would recommend that you engage in practices that help sustain you and stay connected to yourself and to energy and a source that.... If you can claim a source that's greater than yourself, that will help you to be in this world, as the Word says, "Be not of this world." Because the work is taxing and laborious, challenging. You can feel hopeless. It's vast. I'm doing my best to be in the line of the folks who came before me who've done movement work to move us forward. I think about all the civil rights pioneers and people who labored in the fields. Do whatever you need to do if you are called to this work to sustain yourself and to keep yourself rooted in love.

Because that is the foundation for keeping yourself whole, keeping yourself healthy, and for actually doing work that is transformative and sustainable. It's not work that you can do in your own strength. You have to be able to find those sustaining practices that are going to help you stay grounded along the way and keep you from burning out and giving up.

There was power in her words. In my head I was answering the questions. Zora had me reflecting on how and why I chose to do this work. I asked her: "Before we wrap up, do you have any parting words?" Without hesitation, she said:

What just came to me is a scripture that says, "To whom much is given, much is required." If you find yourself in this place, it is a result of what you have been given along the way. However, you may feel about yourself in the role, you're in it. You've been given a lot. You have a lot that's expected of you. But that doesn't mean you've got to work yourself to death. It means working from a place of gratitude and groundedness and discerning what it is you have been called there to do.

That takes a commitment to carving out time to be mindful, to be prayerful, intentional, to be quiet and still so that you can discern your direction and your approach to the work. You are staying in an alignment with what you've been called there to do. So: how to be in the world, but not of the world. Remembering that you have been given much, so much is required of you to give.

A Portrait of Dhabia

I'd been looking forward to my conversation with Dhabia, both to interview her about her experience during the double pandemic and also to finally have dinner at this pan fusion seafood restaurant I'd been desperately wanting to try. Dhabia was my brunch buddy, restaurant hopper, and part of my COVID pod squad.

We arrived at the same time. As usual, Dhabia looked like she'd stepped off the page of *Vogue* and danced over to the cover of *Essence*. Her dress accentuated her curves. Her Chanel bag dangled from her right shoulder and swayed with the rhythm of her steps. The sun was slowly setting. However, there was enough light to showcase the deep blonde highlights that enhanced her shoulder-length dark brown hair, which gracefully moved with the wind. Her chestnut-colored skin glowed as if she'd just returned from a Caribbean vacation. I thought, "I've got to ask her what foundation she's wearing," and then I noticed that Dhabia didn't have a mask on. I gently grabbed her elbow to stop her from entering the restaurant and asked, "Do you have a mask?" The smile on her face disappeared and she furrowed her brow and pursed her lips. She quickly rummaged through her bag, looked up and muttered an expletive. I reassured her, "No worries. I have more in my car. Take my keys and grab one. They're in the back seat. I'll let them know we're here and meet you inside."

The restaurant had just opened, and it was empty. The dark wood of the furniture, the tea lights on each table, and the fireplace along the back wall created a cozy feeling. My mood immediately lightened as I settled myself into the booth and waited for Dhabia. Slightly frazzled, she approached the table and handed me my keys. As she sat down across from me, she said, "I can't believe that I still forget to grab a mask when I'm leaving the house." Our server suddenly appeared with menus in hand and said, "Looks like you need a drink. Can I get you something to get you started?" The spicy margarita was beckoning me to indulge.

We put in our drink order, and I skipped the pleasantries and moved right into the conversation: "Before we get started, do you mind if I record our conversation?" While asking the question, I removed my cell phone from my bag and put it between us on the table. Dhabia looked up from the menu and nodded her head in assent. I hit record and began the interview:

As you know, I'm looking to explore the perceptions and experience of Black women who are diversity practitioners at an Ivy League institution during the dual pandemic of COVID-19 and the racial reckoning of 2020 and 2021. You're one of the two women I'm interviewing for this project. We can stop to order and eat as needed. So, to get us started: Can you tell me in your own words how would you describe the dual pandemic?

Dhabia leaned back in her chair. I could tell she was thinking about what I just asked her. She replied:

I'm sure folks have said these words before, so I'm going to keep going until I find a word that really captures what I'm feeling. I guess I'll start by saying draining and in some ways, cathartic. It clarified things for a lot of folks. Like storms that come to clear the path. I think that might be a great way of describing what that was, because it was truly a storm. And it cleared up some things too, even as it complicated some things. I can elaborate if you want me to.

I did, so I asked her, "Can you elaborate on the word cathartic?" She replied:

Yeah, I think we all needed a break, and the break came at the expense of racial injustice. So, we traded in one thing for another, not that it ever was not around, but we got to be home, we got to rest a little bit. Even amidst worry, there was some peace. I think we all got to think about our homes in a way that we haven't in a long time. Things were sold out. Everyone's on the same train of thought, stocking up on food and I'm like, "I'm going to garden!" Seeds are sold out. I'm like, "Oh, so we are all on the same page?" Everyone started thinking about same things at the same time to keep themselves sane. Hammocks were sold out. People started redoing their backyards. So, I'm thinking, everyone's starting to think about their homes and their spaces and then making it comfortable. But at the same time, we're also dealing with racial injustice with that peace that you may find being at home and working from home: It grinds to a halt.

Once she got started, the words began to flow. Our server patiently waited behind her chair and, when Dhabia paused to take a break, inserted herself and took our order. Once she was gone, Dhabia immediately picked up where she left off: "You know, just trying to navigate it all I think was a difficult experience. So, while there were many gains in the process, I think you realize then what matters to you.... Right?" She looked at me intently, leaning her head to the side looking for me to affirm her. I nodded my head in agreement, and she continued:

Like, how do you feel not having to deal with your coworkers every single day, at least in person? And the peace, and how you can focus on just the work, and then you ask yourself how much of your day to day was just politics, and not the work? It's over. And who are you when you can just get the work done?

It was a rhetorical question, because she continued speaking without waiting for an answer: "You know now that with the absence of the toxicity of the workplace, you reflect on how you actually feel about your job. So, I think that was interesting for me."

She was still thinking about it, and I took advantage of the deep sigh that escaped her lips to ask another question: "Can you expound on the toxicity of the workplace?" Upon hearing that question, she perked up:

Oh yeah, yeah. So, I mean...can I say this? I'm lucky. I feel like I'm at a place that's not as toxic as it could be. Even though I literally am in a place where I'm the only self-identified Black person within my department. But I've always been a person that wants to just get the work done, so this was a dream for me. I can literally just do my meetings and carry on. And my meetings are of a nature where I don't have to even deal with my coworkers in those meetings, so it was just doing the work and leaving Zoom. And even though that was heavy too, it took away all the posturing, the performance that comes with having to be a Black woman in the workplace on a day-to-day basis. And that in itself was a relief.

Nodding in agreement, I intently waited for her to continue her train of thought.

I think that Black women don't care for themselves as much. And we know this, with the research. But I think it's important that we were in our homes for a little bit, and we got to figure out, do you like how you're living? We barely see our spaces. We didn't have time to really think about "I don't like my bed, it's uncomfortable," or "I need a desk in here," or "I want a candle for that corner of the room." No one knew that until, or at least as acutely, until we were home so much. So, I think it's important for us to have had that moment away from the workplace to kind of assess how we felt. Holistic wellness was being dealt with in a way that I don't think we've been able to otherwise.

Her words resonated with me, and I leaned back into the leather of the booth and let it embrace me: "Holistic wellness, I like that." Not wanting to dwell on that thought and needing to move the conversation along, I asked, "How did the death of George Floyd and the ensuing protest impact your life, personally and professionally?" Dhabia took a sip of her drink and laughed:

Oh, Jesus. I'm a compartmentalizer. So, as much as I deeply felt it, I didn't think I would really feel it... and suddenly I started feeling. And I was like, "This is odd." We've been through this before.... I grew up close to where Sean Bell was murdered in Queens. I've been through all this. The police outside of Jamaica Avenue Courtroom...when the day of the verdict came in.

Dhabia stopped talking, took a deep breath, and continued:

I knew these things, so why am I feeling this way? I thought I would be able to have a handle on it this time. And what exacerbated it for me is that I was living in a house with three people—my South Asian roommate and her boyfriend and my Croatian roommate. We would hang out all the time. And as I'm deeply grappling with this content, they're carrying on with their lives. And that really upset me because I'm like, "Oh, this is it. So, we're really in different worlds." They weren't callous, and I do think that they kind of listened in on it, but they were not experiencing it the same way I was. And that took a toll on me, that I really felt alone in this. And that I couldn't really even express my frustrations in my own home, because as nice as the candles were and all of that, I still couldn't even speak freely [and] be like, "This is bullshit." Because I don't even know where they stood...honestly. So that, personally, was hard. I followed the whole thing. I was glued to CNN the entire time. If I'm honest, I was happy when the looting started.

Dhabia looked me in the eyes and said:

And you can quote me on that. I was delighted. I stayed up all night. And I was like, "Get all the shit you can." And this is weird for me, as a politically correct Black girl in White spaces, but I was excited for everyone out there. I'm looking at who was getting a purse, a handbag. I think I even posted about it saying, "I would like a handbag, or my shoe size is..." I was joking about it, but I wanted people to know that I was in support of the looting that was going on. Because I think that sometimes that's the most freedom that we will ever see. And I was happy for them to get that.

I slowly nodded, affirming her statement, and said, "Wow, that's deep." Dhabia waited to see whether I was finished with my thought, and when she realized I wasn't going to say anything else, she continued:

One thing I'll add to this—which was personal—is about my little sister who I didn't know was justice oriented. We ended up having a conversation. We never had these types of conversations...because I don't hold back, so I don't talk to my family about race. She shocked me, because she did a Black Lives Matter blueprint for protesting on our block. She drew the street! She said, "First, we'll protest." Then what I did is I put her on Instagram, because I was shocked, and people were commenting, "Yeah!" They were supporting her. I didn't know she was so aware. It was shocking to me that she was ready to...protest with this agenda, "Plans for Black Lives Matter." And she goes to school, acts very nicely, and then comes home to this plan. So, I'm like, "How is she processing all of this?" So yeah, that's the personal.

And then professionally.... Oh yeah, I got in a little row, now that I'm thinking about it. There was conversation about, "We should do something at work, blah, blah, blah." And there was not resistance per se, but there was a conversation around supporting a group of folks who wanted to close down the office for a day to support the Black Lives Matter movement. And they were like, "Can we just put a message up or something on our website instead?" And I remember them saying this directly to me.... I was very angry, and clearly I was raw and emotional, but I was like, "Y'all making it complicated. It's really not that complicated." And everyone was kind of like, "Ooh." Because people wanted to hear from me as the party-line Black woman. And I didn't know what to say to them. Everyone's just trying to share but trying to be as PC as possible. My institution is good at that. But I was questioning how many people really cared. Some said like, "Oh, yeah. I heard a Black guy has a sign up in my neighborhood. Someone engaged me in a conversation about it when I was walking." So, once again it was very performative. And I still don't know where people really stand. I don't trust any of them.

But they at least tried. Some offices I know, departments and places of business, didn't even bother. So, I don't know which one's worse. Pretending that you care, or actually not even trying to pretend? I guess I could give them credit for trying their best in that moment. One of my colleagues' daughters was writing letters at home as some sort of a project.

Sure, there were some microaggressions, and I blocked them out of my mind to survive this. But I was just really actually happy to be, even though I was in a weird space, in my home. I was just happy not to see these people every day. I really didn't care where they were at. Because I was just like, "I'm in my bubble and I don't have to see anybody." Even amidst all of the trauma...it still was better than having to go to work and deal with this at the same time.

Dhabia said it with resolve, but the heaviness of that statement permeated the space. I asked, "What about COVID? How did it impact you personally and professionally?" Dhabia replied:

Oh, well, so my mom had COVID because she kept taking public transportation to work. She worked at a homeless shelter through the New York City Police Department. And I was like, "This is not a good idea. Don't take the train to work." She wasn't listening, so there was that. Until about March or April, she was just focused on her God. And I was like, "Whatever." I actually decided, this is probably capitalism at work, or maybe...what's the word for it? Maybe I've been a product of this environment too long.

After she made that statement, she frowned and continued:

But there were these COVID funds where you could get extra money for writing a letter. And I was like, "Oh, my mother has COVID." So, I'm going to write the city that I live in and my institution around this topic. And, I needed it, it wasn't like I was faking, but I knew strategically...this is a good time do it. And I was like, "Wow." Even amidst pain and frustration, I was still typing away, playing the game.

I thought I knew what she was saying but I checked for clarification: "Do you think the institution prepared you to do that?" She looked up at me confidently and said:

Well, yeah! I don't know where else I would have learned that, but I know that we're good at commodifying our pain. We've been taught to do that. In fact, I was just meeting with a student the other day about the Rhodes Scholarship, and I was like, "I hate to commodify your pain, but if there's ever a time to, this is the moment." So, we know when and where to do it. And it feels icky...but I'm like, if it means that my little sister and I would be okay, and she can get extra money for after school, whatever the situation is, yeah, I'll do it.

I could tell she had unlocked a vault in one of her compartments, so I just sat back and listened as she said: "I'm going to go back to the professional if you don't mind?" I didn't think Dhabia was asking for permission, so I just let her continue her train of thought:

I encountered a situation at the very beginning of the pandemic. It's not part of my work, but I'm really close to the first-gen, low-income [FGLI] students on my campus. In the spring of 2020, they got to work quickly, because they felt that they were displaced, and I didn't even think about it. Honestly, even as someone who was a FGLI college student, I didn't think, "Oh my God, what are they going to do." I thought about every other historically marginalized student, but I didn't think, "Wow, there's some students who are going back into toxic environments." That was not the first thing on my mind when they said, "You all have to go." All of that kind of washed over me and days later, I'm like, "Wow, there are people who are going back to places that they never thought they would ever have to see again and have to live there again." And now I'm realizing this is a place where they experience more freedom, and how hard that must be for the soul having to leave so abruptly.

We were rallying with alumni groups. I wasn't on the FGLI alumni board yet at that point, but I was liaising with our first-gen alumni groups and students on how we could raise money. And they raised a lot of money through the alumni, because that was a group of folks who could understand what it could be like at my institution during the COVID shutdown. So, whether they're here or not, they were like, "Look what you did to these kids." So, a lot of money started rolling in to help FGLI students. I was speaking to two students in our last few days of meeting before we had to shut down, and they were talking about their ranch that they're going back to, their 10-bedroom ranch in Texas. And then there was another student who was talking about, "I'm going back to a two-bedroom apartment in Brooklyn. And my brother already took over my room." There was a stark difference between the two experiences. One is going back to a mansion, and another is going back to a hovel. And what does that mean for how you conduct your work in an academic setting in these two residences?

That was a powerful question. I knew it was rhetorical and she wasn't looking for the answer, so I took advantage of the silence and asked, "Do you think there was a difference? Do you think your positionality had you respond to the students in a way that your other coworkers could not?" Dhabia didn't skip a beat:

Oh, yeah. No one was probably reaching out to them while they were crying, all through the pandemic. I had many crying Zoom calls. I cried myself. One of my Asian American students was like, "We keep moving. My family was in the sticks of Indiana, but we had to move because my father keeps trying to find a job in different places. We keep changing states." This was the situation for so many of my students. And it was like, "What the hell?"

So, yeah, I definitely shouldered a burden that was different from my peers. They were chilling at home; they were in their lake houses. And I was here trying to carry a population of students on my shoulders. And I had no.... I was not equipped to do so, but the best I could do was listen and cry with them, as we cried together about the situation.

And I will say, I did advocate. For example, one of the things that came up was the students who didn't stay on campus and were able to leave and get away were going to get an extra two summer classes when we returned to campus, but the people who stayed wouldn't? So, I'm asking, "Are we furthering the inequalities and inequities that are built into the system already, with the students who probably need the extra two classes, but because they stayed, they'll be two classes behind those who could afford to leave campus?" I kept raising that issue. I'm asking, "This is not bizarre to anybody?" And they're like, "That's a good point!" Because no one was thinking of this as a problem in terms of pipelines, in terms of the overlap between potentially some of our students who are from lower [socioeconomic status], and them being the least academically prepared in the first place. And then you're going to give a bonus two classes to people who could afford to leave?

What the heck? Who thought of this? I don't want to blame anyone. I'm sure people didn't intentionally set out to marginalize a subset of students.... You could think about so many different lenses of students. And I think that as I grow as a professional, if something like this ever happens again, in a boardroom meeting, I would say, "Let's talk about every demographic of students that we have in this community, and let's go through one by one, and tell me how this decision will impact them. Individuals, LGBTQIA+, Black, White, Hispanic, South Asian, Indigenous, etc. It becomes something with so much weight. Let's go through everybody we've got to see how this would actually impact them." Because I think that was missed with this conversation. People didn't think about, "Oh, how does this make sense for everybody on campus?" So, that was a professional challenge.

I wanted to get in more questions. As she stopped to take a bite of her food, I asked, "During COVID, do you think there were ways in which your work and positionality were impacted because you were at an Ivy League institution?" Dhabia replied:

Yeah, we weren't furloughed, and that was something on my mind. I heard a lot of people saying that they were. And I had to kind of navigate telling my friends I wasn't, when they were. I'm like, "Shit, I'm still getting my check every week." And there were people who were like, "I'm only working 3 days a week for the next 4 months to make X." And my institution didn't have that problem. And that's a blessing, in a way that I don't know what I would've done if that situation happened to me. Even now, when you think about our testing. My best friend asked me, "Do you think we'll ever have to pay for COVID tests? What do you think?" I'm like, "I don't know, because I get as many tests as I want every day." I can get tested three times a day if I want to, five times a day. And they're around the campus, like candy, and that is a privilege that is unbelievable. And when you're in the bubble, you don't realize how privileged you are. I've never had to pay for a COVID test.

Even information and the news. I knew some shit before CNN News knew some shit. I don't mean it in an espionage way, but I mean my entire department had parents that were doctors, or spouses that were doctors, or were doctors themselves at the medical school and our affiliated hospitals. They were reading the research papers in their spare time and finding out the cutting-edge research on what was working. Even my best friend said, "Y'all left campus before anyone knew what was going on." So, we were way ahead of the ball.

And if anything, I now know that if an asteroid's coming, my institution will know first, maybe even before NASA, so it's great. And I can translate that to my people, but it's also troublesome. Something's happening worldwide, and the information is piecemeal. One would say, I'm sure there are people who would say, "These people don't read and that's why they don't know. The information's accessible." But I don't feel it's just that. I think that there are some nuances.

Dhabia finished her sentence, and our server took advantage of the lull in our conversation to ask if we wanted more drinks. We both said "Yes" at the same time, and that sparked a fit of giggles. The server said, "I'm going to assume you want the same thing." We both vigorously nodded our heads, and when she left, I continued with my questions: "What would you say the impact of the dual pandemics of COVID-19 and the racial reckoning of 2020 had on your work as a diversity administrator?" Dhabia replied:

Yeah, yeah. We all know that there's a disproportionate burden on Black women to be the nannies and the mammies of campus, and I don't know how to escape that. I wonder if there's a way. I wonder if there's a model for those who don't know how to escape it. I would love to hear a case study on a woman who knew about it and chose not to do it. But I don't know anyone who doesn't. I have to say I'm thankful for the women who shepherded me through my journey, but this is a burden you shouldn't have to handle as a Black woman.

I think about the Black women who saved me through my own grad student experience. I couldn't have gotten through without them, and I feel bad that I dumped my shit on them on a day-to-day basis. So yeah, that's what I think about. And I think about the students who come into my office, and sometimes it's a lot. Sometimes I'm like, "Fuck. I really want to just have lunch," and I'm getting a text about a panic attack.

Even when I'm like, "I do not want to do this right now," but I know that there were people who did it for me, and this is my way of paying it forward. And I will never say no, even if I want to. And I don't know how to reconcile that, I don't know what to do with that information, but I'm thankful that the people that I went to didn't say no to me, because I don't know where I would be without them.

She seemed sullen after making that statement, which made me interject: "You know there are subtle and not subtle ways that race and gender create double obstacles for Black women in our field, which leads to enormous stress. Did you experience that phenomenon?" Dhabia let out a chuckle:

This is always my soapbox, my bone to pick. I know that a lot of Black women were living by themselves. And I say, "Great that you can afford to live in a major urban city by yourself," which is a triumph in one light, but a tragedy in another, because why the hell are you alone during the pandemic? There's research on that, days and nights by yourself isn't good, what the hell? It's horrible.

And I would imagine that first, we'd want to have Black men with us, and they were nowhere to be found. I don't know if that means anything to anybody. And I'm thankful for the ones that were around, because they were needed, just to even play cards, or take a walk, or go to a grocery store. I would say, even the raggedy ones I know.... I ran out of bottled water in my house one day. And I was terrified to go back to the grocery store. A male friend was at my house earlier that day. And that afternoon he called me and said, "I'm outside." And I said, "Oh, did you forget something? Because I already set up my meetings for the afternoon." And he said, "No, I just dropped off a case of water at the stairs and a bacon, egg, and cheese sandwich."

And I was so blown away by that act of kindness, because I didn't say I needed water, I didn't.... He just, I guess, noticed. It was just nice for him to double back and do that. And I wish that one act wasn't a big deal to me, because...I haven't seen it since, and I don't know many Black women that had that. And even that little crumb of care was more than we ever get. And I hold it at a premium in a way that I can.

I could tell a lot was coming up for her, so I just let her continue talking.

I actually got closer to people. There are people who I had no time for during the day. But during the pandemic, I had plenty of time to talk to people. Become one with nature. It reminded me...of when I lived abroad. And now I'm realizing I really don't want to do this shit anymore. And however, I need to find a way to get off this treadmill come hell or high water, by land or by sea, I'm not doing this the rest of my life. And that doesn't mean I'm not doing it in terms of the work. I will do the work forever, but not under the duress, the stress.

If I have to marry rich.... I hope I wouldn't have to go that far. But I don't care what I have to do, but I'm not interested in back-breaking labor for 60 years. You get a watch and a plaque. I refuse to do it, and I'm going to find a way out of it one way or another, or I'm just going to leave the country.

Either way, I now know that this is not normal. I think we all know that it's not normal, what we are doing, and it shouldn't ever be normal again, even as capitalism pushes us to make it normal again. It should never be normal. The burden and the load you are taking on every single day as Black female diversity administrators, hell, Black women who are professionals. I think that Black females have to put on...armor...and it's hard to take it off, and we're constantly fighting against it.

For example, some people when they completely let go, they have a hard time getting back on track. And then there were people who couldn't let go, and thought it was business as usual. And I find...I don't know, I would like to research the percentage of Black women who fell into the business as usual. For those of us who wanted to let go, it took a while for us to really drop the armor. I recognize that this is a different terrain, and we need to try something different in this moment.

I thought about myself and decided to be vulnerable in the moment:

It did take a while for me to put down the armor. And I'll admit I never let it out of my sight. I was prepared to put it back on in a moment's notice to protect myself. I don't know if that's good or bad.

Trailing off, I realized that this conversation wasn't about me, so I said:

You talked about doing research. We are the research. We are living the research in real time, as Black women who are diversity practitioners in higher education. With that in mind, what would you say to a woman who's going to come into this work, based on your experience pre-COVID, COVID, right now?

Dhabia replied:

You know, I said this as a whisper before COVID, but now it's turned into a roar. Don't let the opportunity slip by you. It's great work, you get to help a lot of people. But the greatest work is getting yourself through it, through your life at home. And you can't do that if you make this thing your entire identity. You have to constantly be asking yourself, "Who am I without this job?" Like, "Who are you without your admin experience? Who are you without being this prominent symbolic person on campus?" And figure that out so that you can let go and be free. Because if you're letting your job define you, you're already in a world of trouble, because they will use that, and they will run with it, and they will make sure that you feel that way, and underscore it. But you got to make sure that you can walk away at any point, and that's hard.

And the hardest part is probably not the institution, it's the students. And that's something I haven't fully clarified just yet because I know they can still find me on campus or off. I know, sadly, there'll always be another Black woman who will give up her life and body to service them. But I recognize now that it's just powerful to show them that I can walk away, and that they can walk away too.

So that's what they need to see, they need to see me being like, "I'm not doing this shit anymore. I'm actually taking a day off." And they need to see that so that they have the permission to do so themselves. So, show your vulnerability, show that things are rough. I think that Black women as a collective, we need to let down our armor, because people have gotten very, very comfortable, too comfortable with us being superwomen. And we need to make sure that we humanize ourselves again, because no one else will.

Her words moved me to say:

Man, you dropped a gem. So, you're saying to the woman who just accepted the role, she got the offer letter, she's going to the top Ivy League institution and the word diversity is somewhere in her job title. What do you say to her? What are you telling her to do?

Dhabia replied, "I'll tell her...what my White supervisor told me: 'Once your 90 days are over, start scheduling your vacation.'"

CONCLUSION

Thomas and Jackson (2007) posited that Black women in predominately white institutions lack the necessary support to navigate the burden of role overload as it relates to their racial and gender identity. The portraits of Zora and Dhabia reveal "the subtle and not-so-subtle ways that race and gender stereotypes combined can create double obstacles for Black women in higher education, which in turn can lead to a sense of hopelessness and stress" (Thomas and Jackson, 2007).

Despite the mental and physical taxation on their bodies, the women in this chapter had found pockets of peace and joy amid the turmoil caused by COVID-19 and the amplified racism within the United States. Leaning in to spiritual practices, a commitment to well-being, and different modalities of self-care, the two women in this chapter exemplify what it means to be resilient in the face of uncertainty and recurring trauma.

Diversity work is not for the faint of heart, yet it is a calling for many. For Black women in the field, entering the field, or contemplating the field, remember the advice given by Zora: "Be mindful, be prayerful, be intentional, be quiet, and be still so that you can discern your direction and your approach to the work." And in the words of Dhabia: "Start scheduling that vacation!"

ACKNOWLEDGMENT

This research received no specific grant from any funding agency in the public, commercial, or not-for-profit sectors.

REFERENCES

Collins, P. H. (2001). Defining Black feminist thought. *Race Critical Theories,* 152-175.

Delgado, R. (1989). Storytelling for Oppositionists and Others: A Plea for Narrative. *Michigan Law Review*, *87*(8), 2411–2441. doi:10.2307/1289308

Hackmann, D. G. (2002). Using portraiture in educational leadership research. *International Journal of Leadership in Education*, *5*(1), 51–60. doi:10.1080/13603120110057109

Lawrence-Lightfoot, S., & Davis, J. H. (2002). *The art and science of portraiture*. Jossey-Bass.

Thomas, V. G., & Jackson, J. A. (2007). The education of African American girls and women: Past to present. *The Journal of Negro Education*, *76*(3), 357–372.

Wallace, S. L., Moore, S. E., Wilson, L. L., & Hart, B. G. (2012). African American women in the academy: Quelling the myth of presumed incompetence. In G. Gutierrez y Muhs, Y. Niemann, C. González, & A. Harris (Eds.), *Presumed incompetent: The intersections of race and class for women in academia,* (pp. 421–438). University Press of Colorado. doi:10.2307/j.ctt4cgr3k.38

Whitaker, M. C., & Grollman, E. A. (Eds.). (2018). *Counternarratives from women of color academics: Bravery, vulnerability, and resistance,* (1st ed.). Routledge., doi:10.4324/9780429465505

Willis, J. M. (2019). *Pushing through despite the bullshit: Black women graduate students in higher education at historically White institutions* (Publication No. 13862212) [Doctoral dissertation]. California State University, USA.

ADDITIONAL READING

Chance, N. L. (2022). Resilient leadership: A phenomenological exploration into how Black women in higher education leadership navigate cultural adversity. *Journal of Humanistic Psychology, 62*(1), 44–78. doi:10.1177/00221678211003000

Golden, M. (2021). *The strong Black woman: How a myth endangers the physical and mental health of Black women*. Mango Publishing.

Jones, C. (2006). Falling between the cracks: What diversity means for Black women in higher education. *Policy Futures in Education, 4*(2), 145–159. doi:10.2304/pfie.2006.4.2.145

Lightsey, D. (2020). *A phoenix first must burn—How Black women in higher education administration implement the reactionary principle of professionally clapping back: A cognitive process to manage workplace microaggressions* (Publication No. 28088653.) [Doctoral dissertation]. University of Southern California, USA.

Love, R. (2021). *We are not the same: The experiences of Black women multicultural directors at predominantly White institutions* (Publication No. 28722543) [Doctoral dissertation]. Colorado State University, USA.

Njoku, A., & Evans, M. (2022). Black women faculty and administrators navigating COVID-19, social unrest, and academia: Challenges and strategies. *International Journal of Environmental Research and Public Health, 19*(4), 2220. doi:10.3390/ijerph19042220 PMID:35206408

West, N. M. (2021). Embodying Black feminist epistemology to make green grass grow: The transition from administrator to academic for a Black woman in student affairs. *Journal of Diversity in Higher Education, 10* (1037),0000-375.

KEY TERMS AND DEFINITIONS

Authenticity: The ability to be true to oneself.
Black Women: Women who self-identify as has having a heritage within the African diaspora.

Faith: Trust or confidence in a higher being.

Liberation: To be free from physical, psychological, and emotional encumbrances.

Resilience: The ability to overcome, bounce back, and recover.

Self-Care: Doing things to take care of the mind, body, and spirit—activities that support a healthy lifestyle.

Spirituality: A belief or connection to a higher power or something beyond oneself.

Chapter 6
Of Protest and Paradox:
Leading DEI in Minnesota

Lauren L. Jones
https://orcid.org/0000-0002-4219-5665
University of Minnesota, USA

ABSTRACT

This chapter glances into the experience of leading diversity, equity, and inclusion (DEI) work while living in Minneapolis before, during, and after the murder of George Floyd, the subsequent uprisings, and racial reckoning of 2020. Ironically, the progressive state of Minnesota has been the site of multiple state-involved murders while also consistently voting Democrats into the White House and U.S. congress. This Minnesota paradox creates a unique place for DEI work. The author explores theories of white guilt and white saviorism, provides context about the racial and social environment of Minnesota, and provides recommendations for Black women DEI practitioners and those that employ them.

INTRODUCTION

The events of summer 2020 changed significantly for the diversity, equity, and inclusion (DEI) field and those who work in it. In this chapter, I revisit the murder of George Floyd and the subsequent events. In recalling my experiences since moving to Minnesota, I introduce important contextual information about the Twin Cities and Minnesota that have contributed to today's sociopolitical environment. This chapter will explore tenets of whiteness that make DEI work uniquely difficult in liberal communities and ways that I have worked with and against those norms. I talk about my challenges as a Black woman, how I have grown, and how I have seen the industry change since 2020. Finally, I offer recommendations for Black women who work in DEI as well as the organizations that employ them. While my work is within the higher education setting, many of these lessons are widely applicable to different types of organizations. This is a critical chapter for people trying to make sense of the last couple of years and how they can move forward with a more grounded approach to racial and social justice work.

DOI: 10.4018/978-1-6684-3564-9.ch006

BACKGROUND

On May 25th, 2020, police were dispatched to Cup Foods, a convenience store on Minneapolis' south side, regarding a counterfeit $20 bill. At the scene, police apprehended and handcuffed George Floyd, a 46-year-old Black man who had moved to Minnesota in 2014. While Floyd was handcuffed, face down on the ground, Derek Chauvin, a 19-year veteran officer, forced his knee into Floyd's neck and kept it there for over nine minutes. Floyd repeatedly yelled that he was not able to breathe and was in pain. An ambulance would eventually respond, but Chauvin kept his knee in Floyd's neck a whole minute after they arrived. Floyd had lost consciousness and would be pronounced dead approximately one hour later (BBC, 2020).

If not for a number of key circumstances, the incident may not have been more than a blip on the radar. First, the time of year meant that there was enough light to see at night and warm enough that people could watch and, later, protest. Second, the pandemic meant that many people were at or near home while on lockdown. Third, it was the latest in a string of racist incidents that year that ended with innocent Black people dying. In February 2020, Ahmaud Arbery was jogging in a neighborhood in Glynn County, Georgia. Three white men would later be convicted of his murder, largely because it was caught on video. The following month, Breonna Taylor was fatally shot in her own apartment in a botched police raid in Louisville, KY. No charges were initially filed against the officer, causing unrest and anger across the world. By the time George Floyd was murdered, everything seemed to come to a head. By May 26, 2020, local protestors were already in the streets. Their anger was further provoked by the militarized police presence. Journalists and civilians were injured in the chaos. Many businesses and some residences were damaged or burned to the ground. The protests would spread across the world and last weeks. By June 3rd, over 200 US cities had imposed curfews, and over 62,000 national guard personnel had been deployed (Sternlicht, 2020; Warren and Hadden, 2020). Professional athletes and celebrities joined protests. Major media outlets provided round-the-clock coverage. And the biggest corporations in the world vowed to stamp out racism in their organizations. It was the wildest summer I had ever experienced.

Minnesota, an American Paradox

Minnesota is, as many here will say, *interesting*. Often, Minneapolis, St. Paul, and the surrounding suburbs are named as top places to live, work, or raise children (U.S. News & World Report, 2022). There is some truth in these declarations. There are what seem to be endless outdoor activities, cultural events, and Fortune 500 companies in the metro area. But there are also other truths, those that led to the murders of George Floyd, Daunte Wright, and Philando Castile. This is part of what University of Minnesota economist Dr. Samuel Myers, Jr. calls "the Minnesota Paradox": it is the best state for some but also has some of the worst social and economic racial gaps in the country (Myers, n.d.). While White citizens enjoy the lakes, fresh air, and abundant employment opportunities, Black and other citizens of color contend with food deserts (Jackson, 2020), racial covenants (Mapping Prejudice, n.d.), and high incarceration rates (Minnesota Department of Corrections, 2020).

Recognizing the vast disparities, The Mapping Prejudice project has worked since 2016 to identify one source of the structural racism here: housing. The initiative, led by historians, librarians, geographers, digital humanists, and community activists, has worked to expose racial covenants, which real estate developers used in the early 20th century to keep people of color out of neighborhoods (Mapping

Prejudice, n.d.). One such covenant read that the particular "*premises shall not at any time be conveyed, mortgaged or leased to any person or persons of Chinese, Japanese, Moorish, Turkish, Negro, Mongolian or African blood or descent*" (Mapping Prejudice, n.d.). As a result, the most desirable neighborhoods were kept all white, allowing white Minnesotans to accumulate and inherit wealth over generations.

Meanwhile, Black residents were excluded, harassed, and displaced. In Minneapolis, the City Council argued for years over whether they should pass an open housing law, which would finally allow Black and other residents of color to live wherever they wanted, whether as renters or owners. In 1958, instead of passing housing equity legislation, an Interim Commission on Housing Discrimination in Minnesota proclaimed that an education campaign focused on tolerance was needed and that "the Negro people can recognize the need for and actually practice patience, great patience" (Montrie, 2022, pg. 137). When an anti-discrimination law finally was passed in 1962, it was met with much resistance. Opponents took the teeth out of the law by adding exceptions, and local realtor groups argued that the law was designed for race-mixing, effectively lobbying to limit the budget of the agency in charge of enforcing the law (Montrie, 2022). The racist real estate, rental, and loan practices, along with federal redlining, were effective in restricting Black Minneapolitans to areas that would be deemed as "blighted." This classification made these areas subject to redevelopment projects, including new highways.

Like many American cities, Minneapolis and St. Paul built major highways through former Black communities, displacing hundreds of families and diminishing much of the wealth they had accumulated via homeownership (Montrie, 2022; Restorative Rondo, 2020). In St. Paul, the Rondo neighborhood was home to about 80% of that city's Black population by the 1950s, in addition to many residents of other races. The community thrived, establishing the St. Paul NAACP, multiple Black newspapers, and several important social clubs. The construction of I-94 from 1956-1968 led to the demolition of more than 700 Black owned homes, and 300 Black owned businesses, in addition to churches, schools, and community centers. The community was irreparably fractured (Montrie, 2022). While white Rondo residents were able to find new homes easily, Black and mixed families encountered discrimination. Many of those displaced as well as their children are still wont to tell stories about their losses and former community. In 1983, an annual celebration known as Rondo Days was initiated to celebrate the history and ongoing legacy of the community (Montrie, 2022; McClure, 2022).

In Minneapolis, the construction of interstate 35W disrupted the lives of Black residents in the Central community on the city's south side. There, Black businesses dominated the 38th street corridor, where the Minnesota Spokesman-Recorder, Minnesota's first Black-owned newspaper, is still headquartered (Onile-Ere, 2021). It is one of the few neighborhoods where Blacks were permitted to live in the city and the area includes the corner where George Floyd was murdered, 38th and Chicago Avenue. Donofrio (2020) lays out a stunning set of historical facts and oral history about the planning and construction of the highway and how it points to a logic based on racism. For example, interviews indicate that Black residents from the neighborhood perceived 35W as a dividing line between White and Black residents. Maps from the federal government that highlight redlined districts, as well as appraisers' descriptions of the neighborhood confirm their beliefs: the Federal Housing Administration encouraged the building of high-speed traffic arteries to shield desirable neighborhoods from "inharmonious racial groups" (Federal Housing Administration as cited in Donofrio, para. 11).

George Floyd was murdered in this area, right on the border of two neighborhoods, Central and Powderhorn. Today, Central is 36% Hispanic, 31% White and 27% Black. Powderhorn is currently 48% White, 30% Hispanic, and 13% Black, and (City of Minneapolis, 2022). In a beautiful essay in Vanity Fair, Safy-Hallan Farah (2020) details her experience growing up in this area. She points out the anti-Blackness she saw and felt from Whites and non-Black people of color, and even within her own community, the Somalis. This same racism and anti-Blackness are deeply connected to the murder of George Floyd. As a Black person in this city, I experience this every day, in the food desert of North Minneapolis, and in a historically White institution that is grappling with shifting attitudes and demographics. These histories and current day realities make my work both incredibly difficult and incredibly meaningful. The Twin Cities, liberal bastion of the north, is, in many ways, a perfect microcosm of American race relations.

White Americans relationship to race and racism has always been fraught. After the election of Donald Trump, White liberals seemed to struggle to reconcile what they were seeing with what they thought America was. On MSNBC, for example, a reliably liberal news source, pundits repeatedly decried to viewers that "this is not who we are" and "we're better than this" (Bell, 2019). After the two-term election of Barack Obama, they deemed racism as a fringe belief, one confined to rural and Southern America. The stories of coming from Black America, however, have never corroborated this. We have continued to navigate systemic racism since our arrival to this country. There has seemingly always been a gap between our reality and the stories that White America believes about itself. In his recent book, sociologist Victor E. Ray (2022) addresses this phenomenon by explaining the hierarchies of credibility. Ray (2022) says, "those in power are deemed purveyors of truth, while marginalized people are disbelieved, even about their own experiences" (pg. 86). Critical race theory posits that Black Americans are experts on the racism we see, feel, and experience each day (Ray, 2022), even in places that are considered progressive. As Malcolm X proclaimed, the U.S. South begins at the Canadian border.

GOOD WHITE INTENTIONS

The aforementioned difficult social realities have been catnip for the culture of civic engagement and philanthropy in the Minneapolis-St. Paul metro. Dozens of nonprofits and governmental programs exist with the goal of creating equity between White and non-White residents. Organizations like the Facilitating Racial Equity Collaborative, Voices for Racial Justice, and Black Visions exist solely to support racial justice and equity in the area. Other organizations such as the Bush Foundation, Wilder Foundation, and the local YWCA have broader missions but contribute massive resources to combat racial disparities. Several of these organizations received millions in donations after the murder of George Floyd (Bui, 2020).

One of the state's largest nonprofits is Lutheran Social Services (LSS), which serves 1 in 65 Minnesotans with their $208m annual budget (Lutheran Social Service, n.d.). The Lutheran influence is deep. Minnesota has the largest Lutheran presence in the country, with just under 700K members in the state. Stemming from the immigration waves from Scandinavia and Germany, Minnesota boasts five private Lutheran colleges, one of the world's largest Lutheran seminaries, the National Lutheran Choir, and the publishing house of the Evangelical Lutheran Church of America (Hopfensperger, 2016). The Lutheran ideals of dignity and justice represent social services in Minnesota, and, to a large extent, exemplify what Minnesotans think of themselves AKA Good White Intentions. Unfortunately, the desire to do and appear good have not led to better conditions for Black residents in Minnesota.

The state consistently votes for democratic presidents and senators, especially in the metro area, and most of the officers involved in killing unarmed citizens in the last few years have been convicted. And yet, the inequities persist. The Good White Intentions are simply not enough, or are perhaps, just a façade. Mere months after George Floyd, Daunte Wright was killed by an officer in Brooklyn Center, several miles north of my home in North Minneapolis. These are such difficult realities to reconcile.

Black people from places like Chicago, Detroit, and Gary moved to the Twin Cities and Minnesota over the last four decades (Biewen, 1997) because the jobs were plentiful and because, in case they fell on hard times, the social safety net was strong. Between 2010 and 2020, the Black/African American population in Minnesota grew by almost 55% (Minnesota Employment and Economic Development, 2022). This includes recent immigrants from African countries such as Somalia, Ethiopia, and Liberia. While we represent only about 6% of the state, Black people are 19% of the population of Minneapolis and nearly 16% of those in St. Paul (U.S. Census, 2021).

The high voter turnout (U.S. Census, 2020), low unemployment (U.S. Bureau of Labor Statistics, 2022), strong culture of volunteerism (AmeriCorps, n.d.), high education rates (Federal Reserve of St. Louis, 2021), and generous government support structures would seem to point to a state that is committed to values like racial justice. However, as history shows, it points to a culture of White guilt, White urgency, and White saviorism (all which I define shortly). These three phenomena, while not unique to Minnesota, have contributed to a difficult yet compelling place to be a DEI practitioner.

RACE AND RACISM IN MINNESOTA

There is a high a high turnover rate for professionals of color in the Twin Cities area (Schubert, 2018). In 2016, the Star Tribune showed that sixty percent of professionals of color surveyed were planning to leave the state in three to five years (p. 01A). The focus group participants cited having an outsider status and the pressure to assimilate [to White dominant culture] as reasons that they leave.

Another reason why professionals of color leave the profession in Minneapolis is the less than warm reception they get from Minnesotans who were born/raised here is what is often called "Minnesota Nice." Minnesota Nice is defined conversely as both polite to a fault and overly passive-aggressive; it includes being non-confrontational and socially guarded, making it hard to form relationships and discuss hard topics such as racism (Moen, 2019). People who move to the area from out of state find this phenomenon difficult to navigate, especially professionals of color who have multiple challenges to overcome. Instead of trying to conquer it, many simply gain their professional experience, then leave. This culture of transience makes it difficult to sustain a strong Black middle class or create meaningful policy change. The cities of Minneapolis and St. Paul have created initiatives to address the transience issue, but no data is yet available to determine whether they are working.

As I consider whether I will stay here for the long haul, I think about how this particular brand of racism will impact me, my career, my household, and my relationships. I suspect I will move away in a few years, but only time will tell. One thing I know for sure, is that to be a Black person immersed in a culture of White Guilt is exhausting.

White Guilt

In Helms' (1995) White identity development model, she identified six identity statuses (formerly called stages) of how White people respond to racial situations in their environment. The second status, known as disintegration, is where the White person learns about race-based privilege and oppression, experiences dissonance about our realities, and may encounter more people of color. The fourth status is pseudo-independence, wherein the White individual begins to understand race and racism intellectually and often attempts to form relationships with people of color. Both of these statuses can lead to complex feelings, including guilt (Helms, 1995).

Guilt is the emotion of responsibility or remorse for some offense, real or imagined (Dictionary.com, 2022). White guilt is the result of the cognitive dissonance Whites experience when learning about the incongruencies of race and racism. Seeing the murders of innocent Black people happen in your own state that you believed was progressive and "not racist" is certainly difficult to reconcile. Tatum (1996) theorized that the lack of White role models who champion racial justice could contribute to feelings of White guilt (as cited in Arminio, 2001). In Minnesota, there are many organizations, classrooms, and programs being led by well-intentioned but poorly equipped White people. However, the key social indicators for racial equity have barely moved.

White Savior Complex

Dr. Amy C. Finnegan (2022) defines the White Savior Complex (WSC) as a network of relationships and resources guided by an ideology that centers White bodies as essential helpers in responding to social problems. Generally, privileged White people (unconsciously) utilize the WSC to conciliate their White guilt. In Minnesota, the average White family is doing better than White families across the country, while the average Black household is doing worse. This includes data about income, poverty, and education. For example, the median household income for Black people in the seven-county metro area was $38,822, while for Whites, it was $86,783 (O'Neill, 2020). Additionally, the high school graduation rate for Black students stands at 67%, while for Whites, it is 88% (Morrissette, 2021). Many other data points support the Minnesota Paradox theory. The relative privilege of Whites in the state, along with a strong democratic base and Lutheran values, seems to have led to the complex system of nonprofits and government-sponsored programs designed to alleviate racial disparities.

Finnegan (2022) names this part of the WSC as a pursuit to find purpose. It is about being right and good—and it is about reaching out to assist others while avoiding examination of oneself and the conditions that enable suffering in the first place. But charity is no substitute for justice. Funneling money and resources into organizations without changing policies and shifting power is a futile exercise of pride.

White Urgency

After George Floyd's murder went viral, the panic seemed to set in. Minnesota was, once again, on the world stage as a place where racism was allowed to flourish. How could we, the reliable liberal state, be both good and also *racist*? As Robin DiAngelo points out in her book, White Fragility,:

"Racists were those white people in the South, smiling and picnicking at the base of lynching trees, store owners posting Whites Only signs over drinking fountains and good ol' boys beating innocent children such as Emmitt Till to death" (p. 72-73)

White Minnesotans were in a panic. Donations poured in to organizations that promised to help. Narratives were constructed (or re-published) about how the state and metro area were full of racial inconsistencies. I was part of many conversations with White colleagues who, once they moved past their shock and anger, jumped into action mode. But there was often a lack of substantive processing, organizing, or intention. In their place was instead an intense feeling of urgency.

One of the tenets of White supremacy culture is urgency. This can be defined as the intense desire and need White people have for quick action and resolution to racial injustice, often asked of people of color. Instead of taking time to reflect, build relationships, and come to a consensus, White supremacy urges us to make quick decisions and create visible results. This kind of approach has many drawbacks. Among other things, it privileges those who process information quickly, utilizes shame, guilt, and self-righteousness to manipulate quick decisions, and leads to mental, physical, and spiritual burnout (Okun, 2022). White urgency is particularly painful for folks who have been experiencing and talking about racism for decades. Berila (2020) notes that this urgent energy stems from Whites not having the ability to sit with their pain and ignorance. It is a stark reminder that those who are coded as White can enter or exit the fight for racial justice whenever it pleases them (Berila, 2020). Many of us have experienced the disengagement of our White colleagues when the topic of racial justice becomes overwhelming or is no longer in the headlines.

White Urgency in Action

While racial justice is important and urgent, we cannot expect to dismantle a 400+-year-old problem with a 3-year strategic plan. This is not how DEI works (or rather, it shouldn't). In many meetings at my institution, I often say that we will lead this work with intention because doing something right is better than doing it fast. Resisting White urgency has been an important touchstone for me in this work. I have made it a point to center equity, liberation, and community healing in my work. These take significant time and collaboration. I have had to contend with white urgency a couple of times in my career.

In the immediate wake of George Floyd's murder, the inboxes I had on social media, text messages, and my email exploded. The requests were diverse, examples include asking me to:

- Facilitate processing spaces with students
- Expand the scope of our climate assessment to include alumni
- Help craft several messages that would go out to the entire school community
- Advise a statistics student about how he could professionally contribute to justice work

Truth be told I wasn't mad about most of these requests, they were part of my job anyway. However, the speed and volume at which they were coming was unfamiliar and overwhelming. In addition, open letters were being posted from multiple groups of students and faculty. The letters were primarily directed to the dean but also to other members of the leadership team, which I was not a part of at the time. But many of the demands included actions that would fall under my purview. Direct or indirect, the pressure was on me and other DEI leaders to create major changes.

The second meeting of the DEI strategic planning committee was held about two weeks after the murder of George Floyd. There was a lot of emotion in the room. While it was a very mixed group, the most fervor came from the white women in the Zoom room. They expressed frustration about us having a White consultant facilitating the meetings, asked how we would respond to the flurry of demands from the school community, and called for clarity about how we would be using our time. I worked hard to maintain my composure in one of the most intense meetings of my life. As a Black woman in a White institution, I simply do not have the privilege to be that emotional in public. Even if it is my community that is the one most impacted. We forged ahead, through tension and disagreements. Throughout the following year, I repeatedly had to remind the committee that we would focus on intention over speed in our planning. Eventually, with skillful and patient facilitation, through many uncomfortable conversations, we were able to focus and create a strong strategic plan that centers antiracism.

MY MINNESOTA STORY

I had moved to Minnesota in July 2017 to work at the University of Minnesota and, ironically, to heal. I had spent the six years prior in the Deep South. I officially began doing DEI work in 2014 at a small university in South Carolina. I was overworked and underpaid, but like most young student affairs professionals, I was focused on the work and the difference I could make for students. I helped organize free HIV testing, taught leadership courses, and managed mentorship programs, among other responsibilities. And I made a salary of $34,000 per year. There was no route to a higher salary in that role. The state of South Carolina (along with several other states) was suing the federal government over proposed changes to the Fair Labor Standards Act (FLSA), which would have brought my salary up to the minimum of $47,000.

This all came to a head in 2016 when, amidst the political chaos of the year, I was forced to have emergency surgery. I spent several days in the hospital and six weeks in bed recovering. The doctors told me I would need regular check-ins and more surgeries in the future. Even with insurance, my salary was not enough to cover the ongoing costs. It felt like I was being betrayed by my body, my institution, the state, and the country. I spent much of that spring in tears. My body was healing, but my heart was breaking.

More hot angry tears came after the 2016 election. I couldn't believe it. What had felt like a yearlong joke had become all too real. The murders of Walter Scott and the nine parishioners in the Charleston massacre hadn't made a bit of difference to White voters in South Carolina. They could not bring themselves to vote for a democrat, let alone a woman named Clinton. I no longer felt safe in rural South Carolina. I had become used to seeing confederate flags and memorials every day, but after the 2016 election, I felt downright targeted for trying to dismantle racism, sexism, and homophobia in this state. Besides, I was broke, and there were no opportunities for advancement. I applied for jobs back in the Midwest, so I could be closer to my family and continue my convalescence. I spent about six months applying for jobs and interviewing while the country continued to devolve into chaos. When I was finally offered a DEI role in Minneapolis, I took it almost immediately. I was excited but cautious.

At that point, I had never spent more than a summer in Minnesota, visiting family and working retail as a teen. My experiences had been mixed. By 2017 Minnesota was already being put on the map for its racism. Philando Castile was killed in summer 2016, and the officer responsible, another man of color, was acquitted in June 2017. This was on my mind as I contemplated my next steps. Still, it seemed that Minnesota had to be an improvement over my life in South Carolina.

Spring 2020

I began my life as a staff member at the University of Minnesota in summer of 2017, where I am also working on my Ph.D. The University of Minnesota Twin-Cities is located in Minneapolis and St. Paul, on both sides of the Mississippi River in Minnesota. It is the flagship of the University of Minnesota system, a land-grant institution that is part of the Big 10 conference. Boasting over 50,000 students and 20,000 employees, the university is one of five universities in the nation with an engineering school, medical school, law school, veterinary medicine school, and agricultural school all on one campus (University of Minnesota, n.d.).

Up until 2020, my work was in student services, mostly focused on supporting students of color and educating people within the school on DEI topics. I was on vacation when George Floyd was murdered. I had just finished the planning and implementation of our first virtual commencement. Managing the speakers, graduates, and regalia for the event had been a monumental task, and I was completely spent. But it felt so good to be done, and I needed this time away to recoup.

My now husband and I had driven several hours north to the Duluth, Minnesota area to an Airbnb on a lake. By that evening, I was reading stories about a man dying in the custody of the Minnesota Police Department. "Shit," I thought. Not another one. By this time in 2020, in addition to the pandemic, there had been multiple stories of innocent Black lives being stolen. Breonna Taylor and Ahmaud Arbery were now names and hashtags I heard and read daily. And now I had learned a new name and hashtag: George Floyd. We watched our social media feeds fill up with news from back home. Behind moments of joy and respite, we worried about what we might return to. As it turned out, it would be so much worse than we could have imagined. But somehow, eventually, also, so much better.

Two weeks before Derek Chauvin forced his knee into George Floyd's neck, I had hosted the first DEI strategic planning meeting for our college. I contracted with an external consultant to facilitate the meetings. She had previously worked at the university and was well respected. I worked strategically, knowing that some people in our school would trust this White woman with a Ph.D. more than me, a young, Black, student affairs professional. Rosette and Livingston (2012) found that White people were perceived as more effective leaders and that Black men and White women benefitted from the dominant aspects of their identities, in comparison to Black women. I knew my identities were not in my favor. I also recognized that I wasn't willing to expend the emotional labor needed to facilitate the project. It was a strategic compromise that I was willing to make for long-term progress. The meeting went on without incident: we got to know each other, set some guidelines for our work together, and scheduled the next meeting. Before we could gather a second time, the ground beneath us would shift.

Floyd's murder prompted confusion and fervor among White people. I was getting emails, calls, texts, and meeting requests from everywhere, from former co-workers and classmates, but also people I barely knew. "Are you okay?" "I'm here for you." "What do you need?" "What books should I be reading?!" Minneapolis had always had an ethos of White guilt to me. That energy had turned into a desperate cry for affirmation from Black Americans. "*Aren't we the good ones? We're not racist*!!" it seemed to scream. In her book *But I'm not racist!* Obear (2017) writes about Whites' tendency to get caught in a swirl of unproductive emotions and concern about being a good or bad person. As DiAngelo (2018) points out, when faced with the realities of racism, White people can demonstrate a multitude of reactions, including anger, emotional incapacitation, guilt, and cognitive dissonance (p. 101). I saw all of these in a very short span of time. Their intensity matched what was happening in the city. As the city burned, brave multiracial coalitions of organizers convened to create change.

The one demand from protestors here that was perhaps the loudest and most shocking was to defund the police. But it was not surprising to anyone here. The movement for abolition and police accountability was already well underway by 2020. In December 2017, months after Jeronimo Yanez was acquitted for the killing of Philando Castile, a group of organizers, artists, activists, and scholars called MPD150 released a report called "Enough is Enough." The document provided a history lesson as well as a performance review of the Minneapolis Police Department (MPD) on the 150th anniversary of its founding. Their stated purpose is to help dissolve the MPD (MPD150, n.d.). Reclaim the Block, established in 2018, has a similar mission around divestment from policing and redirecting resources to community-led health and safety efforts (Reclaim the Block, 2019). Having organizations already doing this work made it easier to mobilize and support a strong united message in 2020. "Defund the police" messaging was heard around the world. Within our individual organizations in the area, however, our concerns were different.

Within the college where I worked, we were managing multiple crises. Inside the metaphorical house, open letters signed by faculty and students called for change and accountability, up to the resignation of our dean. They asked for changes to our hiring and student recruitment strategies, more scholarship funds for Black students, and culture change. Externally, we received critiques from alumni of color who had experienced racism during their time in the school. At the university level, Black students were also fed up. The student body, led by a Black woman for the first time that year, demanded that the university cut ties with MPD. They cited both a misalignment with university values as well as specific incidents that had left Black students feeling targeted (Chang, 2020).

As a Black woman, I was scared, angry, and so incredibly tired. As a DEI practitioner, I was being asked what we, as a school, should be doing. It was frantic, chaotic, and non-stop for months. I had a hard time processing it all.

I had previously asked for a graduate assistant to support the work I was doing. I was told that it was not in the budget. Suddenly, after the murder of George Floyd, I was approved to hire a full-time coordinator. We posted a job description and kept working on our strategic plan. What had been perhaps thought of as a side project suddenly became the critical proof the school needed to shield us (them) from critique. I was three years into the job, I had already spent plenty of time agonizing over how I might be being tokenized. Token hires uphold systems of oppression by distorting the discriminatory nature of an organization and contributing to the myth of meritocracy (Danaher and Branscombe, 2010). In retrospect, I do think my initial hire was based in Good White Intentions. I also recognize how I have been empowered to lead change since 2020. Holding that tension, I see how under the right circumstances, transformation is possible.

At any rate, I am profoundly introverted, and I was anxious about the new spotlight. I also found myself excited about the flood of support I was receiving. What might this mean for the DEI strategic plan? For our school and university? For my career? I struggled to reconcile what felt like very conflicting thoughts. The difficult truth is that White guilt, saviorism, and urgency all played key parts in what was happening to me and my work.

DOING DEI WORK IN MINNESOTA

All the above circumstances have led to a strong job market in Minnesota for DEI practitioners. Whether in K-12, higher education, healthcare, nonprofits, consulting, or corporate settings, the DEI jobs are abundant. They come with great pay and benefits and usually job security. What they do not have, however, is strong supervision. The ethos of White guilt seems to make White supervisors incapable of providing sincere feedback to employees of color. Instead of receiving specific feedback on how they can improve their work, employees of color who report to progressive White supervisors may hear all positive reviews. They probably fear being called or thought of as racist and may feel unequipped for DEI work. They therefore offer very little critique to Black employees. This is problematic for several reasons, two of which I will name.

First, while having lived experiences of oppression does provide some level of expertise, it is not enough to prepare one for working full-time as a DEI practitioner. Those of us who do this work professionally recognize the time and energy it takes to learn the theories, history, and skills needed to be competent while simultaneously deconstructing internalized oppression. This is a huge commitment that requires constant learning and support from both peers and mentors.

Secondly, while positive feedback can be good for individual morale, it does not help the practitioner to learn and grow. Instead, many of us have come to rely on our professional networks for learning and development. Attending conferences, informal lunches, and on-campus collectives have been critical to my growth, especially in disciplines that were new to me, such as tribal relations. I have connected with dozens of scholars and practitioners digitally and in person across the metropolitan area. They have all kinds of specializations, from disability justice to assessment to raising anti-racist children. The Minneapolis area has become a nucleus of learning and practice for social justice and organizing.

MOVING FORWARD SINCE 2020

In fall 2020, I was able to add a team member to my office, and in Spring of 2022, I hired a third. The work that we are doing centers antiracism and, more broadly, anti-oppression. By and large, the college has enthusiastically embraced this shift. Our community of faculty, staff, and students have had many difficult conversations and workshops about White supremacy, racism, and systemic oppression. These were not words most of us were comfortable uttering out loud prior to 2020. More importantly, these conversations have led to measurable impacts in Human Resources processes, communications, fundraising, classrooms, and events. We still have much work to do, but the atmosphere has shifted in the school, and I am excited to be a part of it.

At the university level, more support has been put in place to hire and retain faculty of color and to help students of color succeed. For example, in the fall of 2020, the Gopher Equity Project was launched with the goal of improving campus climate. The training modules include topics such as power, privilege, and oppression and are required for first-year students, but all students and employees have access (Machtig, 2020). In February 2021, the University system introduced a program to cover tuition costs for students coming from households making less than $50,000 per year (Nietzel, 2021). In November 2021, the University announced that it would provide tuition coverage for Native students who belonged to one of the state's 11 federally recognized tribes (Kraker, 2021). Additional efforts include new DEI staff in many areas, the renaming of buildings, and new scholarships.

I recognize that change happens very slowly in higher education, but I would like to see more support specifically for Black students and employees. However, considering the recent pushback we have seen against Critical Race Theory and affirmative action, it seems unlikely. Just this month, the Vice Chair of our University Board of Regents asked one of the system chancellors if "too much diversity" was the reason for declining enrollment on her campus. After much backlash, he has stepped down from his Vice Chair role but will complete his term on the board (KSTP, 2022).

In Minneapolis, one of the most noticeable changes is the overall operations of MPD since 2020. In my neighborhood, I saw significantly less police presence and response. Hundreds of officers resigned, and the City has compensated at least 60 of them for claims of PTSD due to the uprising (CBS News, 2021). A measure that was placed on the 2022 ballot to dismantle the MPD narrowly failed. Instead, city leaders are supporting a new Office of Community Safety, under which MPD will fall, along with the fire department and emergency management (Goyette, 2022). Based on the actions of the new Commissioner, I am not hopeful about the new direction.

Chauvin, the primary officer responsible for Floyd's murder, has been convicted on state murder charges and plead guilty to federal charges. He is currently serving a 22 ½ years in prison for the state charges and awaiting sentencing for the federal charges. The other three were also convicted earlier this year at the federal level and will serve between 2 ½ and 3 ½ years for the federal charge of violating Floyd's civil rights. Two of the other officers, Thomas Lane and J. Alexander Kueng have plead guilty to the state charge aiding and abetting second degree manslaughter and the final officer, Tou Thao is still in legal proceedings at the state level. (Forliti, 2022). Minneapolis leadership seems determined to pour more resources into policing (Ibrahim, 2022), even after the state's Department of Human Rights found a pattern of racial discrimination (Simon, 2022).

Personally, I have been stretched in multiple ways over the last two and a half years. Politically and intellectually, I have had to hold and reconcile competing truths: there are criminals who may enact harm AND policing and prisons are not and cannot be sustainable or antiracist solutions. Before, I was only learning about abolition and how we could use it to address structural harm. As I watched the city burn and the MPD and mayor fail us, I understood that we simply could not reform our way out of this. I have been learning about and advocating for the abolition of prisons and policing since then. Believe it or not, this is still an unpopular opinion in the state and even much of the Twin Cities metropolitan area. In November 2021 for example, a ballot initiative to disband the Minneapolis Police Department failed, with 56% of voters voting against it. The plan was to create a new Department of Public Safety that was "public-health oriented" (Kaste, 2021). The outcome was difficult to process, but it is also important to recognize that 44% of voters asked for something different and better. I am cautiously optimistic about what the next fifteen years will bring in the city and state.

On the professional side, I learned about strategic planning, budgeting, supervision, and change management which was accelerated because of the murder of George Floyd. So many of us were asked to show up in new ways in response to the uprisings. For example, I had been talking about race in my work, but rarely racism. In the fall of 2020, at our new student orientation, I did a presentation for our new students about race and racism in Minnesota. I had been taught that orientation was supposed to have an energetic and positive tone, so this was very much out of my element. At the same time, it was a huge elephant in the room, one that we could not ignore. I was also asked to present at a national conference about our work and response to the uprisings.

I held multiple spaces for our Black community members, something that would have been difficult to justify under different circumstances. And this all happened while I was processing my own anger, grief, and confusion. I was overwhelmed but kept going. The doors that have opened for me since have been difficult to reconcile but also affirming. I wish that George Floyd hadn't died. But his murder sparked critical change that was way overdue. I now use my opportunities to talk about collective care, abolition, and public health, in addition to the standard DEI topics.

Because my politic has shifted over the last several years, I found myself spending a significant amount of time thinking about my future in the field. It is becoming increasingly clear that I will not feel comfortable in White institutions for much longer. There are things that I believe simply will never align with White power structures. I made the decision early in 2022 to form my own LLC, under which I have been consulting with higher education institutions, nonprofits, and government offices. I am close to completing my Ph.D. and will explore my options when that time comes. More than anything, the last two years have taught me that our time here is limited, and we need the freedom to be ourselves all the time.

Changes in the Field

The industry has changed significantly since 2020 as well. Between March and May of 2020, as a result of the pandemic, organizations had been pulling back on DEI investment, with DEI job postings falling at twice the rate of overall openings. By August, DEI openings had risen by 55 percent (Glassdoor, as cited in Maurer, 2020). After demands for racial justice, it seemed that every industry wanted DEI practitioner expertise or, at least, wanted to appear as if they did. Many people from different fields declared themselves DEI speakers and consultants and were (are) paid very well. Books by Ibram X. Kendi, *How to be an Anti-Racist* and Robin DiAngelo, *White Fragility,* flew off the shelves. There were a number of webinars, articles, and tv segments attempted to explain race, racism, and how to be antiracist.

I found myself frustrated by this rapid expansion of DEI work. In my opinion, this was a form of urgency. My concern is people who are not qualified going into organizations to "fix" racism. In the worst-case scenario, they do more harm and leave people with the impression that DEI work is rhetorical when in fact it is based in deep knowledge about systems and organizational change. Again, White guilt and urgency cause leaders to employ the right identities instead of the right skill set. This has made me think and work harder to prove that we can produce outcomes instead of just book clubs and speeches. I am disappointed in some of what I have seen but also, I made it a priority to look deeper into theories, strategic partnerships, and leadership development. I realized that our entire organization must be on board for us to see real transformation. Big-name consultants or guest lecturers cannot repair an institution. We must do it ourselves, day-by-day, one person, process, and policy at a time.

RECOMMENDATIONS FOR BLACK WOMEN DEI PRACTITIONERS

The events since 2020 have six key implications for Black women as DEI practitioners, as well as those in broader leadership positions. The first implication is of my own wellness and the ability to work from home. I am a huge proponent of remote work for Black women. Working from home alleviated stress for me. Prior to the pandemic, I experienced anxiety around driving in Minneapolis due to both regular inclement weather and the threat of the police. I also hated the small talk and microaggressions and feeling isolated as the only Black person in the office. The quarantine order due to the COVID-19 pandemic allowed me more control over my time and the freedom to be Black all day in my Black household. I felt a weight leave my body. Studies indicate that Black people are more interested in working remotely but less likely to have the option (Gould & Kandra, 2021; Future Forum, 2022). Organizations that want to support and retain Black women, especially those in emotionally taxing jobs like DEI, should be sure to offer remote or hybrid work options.

A second implication is that as DEI practitioners, we should think broader than our own organizations. Our work is situated in multiple layered contexts that deeply impact our work. We live and work in cities with long and complicated histories, within states and regions that are also complex and dynamic. Communities, especially those that are oppressed, often have long memories. I knew some of that context before George Floyd was murdered, but not all of it. Spend time learning about the city, state, and region in which you are working. What is the history of oppression and how have local communities responded? What organizations are doing grassroots work to stabilize the marginalized communities? Tapping into those networks personally and professionally will better equip the organization and its stakeholders to mobilize in a crisis. For example, healthcare organizations that understand the community will have translators, clergy, and prayer spaces ready for patients with a variety of language and faith needs. A school that is in relationship with the community can facilitate internships, host guest speakers, and advocate for policy change with the legislature. A school that is not connected to the surrounding community will only perpetuate more harm and inequities.

Next, practitioners should not assume that positions in liberal enclaves will be easier, better, or more developmental. While jobs in conservative locations can prove to be politically constraining, the progressive ones have many unseen challenges. The emotional labor of trying to navigate White guilt and passive aggression can be overwhelming. Instead, we must fortify ourselves for this work, no matter the location. I have grounded myself by constantly learning and by building a strong community around me.

Another implication is that practitioners must be intentional about creating networks of other DEI professionals. Prior to 2020, I found myself craving the company and consult of other experienced DEI professionals. I needed to process events, talk through my ideas, and get honest feedback. Thankfully, my student affairs network helped me to connect even before I arrived on campus. We all need others in the field to serve as confidantes, thought partners, and cheerleaders. For those of us who are single, new to the area, and/or doing the work as a single-person team, this is even more important.

In conjunction with support, practitioners should help our White supervisors, many of whom have a less in-depth understanding of privilege, power, and oppression, to supervise us. Managing up is a skill I have had to learn, and I think it is absolutely necessary for Black women in this field. We need to learn to set expectations as well as boundaries for our success and well-being. For example, early on in a supervising relationship, we can advise our supervisors about our work and learning styles, how we best receive feedback, and long-term career goals. This should set the supervisor up well to advise, support, and challenge you throughout the relationship. Of course, a supervising relationship does require boundaries, and we will have professional needs that cannot be met by them or even our larger networks. This is where sister circles become important.

A final implication for Black women practitioners is the use of sister circles. Sister circles are one way that Black women have been able to support each other's success. Scholars in industries such as psychology and higher education have used sister circles as a retention tool (Palmer, 2021; Linnaberry, et al, 2004). Black womanhood is a very specific experience that only we can fully understand. It is critical that we are in deep community with each other. It can be through book clubs, writing groups, or sororities, but we absolutely need each other, especially in DEI work. I have used my doctoral classes, Greek life, and *MeetUp* groups to meet other Black women in the area. We share tips about hair stylists, school districts, and places of worship. We show up for each other in times of distress and challenge each other when we need an extra push. "We all we got" is not only a fact of life for Black women but a war cry. We need each other in this hostile and violent world.

RECOMMENDATIONS FOR ORGANIZATIONS

As public health practitioners will tell you, the way to fix a problem is by going upstream to find the source (Shah, 2021). Racism and oppression are perpetuated primarily not by individuals but through policies and practices. There are three key ways organizations can support Black women who are doing DEI work. One of the most important steps is to invest in this work. The nature of DEI work means that many of us become burnt out within a few years. One Wall Street Journal article indicated that chief diversity officers' average tenure in the job is about three years (Cutter & Webber, 2021). Anything that we want to last requires investment. Organizations need to invest in Black women and in DEI work via professional development, support staff, technology, and equitable compensation. Having a single person doing DEI work sends the signal that the organization is performative and disinterested. Instead, fully staffed units should be able to provide assessment, training, employee/community engagement, and real change. This requires commitment from leaders, a sustained budget, and dedicated time from everyone in the organization.

Another recommendation is that we move on from the basics of DEI. Racial justice is something we have waited and asked for far too long. Instead of implicit bias trainings, organizations should boldly address systemic oppression. Systemic oppression can include racial aggression, wage disparities, and all White leadership teams. DEI leaders are change agents: we want to do that work but need the freedom and organizational power to do it. While the political climate may not be ideal, the time is now. Recruit DEI professionals who are courageous and intelligent enough to address root problems instead of those who want to collect a paycheck for showing up.

Finally, I would advocate for more flexible work options, especially for Black women. Bloomberg reports that in 2021, 26% more of Black knowledge workers reported feeling that they were treated fairly at work as compared to 2020 (Boyle, 2021). This may be because many of us were working from home and free from daily microaggressions. Bloomberg also noted that a higher proportion of Black employees wanted mostly or fully remote work going forward, as compared to their White peers (Boyle, 2021). Professional Black women wanted the freedom to be ourselves, to grieve with other Black people, and not be forced to perform friendliness or look "presentable" for the office (Onwuamaegbu, 2021). Code-switching, or shifting speech and behavior patterns to fit in with dominant norms, has been shown to contribute to burnout (McCluney et al., 2019) and emotional exhaustion and attrition (Hewlin, 2009). This data, of course, does not even account for those of us doing DEI work and the emotional labor that we expend. For me, the benefits of the work have outweighed the costs, and my team has been incredibly productive and successful while working from home.

CONCLUSION

George Floyd's story shook the world. The millions of people who took to the streets in the wake of his murder were unified in their anger and cries for justice. The protests and the pandemic also transformed the profession of DEI profoundly. It is no longer enough to recruit Black people into your organization and urge them to join employee resource groups for support. Working people are organizing for equitable compensation, paid leave, hybrid options, and more.

The DEI space is incredibly en vogue at the moment, but too many of us are focused on individual success. If your cousins, grandmas, and aunties cannot understand and benefit from your work, is it really making a difference? Going forward, DEI should refrain from making "the business case" for diversity. The mission, at least for healthcare, education, government, and nonprofits, should be around equity, justice, and liberation. This means including different ways of knowing, working with and within marginalized communities, and looking for sustainable solutions. It means accessible systems, long-term commitments, and giving everyone an opportunity to thrive. Ultimately, I believe we should be working ourselves out of a job. What might you have been if not for oppression?

ACKNOWLEDGMENT

This research received no specific grant from any funding agency in the public, commercial, or not-for-profit sector.

REFERENCES

AmeriCorps. (n.d.) Volunteering in America: Rankings. *Americorps/* https://americorps.gov/sites/default/files/document/Volunteering_in_America_Rankings_508.pdf

Arminio, J. (2001). Exploring the nature of race-related guilt. *Journal of Multicultural Counseling and Development*, *29*(4), 239–252. doi:10.1002/j.2161-1912.2001.tb00467.x

Bell, K. (2019). "This is not who we are": Progressive media and post-race in the new era of overt racism. *Communication, Culture & Critique*, *12*(1), 1–17. doi:10.1093/ccc/tcz005

Berila, B. (2020, June 23). White urgency to end racism: Why now? *Open Democracy*. https://www.opendemocracy.net/en/transformation/white-urgency-end-racism-why-now/

Biewen, J. (1997, August 19). Moving up: Part one. *Minnesota Public Radio*. http://news.minnesota.publicradio.org/features/199708/19_biewenj_migration/

Boyle, M. (2021, October 6). Remote Work Has Vastly Improved the Black Worker Experience: A survey finds that Black employees in white collar jobs feel more valued and supported working from home. *Bloomberg*. https://www.bloomberg.com/news/articles/2021-10-05/return-to-office-black-workers-are-happier-more-valued-working-from-home

British Broadcasting Corporation. (2020). George Floyd: What happened in the final moments of his life. *BBC*. https://www.bbc.com/news/world-us-canada-52861726

Bui, T. (2020, July 8). Minnesota racial-justice groups with sudden influx of money face new scrutiny. *MinnPost*. https://www.minnpost.com/community-sketchbook/2020/07/racial-justice-groups-with-sudden-influx-of-money-face-new-scrutiny/

CBS News. (2021, September 24). 'These officers have suffered': Ex-MPD officers, many citing PTSD, get six-figure settlements from city. *CBS*. https://www.cbsnews.com/minnesota/news/these-officers-have-suffered-ex-mpd-officers-many-citing-ptsd-get-six-figure-settlements-from-city/

Chang, A. (2020, May 28). Student actions prompt UMN to rethink its relationship with Minneapolis police. *National Public Radio*. https://www.npr.org/2020/05/28/864469597/student-actions-prompt-umn-to-rethink-its-relationship-with-minneapolis-police

Cutter, C., & Webber, L. (2021, July 13). Demand for Chief Diversity Officers Is High. So Is Turnover. *Wall Street Journal*. https://www.wsj.com/articles/demand-for-chief-diversity-officers-is-high-so-is-turnover-11594638000?page=3

Danaher, K., & Branscombe, N. (2010). Maintaining the system with tokenism: Bolstering individual mobility beliefs and identification with a discriminatory organization. *British Journal of Social Psychology*, *49*(2), 343–362. doi:10.1348/014466609X457530 PMID:19646326

DiAngelo, R., & Dyson, M. (2018). *White fragility: Why it's so hard for White people to talk about racism*. Beacon Press.

Dictionary.com. (2022). Guilt. *Dictionary.com LLC*. https://www.dictionary.com/browse/guilt#:~:text=the%20fact%20or%20state%20of.%2C%20whether%20real%20or%20imagined

Donofrio, G. (2020, December 4). Racial dividing line. *Human Toll 35W*. https://humantoll35w.org/essays/racial-dividing-line/

Farah, S. (2020, June 11). George Floyd Was Killed in My Neighborhood. *Vanity Fair*. https://www.vanityfair.com/style/2020/06/growing-up-in-george-floyds-minneapolis-neighborhood

Federal Reserve Economic Data. (2021). Annual educational attainment: Bachelor's degree or higher by state. *Federal Reserve Bank of St. Louis*. https://fred.stlouisfed.org/release/tables?eid=391444&rid=330

Finnegan, A. C. (2022). Growing Up White Saviors. *Journal of Applied Social Science*, *16*(3), 617–636. doi:10.1177/19367244221082023

Forliti, A. (2022, October 22). Ex-cop Kueng cop pleads guilty in George Floyd killing. *Associated Press*. https://apnews.com/article/death-of-george-floyd-j-alexander-kueng-thomas-lane-tou-thao-e9d40eae8ac193e61f07004323a3193d

Future Forum. (2022). Desire for flexibility intensifies among knowledge workers—and they're willing to walk to get it. *Future Forum by Slack*. https://futureforum.com/wp-content/uploads/2022/07/Future-Forum-Pulse-Report-Summer-2022.pdf

Gould, E., & Kandra, J. (2021, June 2) Only one in five workers are working from home due to COVID, Black and Hispanic workers are less likely to be able to telework. *Economic Policy Institute Working Economics Blog*. https://www.epi.org/blog/only-one-in-five-workers-are-working-from-home-due-to-covid-black-and-hispanic-workers-are-less-likely-to-be-able-to-telework/

Goyette, J. (2022, September 15). New Minneapolis Public Safety Commissioner seeks $1M budget. *Fox 9 KMSP*. https://www.fox9.com/news/minneapolis-public-safety-commissioner-budget

Helms, J. E. (Ed.). (1990). *Black and White racial identity: Theory, research and practice*. Greenwood Press.

Helms, J. E. (1995). An update of Helms's White and people of color racial identity models. In J.G. Ponterotto, J.M. Casas, L.A., Suzuki, C.M. Alexander, eds. Handbook of multicultural counseling. Thousand Oaks, CA: Sage.

Hewlin, P. F. (2009). Wearing the cloak. *The Journal of Applied Psychology, 94*(3), 727–741. doi:10.1037/a0015228 PMID:19450009

Hopfensperger, J. (2016, December 11). Minnesotans renew bond with Luther to revive faith. *Star Tribune.* https://infoweb-newsbank-com.ezp2.lib.umn.edu/apps/news/document-view?p=AWNB&docref=news/16147DA536F492B0

Ibrahim, M. (2022 September 15). A snapshot of Mayor Jacob Frey's proposed police budget. *MinnPost.* https://www.minnpost.com/public-safety/2022/09/a-snapshot-of-mayor-jacob-freys-proposed-police-budget/

Jackson, K. (2020, June 24). For Minnesotans of color, a new food desert underscored disparities. *TPT Originals.* https://www.tptoriginals.org/for-minnesotans-of-color-a-new-food-desert-underscores-disparities/

Kaste, M. (2021, November 3). Minneapolis voters reject a measure to replace the city's police department. *National Public Radio.* https://www.npr.org/2021/11/02/1051617581/minneapolis-police-vote

Kraker, D. (2021, November 1). U of M to offer free tuition to many Native American students. *MPR News.* https://www.mprnews.org/story/2021/11/01/u-to-offer-free-tuition-to-many-native-american-students

KSTP. (2022, October 25). U of M Regent Sviggum resigns as vice chair after 'too diverse' question, will finish board term. *KSTP Eyewitness News.* https://kstp.com/kstp-news/top-news/u-of-m-regent-sviggum-resigns-as-vice-chair-after-too-diverse-question-will-finish-board-term/

Linnabery, E., Stuhlmacher, A. F., & Towler, A. (2014). From whence cometh their strength: Social support, coping, and well-being of Black women professionals. *Cultural Diversity & Ethnic Minority Psychology, 20*(4), 541–549. http://dx.doi.org.ezp1.lib.umn.edu/10.1037/a0037873. doi:10.1037/a0037873 PMID:25313433

Lutheran Social Service of Minnesota. (n.d.). Responding to Minnesota's changing needs. *LSSM.* https://www.lssmn.org/about-lss

Machtig, A. (2020, October 16). University launches new equity training amid ongoing racial justice calls. *The Minnesota Daily.* https://mndaily.com/263065/news/university-launches-new-equity-training-amid-ongoing-racial-justice-calls/

Mapping Prejudice. (n.d.). *Visualizing the hidden histories of race and privilege in the built environment.* https://mappingprejudice.umn.edu/

Mapping Prejudice. (n.d.). *What is a covenant?* https://mappingprejudice.umn.edu/racial-covenants/what-is-a-covenant

Maurer, R. (2020). New DE&I roles spike after racial justice protests. *Society for Human Resource Management (SHRM).* https://www.shrm.org/resourcesandtools/hr-topics/talent-acquisition/pages/new-dei-roles-spike-after-racial-justice-protests.aspx

McCluney, C. L., Robotham, K., Lee, S., Smith, R., & Durkee, M. (2020). The costs of code-switching. *Harvard Business Review.* https://hbr.org/2019/11/the-costs-of-codeswitching

McClure, J. (2022). Rondo Neighborhood. *Saint Paul Historical.* https://saintpaulhistorical.com/items/show/160

Minnesota Department of Corrections. (2020). *Adult prison population summary.* https://mn.gov/doc/assets/Adult%20Prison%20Population%20Summary%201-1-2020_tcm1089-418232.pdf

Minnesota Employment and Economic Development. (2022). Minnesota's Black Labor Force: An analysis of demographic, economic, and educational trends, and disparities. *DEED Labor Market Information Office.* https://mn.gov/deed/assets/black-african-american-data-report-acc_tcm1045-539222.pdf

Moen, M. (2019, November 21). Ask a 'sotan: Revisiting 'Minnesota Nice'. *MPRN News.* https://www.mprnews.org/story/2019/11/21/ask-a-sotan-revisiting-minnesota-nice

Montrie, C. (2022). *Whiteness in plain view: A history of racial exclusion in Minnesota.* Minnesota Historical Society Press.

Morrissette, M. (2021, January 27). How does Minnesota compare to other states in education? *Women's Press.* https://www.womenspress.com/how-does-minnesota-compare-to-other-states-in-education/

MPD150. (n.d.). About. *MPD150.* https://www.mpd150.com/about/

Myers, S., Jr. (n.d.). *The Minnesota Paradox.* University of Minnesota. https://www.hhh.umn.edu/research-centers/roy-wilkins-center-human-relations-and-social-justice/minnesota-paradox

Nietzel, M. T. (2021 February 13). University of Minnesota will offer free tuition to lower income students. *Forbes.* https://www.forbes.com/sites/michaeltnietzel/2021/02/13/university-of-minnesota-will-offer-free-tuition-to-lower-income-students/?sh=526f83851611

O'Neill, T. (2020). *Income and poverty in the Twin Cities metro area.* https://mn.gov/deed/newscenter/publications/review/december-2020/twincities-income-poverty.jsp

Obear, K. (2017). *But I'm not racist: Tools for well-meaning whites.* The Difference Press.

Okun, T. (2022). Sense of Urgency. *White Supremacy Culture*. https://www.whitesupremacyculture.info/urgency.html

Onile-Ere, B. (2021, November 15). Minnesota untold: I-35w freeway uprooted and divided African American business district. *Fox 9*. https://www.fox9.com/news/how-the-construction-of-i-35w-tore-apart-black-communities-in-minneapolis

Onwuamaegbu, N. (2021, July 24). Many Black women felt relieved to work from home, free from microaggressions. Now they're told to come back. *The Washington Post*. https://www.washingtonpost.com/lifestyle/2021/07/24/black-women-office-work-home/

Palmer, D. (2021). I Got a Lot to Be Mad About: Sista Circles as a Counterspace for Black Women Doctoral Students.

Prather, S. (2016, September 25). Racial Chill Spurs Quiet Brain Drain // Professionals of color cite outsider status as reason to leave. *Star Tribune*. https://www.startribune.com/twin-cities-businesses-ask-why-professionals-of-color-leave/394688601/?refresh=true

Ray, V. (2022). *On critical race theory: Why it matters & why you should care* (1st ed.). Random House.

Reclaim the Block. (2019). *About Reclaim the Block*. https://www.reclaimtheblock.org/home/#about

Rosette, A. S., & Livingston, R. W. (2012). Failure is not an option for Black women: Effects of organizational performance on leaders with single versus dual-subordinate identities. *Journal of Experimental Social Psychology*, *48*(5), 1162–1167. doi:10.1016/j.jesp.2012.05.002

Schubert, K. (2018, August 31). Entrepreneur works to curb Minnesota's POC retention problem. https://spokesman-recorder.com/2018/08/31/entrepreneur-works-to-curb-minnesotas-poc-brain-drain/

Shah, H. (2021, June 3). Addressing the social determinants of health upstream. *Loma Linda University Health*. https://ihpl.llu.edu/blog/addressing-social-determinants-health-upstream

Simon, A. (2022, April 28). Here's what the Department of Human Rights discovered while investigating the MPD. *Kare 11*. https://www.kare11.com/article/news/local/minneapolis-police-department-human-rights-investigation/89-82ed0eeb-ac93-4c8d-a55c-7f887eb63c9c

Sternlicht, A. (2020, June 2). Over 4,400 Arrests, 62,000 National Guard Troops Deployed: George Floyd Protests By The Numbers. *Forbes*. https://www.forbes.com/sites/alexandrasternlicht/2020/06/02/over-4400-arrests-62000-national-guard-troops-deployed-george-floyd-protests-by-the-numbers/?sh=67e5b954d4fe

Terrill, W., & Reisig, M. (2003). Neighborhood Context and Police Use of Force. *Journal of Research in Crime and Delinquency*, *40*(3), 291–321. doi:10.1177/0022427803253800

University of Minnesota. (n.d.). *About us*. https://twin-cities.umn.edu/about-us

U.S. Bureau of Labor Statistics. (2022). Unemployment rates for states. *USBLS.* https://www.bls.gov/web/laus/laumstrk.htm

U.S. Census Bureau. (2020). Reported voting and registration for states: November 2020. *U.S. Department of Commerce.* https://www.census.gov/data/tables/time-series/demo/voting-and-registration/p20-585.html

U.S. Census Bureau. (2021). Quick facts: Minneapolis city, Minnesota. *U.S. Department of Commerce.* https://www.census.gov/quickfacts/minneapoliscityminnesota

U.S. Census Bureau. (2021). Quick facts: Saint Paul city, Minnesota. *U.S. Department of Commerce.* https://www.census.gov/quickfacts/stpaulcityminnesota

U.S. News and World Report (2022) Best Places to live in the U.S. in 2022-2023. *US News.* https://realestate.usnews.com/places/rankings/best-places-to-live

Warren, K., & Hadden, J. (2020, June 4). How all 50 states are responding to the George Floyd protests, from imposing curfews to calling in the National Guard. *Business Insider.* https://www.businessinsider.com/us-states-response-george-floyd-protests-curfews-national-guard-2020-6

Yorth Group. (2020). Restorative Rondo: Building equity for all. https://reconnectrondo.com/wp-content/uploads/2021/01/Rondo-Past-Prosperity-Study.pdf

ADDITIONAL READING

Feagin, J. (2020). *The white racial frame: Centuries of racial framing and counter-framing,* (3rd ed.). Routledge. doi:10.4324/9780429353246

Grunewald, R., & Nath, A. (2019). A Statewide Crisis: Minnesota's education achievement gaps. *Federal Reserve Bank of Minneapolis.* https://www.minneapolisfed.org/~/media/assets/pages/education-acheivement-gaps/achievement-gaps-mn-report.pdf?la=en

Hankin-Redmon, E. (2020, January 20). How Near North came to be one of Minneapolis' largest black communities. *MinnPost.* https://www.minnpost.com/mnopedia/2020/01/how-near-north-came-to-be-one-of-minneapolis-largest-black-communities/#:~:text=By%201960%2C%20one%20third%20of,Americans%20lived%20in%20Near%20North.&text=The%20Near%20North%20community%20of,presence%20since%20the%20early%201900s

Jacobs, W., Taiwo, W., & August, A. (2021). *Sparked: George Floyd, racism, and the progressive illusion.* Minnesota Historical Society Press.

Mills, C. W., & Shelby, T. (2022). The racial contract (Twenty-fifth anniversary ed.). Cornell University Press.

Omi, M., Winant, H., & Ebrary, Inc. (2014). *Racial formation in the United States,* (Third ed.). New York, NY: Routledge.

Urban League Twin Cities. (2022). State of Black Minnesota Report 2021. *ULTCMM.* https://ultcmn.org/wp-content/uploads/2022/04/SOBM-Report-2021-Final-rev.03.17.22-1.pdf

KEY TERMS AND DEFINITIONS

White Guilt: the emotional response White individuals and groups can experience after learning about the historical and contemporary impacts of racism on people of color

White Urgency: the intense desire and need White people have for quick action and resolution to racial injustice, often asked of people of color

White Savior Complex: the systems and structures that white liberals use to alleviate White guilt, including the charities, mission trips, and organizations that operate primarily in communities of color. Often solutions are made without community input, do not address policies or systemic oppression, and lack sustainability.

Minnesota Paradox: the phenomenon in Minnesota of having a thriving White populace but massive inequities for people of color who live in the same state. Particularly looks at gaps in employment income, education, home ownership, wealth, health, and incarceration

Chapter 7
Training in Diversity, Inclusion, and Equitable Mindfulness

Tiara A. Cash
https://orcid.org/0000-0002-3681-5274
Crowned Vitta LLC, USA

Tristen Brenaé Johnson
https://orcid.org/0000-0001-9708-9600
The Tristen Johnson, LLC, USA

ABSTRACT

This chapter explores how two Black women working as diversity, equity, and inclusion (DEI) independent consultants teamed up to create the Training in Diversity, Inclusion, and Equitable Mindfulness (TDIEM) workshop series. TDIEM workshops are interactive educational sessions that teach DEI concepts through the lens of Equitable Mindfulness. Equitable Mindfulness utilizes the application of mindfulness (present moment experience) for everyone– removing personal and systematic barriers that work against inclusivity and transformative change within themselves and within the communities they work within (Cash et al., 2021). Here the authors discuss Black women's positions as DEI workers as well as the history of mindfulness, outline the TDIEM workshop series, present challenges to collaborating and facilitating this curriculum in White spaces, and offer recommendations for practice for other Black women DEI practitioners to use for future work in White spaces.

INTRODUCTION

Our current contemporary ideas about diversity, equity, and inclusion (DEI) work have long been heralded by the prior efforts and labor of Black women or people of color (Edgehill, 2007). These efforts and labor range from Ida B. Wells-Barnett, (a journalist in the late nineteenth to the early twentieth centuries who led a national anti-lynching crusade and founded a Black women's suffrage organization in Chicago, Illinois), to Tamika Mallory, (a twenty-first century civil rights activist who was one of the

DOI: 10.4018/978-1-6684-3564-9.ch007

leading voices in the nation-wide protest of the murder of George Floyd, the co-founder of the 2017 Women's March, and co-founder of the non-profit organization Until Freedom). The fight for diversity and inclusion is far from over.

This work - while extremely rewarding - can also be equally taxing. While shedding light on experiences, concepts, and theories surrounding the current and historical underpinnings of oppression within the western world, the pressuring weight of educating and expression usually falls on the diversity and inclusion facilitators, especially if they are Black women. Importantly, the work itself is also taxing on the participants. Holding space - inviting an individual into one's own mindfulness practice by seeing, hearing, and holding what they need to express, and using mindful listening and heartfelt compassion without giving advice or attempting to solve problems (Cash et al., 2021, pg. 13) - for critically examining long-standing concepts of colonialism, colorism, and capitalism can feel burdensome. Imagine then if there were a tool to support both DEI facilitators and participants while investigating these hot-button concepts.

The Training in Diversity, Inclusion, & Equitable Mindfulness Series (TDIEM) workshops are interactive diversity, equity, and inclusion (DEI) educational sessions that teach DEI concepts while grounding in the framework of Equitable Mindfulness (EM) (Cash et al., 2021). Conceptualizing DEI topics, especially difficult ones, can be enhanced with the practice of Equitable Mindfulness, as this framework presents the concept of mindfulness (present moment experience) to *everyone*, while being active to remove personal and systematic barriers that work against inclusivity and transformative change within a respective community. TDIEM is a collaborative effort between Dr. Tristen Johnson and Tiara Cash. The Tristen Johnson, LLC is a business dedicated to education and training centered on DEI. Crowned Vitta LLC is a company focused on concepts of mindfulness, meta-awareness, and meaningful self-relationships and relationships with others. For the purposes of the chapter, we will use "we" when speaking about our work together as a partnership. We have worked together to create curriculum for a number of non-profit, corporate, and higher education institutions by coaching them on how to hold space for each other in equitable ways while utilizing the educational and theoretical expertise of the authors' backgrounds.

This chapter aims to inform the literature through three main pillars: background diversity and inclusion and the TDIEM program, narrative and challenges of the authors' experiences with TDIEM, and recommendations for further practice. The background section, or literature review, begins with a discussion about diversity and inclusion and the need for organizations to have both to be successful. It then provides a historical overview of mindfulness and finishes with a conversation about Equitable Mindfulness and how it relates to DEI, especially in group facilitation settings. Then, the background transitions into a general overview of the conceptual framework, Black feminism to showcase that our experiences navigating the world as Black women give us the skills needed to not only be diversity practitioners but to facilitate difficult conversations about DEI. Following the conceptual framework is the narrative section centering the authors' experiences working together as business partners and providing the TDIEM curriculum to employees of historically White non-profit organizations or student groups at historically White institutions (HWIs) of higher education. Finally, the authors will provide recommendations for practice for Black Women DEI practitioners who are looking for new ways to both center themselves and to engage participants in HWIs.

BACKGROUND

This literature review begins with a discussion around the difference between diversity and inclusion, two of the key components of the TDIEM series. Then, a historical perspective of mindfulness is presented and following that is an overview of the creation of the Equitable Mindfulness Framework. Finally, Black feminism is briefly introduced as a conceptual framework to explain the importance of Black women's ways of knowing. Understanding Black women's positionality in how we make meaning of our lives, how we share our stories, and how we use our experiences as a mechanism of survival in any White dominated space is key to understanding why we, the authors, intentionally designed the TDIEM curriculum the way we did.

What Is Diversity?

The COVID-19 Pandemic exacerbated the health inequities that disproportionately negatively impact the Black, Hispanic/Latino, and Indigenous communities. At the onset, these communities died at higher rates of the virus than other racial/ethnic groups in the United States (Center for Disease Control, 2020). As COVID-19 rapidly took the lives of communities of color, another pandemic was taking the lives of Black people, the racial pandemic in the criminal justice system. The world watched the eight minutes and forty-two second video of former Minneapolis, Minnesota police officer kneeling on the neck of George Floyd, a Black man, killing him in May of 2020. The video of Floyd's murder circulated around the globe sparking worldwide protests for police reform, the arrest of the officer who killed Floyd, and for the saving of Black lives (CNN, 2020). Floyd's murder came two weeks after the video was released of three men in Georgia shooting another Black man, Ahmaud Arbery, who was jogging down the street. Arbery was killed in February of 2020. The national attention of Floyd and Arbery's murders helped bring to light another wrongful police killing of a Black woman, Breonna Taylor that happened in March 2020.

In the wake of these murders, corporate America, higher education institutions, and healthcare systems pledged new commitments and held listening sessions for diversity, equity, and inclusion (DEI) in their organizations. These new commitments included donating money to Black organizations or racial equity initiatives, hiring a specific number of Black employees into leadership roles, and increased spending with Black diverse suppliers (Feiner, 2021; Ngyuen, 2021). Newkirk (2020) noted that because the COVID-19 pandemic caused the country to quarantine or "shelter in place," people had no choice but to reckon with the harsh realities of racial injustice. Although these situations were not the first time unarmed Black people have been murdered by law enforcement or vigilantes, it was these highly publicized deaths that set the course for the radical change in addressing DEI concerns in institutions. Their response to the racial pandemic of 2020 - swift publications of diversity statements, hiring more Black staff, and the intense focus on DEI issues - is also not the first time organizations recommitted to increasing DEI measures after a major event. Newkirk (2020) noted that elite organizations "maintain racial custom and tradition in their hiring until they are publicly shamed or otherwise coerced into widening access to people of color" (p. 18). This portion of the literature review will provide a brief high-level overview of the push for diversity across the U.S. beginning in the 1960s until now. Following the discussion around diversity comes a conversation about inclusion, the shift from more than just representation in organizations.

Diversity Origins

According to Johnson (2021b), "diversity has been difficult to define" (p. 242). For the purposes of this review, we will follow Merriam-Webster's definition of diversity, "the quality or state of having many different forms, types, ideas, etc... the state of having people who are different races or who have different cultures in a group or organization" (para. 1). National conversations around diversity began in the 1950s and 1960s in the midst of the Civil Rights Movement (CRM). Black Americans across the country fought against their second-class citizenship and demanded equal rights within a number of social organization structures such as voting, employment access, education, healthcare and more (Anti-defamation League, n.d.). While former President John F. Kennedy began the call for "affirmative action" in 1961 requiring federal contractors to "treat applicants fairly without regard to race, color, religion, sex, or national origin" (AAAED, 2021, para. 1), President Lyndon B. Johnson expanded this call with the Civil Rights Act of 1964. The Civil Rights Act of 1964 outlawed discrimination in all sectors - including but not limited to employment and voting rights - paving the way for more Black Americans to join the work force and enroll in institutions of higher education. Then in 1967, President Johnson developed the National Advisory Commission on Civil Disorders to address the racial unrest happening in major U.S. cities which acknowledged that racism was the impetus for the issues affecting Black people in the U.S. (Center for Homeland Security Digital Library, n.d.; Newkirk, 2020). According to Newkirk (2020), the Commission "recommended the inclusion of African Americans in institutions that had historically excluded them...it highlighted the need to address the shameful legacy of slavery and Jim Crow" (p. 3). This move inadvertently excluded other groups of color (Newkirk, 2020). Under the Reagan Administration, however, these newly formed programs to help Black Americans advance were immediately cut off (Newkirk, 2020).

Diversity Today

Today, the conversation about diversity has expanded to other racial/ethnic minority groups and other social identity groups like the LGBTQIA+ community and people with disabilities. According to Marquis et al. (2008), diversity is crucial for organizations because it provides opportunities to tap into the unique perspectives and skills of employees from culturally diverse backgrounds and requires "fundamental organizational change" (p. 1). Although diversity is a hot word across various industries, there are still major discrepancies in leadership organization, especially in HWIs. For example, corporate America ties diversity to their business goals and spends millions of dollars annually on diversity initiatives, consultants, and trainings (Flory et al., 2021; Newkirk, 2019), but Black and other people of color are still underrepresented in senior leadership roles and underpaid compared to their White counterparts (Miller, 2020; Newkirk, 2019; Newkirk, 2020). In higher education, administrators and faculty of color remain underrepresented and some find it hard to climb the proverbial ladder to leadership (Johnson, 2021a; Newkirk, 2020; Smith, 2020).

When companies and institutions lack diversity, members from historically marginalized groups are often singular or one of few from their social identity groups (Johnson, 2021a; Smith, 2020). Being the only one can lead to tokenism (Sobers, 2014). Tokenism is when an organization hires one or a small number of members of an underrepresented group to give the appearance that their organization is diverse. When employees feel tokenized, it can impact their overall self-worth and their performance in their positions (Nathoo, 2021). People who are underrepresented in the workplace may feel a level of increased scrutiny from the dominant group (Phelps, 2016). Tokenism can also restrict the mobility of members from historically marginalized communities in work environments because they are expected to perform stereotypical job responsibilities that have historically been assigned to that social identity group (Phelps, 2016). Institutions must ensure that their workforce is infused with people from multiple visible and invisible social identity groups to ensure the success of their organizations.

Some companies compete to prove themselves in the area of diversity and inclusion and submit their institutional data for third-party review. DiversityInc, founded in 1998, is "the "dominant 'diversity' publication" that collects diversity and inclusion data from thousands of organizations across the country. They partner with corporate entities to conduct a "metrics driven" diversity assessment of the environment of that institution (DiversityInc, n.d.). Every year, the results of a competitive assessment are published in: "Top 50 Companies for Diversity List" with each participating company receiving a free "report card" on their status in six key areas of diversity and inclusion management. DiversityInc uses survey data from "companies with at least 750 employees in the U.S." where "[c]ompanies are evaluated within the context of their own industries." DiversityInc provides a Top 50 List for Corporate America but also evaluates other industries such as healthcare with the Top Hospitals and Health Systems list. This assessment measures six areas: human capital diversity metrics, leadership accountability, talent programs, workplace practices, supplier diversity, and philanthropy. Companies use their data to "keep up with quickly evolving best practices" and for continued growth in the area of diversity.

Diversity is just one facet of what organizations need to be successful. Grievances of "diverse" employees stem from not feeling included at their institutions (Johnson, 2021a; Mcgirt, 2016; Smith, 2020; Nzinga, 2020). It is not enough to just have diversity in companies. Institutions must foster an inclusive environment. It is important to note that diversity and inclusion are not synonymous and both are needed. The following section will cover inclusion and how organizations can benefit from fostering a sense of belonging for team members to be successful.

From Diversity to Inclusion

While diversity is one component of what organizations need to be successful, it alone will not suffice. Institutions must also practice inclusion (Ferdman & Deane, 2014). It is at the intersection of diversity and inclusion where the business benefits of inclusive environments come into play: innovation, productivity, revenue, and creativity (Cole, 2020; Ferdman & Deane, 2014). Inclusion is defined as "the act of including; the state of being included" (Merriam-Webster Dictionary, n.d., para. 1). Ferdman (2014) said that inclusion is unique to an individual's experience and influenced by the interactions they have with those around them. Winters (2014) defined inclusion as fostering an environment "that acknowledges, welcomes, and accepts different approaches, styles, perspectives, and experiences, so as to allow all to reach their potential and results in enhanced organizational success" (p. 206). Inclusion being an 'act' is what all three definitions have in common. It is an intentional act that works synergistically with diversity.

Diversity and inclusion are often used interchangeably. However, it is important to distinguish the two (Winters, 2014). Diversity allows for a variety of identities and perspectives to come to the table and inclusion is the value and appreciation of differences that help elevate organizations (Ferdman, 2014; Winters, 2014). Creating inclusive workplace environments has been difficult. HWI's cultural norms, for example, have practiced exclusionary behaviors towards members from underrepresented groups (Winter, 2014). The way to rid institutions of exclusionary practices is by "removing obstacles that cause exclusion and marginalization" through inclusive leadership (Booysen, 2014, p. 298). Establishing inclusion in institutional or corporate cultural norms begins with a top-down approach through the organization (Newkirk, 2020).

Engaging in inclusive conversations is important and has come to the forefront of workplace priorities after the heightened racial pandemic of summer 2020. One way leaders can begin to develop inclusive environments and cultural norms is by "being open to and valuing new ways of thinking generated by diverse talent" (Newkirk, 2020, p. 224). This can be done by creating a space for inclusive conversations. Inclusive conversations are opportunities for members of different social identities and backgrounds to discuss a range of topics with the goal of equitable outcomes (Winters, 2020a). The key components of inclusive conversations are as follows:

- Consider power dynamics and systems of inequity;
- Require the courage to critically self-reflect;
- Acknowledge what you don't know; and
- Embrace a willingness to learn. (Winters, 2020a, p. 5).

If institutions are unwilling to have inclusive conversations in the workplace, Winters (2020a) posited that achieving equity, inclusion, and belonging is unattainable. The Training in Diversity, Inclusion, & Equitable Mindfulness (TDIEM) series incorporates inclusive conversations into the curriculum for organizations. More about this will be covered in the narrative section of this chapter.

It's widely recognized that both diversity and inclusion are needed for organizations to succeed, but there is still more work to be done to achieve the goals of inclusion. The TDIEM series allows for the removal of barriers to inclusive practice and allows us to hold space in unbiased ways using the Equitable Mindfulness Framework. The following section will explore the concepts of mindfulness and the history behind it and then highlight Equitable Mindfulness and how it is used as a tool for more open and inclusive conversations in educational training sessions.

Why Mindfulness? A Brief Introduction

Mindfulness, the practice of present moment experience, is an ancient concept shared by many cultures and wisdom traditions globally. This universal practice has been described as "inherent to the fabric of human existence" (Cash et al., 2021). There are many ways to practice mindfulness, both formally and informally. These practices include: breath awareness, meditation, yoga, and being mindful of the present moment through focusing practices. Research has long shown that these practices can be utilized to improve balance, mood, and equanimity (Rogers, 2016); self-compassion and kindness towards others (Pipe & Bortz, 2009); and, increased resilience, increased positive affect, and decreased negative affect (Montero-Marin et al., 2015). Yet, the monetizing and popularity of this work in the west has centered mainly on White/Western, Educated, Industrialized, Rich, and Democratic (WEIRD) populations. As such, mindfulness has been popularized as a tool for self enhancement specific to personal healing and wellness. Although these personal gains are important, how have and can these practices be used at the macro-level (i.e., societal, collective, and institutional levels)?

Recent research and conversations on the practices of mindfulness have circled these concepts back to the parts of their original understandings: grounded in a broader societal perspective with inherent relations to justice and equity. As practitioners and researchers have explored this intersection, the practices of mindfulness can be explicated as being used in personal, interpersonal, and institutional levels (Gueci and Cash, 2020), while inherently principled as anti-oppressive and anti-racist (Cannon, 2016; Berila, 2015; Cash et al., 2021). These concepts are being used in pedagogy, schools of law, and in social work to support teachers, lawyers, and practitioners (Gonzalez, 2017; Berilia, 2015; Wong, 2004).

Critically, the practice of mindfulness is also implemented in cultures spanning the globe - in East and South Asia, Africa, the African diaspora, current and ancient Indigenous cultures around the world, and in older civilizations in Europe (Hanson, McLeod, & Ross, 2017; Le & Shim 2014; Nussbaum, 2013; Phillips, 1990). Historically used in many global majority societies (i.e., the non-White majority of the globe - Henrich, J., Heine, S., & Norenzayan, A., 2010), mindfulness has been integral to the survival of people of color and systemically marginalized individuals. Specifically, for Black women, these practices have gone unrecognized by many scholars, but are often at the basis of daily functioning. For example, when Black women have been faced with situations of racial discrimination and microaggressions, there has been a long standing history of them "focusing on their breath" (Streeter, 2020). These non-formal practices have been passed down as coping mechanisms which have allowed us to survive. And yet, in these mindfulness spaces there has been a deficit of Black women practitioners, although we know that Black women have used these practices for centuries (Magee, 2016). The interchange of this theoretical background with the missing components of the Global majority within the current western, secular mindfulness applications conceptualizes the creation of the novel framework, Equitable Mindfulness.

Equitable Mindfulness

Equitable Mindfulness is defined as presenting the concept of mindfulness to everyone, while being active in our respective communities by removing personal and systematic barriers that work against inclusivity and transformative change (Cash et al., 2021). Created by Cash at the Center for Mindfulness, Compassion, and Resilience at Arizona State University, Equitable Mindfulness is functionalized by three pillars: Personal protection, mindful activation for systemic change and the sustainability of practice, and creating robust programming with the population in mind.

Personal protection is a key pillar dedicated to individuals and communities who have been historically and systematically marginalized. As mentioned in the brief introduction, mindfulness has been used by many global majority cultures, formally and informally. This pillar recognizes the oppressive systems and states of burden that those who are oppressed within these systems face. By utilizing the practices of mindfulness, individuals and communities who have been systematically marginalized and oppressed can decrease personal harm by making choices in how they would like to engage within these systems. This pillar is not built on passively numbing the realities of today's world. Instead, it is dedicated to both acknowledging these realities and giving members of systematically marginalized communities tools to engage at their own discretion and to protect themselves mentally, emotionally, and spiritually if they choose to do so.

Mindful activation for systemic change and the sustainability of practice begins to move this concept from the personal to the interpersonal and institutional. By having a formal and routine mindfulness practice, individuals are better able to sustain the solidarity and justice work that go into anti-oppressive and anti-racist movements. The practice of mindfulness allows for an individual to re-charge and to rest, giving them better access to hold space (i.e., inviting an individual into one's mindfulness practice by seeing, hearing, and holding what they need - Cash et al., 2021) and to engage in institutional movements for systemic change.

Finally, programming with the population in mind is specific to mindfulness practitioners who would like to utilize mindfulness to support organizations and communities. This pillar asks for practitioners themselves to be driven by DEI concepts, understanding that each demographic that they teach/practice mindfulness to/with are different and have their own experiences around these practices. For example, if a mindfulness practitioner were to go to the US South and talk about mindfulness, they would include practices of prayer or familial practices of mindfully cooking (picture grandma over the stove stirring the pot while humming). Alternatively, if they were to go to an indigenous group and talk about mindfulness they could use examples of ceremony or pow wows. These distinctions are important and are often overlooked in the current examples of mindfulness research and pedagogy.

Equitable Mindfulness also utilizes a model created for conversations around DEI concepts. This model includes four constructs: mindfulness practice; land (historical and ancestral acknowledgments); community agreements; and narrative sharing (Cash et al., 2021). This model's importance centers on the concepts of individual participants within the conversation holding space and actively bridging *(i.e., Relating to other groups based on deep listening, empathetic space, and recognition of suffering. Rejects the concept of "them" while recognizing unique differences. An intentional rejection of othering (the act of making someone feel as if they are not a part of a group; (Hass Institute, 2019, Cash et al., 2021)), while the facilitator of the conversion creates a brave container (i.e. an action initiated by the facilitator and continued and managed by the participants to intentionally create a space of conversation and community while grounded in principles of mindfulness and bridging, Cash et al., 2021).

Implications

Currently, the Equitable Mindfulness Framework is being used independently with higher education institutions, non-profits, boards, and corporate businesses. The practices, in effect, teach the concept of mindfulness, talk about the origins of equity and inclusion within the practices, and then give experiential space for individuals to practice mindfulness techniques of discovering their own implicit bias, relationship to "others", and compassion towards collectives. The work has gained qualitative and narrative based acceptance (Cash et al., 2021) and the Equitable Mindfulness model has been submitted for extensive peer review (Bautista et al., under review). With the experiential gains that Cash and the partnership of Cash and Johnson (i.e., the TDIEM series) have seen (e.g., a more concrete understanding of how someone's personal, social and cultural lenses effect their relationship to DEI) we are excited about the potential that this work has in DEI spaces. The implications of Equitable Mindfulness for other DEI sources is a collaborative effort of mindfulness to support the personal awareness and learning that comes with DEI workshops, events, and trainings.

Conceptual Framework - A Black Feminist Perspective

In 1977, a group of self-proclaimed Black feminists wrote *The Combahee River Collective Statement* (CRC). The CRC was a statement that gave voice to Black women's positionality as "other" in the United States. In the statement, the women spoke to the "interlocking oppression" that affects Black women (Taylor, 2017). Black women do not only experience racism, sexism, classism, or homophobia; the combinations of all of these systems of oppression can simultaneously impact Black women. The CRC "was crucial to understanding the particular experiences of Black women as compared to White women and Black men, and created entry points for Black women to engage in politics" (Taylor, 2017,

p. 92). The CRC wrote their own narratives from their unique positionality as people who held multiple marginalized identities. Although the CRC were not the first group to name Black women's positions in the U.S., (authors like Collins (2000) have documented Black women who similarly described and named their own experiences since enslavement), they are the foundation that helps us as the authors understand our Black feminism and the importance of using our voice in the TDIEM training sessions.

Brittney Cooper (2018) eloquently described herself as a Black Feminist, "capital B, capital F" because she "learned her feminism from Black women" (p. 34). She goes on to define her "feminist theory and praxis" as "the particular ways Black women have understood, thought about, and written about the problems of racism and sexism across space and time" (p. 34). Black feminism is a practice rooted in the intellectual, political, and social spheres of dominance that have shaped Black women's lived experiences throughout history in the U.S. Black Feminists are activists for Black women's advancement and freedom. Evans-Winters (2019) further explained this perspective by acknowledging that Black women know what they know from the shared stories told by other Black women, their own lived interactions with the world, and that the needs of Black women diverge from those of Black men and White women.

Every Black woman "does" feminism in her own way and not all Black women share the same experiences (Collins, 2000). However, one concept of Black feminism is for Black women to, in the words of Cooper (2018), "get free or die trying" (p. 35). Meaning, Black women should fight for their voices to be heard, fight for their rights, and fight to be free rather than not fight at all. Because Black women have been the most oppressed in society, their freedom is the key to freeing the entire society (Taylor, 2017). Black Feminists such as the women who wrote the CRC and Audre Lorde remind us that "the personal is political" (Lorde, 1984, p. 113) and that Black women's positionality in the U.S. cannot be separated from the politics of the country. Black women's social identities and their experiences are wrapped in the political arena in areas such as criminal justice reform, healthcare, women's rights, LGBTQIA+ rights, etc.

The development and curriculum design of the TDIEM series stems from a Black Feminist perspective. We, the authors, have the lived experiences as Black women that put us in a unique position to build a customized training series like TDIEM. Black feminism opens the doors for us to be "producers of knowledge" (Evans-Winters, 2019, p. 17) by using what we know about the interlocking systems of oppression (as well as our own lived experiences with oppression) to teach participants about power, subjugation, and the importance of dismantling those systems in order for their organizations to progress.

THE DEVELOPMENT OF TDIEM

The Perfect (Brain)storm

TDIEM was built by two Black women who had gained expertise in their fields (DEI and mindfulness) and who wanted to utilize this expertise together to serve organizations that want outside help in the realm of DEI. Our partnership began over two years ago when, as friends, we discussed our journeys to exit the traditional corporate organizational systems and proceed into a personal small business setting where we could create curriculum that aims to give people the tools to try to begin pushing back against the ills of modern western society. After speaking about our work and our passions, we realized that we had complementing interests! This initial conversation grew to be the blueprint or a brainstorming session for the TDIEM series. We both had experience of people incorporating mindfulness activities in past DEI training sessions that we attended. We knew this component was important. As Hayles (2014) pointed out, mindfulness is an integral component of managing contentious conversations. In retrospect, we believed the activities we participated in were missing a lens of equity and anti-oppression, two critical aspects that the Equitable Mindfulness Framework now provides.

After this initial brainstorm, we received our first TDIEM commission. We were asked to go to Arkansas to present a diversity training for a non-profit organization that employed Head Start educators and case management service employees. The two of us put our brains and hearts together, created a curriculum, flew to Arkansas, and presented to a room of more than one-hundred participants of multi-ethnicities and backgrounds. The response was astounding. Participants came up to us following the presentation asking for more advice and how we thought of creating this work together. At that moment, we realized we had created something special.

Curriculum Design

Dr. Johnson researches, writes, and develops the diversity and inclusion portion of the curriculum, and Cash respectively does the same for the Equitable Mindfulness (EM) components. Johnson outlines and scripts the DEI portion and then sends it to Cash for review. Cash then develops the EM activities to emphasize concepts in the DEI curriculum or sets up a new section of the DEI curriculum. The trainings are built on the concept and framework of Equitable Mindfulness, which roots the participants in mindful practices while engaging deeply in the curriculum. As such, our "training" is really education for life. The participants receive a customized curriculum rooted in research and practice that encourages a larger picture perspective from mindfulness regarding the importance of the DEI topics covered to support participants' engagement in ongoing life-long learning. Below, we briefly outline the DEI and EM development process.

Diversity and Inclusion Curriculum - Johnson's Narrative

During the initial meeting, potential clients provide us with an overview of the DEI educational needs of their organization. I (Dr. Johnson) then conduct extensive research on that particular topic to use as I build a customized curriculum for their group. For example, TDIEM offers a two-part session on anti-racism lasting two and a half hours. Anti-racism means to actively work against racism in one's everyday life, organizational cultures, healthcare, or any system that has historically upheld racist practices and policies (Kendi, 2019). In order for me to build that education, I had to read a number of articles, books, and news articles centered around capitalism, the social construction of race, slavery, scientific racism, colonialism, anti-racism, and more. I then take the knowledge I gained from my research, the knowledge of my own life experiences with misogynoir (Bailey, 2021) (anti-Black misogyny towards Black women), and my skills in content development for adult learners, and build a customized training. Because the TDIEM anti-racism education is one of our most requested sessions, I keep the original core content and then develop additions to the training that best fit the needs of each company's culture.

We discussed diversity being an essential component of organizations. We have also outlined how inclusion is a practice that is interconnected with the culture of the organization. The TDIEM series not only encourages diversity and the creation of an open space for inclusion, it also encourages our participants to use DEI to reflect on the way they interact with people from culturally different backgrounds and the cultural norms of their organizations. I build specific discussion questions and activities to help them do this and that gives participants ownership and agency in their own learning. I found that discussions and small group activities work best for some historically White organizations that Cash and I worked with previously. I speak more to this in the challenges section of this chapter under the topic, "White fragility" (DiAngelo, 2018). So, I design trainings like anti-racism that often stir controversial conversation topics, in a way that members of different social identity groups can find relatable. After they learn those core pieces, I conclude the curriculum with action steps. Each participant is then responsible for creating action plans and accountability plans using the information they learned to begin to make changes derived from the action plans in their organization.

Equitable Mindfulness Curriculum - Cash's Narrative

One of the most notable novel aspects of our TDIEM curriculum is the addition of an explicit Equitable Mindfulness component. These mindfulness practices are built directly into the TDIEM curriculum concurrent to the DEI work and centered on the foundations of the Equitable Mindfulness Framework previously described. These intentionally designed components include an exploration of implicit bias through self-introspective practices, relating to one another's differences and similarities through meditation, grounding in marginalism through mindfulness, and many other ways of contemplating DEI principals through mindful awareness. These moments of reflection are also known as "intentional pauses." By incorporating intentional pauses during contentious conversations and practice, we found that participants have a chance to engage with the material more fully and with more respect for the container (which includes the facilitators and the participants). Mindfulness, the practice of present moment experience, also gives our participants the opportunity to look inward when they feel they have been triggered instead of reacting to the trigger by expressing that emotion outward to another person. This has been a game-changer in this work.

It is important to note a few points for those who might be considering adding a mindfulness component into their DEI curriculum. First, the practices of mindfulness should not be used as a Band-Aid. These practices are included to support and uplift participants in their self-discovery and relationship to justice, equity, and inclusion. This means that when incorporating these mindfulness practices, they should come from a facilitator who has a mindfulness practice of their own, and that the focus of the inclusion of mindfulness should only be "planting a seed." By the facilitator having personal experience with a mindfulness practice, the work of sharing these concepts as an experiential process is more clear. As mindfulness is a personal practice, the understanding passed from the facilitator should additionally, and importantly, incorporate how to approach these practices without the cultural baggage of colonial, oppressive, or misogynistic orientations. Planting a seed of mindfulness means that a facilitator shares the tools and practices for their own sake, without being attached to the specific outcome of those practices. As most colonial, oppressive education tools have shown us, there is usually a direct relationship between the teacher/facilitator/practitioner's success and the participant's success – meaning there is more focus on the outcome instead of the process. Here, the focus is not on personal gain, but instead what the student's might experience during the process as a successful outcome. The goal is to share mindfulness with the understanding, unequivocally, that the participants will utilize these tools as they see fit when they need to - both during their time within the container and when they leave back into the "real world." With this understanding, the facilitator, too, is practicing mindfulness of the present moment and not attached to a future outcome.

We, Cash and Johnson, utilize these practices as intentional pauses, which means that we pre-plan inclusions of mindfulness into our curriculum, and we are constantly aware of maintaining the container during our sessions so that when the participants need the chance to pause, we can respond mindfully. It is important to have this open awareness and to maintain a compassionate relationship with the participants and the container so that the response can be authentic. We have found that the work of understanding DEI concepts from participant's lenses has been enhanced with these inclusions and opportunities.

Radical Empathy

Merriam-Webster defines empathy as "the action of understanding, being aware of, being sensitive to, and vicariously experiencing the feelings, thoughts, and experience of another of either the past or present without having the feelings, thoughts, and experience fully communicated in an objectively explicit manner" (para. 1). Winters (2020a) posited that empathy is essential to building trust among culturally diverse groups of people and is key to inclusion. Meaning, the art of putting yourself in someone else's position or seeing their experience from their perspective. However, we incorporate radical empathy into our curriculum which is an extension of the traditional empathy mentioned. Radical empathy moves this a bit further to understand the cultural, social, and dynamic nuances of these experiences - realizing that although we can attempt to put ourselves in another's shoes, we will never truly understand how they operate within the world or their perspective. This also takes into account that although we can respond to possible actions through the perspective of the person that we are providing empathy for, there will be circumstances where our own lived experiences do not, and cannot, conceptualize the other person's lived experiences. This is radical in the sense that we are attempting to both understand the person's perspective from within a solidarity-oriented stance to provide true empathy to the person whose perspective we are taking. Empathy in action in a training, workshop, or educational session can look like:

- "acknowledge the situation" that happened;
- "share how you feel";
- "show gratitude that the person trusted you enough to share" their experience or perspective; and
- "show genuine interest and concern" (Winters, 2020a, p. 103).

In the TDIEM curriculum, radical empathy is a core concept woven into the fabric of every session.

In addition, we encourage participants to lean into the words and feelings that we both share as facilitators and the words of their team members who are in the session with them. We do this by thanking participants for sharing their perspectives, asking follow up questions about their experiences, and holding a mindful space for them. If the conversation is triggering, we take a moment to pause, sit, and reflect on that person's story as a way to practice radical empathy. If a participant shares something emotional or personal, often the person might leave the session feeling that sharing caused more harm. As such, by incorporating the moment of silence, we acknowledge the statement again within the body of the group, we connect it to others' experiences, we ask other participants how the comments shared personally impacted them, and then provide space for others to share. This engages everyone in understanding how to move through a sensitive moment.

CHALLENGES

Building the curriculum is one component of our experience as Black women DEI practitioners. As with any partnership there are challenges, and this narrative style discussion that follows explores the top challenges we've faced in delivering this curriculum. It is important that while we explain, uplift, and expand on the impacts that the TDIEM partnership has created, we are also transparent about challenges that have risen over the past couple of years. Those challenges include: the facilitation process, White fragility in training spaces, and budget.

Facilitation

In the discussion about the creation of our partnership, we mentioned that our first session was in-person in front of more than one hundred participants. That initial workshop was in February 2020, one month before the world shut down due to the COVID-19 pandemic. During the COVID-19 pandemic closures, Cash moved to Canada to begin her doctoral work. We were now limited to facilitating for teams virtually via the Zoom platform. Although the COVID-19 pandemic showed the world that communication could happen instantaneously and still is done well through video means, Zoom created challenges for us. We found that because these sessions with certain groups were not in person, university students, for example, felt they had a choice to attend or not to attend. This made it difficult when the teams that had major conflicts surrounding diversity and inclusion were not all in the training sessions to work on the conflicts the company hired us to help them navigate through. With Zoom, individuals are also allowed to keep their cameras off. While this is great for the choice of comfort and inclusivity - when dealing with difficult topics such as DEI concepts - there is a need to see one's face and reactions to help hold space for what is coming through at the time.

Additionally, facilitating while Black and a woman takes a toll on us. We often have to hold conversations in these White spaces about racism and the horrors of the systemic violence that plagues Black, Brown, and Indigenous bodies. This connects back to our conceptual framework of Black feminism. Our identities are political. Our identities are tied to the work that we do. There is a form of Black fatigue that comes with this. Winters (2020b) defined Black fatigue as "repeated variations of stress that result in extreme exhaustion and cause mental, physical, and spiritual maladies that are passed down from generation to generation" (p. 1). Not only is facilitating our content triggering for us, it is even more triggering when events like the killing of unarmed Black people by police continue to happen around us nationally. One way we experienced Black fatigue outside of facilitating for historically White spaces was after George Floyd's murder. We created a fundraiser workshop session titled "Black, Breathe, Repeat" (BBR) specifically for Black people to participate in mindfulness meditation exercises while simultaneously processing the national outrage of Floyd's murder. Even in situations like BBR where we knew Black fatigue would show up, we still showed up as support for those who joined us. As we will mention later in our recommendations, one way to navigate these challenges is to practice what we preach. Meaning, we make sure to have our own mindfulness practice and to engage in Black joy to help mitigate some of the stressors that come with being Black women DEI facilitators.

White Fear/White Fragility

In our experience as individual consultants, we have learned that training sessions do not always work for everyone. During our time as partners facilitating TDIEM, we found that some White participants were defensive or silent during conversations that particularly centered on race and racism. DiAngelo (2018) named these actions as parts of a larger concept called "White fragility." White fragility is the emotional and physical (usually defensive) response that White people get when in conversations about race and racism (DiAngelo, 2018). White fragility helps White people "repel the challenge [of being confronted about their race], return to [their] racial comfort, and maintain dominance within the [socially constructed] racial hierarchy" (DiAngelo, 2018, p. 2). While DiAngelo (2018) is not the first to "call out" White folks for their disengagement with their racial identity and race issues - Black people and Black women in particular have done this for centuries - her term "White fragility" gave Cash and I a blanket term to use when we facilitate sessions where this behavior is presented.

There were moments during a few of our sessions where White fragility was at play. Some White participants would use the art of silence - which we teach them to do as a practice of Equitable Mindfulness - but they would utilize silence as a tool instead to avoid the DEI work rather than a tool to hold space. One particular participant, a White male, in a session we developed for a non-profit organization in the Midwest did not participate or speak during the entire workshop. Even when we sent the participants to Zoom break-out rooms for group work, many of his teammates after the session informed us that he did not contribute to any of the discussion or to the creation of action plans. They noticed him rolling his eyes and he eventually turned his camera off. These actions distract from the learning and development of other participants and from their own personal development.

Budget

In the diversity portion of the literature review, we presented a short discussion on the millions of dollars companies spend annually on DEI initiatives and staff positions. During our time as partners, we learned that all budgets are not created equal, meaning, small non-profits or institutions of higher education do not have the same revenue flow as large corporations. Usually non-profits' and higher education institutions' (depending on the size of the school) budgets are smaller. We understand budget constraints but we also recognize that our consulting work is what helps sustain us. The time investment it requires to research and then design curriculum to facilitate is how we determine our consulting fees. Sometimes, an organization has a complex request for the work they want us to do but can only afford to pay us for a fraction of it. That puts us in a difficult position to either negotiate or respectfully decline the offer.

As Black women DEI practitioners, we learned quickly that a few things were going to be important in our journey with this work. Negotiating fees and finding the best price range with clients is one of them. However, one of the main challenges with facilitating as Black women accompanied by our "younger-looking" faces is the attempt of White-owned businesses to devalue our work. We experienced a time when a potential White male client blatantly offered us a rate that was disrespectful to us as "younger" Black women but also to the work of DEI. He came to us (from a word-of-mouth recommendation) and asked if we could do two full-day training sessions for minimal pay. We were shocked but not surprised. As soon as the Zoom call began, his tone changed when he saw us. Cash showed up with braids in her hair and Dr. Johnson was on with her locs and shirt that read "Sandra Bland" on it. He spoke condescendingly to us and questioned our expertise in the field. However, we remembered how the system plays into our role as facilitators. One important aspect of utilizing Equitable Mindfulness for ourselves and in our own work is understanding oppressive systems for what they are and using our breath to take the time needed to respond instead of react. Using the technique of the breath we were able to remind ourselves of our important role in this work. We kindly declined the offer and chose to utilize that time for someone who was willing to support their own company with payment that showed they cared about the work we were producing. We also did not want to work with someone who showed that he was not really ready for the type of conversations we were going to bring to his team.

RECOMMENDATIONS FOR PRACTICE

Our commitment to DEI work is life-long. The challenges we presented in the previous section are only a glimpse of what we have had to navigate in this facilitation partnership. Those challenges helped us grow in this work and have been the catalyst for the following recommendations to assist others in persevering within any situation. These recommendations include: remedying facilitation challenges virtually, managing White fragility, negotiating fees, and Equitable Mindfulness advice for participants and also specifically for Black women DEI practitioners.

Recommendation 1 - Remedying Virtual Facilitation Challenges

Navigating DEI workshops in a virtual space is not easy. You lose the in-person community building that groups experience when we are all together in one room. Virtually, participants can actively or passively disengage with the facilitator and group thus disrupting the community building process. Equitable Mindfulness allows us to build that community from the opening of each session. Cash leads an opening meditation followed by a land, historical and ancestral acknowledgement called "Three Breaths, Three Thank Yous" practice that honors the land and its people, those who have traditionally not been honored in these spaces (i.e., enslaved and indentured), and ancestors/ourselves. As she opens the container for learning, we are ultimately challenging the participants right from the beginning to lean into the session and into any potential discomfort. Dr. Johnson designs the curriculum in a way where the participants have buy-in in for their learning and different opportunities for engagement like poll questions, writing activities, breakout rooms with activities and discussions, Google Jamboard collaboration working groups, and more. Our take-away: research on effective ways to engage different types of learners works best when planning trainings virtually.

Recommendation 2 - Managing White Fear/Fragility in Training Space

The next recommendation is to manage White fear/fragility in a training space. We recognize that historically, Black women have been at the center of managing White fear, and here are a couple examples: Black women were excluded from the suffrage movement in the 19th and 20th centuries and Sojourner Truth, a former enslaved woman, used her voice as an activist to call out that exclusion from White women who were leading the movement. Stacey Abrams and her team in Atlanta, Georgia flipped the state of Georgia blue in the 2020 presidential election. Black women have proven to be change makers in the face of White fragility and supremacy. We are no different. As Black women, we learned from an early age how to manage fear (Cooper, 2018) because of our own life experiences in a world where we had to make hard choices out of fear. Cooper (2018) calls this "surviving and thriving" (p. 207). In training sessions, we acknowledge that fear might be present in the space. We never run from or alter our curriculum because of it, though. Instead, we embrace our fears and help participants work through their own discomforts, especially if their fear is holding the rest of the group back from their learning.

Normalize Fear

As mentioned above, Black women have been at the forefront of holding spaces and managing White fear. Because of this, we have been the ones who usually carry the burden in spaces where participants are challenged by concepts around DEI. One way of managing this is to normalize it for everyone by letting participants know at the forefront that fear, anger, etc. is a part of the process. One thing that we also make sure to incorporate is the idea that many of us have been dealing with fear and anger most of our lives (i.e, BIPOC individuals). As such, it is important to share that burden and to normalize the fact that this is a part of the collective healing process.

Ask Participants to Hold Fear

One of the benefits of having mindfulness practices as a part of our curriculum is the opportunity to utilize them when participants have emotions that they tend to run from. Here, we make it a point to ask participants to not run from emotions, but to "sit with them." In summary, by asking participants to hold their own fear, we give them the opportunity to learn from the emotion and to see what cognitive appraisals (i.e., a person's interpretation of the situation) arise.

Recommendation 3 - Negotiating Fees

Negotiating salary or fees for Black women is challenging. Historically, Black women have been offered the lowest paying jobs or no money at all for their labor (Davis, 1981). Racial biases play a role in the low salary offers Black people receive in the workforce (Oliver, 2020). Black people are least likely to negotiate their salaries or will negotiate a lower payment than a White counterpart (Hernadez, et al., 2019). As mentioned in the budget challenge, we experienced racial bias first-hand in our interaction with the White male who offered to pay us only a small fee for our services. We respectfully declined his offer but that situation prompted us to see the value in who we are as people and the value in the intellectual knowledge that we possess. We encourage other Black women to map out the amount of time it is going to take-to prepare a full-training session. This includes the amount of time it takes to research and analyze the literature, develop curriculum, create activities, facilitate, and to determine whether the session will be virtual or in-person. Also consider the number of people who will attend your session because the more people, the more difficult it will be to manage.

We recommend that Black women set fees for their trainings prior to meeting with potential clients. As mentioned above, consider setting a price for the time needed to research and build the curriculum, as well as the length of the scheduled training sessions. Let clients know your fees and then, determine if negotiation is necessary. Do not be afraid to respectfully decline an invitation to work with the potential client if the money or the task is not a good fit.

Recommendation 4 - Equitable Mindfulness

The final recommendation centers on Equitable Mindfulness and how to utilize this framework in facilitation and in survival as Black Women DEI practitioners. The first set of recommendations are specific to using these practices in HWIs and demographic-specific spaces (i.e. spaces that are created for a specific demographic such as BIPOC), and the second set are specific for Black Women DEI practitioners.

EM Specific for incorporating Into HWIs and in Demographic-specific Groups

Have a practice of your own - The most important thing you can do to be the best advocate and service provider of this information is to have a practice of mindfulness yourself! As mentioned before in the narrative section, sharing these practices can be an oppressive activity in vulnerable populations if you do not model the practices yourself.

Find a cultural connection - Culturally, many people have a connection to something they can relate to with mindfulness, such as prayer, cooking rituals, ceremonies, and practices of silence. Aim to be demographic-specific by utilizing ways to connect using words, phrases, and symbols that a person might already recognize.

Plant the seed - As mentioned, if you choose to share this framework with others, your only job is to plant the seed. It's the other person's job to water it and cultivate its growth. In other words, however your participants/students/community come to this practice, you meet them there. Expectations of how they are supposed to receive this information will only result in disappointment for you or resistance from them. Their outcome is not tied to you. Your role is only to share your tools and your practice-based informed perspectives.

EM Specific for Black Women DEI Practitioners Looking to Use EM as a Tool

Have a personal practice - This is being mentioned again here because of its importance. However, here, it is not for the sake of the participants, but for the sake of you - the Black Woman DEI practitioner. As mentioned, one of the pillars of Equitable Mindfulness is Personal protection. We implore you to utilize mindfulness as a practice for your own survival. By having a safe space within your own consciousness to come back to in silence or in mindful action, you give yourself an opportunity to heal. This part of our recommendation is pivotal as we recognize the sheer weight and burden that we as Black Women carry. As such, it is important to have spaces of healing and joy. If you do not already have a practice, find one that fits and use it!

Say no - One of the challenges that we receive as Black Women is the idea that we are constantly available for the needs of others. This simply isn't true. For many reasons - budgetary, time, or simply because we don't want to - we need to be comfortable saying "no." As much as we consider this a tool of self-care it is also an Equitable Mindfulness practice. Saying "no" is being mindful of your present capacity while giving yourself the opportunity of choice - which is a huge component to mindfulness practice.

Not compromising our positions - We come with knowledge and know what we are doing. Do not second guess your abilities simply because someone tells you your fees are too high or you experience push-back in your sessions. Stand firm and facilitate a space where productive and equitable dialogue can occur.

Embrace the collaboration between Black women doing DEI work - The more of us we have to lean on, the more opportunity for support and networking. Support each other outside of DEI space. When life is happening in the world, we call each other. We HOLD space for each other. Oftentimes, we do not recognize this as a mindfulness technique.

Find JOY - Last, but certainly not least, is the recommendation to constantly find joy! This joy may be individual like dancing, singing, cooking, etc. Or, the joy you find may be communal. Studies have shown that our relationship to our identity groups are a direct path to well-being (Branscombe, Schmitt, & Harvey, 1999). As such, as much as you can, check in with your Black friends. Laugh with them! Find joy in spaces together and be present in these moments while doing it.

CONCLUSION

The TDIEM partnership has provided us the opportunity to hone our skills as DEI practitioners in a robust field that continues to grow. Our identities as Black women place us in a unique position to facilitate difficult conversations around diversity and inclusion. We encourage our clients to use the tools we have provided them in sessions and to incorporate them into their daily practices. Organizations must be willing to not only promote diversity by ensuring representation of multiple visible and invisible social identities but to practice the art of inclusion, using Equitable Mindfulness as the anchor.

We want to leave you with a simple mantra that Cash created for us, by us! A mantra is a mindfulness tool that can be repeated silently or aloud to help ground us and focus on an intention. We challenge you to use this mantra when you are in need of some good, Black joy and a reminder of just how much melanin magic you provide as a Black Woman DEI practitioner.

My Black Is Beautiful Mantra

Created By: Tiara Cash

I am a product of strength and love.

My Black is beautiful.

I am deserving of all good things.

My Black is worthy.

I am an instrument of truth and prosperity.

My Black is a changemaker.

I am, just that, and don't need to be anything other than what I am.

My Black is divine, cosmic, and universal. ©

REFERENCES

American Association for Access, Equity, and Diversity. (2021). Affirmative action policies throughout history. *AAAED*. https://www.aaaed.org/aaaed/History_of_Affirmative_Action.asp

Anti-defamation League. (n.d.). Civil Rights Movement. *ADL*. https://www.adl.org/education/resources/backgrounders/civil-rights-movement

Bailey, M. (2021). *Misogynoir transformed: Black women's digital resistance*. NYU Press. doi:10.18574/nyu/9781479803392.001.0001

Bautista, T. G., Cash, T. A., Meyerhoefer, T., & Pipe, T. B. (2022). Equitable Mindfulness: The Practice of Mindfulness for All. *Journal of Community Psychology*. doi:10.1002/jcop.22821

Berila, B. (2015). *Integrating mindfulness into anti-oppression pedagogy: Social justice in higher education*. Routledge., doi:10.4324/9781315721033

Booysen, L. (2014). The development of inclusive leadership practice and processes. In B. M. Ferdman & B. N. Deane (Eds.), *Diversity at work: The practice of inclusion,* (pp. 296–329). Jossey-Bass.

Branscombe, N. R., Schmitt, M. T., & Harvey, R. D. (1999). Perceiving pervasive discrimination among African Americans: Implications for group identification and well-being. *Journal of Personality and Social Psychology*, *77*(1), 135–149. doi:10.1037/0022-3514.77.1.135

Cannon, J. (2016). Education as the practice of freedom: A social justice proposal for mindfulness educators. In R. Purser, D. Forbes, & A. Burke (Eds.), *Handbook of Mindfulness,* (pp. 397–409). Springer., doi:10.1007/978-3-319-44019-4_26

Cash, T. A., Gueci, N., & Pipe, T. (2021). Equitable Mindfulness: A framework for transformative conversations in higher education. *Building Healthy Academic Communities Journal*, *5*(1), 9–21. doi:10.18061/bhac.v5i1.7770

Center for Disease Control. (2020). Disparities in death from COVID-19: Racial and ethnic health disparities. *CDC*. https://www.cdc.gov/coronavirus/2019-ncov/community/health-equity/racial-ethnic-disparities/disparities-deaths.html

CNN. (2020). Protests across the globe after George Floyd's death. *CNN*. https://www.cnn.com/2020/06/06/world/gallery/intl-george-floyd-protests/index.html

Cole, B. M. (2020). 8 reasons why diversity and inclusion are essential to business success. *Forbes*. https://www.forbes.com/sites/biancamillercole/2020/09/15/8-reasons-why-diversity-and-inclusion-are-essential-to-business-success/?sh=22d25fc21824

Collins, P. H. (2000). *Black feminist thought: Knowledge, consciousness, and the politics of empowerment,* (2nd ed.). Routledge.

Cooper, B. (2018). *Eloquent rage: A Black Feminist discovers her superpower*. Macmillan Publishing Group, LLC.

Davis, A. Y. (1981). *Women, race, and class.* Random House.

DiAngelo, R. (2018). *White fragility: What it's so hard for White people to talk about racism.* Beacon Press.

DiversityInc. (n.d.). Overview of the Top 50 companies for diversity. *Diversity Inc.* https://www.diversityinc.com/about-the-diversityinc-top-50-process/

Edgehill, V. E. (2007). Historical patterns of institutional diversity: Black women in race -specific positions on predominantly White college campuses (Order No. 3283238) [Doctoral Dissertation]. Howard University, USA.

Evans-Winters, V. E. (2019). *Black feminism in qualitative inquiry: Mosaic for writing our daughter's body.* Routledge. doi:10.4324/9781351046077

Feiner, L. (2021). Tech companies made big pledges to fight racism last year – here's how they're doing so far. *CNBC.* https://www.cnbc.com/2021/06/06/tech-industry-2020-anti-racism-commitments-progress-check.html

Ferdman, B. M. (2014). The practice of inclusion in diverse organizations: Toward a systemic and inclusive framework. In B. M. Ferdman & B. N. Deane (Eds.), *Diversity at work: The practice of inclusion,* (pp. 3–54). Jossey-Bass.

Ferdman, B. M., & Deane, B. R. (2014). *Diversity at work: The practice of inclusion.* Jossey-Bass.

Flory, J. A., Leibbrandt, A., Rott, C., & Stoddard, O. (2021). Increasing workplace diversity: Evidence from a recruiting experiment at a Fortune 500 Company. *Journal of Human Resources, 56*(1), 73–N.PAG. https://doi-org.libproxy.lib.ilstu.edu/10.3368/jhr.56.1.0518-9489R1

Gonzalez, T. (2017). Root to rise: Mindful lawyering for social justice. *NYU Rev. L. & Soc. Change, 41,* 91.

Gueci, N., & Cash, T. (2020, March 10). *The Expansive Model of Mindfulness.* LinkedIn. https://www.linkedin.com/pulse/expansive-model-mindfulness-nika-gueci-tiara-cash-nika-gueci/

Haas Institute. (2019). Whole Story, & Studio Pathways. The Circle of Human Concern. https://haasinstitute.berkeley.edu/sites/default/files/expanding_belonging_-_the_circle_of_human_concern.pdf

Hanson, K., McLeod, C., & Ross, M. (2017). Mindfulness and Nature. A mindful teaching community: Possibilities for teacher professional learning, 89.

Hayles, V. R. (2014). Communicating about diversity and inclusion. In B. M. Ferdman & B. N. Deane (Eds.), *Diversity at work: The practice of inclusion,* (pp. 55–90). Jossey-Bass.

Henrich, J., Heine, S., & Norenzayan, A. (2010). The weirdest people in the world? *Behavioral and Brain Sciences, 33*(2-3), 61–83. doi:10.1017/S0140525X0999152X

Hernandez, M., Avery, D. R., Volpone, S. D., & Kaiser, C. R. (2019). Bargaining while Black: The role of race in salary negotiations. *The Journal of Applied Psychology, 104*(4), 581–592. doi:10.1037/apl0000363

Homeland Security Digital Library. (n.d.). Report on the National Advisory Commission on Civil Disorders: Summary of report. https://www.hsdl.org/?abstract&did=35837

Johnson, T. B. (2021a). *The experiences of Black women in diversity roles at 4-year predominantly White institutions* (Order No. 28150595) [Doctoral Dissertation]. Illinois State University, USA.

Johnson, T. B. (2021b). Perspectives from a multicultural affairs office professional: Diversity education during COVID-19. In L. Kyei-Blankson, J. Blankson, & E. Ntuli (Eds.), *Handbook of research on inequities in online education during global crisis,* (pp. 240–259). IGI Global. doi:10.4018/978-1-7998-6533-9.ch013

Kendi, I. X. (2019). *How to be an anti-racist.* One World.

Le, T. N., & Shim, P. (2014). Mindfulness and the Aloha response. *Journal of Indigenous Social Development, 3*(2).

Lorde, A. (1984). *Sister outsider.* Ten Speed Press.

Magee, R. V. (2016). Teaching mindfulness with mindfulness of race and other forms of diversity. In D. McCown, D. Reibel, & M. Micozzi (Eds.), *Resources for Teaching Mindfulness.* Springer., doi:10.1007/978-3-319-30100-6_12

Marquis, J. P., Lim, N., Scott, L. M., Harrell, M. C., & Kavanagh, J. (2008). *Managing diversity in corporate America: An exploratory Analysis.* RAND Corporation. https://www.jstor.org/stable/10.7249/op206rc.6

Mcgirt, E. (2016). The subtle ways people of color feel excluded at work. *Fortune.* https://fortune.com/2016/10/06/inclusion-diversity-employers-race/

Merriam-Webster Dictionary. (n.d.). *Diversity.* https://www.merriam-webster.com/dictionary/diversity

Merriam-Webster Dictionary. (n.d.). *Inclusion.* https://www.merriam-webster.com/dictionary/inclusion

Miller, S. (2020). Black workers still earn less than their white counterparts. https://www.shrm.org/resourcesandtools/hr-topics/compensation/pages/racial-wage-gaps-persistence-poses-challenge.aspx

Montero-Marin, J., Tops, M., Manzanera, R., Piva Demarzo, M., Álvarez de Mon, M., & García Campayo, J. (2015). Mindfulness, resilience, and burnout subtypes in primary care physicians: The possible mediating role of positive and negative affect. *Frontiers in Psychology, 6,* 1895. doi:10.3389/fpsyg.2015.01895

Nathoo, Z. (2021). In homogeneous organisations, even the most talented hires can feel tokenised. It's a problem that hits everyone hard. *BBC.* https://www.bbc.com/worklife/article/20210902-why-diverse-hires-cant-always-escape-tokenism

Newkirk, P. (2019). Diversity has become a booming business. So, where are the results? https://time.com/5696943/diversity-business/

Newkirk, P. (2020). *Diversity inc.: The fight for racial equality in the workplace.* Bold Type Books.

Ngyuen, J. (2021). A year later, how are corporations doing on promises they made to fight for racial justice? https://www.marketplace.org/2021/05/24/a-year-later-how-are-corporations-doing-on-promises-they-made-to-fight-for-racial-justice/

Nussbaum, B. (2013). African culture and Ubuntu reflections of a South African in America. *World Business Academy*, *17*(1), 1–12.

Nzinga, S. M. (2020). *Lean semesters: How higher education reproduces inequity*. Johns Hopkins University Press.

Oliver, B. (2020). I went on 100 interviews in 8 months: This is what it's like to negotiate your salary as a Black woman. *CNBC*. https://www.cnbc.com/2020/03/31/what-its-like-to-negotiate-salary-as-a-black-woman-equal-pay-day.html

Phelps, P. M. (2016). *An examination of the effects of tokenism for female command officers in law enforcement* (Order No. 10239943) [Doctoral Dissertation]. Capella University, USA.

Phillips, F. B. (1990). NTU psychotherapy: An Afrocentric approach. *The Journal of Black Psychology*, *17*(1), 55–74. doi:10.1177/00957984900171005

Pipe, T. B., & Bortz, J. J. (2009). Mindful leadership as healing practice: Nurturing self to serve others. *International Journal for Human Caring*, *13*(2), 34–38. doi:10.20467/1091-5710.13.2.34

Rogers, H. B. (2016). *The mindful twenty-something*. New Harbinger.

Smith, D. E. (2020). *Black while leading: Unmasking the anti-Black lived experiences of senior-level black men administrators at historically White institutions* (Order No. 28150659) [Doctoral Dissertation]. Illinois State University, USA.

Sobers, S. T. (2014). *Can I get a witness?: The resilience of four Black women senior student affairs administrators at predominantly White institutions* (Order No. 3625189) [Doctoral Dissertation]. Illinois State University, USA.

Streeter, C. (2020). Breathing Power and Poise. *Australasian Journal of American Studies*, *39*(1), 5–46. https://www.jstor.org/stable/10.2307/26972999

Taylor, K. Y. (2017). *How we get free: Black feminism and the Combahee River Collective*. Haymarket Books.

Winters, M. F. (2014). From diversity to inclusion: An inclusion equation. In B. M. Ferdman & B. N. Deane (Eds.), *Diversity at work: The practice of inclusion*, (pp. 205–228). Jossey-Bass.

Winters, M. F. (2020a). *Inclusive conversations*. Berrett-Koehler Publishers, Inc.

Winters, M. F. (2020b). *Black fatigue: How racism erodes the mind, body, and spirit*. Berrett-Koehler Publishers, Inc.

Wong, Y. L. R. (2004). Knowing through discomfort: A mindfulness-based critical social work pedagogy. *Critical Social Work*, *5*(1), 1–19.

ADDITIONAL READING

Ahmed, S. (2012). *On being included: Racism and diversity in institutional life*. Duke University Press.

Cooper, B. (2017). *Beyond respectability: Women, gender, and sexuality in American history*. University of Illinois Press. doi:10.5406/illinois/9780252040993.001.0001

Healthy People 2030. (n.d.). Social determinants of health. https://health.gov/healthypeople/objectives-and-data/social-determinants-health

Hooks, B. (2015) Feminist theory: From margin to center, (3rd edition). Routledge.

Hooks, B. (2015). *Talking Back: Thinking feminist, thinking Black*. New edition. Routledge.

Hooks, B. (2015). *Yearning: Race, gender, and cultural politics*. Routledge.

Londrell. (2017). *Eternal sunshine*. CreateSpace Independent Publishing Platform.

Prats, J. M. (2021). Diversity Initiatives and the backlash of reverse discrimination claims. *The Florida Bar Journal*, *95*(5), 42–46.

St. Pierre, M. A. (1991). Reaganomics and its implications for African-American family life. *Journal of Black Studies*, *21*(3), 325–340. doi:10.1177/002193479102100307

Ward, M. (2021). DEI trailblazers: 16 diversity executives transforming the workplace in post-George Floyd corporate America. *Business Insider*. Https://Www.Businessinsider.Com/Diversity-Executives-Transforming-Corporate-America-Post-George-Floyd-2021#Cynthia-Bowman-Chief-Diversity-And-Inclusion-And-Talent-Acquisition-Officer-At-Bank-Of-America-16

Williams, D. (2013). *Strategic diversity leadership: Activating change and transformation in higher education*. Stylus Publishing, LLC.

Williams, R. V. (2002). *Being Black: Zen and the art of living with fearlessness and grace*. Penguin Books.

KEY TERMS AND DEFINITIONS

Anti-Racism: The act of working against the institution of racism in all facets of society.

Black Fatigue: The emotional stress that impacts the overall health of Black people caused by racism.

Black Feminism: Centers the experiences of Black women and their positionality in the social and political context as they have historically been ostracized from conversations surrounding feminism.

Brave Container: An action initiated by the facilitator and continued and managed by the participants to intentionally create a space of conversation and community. Grounded in principles of mindfulness and bridging (see below), this is a departure from the traditional role of the facilitator and the associated power gradient in workshops

Bridging: Relating to other groups based on deep listening, empathetic space, and recognition of suffering. Rejects the concept of "them" while recognizing unique differences. An intentional rejection of othering.

Equitable Mindfulness: Presenting the concept of mindfulness to everyone, while being active in our respective communities, removing personal and systemic barriers that work against inclusivity and transformative change

Global Majority: An attempt to move away from the term 'minority', Global Majority includes the non-White majority of the world.

Holding Space: Inviting an individual into one's own mindfulness practice by seeing, hearing, and holding what they need to express, and using mindful listening and heartfelt compassion without giving advice or attempting to solve problems

Tokenism: The practice of making only symbolic gestures in order to give the appearance of equality.

White Fragility: The way in which White people deflect or become defensive when confronted with uncomfortable conversations surrounding race and racism.

Chapter 8
Black Women, Emotional Intelligence, and Organizational Opportunities for Growth

Adela E. Jiménez
https://orcid.org/0000-0002-6716-2261
Independent Researcher, USA

Charnise Virgil Moore
https://orcid.org/0000-0003-4262-0374
Independent Researcher, USA

ABSTRACT

Since the end of 2019, the world has been trying to identify ways to deal with the dual pandemics of COVID-19 and the racial reckoning that arose during the summer of 2020. Organizations have scrambled to re-energize diversity, equity, and inclusion (DEI) initiatives. The questions to be asked are why are organizations focusing their efforts on DEI initiatives, and how can they be successful? This chapter introduces and examines emotional intelligence as a vehicle leveraged by both authors and many other Black women, including Black diversity, equity, and inclusion (DEI) practitioners, as a means for advancement within their organizations. The authors further offer that in order for organizations to achieve equity and inclusion, emotional intelligence is a required baseline, and the support of DEI practitioners in this arena will create an array of positive effects, such as a harmonious work environment, self-actualized individuals including Black women, and thus personal, community, and organizational success.

"The most common way people give up their power is by thinking they don't have any."— Alice Walker

Energized by the process of improving, we find passion in learning new facts, exploring new ideas, and applying what we have learned in various environments. Dr. Jiménez, a true people-enthusiast, and Dr.

DOI: 10.4018/978-1-6684-3564-9.ch008

Moore, an advocate for women's and girls' rights, approach writing this piece with the same curiosity and expectation that it will drive change for those who generously take the time to experience this learning.

As two Black women, the authors, one a Black Hispanic and the other an African American, have both experienced the intersectionality of being a woman and being Black and the undermining that takes place at both levels. The concept of intersectionality speaks about the double burden Black women often experience when discriminated against based on race and gender (Crenshaw, 1989). Black women's experiences are not merely one or the other; they are both Black and female. Regrettably, a framework does not exist to address the meeting of these two dimensions, creating an environment that obscures their existence and ends with them feeling isolated. Thus, having to succeed within norms established without consideration for their needs and experiences often creates personal, professional, and emotional challenges.

INTRODUCTION

A significant emotional event (SEE) is an experience that disrupts one's emotional, spiritual, and physical being (Massey, 2014). In essence, such an event causes one to 'see,' that is, to consider, examine, and possibly change behaviors and even value systems. A SEE disrupts one's patterns, causing changes in thought processes and behaviors.

For the last two and a half years, the world has been trying to identify ways to deal with the significant emotional events of COVID-19 and the racial reckoning spurred on by the killing of George Floyd in the summer of 2020. We refer to both of these events as pandemics. This dual pandemic has pushed us to alter our behaviors and, in some cases, our value systems to address the environmental, economic, and social impact of both. For Black women (BW), this dual pandemic exacerbates the already tenuous environments in which they live and operate, adding more landmines to already complicated minefields. Although not literal, these minefields, especially the ones encountered in their work environments, contain landmines that are as dangerous and deadly as those in the war zone.

Due to the so-called 'awakening' caused by this dual pandemic, organizations have scrambled to re-energize initiatives in hopes of addressing diversity, equity, and inclusion (DEI) challenges with the underlay of COVID-19 (Middaugh, 2021; Talan, 2022). The challenge remains in just that: organizations have decided to re-energize initiatives instead of rebuilding or developing initiatives with the new information provided by the current times. This is a challenge not only because it can be argued that organizations never fully honed or developed adequate infrastructures to support initiatives that address DEI but also because re-energizing initiatives would require organizations to develop avenues for discourse, learning, and reflection. It is the experience of many BW that although organizations have engaged in these DEI initiatives, even hiring numbers of DEI practitioners, BW are still waiting to see and feel improvement in this realm (Jackson, 2022). Many DEI hires experience issues because they are relegated to developing, communicating, and enforcing diversity-related initiatives in an environment that does not grant them the power to operate (Drake-Clark, 2009). Sadly, this speaks to the organizational culture manifested through company messaging, leadership behaviors, and employee interactions. Through this chapter, we explore the current state of emotional intelligence (EI) within organizations, the experience of BW within these organizations, and also provide recommendations for organizations to close the gap.

THE IMPACT OF THE DUAL PANDEMIC ON BLACK WOMEN

The word pandemic originates from a combination of the Greek words' pan + demos,' which means 'all + people.' Indeed, we, 'all people,' have been affected by the COVID-19 pandemic and the social unrest due to the murder of George Floyd, the dual pandemic. The COVID-19 pandemic has directly or indirectly affected some family members, friends, and even those we may not have known personally, thus affecting our psyche. There have been other outbreaks in the last 100 years, such as six cholera outbreaks (1899-1923); Spanish and Asian flu (1918-1959); and most recently, SARS; Swine Flu; and MERS. However, because of global integration and the ease of travel, COVID-19 has spread rapidly, wreaking havoc around the world.

Although, as humans, we are reluctant to change, the COVID-19 pandemic has forced us to do just that, to change and change rapidly. COVID-19 has interrupted our routines, causing us to look at our lives to determine what is truly important. Families have had to make financial adjustments that have noticeably impacted their lifestyles. Some parents have had to change their work routines (start, stop, breaks, etc.) to take care of their children, which in many cases even meant becoming teachers. Others have had to change jobs and even start new businesses to meet their family's needs. In addition, individuals have been experiencing high levels of stress, anxiety, frustration, and anger, due to the uncertainty of their current environment, the constant barrage of news related to the virus, and the fear related to the risk of contagion (Abdel-Fattah, 2020; Duan & Zhu, 2020).

For BW, the COVID-19 pandemic, in some instances, rather than creating inequalities, highlighted them (Hammonds, 2021). For example, in early 2022, the CDC reported that deaths in the Black community related to COVID-19 accounted for a higher share when compared to the overall Black population (13.9% versus 12.5%). Other factors to consider are the statistics related to health insurance, which indicate that as of 2021, 11.2% of Black Americans had no health insurance when compared to only 7.8% of Whites and are therefore less able to address the higher incidences of obesity, diabetes, hypertension, and other comorbidities (Wiley et al., 2022). Furthermore, Black Americans are more likely to work as essential workers, holding jobs in sanitation, transportation, and warehouses, and operating as delivery workers, residential facility workers, and community-based services workers, all of which expose them more to COVID-19 (Banks, 2019; McNicholas & Poydock, 2020). In fact, Black workers make up 17% of essential workers, including Black mothers who are, in most cases, 80% of the time, the primary breadwinners for their families (Banks, 2019; Gould & Wilson, 2020) but who earn 70% less than White households (Carrazana, 2020).

Two issues emerge from this dynamic: first, the reality and effect of these statistics added extreme stress to the lives of BW, who had to continue working while managing all the emotions associated with the pandemic. Sun et al. (2021) remind us that behaviors drive job performance and that emotions underpin those behaviors. Second, while most of America adjusted to stay-at-home orders, essential workers, often BW, continued working their regular schedules, creating a greater risk of exposure for themselves and their families. The increased risks of exposure to COVID-19, lower prevalence of health insurance coverage, higher comorbidities and death rates, and our country's response to it further highlighted, as posited by Carrazana (2020), the structural and institutional racism that exists and reinforced social, economic, and health inequities.

In the mists of grappling with COVID-19, the cruel death of George Floyd took place. The way the police officer involved showed no regard for another human being, by placing his knee on the neck of George Floyd until he could no longer breathe, sent shock waves throughout the world. This act caused another pandemic to rise. Throughout the streets in the US and the world, individuals protested and demanded that race no longer be treated as divisive but unifying. This opposing view would only take foot if the population in power were willing to confront the racism in our environment and within themselves and if they began to see, appreciate, and celebrate the contributions of people of color, including BW.

So, the question becomes: where do we go from here? A survey titled "Black Women Thriving (BWT)" indicated that 88% of BW experience burnout on the job, especially when they do not have supportive environments (Hines & Fitts, 2022). To answer this question, organizations have decided to institute several DEI initiatives. These organizations must determine, however, the fundamental drivers or reasons for these initiatives. The authors believe there to be three potential reasons. The first reason may be that they follow a trend seen throughout corporate America in response to an uprise that demanded racial justice. A second reason may be because organizations with diverse teams have (1) 22% greater productivity and lower turnover, (2) are twice as likely to meet or exceed financial targets as those without, (3) are six times more likely to be innovative and agile, and (4) are eight times more likely to achieve better business outcomes (Deloitte, 2018). Finally, the third reason may be because they see themselves as living organisms or teal organizations (Laloux, 2014), always ready to learn and adapt. Laloux (2014) posited that teal organizations create environments where harmony within oneself, the immediate community, the organization, and the world is the goal. Teal organizations invite all their stakeholders, including BW, to share their whole selves, their authentic selves, with the expectation that their uniqueness will be celebrated. However, the question remains: Why are organizations focusing on DEI initiatives? It is essential to identify the underlining reason, for it sets the stage for how much these organizations would be willing to invest and how far they would be willing to go to achieve true harmony.

CONCEPTUALIZATION OF EMOTIONAL INTELLIGENCE

Mayer et al. (2011) said that EI is "the mental ability that lurks amidst the emotions" (p. 544) and is defined by Verma et al. (2017) and Boyatzis and Sala (2004) as the capability of an individual to adapt to his environment by recognizing and discriminating between their own emotions and those of others to achieve superior performance in life and work. Therefore, we posit that EI is a necessary foundation for those organizations that see themselves as teal organizations.

When emotions are addressed in a healthy and safe environment where EI is the norm, individuals grow and improve their social lives, work, and, ultimately, the organization's output. Taking an active approach to comprehending one another's emotions and concerns will draw people together. This new collaborative and caring environment will develop trust amongst the team, resulting in efficiency, better decision-making, and, ultimately, better job performance.

Daniel Goleman greatly popularized EI in a book he wrote n 1995 entitled *Emotional Intelligence-Why it can matter more than IQ*. Goleman (2005) defines EI as a set of skills and competencies that enhances managerial performance and leadership. Two distinct areas emerge when studying EI. The first, says Goleman (2005), is self-management, further defined by the dimensions of self-awareness, self-regulation, and self-motivation. The second is social management, further defined by empathy and social skills dimensions. We define each one of these five dimensions of EI below.

Self-Awareness

Self-awareness is the ability to truthfully identify one's emotions as they occur, looking inwardly as opposed to focusing on one's surroundings, and is crucial in alerting a person to their strengths and opportunities for growth (Carver, 2012; Goleman, 2005; Schutte et al., 1998; Serrat, 2017; Yahaya et al., 2012). Nevertheless, so often, people go through life without checking for blind spots, that area around a car that a driver cannot see by looking in the rearview or side mirrors (the usual and expected), without turning their head and therefore taking their eye off the road (look inwardly). Blind spots can therefore be dangerous. So, self-aware individuals work to mitigate that danger by constantly checking inwardly, seeking feedback, and having a realistic understanding of themselves.

Self-Regulation

Self-regulation is the ability to manage and take responsibility for one's actions in every situation (Goleman, 2005). It is not about suppressing emotions; on the contrary, it is about honoring them while not allowing them to overwhelm one. This process happens by suspending judgment, becoming comfortable with ambiguity, redirecting impulses and moods, and taking responsibility for the outcome of one's actions. Self-regulation is about how we act instead of react in response to the emotions we experience. White (1890) wrote that the real greatness of a person is measured by the power of the emotions that they control and not by the power of those that control them.

Self-Motivation

Self-motivation is the ability to doggedly pursue an objective despite the challenges that one may encounter (Goleman, 2005). In the case of leaders, their intense drive for achievement and organizational commitment originates in intrinsic versus extrinsic values and rewards. Self-motivated individuals set challenging goals and take calculated risks while remaining focused on their goals. In addition, they have an internal curiosity that pushes them to learn what drives them to accomplish their goals.

Empathy

Empathy is a careful mix of cognitive empathy (understanding someone else's viewpoint), emotional empathy (feeling with another), and empathic concern (being able to capture what someone else needs of them at the moment), as posited by Goleman (2013). Simply put, empathy is being able to understand the emotions that others are experiencing by picking up on the subtle signals expressed by them and then being willing to experience those emotions alongside them. In addition, a hallmark of empathy is a sincere inquisitive interest in others with the goal to serve. Finally, empathy leads to an appreciation of all differences, including gender, race, and cultural differences.

Social Skills

Social skill is the ability to use effective communication to negotiate and resolve conflicts to guide people toward achieving their goals (Goleman, 2005). Developing social skills requires individuals to form networking groups beyond their immediate comfort zone, which leads to identifying and being willing to remove any barriers that would not support a harmonious environment. Individuals with high social skills emerge as natural leaders drawing others into active participation in task completion.

IMPORTANCE OF EMOTIONAL INTELLIGENCE IN ORGANIZATIONS

Research has shown that EI, which is the way individuals recognize, understand, and manage their emotions, is a variable that significantly affects organizational behaviors and outcomes (Ashkanasy & Daus, 2005; Cote & Miners, 2006; Mohamad & Jais, 2016; Newman et al., 2010). An example of such is a study whose objective was to examine whether training in this area would improve the EI levels of project managers in an organization in the UK. The study's results indicated a positive effect on the managers regarding emotional ability, understanding of emotions, teamwork, and conflict management. Moreover, this was the case six months after the training was completed (Clarke, 2010). Therefore, having high levels of EI in an organization's workforce is even more critical during pandemic times since it assists in understanding how stress and anxiety can be better managed (Extremera, 2020). Abdel-Fattah (2020) agrees, stating that EI is essential when dealing with a crisis. He goes on to say that individuals with high EI can assess a situation and move forward to address and solve the issue at hand.

Organizations must ensure that EI training takes place to improve leaders' self-management and social management skills, suggest Sadovyy et al. (2021) and Sellie-Dosunmu (2016). We offer that those organizations with high EI leaders will indeed create an array of positive effects, such as a harmonious work environment, self-actualized individuals (including BW), and thus personal, community, and organizational success.

As Lencioni (2020) suggested, these leaders will be motivated by responsibility-centered leadership or a deontological approach that shows their decision-making is based on duty and strong ethics. Alternatively, reward-centered leaders, who take on a teleological approach to leadership, take the attitude that others should serve them. Therefore, they avoid unpleasant tasks to the detriment of employees and the organization. Much like responsibility-centered leaders, teal organizations do the right thing for the right reasons, following a deontological approach.

BLACK WOMEN IN THE WORKPLACE

An immigrant from Cape Verde originally wrote the following words. However, they reflect the sentiments of BW in every environment: "being present and yet not visible, being visible and yet not present" (Freire, 2005, p. 11). This statement is substantiated by the results of the BWT survey, which indicated that 75% of BW say that their organization does not take full advantage of their skills. They are simply hired to meet the diversity count in many cases ("being present, yet not visible") but are not being appreciated ("being visible and yet not present.") BW experience this every day, and yet they perform their jobs. They juggle others' expectations while remaining true to themselves.

While juggling the challenges that arise from not being seen or appreciated, they can still tap into their empathy muscle in the hopes of establishing good relationships. The BWT survey findings suggest that though BW do not have equal access to opportunities, power, and organizational resources, they still seek to feel connected to their team, managers, and leadership. For example, one respondent to the

BWT survey stated it this way "I [want] an opportunity to be included in certain conversations… New relationships are being built. I just want to be in the mix." (Hines & Fitts, 2022).

Just as in military operations, where the object is to rapidly clear a path through a minefield, we propose that EI can be the tool to clear that path in organizations. Organizations seeking change using EI as the guide will look within and address the issues identified, specifically concerning BW. As a result, these organizations will be motivated to do the right thing arriving at a place of empathy, leading ultimately to harmonious relationships and environments.

RELATIONSHIP BETWEEN EI, ORGANIZATIONS, AND BLACK WOMEN

Becoming emotionally intelligent is a cyclical process that starts with understanding the different layers that affect us and how this impacts others (see Figure 1). It is furthermore the capacity to be vulnerable enough to share or explain to others what one is experiencing and the source of our mood. Individuals will aid this process by engaging in effective communications that will assist in resolving conflicts and thus enhancing relationships.

Figure 1. Cyclical Nature of Emotional Intelligence
(Jiménez, 2021)

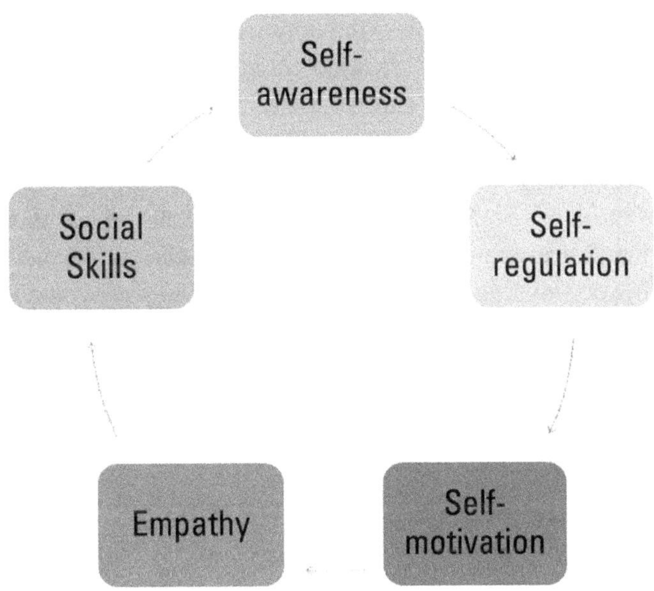

The good news is that, unlike IQ, which measures a person's ability to use information and logic to answer questions and does not show much improvement past adolescence, EI can be improved by practicing behaviors that then become second nature (Bradberry & Greaves, 2015; Cotruş et al., 2012). So, should organizations set the environment for EI to flourish? Research supports this approach. The improvement of EI competencies of senior leaders results in the creation of inspiring, nurturing, and empathetic environments for their mid-level leaders, who in turn influence front-line workers, therefore contributing to an enhanced job and organizational performance (Alonazi, 2020; Amina et al., 2021; Heckemann et al., 2015; Prezerakos, 2018; Webb, 2009). In addition, EI, focusing on empathy and social skills, can assist organizations in bridging cultural divides and lessen the stress created by the same (Laloux, 2014 & Sellie-Dosunmu, 2016).

In the case of BW, this stress is heightened by the necessity to navigate in mostly White spaces. The BWT survey revealed that the burnout experienced by BW is driven primarily by the microaggressions they experience daily (Hines & Fitts, 2022). Additionally, BW report feeling as though they are always in a fish tank, where their every gesture is scrutinized, every word is analyzed and every move criticized. BW have had to compartmentalize their experiences to prevent negative assertions about their actions (loud, aggressive, bossy) from tarnishing their true identity (Motro et al., 2022). BW are always on stage, acting the part that the dominant culture has relegated them to play, and they must do so to succeed.

The problem with this approach is that although BW may succeed in the role they have been assigned, dimming their light does not set them up to thrive, and neither does the organization (Cheeks, 2018). Organizations are being derelict in their duties to produce the highest return on their investment by hiring BW but not setting the stage for them to thrive. What are organizations willing to do to address this problem?

There are two schools of thought; one espouses that it is not the responsibility of Black people, indeed BW, to educate the majority about the issues and possible solutions. The other is that collaboration between Black people, and the majority is the only way to improve the current conditions. We agree that it is not the duty of BW to educate, especially since BW have no actual control over what the majority does. However, we suggest that collaboration is the only way to improve the current environment. We are not naïve enough to believe such a transformation could take place without dismantling the current power structure. Ultimately, as identified by Freire (2005), "only power that springs from the weakness of the oppressed will be sufficiently strong to free both" (p. 44).

Dancing alone can allow one to have a good time, but when done with someone else, although one is not able to select all of the songs or moves, the experience is richer. When those two individuals who took the opportunity to dance meet again, a smile looms over their faces. No, one individual cannot force another to dance, but BW keep inviting others to dance because they know the joy it brings. Therefore, we invite these organizations that have loudly proclaimed their interest in true diversity, equity, and inclusion to accept the invitation to dance and effectuate change that will bring joy and a harmonious environment for all.

RECOMMENDATIONS FOR ADDRESSING THE INCLUSION GAP WITH BW

Organizations, as we stated earlier, have engaged in hiring several BW to have a diverse workforce, but they have fallen short of the inclusion goal. This section explores how BW currently see themselves in the workplace and how organizations interact with them. Then, based on our experience, we offer recommendations on how organizations should interact and effectively include BW in the organizational culture using the EI framework.

Self-Awareness Model

Self-awareness is the first dimension of EI (see Table 1). Ask any BW in your organization how she is perceived in the workplace, and you will find that she feels seen but not heard. BW expend so much energy managing how others see them that it often creates isolation. A survey commissioned by Cigna reported that African American workers, including BW, feel 5% more isolated than their White counterparts (Hunter-Gadsden, 2020). The majority group sees this as BW being antagonistic and separatist when they are just trying to protect themselves. This focus on protection, rather than simply being a contributing team member, creates an energy drain.

Table 1. Self-awareness, closing the gap

Self-awareness			
Desired Outcome	**How Black Women See Themselves**	**How Organizations Threaten Black Women**	**Closing the Gap**
Conscious awareness of one's internal state	A low point for BW who have been taught to ignore their internal feelings.	Limited understanding of implicit bias against BW.	Creating safe structures for appropriate expression and dialogue around the work experiences of BW.
Getting to know and appreciate oneself	BW have learned to appreciate themselves despite the lack of frequency of external reassurance.	The belief is that the organization's majority is the norm and standard.	Incorporate BW work experiences in DEI programs/ initiatives and foster a better sense of community.
Awareness of how others see you	Keenly aware of how others view them.	Not aware or interested in the way others see them, especially BW, because they believe they are the norm. So, they speak without awareness of how their statements affect BW (e.g., commenting on their hair and fashion).	Leverage tools/resources to initiate feedback & dialogue with BW on how they view leadership and the organization.
Self-confident	Self-confidence leads BW to be ambitious.	Although they benefit from hiring self-confident BW, they stifle their growth, believing that BW are advancing too quickly.	Creating opportunities for advancement will lead to more confident, diverse, and productive teams and work culture.

So, how can organizations leverage EI to ensure they are aware of their impact on BW and provide benefits to the organization? Suppose an organization is looking to start a new chapter. In that case, it must abandon the mindset that hiring a DEI leader or holding a focus group on improving racial dialogue is the answer to the problem. Hiring a DEI practitioner without active and thoughtful engagement and commitment by executive leadership is not only a recipe for disaster but also further perpetuates the issue that this chapter and book look to overcome: hostile environments that do not acknowledge and appreciate BW holistically. Instead, your organizations should look at where their workforce is today. What are your demographics? How do the BW in your organization share their thoughts, ideas, and opinions? What resources are available to BW and how many and how often do they use those resources? Understanding the answer to these questions will help identify your potential first steps in incorporating

EI in your organization. Communicate your desire to learn and build EI while sharing that you are not the expert but are committed to improvement. Following this approach will go a long way in initiating dialogue and becoming self-aware of the areas for improvement. Once you have received BW's feedback, work towards creating those resources and structures for them to utilize. Be transparent with your intentions and frequently reassess to determine effectiveness. Checking in with BW to say, "how is that new resource we added?", actively listening to the feedback, and readjusting as needed will enhance the organization's self-awareness. Without taking stalk of all of the workforce, organizations are inevitably leaving valuable information on the table.

As Black women who have worked in primarily white organizations, both authors have experienced organizations that embraced self-awareness and others that did not. For example, author Moore previously worked in an organization that showed commitment to diversity, equity, inclusion, and belonging by implementing an annual diversity program with a new cohort established each year that met monthly to explore complex topics. The program gathered staff and leaders from all departments and positions to cultivate understanding and empathy amongst the organization's employees. Thus, participants benefited from group dialogue with others who differ from them based on race or gender, allowing them to contribute their own experiences and truth and hear and appreciate the experiences of others.

In contrast, author Jiménez's experiences include working in an organization with no established DEI efforts to allow organizations and its employees to learn from or share their own experiences and truth. The lack of a safe space for expression and learning led many BW employees to form groups and circles amongst themselves to find comradery and support. The authors purport that organizations that actively engage employees in DEI efforts have less frustration expressed by BW employees. In contrast, organizations with no DEI efforts often have BW complaining within their safe circles.

Self-Regulation Model

The next dimension in the EI framework is self-regulation (see Table 2). This dimension of EI is the dimension that most closely aligns with the responsible actions needed to make a behavior change. For BW, the constant negative stimuli must be met with self-regulation: resisting the impulse to react but rather to act. In cases where statements such as *You are so eloquent and well-prepared; You are too animated when speaking; You lean into the camera when on ZOOM*, are directed at BW, they must refrain from responding. While you may just now be considering the impact behind the aforementioned statements, most BW in your organization hear them daily, albeit every moment and interaction. BW refrain from responding with the same level of disrespect as they recognize these statements as code for diminishing their presence.

This constant assault on BW often leads them to experience imposter syndrome, which is when a woman starts to question her talents and accomplishments and lives in constant fear of being exposed as a fraud. So, despite this constant assault, BW must choose to act instead of reacting to these assaults, put on a brave face and show up. Every. Single. Workday. What can be an effective approach for BW is to do your best on every project. Once BW have done their best, they should remind themselves that while the group may perceive them differently, it is just their thought and opinion, which is not based on reality.

Table 2. Self-regulation, closing the gap

Self-regulation			
Desired Outcomes	**How Black Women See Themselves**	**How Organizations Threaten Black Women**	**Closing the Gap**
Responsible	High standards and personal accountability to the point of suffering from imposter syndrome.	No personal accountability for the work environment that does not elevate BW.	Awareness that there is no opportunity for an emotionally intelligent organization without acknowledging and taking responsibility for all workforce members, recognizing that all are critical to its overall success and culture.
No knee-jerk reaction; instead, thoughtful action	Assess their environment quickly and engage in behavioral adjustments to fit in, as with code-switching.	Because the majority is not BW, they take no time to process information and therefore react instead of act.	Organizations must engage in deep thought and develop goals and action plans that show inclusivity to all.
Successful amid change and ambiguity	Adaptability comes as second nature to BW as they must be ready to fulfill others' whims from moment to moment.	There is little to no consideration to adapt due to organizations holding systemic power. They set the tone rather than adapt to it.	Organizations must constantly reassess themselves and adapt to the changing workforce.
Acting with integrity	It is unreasonable to expect BW to leave parts of themselves at the door.	Even though the mission statement states it, strong morals are not usually viewed from the perspective of BW.	Authentically consider the best ways to improve your organizational culture, keeping in mind that acting with integrity should leave BW feeling safer in the workplace.

Organizations can self-regulate by acknowledging that they have the power to act and change their own culture. Self-regulation begins with the willingness to reframe your thoughts. Reframing one's thoughts consists of questioning every thought, recognizing that thoughts are just a mental event and that having one does not equate to the truth. Every thought is not the truth, including the maxims often voiced about BW. So, consider new ways to interact with and respond to BW in your organization. Nothing will change by denying differences or being intimidated to have dialogue. If your organization is to become emotionally intelligent, it must consider the experiences of BW and create safe spaces for discourse, learning, and improvement.

Self-Motivation Model

The third dimension of EI is self-motivation (see Table 3). This dimension centers around remaining focused on a goal regardless of the present perils, distractions, and challenges. Organizations must then be willing to dismantle, if necessary, their legacy approaches in addressing DEI issues. New approaches to meet new needs must be developed. Therein lies the challenge. Zippia (2022) reports that 81.3% of chief diversity officers identify as White, leading to the creation of DEI initiatives, says Brownlee (2022), without the input of the population it seeks to involve and expect this minority population to just rubber-stamp the initiatives.

Table 3. Self-motivation, closing the gap

Self-motivation			
Desired Outcome	**How Black Women See Themselves**	**How Organizations Threaten Black Women**	**Closing the Gap**
Focused on destination	BW show high levels of resilience. They are determined to succeed despite having worse experiences at work than any other group.	Lack of concern and no acknowledgment of how or why BW succeed in their roles. Instead, hard work is rewarded with more responsibility and no advancement.	Organizations to focus on BW by acknowledging when work has met and exceeded expectations, not only via one-on-one dialogue but also among peers and leadership teams.
Steady aim	BW are not often derailed from their goals or responsibilities. Instead, they are known to stay the course even while facing opposition and setbacks.	Organizations have historically created dialogue around DEI efforts but often lose focus.	Organizations should fully commit to DEI once they have announced it as an important part of their culture. A shift in priorities should not necessitate a reduction in DEI efforts.
Internal curiosity	High investment by BW to identify their genuine interest since they usually do not find true mentors. BW value being around people they can learn from – a growth mindset.	Lack of interest in identifying BW's motivators and career goals.	Organizations should lean into identifying the motivators and goals of BW and provide cross-training opportunities that will lead to agile and thriving organizations.
Focus on hope instead of fear	BW operate by giving the organization the benefit of the doubt when they encounter negative situations.	Organizations are quick to label BW with personal adjectives such as aggressive, combative, and angry, which colors their appreciation for BW's job output. As a result, the feedback becomes personal.	Commitment should be made to identify opportunities for the mentoring, coaching, and feedback of BW related to job function. This approach instills hope in BW, lessening the chance for turnover.

One example of BW having self-motivation is a consistent theme that Moore has seen in organizations where she has worked and schools where she has attended. BW often come together to form a circle of support for themselves and others. This circle is not a physical one often seen by the organization but is more frequently a collection of BW gathering together outside the organization to share knowledge, experiences, and tips for maneuvering through and advancing. Organizations may ask why BW form these circles. The answer is simple; no other support structures are in place to offer clear feedback, mentorship, or guidance for BW. These structures mainly exist for other groups. Therefore, it is clear that the power resides with the majority group. Unless this group moves away from this form of false generosity (saying it is 'acting' like it but not actually relinquishing power), progress will never go beyond an attempt (Freire, 2005).

Our recommendation for organizations concerning self-motivation is to create programs in partnership with their workforce. While these programs will help BW, they will also improve your organization's culture by including their perspectives. All teams and staff benefit from coaching, mentorship, and feedback, but sadly BW are less likely to receive such investment even though they significantly contribute to the organization (Lean In, 2022). It is also essential to keep in mind that EI starts with the individual. Therefore, investing time, energy, and money in personal development is of great value to leaders (Scazzero, 2015). Steps taken by leaders to become emotionally intelligent will serve as motivation for everyone in the organization. Suppose leaders and staff find that the organization has emphasized EI development and can articulate and experience the benefits of staying focused on a goal despite the challenges. In that case, this will motivate the entire organization to push through the challenges such a realization brings. When the entire organization leads in a way that shows intention and direction, in this instance, acknowledging and mentoring BW, it will become the norm.

Empathy Model

The fourth dimension of EI is empathy (see Table 4), which is vastly different from sympathy. Empathy is more than just being sorry about another person's issues; it is being able to understand by feeling. Therefore, please do not expect BW to give their all to an organization that shows no concern for them during challenging times. For example, since COVID-19, there have been countless news stories of racial injustices experienced by Black Americans. Although these stories may seem unrelated to BW in your organizations, that is likely not the case. Most people hear these news stories and continue to go about the rest of their day. However, for BW, these stories put the spotlight on the structural racism that is in place in society and can be debilitating for BW. Let us look at an example. In March 2020, Breonna Taylor was asleep in her home in the middle of the night when Louisville police officers conducted a no-knock warrant and forcibly entered her home, resulting in her death without any responsibility being born by the police officers. While this may seem like a situation not worthy of organizational empathy, for BW it is another reminder that their home could be invaded without cause, that they could be murdered, and that no one would be brought to justice. This leaves BW feeling vulnerable and uncertain of their place in the organization, especially in an organization that has done little to show that BW are valuable to its culture and community.

While some organizations pledged to become social justice advocates and develop DEI programs, others did very little in the wake of George Floyd and Breonna Taylor's murders. These organizations that did nothing likely had BW and Black employees talking not only about the social injustices in the world but also about the lack of dialogue and effort put forth by their organization. Both authors know this to be true because they engaged in these conversations in different settings. The lack of commitment to DEI work and, more importantly, to BW and Black employees speaks volumes and does not go unnoticed.

Table 4. Empathy, closing the gap

Empathy			
Desired Outcome	**How Black Women See Themselves**	**How Organizations Threaten Black Women**	**Closing the Gap**
See the individual and hear the individual	Assign bias and microaggressions to ignorance and are still able to establish productive relationships with coworkers.	BW are frequently associated with negative stereotypes. For example, they are four times more likely to receive comments about their speech than White women.	Acknowledge and leverage the different lives, experiences, and perspectives that BW bring to solving the various challenges that arise within an organization.
Listen with the aim to serve	Often absorb information to improve their performance and that of others.	Not listening to BW and their needs. Although more than 80% call themselves allies, people of color do not believe these "allies" actually help when they should.	Create measurable goals and objectives to assist BW in meeting their personal and professional goals
Inquisitive interest in others	Must create meaningful relationships with peers and leaders to succeed in their roles.	Unaware of microaggressions and biases against BW.	Take an active interest in the personal and professional growth of BW. This leads BW to feel confident of their fit within the organization.

We challenge organizations to be empathetic and to develop active listening skills. In doing so, the organization will be able to feel the pain through the voices and lives of BW. Thus, creating opportunities for genuine connection and dialogue, ultimately leading to excellent job performance. This is not to say that all BW will want to dialogue on these matters, but creating a forum for it to take place would go a long way.

During the Breonna Taylor and George Floyd trials, many organizations came forward with either internal or external communications that showed their support for grieving communities and populations. In contrast, others continued or initiated DEI programs. For example, some organizations implemented rest days to allow staff to be home and not focus on work demands while the nation was grappling with race relations. Other organizations added additional resources to their Employee Assistance Program, which offers tools to assist in dealing with everyday struggles through counseling. These and other initiatives can show an organization's empathy.

Social Skills Model

The final dimension of EI is social skill (see Table 5), which requires the organization to form bonds with BW, which will assist in changing the organization's culture to be more inclusive. It is important to note that the only dimension that focuses solely on effective communication is social skill. Most of us are familiar with the verbal and non-verbal model of the 7-38-55% communication rule, which purports that only seven percent of communication is verbal. In comparison, the other 93% is non-verbal, 38% is related to tone, and 55% is related to facial cues (Mehrabian, 1967). This communication formula has become a maxim, although Mehrabian (1967) advised against it. Moreover, in becoming a maxim, all are judged by it even though it did not consider race, culture, or gender. BW communicate differently, their tone is different from that of the majority, and their facial expressions are also different when they communicate. So, although they may be using the exact words as those of their White colleagues, because 93% of communication has been assigned to tone and facial cues, BW are viewed as hostile, illogical, and aggressive (Motro, 2022). This setting forces BW to have to choose between 'acting the White role' if they want to have successful relationships within that space or being courageous and their authentic selves while recognizing that doing so may stunt their growth within the organization. Code-switching in the workplace is a relevant example of acting in the white role. Jiménez shares that, to be honest, she has had to do this daily within organizations where she has worked to be viewed as a professional. Meanwhile, her white male coworkers have used profanity and shown their disagreement through tone, facial expression, or crossed arms. As BW, we know that if we showed just one of those traits, it could significantly jeopardize our career.

Table 5. Social skills, closing the gap

Social Skills			
Desired Outcome	**How Black Women See Themselves**	**How Organizations Threaten Black Women**	**Closing the Gap**
Influence other's emotions	Serve as a sounding board for their peers and provide feedback and reinforcement.	Organizations often lack structures that support positive reinforcement and feedback to BW.	Organizations have the opportunity to lead in providing positive reinforcement to BW. Black women (and all staff) should be commended in public and corrected in private. This helps to influence the emotions, ideas, and opinions of others concerning BW.
Everyone contributes and is heard	Black women create safe spaces to participate with their peers.	Organizations have a history of acknowledging the voices and perspectives of most staff while diminishing the perspectives of BW.	Ensure structures and executive (HR) leaders are in place that recognize and can practice the importance of hearing and seeing BW.
Effective negotiation skills	BW negotiate by ensuring that the majority group does not experience much discomfort.	Organizations deem themselves great in this area because again, the needs of BW are not given the same value as their White female counterparts.	Conflict resolution tools are essential when instituting EI and will serve to address and elevate all, including BW.
Strong lasting relationships	Black women often look to develop working relationships but are often overlooked when opportunities are created for bonding.	Organizations typically lack lasting solid relationships with BW as their time together is more surface-level and transactional.	Organizations must take the time to invest in developing authentic relationships with BW. Such relationships can often lead to a sense of belonging, community, and connectivity to an organization and its teams.

What does this mean? Organizations must take on the responsibility of learning and opening up the norms for what is effective communication. In other words, they must engage in cultural competency training, which calls for valuing diversity, a willingness to engage in a cultural self-assessment, the consciousness of the dynamics of cultural interaction, institutionalization of cultural knowledge, and the development of adaptations to diversity (Cross et al., 1989). By widening this norm, BW will be considered partners in all facets of the organization and would be brought to the table not solely to solicit feedback on DEI initiatives but also to develop and plan strategic growth. Incorporating this level of social skill will lead to a change in the organization's culture, where this approach will no longer be a part of a DEI objective but of the organization as a whole.

FUTURE RESEARCH DIRECTIONS

The authors acknowledge that DEI initiatives, closing gaps between the organization and BW, and changing organizational culture can be challenging. However, it is essential for organizational growth and the inclusion of perspectives from BW. Future research should focus on those organizations that have committed themselves to genuine DEI initiatives and programs, and improvement of their culture to share best practices. The objective of this future research should be to identify areas of growth while also identifying strengths, weaknesses, opportunities, and threats. A SWOT analysis can paint a vivid picture of how far organizations have come and where they should set goals. As a secondary objective, future research should also look to assess the perspectives of BW. The BWT survey has proven to be an exceptional piece of research that also offers a valuable research tool. Future researchers should utilize the same survey tool to identify if and how the perspectives of BW have changed over time. The results of this cyclical process could lead to large-scale improvements within organizations.

CONCLUSION

Again, we ask the question, why is your organization focusing efforts on DEI initiatives and increasing or hiring DEI practitioners? Are they simply following the trend seen throughout corporate America? Are they looking to achieve better business outcomes? Or are they wanting to do the right thing for the right reasons? Earlier, we established the concept of organizations being living organisms or Teal organizations. This concept does not allow organizations to move like the Titanic, unable to steer away quickly from an iceberg but instead to take in information as it happens and adjust the course of action to avoid the iceberg, which in this instance is the dual pandemics and the treatment of BW.

Moreover, these teal organizations ensure that the work environment is one where every individual, including BW and DEI practitioners, feel appreciated for their uniqueness and experiences. Sadly, BW continue to feel isolated, are granted fewer opportunities to be mentored by senior leaders, and are more likely to experience prejudice and microaggressions. Therefore, there is a need for even more support networks and positive racial socialization (Coqual, 2019; Terhune, 2008). The case is even direr for BW who must operate in an environment that does not see their uniqueness and does not account for the effects of their social, racial, and economic challenges (Ashley, 2014).

EI, with its aim of long-lasting, fruitful relationships, is the vehicle we offer to assist in building better relationships with BW. EI is a learned ability, as evidenced by a two-sample study by Sala (2002). The first sample found an 11% increase in EI scores of Brazilian managers and HR consultants after eight months of training. The second sample, a large US government accounting organization, found a 24% increase in EI scores after 14 months of training.

The development of EI is a process that requires a commitment to looking internally to identify the blind spots in your sphere of control, whether personal or professional. Once identified, not reacting to the information but pausing to develop a thoughtful action to address the issues. Once self-management is in place, the dimensions of social management, empathy, and social skill, will ensure lasting relationships. Organizations must sign up for this same process, for once they do, they will be able to see everyone in their organization. There is a pervasive thought that "not seeing race or color" signifies an unbiased person or organization. We challenge that concept and suggest that seeing a BW's race and acknowledging her lived experience is essential to the EI of the organization and its overall success.

Earlier, we shared the quote from Freire (2005) that indicated that the oppressed must utilize their power if a change is to occur. So, DEI practitioners can continue to move forward even while working within an environment that does not fully understand or care to understand the challenges that are before them. BW and BW DEI practitioners can develop programs that are informed by their own shared experiences of being a woman and Black to assist other BW and those who may care to increase their cultural knowledge (Drake-Clark, 2009). This does not provide a pass to organizations' responsibility to bridge the gap between how BW see themselves and how organizations threaten their uniqueness. Instead, it is an opportunity for BW and DEI practitioners to remain focused on a goal and not be demotivated. Remember that EI is the bridge to close that gap. It calls for organizations to provide a safe space for

BW to show up as authentic, unique individuals, ensuring that their differences are celebrated instead of seeking a monolithic environment. EI and its five dimensions of self-awareness, self-regulation, self-motivation, empathy, and social skill are your tools to manage, incorporate, and uplift your organization. Be sincere in your efforts, and let EI lead you.

ACKNOWLEDGMENT

This research received no specific grant from any funding agency in the public, commercial, or not-for-profit sectors.

REFERENCES

Abdel-Fattah. (2020). Emotional intelligence and emotional stability in crises. *Journal of Psychiatry and Psychiatric Disorders*, *4*(2), 56–52. doi:10.26502/jppd. 2572-519X0090

Alonazi, W. B. (2020). The impact of emotional intelligence on job performance during covid-19 crisis: A cross-sectional analysis. *Psychology Research and Behavior Management*, *13*, 749–757. doi:10.2147/PRBM.S263656

Amina, A., Hadi, N. U., Waheed, A., & Fayyaz, H. (2021). The effect of leader mindfulness on employee job performance: Investigating the mediating and moderating role of leader-member exchange and organization culture. *Journal of Behavioral Sciences*, *31*(2), 138–165.

Ashkanasy, N., & Daus, C. (2005). Rumors of the death of emotional intelligence in organizational behavior are vastly exaggerated. *Journal of Organizational Behavior*, *26*(4), 441–452. doi:10.1002/job.320

Ashley, W. (2014). The angry black woman: The impact of pejorative stereotypes on psychotherapy with black women. *Social Work in Public Health*, *29*(1), 27–34. doi:10.1080/19371918.2011.619449

Banks, N. (2019, February 19). *Black women's labor market history reveals deep-seated race and gender discrimination.* Economic policy institute. https://www.epi.org/blog/black-womens-labor-market-history-reveals-deep-seated-race-and-gender-discrimination/

Boyatzis, R., & Sala, F. (2004). Assessing emotional intelligence competencies. In Glenn Geher (Ed.), *The measurement of emotional intelligence*. https://www.eiconsortium.org/pdf/Assessing_Emotional_Intelligencc_Competencies.pdf

Bradberry, T., & Greaves, J. (2015). *Analysis & review of emotional intelligence 2.0.* Eureka Books.

Brownlee, D. (2022, August 11). DEI tragically fails many black professionals. *Forbes*. https://www.forbes.com/sites/danabrownlee/2022/08/11/this-is-why-corporate-dei-tragically-fails-many-black-professionals/?sh=a3549e7efbcc

Carrazana, C. (2020, August 10). When systemic racism meets the coronavirus, Black women suffer economically. *The 19th News(letter)*. https://19thnews.org/2020/08/black-women-economy-coronavirus-systemic-racism/

Carver, C. S. (2012). Self-awareness. In M. R. Leary, & J. P. Tangney (Eds.), *Handbook of self and identity* (pp. 50–68). The Guilford Press. Centers for Disease Control and Prevention. COVID Data Tracker. Atlanta, GA: US Department of Health and Human Services. https://covid.cdc.gov/covid-data-tracker

Cheeks, M. (2018). How Black Women Describe Navigating Race and Gender in the Workplace. *Harvard Business Review*.

Clarke, N. (2010). The impact of a training program designed to target the emotional intelligence abilities of project managers. *International Journal of Project Management*, *28*(5), 461–468. doi:10.1016/j.ijproman.2009.08.004

Coqual, (2019). Being black in corporate America: an intersectional exploration. *Coqual*. https://coqual.org/reports/being-black-in-corporate-america-an-intersectional-exploration/

Cote, S., & Miners, C. T. (2006). Emotional intelligence, cognitive intelligence, and job performance. *Administrative Science Quarterly*, *51*(1), 1–28. doi:10.2189/ asqu.51.1.1

Cotruș, A., Stanciu, C., & Bulborea, A. (2012). EQ vs. IQ which is most important in the success or failure of a student? *Social and Behavioral Sciences*, *46*, 5211–5213. doi:10.1016/j.sbspro.2012.06.411

Crenshaw, K. (1989). Demarginalizing the Intersection of Race and Sex: A Black Feminist Critique of Antidiscrimination Doctrine, Feminist Theory and Antiracist Politics. *University of Chicago Legal Forum*, *1*(8).

Cross, T., Bazron, B., Dennis, K., & Isaacs, M. (1989). *Towards a culturally competent system of care: A monograph on effective services for minority children who are severely emotionally disturbed*. https://eric.ed.gov/?id=ED330171

Deloite (2018). *Inclusive Mobility: How Mobilizing a Diverse Workforce Can Drive Business Performance*. https://www2.deloitte.com/us/en/pages/tax/articles/inclusive-mobility-diverse-workforce-drive-business-performance.html

Drake-Clark, D. (2009). *Discrimination happens without effort: How Balck Women Human Resources Managers Negotiate Diversity in a Corporation*. [Unpublished doctoral dissertation]. The University of Georgia, USA.

Duan, L., & Zhu, G. (2020). Psychological interventions for people affected by the COVID-19 epidemic. *The Lancet. Psychiatry*, *7*, 300–302. doi:10.1016/S2215-0366(20)30073-0

Extremera, N. (2020). Coping with the stress caused by the COVID-19 pandemic: Future research agenda based on emotional intelligence. *International Journal of Social Psychology*, *35*(3), 631–638. doi:10.1080/02134748.2020. 1783857

Freire, P. (2005). *The pedagogy of the oppressed*. Continuum International Publishing Group.

Goleman, D. (2005). *Emotional intelligence: Why it can matter more than IQ*, (3rd ed.). Bantam.

Goleman, D. (2013). The focused leader. *Harvard Business Review, 91*(12), 50–60.

Gould, E., & Wilson, V. (2020, June 1). Black workers face two of the most lethal preexisting conditions for coronavirus—racism and economic inequality. *Economic policy institute*. https://www.epi.org/publication/black-workers-covid/

Hammonds, E. (2021). A Moment or a Movement? The Pandemic, Political Upheaval, and Racial Reckoning. *Journal of Women in Culture and Society, 47*(1).

Heckemann, B., Schols, J., & Halfens, R. (2015). A reflective framework to foster emotionally intelligent leadership in nursing. *Journal of Nursing Management, 23*(6), 744–753. doi:10.1111/jonm.12204

Hines, E., & Fitts, M. (2022). *Black Women Thriving. Every Level Leadership*. https://everylevelleads.com/bwt/

Hunter-Gadsden, L. (2020). Why People Of Color Feel The Loneliest At Work. *Forbes magazine*. https://www.forbes.com/sites/nextavenue/2020/05/19/why-people-of-color-feel-the-loneliest-at-work/?sh=632797281ad8

In, L. (2022). *The state of black women in corporate America*. https://leanin.org/research/state-of-black-women-in-corporate-america/introduction#!

Jackson, A. (2022). *Black women are in 'survival mode' at work—and company diversity efforts' fall short'*. https://www.cnbc.com/2022/07/01/company-diversity-efforts-to-support-black-women-fall-short.html

Laloux, F. (2014). *Reinventing organizations: A guide to creating organizations inspired by the next stage of human consciousness*. Nelson Parker.

Lencioni, P. (2020). *The motive*. John Wiley & Sons, Inc.

Massey, M. (2014, June 27). [EnterpriseMediaVideo]. *What You Are Is Where You Were When... AGAIN!* [Video]. YouTube: https://www.youtube.com/watch?v=l6rPiehHQu8

Mayer, J., Salovey, P., Caruso, D., & Cherkasskiy, L. (2011). Emotional intelligence. In R. Sternberg & S. Kaufman (Eds.), *The Cambridge handbook of intelligence, Cambridge handbooks in psychology* (pp. 528–549). Cambridge University Press. doi:10.1017/CBO9780511977244.027

McKinsey & Company. (2021). *Women in the Workplace 2021*. https://www.mckinscy.com/fcaturcd-insights/divcrsity-and-inclusion/women-in-the-workplace?cid=eml-web

McNicholas, C., & Poydock, M. (2020). Who are Essential Workers: A Comprehensive Look at Their Wages, Demographics, and Unionization Rates. *Economic Policy Institute*. https://www.epi.org/blog/who-are-essential-workers-a-comprehensive-look-at-their-wages-demographics-and-unionization-rates/

Mehrabian, A. (1967). *Mehrabian's Communication Theory: Verbal, Non-Verbal, Body Language*. https://www.bl.uk/people/albert-mehrabian

Middaugh, D. (2021). Leading the Pack in Tough Times. *Medsurg Nursing*, *30*(3), 212–215.

Mohamad, M., & Jais, J. (2016). Emotional intelligence and job performance: A study among Malaysian teachers. *Procedia Economics and Finance*, *35*, 674–682. doi:10.1016/S2212-5671(16)00083-6

Motro, D., Evans, J., Ellis, A., & Beson, L. (2022). The "Angry Black Woman" Stereotype at Work. *Harvard Business Review*.

Newman, D., Joseph, D., & MacCann, C. (2010). Emotional intelligence and job performance: The importance of emotion regulation and emotional labor context. *Industrial and Organizational Psychology: Perspectives on Science and Practice*, *3*(2), 159–164. doi:10. 1111/j.1754-9434.2010.01218.x

Prezerakos, P. E. (2018). Nurse managers' emotional intelligence and effective leadership: A review of the current evidence. *The Open Nursing Journal*, *12*, 86–92. doi:10.2174/1874434601812010086

Sadovyy, M., Sánchez-Gómez, M., & Bresó, E. (2021). COVID-19: How the stress generated by the pandemic may affect work performance through the moderating role of emotional intelligence: Corrigendum. *Personality and Individual Differences*, *182*, 1–9. doi:10.1016/j.paid.2021.111092

Sala, F. (2002). *Do programs designed to increase emotional intelligence at work-work?* https://www.eiconsortium.org/reports/do_ei_programs_work.html

Scazzero, P. (2015). *The emotionally healthy leader*. Zondervan.

Schutte, N., Malouff, J., Hall, L., Haggerty, D., Cooper, J., Golden, C., & Dornheim, L. (1998). Development and validation of a measure of emotional intelligence. *Personality and Individual Differences*, *25*(2), 67–177. doi:10.1016/ S0191-8869(98)00001

Sellie-Dosunmu, M. (2016). Using emotional intelligence in the workplace. *Association For Talent Development*, *33*, 1612. doi:10.1080/09669582.2020.1758708

Serrat, O. (2017). *Understanding and developing emotional intelligence. Knowledge solutions*. Springer. doi:10.1007/978-981-10-0983-9_37

Statistica (2022). Percentage of people without health insurance in the United States from 2010 to 2021 by ethnicity. https://www.statista.com/statistics/200970/percentage-of-americans-without-health-insurance-by-race-ethnicity/

Sun, H., Wang, S., Wang, W., Han, G., Liu, Z., Wu, Q., & Pang, X. (2021). Correlation between emotional intelligence and negative emotions of front-line nurses during the COVID-19 epidemic: A cross-sectional study. *Journal of Clinical Nursing*, *30*(3-4), 385–396. doi:10.1111/jocn.15548

Talan, T. (2022, August 9). *Diversity, Equity, and Inclusion: When values become actions*. McCormick Center For Early Childhood Leadership, At National Louis University. https://mccormickcenter.nl.edu/library/dei-iposter-080922/

Terhune, C. P. (2008). Coping in Isolation: The Experiences of Black Women in White Communities. *Journal of Black Studies*, *38*(4), 547–564. doi:10.1177/0021934706288144

Verma, S., Aggarwal, A., & Bansal, H. (2017). The Relationship between Emotional Intelligence (EQ) and adversity quotient (AQ). *Journal of Business and Management*, *19*, 49–53. doi:10.9790/487X-1901024953

Webb, K. S. (2009). Why emotional intelligence should matter to management: A survey of the literature. *Advanced Management Journal*, *74*(2), 32–41.

White, E. (1890). *Patriarchs and Prophets*. Review and Herald Publishing Association.

Wiley, Z., Kubes, J., Cobb, J., Jacob, J., Franks, N., Plantinga, L., & Lea, J. (2022). Age, Comorbid Conditions, and Racial Disparities in COVID-19 Outcomes. *Journal of Racial and Ethnic Health Disparities*, (9), 117–123.

Zippia (2022). Chief diversity officer demographics and statistics in the US. *Zippa.* https://www.zippia.com/chief-diversity-officer-jobs/demographics/

ADDITIONAL READING

Bradberry, T., & Greaves, J. (2009). *Emotional Intelligence 2.0.* TalenSmart.

Erkayiran, O., & Demirkiran, F. (2018). The impact of improving emotional intelligence skills training on nursing students' interpersonal relationship styles: A quasi-experimental study. *International Journal of Caring Sciences*, *11*(3), 1–12.

Goleman, D., McKee, A., & Achor, S. (2018). *Everyday Emotional Intelligence.* Harvard Business Review Press.

Ioannidou, F., & Konstantikaki, V. (2008). Empathy and emotional intelligence: What is it really about? *International Journal of Caring Sciences*, *1*(3), 118–127.

Karimi, J. (2014). Effects of emotional intelligence on employee performance in the hotel industry in Kenya. *International Journal of Business and Management*, *2*(12), 6–14.

Munir, M., & Azam, R. (2019). Emotional Intelligence and Employee Performance: An Intervention Based Experimental Study. *Journal of Business & Economics*, *9*(2), 1–19.

Wilkinson, B. (2021). *The diversity gap: where good intentions meet true cultural change*. HarperCollins Leadership.

KEY TERMS AND DEFINITIONS

Active Listening: Capturing not only the words but also the thoughts and feelings that come from communicating in order to understand rather than to respond.

Black Women (BW): Individuals who self-identify as Black and female regardless of race, ethnicity, and gender.

Code-Switching: Alteration of one's true self through the use of different vernacular, body language, or tone to suit the majority.

Conflict Resolution: The process that two or more individuals engage in to address and resolve an issue.

Emotional Intelligence: Capacity to recognize, understand and manage the emotions behind facial, voice, and physical cues of oneself and others.

Emotional Intelligence in Organizations: Ability to self-reflect and be appreciative and inclusive of diversity.

Essential Workers: Employees who are deemed necessary for the continuation of community services, specifically during the COVID-19 pandemic.

Inclusion: A setting where marginalized or individuals in the minority are and feel appreciated and free to participate and thrive in all activities.

Organizational Culture: Values, beliefs, and actions of an organization that drives employee interactions, workplace ethics, and organizational effectiveness.

Safe Spaces: Physical and social environments that allow individuals to express themselves without fear of retaliation or isolation.

Chapter 9
Deconstructing Standards of Whiteness to Establish the Power of Black Women

Norka Blackman-Richards
https://orcid.org/0000-0002-7431-7014
Queens College, USA

Jilma V. Jiménez
https://orcid.org/0000-0003-4822-898X
Independent Researcher, USA

Eleonor Pusey-Reid
https://orcid.org/0000-0003-4069-4898
MGH Institute of Health Professions, USA

ABSTRACT

This chapter will examine standards of whiteness that are embedded in current organizational cultures and how these standards impact Black women (BW) in the workplace; particularly after the dual pandemics of COVID-19 and the racial reckoning of 2020. The authors widen the perspective beyond the confines of diversity, equity, and inclusion (DEI) as a role, to discuss cultural issues that universally diminish the power of BW, and that DEI practitioners should inherently be charged to recognize, name, and be empowered to eradicate. The work introduces microdevaluation as a construct encompassing an array of racial aggressions often experienced by BW in public settings. The authors further examine the effects on innovation caused by the lack of inclusion of the voice of the BW within organizations. The chapter ends by providing recommendations that organizations and institutions must adapt in order to transform and achieve equity for BW and reap the benefits afforded by diversity and inclusion.

DOI: 10.4018/978-1-6684-3564-9.ch009

It's not about supplication; it's about power. It's not about asking, it's about demanding. It's not about convincing those who are currently in power, it's about changing the very face of power itself. - Kimberlé Williams Crenshaw (1991)

INTRODUCTION

In the aftermath of the public murder of Mr. George Floyd and the racial reckoning of the Summer of 2020, many companies sought to appoint diversity, equity, and inclusion (DEI) leaders. The primary role of these DEI leaders is to ensure that the companies' DEI strategies are being followed. They have also been tasked with changing organizational cultures while serving top leadership, employees, and even external partners. Many companies have since appointed Black women (BW) to DEI roles. As an example, in the inaugural Elite 100 Black Women leaders list by Diversity Woman Media more than 35% of the BW listed were in DEI roles (Sykes, 2021). Built on their race and gender identity, BW DEI leaders offer the institution the benefit of credibility to their commitment to diversity and inclusion. However, it is that same racial and gender identity that puts them at peril within organizational cultures that have not done the necessary work to support their leadership. Therefore, the BW DEI leaders are left to walk a tightrope, balancing what's best for the company's profile and brand, while supporting people within their ranks, at the exclusion of themselves. Many have felt the burden to fix a system where they are themselves the victims and to do so in a manner that is acceptable to their offenders. This burden shows up in many ways, such as in having to educate on matters related to appropriate and inclusive behaviors, as well as historical factors that make certain language and behaviors inappropriate or non-supportive of inclusion. To be effective the BW DEI leaders must be empowered to call out problematic and systemic behaviors. But when raising her voice, she runs the risk of being seen as militant or of being ascribed negative stereotypes. The authors include a historical view of the ways in which BW have been diminished through tropes as well as the effects that these have had in achieving parity of representation. The authors then challenge the notion that BW are guests at "the table" and offer a new construct of micro-devaluation. Lastly, the authors discuss the lost opportunities to institutions that do not have diverse work cultures and offer recommendations to elevate the voice and power of all BW within the workforce, especially of BW DEI practitioners.

The authors choose to define BW's power as fearlessness in the face of obstacles, having the courage and willingness to confront any adversary to achieve an intended goal that will break barriers. Poet Audre Lorde (1984) has referred to Black womanhood as "dark, ancient, and deep" (p. 37). The authors believe that this ancestral power is the immense capacity that BW have displayed, for centuries, to defy the odds against all prognostications. This power is enveloped in ancestral knowledge and will, gleaned from our ancestors - our grandmothers, mothers, and aunts - to overcome obstacles. We carry a "legacy that resists and ensures our survival" (Harris, 2020, para. 6). It is this capacity that corporations, institutions, and governments need to harness as a vital resource.

The authors choose to define DEI as the inclusivity, representation, and contribution of all voices. Inclusivity is centered on equitable investments in all human capital. The authors also believe that in the 21st Century, companies, institutions, and governments will lack the ability to thrive without the level of innovation that only inclusivity can bring. Thus, harnessing diverse talent is critical to organizational, institutional, and global survival and success.

The authors, a higher education administrator, an engineering consulting executive, and an associate professor in healthcare, come to this work as BW whose Blackness predates their given names and their professional achievements. Their perspectives are informed by decades of professional labor and barrier-breaking DEI participation in predominantly White institutions and corporations. Within these spaces, they have observed, experienced, and endured the White standard (WS). The authors define the WS as the Eurocentric ideology where cultural norms, views, and esthetics are considered to be above reproach, superior, and thus imposed on others, particularly on BW. The totality of the WS is born out of imperialism, colonialism, and the enduring White supremacy that is prevalent and persists to this day. White standards (WSs) and the dominance of Whiteness have been established as norms (beauty, mannerisms, expressions) and socialized and normalized as the status quo, which enables White ideologies to remain the neutral, universal, and preferred practice (Ray, 2019).

As BW born in Latin America, specifically the country of Panama, all three authors reaffirm the words of the Black Panamanian poet, Dash Harris, "I am Negra. Black, wherever I go" (Harris, 2020). As members of a minoritized ethnic group, the authors have endured colorism, texturism, and featurism, and recognize these as manifestations of the same structural and systemic racism endured by our sisters in the global African Diaspora.

BACKGROUND

"Black women have on one hand always been highly visible, and so, on the other hand, have been rendered invisible through the depersonalization of racism" - Audre Lorde (1984)

Stereotypes and Tropes

For centuries BW have had to endure racialized labels, tropes, and derogatory terms stemming from a legacy of racism and sexism (Mgadmi, 2009). These labels are founded in stereotypical images of Black womanhood that seek to minimize their humanity and devalue their contributions. Black women have often been depicted as "the nurturing mammies" according to Kayembe (2021), who highlights that, "the 'mammy' trope frames BW as subordinate, gentle, sage advisors; warm maternal-like figures the ever-vigilant caretaker of the children of her White employers" (para. 1). Black women living in poverty and needing the help of the state to survive have been called, "welfare mothers"...depicted by society as lazy, promiscuous women who are unable to socialize their children adequately…bad mothers who do not provide an appropriate role model for their children because of their unemployment" (Sparks, 1998, p.2). Assertive BW, who dare to question the status quo or who would not accept silencing, have been called the "angry Black woman," which as described by Ashley (2014) "presumes all BW to be irate, irrational, hostile, and negative despite the circumstances." Black women have also been burdened by the unhealthy stereotype of the "strong Black woman", defined by Donovan and West (2015) as the "perception that Black women are naturally strong, resilient, self-contained, and self-sacrificing" (p. 4) which when internalized, limits their ability to ask for and accept help, but instead, feel solely responsible for carrying the world on their shoulders.

In addition to these stereotypes, BW have also endured the rejection of their physical characteristics. Black women have endured colorism, which entails skin tone gradations and preferences, "ordered from light to dark or white to black, that in the Western world, are also based on ideas of racial or color hierarchy" (Dixon & Telles, 2017). Furthermore, BW have endured texturism, which Shepherd (2018) defines as, "texture discrimination by the prejudicial or preferential treatment of people with afro-textured hair based solely on the texture of their curls." Black women have similarly endured featurism, which Faal (2021) describes as, a "preference for Eurocentric features." The world insists on wanting to degrade and "fix" BW's bodies to fit WSs, yet White women are celebrated when they imitate BW's hairstyles and undergo surgery to enhance physical features (lips, hips, butt, breasts) to look like BW. They take from us to erase us and render us invisible. This "fixing" is also present in professional settings and further manifested when BW prove themselves to be over-, or best qualified. It is the confluence of these stereotypes and tropes that have diminished the voices and contributions of BW in the labor force. These stereotypes are also at play in the failure to experience economic equity for those who surmount the barriers.

Pay Inequities

The 2020 United States (U.S.) Census Bureau reports that women in the U.S. make up 50.5% of the population (U.S. Census Bureau, 2021). While women of color comprised 20.3% of the people of that segment, BW comprises 12.9% percent of that population (U.S. Census Bureau, 2020). While BW make up a significant portion of the population of women of color, the U.S. Department of Labor also reports that BW's earnings are 63.0% of that of White, non-Hispanic men. In comparison, White, non-Hispanic women earn 78.7% of White, non-Hispanic men's earnings, and Asian women earn 87.1%. However, this earning gap is not due to lower or less advanced professional degrees on the part of BW. The Department of Labor reported that even with advanced degrees BW's median weekly earnings are less than those of White men with bachelor's degrees (Roux, 2021). Furthermore, studies show that BW as a group are currently the most educated demographic in the U.S. (Thompson, 2019). The Institute for Women Policy Research (2017) reports that BW are also the most active participants in the labor force. Yet, at our current pace, pay equity will not be achieved for BW or other women of color, until centuries later. Pay equity is expected to arrive for White women in 2059, while for BW -- the currently most educated and participatory group in the labor force -- it is projected that they will not see equity in pay until 2124.

The stark reality is that the above equity pay gaps are reflective of the depths of structural and systemic racism. The educational achievements and professional contributions of BW as a group are still not enough to land them in a place of equity. In addition, this adds to the racialized emotional, psychological, and social harm Black people, and in particular BW, continue to endure in the workplace, in public arenas, and even on platforms of power.

Micro-Colonialism

Black women are positioned to be invisible and excluded from the conversation that speaks to their unique experiences of being unable to be their authentic selves because they get absorbed into other significant movements such as feminism and antiracism. This invisibility becomes actualized because the people in power consider the prototypical woman as a White woman and a prototypical Black person as a Black man (Coles & Pasek, 2020). Coles and Pasek (2020) argue that this under-differentiation erases the recognition of the unique forms of oppression experienced by BW. As a result, we are unrecognized as women and as humans, confirming our invisibility and exclusion.

United Kingdom based psychologist, Guilaine Kinouani (2021) uses the term "micro-colonialism" to define the "everyday intrusions and breaches of boundaries, physical or psychological, such as invasions of privacy or personal space Black people continue to experience within White spaces'' (p.111). Workplaces, including platforms of power, have become "micro-colonies'', where invasions of privacy and personal space continue to target BW. Proof of this is that structural injustices seem to have also worsened, as Jameel & Yerardi (2019) pointed out that while workplace discrimination is illegal it continues to be a problem. Perhaps injustice is now more visible, or we are more willing to call it out because of our collective and increased conscious awareness of it, but it has always existed.

The authors acknowledge that many BW - even some in roles as DEI practitioners - have internalized the WS because Whiteness has always been imposed as the rule and expectation (Rabelo et al., 2021). They also acknowledge that this internalization is often a mechanism of survival to gain access to and secure resources and opportunities. As a DEI practitioner leading a higher education opportunity program that serves equity-needing students, author Blackman-Richards often has to advocate for resources. She has encountered some of her greatest allies and co-conspirators in women of all ethnicities. These allies and co-conspirators are brilliant, have done the internal work, and have become adept at making a system filled with structural barriers work to the advantage of the disadvantaged. On the other hand, pushback, and reluctance to create pathways of equity sometimes comes from the least expected places, other women of color who in their DEI roles have the power to allocate resources. These women often see themselves as "protectors" of the institution; they become gatekeepers. They do not understand that their role includes repairing harm. Blackman-Richards has come to understand this behavior as a misguided form of professional survival that translates as co-signing to the WS. By keeping resources away from the same people they are hired to represent and advocate for, women of color who have internalized the WS believe they can secure their jobs and positions of power by upholding the status quo. Toni Morrison often reminded her students of the following, "When you get these jobs that you have been so brilliantly trained for, just remember that your real job is that if you are free, you need to free someone else. This is not just a grab-bag candy game" (Houston, 2003, para.11). At the same time, this lack of ability to see the DEI role as an opportunity to liberate others, can be linked to "the colonized sense of self [that leads] to the internalization of racial myths and constructions such as the inferiority of Black and Brown people" (Kinouani, 2021 p. 68). The most dangerous effect of the WS is that it seeks to disempower. It disempowers some BW by making them feel that while at the table they must continue to uphold oppressive norms as a form of gratitude, keeping them off the table altogether, or when at the table treating them as guests and not as owners and full participants. What we now know is that although the DEI Industry was created in an effort to address structural inequities and its multi-million-dollar obsessive focus on implicit bias (Zelevansky, 2019), it has been incapable of making workplaces more equitable or inclusive of all voices.

WE ARE NOT GUESTS

"Guests are invited to distract attention from the real aim of parties" — Noha Alaa El-Din, Norina Luciano

Does requesting a place at the majoritized table perpetuate the notion that we are guests in their spaces and bound to remain within the WS's creative and innovative boundaries? When we are invited to tables and treated as guests, it creates a sense of unbelonging. When we work at institutions where we understand that our positions/roles are contingent upon us complying with the WS, we are limited to playing within the confines of the set sandbox. Black women DEI practitioners are brought to the table to give the appearance of diversity and inclusion without having a voice or say.

In their professional experiences, the authors have been invited to tables to be the face and representation of DEI. However, at these tables, their contributions are not sought after or even welcomed. They realized that the agendas were already set, and the institution or organization benefited from their presence to add to its credibility but not because there was intent for real change to take place. During a speech at Spelman College, the CEO of the drugstore chain Walgreens Boots Alliance, Rosalind "Roz" Brewer, shared that she was once invited as the keynote speaker at an exclusive CEO roundtable in New York City. During the reception, she recalled introducing herself as the CEO of Sam's Club, yet a fellow CEO proceeded to ask her if she was there as the lead for marketing. Brewer's experience speaks to the shared experience of many BW that are treated as a guest at the table of the organizations, institutions, and corporations where they are leaders. They are continuously led to feel as if they do not belong at the table or in those spaces (Connley, 2021). The need placed on BW by the WS to consistently prove that they are ready, worthy, trained, etc., is a sign of unbelonging. Many feel that as BW, they are on a treadmill that is constantly moving to force them to belong, comply, or code-switch (McCluney et al., 2019) in order to navigate spaces that might not be able or fully willing to receive their authentic selves.

We are keenly aware of how BW are scrutinized and punished for showing up in any form of their authentic selves and how this interferes with their contributions because it is inextricably linked to how others view them (Rabelo et al., 2021; Ray, 2019). These imposed standards on BW are deeply rooted in White supremacy and have become a functioning part of a power dynamic used to constrain contributions and potential (Byrd, 2012; Coles & Pasek, 2020). In this system of power, Whiteness ends up dictating how BW's bodies are evaluated, recognized and scrutinized. Power dynamics enable White people to maintain their structures and privileges at the expense of BW's agency and dignity (Rabelo et al., 2021).

A Black woman herself, Melonie Parker (2022), Chief Diversity Officer for Google, stated in her white paper that for many people, their jobs are more than a source of income. It is a place of community, meaning, and purpose. Companies, institutions, and organizations are claiming to understand the importance of a healthy workplace and creating a sense of belonging, but this has not become a reality for Black employees, and trust continues to be eroded (Parker, 2022). Black Women experience feeling unseen. This is inextricably linked to a lack of belonging, feeling that they do not matter, or a lack of social connections within those spaces.

The perpetual state of feeling like a guest in our workplaces, while sitting at the table deprives us of that fundamental human need for belonging, which is an essential resource for health and well-being (Carr et al., 2019; Caxaj & Berman, 2010). This lack of a sense of belonging can lead to feelings of isolation, which negatively impacts people's work commitment, performance, engagement, and turnover (Carr et al., 2019).

Black women are not easily discouraged. Their tendency is to believe in their ability to grow and to make decisions that reflect their convictions, capabilities, worth, and potential. They possess unique strengths that are assets to their relationships and workspaces (Bradley Smith, 2021). They should hold firm to the unnegotiable principle of "Nothing about Us without Us''. They need to be present to provide insights into particular inequities that will allow for a more comprehensive understanding of the complexities faced, and the bringing about of equity and access-based solutions.

THE MICRO-DEVALUATION OF BLACK WOMEN

"The Black female is assaulted in her tender years by all those joint forces of nature at the same time she is caught in the tripartite crossfire of masculine prejudice, White illogical hate, and Black lack of power. The fact that the adult American Negro female emerges as a formidable character is often met with amazement, distaste, and even belligerence. It is seldom accepted as an inevitable outcome of the struggle won by survivors and deserves respect if not enthusiastic admiration," —Maya Angelou, I Know Why the Caged Bird Sings, (1969)

The public murder of George Floyd reignited and globally extended the Black Lives Matter movement and also sparked the resurgence of the DEI Industry with a $50 Billion investment (Jan et al., 2021). After making public anti-racist statements, institutions and corporations renewed their commitment to DEI. Sadly, these commitments amounted to largely ineffective diversity training, and the openings of spaces for one or two DEI positions to sit at executive tables, but there have been very few significant changes in our systemic culture of racism, exclusion, and anti-Blackness. The WSs of deservedness still prevail. Proof of this is that Black people [especially women] continue to experience hostile workplaces (Jameel et al., 2019). These workplaces are steeped in traditional notions that reinforce standards for which some bodies, intellects, and identities are more desirable and capable (i.e., White, heterosexual, able-bodied men) than others. These standards put pressure on BW to perform in order to fit those identities (McCluney & Rabelo 2019). Working daily under WSs forces BW to constantly negotiate the intersectionality of being female and Black to prove worth, desirability, and deservedness, while often being overqualified. As a result, BW must consistently recreate and rewrite these notions, "become self-defined and self-determining within intersecting oppressions" (Collins 2002).

INTERSECTIONALITY AND BLACK WOMEN

"There is no such thing as a single-issue struggle because we do not live single-issue lives" - Audre Lorde

Racialization is an exclusionary colonizing phenomenon that seeks to further oppress BW across intersectionalized conditions of gender, race, and class. Black women, at their intersections, bear the additional burdens of living in and navigating the societies that oppress them (Crenshaw, 1991). But many professional BW must also work for corporations and institutions that perpetuate oppression by not recognizing their humanity and the self-agency and power that comes with it. Instead, BW are continually measured by the established WSs, and demands are placed upon them to acquiesce to these standards in order to succeed. The outcome of this measurement to meet the demands of WS is that it ultimately excludes BW from places of power.

Regardless of their position or platform of power, BW in predominantly White spaces are challenged to adapt to the WS. Congresswoman Maxine Waters, a public servant for over 45 years in the U.S. House of Representatives, is one of the most powerful Black politicians in America, but she has also experienced the devaluation and microaggressions frequently experienced by BW in White spaces (Mena & Vaccaro, 2017). On March 28, 2017, Waters was thrust against the sharp White gaze when she was disrespected by TV commentator Bill O'Reilly who stated after a news clip of her: "I didn't hear a word she said, I was looking at the James Brown wig" (Edes & Taylor, 2017, para. 3). Black women's bodies (how we look and dress), hair, mannerism (how we talk and move), and racial imagery do not blend easily within the larger power structures of the WS, and we are continuously filtered through the lenses of sexism and racism.

In this new era of racial reckoning, BW are not conforming or internalizing, but choosing to operate within their own standards and values in White spaces. Black women are choosing not to conform to the Eurocentric standard imposed through White rules (control of our demeanor and expression that makes folks uncomfortable) and White beauty standards (colorism, texturism, and featurism). Black women are amplifying their collective voice to elevate their individual and shared experiences into a larger public discourse (Rabelo et al., 2021; Ray, 2019). Not all states in the U.S have laws that ban race-related hair discrimination. As practitioners we sometimes find ourselves addressing these issues and advocating on behalf of Black staff or students.

On June 21, 2022, Francia Márquez Mina, a dark-skinned Afro-descendant woman with naturally textured hair who dresses in colorful Afro-representative attire, was elected as the first Black woman Vice-president of the country of Colombia, and the second Black woman in Latin America to ascend to that position. Marquez' language has been intentionally inclusive of gender, ethnicities, and LGBTQI+, a fact that baffles and bothers her opponents (Morales, 2022). Marquez, the winner of the 2018 Goldman Environmental Award, is also a lawyer, a feminist, and human rights activist. During her campaign, Marquez had to navigate the contentious and often dangerous political waters of Colombia. Besides death threats, she also had to deal with publicly racialized assaults (Daniels, 2022). One incident, in particular, occurred when a White-presenting female singer, whose artistic name is Marbelle -- known for generating political controversy with her online tweets -- crossed the line of opinion to racialized assaults on Twitter. Marbelle referred to Márquez as "King Kong". Marbelle's tweet was retweeted by a member of Márquez' own political party, further validating the racist assault. The public outcry on Twitter and in the media forced the singer to delete her post, but by then the screen shot of the tweet had become viral.

Márquez responded to the tweet:

"Racism not only hurts, it also kills. Racism doesn't only hurt us, but it also damages those who express it because it doesn't allow us to construct from a place of love and difference. Sending an ancestral hug for healing to Marbelle, let's begin to construct from a place of difference." (@FranciaMarquezM, March 30th, 2022)

Marbelle responded to Márquez' tweet:

"Keep your ancestral hug! I do not trust you nor do you represent me in any way (all caps)..." (@ Marbelle, 30th, 2022)

Three lawsuits were lodged against the singer in the office of the Attorney General of Colombia, sponsors removed their financial backing from a major concert that was later canceled. The incident also opened a months-long first-ever national debate in Colombia, about race, racism, and inclusivity.

Another example of the difficulties that BW must traverse as a result of the intersectionality of their race and gender was displayed following the announcement of the retirement of Justice Stephen Breyer, on January 28th, 2022. The U.S. President Joseph Biden announced to the world that his Supreme Court nominee would be a Black woman (Shear & Savage, 2022). Because his announcement would upset the traditional order of things, in other words, WSs, it was met with widespread criticism and skepticism.

Was female and Black the only qualifications for the highest judicial seat in the land? many dared to ask. This nomination would break the 233 years-old order of White men comprising the majority of the Supreme Court. The announcement should have served to debunk standards of Whiteness surrounding who was deserving of the role, Adeniran (2022) states, "Black women are frequently the last racial and/or gender demographic segment of the population to achieve representation in places of honor and power, even when they are equally or more qualified" (p.189). In the New York Times, Shear and Savage (2022) reported that Brown Jackson belonged to a pool of elite BW judges, "a rarefied group of well-credentialed Black women who have elite educations and experience on the bench" (para. 3).

When compared to the current supreme justices, President Biden's nominee, Judge Ketanji Brown Jackson was over-credentialed, and her professional experience rendered her over-qualified. In March 2022, The Washington Post published a diagram comparing and contrasting the education and professional experiences of Brown Jackson with all other supreme justices. Justice Brown Jackson, with a Harvard degree, outranked her justice peers in court experience, with Justice Amy Barret, one of two White female justices, ranking as the least experienced of the group (Blanco & Tan, 2022). To many in Black Indigenous People of Color (BIPOC) Communities, Judge Brown Jackson was not an anomaly; they themselves represent or know of Black female professionals who are over-credentialed and over-qualified. In truth, there was unreadiness for the sight of Judge Brown Jackson, a dark-skinned African American woman showing up at her confirmation senate hearings with her tightly coiled sister locks (McGrady, 2022). With this act, Justice Brown Jackson, whose Swahili name Ketanji Oyika, means "lovely one", challenged the WS. This was evidenced as the world watched Judge Brown Jackson experience every level of racial aggression on the taxonomy of microaggressions proposed by Sue et al. (2008).

Microaggressions, as defined and originally coined by Pierce are "subtle, innocuous, preconscious, or unconscious degradations and putdowns, often kinetic but capable of being verbal and/or kinetic (1970). In the book Microaggressions in Everyday Life, Sue (2010), proposes a taxonomy of microaggressions that can be manifested in verbal, nonverbal, and environmental ways via microinsults, microassaults, and microinvalidations (see figure 1).

Figure 1. Microaggressions Taxonomy
(Sue 2010, p. 30).

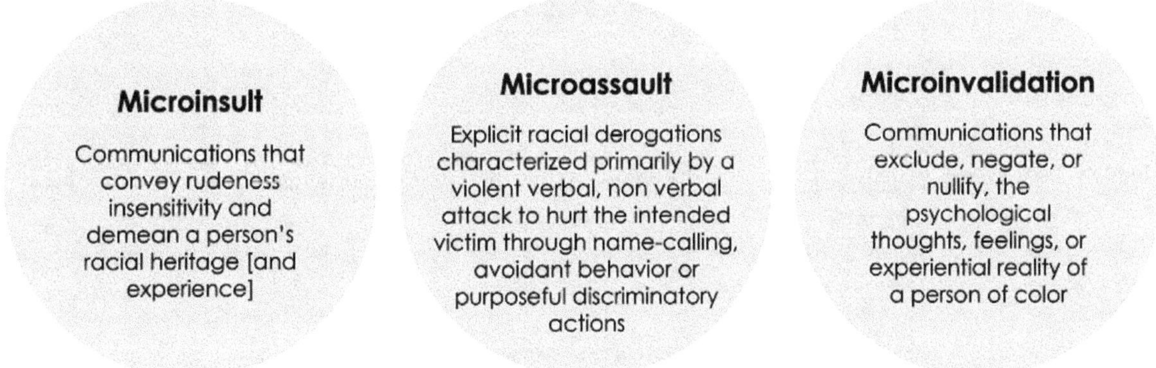

The line of questioning Justice Brown Jackson endured during her three-day public hearings was not only driven by differences in political ideology but also deeply held racial misconceptions and perceptions, fueled by the construct that Whiteness -- regardless of qualifications -- is the only standard for access to places of power like the U.S. Supreme Court. Using verbal attacks riddled with manifestations of microinsults, microassaults, and microinvalidations, a majority of White, male legislators attempted to discredit Brown Jackson's rulings and professional experience, achievement, and contributions.

The public devaluations of Congresswoman Maxine Waters, Vice-president Francia Marquez Mina, and Justice Ketanji Brown Jackson are representative of what too many BW experience throughout their careers in professional settings. More than political theater, Water, Marquez, and Brown Jackson experienced "microdevaluations" of their humanity and professional achievements.

The authors posit that the public experiences of microaggression against women, BW in particular, in professional and power arenas are "microdevaluations." They define microdevaluations as the sum total of microassaults, microinsults, and microinvalidations; a concerted effort to consciously make a public case to try to prove professional inferiority, undesirability, and unworthiness (see figure 2). As BW DEI practitioners, when facing microaggression in the workplace the authors sometimes find themselves having limited capacity to respond. Their limitation is due to the dual roles of representing both the organization and advocating for staff. The conflict for many DEI practitioners is that they can become gatekeepers for the institution while fully aware of the need to address a culture of microaggression. It should not be the burden of the minority to educate the majority but in these cases, the authors make a conscious choice to help create safe and brave spaces for further exploration. This has come at the cost of having to deal with human resources operatives or direct supervisors who prefer that they just "manage passively" and not create any waves. However, the author's experience has taught them that brave spaces especially allow for difficult but needed conversations to confront insults/aggressions and devaluations. The authors believe that the breaking of cycles and the beginning of healing begins with each and every one of us.

Figure 2. Microdevaluation within the Microaggressions Taxonomy
(Blackman-Richards, Jiménez & Pusey-Reid)

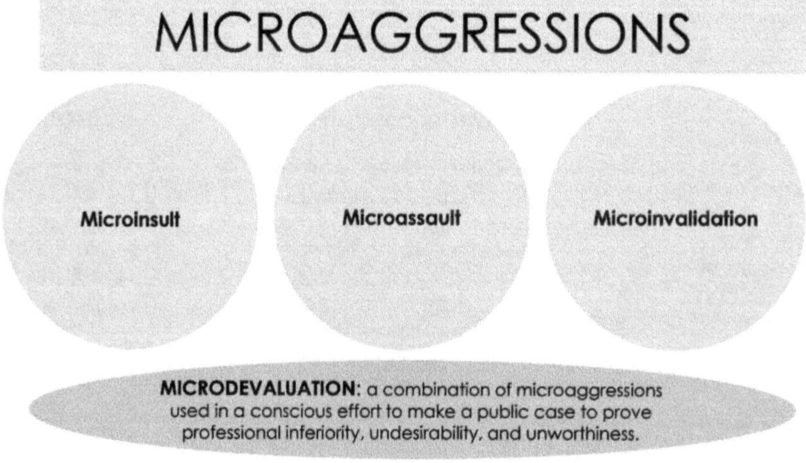

KILLING OUR ENERGIES

"You need a lot of ideas in the room, and you need a lot of perspectives in the room. Perspectives are born from experiences. Experiences are born from a lot of different people in the room… Innovation is the dominant competitive parameter around all markets" – Carla Harris (Lewis, 2021)

Fueled by technology and driven by data, the digital era in which we live always calls for two things: "better" and "more" (Oberholzer-Gee). Better products, better services, better decisions, and more sales, more revenues, and more profitability. Technological advances are happening at such great speeds that they are continually pushing the boundaries of what is possible. While this is an era full of promise, it also is a time of increased pressure on companies who want to establish or maintain a competitive advantage. To survive within the global economy, these companies must continue to reinvent themselves, ever revamping their service offerings to meet growing client expectations. It is this need for reinvention that has made innovation a key pillar in most companies' strategic plans. While the concept of innovation is clear, embedding innovation into a company's culture is not. Who teaches us to innovate? Isn't innovation reserved for the Einstein types? There are lots of new products led by the intellectual elites, but this is not the only type of innovation that companies are yearning for. What they seek is a team that will innovate their processes day in and day out, always making small improvements that make their delivery and operations more efficient. New delivery models, new services, and new processes – are all geared toward the achievement of better business results (Boston Consulting Group, 2021).

Long before the COVID-19 pandemic or the murder of George Floyd, there was overwhelming evidence of a strong correlation between innovation, improved financial performance, and diversity. A McKinsey & Company study found that companies within the top 25% of gender and ethnic diversity produced better financial results. Gender diversity produced a 25% improvement, while ethnic/racial diversity produced an even greater improvement: 36% (Dixon-Fyle, et.al. 2020). This and several other studies have observed benefits to cognitive thinking and innovation spurred on by the diversity within groups. Conversely, when there are lower levels of diversity, employees of historically excluded groups are creatively inhibited (University of North Carolina Pembroke, 2021). But diversity alone is not sufficient to produce the desired results. Rather, it is achieving inclusion within diverse teams that spurs on the desired thought diversity that leads to innovation. Without a sense of inclusion or belonging, people of color (Steele & Aronson, 1995) and women (Inzlicht & Ben-Zeev, 2000) operate under the fear of confirming negative stereotypes about their groups. Inclusion and belonging, however, have been associated with higher levels of performance and even improved health metrics (Walton & Cohen, 2011).

Knowing that diversity was linked to better business performance, in and of itself was not good enough to move the needle. The viewing of Mr. Floyd's public execution horrified company executives, but also provided what some would hope to be the catalyst for moving towards the key objective of growing the diversity of their teams; and thus, reaping the desired business results. So, in the weeks that followed, companies worked hard and fast at producing DEI statements, setting new diversity targets, and even making financial contributions to DEI causes. But the speed of the results in no wise has matched the speed of the published statements, especially as it relates to BW.

Why Aren't We Seeing the Results of DEI Targets for Black Women?

After billions of dollars invested within the DEI industry since 2020, the intended results have not followed because there is inconsistency in target setting and measurement of DEI results, and because in certain cases this work has been relegated to volunteer groups within institutions. For instance, of the three dimensions of DEI – Diversity offers the clearest set of actions necessary to achieve targets and the simplest way of measuring achievements. When employee demographic data indicates a lack of diversity, a company can concentrate its energies on hiring diverse talent. In that sense, diversity is simply a numbers game; representation is either present or not. Given the clear path to increasing diversity, during the 2020 Summer of Racial Reckoning, corporations and organizations adopted specific targets for racial/ethnic and gender diversity. Some set goals like doubling Black representation at the level of partners and managing directors (KPMG, 2021) or increasing representation of women in global leadership roles to 45% to reach gender parity in leadership roles by the end of 2030 (McDonald's, 2022).

Since 2020 women gained ground in representation at all levels within the corporate pipeline, and this is what the industry wants to achieve. However, this trend does not extend to women of color, who saw a decline in representation at every level (Burns et. al., 2021). Fifty-four percent of BW still report being the "only" within their groups and are significantly underrepresented in senior leadership positions. While BW represents 7.4% of the US population, the Lean In study found that they held just 1.6% and 1.4% of the Vice-president and C-Suite roles; respectively. This is in stark difference to White men, who represent 35% of the U.S. population and hold 57%, and 68% of the Vice-president and C-Suite roles; respectively (Lean In, 2020). When setting diversity goals, few companies adopted diversity targets specific to BW. Hence, it is plausible to meet both – African American/Black and gender goals without increasing the representation of BW. Improving the representation of BW in the workforce will require specific goals around this specific demographic.

Unlike diversity, the paths and measurements necessary to achieve equity and inclusion are far more nuanced. Sample inclusion goals within the workforce are statements like "Engaging everyone in our firm to foster an environment of … inclusion" (KPMG, 2021, p. 5). But, without a clear path and metric, these types of goals are far more difficult to achieve. A common approach to foster inclusion is Implicit Bias Training. Since 2020, the amount of implicit bias training has increased substantially (Thomas et al., 2021), but there is mixed evidence around the effectiveness of this type of training. A recent panel of experts assembled by the National Institutes of Health (NIH) reported that mandatory and one-time training sessions were not effective at dismantling implicit bias and could produce negative consequences (NIH, 2021). They noted that these types of training could give the impression that mere participation in the training renders participants no longer vulnerable to the influences of said bias.

Another widely adopted inclusion approach is the creation of employee networks. As such, African American/Black and Women networks have become frequent within workplaces. But individually or combined, these are not equipped to focus on the matters affecting the inclusion of the double "only" status of BW. Therefore, it is not surprising that since 2020, BW report having the worst experiences of any other group within the workplace, with the highest and the widest level of microaggressions and the lowest level of support and advocacy from their managers (Lean In, 2020).

Most of the metrics of inclusion and belonging rely on employee survey data. Employers ask employees to report their individual feelings of inclusion and belonging during interactions and relationships within their team. And while the data does a good job of reporting the individual's sentiments, it only offers one side of inclusion. Inclusion, however, is a two-sided coin. There is a component to inclusion that relies on the group and not just the individual. If a group decides to exclude an individual, there is little that the individual can do to penetrate and change that decision. This is a significant factor for BW, who report that they operate in an "outsider within" status at greater proportions than any other group, leaving them more vulnerable while navigating matters of office politics alone (Collins, 2019).

A frequent tactic that groups employ to exclude and ultimately justify the action is the use of labels. Labels have the effect of devaluing and dehumanizing an individual (Brown, 2018); thus, they reduce them to tropes that can be eliminated or excluded. This scenario is particularly effective in cases where BW are in positions of power where they may be called on to challenge their teams to move past their comfort zone. When it comes to BW, telltale signs of this kind of group elimination and exclusion tactics are references to her speaking abilities (e.g. articulate, eloquent) coupled with negative emotions (e.g. aggressive); which are evocative of the "Angry BW" trope. In these cases, BW leaders are "othered" by their teams, and unless they rely on good support from their leaders and Human Resources departments, it puts their leadership at stake (Burns et al., 2021). Therefore, groups must also be accountable for their responsibilities towards inclusion. Leaders must also be held accountable, especially as it relates to the inclusion of new members and BW in their teams. Carla Harris, Vice Chairman and Managing Director at Morgan Stanley, says, "When you bring new people into your organization, you need to over-index to ensure their inclusion" (Dodd, 2018).

Equity, on the other hand, is a measure of power dynamics. It is widely known that both men and women respond negatively to women in leadership positions (St. Catherine University, 2021). This factor is heightened even further for BW, who report not experiencing the same treatment as White women when engaging in similar conduct.

The work flexibility provided by the pandemic and the heightened calls for DEI after the 2020 Summer of racial reckoning have not produced the expected results, particularly as it relates to BW. In fact, BW's representation has decreased at all levels, and they are having the worst experiences at work (Lean In, 2020). No surprise that BW are pessimistic about their companies' commitment to DEI (Thomas, 2021).

THE EFFECTS OF INNOVATION

"Diversity further enables nonlinear novel thinking and adaptability that innovation requires," -Stuart R. Levine

When working within environments where they are underrepresented, not supported, microaggressed, and microdevaluated, BW seek security and psychological safety as their most pressing needs. Chasing safety is antithetical to innovation. To innovate, to propose something that has never been done before, something that may be criticized, and may even be shot down, requires a combination of courage and vulnerability. This cannot happen within a place where the greatest pressing need is for safety. When there is a need for safety and the protection of their identities, some BW rely on "code switching" or WS adaptations – activities and practices geared at fitting in. Fitting in becomes the objective, not because they do not like who they are, but because they feel that downplaying who they are is necessary to surviving within the space. But fitting in depletes energy. It is energy that conjures constant second-guessing of how their thoughts or comments will be perceived. While trying to focus an inordinate amount of time on figuring out how to slip the idea into the conversation so that it is evaluated on its merit and not undervalued because of whom it is coming from.

Expending their energies trying to fit in leaves less – if any – energy for higher-level functions such as innovation. The Maslow Hierarchy of Needs has been reinterpreted for several areas including employment. As seen in figure 3, after pay/financial reward, safety is the next level on the pyramid. Without safety, most BW are not empowered to operate at the belonging, self-esteem, and self-actualization levels where they can contribute to the innovation paradigm.

Figure 3. Hierarchy of needs
(Adapted from Columbus Chamber of Commerce, 2021)

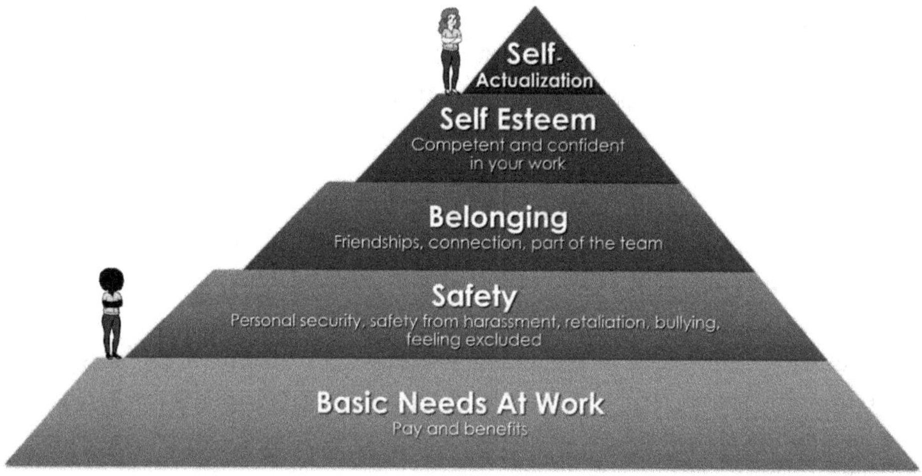

Even in the absence of safety, some BW tend to push past their own feelings of belonging and self-esteem to contribute to the innovation paradigm. These women draw from their internal resources the courage to share their thoughts. This courage is sometimes rewarded; however, the effectiveness of their contributions is held hostage by the group's level of inclusion of the BW. When a group chooses to withhold the inclusion of an individual, they withhold positive intent and do not offer the benefit of the doubt. In these settings, despite the Black Woman's efforts in posturing her comments, they tend to be misunderstood, and in some cases, this even leaves the Black woman in a worse position within the team than if she had remained silent. As long as BW do not feel such psychological and identity safety, or that their jobs and positions are secure, it is unlikely that the industry will benefit from the power of their contributions, and the full diversity of thought that generates innovation and improved business results.

The lack of safety felt by BW in their places of work is probably confirmed by the disparities in the number of employees wanting to return to the office. A recent survey found that only 3% of Black knowledge workers wanted to return to full-time office work, in comparison to 21% of White workers (Subramanian & Gilbert, 2021).

Why Black Women Don't Want to Go Back

As previously mentioned, more than half of BW are still the "only" within their teams (Lean In, 2020). When the "only" BW work under an enormous amount of pressure, they tend to feel that they are overly scrutinized (Lean In, 2020). This scrutiny goes far beyond the elements of their work to include their person and things, such as their hair, their clothing, their mannerisms, and even the foods they eat for lunch. Working from home provides some cover. It allows BW mental space to concentrate on those areas of their work they can control without having to concentrate on the parts they cannot control, such as the bias associated with their gender and racial identities.

Frequently cited reasons BW do not want to return to full-time in-person work are: cannot be themselves, physical appearance, and White centering. The authors discuss each of these below.

Cannot Be Themselves

Many BW feel that they cannot express emotions or be themselves at work because they are held bound within the "guests construct." Differences in expression are typically viewed as threatening. So, fearing being labeled angry or aggressive – they adopt other personas throughout the day at work. This is mentally and emotionally exhausting.

Although BW are no more prone to experiencing anger than any other population, they are frequently described as angry; especially by White women (Williams, 2022) - a description seldom used to describe women from other racial/ethnic backgrounds. Studies show that anger is an emotion frequently expressed in the workplace, but when BW express anger, non-Black people are more likely to attribute the anger to their personality rather than the situation inciting the emotion (Motro, 2022). This stereotype poses career limitations on BW. To flee the "angry" label, BW feel the burden of always pretending to be friendly and content. Other women reported that the fear of being labeled as angry left them having to frequently conceal their emotions. This led to their supervisors or teams describing them as disengaged or too passive.

Moreover, BW's "body language" and "tone" are frequently evaluated, especially by White women, categorizing their tone of voice, known as Tone Policing (Barratt, 2020). Such unwelcome evaluations are also accompanied by frequent comments about their language and speech dexterity. McKinsey's (2021) study found that 25% of BW have heard someone in their workplace express surprise at their language skill in comparison to ten percent of White women (Burns et al., 2021). Working from home lessens exposure to these types of insensitivities.

Prior to the pandemic, a lot of companies were adapting open-concept office spaces. Moving away from even cubicles, spaces were designed to be wide open and intended to foster collaboration. However, in an environment that operates under the construct of "Micro-colonialism" posited by Kinouani (2021), where BW's identities were not secure, these spaces proved to be an even greater challenge for BW; forcing them to spend their entire day in an environment prone to microaggression that felt like being under a microscope. But there is nothing "micro" about microaggressions. As Madia Logan, founder of Logan PR puts it "we shouldn't even call them microaggressions. We should think of them as paper cuts." She goes on to liken each slight to a cut that "hurt like hell" yet "you're bleeding just a lil" (Logan 2022, para. 1, 3 & 5) and leaves you protecting and readjusting natural movements because of your need to protect yourself against the ongoing pain.

Working from home has afforded BW more opportunities to be themselves throughout the day while lessening their exposure to microaggressions; creating a significant reason why BW do not want to go back to the office.

Physical Appearance

A recent Harvard Business Review study found that 79% of women of color reported having to alter their appearance or demeanor to fit in work (Williams, 2022). Prior to remote working, BW spent a lot of time and resources on their appearance as a way to address the established WSs that corporate and academic settings have established. As previously mentioned, these visual standards of "professionalism" are antithetical to the ethnic and racial preferences of many BW.

One of the authors, Jiménez, attended a recent National Transportation Conference, where a CEO of a large metropolitan transit agency recounted an experience that gave her greater insights into the burden of physical appearance that Black people face. Several hundred employees were on a virtual call when one of her reports - an older White male - noticed a peculiar difference between the attendees. He said, "Have you noticed that all the Black people are wearing professional attire, while none of the White people are?" At first, she did not believe the observation, so she swiped through several screens, only to confirm that it was true. The attire of all the Black people was noticeably professional in comparison to all the White people, who as she described, were mostly wearing sweat suits and loungewear. The official went on to describe her surprise and confessed that she had not realized the pressures that Black people face around their appearance – pressure that is manifested even when attending virtual meetings.

White Centering

A working manifestation of the WS, White Centering refers to a phenomenon of White people judging situations through their own feelings. Even the recent racial reckonings of the Summer of 2020 were largely White centered in some media outlets, through White people's feelings, emotions, and even their own guilt over those of Black people or People of Color (POC) who are directly affected by racial discrimination (Barkataki, 2019). White centering also extends to describe what POC feel is a burden to have to craft their comments and messages around the feelings of their White colleagues. Some POC noted they would not mind "White Centering" their messages if in fact, White people took the same amount of thought to carefully consider their speech before ventilating them. Yet this type of sensitivity was rarely experienced.

At the same Transportation conference, Jiménez attended a panel discussion of a diverse group of prominent women leaders within the Transportation Industry. All of these women led large organizations and/or carried the title of CEO. After a robust discussion on gender roles, and the advancement of women and underrepresented groups within the industry, the moderator announced a quick-fire round, where she would ask seemingly easy and light-hearted questions of the panelists. The moderator, a high-ranking, politically appointed BW, asked a White woman panelist to share the preferred decade she would like to go back to. After thinking about it briefly, the panelist responded, "I'd like to go back to the 1940s." When asked the reason behind her selection, she stated her love for the music and the fashion, and that "overall, the 1940s were so cool." The audience of roughly 400 attendees was silent. No quips, no "oh yeah" were heard. Jiménez secretly wondered if the responder had noticed the irony of her response, given the prior discussion around the advancement of women, an underrepresented group within the industry. Had she even considered the impact of her wish on the Black female moderator? In the 1940s, Jim Crow laws ruled the day in America. Segregation was so prevalent, that the chances of a BW being able to sit next to her or moderate a session was highly unlikely. Jiménez chalked the experience up to another time when a White person did not consider their words or their thoughts before speaking.

THERE IS HOPE

"Keep hope alive!" - Jesse Jackson (1988)

Unbeknownst to Jiménez, at the same event, seated across from her at the same table, were two staff members of the official who wanted to go back to the 1940s. Both were White. As the session concluded, she overheard them commenting about their leader's response to the quick-fire question. One of them said "I like her, but I wish someone were to grab her and coach her. How could it be that her response was from the 1940s? Did she think of what she was saying? What was happening in the 1940s?" The other woman agreed, and they went on to discuss the insensitivity of the response, noting the difficulties that the moderator, and many members of her team, would have felt if they had to go back to the 1940s. This discussion gave Jiménez hope. The efforts towards raising the consciousness of bias and discrimination are beginning to provide positive returns. Some White people are "getting it." But getting it is not the same as doing something about it. More than 80% of White people consider themselves to be "Allies" to POC at work, yet just slightly over one-quarter of BW feel they have strong allies in the workplace (Lean In, 2020).

The pace of innovation is tied to inclusion. As companies seek to re-introduce workers into the office and to re-ignite collaboration, one voice must not be left behind – the voice of the BW. Getting full advantage of the unique perspectives and contributions that the BW brings to the team will require the dismantling of institutional norms and WS that undergird the negative experiences that BW currently face within their organizations. This effort is an invitation for institutions and organizations to embrace and include the contributions and perspectives of BW.

RECOMMENDATIONS

Institutional and Cultural Shifts Needed to Make DEI Relevant

"The best way to get the best out of people is to not force them to be something other than they naturally are. Now, what do they have to be? They have to be respectful." – Ursula Burns (Strategies for Influence)

While the concept of DEI is not new, the work of deconstructing WS is just beginning. The necessary cultural shifts require higher levels of awareness and education within the majoritized population. The Black woman DEI leader, as an individual, is not by herself able to fix inequities and transform cultures. This work requires a partnership that the authors are actively seeking to establish within their institutions. There are several actions that institutions can take to create a culture that is respectful and supportive of BW and move away from the WS. Some of these are listed below.

1. **Empower and strengthen the role of DEI Practitioners**: DEI practitioners need not only be granted titles and paraded as institutional panaceas. Sadly, this type of performative showcasing only translates into DEI leaders re-enacting exclusionary and gatekeeping practices for the organization or institution. They also cannot be attached to Human Resources departments and have no power of their own to accomplish change. Their roles must be elevated, prioritized, and given a budget commensurate to accomplishing organizational goals. The role of DEI should also not begin and end with an annual conference on bias training; there is a need for work that is intentional and

strategic in order to center DEI and solidify it as part of institutional culture. The voices, expertise, and roles of DEI Practitioners must be empowered, elevated, and respected for real organizational and institutional shifts to begin to take place.

2. **Confront the Issue:** Bias and discrimination against BW in the workforce can only be eradicated if it is confronted. Spaces for truthful conversations for people to hold each other accountable, learn, and heal should never be avoided but instead created, appreciated, and honored.
3. **Interrogate the Norm:** Companies must challenge the existing standards that hold White preferences or ways of doing things as "the norm". BW, should not be treated as up-and-comers within the team that need to be coached till they achieve the appropriate level of WS. Often, they are expected to strip their natural and cultural identities as a bar they must cross prior to being recognized for their brilliance.
4. **Amplify BW's Voices:** Carla Harris makes the distinction between mentoring and sponsoring. A mentor shows the way and serves as a guide - a sounding board for reflection and strategizing the next steps. A sponsor goes into the room and when the opportunity arises mentions your name as the woman for the job. He or she knows your qualifications and can stand by your record. BW need both mentors and sponsors. Training and mentoring will not achieve diversity if we do not sponsor BW and create opportunities to include them. A recent McKinsey study found that more than 67% of Black employees report they do not have a sponsor at their organization, even though 87% of companies report having a sponsorship program in place (Hancock, 2021).
5. **Protect BW**: Companies must plan and protect the investments made towards increasing the leadership of BW. Allowing them to serve in certain roles without providing cover and support is ineffective. Human Resources departments, institutional and corporate leaders must learn to assess and deal with discriminatory treatment towards BW. Equality of protection is not the same as equity of protection. Equity demands additional treatments and protections for BW.
6. **Acknowledge that White ignorance is no longer acceptable or justifiable:** Often, when called out for using insensitive language around People of Color (POC), White people sight ignorance, not knowing that the language was offensive. But considering all the body of evidence available around discrimination of POC and especially BW in the workforce, ignorance is no longer a justifiable response for individuals, institutions and organizations. Institutions and organizations must be accountable for working to increase the cultural awareness of all their staff. White employees must receive ongoing sensitivity and cultural awareness and learn to think about the impact of their comments before ventilating them. To perpetuate harsh and inhospitable conditions for BW should no longer be accepted or tolerated. If adopted, this recommendation will produce discomfort for the majority classes, however, discomfort is the first step towards progress. Additionally, companies should enact zero tolerance policies for microaggressions. Perpetuating the "Angry Black Woman" trope, which is a chief microaggression against BW, should not be allowed within workplaces or teams.

CONCLUSION

This chapter examined the impact of White standards and norms that are embedded in current organizational cultures and how these standards impact BW. It widens the perspective beyond the confines of DEI roles, and discusses microdevaluation, as a new construct frequently experienced by BW in leadership roles. Examples are provided to explicate the complexities experienced by BW in DEI roles and data is used to underscore inequities that exist despite all the huge investments in DEI. The chapter further examines the effects on innovation caused by the lack of inclusion of the voices of BW within organizations. Finally, it offers recommendations to organizations and institutions that genuinely seek to change cultural norms and practices to achieve their stated DEI objectives. The adoption of these recommendations would allow institutions the ability to derive the full benefits of BW DEI practitioners beyond the credibility of their race and gender.

ACKNOWLEDGMENT

This research received no specific grant from any funding agency in the public, commercial, or not-for-profit sectors.

REFERENCES

Adeniran, R. K. (2022). Black women and microaggression: The confirmation hearing of associate justice Ketanji Brown Jackson. *Holistic Nursing Practice*, *36*(4), 189–191. doi:10.1097/HNP.0000000000000533 PMID:35708554

Angelou, M. (1979). *I know why the caged bird sings*. Random House.

Ashley, W. (2014). The angry Black woman: The impact of pejorative stereotypes on psychotherapy with Black women. *Social Work in Public Health*, *29*(1), 27–34. doi:10.1080/19371918.2011.619449 PMID:24188294

BallotPedia. (2022). Maxine Waters. *Ballotpedia*. https://ballotpedia.org/Maxine_Waters#Committee_assignments

Barkataki, S. (2019, July 26). *Why the heck are you white centering and what to do about it*. https://www.susannabarkataki.com/post/why-the-heck-are-you-white-centering-and-what-to-do-about-it

Barratt, B. (2020, June 19). The microaggressions towards black women you might be complicit in at work. *Forbes*. https://www.forbes.com/sites/biancabarratt/2020/06/19/themicroaggressions-towards-black-women-you-might-be-complicit-in-at-work/?sh=fe1cf542bda5-

Blanco, A. & Tan, S. (2022, March 20). How Ketanji Brown Jackson's path to the supreme court differs from the current justices. *The Washington Post*. https://www.washingtonpost.com/politics/interactive/2022/ketanji-brown-jackson-school-career/

Boston Consulting Group (2021, May). The race for innovation. https://media-publications.bcg.com/BCG-Executive-Perspectives-Race-for-Innovation.pdf

Bradley Smith, S. (2021, March 5). How a lack of sponsorship keeps black women out of the c-suite. *Harvard Business Review*. https://hbr.org/2021/03/how-a-lack-of-sponsorship-keeps-black-women-out-of-the-c-suite

Brown, B. (2018, March 17). Dehumanizing always starts with language.https://brenebrown.com/articles/2018/05/17/dehumanizing-always-starts-with-language/

Burns, T., Huang, J., Krivkovich, A., Yee, L., Rambachan, I. & Trkulja, T. (2021).Women in the workplace 2021. McKinsey & Company. https://www.mckinsey.com/featured-insights/diversity-and-inclusion/women-in-the-workplace

Burns, U. (n.d). Strategies for Influence coaching quotes and tips. https://strategiesforinfluence.com/ursula-burns-coaching-advice/

Byrd, M. Y. (2012). Critical race theory: A framework for examining social identity

Carr, E. W., Reece, A., Rosen Kellerman, G. & Robichaux, A. (2019, December 16). The value of belonging at work. *Harvard Business Review.* https://hbr.org/2019/12/the-value-of-belonging-at-work

Caxaj, C. S. & Berman, H. (2010). Belonging among newcomer youths: Intersecting experiences of inclusion and exclusion. *Advances in Nursing Science, 33*(4), E17-E30. doi:10.1097/ANS.0b013e3181fb2f0f

Coles, S. M., & Pasek, J. (2020). Intersectional invisibility revisited: How group prototypes lead to the erasure and exclusion of Black women. *Translational Issues in Psychological Science, 6*(4), 314–324. doi:10.1037/tps0000256

Collins, P. H. (2002). *Black feminist thought: Knowledge, consciousness, and the politics of empowerment.* Routledge.

Collins, P. H. (2019). *Intersectionality as critical social theory.* Duke University Press.

Collins, P. H., & Bilge, S. (2020). *Intersectionality.* John Wiley & Sons.

Columbus Chamber of Commerce (2021, August 18). Address the great resignation using psychological safety. https://columbus.org/address-the-great-resignation-using-psychological-safety/

Connley, C. (2021). Walgreens' new ceo roz brewer on bias in the c-suite: 'When you're a black woman, you get mistaken a lot'. CNBC. https://www.cnbc.com/2021/01/27/walgreens-new-ceo-roz-brewer-on-dealing-with-bias-in-the-c-suite.html

Crenshaw, K. (1991). Mapping the margins: Intersectionality, identity politics, and violence against women of color. Stanford Law Review, 43(6), 1241–1299

Daniels, J. P. (2022, May 25). She represents me: the black woman making political history in Colombia. *The Guardian.* https://www.theguardian.com/global-development/2022/may/25/francia-marquez-colombia-vice-president-black-candidate

Diversity of Black Women in Positions of Leadership *Handbook of research on workforce diversity in a global society: Technologies and concepts.* IGI Global.

Dixon, A. R. & Telles, E. E. (2017). Skin color and colorism: Global research, concepts and measurements. *Annual Review of Sociology, 43,* 405-424. doi:10.1146/annurev-soc-060116-053315

Dixon-Fyle, S., Dolan, K.,Hunt, D. V. & Prince, S. (2020). Diversity wins: How inclusion matters. https://www.mckinsey.com/featured-insights/diversity-and-inclusion/diversity-wins-how-inclusion-matters

Dodd, B. (2018). 44 leadership quotes from Carla Harris – 2018 global leadership summit. https://briandoddonleadership.com/2018/08/10/44-leadership-quotes-from-carla-harris-2018-global-leadership-summit/

Domínguez, S. & Embrick, D. G. (2020). Racial microaggressions: Bridging psychology and sociology and future research considerations. *Sociology Compass, 14*(8), e12803. doi:10.1111/soc4.12803

Donovan, R. A., & West, L. M. (2015). Stress and mental health: Moderating role of the strong black woman stereotype. *Journal of Black Psychology, 41*(4), 384–396. doi:10.1177/0095798414543014

Edes, A., & Taylor, J. (2017). #BlackWomenAtWork: Women speak out after criticism of journalist, congresswoman. *NPR*. https://www.npr.org/2017/03/29/521954040/-blackwomenatwork-women-speak-out-aftercriticism-of-journalist-congresswoman

Hancock, B., Williams, M., Manyika, J., Yee, L. & Wong, J. (2021, February 21). Race in the workplace: *The Black experience in the US private sector*. McKinsey & Company. https://www.mckinsey.com/featured-insights/diversity-and-inclusion/race-in-the-workplace-the-black-experience-in-the-us-private-sector

Harris, D. (2020). No, I am not a proud latina. The future of latinidad. *Refinery 29*. https://www.refinery29.com/en-us/latinx-identity-black-history-personal-essay

Houston, P. (2003). The truest eye. Toni Morrison on love, writing, the greater good. *Oprah Magazine*. https://www.oprah.com/omagazine/toni-morrison-talks-love/all

Institute for Women Policy Research (2017, November 21). Women's median earnings as a percent of men's, 1985-2016 (full-time, year-round workers) with projections for pay equity, by race/ethnicity. https://iwpr.org/iwpr-general/womens-median-earnings-as-a-percent-of-mens-1985-2016-full-time-year-round-workers-with-projections-for-pay-equity-by-race-ethnicity/

Inzlicht, M., & Ben-Zeev, T. (2000). A threatening intellectual environment: Why females are susceptible to experiencing problem-solving deficits in the presence of males. Psychological Science, 11(5), 365–371.

Jameel, M.& Yerardi, J. (2019, February 28).Workplace discrimination is Illegal. But our data shows it's still a problem. *Vox Magazine & Center for Public Integrity*. https://www.vox.com/policy-and-politics/2019/2/28/18241973/workplace-discrimination-cpi-investigation-eeoc

Jan, T., McGregor, J. & Hoyer, M. (2021, August 23). Corporate america's $50 billion promise. *The Washington Post*. https://www.washingtonpost.com/business/interactive/2021/george-floyd-corporate-america-racial-justice/

Kayembe, B. (2021). Why are we still depicting black women as mammies? https://shado-mag.com/all/why-are-we-still-depicting-black-women-as-mammies/

Kinouani, G.(2021). *Living while black: The essential guide to overcoming Racial trauma*. Penguin Random House.

KPMG. (2021). Diversity, equity and inclusion: 2021 U.S. *DEI transparency report*. https://www.kpmg.us/content/dam/global/pdfs/2021/kpmg-us-2021-dei-report.pdf

Lean In (2020). The state of black women in corporate america. https://media.sgff.io/sgff_r1eHetbDYb/2020-08-13/1597343917539/Lean_In_-_State_of_Black_Women_in_Corporate_America_Report_1.pdf

Lewis, B. (2021). Diversity is no longer just a moral imperative, it's also critical for business. https://www.procore.com/jobsite/diversity-is-no-longer-just-a-moral-imperative-its-also-critical-for-business/#:~:text=If%20you%20need%20a%20lot%20of%20perspectives%2C%20you%20need%20a,experiences%20are%20born%20from%20people.%E2%80%9D

Logan, M. (2022, July 18). Linkedln post. *LinkedIn*. https://www.linkedin.com/posts/madialogan_womenintheworkplace-protips-50ways-activity-6953382501763452928-XSL5/?utm_source=linkedin_share&utm_medium=ios_app

Lorde, A. (1984). *Sister outsider: Speeches and essays*. Crossing Press.

MacDonald (2022). Diversity, equity and inclusion. https://corporate.mcdonalds.com/corpmcd/our-purpose-and-impact/jobs-inclusion-and-empowerment/diversity-and-inclusion.html

McCluney, C. L. & Rabelo, V. C. (2019). Conditions of visibility: An intersectional examination of black women's belongingness and distinctiveness at work. *Journal of Vocational Behavior, 113,* 143-152. doi:10.1016/j.jvb.2018.09.008

McCluney, C. L., Robotham, K., Lee, S., Smith, R. & Durkee, M. (2019). The costs of code-switching. *Harvard Business Review*. https://hbr.org/2019/11/the-costs-of-codeswitching

McGrady, C. (2022, April 8). What Ketanji Brown Jackson's sisterlocks mean to black women. The Washington Post. https://www.washingtonpost.com/lifestyle/2022/04/08/ketanji-brown-jackson-hair-sisterlocks/

Mena, J. A., & Vaccaro, A. (2017). I've struggled, I've battled. Invisibility microaggressions experienced by women of color at a predominantly white institution. NASPA Journal About Women in Higher Education, 10(3), 301-318. . doi:10.1080/19407882.2017.1347047

Mgadmi, M. (2009). Black women's identity: Stereotypes, respectability and passionlessness (1890-1930). *Revue LISA/LISA e-journal*, 7(1), 40-55.

Morales, Isabel. Fighting for the visibility of the "nobodies": Francia Marquez. Panoramas A Wider Perspective. University of Pittsburgh.

Motro, D., Evans, J. B., Ellis, A., & Benson, L. (2022). Race and reactions to women's expressions of anger at work: Examining the effects of the "angry Black woman" stereotype. *The Journal of applied psychology, 107*(1), 142–152. doi:10.1037/apl0000884

National Institutes of Health [NIH]. (2021). Scientific workforce diversity seminar series (SWDSS). seminar proceedings. *National Institutes of Health*. https://diversity.nih.gov/sites/coswd/files/images/NIH_COSWD_SWDSS_Implicit_Bias_Proceedings_508.pdf

Oberholzer-Gee, F. (2021, May-June). Eliminate strategic overload: How to select fewer initiatives with greater impact. *Harvard Business Review*. https://hbr.org/2021/05/eliminate-strategic-overload

Parker, M. (2022, June 8). Beyond employee well-being: Creating a sense of belonging in the workplace. *Harvard Business Review*. https://hbr.org/resources/pdfs/comm/google/BeyondEmployeeWell-Being.pdf

Pierce, C. (1970). Offensive mechanisms. In F. B. Barbour (Ed.), The black seventies. Porter Sargent Publisher.

Rabelo, V. C., Robotham, K. & McCluney, C. (2021). "Against a sharp white background": How Black women experience the white gaze at work. *Gender, Work & Organization*, 28(5), 1840-1858. doi:10.1111/gwao.12564

Ray, V. (2019). A theory of racialized organizations. *American Sociological Review*. 84(1), 26–53. doi:10.1177/0003122418822335

Roux, M. (2021, August 3) Five facts about black women in the labor force. *The U.S. Department of Labor Blog*. https://blog.dol.gov/2021/08/03/5-facts-about-black-women-in-the-labor-force

Shear, M. D. & Savage, C. (2022, January 26). Biden expected to nominate a black woman to the supreme court. *The New York Times*. https://www.nytimes.com/2022/01/26/us/politics/supreme-court-nominee-black-woman.html

Shepherd, J. M. (2018). *Don't touch my crown: Texturism as an extension of colorism in the natural hair community*. Thesis. Master of Arts in Mass Communications. Texas State University.

Sparks, E. (1998). *Against all odds: Resistance and resilience in African American welfare mothers*. Wellesley College.

St. Catherine University (2021, April 16). Overcome barriers to female leadership. https://www.stkate.edu/academics/women-in-leadership-degrees/barriers-to-female-leadership

Steele, C.M., & Aronson, J. (1995). Stereotype threat and the intellectual test performance of African Americans. Journal of Personality and Social Psychology, 69, 797–811.

Subramanian, S. & Gilbert, T (2021, March 11). A new era of workplace inclusion: Moving from retrofit to redesign. *Future Forum*.https://futureforum.com/2021/03/11/dismantling-the-office-moving-from-retrofit-to-redesign/

Sue, D. W. (2010). *Microaggressions in everyday life: Race, gender & sexual orientation*. John Wiley & Sons, Inc.

Sue, D. W., Capodilupo, C. M., & Holder, A. M. B. (2008). Racial microaggressions in the life experience of Black Americans. *Professional Psychology: Research and Practice, 39*(3), 329–336. doi:10.1037/0735-7028.39.3.329

Sykes, T. A. (2021). The elite 100: A tribute to black women executives: The change is here. *Diversity Woman Media*. https://www.diversitywoman.com/the-elite-100-a-tribute-to-black-women-executives-2/

Thomas, R., Cooper, M., McShane Urban, K., Cardazone, G., Bohrer, A., Mahajan, S., Yee, L., Krivkovich, A., Haung, J., Rambachan, I., Burns, T., & Trkulja, T. (2021). Women in the workplace. *McKinsey & Company*. https://wiw-report.s3.amazonaws.com/Women_in_the_Workplace_2021.pdf

Thompson, S. (2019). Despite being the most educated, black women earn less money at work, in entrepreneurship and venture capital: here are three ways to fix it: when black women win, we all win. https://www.inc.com/sonia-thompson/black-women-equal-pay-equity-how-to-make-progress.html

United States Census Bureau. (2020). Annual estimates of the resident population by sex, race, and hispanic origin [Data set]. 2019 Population Estimates by Age, Sex, Race, and Hispanic Origin. https://www.census.gov/newsroom/press-kits/2020/population-estimates-detailed.html

United States Census Bureau. (2021). QuickFacts. USCB. https://www.census.gov/quickfacts/fact/table/US/LFE046220

University of North Carolina Pembroke. (2021). Why diversity and inclusion are good for business. https://online.uncp.edu/articles/mba/diversity-and-inclusion-good-for-business.aspx

Walton, G. M., & Cohen, G. L. (2011). A brief social-belonging intervention improvesacademic and health outcomes of minority students. Science, 331(6023), 1447–1451.

Williams, J. C., Andrews, O. & Boginsky, M. (2022). Why many women of color don't want to return to the office. https://hbr.org/2022/05/why-many-women-of-color-dont-want-to-return-to-the-office

Williams, M. T., Skinta, M. D., & Martin-Willett, R. (2021). After pierce and sue: A revised racial microaggressions taxonomy. *Perspectives on Psychological Science, 16*(5), 991–1007. doi:10.1177/1745691621994247

Zelevansky, N. (2019). The big business of unconscious bias. *The New York Times*.

ADDITIONAL READING

Davis, A. Y. (1990). *Women, culture, and politics.* Vintage.

Harts, M. (2021). *Right within: How to heal from racial trauma in the workplace.* Seal Press.

Kendall, M. (2020). *Hood feminism: Notes from the women the movement forgot.* Viking.

Kinouani, G. (2022). *Living while black: Using joy, beauty and connection to heal racial trauma.* Beacon Press.

Oluo, I. (2020). *Mediocre: The dangerous legacy of white male America.* Seal Press.

KEY TERMS AND DEFINITIONS

Black Women's Power: Behavior exemplified by BW when demonstrating fearlessness in the face of obstacles; having the courage and willingness to confront any adversary to achieve an intended goal that will break barriers.

Code Switching: The adaptation of behavior, language or appearance to fit the White standard or norm.

DEI: Inclusivity, representation and contributions of all voices. Inclusivity is centered on equitable investments of all human capital.

Innovation: Continual micro and macro improvements in products or processes.

Microdevaluations: The sum total of microassaults, microinsults and microinvalidations that constitute a concerted effort to try to publicly prove professional inferiority.

Microinvalidation: Communications that exclude, negate or nullify the psychological thoughts, feelings or experiences of a person of color.

White Standard: The Eurocentric ideology where cultural norms, views, and aesthetics are considered to be above reproach, superior, and thus imposed on people of color.

Chapter 10
Black, White, and Everything in Between:
Trials of a Black DEI Professional in PWIs

Stephanie Reed
Aspire2Higher Personal and Professional Development, Inc., USA

ABSTRACT

With this chapter, the author sheds light on the experiences of a Black woman hired to create, administer, and manage the day-to-day needs of diversity offices at two small, white private liberal arts universities. The chapter will include insights on the very racism and implicit bias the author experienced, reported, and helped diminish. The chapter also describes the seemingly impossible task of managing change and transformation on private institutions rooted in white supremacist traditions and built upon a history of exclusion. To do this, the author shares personal narratives from colleagues collected via online surveys. The author describes the personal angst experienced while collecting, reporting, and managing the many micro-aggressions, experiences with racism, transphobia, and other reported biases. The author considers the mental gymnastics necessary to serve the needs of the institution and attempt to protect personal integrity and sanity.

INTRODUCTION

"An educator in a system of oppression is either a revolutionary, or an oppressor." – Lerone Bennett, Jr.

This quote explicitly expresses what I experienced and struggled to name during my career, as a Black woman who leads diversity, equity and inclusion efforts in higher education. It is not, however, how I felt when I began my career. Starting a career in higher education (HE) as a young, Black professional at a large, Division 1, predominantly White institution (PWI) was exhilarating for me. As a proud alumna of a historically Black college/university (HBCU) with a master's degree in higher education, working at a flagship PWI was an intentional decision. I wanted to serve students of color (SOC) and first-generation

DOI: 10.4018/978-1-6684-3564-9.ch010

students who "missed out" on the supportive and loving environment offered at an HBCU. While I worked in an unrelated role, I was asked to assist with diversity, equity, and inclusion (DEI) initiatives.

I worked collaboratively with other departments on university DEI initiatives, which is how I gained experience in diversity work in higher education. As a young, Black woman and new professional, I felt marginalized as an employee of the institution. Research suggests that Black faculty and staff "...discuss disparate treatment in workloads, in expectations regarding how they express themselves, and in the need to establish their position as a part of the team" (Turner & Grauerholz, 2017, p. 217). However, young professionals who seek a sense of community can often foster it when working with Black faculty and staff members, as well as when serving SOC through volunteer DEI experiences.

Nonetheless, after serving at an institution with few Black, Indigenous, and People of Color (BIPOC) administrative leaders for mentorship and support, a young, Black professional might experience waning motivation. In my professional journey as a Black woman DEI administrator, unfortunately, I often resigned from positions shortly after my motivation decreased while in the role. Thereafter, my decisions to resign were accompanied by feelings of guilt, which I learned was a feeling often shared with other Black higher education professionals, after discussions regarding their trepidations about leaving roles.

One of my sentiments frequently expressed in conversations with other Black higher education professionals was regarding leaving the Black students I, so intently, cared to serve and support. Therefore, I contemplated continuing my career at an HBCU, instead, given the consideration that HBCUs, reportedly, have a strong sense of community infused into the culture of the campus, to ensure student success. There is a presumption that working at an HBCU is more manageable for BIPOC HE professionals than working at a PWI. There has also been research to suggest that Black women, who work on HBCU campuses, have more support among colleagues (Becks-Moody, 2004). In a study of African American women administrators in higher education, Becks-Moody (2004) stated, "[t]he women at the HBCUs did not experience racism from their counterparts. However, they reported being treated differently by counterparts from other universities and the governing board" (p. 267). Black women DEI professionals in HE are likely unable to find reprieve if they seek new work on an HBCU campus. Perhaps they would simply be trading one set of challenges for another if they sought new work on HBCU campuses.

Another sentiment expressed in my debates and discussions with other Black HE professionals, and more specifically, with other Black women DEI administrators, was the sentiment expressed in the opening quote. In his dissertation research on racial socialization and anti-Blackness in post-secondary educators, Damon Lamont Dees, Jr. (2019) referred to Lerone Bennett, Jr.'s famous quote, "An educator in a system of oppression is either a revolutionary, or an oppressor" (p. 4). Dees, Jr.'s dissertation, like the sentiments expressed in this quote, discussed the dichotomous feelings of Black educators in higher education when faced with the racism that is prevalent in higher education.

One common, all too frequent student incident report, I often handled as a DEI professional, was the pejorative use of racial epithets, most frequently from student to another student. Greta Anderson (2020) described one such case in an article titled *The Emotional Toll of Racism*. Anderson (2020) summarized the incident and said,

*Lofton, who is Black, asked her macroeconomics professor a question during class and heard someone sitting behind her say, 'I guess n****rs don't understand.' Lofton, 'completely shocked' to hear a racial slur used so casually, said nothing, and neither did her professor, who Lofton said paused and appeared to have heard the comment (p. 15).*

This type of incident periodically occurred on each PWI campus where I served as the DEI Director. In each role I held, these incidents required an investigation, intervention, advocacy, education, and support from my department. Managing and investigating these incidents, as a member of a marginalized community, while supporting the involved student and faculty member was emotionally draining. Consequently, I felt unsupported when doing this work on each PWI campus and could not mitigate the subsequent conflicting feelings, particularly when these and other incidents commonly occurred. Thus, even as I changed campus locations in my career as a DEI professional, I experienced burnout in each DEI role and strongly considered resigning from my post.

As a result of burnout, Black higher education professionals often reflect about the congruency between their work and their personal values, without the support of a mentor who could empathize with their experiences. Findings from a study by Davis & Maldonado (2015) regarding the leadership development of African American women in higher education, supports this assertion by stating that, "women faced exclusion from social networks…" (p. 59). Research from West (2021) similarly states, "…lack of access to culturally similar and/or conscious mentors, colleagues, and supervisors, which leads to feelings of loneliness and unsupportive work environments" (p. 1). As a Black woman DEI professional on PWI campuses, my experience aligns with what this research has found. In my many years as a DEI administrator on PWI campuses, I never had a Black woman in a leadership role on my campus to provide guidance or mentorship.

Overall, this chapter examines the professional experiences of a DEI mid-level professional within several private PWIs. The personal narratives of colleagues and my professional challenges, which ultimately led to my exit from HE, are the focal point of this manuscript. With this, we explore experiences regarding managing diversity work at a PWI, which includes receiving, managing, and investigating reports of bias and racism, as a Black DEI professional. For the remainder of the chapter, my experiences as a Black, cisgender, and female-identifying DEI practitioner are explored. Also, the personal narratives of other Black HE professionals who work in private, White liberal arts universities are included. The objectives of this chapter include the following:

- Offer insights and reflections regarding the difficulties faced by Black DEI professionals working in private liberal arts colleges and universities.
- Describe the inherent duplicity in a Black woman being charged to affect change and provide transformative DEI leadership on PWI campuses.
- Call attention to the experiences of Black and HE professionals of other marginalized identities who received coded and biased feedback and lacked the necessary supports to advocate for themselves.

BACKGROUND

During the 1960s and 1970s, The Black Campus Movement made a plethora of inroads for DEI work, in its purposeful and powerful activism (Rogers, 2009). In its early period, diversity work in HE had a central focus on nondiscrimination, affirmative action, and increasing access to post-secondary education, particularly for federally protected groups. It slowly expanded out of the Black Campus Movement, through an emergence of Black Student Unions and, eventually, to include LGBTQ+ education. A focus on multicultural competence and culturally relevant course content is evidence of universities linking diversity work to individual student outcomes, as well as institutional and societal benefits (Nixon, 2013).

Over time, diversity work—currently known as DEI work—has developed into a robust and complex industry. Presently, the DEI industry encompasses a broader focus and has taken a more wholistic and multidimensional approach to the work. The National Association of Chief Diversity Officers in Higher Education (Worthington et al., 2020) released a report which outlines standards of professional practice. In this report, they offer a Three-Dimensional Model of Higher Education Diversity, adapted from Worthington et al. (2012) to illustrate, in their words, "the multitude of dimensions of social identity characteristics inherent to the work of diversity in higher education" (p. 7). I also experienced my work evolve to include data-driven program development, strategic planning, institution-wide commitments to equity in the curriculum and co-curricular programmatic goals and outcomes, bias reporting and bias response teams, inclusive excellence leadership models, and more. Authors of the NADOHE (2020) stated, "when current missions and historical contexts reflect exclusionary practices, CDOs declare their commitment to...work from comprehensive definitions of equity, diversity & inclusion…towards organizational change" (p. 8). As such, DEI work has had to expand, and become more interdisciplinary in nature. The management and functions of DEI work varies, based on the size and types of institutions. It has been argued that institutional commitment to DEI work and diversity, as a value, is evidenced in how resources are allocated to support and operationalize the work (Greene & Paul, 2021).

Considering the complexity of DEI work, the professionals who occupy these roles must possess specialized knowledge and skills (Howard-Hamilton, 2003). Amid the steady growth of the DEI industry, women, higher education DEI professionals face numerous challenges in their work. Most recently, West (2021) stated, "Black women postsecondary administrators and faculty continue to face a wide array of significant workplace challenges…" (p. 1). As aforementioned, working as a Black DEI professional presents a particular set of challenges. One of the challenges specific to Black DEI professionals in higher education is the constant struggle to maintain psychological safety when conducting DEI work and in their work environments. Many Black women HE professionals, including those who work as DEI administrators on White campuses, must navigate White supremacy culture. In Okun and Jones' (2000) research, they identified several characteristics of White supremacy culture, one of which is the "right to comfort" (p. 25). Research from Dr. Wilma J. Henry and Nicole M. Glenn (2009) describes the oppressive conditions on PWI campuses coupled with the lack of critical mass as creating an interlocking system of barriers that Black women HE leaders navigate.

As Black HE professionals persevere through and navigate the trials and tribulations of toxic work environments, they are often met with disparate opportunities for promotion and tenure, as both faculty and administrative staff. When they can ascend to a senior-level position, and the complexity of the work increases, the network of support becomes smaller (Davis & Maldonado, 2015; West, 2021). Simultaneously, stress and imposter syndrome, coupled with a devaluing and disrespect of Black HE professionals' knowledge, credentials, experience, and scholarly work, are constantly present in the classroom and in senior-level positions (Harris, 2020). For instance, the most senior role in HE DEI work is the Chief Diversity Officer (CDO). In the 2020 report from NADOHE, task force members and authors outlined the Standards of Professional Practice for Chief Diversity Officers in Higher Education and stated, "… the work of CDOs can be inherently fraught with challenges, threats, incongruities, and conflicts…" (p. 6). Thus even at the highest administrative level of DEI work in HE, when the administrator has earned some power and influence, they are still met with these difficulties.

Much of the research on Black women professionals in HE on PWI campuses details the hostile, isolating, and systemically racist environments through case studies and dissertation research (Lloyd-Jones, 2009; Maraña, 2016). One of the most striking examples of the systemic racist treatment of Black women in HE is that of the tenure saga of Dr. Nikole Hannah Jones. What should have been an internal, common, institutional process, played out, nationally, as televised history for the world to scrutinize. Dr. Hannah Jones was not granted tenure when she was offered a prestigious faculty chair position at her alma mater, a PWI, whereas all the preceding appointees were provided tenure with this appointment. Ultimately, Dr. Hannah Jones declined the coveted position for another faculty appointment—with tenure—at Howard University, an HBCU. Unfortunately, given the media frenzy surrounding this tenure case, it is more widely known that there are countless other examples, such as this of the renowned scholar, Dr. Hannah Jones. It should be no surprise that non-White people of multiple marginalized intersectional identities are exasperated by toxic and harmful HE environments.

The most challenging things about being a Black HE professional working on the campus of a PWI, for me, have been the invisible labor, (which can be understood to mean unrecognized work that BIPOC educators must do to support BIPOC students), feelings of guilt, despondency, and resentment. These feelings are associated with the countless times Black faculty and staff must witness the marginalization, persistent microaggressions, gaslighting, and racist experiences imposed upon students who are BIPOC, LGBTQ+ and, otherwise, minoritized. Furthermore, it is considerably more challenging to serve as the DEI administrator who is responsible for managing the reports of microaggressions, bias incidents, racial tensions, and campus climate, especially while also serving as a support person to the aforementioned student populations. In a book titled *Dismantling Race in Higher Education*, contributing author, Sara Ahmed (2018), described the idea that in HE, women of color become symbols of diversity who must "do diversity" and "be diversity" (p. 338). This statement encapsulates how Black women are tokenized, propped up, counted as double minorities, how they nurture and support other minorities, teach diversity, and model inclusion, while we hope for our own!

MAIN FOCUS OF THE CHAPTER

Being a DEI professional at a majority and historically White, private institution can be both challenging and frustrating. The following sections of this chapter encompass personal narratives and brief testimonies that detail the challenging work of Black DEI higher education professionals, my lived experiences, and accounts of other Black HE professionals. These stories detail experiences concerning anti-Blackness, othering, and systems of White supremacist frameworks used to judge the merits of Black women as well as other faculty, staff, and administrators of color. These experiences are framed within the larger context of the history, traditions, and ethos of campuses founded upon institutionalized White supremacy culture.

Thus, the central focus of this chapter is to critically examine my lived experiences in the DEI realm of HE. Specifically, I explore my journey while considering the challenging circumstances discussed throughout the chapter and the overwhelming feelings associated with navigating these happenings. Also, by including parts of my own story in parallel to other Black women in HE, I further demonstrate how the issues described have both socially persisted over time and how my experiences have been shared by other Black women in the field.

A Google form was created to circulate a brief survey to former colleagues to collect personal narratives, using social media platforms to reach them. Each narrative was examined, considering issues that compound Black HE professionals at White institutions and lead to feelings of isolation, exhaustion from invisible labor, and negotiation of their racial identities while navigating microaggressions and instances of bias.

Issues, Controversies, and Problems

I provide insight, as a Black DEI practitioner, through my personal reflections on the complicated struggles to collect, report, and manage campus reports of ongoing microaggressions, bias in the curricula, teaching practices, and persistent marginalization of both my Black colleagues and many marginalized students. Additionally, I describe the challenge to maintain the mental fortitude necessary to process my feelings and synthesize this data for use in institutional policy and practice. Furthermore, to provide examples of the microinvalidations, biased feedback, and disparate treatment Black women face and report, personal narratives from other Black women in higher education are also shared.

Some of the issues discussed in this section include:

- Biased and coded feedback about Black HE professionals regarding their professionalism and work performance.
- Being a Black DEI administrator who works to disrupt and remove bias, racism, and White supremacist culture from university and college campuses while also being subject to the same bias, racism, etc.
- The contradictions between the expectation to fully devote oneself to their work and the harsh experiences of working as a Black DEI professional on these campuses.

With approximately thirteen years of professional experience in HE, ten of which were worked as a director of two DEI offices, I was able to consider the challenges discussed in this chapter. Also, after careful reflection and consideration of the literature regarding this subject, I found my assertions were supported. Through the lens of an African American woman, who graduated from an HBCU, I have personal consternations and made many observations about the issues discussed. Out of these consternations and observations, arises a complicated perspective and position; my perception of the DEI HE industry is that these problems and controversial matters are ingrained into the culture of PWI campuses. They are, however, more saliently felt and experienced by Black DEI professionals as well as BIPOC higher education faculty and staff members in a variety of other roles. Reflecting on my 13 years of higher education and DEI experience was also done, considering the evolving frames and models that have undergirded DEI work overtime. Recognizing the persistence of the stated issues in DEI higher education work has led to a desire to deepen my understanding of the lived experiences of other Black women who function as DEI administrators.

I was a graduate student preparing to enter the HE profession during the emergence of the theoretical frameworks known as Multiculturalism and Multicultural Competence. At that time, much of the literature regarding multicultural competence in student affairs theory was being authored by one of my graduate school professors, Dr. John A. Mueller. In his book, *Multicultural Competence in Student Affairs*, the authors defined multicultural competence as "a necessary prerequisite to efficacious and multiculturally relevant practices at colleges and universities" (Pope et al., 2019, p. 2). It was refreshing and exciting to learn directly from a scholar who contributed significant work to the field of higher education.

Shortly after finishing graduate school, I entered the HE field armed with the knowledge of multicultural counseling theory. The philosophies, therein, fueled my confidence and reassured me of my value and usefulness, to all students, for the first few years I worked. Not long after starting, however, my rose-colored glasses were quickly removed when I observed how Black students segregated for self-preservation at institutions for which I worked. As career transitions moved me to different college campuses, which eventually landed me in the world of diversity work, I realized that Black faculty and staff's experiences mirrored that of the Black students.

Over time, I understood that learning about the theories from graduate school did not prepare me to fight the racialized battles happening around me every day. Those battles helped me exercise my agency as the DEI leader on these PWI campuses, and ultimately helped improve the academic and campus experiences of BIPOC as well as other underrepresented students. These battles also involved White faculty and all White senior level administrators who managed institutional traditions, policies, and practices, which often cause BIPOC faculty, staff, and students to experience hostile and racist learning and work environments.

Higher education DEI work is evolving with the sociocultural and sociopolitical tides. However, one thing has remained as an undercurrent throughout its evolution: the persistence and centrality of Whiteness in the historical practices of higher education. Thus, while higher education shifted its DEI focus from the Black Campus Movements to access and inclusion, universities have slowly led social change. Further, the work regarding issues of gender, religion, sexual orientation, and other identity groups emerged to the forefront (Nixon 2013; Rogers, 2010). The trials, challenges, and struggles of Black DEI professionals in higher education can be characterized by a passage from the foreword of the book *Dismantling Race in Higher Education* (Arday & Mirza, 2018). The foreword, written by Paul Warmington, describes the evolving shift in DEI in higher education by stating," For it is no longer possible to slap on a dash of paint or plaster to disguise the stratification of our higher education system… And it is no longer possible to gloss over the racialised disparities in undergraduate attainment or the blocked pipelines to work…" (Arday & Mirza, 2018, p. ix).

Warmington highlighted the need for DEI work in higher education to stop "covering up" its racist practices and differential treatment of its BIPOC faculty, staff, and students. He further described the need for DEI work in HE to shift away from "glossing over" and towards actually doing the work to address and resolve the disparities.

More Issues, Controversies, and Problems

To illuminate how the problems stated in the existing literature show up on PWI campuses and in the lived experiences of Black women, I share personal narratives from three Black women survey respondents. I highlight these three Black women because, of the survey respondents, their feedback most closely aligned with the book's intent to amplify Black women who work as DEI professionals in higher education. Upon receiving and examining responses to the social media survey, some trends emerged. Five themes are used to share the personal narratives of three Black women survey respondents, in tandem with the details of my lived experiences as a Black woman and DEI professional. In coordination with the stated objectives of the chapter, the themes have been organized into the following five categories:

1. Fake Love
2. Under the Guise of Constructive Criticism

3. Tokenized, Villainized and Weaponized
4. Faculty Distinction
5. Bring your Full Self to Work

Fake Love

This section discusses the warm welcome I received when I was first employed as a DEI practitioner. On the campus of each PWI, where I served as the DEI Director and sole DEI professional on the campus, their communities were described as close-knit, collaborative, and inclusive. On each campus, the organizational structure or, more specifically, the placement of departments on the organizational chart, was integral to how people interacted with one another across the organization. Early in my career, there were intentional efforts made by a variety of campus partners, including staff and faculty units, to engage with my department and express both interest and gratitude.

Over time, my White colleagues made an effort to get to know me. They often spoke to me about their appreciation of the work I was doing on campus. As the DEI work evolved and the impacts of that work reached across the organizational structures, divisions, or silos, their "love" for me and my work dissipated. The deterioration of the "love" can be characterized by the faculty's multiple attempts to intimidate me. Some instances included reaching out to my boss to complain about our interactions, scheduling unnecessary meetings to interrogate me about my work, and the constant scrutiny and policing of my communication style. What I learned was that this love was not genuine from many of the faculty and staff, and if it was, the love was conditional. Although faculty members loved the work I was doing with students regarding diversity, equity, and inclusion, they were uninterested in doing that work in their academic departments.

What stood out about these circumstances was that my work often involved many departments, both academic and student services, and when that work required a conversation or intervention with a student services department, the department's administrators were more receptive to the experience. For example, I spoke on a student run podcast one year when I oversaw a DEI office at one of my former private PWIs. I was asked to describe my role as the DEI administrator on campus, to which I replied that most of my work is done behind-the-scenes. I mentioned that some of my behind-the-scenes work included advocating for students to university leadership. I discussed how class attendance policies might serve as a barrier to student success for underrepresented students because, for instance, we knew that our underrepresented student populations worked close to 30 hours a week. The podcast circulated among faculty, because there were a few faculty members who were uncomfortable and unhappy with my tone and reference to "their" attendance policy.

Not long after, I received a scolding email from an academic administrator. In the following weeks, I met with several faculty members, along with my supervisor where a space was created for faculty to air their grievances regarding the podcast. During this incident, the feelings and thoughts of all faculty members involved, all of whom were White, were centered in all communications. Interestingly, there was a Black faculty member present for the sit-down meeting, and they expressed a sentiment opposite from the White faculty. The Black faculty member articulately and carefully expressed that when they listened to the podcast (even after being prompted to do so by an upset White academic colleague), they interpreted my use of absence policies as an example and not a critique of our institution's actual policy. This is also what I communicated when the issue was initially raised by faculty. This explanation (from me) and perception of the situation (from the Black faculty member) was disregarded and deemed insufficient, given how I spoke on the podcast and my word choice made them uncomfortable. I was asked to be more careful when speaking on a public forum. Further, I was told, in the meeting, by the Vice President for Academic Affairs, that our attendance policy would never change and I should refrain from speaking on it to avoid giving the impression that it might.

It was clear to me that, regarding this matter, the perspectives and feelings of their DEI leader (me) and their Black colleague were not valued. Considering this situation, the overarching sentiment was clear: I was not to question or speak on an academic matter when I was not an academic. Their right to comfort overrode any ideas, thoughts, and levels of comfort I might have had. This is an example of how the characteristics of White supremacy culture (Okun, 2000) is exhibited, particularly when the DEI leader involved is a Black woman. Several of the faculty members involved in this example also happened to be the same faculty members who lauded my work in the past and expressed "fake love" towards me.

Even when the work history of Black women HE professionals is highly regarded and they ascend to more senior-level roles within PWIs, they are continually lambasted and confronted with microaggressions and overtly harsh critiques of their work. Lloyd-Jones' (2009) case study regarding senior level African American women in PWIs discusses a similar story. The following is a personal narrative from a survey participant, who self-identifies as Black or African American. When asked how frequently they believed, felt, or perceived that the feedback they received, from White colleagues and White direct reports, was coded or biased, the participant responded they often felt this way. The following Black female DEI professional has a long tenure in HE diversity work and transitioned from Director of Multicultural Affairs to Assistant Dean for Multicultural Affairs to Associate Dean of Institutional Diversity. The advancements in her career were coupled with a long history of micro aggressive encounters, the questioning of her knowledge and expertise, and other biased and oppressive experiences. She said,

...a student asked to meet with me regarding a program that she and others were planning, in recognition of Holocaust Remembrance Day. Upon meeting, the student shared the plan for the program and that, through study, that she was very knowledgeable of the Holocaust. I engaged in the conversation, sharing what I'd been learning and just off the top of my head, and with no ill intent, wondered aloud of just what would make Hitler and his cronies commit such atrocities?!

The question really wasn't one for the student to address or explain, and she didn't offer any response; it was really a rhetorical question like one would ask (wonder) of any senselessness. The student left saying she would share the flyer and information about the program. A day or so later, I was contacted by the head of Human Resources (HR) informing that a complaint had been filed against me by the student! The student shared our conversation with a faculty advisor who found my "query" to be anti-Semitic and encouraged the student to file a complaint with the provost (to whom I reported) and to HR. Other faculty of Jewish ancestry also either met with or shared their outrage and support of the complaint with the head of HR via emails. HR proceeded with an investigation that lasted about two or three weeks, meeting with and interviewing/questioning me on at least two occasions about the conversations that I had with the student, and I shared that the student never indicated to me that she was upset by our conversation. Irrespective of this fact, the head of HR wrote me up! To make matters worse, the university's General Council and the head of HR agreed that this "offense" didn't rise to a level requiring the Civility Flag to be lowered, several Jewish members of the university community INSISTED that it be lowered and threatened to call in the ADL, an organization dedicated to "stop[ing] the defamation of the Jewish people, and to secure justice and fair treatment to all" (ADL, n.d., para. 1). The VP of EM[enrollment management] gave in to the pressure and did as they wanted [lowering the civility flag].

Needless to say, but I was PISSED and angry at the whole damned process. What did they mean by lower[ing] "the flag" on the head of Diversity?! I was the one who truly supported all folks on that campus, including Jewish students. I, a Black woman, the institution's head DEI professional, endured a process that was originally designed to foster inclusion, by holding people accountable and creating space for carefully facilitated dialogue, when it was decided to "lower the civility flag" with no institutional support. In this instance, I was alleged to have enacted the incivility and, for me, going through this process was highly stressful, arduous, and emotionally challenging."

In these types of cases, the DEI professional is usually the one to provide support and advocacy for all parties involved, especially when the "civility flag" is lowered on campus. Therefore, who advocates for the needs of the DEI professional when that flag is lowered on us? Are we not also valued members of the community, whose thoughts and lived experiences should be affirmed and included in the same ways that other campus community members are?

Under the Guise of Constructive Criticism

Another emergent theme from the survey responses developed because several respondents expressed having difficulty processing and reacting to feedback from White colleagues and, more specifically, White managers or supervisors. The expressed difficulty in explicitly naming the feedback as either racist, biased, or based in White supremist frames of understanding professionalism was due to the feedback being delivered using formal feedback or evaluation processes. As such, Black HE professional experienced these moments as a "guise" for giving a colleague or direct report "constructive criticism" but they were received by the recipients as coded or racist. Next, I outline and describe some of the feedback received by BIPOC faculty or staff at the PWIs where I served as the lead DEI administrator. Also included are personal narratives from several BIPOC HE professionals, in addition to my own, which detail our experiences regarding coded and biased feedback we have received.

Early in my career, there was a situation during which I received coded feedback from a direct report. The feedback included comments regarding how I presented myself in meetings as "Steph, the Philly girl" and "Miss Stephanie Reed, the DEI Director" at other times. I interpreted this as a comparison between my intersecting identities and as a judgment of how I expressed myself in meetings. During staff or committee meetings, my supervisor often remarked about who he "observed in the meeting", based on what discussed and how I spoke. In other words, he examined my speech, body language, and expressions to determine and take note of when I switched my style of speech and demeanor between the more professional *Ms. Reed* and "less professional" *Steph Reed*. This is an example of coded feedback. It demonstrated the hypocrisy of being told to be my full self while at work and then having my identity used against me. This feedback was code for the "unprofessionalism" in my Blackness, versus my work persona. This feedback could also be interpreted or understood as an assertion of male privilege and misogynoir, considering my supervisor was a male. Further, a colleague who observed and directly heard the feedback given to me by my supervisor shared with me that they were profoundly disturbed by the exchanges.

Comparatively, the experiences of other BIPOC HE professionals, who work specifically on private and predominantly White campuses, was explored. A six-question survey was distributed to collect the experiences of other BIPOC HE professionals. One question asked participants to use a Likert scale to rate how frequently they felt or believed they received coded or biased feedback. The choices were on a scale of 1-5, with1 being "Hardly Ever" and 5 indicating that they "Always" felt or believed they received coded or biased feedback. The responses to the social media survey gathered a variety of experiences and allowed for a comparison to my experiences. With the personal narratives of others, I can offer multiple perspectives as well as explore and analyze the experiences of colleagues on other campuses alongside my own.

Below is the personal narrative of a HE professional who identifies as Hispanic/Latinx. When asked on the survey about coded feedback, their response was "3"—they sometimes felt or believed that they received coded or biased feedback. They said,

I have found that when reporting to, specifically, cis, heterosexual White men, there was a disregard for considering my identities in how they provided and delivered feedback. It felt like they forgot and feel this likely was informed by me being White passing…

I also find when interacting with or presenting ideas to coworkers of privileged identities (mostly cis White men and women) informed by research or experience of marginalized communities, there is an immediate resistance and a questioning of why the idea is relevant or necessary. I was often asked how this idea/project/program was inclusive versus exclusive because it seemed to only benefit one group. We neglect that there is opportunity for all to learn, whether they hold the identities or not. Just because you have not experienced it, does not make it less valid…

Below is another example and personal narrative provided by a survey respondent, who identifies as Black/African American. When asked on the survey about coded feedback, their response was "4"—they often felt or believed that they received coded or biased feedback. They said,

When it came time for my annual review, I was scored a 2/3 for most of the sections because a 3 means that you're perfect without room for improvement, according to my chair and director. They, essentially, told me that they needed to critique me now because it would seem out of place for them to do this in my third year. They emphasized that it had also been done to them. There were areas that they scored me that they had no real knowledge of because they were not present. There was no discussion about the section but they scored me under the maximum of 3 because they could. Those scores were tied to my merit increase, which I earned. Fast forward a few months, my director attempted to reduce my merit increase by 50%, because a colleague would not receive hers (department rules) and for the purposes of equity, based on gender and race, he wanted to keep our salaries exactly the same. Our director is a Black man who operates as an agent of White supremacy. He makes intentional strides to sabotage the work that we do in order to minimize our impact and effort.

This following example is from a BIPOC professional who identifies as Black/African American. When this respondent was asked on the survey about coded feedback, their response was "2"—they seldom felt or believed that they received coded or biased feedback. However, they discussed examples of when they did receive this feedback. They said,

I typically saw this around the amount of work that was placed on me (as a Black woman) and other Black women. When providing feedback about the amount of work being too much or inequitable, I was often

met with phrases like 'you can do it! 'If anyone can do it, you can,' etc. This is harmful and often tied to the amount of labor Black women must do to be recognized and taken seriously on the job. This feedback came from my VP, who was a White man....while not from a superior, I did receive coded feedback from colleagues around the creation of the Black Student Union and the Latin Student Union. I was met with coded language like 'divisive' and 'exclusive' when discussing these groups. There was also a clear lack of knowledge around why these types of groups were important for students, especially those at PWIs.

The final personal narrative is from a survey respondent who identifies as Black/African American. When asked on the survey about receiving coded feedback, their response was also "4"—they often felt or believed that they received coded or biased feedback. They said,

September 2017, I had been in the role of Academic Advisor for X University's School of Professional Studies program (adult learners) for five years...had been promoted a few times, was well liked and respected by my peers, students, alumni, and board members. The SPS program was comprised of three staff members: myself as the Academic Advisor; an Admissions Counselor; and a White woman (who we'll name Mandy) whose title, at that time, I cannot recall,...(but it was on the same level as my own). We, all three, worked together in the SPS program but each reported to different managers. A few days prior to Labor Day 2017, I had submitted a vacation request... My direct manager, a White woman, approved my vacation request with no questions or issues. However, once Mandy discovered that I was going to be on vacation for two days during the Add/Drop period of the SPS program, she came into my office and confronted me on the timing of my request. She very sternly told me that she did not think it was the best decision and that I should always be available to help the students. I sat there too stunned.... Mandy left my office, I immediately sent an email to my manager,... asking for her to intercede on my behalf with this issue.

Once I had a few minutes to digest what had happened, I then went to Mandy's office down the hall and expressed my discontent with her, telling her that I did not appreciate her stepping out of her role and speaking to me as though I reported to her. This interaction lasted no more than 2-3 minutes and I thought that it was over. I received no response from my manager... and I took my vacation, as was approved. Fast forward to two weeks later...still no response from my manager on this issue,... The situation was eventually escalated to the Vice President of Academic Affairs, a White male. In the meeting with the Vice President and my manager, they were both uninterested in hearing about Mandy coming into my office to confront me on my time-off request and they only focused on me circling back to Mandy with my own frustration.

My manager's words to me were that she would have eventually spoken to Mandy on the situation and that I did not give her time. The Vice President's words to me were that he was disappointed that I had not offered an apology for my actions in confronting Mandy. He said to me that I did not appear to be regretful and in my opinion, it was though he was trying to 'break me down.'...both my manager and Vice President made statements to me that they were both doing me a favor by just keeping this as a chat... I felt belittled, ignored, and [singled] out, due to me being a Black woman and Mandy being White.

A common thread in the stories shared in this section is that each situation in which the bias or coded feedback was given, it was delivered by a supervisor.

Tokenized, Villainized, and Weaponized

In this section, I discuss my own experiences with being tokenized, villainized, and weaponized by the universities where I worked as a DEI administrator. This chapter includes several accounts of each issue, the effects of those incidents on me, and how they affected my ability to show up as my full self, maintain professionalism, as well as navigate my capacity to manage my productivity, performance, and professional development. I detailed this earlier in the document with an account of being villainized, from the Black woman and DEI Associate Vice President, whose story was previously shared. While under investigation, she still had to manage all other instances of racism, hate, bias, etc. across the campus community. Additionally, while under the stress of the previous account, she also dealt with this potential case of retaliation and villainization. She said,

...a student of the Muslim faith and of Palestinian ancestry contacted me about the anti-Palestinian remarks made to him by a faculty member who identified himself to the student as being a Zionist. Of the most offensive remarks the faculty member made to the student,... was referring to the student as 'a Palestinian terrorist.' I received the complaint, I wrote up and shared the complaint with the then President, all cabinet members, and the head of HR. An investigation was conducted, but I was never called.... later on campus ...She then informed me that the faculty member who called the student a terrorist was among those complained about me.

My experience was similar, regarding dealing with backlash from exposing racism, interrupting it, and calling it out. I was teaching students how to do the same while helping all students find and amplify their voices. Essentially, doing the job I was hired to do, as the DEI Director, highlighted me as the "villain" in all too many tense situations on campus, involving students and faculty. As noted in the earlier podcast-related narrative, the faculty at one institution tended to, first, gain consensus among their faculty peers on any issue they had with the work of my department, particularly as it related to any academic policy or practice, before talking with me. I called this their attempt to "galvanize the troops" before "confronting me" with their objections. Often, these meetings or email exchanges did not encompass a sentiment of understanding but of interrogation and scolding. The communication lacked empathy and was rigid.

Faculty Distinction

There has been a wealth of research conducted regarding the overall experiences of faculty of color in academia. Research from Harris (2020) articulated that "faculty of color face pushback from White students who challenge their authority and intelligence in the classroom because they do not fit a prototypical faculty norm, i.e., White cisgender man" (p. 229). While I may suggest that being a faculty member holds a particular distinction on a college campus, there is literature to document that BIPOC faculty are still subject to lack of support from other Black faculty due to lagging BIPOC representation, disregard of experience and knowledge, microaggressions and micro invalidations (Turner & Grauerholz, 2017).

There is limited literature regarding HE, as it relates to being both a DEI officer for a university and a full faculty member. In this section of the chapter, I explore the notion that it is most effective and impactful for DEI HE professionals to hold a faculty title and position in DEI work on a college campus. We explore this through research and my narratives, as a BIPOC woman and DEI practitioner without a faculty title. Being expected to introduce, manage, and sustain significant organizational transformation within academic units of a university requires the support of faculty and access to the protected process of faculty governance.

There were several occurrences when I was met with strong faculty resistance. The aforementioned podcast narrative was one such time. The diversity and inclusion office was identified as the place where students could escape the traumas of inhabiting hostile learning environments. These hostile environments were often labeled as such, as the result of faculty being unprepared and under-trained to facilitate the difficult conversations around race in their course content. In these situations, which occurred almost weekly, the students sought advice regarding how to fight their discontent through their participation in class discussions, but they would often return to my office diminished, exhausted, and sometimes tearful. Their feelings were less about the course content and dissenting opinions and more about not being seen or heard and their views not being accepted as valid. This, ultimately, meant their lived experiences were not affirmed. Meanwhile, their White student peers not only dominated the discussions, but their lived experiences and perspectives were often validated and accepted as truth. Most times, the BIPOC students just wanted the instructor to be better equipped to include all perspectives, equitably, in class discussions.

In the multiple conversations about what took place in the classrooms on every campus I worked, it was rare that students wanted to do anything about it, due to their fear of retribution from their professor. In the book *Teaching About Race and Racism in the College Classroom*, author Cyndi Kernahan (2019) reminded us of research by Sarah Cavanagh (2016) by pointing out that instructors have a lot of power. In the book, Kernahan outlined how power works by quoting Sarah Cavanagh's research, which states, "we are the ones who decide on the content…and determine grades" (p. 85).

At one institution, I was asked to develop and implement a university-wide system to report and investigate incidents of bias. This new policy and bias reporting system also applied to the classroom, which meant faculty were expected to learn to use it as employees and refer students to it. However, friction arose when faculty realized they could be reported for bias.

At the request of the university president, I created this new policy and reporting system, in partnership with the office of human resources, and sought the involvement of the faculty. I was rebuffed. Their responses were either that they did not have time to be involved or their course loads were all too heavy, and to compensate, they would send "faculty representation" to meetings when time allowed. My work moved forward, and I kept the faculty abreast of progress and decisions through a faculty liaison. However, I never received direct faculty response, nor did any faculty attend the multiple meetings convened to execute this endeavor.

One year later, a campus-wide soft launch event was held to educate the university's community regarding the new policy and resource. In planning the soft launch, we distributed a flow chart, a handout with talking points, and a frequently asked questions section (with answers); all of which had been fully vetted and approved by the senior leadership of the university. Suddenly, on launch day, there were emails sent from faculty to HR, voicing concerns, with attempts to interrupt the launch. HR's response to faculty was that time had been allotted to them to submit their input, and it was ignored. Therefore, the launch proceeded. This created a new sense of urgency among the faculty, and a town hall meeting with the diversity office, faculty members, and human resources was called. It should be noted that on this campus, some staff administrators were asked to teach College 101 and career development required courses, because the faculty did not have the bandwidth to teach all the sections. I was one of those staff members, but this did not give me (or any other staff member) a faculty title or access to faculty governance. I contended that if my role held dual responsibility as a DEI administrator and a full- or part-time professor of a particular discipline, the above process of launching this bias reporting system would have been executed differently.

Having a title and role positioned within an academic unit, college, or school, as a DEI administrator, provides more direct access to faculty governance. Faculty positionality within the institution and how faculty governance benefits and insulates the faculty body demonstrates that having faculty distinction in HE, matters when conducting DEI work. Research conducted by Jeffrey K. Grim et al. (2020) calls this "Legitimacy in Academic Context." In a study of academic diversity officers (ADOs), Grim stated that "ADOs mentioned two types of legitimacy that garnered differential status for ADOs: disciplinary legitimacy and academic standing legitimacy". The article further mentioned, "being able to provide the appropriate framing for faculty… gave DEI initiatives and the ADO legitimacy within the specific academic context" (p. 143).

Furthermore, the findings of this study maintained that what is referred to as "academic standing legitimacy" is achieved by being a faculty member. ADOs who had faculty roles recognized that they had an advantage in executing DEI initiatives.

In some cases, when a DEI officer has background and experience as a staff member and is a member of the faculty with teaching responsibilities, it lends itself to greater impact and success. The faculty distinction is vital to build faculty buy-in and necessary for lasting curricular changes. The distinction is also essential for being supported in efforts to develop or propose pedagogical training, which can introduce significant changes to the classroom experiences of students, particularly students of color.

Bring Your Full Self to Work; Except You, You Must Be Switzerland

Many colleges and universities still do not have a critical mass of diversity on their campuses. Given this, these institutions, even with some representation (including DEI administrator roles), will always be colonial and force assimilation. Thus, DEI work in HE is often exhausting for women of color and BIPOC HE professionals, at large. It has become standard policy and practice at every college and university across the country to encourage employees, at every level of the institution, to bring their full selves to work. Further, this has become part of the English lexicon and is now a social norm and expectation in almost all industries. However, Sarah Ahmed (2018) stated in her work that "when women of color enter the institutions of whiteness, we become symbols of diversity. And we have to do diversity as well as be diversity" (p. 338). Those of us who are DEI administrators on historically and predominantly White academic campuses must be armed with a specialized skillset and demonstrate neutrality, although we may be deeply triggered by our work.

As the DEI administrator on PWI campuses, I managed my struggles with faculty while also being a resource and providing support to faculty of color (who dealt with resistance within their departments and among their faculty colleagues). In the last section, I describe the difficulty of being able to be myself in the workplace as the DEI administrator. I discuss how I struggled to have a sense of belonging on a campus where I created it for so many others. I use examples to shed light on the unwritten expectations, acts of covering, and the exhausting efforts to remain a neutral party during very triggering and high intensity racially charged circumstances.

When I reported to the dean of students early in my DEI career, I handled many requests to be a mediator and facilitator between an all-White staff in the student leadership office and BIPOC students who felt they were treated with bias, when applying for leadership roles. When the BIPOC students were in those roles, they reported feeling as if they were marginalized and harshly judged, in comparison to their

White peers in the same roles. As time went on, a substantial percentage of the Black student population planned a protest. These students sought me out during their planning to ensure their activism was aligned with the student code of conduct. As they were drafting a list of demands, I became painfully aware of all the issues the students were protesting. The protest focused on two issues:

1. The academic deans and faculty making decisions for and about Black students, without involving Black students in the decision-making process.
2. The lack of opportunity for student leadership among BIPOC students in student government and the student programming board.

What followed this series of events was an underlying sentiment of resentment from my more senior colleagues, including my supervisor, the dean of students. There were also contradictory sentiments from faculty colleagues, who reached out to express an appreciation for me in supporting the students in their activism; however, these exchanges felt more like inquisitions than they did innocuous conversations or compliments. There was not any inquiry from campus administrative leaders into my experience as a BIPOC person in the minutia of a highly sensitive racially tense situation. Even after the student newspaper deemed the events a "racial uprising" on what was normally a very quiet campus, there had been no inquiry into how a potential "racial uprising" would affect the DEI professional, who identified as a member of the same race. I had already deeply considered leaving the institution because of the lack of support and growth afforded to me in my role, and I resigned from the university within a year, taking another DEI position at a better financially resourced university (though still not an HBCU). I should acknowledge that I thought the protest was incredibly well done, and I was extremely proud of the students.

Regarding all the issues and controversial situations on many PWI campuses, students are, unfortunately, at the center. They are not highlighted in the beneficial way that centers the needs and experiences of students, however. Students were often caught in the middle of bureaucratic processes littered with the personal biases of faculty and staff. I conclude this section with one last personal narrative from a BIPOC woman and DEI administrator in HE. She declared,

I left that university in mid-August of 2020 after having served for 15-12 years in several capacities, including the initial Title IX Coordinator for 3 years when I was still but an office of one in the Diversity Office, feeling exhausted, unappreciated and ill-supported...I loved, served, supported, and advocated for the students and employees, especially those of color, and gave the best that I had. Since leaving, I must say that it was good to hear from friends and colleagues who shared that at least for the first year of my not being there that not a day went by that someone didn't mention my name regarding all that I had done. As I have said.... Sometimes you have to be silent to be heard and absent to be seen.

SOLUTIONS AND RECOMMENDATIONS

Black women who conduct DEI work in HE face considerable challenges. I suggest that colleges and universities make efforts to provide supports for DEI practitioners. As an industry, HE must acknowledge that the professionals they hire to lead DEI efforts must take measures for self-preservation while doing this work. It would prove beneficial for universities to provide intentionally race-conscious institutional support through programming for their DEI professionals. This should also encompass training for the faculty and staff, at large, to recognize how institutional racism, White supremacy culture, and bias are pervasive. Finally, institutions should operationalize practices to identify and mitigate these challenges. Some additional ways to deal with the issues and problems outlined throughout this chapter include:

- Engage BIPOC alumni, with intentional focus on creating support networks for current BIPOC students.
- Include BIPOC alumni in strategy sessions, to improve teaching practices and programming on campus.
- Build community partnerships that are intentionally collaborative within the local arts community. Given community art tends to operate in very collaborative and co-creative ways, it serves as a potential model for university practice.
- Give attention to these sensitive and potentially controversial issues in HE graduate program coursework, using case studies that center race.

FUTURE RESEARCH DIRECTIONS

Knowing that universities still struggle with issues, such as achieving a critical mass of diversity in this more conscious post-George Floyd era, we can safely say there is room for more work. It is also a common phrase in DEI work that "the work is never finished", and doing this work means we are ushering universities on a DEI journey. As such, there are many opportunities to conduct more research regarding the persistent and evolving barriers to the success of DEI work in higher education. More specifically, research should take a closer look at the experiences of BIPOC women who carry the majority of the work in HE. We suggest research such as:

- Exploring how effective leaders and inclusive institutions, who state they are committed to furthering DEI on their campuses, respond to challenges and tensions that persist.
- Tracking and measuring any differences in the perceptions of DEI work in HE across lived experiences and intersecting identities where the data is stratified across those differences.
- Examining if campus climate assessments and documented reports of bias from BIPOC faculty, staff, and students show disparate numbers.
- Conducting a study that examines if the stated DEI values of the institution match the experiences of BIPOC faculty and staff.

CONCLUSION

Leaders in HE must acknowledge the struggles and barriers that present themselves when engaging in this work as a staff member. Only then can the requisite interventions, such as professional development trainings, organizational restructures, and division cross-trainings take place. The timing of this book, unfortunately, comes shortly after the loss of bell hooks, a pioneering writer on topics such as intersectional feminism and love, as well as the author of *Teaching to Transgress*. The imagery on her book cover and use of the term "La Escalera" deeply impacted me as an educator. This profound book was motivation for me during tough times in the academe. The symbolism in the image of a ladder on the book cover, and the very essence of the book's message, aligned with my "why". The book tells the story of my purpose for working in HE, particularly for PWIs. Ironically, this also describes my reasons for leaving the field of HE. The system that is HE does not want to see the transgression that this book represented.

My work is now HE adjacent. I can freely "teach to transgress" as an independent writer and entrepreneur. However, I cannot sit idly by, observing the oppression of students of color with little power, agency, and ability to advocate for their own needs. Therefore, I began this chapter with the quote from Mr. Lerone Bennett, Jr. I interpret the words of Mr. Bennett as a call to action and, thus, my work will always be to unashamedly pursue the fair treatment of BIPOC students. This quote compels me to show up each day armed to fight the oppressive, White supremist culture interwoven into the fabric and structures of higher education. I close with another quote from Sarah Ahmed whose sentiments reflect my own thoughts concerning DEI work in HE as a Black woman:

"On reflection it was my own experience of diversity work that led me to realize that working in house would not transform that masters house."

ACKNOWLEDGMENT

This research received no specific grant from any funding agency in the public, commercial, or not-for-profit sectors.

REFERENCES

ADL. (n.d.). Our mission. *.ADL.* https://www.adl.org/who-we-are/our-mission

Ahmed, S. (2018). Rocking the boat: Women of colour as diversity workers. In J. Arday & H. S. Mirza (Eds.), *Dismantling race in higher education: Racism, whiteness and decolonising the academy,* (pp. 331–348). Palgrave Macmillan. doi:10.1007/978-3-319-60261-5_19

Anderson, G. (2020). The emotional toll of racism. *Inside Higher Education.* https://www.insidehighered.com/booklet/leadership-pursuit-diversity-equity-and-inclusion

Arday, J., & Mirza, H. S. (Eds.). (2018). *Dismantling race in higher education: Racism, Whiteness and decolonising the academy.* Palgrave Macmillan. doi:10.1007/978-3-319-60261-5

Becks-Moody, G. M. (2004). *African American women administrators in higher education: Exploring the challenges and experiences at Louisiana public colleges and universities* (Publication No. 2074) [Doctoral dissertation]. Louisiana State University, USA.

Davis, D. R., & Maldonado, C. (2015). Shattering the glass ceiling: The leadership development of African American women in higher education. *Advancing Women in Leadership Journal, 35,* 48–64.

Dees, D. L. (2019). *" The help" & the unhelpful educator: An analysis of racial socialization, anti-Blackness, & prosocial behavior in post-secondary educators* [Doctoral dissertation]. California State University, USA.

Flaherty, C. (2021, May 3). Multiple Black professors have resigned in recent years over racism. *Inside Higher Ed.* https://www.insidehighered.com/news/2021/05/03/multiple-black-professors-have-resigned-recent-years-over-racism

Greene, J., & Paul, J. (2021). Diversity university: DEI bloat in the academy. *Heritage Foundation Backgrounder*, (3641).

Grim, J. K., Sánchez-Parkinson, L., Ting, M., & Chavous, T. (2019). The experiences of academic diversity officers at the University of Michigan. *NCID Currents, 1*(1).

Harris, C. H. (2020). Multiracial faculty members' experiences with teaching, research, and service. *Journal of Diversity in Higher Education, 13*(3), 228–239. doi:10.1037/dhe0000123

Henry, W. J., & Glenn, N. M. (2009). Black women employed in the ivory tower: Connecting for success. *Advancing Women in Leadership Journal, 29.*

Hooks, B. (2014). *Teaching to transgress.* Routledge. doi:10.4324/9780203700280

Howard-Hamilton, M. F. (2003). Theoretical frameworks for African American women. *New Directions for Student Services, 2003*(104), 19–27. doi:10.1002s.104

Jones, K., & Okun, T. (2000). White supremacy culture. *Dismantling racism: A workbook for social change groups.* Change Work. https://www.kbtheatre.org/uploads/4/6/5/8/46588037/white_supremacy_culture_1.pdf

Kernahan, C. (2019). *Teaching about race and racism in the college classroom: Notes from a White professor.* West Virginia University Press.

Lloyd-Jones, B. (2009). Implications of race and gender in higher education administration: An African American woman's perspective. *Advances in Developing Human Resources, 11*(5), 606–618. doi:10.1177/1523422309351820

Maraña, J. A. J. (2016). *The lived experiences of women of color chief diversity officers* (Order No. 10250697). ProQuest Dissertations & Theses Global. (1867777302).

Nixon, M. L. (2013). *Women of color chief diversity officers: Their positionality and agency in higher education institutions* (Publication No. 1428435516) [Doctoral dissertation]. University of Washington, USA.

Pope, R. L., Reynolds, A. L., & Mueller, J. A. (2019). *Multicultural competence in student affairs: Advancing social justice and inclusion.* John Wiley & Sons.

Rogers, I. H. (2009). *The Black campus movement: An Afrocentric narrative history of the struggle to diversify higher education, 1965–1972.* Temple University.

Turner, C., & Grauerholz, L. (2017). Introducing the invisible man: Black male professionals in higher education. *Humboldt Journal of Social Relations, 39*(39), 212–227. doi:10.55671/0160-4341.1013

West, N. M. (2021). Embodying Black feminist epistemology to make green grass grow: The transition from administrator to academic for a Black woman in student affairs. *Journal of Diversity in Higher Education.*

Worthington, R. L., Stanley, C. A., & Smith, D. G. (2020). Advancing the professionalization of diversity officers in higher education: Report of the presidential task force on the revision of the NADOHE standards of professional practice. *Journal of Diversity in Higher Education, 13*(1), 1–22. doi:10.1037/dhe0000175

ADDITIONAL READING

Bennett, L. (2003). *Before the Mayflower: A history of Black America.* Johnson Publishing Company Incorporated.

Clark, C., Fasching-Varner, K. J., & Brimhall-Vargas, M. (Eds.). (2012). *Occupying the academy: Just how important is diversity work in higher education?* Rowman & Littlefield.

Hodges, C. R., & Welch, O. M. (2021). *Truth without tears: African American women deans share lessons in leadership.* Harvard Education Press.

Hope, K. K. (Ed.). (2019). *Black women speaking from within: Essays and experiences in higher education.* Peter Lang. doi:10.3726/b14908

Jackson, A. P., & Dorsey, M. R. (2009). *Achieving against the odds: African American professional women in higher education.* AuthorHouse.

Mabokela, R. O., & Green, A. L. (2001). *Sisters of the academy: Emergent Black women scholars in higher education.* Stylus Publishing, LLC.

Robinson-Neal, A. (2009). Exploring diversity in higher education management: History, trends, and implications for community colleges. *International Electronic Journal for Leadership in Learning, 13*(4), n4.

Truehill, M. E. (2021). Black women leaders professional and social experiences in higher education: A review of the research literature. *Journal of Research Initiatives, 5*(3), 3.

Turner, C., & Grauerholz, L. (2017). Introducing the invisible man: Black professionals in higher education. *Humboldt Journal of Social Relations, 39*(39), 212–227. doi:10.55671/0160-4341.1013

Whitford, E. (2020, October 28). Black administrators are too rare at the top ranks of higher education. It's not just a pipeline problem. *Inside Higher Ed.* https://www.insidehighered.com/news/2020/10/28/black-administrators-are-too-rare-top-ranks-higher-education-it%E2%80%99s-not-just-pipeline

Worthington, R. L. (2012). Advancing scholarship for the diversity imperative in higher education: An editorial [Editorial]. *Journal of Diversity in Higher Education, 5*(1), 1–7. doi:10.1037/a0027184

KEY TERMS AND DEFINITIONS

Bias: Prejudicial leaning, treatment, or action that is for, in favor of, or against a person or group based on their perceived membership in a particular group such as race or gender. It is perceived as negative and unfair treatment or judgement.

Coded Language: The replacement of language used to describe racial identity and the way society sees a group of people by using purportedly unbiased terms that conceal explicit or implicit racial acrimony. Fostering fear and anxiety by further dehumanizing and criminalizing a group of people, typically people of color, without the use of words that are overtly racist or biased.

Intersectional: related or referring to intersectionality, when using intersectionality as an approach, framework, or perspective.

Micro-Aggressive: When an environment or set of behaviors within the environment is characterized as having many or frequent micro-aggressions.

Personal Narrative: A story or testimony given by an individual about their lived experiences with a particular subject.

Racial Equity: The act of intentionally and systemically eliminating racial disparities through measurable actions or strategies and outcomes by eradicating any practices, policies, or structures that act as persistent barriers to access and or success.

Racial Identity: How an individual defines their sense of self with respect to being a member of a specific racial group.

Tokenized: When a person, who is BIPOC, is inauthentically included or invited to participate in a group, process or activity, but at face value only. Also, when a BIPOC individual is spotlighted as an example of an oppressed segment of society by an individual or group, giving the false appearance of inclusion, fairness and/or equity.

Chapter 11
Intersectionality in Leadership: Spotlighting the Experiences of Black Women DEI Leaders in Historically White Academic Institutions

Natasha N. Johnson
https://orcid.org/0000-0001-8145-2153
Georgia State University, USA

ABSTRACT

Due to their multiple identities, Black women navigate gendered and racialized pathways to leadership in the US education industry. The journey for Black women in and en route to positions of academic leadership is even more nuanced and multiplicative. Little, though, is known about the effects of their intersecting identities and the structural barriers they encounter in this sphere. To deepen our communal understanding of this phenomenon, this chapter highlights the existing theories and research on the race-gender dyad in the context of academic leadership. Examining the individual and layered effects of race and gender on the professional realities of Black women leaders in higher education, the author spotlights the unique experiences of Black women DEI practitioners and leaders in historically White academic institutions. Given the numerous components at play when Black women lead in predominantly White institutions and settings, this chapter concludes by discussing opportunities to advance relevant research and practice in this arena.

INTRODUCTION

In 2010, Andrew Sherrill, Director of Education, Workforce, and Income Security, United States Government Accountability Office (GAO), provided testimony before the Joint Economic Committee, US Congress, on women's representation, pay, and characteristics in management positions. In his statement, he discussed "issues related to women in management. Although women's representation in the workforce is growing, there remains a need for information about the challenges women face in advancing their careers" (Sherrill, 2010, p. 1). In their more comprehensive report, the Honorable Carolyn B. Maloney,

DOI: 10.4018/978-1-6684-3564-9.ch011

Chair of the Joint Economic Committee, United States Congress, and the Honorable John D. Dingell, House of Representatives, echoed similar sentiments. Based on their estimations,

Female managers earned 81 cents for every dollar earned by male managers in 2007, compared to 79 cents in 2000. The estimated adjusted pay difference varied by industry sector, with female managers' earnings ranging from 78 cents to 87 cents for every dollar earned by male managers in 2007, depending on the industry sector. (US Government Accountability Office, 2010, p. 3).

According to the Center for American Progress, women constitute a majority, at 50.8 percent, of the US population, earning roughly 57 percent of all undergraduate and 59 percent of all graduate degrees (Warner et al., 2018). Yet, although American women hold about 52 percent of all management- and professional-level jobs, they lag considerably behind men in leadership positions across every sector (Dezső et al., 2016; Goethals & Hoyt, 2017; Warner et al., 2018).

What is absent from this body of literature is the consideration of context. Contextual factors, or in this case, the intersection of race, gender, and leadership in traditionally patriarchal spaces, speak to the multiple identities of Black women in varying US educational settings (Evans, 2008; Johnson, 2021, 2022). Without accounting for context, a proper understanding of gender and racial inequities in education leadership remains elusive. An example of this is the consideration of the 'leadership divide.' Burke and Collins (2001) found that despite the notions of political correctness prevalent in North American corporations, the old boy network continues to thrive. The authors also discovered that male employees purposefully generate institutional impediments to freeze women's advancement. At a cultural level, the dominant male network fosters solidarity between males and sexualizes, threatens, marginalizes, controls, and divides females through organizational power structures (Burke & Collins, 2021). Specifically, Burke and Collins (2001) found that male managers tend to perceive the characteristics needed for managerial success as being associated with those generally attributed to men.

This leadership divide is particularly apparent in the field of education large-scale, a sphere in which women comprise a majority of the workforce (Bell & Nkomo, 2001; Hymowitz & Schellhardt, 1986). For Black women in the United States of America, another layer of incongruity lies in the fact that despite their relatively heightened levels of educational attainment (Grogan & Shakeshaft, 2010; Helm, 2016), they generally find themselves at the lower tiers of the organizational pecking order (Betters-Reed & Moore, 1995; Davidson & Burke, 2000; Eagly et al., 2007). This incongruence, coupled with Burke and Collins' finding that male managers may not consider female characteristics essential for managerial success, can negatively influence institutional cultures, climates, and promotional decisions.

Historically, White institutions have worked on actively advancing their focus on diversity, equity, and inclusion practices in their respective organizations (El-Amin, 2022; Showunmi, 2021). Numerous organizations support and even feature diversity practitioners within their workforce. Despite this growing trend, still many traditionally White organizations and institutions still grapple with longstanding, systemic inequities stemming primarily from within. In the aftermath of the dual pandemics of COVID-19 and systemic racism (Johnson, 2023), it is vital for academic institutions to better understand Black women's experiences in and en route to leadership so that they may implement the needed changes to promote more diverse, inclusive, and equitable environments (Johnson, 2023). In light of this, it is increasingly essential to center Black women's paths large-scale – before, during, and after the noted pandemics – across all institutional sectors, public and private (e.g., academia, corporate America, healthcare, public service, etcetera). It is necessary to consider how these spaces converge and continue to impact their ability to perform in institutional settings. Additional research in this capacity offers a prime opportunity for institutional leaders to look inward at organizational cultures, policies, and practices that directly impact the unique journeys and experiences of Black women leaders.

With this piece, I highlight the paths of Black women leaders in historically White academic institutions writ large, and more specifically, the experiences of Black women DEI practitioners in traditionally White institutions. In the sections below, I review the literature regarding the notions of identity and intersectionality manifested within the US higher educational leadership sphere. I argue that by considering the noted contextual dynamics (Hofstede, 2011), we can build upon what we know regarding the race-gender dyad and how it shapes and impacts the unique experiences of Black women in academic leadership (Johnson, 2021, 2022; Ryan et al., 2016; Sabharwal, 2013). Further, as underrepresented leaders, this piece advances the current knowledge base on intersectionality in academic leadership by spotlighting the journeys of Black women who lead in historically White institutional contexts (Breeden, 2021; Clayborne & Hamrick, 2007; Patton, 2010; Patton & Catching, 2009; West, 2019; Yakaboski & Donahoo, 2011).

BACKGROUND: INTERSECTIONALITY, BLACK WOMEN, AND ACADEMIC LEADERSHIP IN CONTEXT

Intersectionality and Academic Leadership

At the root of intersectionality is the premise that people live layered identities derived from social relations, history, and the operation of structured power (Crenshaw, 2013). Anthias (2013) notes that intersectionality approaches:

Provide an important corrective to essentializing identity constructs that homogenize social categories. Although social divisions such as gender, ethnicity and class have been understood through the lens of intersectionality for at least two decades and have had a profound effect on feminist theories in particular, this approach has only recently acquired a more central place in academic and political life. Moreover, intersectionality has now become part of policy initiatives, which have begun to recognize multiple intersecting inequalities. (p. 3)

In other words, "people are members of more than one category or social group and can simultaneously experience advantages and disadvantages related to those different social groups" (Richardson & Loubier, 2008, p. 143).

Despite the growing interest in the standing of Black women as higher educational leaders, there is a sparsity of literature focusing on their representation, notably at top leadership levels (e.g., academic professorships, faculty appointments, college deanships, and presidencies, to name a few). Instead, the research on Black women as administrators is primarily limited to the principalship (Peters, 2012; Reed, 2012) or cloaked in studies on "women and minorities" (see Agosto & Roland, 2018). Since the experiences of women or minority leaders are not homogeneous, we must consider all leaders' distinctive, layered, and intersectional experiences. Various perspectives, including critical race theory (Capper, 2015; Delgado & Stefancic, 2012, 2017), feminist theory (Blackmore, 2013), critical spirituality (Dantley, 2010), and multiculturalism (Santamaría & Santamaría, 2013), have been offered to expose the challenges faced by non-White leaders in higher education. Nonetheless, the theory and research focusing explicitly on Black women's atypical paths to leadership are still emergent. Unless scholars carefully examine the joint impacts of Black women's intersecting identities and structural barriers, implementing "good" policies for equitable leadership opportunities will remain underdeveloped.

Although gains are currently being made in diversifying the demographic profile of academic leaders in the United States of America, males, especially White males, continue to dominate this space (Kellerman et al., 2007; Kulik & Metz, 2015). Indeed, while inroads have been made in capturing and centering the experiences of women and minority leaders in education (Johnson, 2021, 2022), research on Black women in these positions remains grossly underrepresented in the literature. Attesting to the noted limits of extant research, Brown (2018) notes that the voices of many African American women academic leaders have been assigned to the voices of White women and African American men. Rarely are the voices of African American women leaders revealed to solely address the issues and challenges of recruitment and retention faced by African American women to higher-level academic ranks. Neither has credence nor validation been given to the impact of race, gender, and social politics on the recruitment and retention process of African American women in and en route to academic leadership roles.

As such, the significance of identity and intersectionality in leadership should not be underappreciated. As such, and with an emphasis on studies specific to Black women in senior academic leadership roles, this paper adds to the critical conversations around race, gender, and intersectionality, coalesced within the leadership sphere. Examining the individual and compounding effects of gender and race on Black women leaders in academia will undoubtedly lead to meaningful implications and recommendations for improving research, theory, law, policy, and practice in this arena.

Intersectionality, Black Women, and Academic Leadership

Gipson et al. (2017), in their study of women in leadership and leadership styles, asserted that more work must be done to guarantee that those in and promoted to positions of academic leadership are aptly reflective of the generally purported commitment to pluralism and diversity. Yet, the growth and progression of Black women into what has characteristically been a male-dominated realm (Kellerman et al., 2007; Kulik & Metz, 2015) are chief components of the work to increase diversity in leadership. Implications, in this context, include examining the impact of perceptions and evaluations of persons, in leadership roles, with multiple stigmatized identities (Richardson & Loubier, 2008; Rosette et al., 2016; Sawyer et al., 2013).

Cho et al. (2009) conducted a study in which they utilized a critical democratic framework to analyze the perspectives of leaders from various academic institutions across North America. Three primary themes arose from participants' views on the new leader induction program: (1) the role of the leader in streamlining collaborations and partnerships among stakeholders (including faculty, school boards, schools, and communities), (2) the role of the leader in being an effective communicator and imparter of knowledge, and (3) the role of the leader in establishing and maintaining the importance of equity, diversity, and understanding within the community (pp. 125-126). Overwhelmingly, according to Cho et al. (2009), in the ongoing work to improve program philosophy, policy, and practice, there is a need to critically examine the process and outcome of mentorship and induction programs for incoming higher educational leaders (i.e., role models).

Leadership for social justice, according to Whang (2018), "emphasizes that leaders can make efforts to pursue equitable relationships of gender, class, race, culture, etcetera. Therefore, it stresses understanding the "'intersectionality' of multiple biases" (p. 1). Balancing intersectionality (i.e., race and gender) with leadership politics requires advocates for justice to be responsive and not merely reactive. As a result, strengthening social equity in the pursuit and development of leaders remains a deliberate and enduring effort on the part of the justice-based leader. Using control groups, Hogg et al. (2001) and Hogg and van Knippenberg (2003) conducted several experiments examining the interconnection between social identity, group dynamics, and leadership. The authors investigated the relationships between group membership and leader endorsement to connect demographic differences with the notion of the glass ceiling. Further, they concluded that demographic minorities, Black women included, tend to find leading difficult in groups whose prototypes represent the demographic majority.

Using intersectionality theory, Moorosi et al. (2018) presented an analysis of Black women leaders' constructions of success, "shaped by overcoming barriers of their own racialized and gendered histories to being in a position where they can lead in providing an education for their Black communities" (p. 152). Investigating successful leadership practices by three Black women, school principals in the United Kingdom, the United States, and South Africa, their work spotlighted "the overall shortage of literature on Black women in educational leadership, which leaves Black women's experiences on the periphery even in contexts where they are in the majority" (p. 1). As such, the analyses suggested that:

Black women leaders' constructions of success are shaped by overcoming barriers of their own racialized and gendered histories to being in a position where they can lead in providing an education for their Black communities, where they are able to inspire a younger generation of women and to practice leadership that is inclusive, fair, and socially just. (Moorosi et al., 2018, p. 152)

Reinforced here is the stance that in academia, closing the equity gap begins by acknowledging the increased qualifications of women, specifically women of color, to successfully serve in senior-level leadership roles and capacities (Gupton, 2009; Hill et al., 2016; Prime et al., 2009).

Intersectionality and Black Women Leaders in Historically White Academic Institutions

Interestingly and overwhelmingly, the following recurrent terms and themes emerged when making the direct connection between Black women, education, leadership, theory, and research: identity, intersectionality, minorities in leadership, and women in leadership (Falagas et al., 2008, 2008; García-Peñalvo et al., 2010). A large portion of the journal articles accessed through the second search – with Black women leading in academia as the primary area of focus – included terms such as 'labyrinth,' 'complexity,' 'identity,' 'intersectionality,' 'diversity,' 'advantage,' 'contextual' moderators,' 'disadvantage,' 'contradictions,' and 'underrepresented' (Falagas et al., 2008, 2008; García-Peñalvo et al., 2010). As noted at the outset of this piece, numerous scholars agree that research findings on women in leadership, while growing, have been slow-moving (Bruckmüller & Branscombe, 2010; DeWitt, 2016; Reagle & Rhue, 2011; Slaughter, 2015). Moreover, research on Black women in academic leadership has been considerably less progressive (Harper, 2018; O'Meara et al., 2011; Reeves & Guyot, 2017; Sanchez-Hucles & Davis, 2010).

Relevant to Black women leaders in historically White academic institutions is this: identity, equity, and intersectionality in leadership are all interconnected, identity directly impacts one's social reality, which Wing (1997) refers to as the "multiplicative definition of self" (p. 31), and race, ethnicity, and gender manifest as concurrent realities (Howard-Hamilton, 2003; Ngwainmbi, 2004). These factors – and their ensuing ramifications – are further exacerbated in academic leadership, a sphere in which the tenets of equity, diversity, and inclusion are purported. Ospina and Foldy (2009, 2010), in their studies examining the multiple dimensions of leadership, contended that advocacy, bridge-building, and leading for social change are all critical factors in reconstructing the scope of the leadership sphere. According to Day and Antonakis (2012), "issues regarding diversity and leadership have been highlighted as receiving relatively scarce attention in the literature... In particular, the diversity of leaders and followers in terms of culture, gender, race and ethnicity, or sexual orientation has been infrequently addressed" (p. 13). For Black women academic leaders, navigating these boundaries includes exploring the historical cultures, antecedents, and contexts of leadership from a social change perspective (Ospina & Foldy, 2009, 2010).

Wing (1997) and Wing (2003) posit that intersectionality is critical for thinking about how policies, practices, and discourses can be enhanced and transformed. The entrenched policy, legal, and social ramifications justify the need for the advancement of this and other relevant literature. This work begins with acknowledging the current disparities that subsist within the academic sphere. Identifying that this need exists at all (Dhamoon, 2011) is necessary to create new policies promoting equity, inclusion, and belonging in academic leadership. Current studies on the experiences of Black women leaders in higher education, in general, lack conceptual foci that would ultimately clarify matters informing academic policies, programs, practices, and procedures (Brock et al., 2019; Dreachslin & Hobby, 2008; Pratt-Clarke, 2010). The ensuing discourse includes, but is not limited to, the journeys of Black women as they ascend the ladder and assume executive-level positions in academia, especially in primarily White institutions and contexts.

Expanded emphasis on the social aspects of education and the development of academic leaders has meant more attention devoted to investigating the relationships between the school and the community (Ayers et al., 1998). Similarly, more attention is also being paid to the role of academia as a fundamental characteristic of the larger society (i.e., a microcosm). Consequently, increasing emphasis is now being placed on preparing apt leaders capable of understanding and operating from a justice-based perspective. To better understand the path, progression, successes, and barriers of Black women who lead in academic settings, stakeholders must begin by exploring the intersection of race, gender, and equity in leadership. In line with this, Dr. Crenshaw (2013) reminds stakeholders and allies alike that:

Race, gender, and other identity categories are most often treated in mainstream liberal discourse as vestiges of bias or domination-that is, as intrinsically negative frameworks in which social power works to exclude or marginalize those who are different. According to this understanding, our liberatory objective should be to empty such categories of any social significance. Yet implicit in certain strands of feminist and racial liberation movements, for example, is the view that the social power in delineating difference need not be the power of domination; it can instead be the source of political empowerment and social reconstruction. (p. 1)

Given the importance of contextual factors in the leadership sphere (Liden & Antonakis, 2009), the findings of studies of this nature can help increase the number and diversity of leaders in general, Black women leaders in particular.

Recognizing multiple identities and intersecting inequalities is a critical step toward improving equity- and equality-based policy initiatives relevant to Black women who lead in primarily White institutions (Belden, 2017). As such, leaders must establish and uphold cultures that are inclusive of all members of the larger constituency. This charge is significant for those who do not reflect the single-track leadership standard. Infusing intersectionality methods provides stakeholders with the necessary tools to continue disentangling these categories (Equality and Human Rights Commission, 2010). To extend this conversation, I spotlight the experiences of Black women leaders in historically White academic institutions across the four overarching themes below.

Highlighting the Experiences of Black Women Leaders in Historically White Academic Institutions

Theme #1: Negotiating Identity

Scholars are paying more attention to how identities are best conceived and studied, the discursive resources drawn from identity construction processes, and how identities are embedded into power relations. Yet, little is known about how notions of "leadership" and "identity" are connected conceptually, in policy, or in practice. This is, undoubtedly, a significant gap in the study of leadership and leadership identity. According to Eubanks et al. (2012), closing this gap allows us to gain a better understanding of the actors involved in "leading" and "following" and how identity impacts the style that a leader adopts, influences the strategies used, and ultimately, how it shapes the leader's use of power. To this end, Lord and Hall (2003) speak to the dynamics of leadership and issues connected to power imbalances. According to the authors, understanding leadership and power from a psychological perspective can better inform identity-based research and group dynamics in various contexts. In recent years, leader-specific frames have been re-examined through social categorization approaches that focus on people's social identity and roles and the processes that impact perceptions of and expectations about people and groups. For underrepresented leaders, Black women academic leaders, for example, "identity" and "leadership identity" are interconnected and inseparable, making their journeys all the more unique.

The experiences of Black women academic leaders are idiosyncratic, to say the least. Highlighted in *Our presence is resistance: Stories of Black women in senior-level student affairs positions at predominantly White institutions* (Breeden, 2021), Black women continue to make tremendous progress in higher education. Yet, despite current gains, research regarding Black women in senior-level academic positions remains limited. Amplified in this manner are the unique standpoints of Black women in leadership positions at primarily White institutions (PWIs). Breeden (2021) furthers this work by revealing the many nuances of navigating sexism and racism for Black women in senior-level academic positions. Brock et al. (2019), in *Journeys of social justice: Women of color presidents in the academy*, bring the paths of underrepresented women college presidents to the forefront. The authors point to the fact that women of color remain under-represented in senior administrative positions within US academic institutions. They noted that roughly "30% of US college and university presidents are women, and about 4% are women of color. This exclusion and symbolic annihilation represent broader entrenched issues of systemic racism and of institutional inequities" (Brock et al., 2019, p. 1). Study participants responded to this by discussing their experiences, offering guidance and insights, and "reflecting on what it means to create and hold space for self and others in the complex insular world of upper administration in postsecondary education" (Brock et al., 2019, p. 1).

In *Leadership as identity construction: The act of leading people in organisations*, Karp and Helgø (2009) challenge the concept of leadership by emphasizing leadership as identity construction. The reason for this, state the authors, "is because leadership emerges in the interaction between people as the act of recognising and being recognised" (Karp & Helgø, 2009, p. 880). Therefore, leaders' images of themselves are social constructions, and the development of a leadership self (and, thereby, leadership itself) coalesces with the interaction between leaders and followers. Again, the totality of this experience for Black women leaders is neither separable nor mutually exclusive.

Theme #2: Rearticulating Black Women's Academic Leadership Experiences

In *Leading While Black*, Horsford et al. (2021) explored leadership and urban education from a Black epistemological perspective, focusing on the paradox and prospects of Black education leadership in urban contexts. According to the authors, "researchers have written about other Black women education leaders of this era in largely biographical terms, portraying the complexity of their lives and how education intersected with their personal missions" (p. 166). In this way, scholars continue to examine Black academic leadership independently, as race and racism are ubiquitous features of Western, White-dominated societies, and academic institutions are not exempt. Leaders steer the ship and are responsible for implementing policies and mandates. They are also tasked with setting the desired direction, ethos, and culture of their respective universities. Connectedly, Clayborne and Hamrick's (2007) qualitative study of Black women in student affairs administration uncovered "respondents' experiences in light of controlling images of Black women, resistance strategies, and empowerment for activism" (p. 123). The authors' recommendations for practice and future research include "further explorations of culturally informed meanings of leadership and leading, as well as coming to broader understandings of professionals' myriad definitions and fulfillment of leadership" (p. 123).

In *Counter-stories as representations of the racialized experiences of study participants*, Hubain et al. (2016) employed counter-storytelling to construct narratives that "disrupt the master narrative…which often boast an espoused commitment to diversity and social justice" (p. 946). Participants' rearticulated (aka, counter) stories, rooted in the endemic nature of racism in the academy, highlighted their responses to "tokenization, disappointment, feelings of frustration, anger, and racial battle fatigue" (p. 946). Given the little that is known about the experiences of Black women leading in the academy, Patton and Catching (2009) constructed narratives of African American student affairs faculty to focus on their stories through examination and utilization of their personal counter-narratives. Noting the historical underrepresentation of Black leaders within predominantly White institutions (PWIs), the authors spotlighted "the racial profiling that often shapes their experiences" (p. 713), including, but not limited to, dealing with "academic isolation, marginalization of their scholarship, and racial hostility" (p. 713). In response to extant frames that continue controlling the narrative regarding these lived experiences, there is a need to rearticulate Black women's academic leadership journeys (Clayborne & Hamrick, 2007) through counter-stories that serve to broaden collective understanding of this distinct and nuanced phenomenon.

Theme #3: Safe Spaces for Black Women and the Necessity of Community

Underscoring the need for community and safe spaces for Black women leaders in academia, Han and Leonard's (2017) work sought to "challenge Whiteness and institutional racism to promote social justice, dismantle racism to promote better wellbeing for women faculty of color, and move educational communities at large closer toward equitable education, which is a fundamental civil right" (p. 112). As such, they recommend stakeholders – university leaders included – to focus on safe spaces while working to "establish policies and practices to support (recruit, retain, and promote) faculty/leaders of color, not just mainstream academics" (p. 112). Working toward equity, justice, and community implores Patton (2010), involves examining the existence of safe spaces on campus and exploring the impacts of campus culture and climate on faculty and leader retention.

West's (2019) work, spotlighting the need for more knowledge around "the composition of professional counterspaces for Black women employed in higher education" (p. 543), interviewed Black women student affairs administrators who engaged in an annual professional counterspace. Participants described the space and the overall experience as culturally homogeneous, infused with various culturally responsive resources, and using culturally intentional curricula (West, 2019). In this way, these administrators found alignment and unity in the company of their "sister-colleagues." Connectedly, Clayborne and Hamrick's (2007) study shed light on the "intensely relational qualities associated with leadership and leading, mentoring and supervising, and the off-campus nature of most sources for professional support and validation" (p. 123). Reinforced here is the need for community and safe spaces for underrepresented leaders within their institutions so they do not need to turn to external sources for professional support, community, and validation.

Theme #4: Empowering Black Women Leaders in Historically White Academic Institutions and the Role of the Academy as Ally

Despite women's impressive gains in higher education and the workplace over the past 50 years, men vastly outnumber women in leadership, especially in the highest positions. From the halls of Congress to corporate boardrooms, universities to the courts, and religious institutions to philanthropic organizations, men are far more likely than women to be leaders (Hill et al., 2016). What can we do about it now? In academia, at least, empowering Black women leaders in historically White academic institutions begins with allyship. The role of the academy as an ally starts with acknowledging that gender parity does exist and that all shareholders have a role to play in identifying key issues and creating lasting change in this capacity.

Nicol and Yee (2017), authors of *Reclaiming Our Time": Women of Color Faculty and Radical Self-Care in the Academy*, spoke of time as the "currency of love" (p. 154). That is, how one spends one's time indicates who and what that person loves. In academia, one is expected to spend considerable time being of service to others and learning and working so that all can benefit, progress, support themselves and others, and so on. For the underrepresented leader, Black women included, there is often an expectation that one is to allocate one's time "to show commitment and productivity in the service of the university, often at the expense of [one's] health and well-being" (p. 154). Allyship, then, includes being responsive to the need to "establish nonnegotiable habits of radical self-care to cherish [one's] bodies, challenge [one's] minds, and nourish [one's] souls" (p. 154).

Empowering women in academia and student affairs administration (Pasque & Nicholson, 2011; Sax, 2012; Yakaboski & Donahoo, 2011) means advancing extant research on women in academic leadership to ensure social justice and equity are upheld for all constituency members. Pasque and Nicholson (2011), Sax (2012), and Yakaboski and Donahoo (2011) all contend that research on women in student affairs administration increases collective understanding of their experiences and improves college and university retention rates. The authors suggest that the available research on broader conceptualizations of gender has moved the field away from focusing on the experiences and needs of women across race and ethnicity. Thus, more research on Black women in this sphere and greater emphasis on empowerment can aid the greater higher education community by lessening the marginalization of student affairs within and across college and university campuses.

NARRATIVES: FROM THE SOURCE: SPOTLIGHTING THE UNIQUE EXPERIENCES OF BLACK WOMEN DEI LEADERS IN HISTORICALLY WHITE ACADEMIC INSTITUTIONS

What remains absent from the emergent body of research and literature in this sphere are the voices of Black women leaders, generally, and more specifically, Black women DEI practitioners operating in historically White academic institutions. What are the experiences of Black women who lead in historically White Institutions? What are the intersectional leadership experiences of Black women DEI practitioners and leaders in these spaces? How does being a DEI practitioner impact the way these women perceive and manifest their leadership roles? Finally, how does DEI leadership look differently for Black women large-scale? To operationalize the uniqueness of Black women's DEI work in historically White spaces, I unpack these questions, spotlighting the voices and experiences of five Black women DEI practitioners in HWIs below.

What Are the Experiences of Black Women Leaders in HWIs?

Negotiating Identity: Racial equity has taken center stage within the last three years (2020-present). Although roughly $66 billion was pledged to promote racial equity initiatives in the wake of George Floyd's murder, momentum is waning. One question corporate leaders continue to ask is how to tangibly promote a more equitable workplace. A reason why equity continues to evade workplaces is a lack of prioritization on and for the most marginalized employees. Workplaces seeking to foster equitable environments might want to think about adopting new and innovative methods, as explained by Amira Barger in *No, you are not 'over-indexing on Black': Advancing equity is the active process of looking at the systems we have today through the lens of those most disadvantaged by those systems*. Executive VP on the Global Health Sector Team, DEI at Daniel J. Edelman, Amira is a consultant of diversity, equity, inclusion, and belonging (DEIB). In response to the notion of "over-indexing Black," in the context of being employed while Black and what it means to be represented in DEIB spaces while Black, she shares (Barger, 2022):

- A June 2020 survey found that younger Americans were more likely to want an increase in racial representation in advertising, with 55 percent of respondents aged 18-34 in favor of more racial diversity in ads.
- According to 2020 data from SHRM's *The Journey to Equity and Inclusion*, only 13% of White HR professionals agree that discrimination based on race or ethnicity exists in their workplace compared to 49% of Black HR professionals.
- US employment data reported by Statista notes that the Advertising and Promotion industry is 78.7% White, 12.1% Black or African American, 5.2% Asian, and 6.2% Hispanic or Latino.
- McKinsey reports that almost half of Black workers are in three industries with a large frontline presence, with significant underrepresentation, especially in high-growth, high-wage sectors.

- A December 2021 jobs report from the Bureau of Labor Statistics noted that the unemployment rate for Black people increased from 6.5% to 7.1% from November to December. (pp. 2-3)

In a nutshell, asserts Barger, the idea of "over-indexing Black" is a relic and direct consequence of the systemic racism and exclusion at the core of US culture, one built on the backs of Black Americans, yet continues to disenfranchise us in every way possible.

The triage method, for example, is a system adopted in healthcare and medicine. When resources are limited, i.e., during a natural disaster or warzone area, those providing medical care prioritize those with the most severe injuries. This method can also be applied to DEI efforts by concentrating interventions and implementations on employees who serve to benefit the most. Black women experience some of the most serious forms of marginalization; as such, workplaces looking to foster equity must center their needs. Jessica Pharm, MBA, PHR, is an HR Professional; in 2020, she founded *Blackness and the Workplace* with a mission "to empower Black professionals by providing resources, guidance, and support within a safe place to speak truth to power about the uniqueness of our shared experiences and identities" (Pharm, 2022, p. 1). Pharm's background in employee relations, recruitment, training, and employment law and policies speaks to her belief in advocating for and assisting Black professionals as they struggle to negotiate identity while navigating a complex and nuanced American workforce. Seeing the importance of elevating conversations around Black professionals by centering and valuing our experiences in a safe and protected space, Pharm states, "It's very important to me to work for a company who respects me both as an employee and as a person." Going further, she continues:

I am also not dealing with the day-to-day toxicity and microaggressions one experiences as a Black woman in corporate America. I can focus on my job and do it well while protecting my energy and peace. Any company that refuses to acknowledge this truth is not one I wish to work for. (Asare, 2022, p. 2)

Negotiating identity, in this context, means understanding the importance of elevating conversations around the journeys of Black professionals. DEI practitioners and leaders understand the importance of centering and valuing our experiences. This provides all the more reason for institutions to provide safe and protected spaces for them to navigate accordingly.

What Are the Intersectional Leadership Experiences of Black Women DEI Practitioners and Leaders in HWIs?

Rearticulating the Leadership Experiences of Black Women DEI leaders

For Black women DEI practitioners in academia, many of us are in advanced leadership roles, yet we are still unable to fully lead and establish the changes we seek to make. My own experiences as a member of the academy are no different. Pay parity, for example, continues to be a persistent issue for Black women across all occupational spectra. No workplace can ever truly achieve equity or equality without addressing the widening pay gaps that exist. Netta Jenkins, MBA, a leading voice in DEI, was recently named one of the top seven anti-racism consultants in the world by Forbes. She was featured in "CIO Views publication as one of the Top 10 Most Influential Black Women in Business to Follow in 2021" (Jenkins, 2022, p. 1). Speaking to the importance of equity and rearticulating the experiences of Black women leading DEI efforts, she says:

Workplace equity for me means that at the moment I join an organization, my employer has assessed competitive industry data and advises on whether my salary is lower than it should be. It means not asking me to volunteer my precious time without compensation and an explanation of how additional tasks will impact my career. (Asare, 2022, pp. 2-3)

Black women today, says Jenkins, must still demand equal pay for equal work because "unfortunately, we are getting way more work and way less pay" (Asare, 2022, p. 3).

DEI executive Yolanda Collins shares this same sentiment. Collins, a leader with *Employee Resource Groups* with over 20 years of experience, is an advocate for Black employees. Lending her voice to the conversation around parity and representation in the workforce, her stance is that "companies just 'saying' they pay and treat employees equitably is no longer enough" (Collins, 2022, p. 1). Pertinent to the rearticulation of the experiences of Black women DEI leaders, Jenkins and Collins both contend that 60 years later, Equal Employment Opportunity Commission (EEOC) policies are still just as essential and as needed today as they were in the 1960s.

How Does Being a DEI Practitioner and Leader Impact How These Women Perceive and Manifest Their Leadership Roles?

Safe Spaces and the Necessity of Community

Workplace affronts and slights continue to plague Black women's workplace experiences. For example, a Black woman DEI leader in the academy who requested anonymity shared,

Black women experience micro and macro aggressions that are unfamiliar to their male and non-Black peers. Rather than attempt to sweep the transgressions under the rug, colleagues and supervisors should proactively speak out when they witness these events and offer support if a Black female employee confides in them. (Anonymous, 2022, p. 3)

Thus, she concludes, ensuring that institutional policies and practices prioritize the safety and well-being of Black women is vital. Mandy Bynum McLaughlin, creator of the Race Equ(al)ity Index with a focus on data insights, storytelling, strategy design, and venture capital, adds:

There is a felt responsibility to be the voice for everyone because they are a minority representation, which, when added to the emotions felt from simply being in a majority male and/or White room and holding our own, is a lot to take on. The pressure internally and externally to be high performing while navigating microaggressions, the perceptions of Black women's ability to lead constantly being in question, along with the inability to emote anything – let alone anger or frustration – without being labeled aggressive or threatening, are huge factors in what any Black woman might be facing in a leadership role. (Corbett, 2022, p. 2)

Evidencing the importance of safe spaces and the necessity of community via my own research, participants expressed the same feelings across the board. One study participant, in her transition from a K-12 leader to an academic leader in this capacity, revealed:

Being in this position, being an African American female [connecting with] African American females, I think that has served me well because I relate to them, and I share my personal stories with them. And especially when they get to the point where they say, 'I'm not meeting with them unless somebody from the board office comes.' And if I show up to the meeting and they see an African American, oh, it's a done deal. It's resolved. The issue is going to be resolved. (Johnson & Fournillier, 2022, p. 182)

Essential to building community, she talked about the importance of visibility in the effort to create a spirit of collaboration within and beyond one's constituency. DEI leaders must be able to connect with their communities because they need to know that their work is being supported in an inclusive environment – as opposed to "us versus them" cultures and climates.

Empowering Black Women DEI Leaders in HWIs: How Does DEI Leadership Look Differently for Black Women and What Is the Role of the Academy as an Ally?

Empowering Black Women Leaders in Historically White Academic Institutions and the Role of the Academy as Ally

"Diversity, equity, and inclusion are not just a checkmark for good business, it's a way to transform the world (Forbes Media LLC, 2022, p. 1)," says Dr. Nika White, award-winning management and leadership consultant and executive practitioner for DEI efforts across government, business, non-profit, and education, is an advocate for diversity, equity, and inclusion. She helps organizations break barriers and integrate diversity into their business frameworks, and her work has led to her designation by Forbes as a Top10 D&I Trailblazer and a Forbes Books Author. In response to the question regarding empowering Black women DEI leaders and the role of the academy as an ally, she had this to say:

When it comes to building a more inclusive workplace and world, the way forward can feel uncertain and overwhelmingly complex. In the DEI space…we need to know and understand and lay out concrete actions each of us can take to make our contribution, regardless of our place in the change equation. [It is important to be] welcoming and nonjudgmental…and provide a ton of encouragement and support for all of us on our journeys. *(*Forbes Media LLC, 2022, p. 2)

Activist and TV host Lisa Hurley, MA, asserts, "a rising tide lifts all boats. I firmly believe that if one 'solves for Blackness'...if issues that affect Black people, and especially Black women, are prioritized and addressed, then everyone benefits" (Asare, 2022, p. 3). Hurley, an Anthem Award-winning activist whose work focuses on racism, texturism, and destigmatizing introversion, is an advocate for equality, belonging, and neurodiversity. Speaking to the importance of empowering Black women DEI leaders and the role of allies, she adds:

Organizations need to proactively and appropriately sponsor, promote, protect, advocate for and compensate Black women. The focus needs to move beyond mere inclusion. Inclusion is the minimum. As a Black woman, I feel supported and valued when all my abilities, degrees, idiosyncrasies, and intersectionalities are seen and celebrated. (Asare, 2022, p. 3)

Taking stock of this information, recommendations for practice and future research directions are outlined below.

RECOMMENDATION FOR PRACTICE AND FUTURE RESEARCH DIRECTIONS

In *How To Be An Ally For Black Women In The Workplace*, author Holly Corbett offers the following six recommendations:

- **Help Black women feel seen and safe.** From the position of allyship, says Dr. LaNail R. Plummer, founder and CEO of Onyx Therapy Group, this can be achieved by:

Acknowledging what I state and how I state it while not wanting me to mince my words or use semantics that another person is more comfortable with, by not skipping over me during team meetings or allowing another person to repeat my words and giving them credit as if it's the first time the statements have been said, by allowing my lived experience to be held with the same reverence as textbook research, and by respecting my chronological time and work boundaries. (Corbett, 2022, p.3)

Through these simple behaviors, Black women DEI practitioners and leaders can feel valued in their workplace roles. In other words, many necessary changes can be rooted in character and behavioral shifts, not just in response to systemic changes and mandates. Allyship, says Dr. Plummer, "allows me to be me – not a version you want me to or wish I would be" (Corbett, 2022, p. 4).

- **Center Black women.** "Racism is a system that incentivizes and rewards," says McLaughlin (Corbett, 2022, p. 4). "This system is so ingrained into our culture that we don't even realize how often we are perpetuating the harm that we think we are actively trying to undo. It is unintentional" (Corbett, 2022, p. 4), which is why White people working to be allies must constantly learn, listen, and decenter their Whiteness.

Suppose White people are the ones deciding what the most critical allyship steps are to take instead of listening to and acting on the feedback provided by Black women in the academy. In that case, DEI efforts will remain thwarted, and the system will continue to fail those most in need.

- **Be transparent about pay and benefit structures.** "There was a social media post recently where a woman in HR flippantly shared that she gave a Black woman candidate the salary requested, despite it being far less than what the company budgeted," says Dr. Tsoi-A-Fatt Bryant. "Black women have lower salaries than their White counterparts because of issues like this; there aren't allies in place who say, 'No, that's not right.' Give that candidate what was budgeted for the role" (Corbett, 2022, pp. 4-5).
- **Ask these two questions.** "First, I think that every person should ask themselves this question, 'How would I feel if I were the only one in the room?'" (Corbett, 2022, p. 5) says Melva LaJoy Legrand, founder and CEO of LaJoy Plans. The point of this exercise "is that colleagues should actively strive not to engage in behavior that tokenizes the Black women or anyone else that ap-

pears different from the majority because it minimizes what they can truly bring to the table." Next, "it's important to do a temperature check and ask the question [to Black women], 'How are things going?' and be prepared to a) hear the answer and b) thoughtfully follow up if there are areas that need to change."

- **Offer authentic mentorship.** "I think one of the biggest obstacles is finding authentic mentors. Many people say they are willing to mentor but only share the basics," says Dr. Tsoi-A-Fatt Bryant. "They won't give a true peek behind the curtain to lay out what is needed to go higher professionally or what are the potential pitfalls to avoid. I have been in professional relationships as a mentee where I was treated like a charity case—not as a valued staff person with true growth potential" (Corbett, 2022, p. 5).
- **Give DEI leaders the support and resources to create real change.** "Our history has been a cycle of self-fulfilling prophecies. When slavery was outlawed in the US, enslaved people were given zero support to start their lives as free citizens, including even legitimate citizenship," says Bynum McLaughlin. Despite the deeply ingrained and damaging impacts of the lack of support and infrastructure to support formerly enslaved people, Black people in the US still comprise a large percentage of low-income earners. Nevertheless, "our country prefers the narrative depicting Black people as lazy and the reason for their own demise instead of taking responsibility for the marginalizing impacts that resulted from generations of neglect and refusal to recognize African Americans as equal" (Corbett, 2022, pp. 5-6).

We remain hopeful that if allies continue to put in the work, coupled with what we know to be fair and just in the world, we can become the society we believe ourselves to be. Instead of having conversations about providing access or breaking barriers, it will simply be our natural way of conducting ourselves. That is the dream, and while we know it may not be actualized during our lifetimes, we can be heartened by the knowledge that these seeds have been planted. These seeds of equity exist in current and future generations, and we must continue to believe that these next generations can – and will – finally be able to get it right.

Bringing It All Together: Moving the Needle Forward

Connecting the four overarching themes: (1) Negotiating Identity, (2) Rearticulating Black Women's Academic Leadership Experiences, (3) Safe Spaces for Black Women and the Necessity of Community, and (4) Empowering Black Women Leaders in Historically White Academic Institutions and the Role of the Academy as Ally, Iverson (2007), in *Camouflaging Power and Privilege: A Critical Race Analysis of University Diversity Policies*, reminds researchers and stakeholders alike of "four predominant discourses shaping images of people of color: access, disadvantage, marketplace, and democracy. These discourses construct images of people of color as outsiders, at-risk victims, commodities, and change agents" (p. 586). In academia, discourses of this nature converge and "produce realities that situate people of color as outsiders to the institution, at risk before and during participation in education, and dependent on the university for success in higher education" (p. 586). In addition, Parker and Villalpando's (2007) race(cialized) perspective on education leadership offers insight into the "color-blind interpretation of the law and legal policy has had a major ideological and substantive impact on the administrative organization of schools and postsecondary education" (p. 519). It is noteworthy that even in the best of circumstances, well-intentioned attempts to create more inclusive campus environments often reinforce practices that support exclusion and inequity.

From a moral standpoint, academic researchers have been granted a prime opportunity to conduct and execute research that can improve leaders' cultures, climates, performance, and ethics. On a more pragmatic note, "leadership scholars have always been involved in research that aims to contribute to effective leadership. Because ethical leadership and effective leadership are related, the topic of ethical leadership should appeal to scholars with diverse motivations and interests" (Brown & Treviño, 2006, p. 613). Particularly relevant to and for Black women in America, again, is the incongruence, large-scale, that exists between their advanced levels of educational attainment as compared to their relatively low status within organizational leadership spheres (Bell & Nkomo, 2001; Davidson & Burke, 2000; Eagly et al., 2007; Sanchez-Hucles & Davis, 2010). This matter remains a prevalent and pervasive issue across all sectors, institutions, and organizational settings (Helm, 2016).

It is essential to recognize that while no unified theory of leadership currently exists, leadership theory generally emphasizes many outcomes, from how leaders are perceived to how leaders directly impact performance to the specific actions of group members (Day, 2000). For those in and aspiring towards formal positions of headship, "leadership theory has been applied to levels that include events, individuals, dyads, groups, organizations, and political systems; it has focused on immediate and delayed effects; and it often incorporates contextual differences" (Dinh et al., 2014, pp. 55-56). Thus, it is not surprising that leadership encompasses over 60 unique theoretical domains and a wide array of methodological approaches (Dinh et al., 2014). In higher education, a space in which the tenets of equity, inclusion, and diversity are actively purported, the need to study the dynamics of power and privilege, social and critical theory, and how they connect to university policies and practices persists (Iverson, 2007). Moreover, more research on the race-gender dyad, coupled with navigation in academic leadership spaces – particularly those that are 'majority-White' – will lead to essential conversations around representation and inclusion in academic settings (Parker & Villalpando, 2007).

For Black women leaders in higher education, this matter includes addressing, at minimum, their racialized and gendered pathways to leadership. Rhode (2017) reminds relevant stakeholders that factors such as generational inequality, unconscious bias, in-group favoritism, and inhospitable cultures remain obstacles within many leadership spheres. Given Rhode's (2014, 2017) position that confronting these factors is key to addressing the race-gender leadership gap, this piece emphasizes the tenets embedded within equitable, social justice leadership (i.e., identity, equity, and intersectionality) to better appreciate the representation, journeys, and experiences of Black women leaders across all sectors, historically White academic institutions included.

CONCLUSION

This chapter has revealed that the tangible manifestations of justice-based leadership perspectives remain understudied (Berkovich, 2014; Lambert, 2002, 2003; Marshall & Oliva, 2006). Taken together, scholarship in this area illustrates the importance of considering all perspectives regarding matters of equity in leadership. Bogotch (2000) states, "social justice requires an ongoing struggle [i.e., to share power, knowledge, and resources equitably] and cannot be separated from how educational theories and practices are being [re]defined and practiced by professionals within schools, academic disciplines, and governmental circles" (p. 140). This connection between theory and practice, as they relate to the moral use of power, reveals why equity and social justice, as educational frameworks, are relevant in every era (Banai et al., 2011; Dean et al., 2009; Hodges & Welch, 2018).

A testament to such considerations, Day and Antonakis (2012) assert that "there is a need for additional theory building and empirical research directed at the numerous facets involved with diversity and leadership" (p. 13). Within the leadership sphere, there remains a need to provide fresh insights into the roles of race and gender in the experiences of academic leaders (Hodges & Welch, 2018). Scholars must examine Black academics in leadership more thoroughly, as race and racism are pervasive features of Western, White-dominated societies (Horsford et al., 2021). Again, educational institutions are no exception. Moving forward, leaders are responsible for establishing future directions by providing articulable guidelines that are mindful of current issues within the community. This mission includes, but is not limited to, incorporating multicultural centers, strengthening relations with the outside community, and actively supporting inclusivity.

Following the lead of Crenshaw (2013) and others, I contend that advancing social justice leadership theory and research requires scholars and relevant stakeholders to, at minimum, critically examine the numerous foundational assumptions that have defined academic leadership and higher education research over the last 2000 years. The experiences of Black women leading in predominantly White institutions matter. With Black women serving as the primary focus of this piece, I attempt to extend the literature on the links between race, gender, equity, and inclusion within the realm of higher education leadership. Indeed, researchers have made strides in amassing an initial and veritable accounting of the ramifications and implications of being a Black woman leader in academia. In this context, the need for more research spotlighting intersectionality, inclusion, equitability, belonging, and justice is underscored (McCall, 2005; Pignatelli, 1993; Rawls, 2009). To reduce the equity gap in academic leadership, the work to advance research, theory, law, policy, and practice in this arena must continue.

ACKNOWLEDGMENT

This research received no specific grant from any funding agency in the public, commercial, or not-for-profit sectors.

REFERENCES

Allan, E. J. (2003). Constructing women's status: Policy discourses of university women's commission policy reports. *Harvard Educational Review*, *73*(1), 44–72. doi:10.17763/haer.73.1.f61t41j83025vwh7

Anthias, F. (2013). Intersectional what? Social divisions, intersectionality and levels of analysis. *Ethnicities*, *13*(1), 3–19. doi:10.1177/1468796812463547

Asare, J. G. (2022, September 20). *5 Black Women Share What Equity Means To Them*. Forbes. https://www.forbes.com/sites/janicegassam/2022/09/20/5-black-women-share-what-equity-means-to-them/?sh=285e155f71db

Ayers, W., Hunt, J. A., & Quinn, T. (1998). Teaching for social justice. A Democracy and education reader. New Press, 450 West 41st Street, New York, NY 10036.

Banai, A., Ronzoni, M., & Schemmel, C. (Eds.). (2011). *Social justice, global dynamics: Theoretical and empirical perspectives*. Routledge. doi:10.4324/9780203819296

Belden, C. (2017, July 20). Equity vs. equality: An introduction. The Inclusion Solution. Retrieved from http://www.theinclusionsolution.me/equity-vs-equality-introduction

Bell, E., & Nkomo, S. M. (2001). *Our separate ways*. Harvard Business.

Bell, L. A. (2007). Theoretical foundations for social justice education. In M. Adams, L. A. Bell, & P. Griffin (Eds.), *Teaching for diversity and social justice*. Routledge.

Berkovich, I. (2014). A socio-ecological framework of social justice leadership in education. *Journal of Educational Administration, 52*(3), 282–309. doi:10.1108/JEA-12-2012-0131

Betters-Reed, B. L., & Moore, L. L. (1995). Shifting the management development paradigm for women. *Journal of Management Development, 14*(2), 24–38. doi:10.1108/02621719510078876

Blackmore, J. (2013). A feminist critical perspective on educational leadership. *International Journal of Leadership in Education, 16*(2), 139–154. doi:10.1080/13603124.2012.754057

Bogotch, I. E. (2000). Educational leadership and social justice: Theory into practice. *Journal of School Leadership, 12*(2), 138–156. doi:10.1177/105268460201200203

Breeden, R. L. (2021). Our presence is resistance: Stories of Black women in senior-level student affairs positions at predominantly White institutions. *Journal of Women and Gender in Higher Education, 14*(2), 166–186. doi:10.1080/26379112.2021.1948860

Brock, R., Pratt-Clarke, M., & Maes, J. B. (Eds.). (2019). *Journeys of social justice: Women of color presidents in the academy. Peter Lang Incorporated*. International Academic Publishers.

Brown, M. E., & Treviño, L. K. (2006). Ethical leadership: A review and future directions. *The Leadership Quarterly, 17*(6), 595–616. doi:10.1016/j.leaqua.2006.10.004

Brown, N. D. (2018). The impact of leader race and gender on perceptions of organizations in response to corporate error.

Bruckmüller, S., & Branscombe, N. R. (2010). The glass cliff: When and why women are selected as leaders in crisis contexts. *British Journal of Social Psychology, 49*(3), 433–451. doi:10.1348/014466609X466594 PMID:19691915

Burke, S., & Collins, K. M. (2001). Gender differences in leadership styles and management skills. *Women in Management Review, 16*(5), 244–257. doi:10.1108/09649420110395728

Capper, C. A. (2015). The 20th-year anniversary of critical race theory in education: Implications for leading to eliminate racism. *Educational Administration Quarterly, 51*(5), 791–833. doi:10.1177/0013161X15607616

Cho, C., Barrett, S. E., Solomon, R. P., Portelli, J. P., & Mujawamariya, D. (2009). Mentorship and induction: Negotiating a collaborative enterprise or apprenticing for status quo maintenance? *Brock Education, 8*(2), 114–130.

Clapp, J. R. Jr. (2010). Diversity leadership: The rush university medical center experience. *Hospital Topics*, *88*(2), 61–66. doi:10.1080/00185861003768993 PMID:20494886

Clayborne, H. L., & Hamrick, F. (2007). Rearticulating the leadership experiences of African American women in midlevel student affairs administration. *Journal of Student Affairs Research and Practice*, *44*(1), 123–146.

Collins, Y. R. (2022, October). *Home* [LinkedIn page]. LinkedIn. Retrieved October 19, 2022, from https://www.linkedin.com/in/contact-yolandarenee/

Corbett, H. (2022, February 22). *How To Be An Ally For Black Women In The Workplace*. Forbes. https://www.forbes.com/sites/hollycorbett/2022/02/22/how-to-be-an-ally-for-black-women-in-the-workplace/?sh=29dba0983123

Crenshaw, K. (2013). Demarginalizing the intersection of race and sex: A Black feminist critique of antidiscrimination doctrine, feminist theory and antiracist politics. In *Feminist Legal Theories* (pp. 23–51). Routledge.

Crenshaw, K. W. (2013). Mapping the margins: Intersectionality, identity politics, and violence against women of color. In *The Public Nature of Private Violence* (pp. 93–118). Routledge.

Crichlow, W. (2015). Critical race theory: A strategy for framing discussions around social justice and democratic education. Higher Education in Transformation Conference, Dublin, Ireland, 2015, 187-201.

Davidson, M. J., & Burke, R. J. (Eds.). (2000). *Women in management: Current research issues* (Vol. 2). Sage.

Day, D. V., & Antonakis, J. (2012). Leadership: Past, present, and future. *The Nature of Leadership*, 3-25.

Dean, D. R., Bracken, S. J., & Allen, J. K. (2009). *Women in academic leadership: Professional strategies, personal choices*. Stylus Publishing, LLC.

Delgado, R., & Stefancic, J. (2012). *Critical race theory: An introduction*. NYU Press.

Delgado, R., & Stefancic, J. (2017). *Critical race theory: An introduction*. NYU Press.

DeWitt, P. M. (2016). *Collaborative leadership: Six influences that matter most*. Corwin Press.

Dezső, C. L., Ross, D. G., & Uribe, J. (2016). Is there an implicit quota on women in top management? A large-sample statistical analysis. *Strategic Management Journal*, *37*(1), 98–115. doi:10.1002mj.2461

Dhamoon, R. K. (2011). Considerations on mainstreaming intersectionality. *Political Research Quarterly*, *64*(1), 230–243. doi:10.1177/1065912910379227

Dinh, J. E., Lord, R. G., Gardner, W. L., Meuser, J. D., Liden, R. C., & Hu, J. (2014). Leadership theory and research in the new millennium: Current theoretical trends and changing perspectives. *The Leadership Quarterly*, *25*(1), 36–62. doi:10.1016/j.leaqua.2013.11.005

Dreachslin, J. L., & Hobby, F. (2008). Racial and ethnic disparities: Why diversity leadership matters. *Journal of Healthcare Management*, *53*(1), 8–13. doi:10.1097/00115514-200801000-00004 PMID:18283965

Eagly, A. H., Carli, L. L., & Carli, L. L. (2007). *Through the labyrinth: The truth about how women become leaders* (Vol. 11). Harvard Business School Press.

El-Amin, A. (Ed.). (2022). *Implementing Diversity, Equity, Inclusion, and Belonging in Educational Management Practices*. IGI Global., doi:10.4018/978-1-6684-4803-8

Equality and Human Rights Commission. (2010). How fair is Britain? Equality, human rights and good relations in 2010. *The First Triennial Review*, 664.

Eubanks, D. L., Brown, A. D., & Ybema, S. (2012). Leadership, identity, and ethics. *Journal of Business Ethics*, *107*(1), 1–3. doi:10.100710551-012-1295-5

Evans, S. Y. (2008). *Black women in the ivory tower, 1850–1954: An intellectual history*. University Press of Florida. doi:10.5744/florida/9780813032689.001.0001

Falagas, M. E., Kouranos, V. D., Arencibia-Jorge, R., & Karageorgopoulos, D. E. (2008). Comparison of SCImago journal rank indicator with journal impact factor. *The FASEB Journal*, *22*(8), 2623–2628. doi:10.1096/fj.08-107938 PMID:18408168

Falagas, M. E., Pitsouni, E. I., Malietzis, G. A., & Pappas, G. (2008). Comparison of PubMed, Scopus, web of science, and Google scholar: Strengths and weaknesses. *The FASEB Journal*, *22*(2), 338–342. doi:10.1096/fj.07-9492LSF PMID:17884971

Forbes Media, L. L. C. (2022). *Dr. Nika White*. Forbes. https://www.forbes.com/sites/forbesbooksauthors/people/drnikawhite/?sh=33272cf622a4

García-Peñalvo, F. J., de Figuerola, C. G., Merlo, J. A., & Jacsó, P. (2010). Comparison of journal impact rankings in the SCImago Journal & Country Rank and the Journal Citation Reports databases. *Online Information Review*.

Gipson, A. N., Pfaff, D. L., Mendelsohn, D. B., Catenacci, L. T., & Burke, W. W. (2017). Women and leadership: Selection, development, leadership style, and performance. *The Journal of Applied Behavioral Science*, *53*(1), 32–65. doi:10.1177/0021886316687247

Goethals, G. R., & Hoyt, C. L. (2017). *Women and leadership: History, theories, and case studies*. Berkshire Publishing Group LLC.

Grogan, M., & Shakeshaft, C. (2010). *Women and educational leadership* (Vol. 10). John Wiley & Sons.

Gupton, S. L. (2009). Women in educational leadership in the US: Reflections of a 50-year veteran. In Forum on Public Policy Online (Vol. 2009, No. 2). Oxford Round Table. 406 West Florida Avenue, Urbana, IL 61801.

Han, K. T., & Leonard, J. (2017). Why diversity matters in rural America: Women faculty of color challenging Whiteness. *The Urban Review*, *49*(1), 112–139. doi:10.100711256-016-0384-7

Harper, J. (2018). (in review). Webinar recording [Why diversity and inclusion matter. Catalyst.]. *Year*.

Helm, A. (2016, June 5). Black women now the most educated group in US. The Root. Retrieved from https://www.theroot.com/black-women-now-the-most-educated-group-in-us-1790855540

Hill, C., Miller, K., Benson, K., & Handley, G. (2016). *Barriers and bias: The status of women in leadership*. American Association of University Women.

Hodges, C. R., & Welch, O. M. (2018). *Truth without tears: African American women deans share lessons in leadership*. Harvard Education Press.

Hofstede, G. (2011). Dimensionalizing cultures: The Hofstede model in context. *Online Readings in Psychology and Culture*, *2*(1), 2307–0919. doi:10.9707/2307-0919.1014

Hogg, M. A., Fielding, K. S., Johnston, D., Masser, B., Russell, E., & Svensson, A. (2001). *On glass ceilings and demographic disadvantage: Social identity and leadership in small groups. Unpublished manuscript, University of Queensland, Centre for Research on Group Processes.*

Hogg, M. A., & van Knippenberg, D. (2003). Social identity and leadership processes in groups. *Advances in Experimental Social Psychology*, *35*, 1–52. doi:10.1016/S0065-2601(03)01001-3

Horsford, S. D., James-Gallaway, A., & Smith, P. A. (2021). Leading While Black: The Paradox and Prospects of Black Education Leadership in Urban Schools. In Handbook of urban education (pp. 166-177). Routledge.

Howard-Hamilton, M. F. (2003). Theoretical frameworks for African American women. *New Directions for Student Services*, *104*(104), 19–27. doi:10.1002s.104

Hubain, B. S., Allen, E. L., Harris, J. C., & Linder, C. (2016). Counter-stories as representations of the racialized experiences of students of color in higher education and student affairs graduate preparation programs. *International Journal of Qualitative Studies in Education: QSE*, *29*(7), 946–963. doi:10.1080/09518398.2016.1174894

Hymowitz, C., & Schellhardt, T. D. (1986). The glass ceiling: Why women can't seem to break the invisible barrier that blocks them from the top jobs. *The Wall Street Journal*, *24*(1), 1573-1592.

Iverson, S. V. (2007). Camouflaging power and privilege: A critical race analysis of university diversity policies. *Educational Administration Quarterly*, *43*(5), 586–611. doi:10.1177/0013161X07307794

Jenkins, N. (2022, October). *Home* [LinkedIn page]. LinkedIn. Retrieved October 20, 2022, from https://www.linkedin.com/in/nettajenkins/

Johnson, N. N. (2021). Balancing race, gender, and responsibility: Conversations with four Black women in educational leadership in the United States of America. *Educational Management Administration & Leadership*, *49*(4), 624–643. doi:10.1177/1741143221991839

Johnson, N. N. (2022). Central Office Leadership: The Importance of Promoting Diversity, Equity, Inclusion, and Belonging in the Ivory Tower. In A. El-Amin (Ed.), *Implementing Diversity, Equity, Inclusion, and Belonging in Educational Management Practices* (pp. 14–32). IGI Global., doi:10.4018/978-1-6684-4803-8.ch002

Johnson, N. N., & Fournillier, J. B. (2021). Intersectionality and leadership in context: Examining the intricate paths of four Black women in educational leadership in the United States. *International Journal of Leadership in Education*, •••, 1–22. www.tandfonline.com/doi/abs/10.1080/13603124.2020.1818132. doi:10.1080/13603124.2020.1818132

Johnson, N. N., & Fournillier, J. B. (2022). Increasing diversity in leadership: Perspectives of four Black women educational leaders in the context of the United States. *Journal of Educational Administration and History*, *54*(2), 174–192. www.tandfonline.com/doi/full/10.1080/00220620.2021.1985976. doi:10.1080/00220620.2021.1985976

Johnson, T. B. (Ed.). (2023). *The Experiences of Black Women Diversity Practitioners in Historically White Institutions*. IGI Global., doi:10.4018/978-1-6684-3564-9

Karp, T., & Helgø, T. I. (2009). Leadership as identity construction: The act of leading people in organisations: A perspective from the complexity sciences. *Journal of Management Development*, *28*(10), 880–896. doi:10.1108/02621710911000659

Kellerman, B., Rhode, D. L., & O'Connor, S. D. (2007). *Women and leadership: The state of play and strategies for change* (Vol. 141). Jossey-Bass.

Kulik, C. T., & Metz, I. (2015). Women at the top: Will more women in senior roles impact organizational effectiveness? Lambert, L. (2002). A framework for shared leadership. *Educational Leadership*, *59*(8), 37–40.

Lambert, L. (2003). Leadership redefined: An evocative context for teacher leadership. *School Leadership & Management*, *23*(4), 421–430. doi:10.1080/1363243032000150953

Liden, R. C., & Antonakis, J. (2009). Considering context in psychological leadership research. *Human Relations*, *62*(11), 1587–1605. doi:10.1177/0018726709346374

Lord, R., & Hall, R. (2003). Identity, leadership categorization, and leadership schema. *Leadership and power: Identity processes in groups and organizations*, 48-64.

Marshall, C., & Oliva, M. (Eds.). (2006). *Leadership for social justice: Making revolutions in education*. Allyn & Bacon.

McCall, L. (2005). The complexity of intersectionality. *Signs (Chicago, Ill.)*, *30*(3), 1771–1800. doi:10.1086/426800

McLaughlin, M. B. (2022, October). *Home* [LinkedIn page]. LinkedIn. Retrieved October 20, 2022, from https://www.linkedin.com/in/mandybynum/

Moorosi, P., Fuller, K., & Reilly, E. (2018). Leadership and intersectionality: Constructions of successful leadership among Black women school principals in three different contexts. *Management in Education*, *32*(4), 152–159. doi:10.1177/0892020618791006

Ngwainmbi, J. M. (2004). Feminism, feminist scholarship, and social integration of women: The struggle for African-American women. *Journal of International Women's Studies*, *5*(5), 93–104.

Nicol, D. J., & Yee, J. A. (2017). "Reclaiming Our Time": Women of Color Faculty and Radical Self-Care in the Academy. *Feminist Teacher*, *27*(2–3), 133–156. doi:10.5406/femteacher.27.2-3.0133

O'Meara, K., Campbell, C. M., & Martin, A. (2011). Women in academic leadership: Professional strategies, personal choices. *Journal of College Student Development*, *52*(4), 507–509. doi:10.1353/csd.2011.0051

Ospina, S., & Foldy, E. (2009). A critical review of race and ethnicity in the leadership literature: Surfacing context, power and the collective dimensions of leadership. *The Leadership Quarterly*, *20*(6), 876–896. doi:10.1016/j.leaqua.2009.09.005

Ospina, S., & Foldy, E. (2010). Building bridges from the margins: The work of leadership in social change organizations. *The Leadership Quarterly*, *21*(2), 292–307. doi:10.1016/j.leaqua.2010.01.008

Parker, L., & Villalpando, O. (2007). A race(cialized) perspective on education leadership: Critical race theory in educational administration. *Educational Administration Quarterly*, *43*(5), 519–524. doi:10.1177/0013161X07307795

Pasque, P. A., & Nicholson, S. E. (2011). *Empowering women in higher education and student affairs.* Theory, Research, Narratives and Practice from Feminist Perspectives.

Patton, L. D. (2010). Culture centers in higher education: Perspectives on identity, theory, and practice. Stylus Publishing, LLC. PO Box 605, Herndon, VA 20172-0605.

Patton, L. D., & Catching, C. (2009). 'Teaching while Black': Narratives of African American student affairs faculty. *International Journal of Qualitative Studies in Education: QSE*, *22*(6), 713–728. doi:10.1080/09518390903333897

Pharm, J. (2022, October). *Home* [LinkedIn page]. LinkedIn. Retrieved October 19, 2022, from https://www.linkedin.com/in/jessica-pharm/

Pignatelli, F. (1993). Toward a postprogressive theory of education. *The Journal of Educational Foundations*, *7*(3), 7–26.

Pratt-Clarke, M. (2010). *Critical race, feminism, and education: A social justice model.* Springer. doi:10.1057/9780230115378

Prime, J. L., Carter, N. M., & Welbourne, T. M. (2009). Women "take care," men "take charge": Managers' stereotypic perceptions of women and men leaders. *The Psychologist Manager Journal*, *12*(1), 25–49. doi:10.1080/10887150802371799

Rawls, J. (2009). *A theory of justice*. Harvard University Press.

Reagle, J., & Rhue, L. (2011). Gender bias in Wikipedia and Britannica. *International Journal of Communication*, *5*, 21.

Reeves, R. V., & Guyot, K. (2017). *Black women are earning more college degrees, but that alone won't close race gaps*. Social Mobility Memos.

Rhode, D. L. (2014). *What women want: an agenda for the women's movement.* Oxford University Press. doi:10.1093/acprof:osobl/9780199348275.001.0001

Rhode, D. L. (2017). *Women and leadership*. Oxford University Press.

Richardson, A., & Loubier, C. (2008). Intersectionality and leadership. *International Journal of Leadership Studies*, *3*(2), 142–161.

Rosette, A. S., Koval, C. Z., Ma, A., & Livingston, R. (2016). Race matters for women leaders: Intersectional effects on agentic deficiencies and penalties. *The Leadership Quarterly*, *27*(3), 429–445. doi:10.1016/j.leaqua.2016.01.008

Ryan, M. K., Haslam, S. A., Morgenroth, T., Rink, F., Stoker, J., & Peters, K. (2016). Getting on top of the glass cliff: Reviewing a decade of evidence, explanations, and impact. *The Leadership Quarterly*, *27*(3), 446–455. doi:10.1016/j.leaqua.2015.10.008

Sabharwal, M. (2013). From glass ceiling to glass cliff: Women in senior executive service. *Journal of Public Administration: Research and Theory*, *25*(2), 399–426. doi:10.1093/jopart/mut030

Sanchez-Hucles, J. V., & Davis, D. D. (2010). Women and women of color in leadership: Complexity, identity, and intersectionality. *The American Psychologist*, *65*(3), 171–181. doi:10.1037/a0017459 PMID:20350016

Sawyer, K., Salter, N., & Thoroughgood, C. (2013). Studying individual identities is good, but examining intersectionality is better. *Industrial and Organizational Psychology: Perspectives on Science and Practice*, *6*(1), 80–84. doi:10.1111/iops.12012

Sax, L. J. (2012). *Empowering Women in Higher Education and Student Affairs: Theory, Research, Narratives, and Practice From Feminist Perspectives*. Stylus Publishing, LLC.

SCImago Research Group. (2007). SJR-SCImago Journal & Country Rank.

Sherrill, A. (2010). Women in management: Female managers' representation, characteristics, and pay. *United States Government Accountability Office GAO-10-1064T*.

Showunmi, V. (2021, February). A Journey of Difference: The Voices of Women Leaders. [). Frontiers Media SA.]. *Frontiers in Education*, *6*, 548870. doi:10.3389/feduc.2021.548870

Slaughter, A. M. (2015). *Why women still can't have it all*. OneWorld.

US Government Accountability Office. (2010). Women in management: Analysis of female managers' representation, characteristics, and pay.

Warner, J., Ellmann, N., & Boesch, D. (2018, November 20). Women's leadership by the numbers. Center for American Progress. Retrieved from https://www.americanprogress.org/issues/women/reports/2018/11/20/461273/womens-leadership-gap-2/

West, N. M. (2019). In the company of my sister-colleagues: Professional counterspaces for African American women student affairs administrators. *Gender and Education*, *31*(4), 543–559. doi:10.1080/09540253.2018.1533926

Whang, N. Y. (2018). School leadership for social justice and its linkage with perilous politics. *Asia Pacific Education Review*, 1–17.

Wing, A. K. (Ed.). (1997). *Critical race feminism: A reader*. NYU Press.

Wing, A. K. (Ed.). (2003). *Critical race feminism: A reader* (2nd ed.). NYU Press.

Yakaboski, T., & Donahoo, S. (2011). In (re) search of women in student affairs administration. *Empowering women in higher education and student affairs: Theory, research, narratives, and practice from feminist perspectives*, 270-286.

Yukl, G. (2009). Leading organizational learning: Reflections on theory and research. *The Leadership Quarterly*, *20*(1), 49–53. doi:10.1016/j.leaqua.2008.11.006

ADDITIONAL READING

Balzora, S. (2021). When the minority tax is doubled: Being Black and female in academic medicine. *Nature Reviews. Gastroenterology & Hepatology*, *18*(1), 1–1. doi:10.103841575-020-00369-2 PMID:32963339

Bell, M. P., Berry, D., Leopold, J., & Nkomo, S. (2021). Making Black Lives Matter in academia: A Black feminist call for collective action against anti-blackness in the academy. *Gender, Work and Organization*, *28*(S1), 39–57. doi:10.1111/gwao.12555

Funani, L. (1993). The great divide. *Agenda (Durban, South Africa)*, *9*(17), 55–57. doi:10.2307/4065523

Iheduru-Anderson, K., Okoro, F. O., & Moore, S. S. (2022). Diversity and inclusion or tokens? A qualitative study of black women academic nurse leaders in the United States. *Global Qualitative Nursing Research*, *9*, 23333936211073116. doi:10.1177/23333936211073116 PMID:35097160

Jones, R. D., Chapman, C. H., Holliday, E. B., Lalani, N., Wilson, E., Bonner, J. A., ... & Jagsi, R. (2018). Qualitative assessment of academic radiation oncology department chairs' insights on diversity, equity, and inclusion: Progress, challenges, and future aspirations. *International Journal of Radiation Oncology* Biology* Physics, 101*(1), 30-45.

Kearse, L. E., Goll, C. K., Jensen, R. M., Wise, B. J., Witt, A. K., Huemer, K., Korndorffer, J. R. Jr, & Pugh, C. M. (2022). Diversity, equity, and inclusion in presidential leadership of academic medical and surgical societies. *American Journal of Surgery*, *224*(4), 1028–1031. doi:10.1016/j.amjsurg.2022.03.028 PMID:35369971

Livers, A., & Caver, K. (2003). *Leading in black and white: Working across the racial divide in corporate America*. John Wiley & Sons.

Pasque, P. A. (2011). Women of color in higher education: Feminist theoretical perspectives. In *Women of color in higher education: Turbulent past, promising future* (Vol. 9, pp. 21–47). Emerald Group Publishing Limited. doi:10.1108/S1479-3644(2011)0000009007

Smith, E. B., & Nkomo, S. M. (2021). *Our Separate Ways, With a New Preface and Epilogue: Black and White Women and the Struggle for Professional Identity*. Harvard Business Press.

Williams, C. C. (2001). The angry Black woman scholar. *NWSA Journal*, *13*(2), 87–97. doi:10.2979/NWS.2001.13.2.87

KEY TERMS AND DEFINITIONS

Belonging: the sense of fitting in or feeling like one is an important member of a group. When one belongs, one is an official part of a group; there is a sense of compatibility and suiting with specific people and places. A feeling of belonging describes the sense of genuinely fitting or meshing (i.e., with friends, family members, or other sympathetic people).

Diversity: the presence of differences, including race, gender, religion, sexual orientation, ethnicity, nationality, socioeconomic status, language, (dis)ability, age, religious commitment, or political perspective. Populations that have been – and remain – underrepresented and marginalized in the broader society benefit from increased diversity.

Equality: about ensuring all people have the same opportunity to make the most of their lives, abilities, and talents. Equality is also the belief that no one should be viewed as inferior because of intrinsic factors, where they are from, their religious beliefs, or if they have a disability.

Equity: about promoting justice, impartiality, and fairness within institutions or systems' procedures, processes, and distribution of resources. Tackling equity issues requires understanding the root causes of outcome disparities within our society.

Inclusion: an outcome to ensure that those who are diverse are and feel welcomed. Inclusion outcomes are met when people, institutions, and programs are truly inviting to and for all. Inclusion exists when diverse individuals are able to participate fully in development opportunities and decision-making processes within an organization or group.

Inclusivity: the policy or practice of providing all people with equal access to opportunities and resources, especially those who might otherwise be marginalized or excluded, such as people with physical or mental disabilities or those belonging to other minoritized groups.

Lived Experience: refers to personal knowledge about the world gained through direct, first-hand involvement in everyday events rather than through representations constructed by other people. Lived Experience also refers to knowledge of people gained from direct face-to-face interaction rather than through a technological medium.

Navigational Capital: refers to a person's skills and abilities to navigate "social institutions," including, but not limited to, educational spaces large-scale, academic institutions in particular. Navigational capital empowers people – underrepresented people, in particular – to maneuver within unsupportive or hostile environments.

Chapter 12
Footsteps:
Wisdom and Insight Into Navigational Capital for New Black Women Diversity Officers

Toby S. Jenkins
University of South Carolina, USA

Coretta Jenerette
https://orcid.org/0000-0002-9851-4768
University of South Carolina, USA

Michelle L. Bryan
University of South Carolina, USA

Shirley S. Carter
University of South Carolina, USA

ABSTRACT

This chapter is a collaboration between four Black women (Toby, Coretta, Michelle, and Shirley) who currently serve as diversity officers in higher education. Each author has worked in higher education for over 20 years. The authors reflect on and critically assess this lived experience for essential strategies, perspectives, and practices that might be valuable to professionals who are new to the work. The purpose of this chapter is to curate a collection of reflective insights and wisdom derived from the field-from the authors' professional experiences as Black women diversity officers at predominantly White institutions. The chapter serves as a strategic map to help new Black women diversity officers navigate the challenging landscape of diversity, equity, and inclusion (DEI) work in higher education. Each author shares a personal story along with key lessons learned. A list of suggested professional resources is also provided.

DOI: 10.4018/978-1-6684-3564-9.ch012

INTRODUCTION

In the popular allegorical poem, "Footprints in the Sand" (Stevenson, n.d.), a person dreams that they are walking on the beach, reflecting on critical moments in their life. As each life event flashes before their eyes, the person notices two sets of footprints in the sand. One set is their own, and the other set of footprints belongs to a higher, spiritual power. The poem suggests that a spiritual guide is walking with them throughout life, and in the most dire moments, when only one set of footprints is visible, the higher power is actually carrying them. The poem, essentially, speaks to the power and importance of not walking alone in life. For many, within the context of a career, walking with "spiritual support" might involve leaning on a higher power. For others, a "spiritual support" might come in the form of colleagues, mentors, supervisors, friends, peers, or through the work of esteemed (but not personally known) scholars—anyone whose insights give them perspective, wisdom, energy, and the will to keep walking. The purpose of this chapter is to lay those proverbial footprints in the sand for Black women diversity practitioners. Throughout this chapter, we, the authors, provide a collection of reflective insights and wisdom, derived from our experiences as Black women officers at predominantly White institutions (PWI).

CONCEPTUAL FRAMEWORKS

Our critical reflection is conceptually framed through Tara Yosso's (2005) concept of community cultural wealth and Patricia Hill-Collins' (1993, 2002) concept of Black Feminist Thought. First, we use community cultural wealth to document the learned strategies, insights, and wisdom gained from the lived experience of Black women as valuable, assets-professional forms of wealth. We then use Black Feminist Thought as the foundation for constructing knowledge and social consciousness from these lived experiences. Our life stories are not only valuable cultural assets but also critical forms of professional knowledge.

In her work, Yosso (2005) centered the idea of community cultural wealth in "the experiences of people of color in critical historical context [that] reveals accumulated assets and resources in the histories and lives of communities of color" (p. 77). She identifies six forms of "cultural capital" possessed by communities of color that have been essential for their survival (Yosso, 2005). Because of our explicit purpose to help new Black women diversity officers successfully navigate their careers in a culturally meaningful way, we situate this chapter within the realm of navigational capital. Navigational capital represents the skills and abilities to navigate social institutions, particularly organizations not created for communities of color (Yosso, 2005).

Banks-Wallace (2000) asserted that across multiple disciplines, research, scholarship, and practice, aimed at serving Black women, must include more than simply sharing information and facts. Instead, she suggested that "providing a space for renewal or 'breathing fire and life into ourselves' is crucial to improving the health of African American women" (p. 34). For our work, we consider the word "health" to pertain to the totality of a woman's life, including physical health, mental health, the health of a woman's career, or the healthiness of her work environment. Black Feminism scholar, Patricia Hill-Collins (1989) explained:

African American women have many shared experiences and ideas that stem from living in a society that denigrates both women and people of African descent. These experiences provide a unique perspective or standpoint for examining self, community, and society. The commonality of experiences is reflected through the prominence of several characteristic themes within an African American woman's standpoint. Core themes include a legacy of struggle against racism, classism, and sexism that is inextricably linked with a parallel struggle for independence, self-reliance, and self-definition. (p. 35)

Our commonalities, our shared experiences, and the lessons that we learn from them can help us walk confidently and purposefully through tough terrain. Telling these stories to each other (Black women talking to Black women) is also an act of cultural affirmation. We write, as a cultural tradition among Black women, to gather, talk, laugh, and testify as sisters, neighbors, friends, and family. We do this in the theoretical tradition of Black Feminist Thought (BFT), which placed a premium on creating a self-defined lens through which Black women can be seen, heard, and understood (Hill-Collins, 1993). BFT focuses on truth seeking, knowledge construction, and change making, specifically through the lens of Black woman's lived and told experiences. The broader philosophy of Black feminism, which dates back to the 1970's, demands an acknowledgement of the intersectional and full experiences of Black women's lives. Hill-Collins (1993) calls the oppressive intersecting external social forces the matrix of domination. So, to apply a BFT lens involves critically understanding "the ways in which Black women experience the injustices associated with intersecting oppression of race, class, gender, sexuality and nation" (p. 25). But what is most essential in a Black Feminist Thought perspective is the leveraging of the knowledge, strategies, and power that Black women develop, both individually and as a group, through their resistance to oppressive power structures.

This chapter is a collaboration between four Black women (Toby, Coretta, Michelle, and Shirly) who serve as diversity officers in higher education. Each author has worked in higher education for over 20 years, and we each reflected on these lived experiences for important lessons and insights. We critically assess our lived experiences for essential strategies, perspectives, and practices that we believe to be valuable to professionals who might be new to the work. We focus primarily on making visible, not only the challenges often faced by Black women at predominantly White institutions but, also, the strategic, cultural, and creative power that Black women exercise in order to thrive in such spaces. Patterson et al. (2016) noted that creating spaces of affirmation is a critical component of BFT. By sharing our stories and the unique wisdom derived from a shared racial and cultural experience, as Black women, doing diversity work in White institutions, we make visible the feelings, frustrations, experiences, joys, triumphs, and successes that other women have known. We hope that our stories might serve as a cultural mirror and offer other women to see reflections of their own experience in the stories we tell about ours.

FINDING YOUR FOOTING: TOBY'S REFLECTION

A mid-level diversity and inclusion position in student affairs taught me some critical lessons that have continued to guide my path as a DEI administrator. The first day I entered the campus of Penn State University, as Director of the Paul Robeson Cultural Center, I sensed that some people were not excited about me being there. The reception was difficult to digest. I left a campus, where I was a part of a beloved community, to accept this new opportunity. I moved from the extremely diverse Washington,

DC area to a town that was 98% White and located in a snowy valley, within the central Pennsylvania mountains. Here I was, in this place that felt physically, culturally, and psychologically cold to me.

I learned that there were several factors at play that influenced this cold reception. The first issue was a lack of institutional trust. I was hired by an executive leader that the campus did not trust, and I felt guilty by association. At that time, the cultural center director position had a reputation of being an influential and powerful role. There was not an assistant vice president who served as the primary diversity officer in Student Affairs. At the divisional level, the cultural center director was often called to address university-wide issues and policies. The cultural center was also a politically important campus space because of its relationship with student leaders and its role in supporting student activism, during some very high-profile past protests. Understanding that sensitive history was essential and fueled support for internal candidates rather than outside strangers.

Then, there were the age-old issues of ageism and sexism. Some folx on campus (BIPOC and White) couldn't wrap their heads around my being their new colleague. The previous cultural center director, who was a man, was in the role for 25 years and was well-respected. I was a young woman in my twenties. How could I be qualified? Many were convinced that the university administration hired a young professional to control. I stayed at Penn State for five years, and the campus came to not only embrace me, but they also developed a deep respect for my work and professional presence. When I left the university to become a professor, my farewell far outweighed that shady, lackluster welcome. And, while many people's recollections of my time there (including my own) are filled with positive, energetic, transformational memories, that first year felt very lonely.

I share this, because we often jump into discussions about strategies for success without acknowledging that, before we get into budgets, resource allocation, staff, and strategic plans, we must first admit that we are human. We are real people who are excited to achieve a personal goal and earn an opportunity to do good work. However, there are times when we are greeted with suspicion, contempt, and a lack of love. It's challenging to start a job this way, but many of us will have this experience. The field of higher education definitely has its share of cold and passive-aggressive colleagues (Buller & Mary Baldwin College, 2006; Crookston, 2012). This past experience helped me grow, professionally. I learned some valuable lessons, along the way, about finding your footing. I share five of those lessons in the discussion below.

Lesson One: Everything Is Negotiable

This insight came before accepting the job. While a major priority is to ensure that you are compensated adequately and have a full suite of personal benefits, many other agreements can and should be made before accepting the position. There is a well-known belief that many DEI positions are set up to fail, due to a lack of institutional investiture (Harper, 2015; Jenkins, 2016). Often, creating the position is when the institutional commitment ends (Ahmed, 2012). There is no further interest in building a viable department infrastructure with adequate budget, staffing, and institutional footprint, at some institutions. However, the department's budget is often negotiable at the time of hire. In some instances, you might be able to request a permanent budget increase. Suppose financial resources are limited for a significant permanent increase. In that case, one might request a modest permanent bump in budget, combined with a one-time start-up fund to seed several new projects or enhancements.

Another point to remember is that people are a significant resource. As you review the organizational structure of your unit, make sure you have the human resources you will need to be successful. This might require additional requests for full- and part-time staff, half-time graduate assistants, and student employees. Ensure that your office has what it needs to succeed and make a meaningful impact.

Lesson Two: Find Your People

I began this section describing how lonely it was for me as I entered a past position.I learned that students are loud and unapologetic with their love, so it was important that I allowed them to love me. As we move up to senior level-positions, we can lose touch with students, so we must make time to keep them in our inner soul circles. You need them close to ensure that you aren't missing the mark in your work. You need them close, because if students don't know who you are, your work doesn't matter. You need them close, because they might be the only people on campus willing to yell and scream if the institution tries to get rid of you. Regardless of how many drinks you have with colleagues, they probably won't protest, march, sit-in, or cause any ruckus to stand up for you, if you are pushed out. If you rock hard and stand firm for students, students will stand for you.

Also, having peers as your people is a necessity. So, hire them. In those new positions you negotiated, build your village if one does not already exist. Establish a new mindset and energy on campus by hiring professionals who have dynamic visions, incredible skills, and an equal desire to build something incredible. Create a family in your unit where you and your staff feel valued, important, and affirmed.

Lesson Three: Do the Job They Hired You to Do

This lesson required me to understand the power of my voice. As a professional, I speak up in meetings. I, first, observe to know when to speak, whether it is to caution, to analyze a situation, or to teach. But, from my experience, most meetings on a college campus can benefit from DEI knowledge, wisdom, and criticality (Fenwick & Edwards, 2014). I encourage other Black women to contribute. The negative implications of not speaking might affirm some dominant beliefs that just having a [Black woman] present is enough, and there is no need for you to be engaged in leading and changing the institution (Bradley et al., 2018; Parker, 2020). When I say speak up, I am not suggesting that you become confrontational. I mean that offering critical and insightful feedback, guiding and teaching colleagues to view and interpret things differently, and not missing opportunities to step in to address microaggressions are all crucial roles of DEI officers. Developing manuals, trainings, and resources to educate the campus on these things are essential, but modeling it in practice, as a leader, is critical.

Speaking up also takes the shape of marketing and promotion. Give voice to the work of your department. Promote your initiatives widely and ensure that things aren't so quiet that no one is aware of your productivity. The reality is that many will protest for the position to be created and celebrate your arrival. However, a campus can quickly turn on a diversity officer if they feel the work production is lacking (i.e., students become dissatisfied, faculty become critical, staff become cynical, etc.). Constant communication with your campus serves as essential proof of life and validation that the resources allocated were firm investments.

Lesson Four: Conversations Are a Necessary Form of Assessment

Using formal assessment data is a valueable way to figure out the needs of your organization. Thoroughly read program reviews and external reviews for your department or reporting units. Take time to thoughtfully review these units' annual reports so you can appreciate and understand their self-evaluation and make plans to respond to the data. While formal surveys, data, and metrics are increasingly advanced as the most important elements of assessment and analysis, I believe that understanding the needs of any community can not be done without talking to people. Spend at least a semester meeting, talking to, listening to, and dreaming with students, faculty, staff members, and alumni. Ask for their feedback on strengths of your organization and areas of improvement. Encourage them to share their experiences, on campus, and listen to their stories about what relevant DEI issues shaped these experiences. Qualitative assessments give us more than metrics, and they give us a nuanced understanding of the people we serve.

Lesson Five: Establish Priorities Through a Viable Framework

Establishing your priorities requires you to honor the truth of what you hear when you talk to the campus community. First, don't be afraid to stop doing what doesn't work. That is the most radical and revolutionary thing that can happen on a college campus. Some people may even thank you for finally ending a stale program. So, ask the community what's not working and channel those resources (fiscal and human) into something else.

While I use several formal frameworks (Chun & Evans, 2019; Chun & Feagin, 2019; Williams, 2013) for my written plans and documents, I use a very informal approach to how I mentally organize and deal with the work, daily. I simply refer to my main focus areas as flavor, feel, and, flow. Whatever the circumstance, I can always do a quick check of flavor (Who am I being, and how am I acting in this moment?), feel (Does this issue concern the environment, curricula, or a need for professional training?), and flow (Is this a navigational issue? Is there a roadblock that prevents others from advancing? Who does this policy work for and who does this policy work against?)

Flavor is about you. It is about your mindset when approaching the work. Over the past few decades, we have been taught, in DEI, to decenter ourselves and start with data-driven decision-making (Kohl, 2022; Smith, 2020; Williams, 2013). I'm not suggesting that we choose to go with our guts and discard data. I am not saying either you or data. Instead, I am saying both data and you. You will have to interpret the data and translate it into a solution, an initiative, program, or policy. So, it all starts with you. Unfortunately, we don't have enough conversations and aren't given enough space to truly consider questions like, What is my unique contribution to this work? What's special about how I move, professionally? Remembering who you are and bringing that whole person to the table is important.

Diversity officers and other cultural practitioners always have and must continue to embrace the art of giving yourself permission. Permit yourself to dream radical dreams. Sometimes, this radical dreaming may be permitting yourself to do the job they hired you to do. You were hired to help change the institutional climate. Don't be afraid to jump in and take risks that will push the work forward. Do not let pressures of formality, cultures of quiet, or unrealistic ideas of objectivity stop you from what you set out to achieve.

The next area is "feel." Feel is focused on how people live within your institution or organization. The quality of life there. How does it feel for minoritized communities? We have to be concerned about all of the spaces, because regardless of how "woke" the student union building feels, students will leave college if they are having a horrible experience and being demeaned in the classroom. The feel of your institution concerns the campus environment and the education there. We must attend to inclusive education in both the curricular and co-curricular. This also includes how we prepare, support, and evaluate academic instructors and student services staff.

Finally, flow concerns movement. Flow is focused on institutional policies. How are people (or how are they not) moving in and through your organization, department, or institution? When you examine your policies, consider how policies impact a student, faculty, or staff member's ability to navigate the institution successfully. How do policies support or prevent everyone from achieving their aspirations and dreams? Because, at its core, a college campus is all about dreams and aspirations. Movement.

This is serious and important work, but a huge part involves making environments feel more joyful and lovely. Don't forget that, and don't just focus on countering the negative. Create something positive. Enliven the campus. Our jobs are not to simply add light to a dark path. Instead, we are there to guide the organization in a different direction and to walk towards justice and equity.

STANDING ON SOLID GROUND: CORETTA'S REFLECTION

"On Christ, the solid Rock, I stand;

All other ground is sinking sand.

All other ground is sinking sand."

The lines above are from the hymn "My Hope is Built" or "The Solid Rock," by Edward Mote (1797-1874). Although from a hymn, the words are quite applicable and reflect the importance of standing on solid ground, as an academic diversity officer (ADO). If you are not on the solid rock or a strong foundation, sinking might be an appropriate description of your time and effectiveness in the ADO role. I offer a sentinel experience, early in my appointment as an ADO, to set the stage for this discussion. Let me begin with my journey in academia that led me to become an ADO.

After receiving my Ph.D., I completed two postdoctoral fellowships and eventually received tenure at a research-intensive university. Four years later, I had the opportunity to return to my home state to make a difference. I had a history of working on diversity, equity, and inclusion issues, including a successful program of research with a minoritized population, and I was unanimously selected for this position. It was almost as if this position was written just for me. I transitioned to this new position, as a Full Professor and the inaugural Associate Dean of Diversity Equity and Inclusivity.

During, what I would call my "honeymoon phase," I had a significant reality check. A student emailed me and stated that her instructor told her that she could make up a missed assignment. Then, shortly after that, the same instructor came back to the student and said she would no longer be able to make up the clinical assignment. Based on the incomplete assignment, the student would fail the course. The student was passing the course and clinical before this issue. Eventually, the student and her mother arrived at my office to discuss the matter after she could not resolve it with the course faculty. I invited the appropriate assistant dean to join the conversation in, what I thought, would be a joint information-gathering session. This assistant dean was the individual who told the course faculty that the student could not make up the assignment. After hearing the student's perspective, the assistant dean asked a few questions and then, to my surprise, stated her conclusions. Her conclusions were inappropriate and were delivered dismissively and demeaningly, to the student and her mother. I advocated on the student's behalf, as I felt the student was denigrated. I knew the assistant dean was not happy with me, but I felt good about standing up for the student and attempting to help the student navigate the situation.

After our meeting, I was sitting in my office, like the cat who swallowed the canary, when the dean decided to check in. I smiled and said I was doing fine and felt good about a situation where I had just advocated for a student. She, then, revealed that she heard about it and that was why she was there. The instructor, assistant dean, and another faculty member (with whom I had had no interaction) went to the dean about the situation with the student. I was described as a bully, and the assistant dean reported me for not supporting her in front of the student and parent. This conversation took place downstairs, while I was upstairs in my office. The dean burst my bubble of self-satisfaction, and I was in shock! The honeymoon, if there was one, was over. I told the dean that I was astonished and disappointed that she would listen to others talk about me, as a senior leadership team member, without inviting me to be a part of the conversation. There was a prompt apology, but the damage had already been done. I was deflated and disheartened. As an ADO, I was accused of bullying, because I advocated for a student being scolded, inappropriately, in front of her parent.

The student had to petition to remain in the program in the coming weeks. Her petition was approved, but she still needed to repeat the course. The student filed a grievance to have the course grade changed. My only role in the grievance was as the student's witness. Based on policies at the time, I was not allowed to hear any of the case. The Associate Dean of Academics selected the chair of the grievance committee and all the committee members. The student's grievance was not supported, and she had to repeat the course. This course repeat meant another semester of school and everything that went along with it.

The title and big corner office meant nothing. I had no power or influence, and I was distraught, disappointed, depressed, and felt like a failure. After being angry and shedding tears of frustration, I eventually met with myself. All my "Ds" turned into determination. I was determined to be a difference-maker and fulfill the mission that led me to take this position. This situation taught, or retaught, me many powerful lessons. As stated by Maya Angelou, "When someone shows you who they are, believe them the first time." To be successful as an ADO, I needed to garner support with resources and people, implement strategies to overcome pushback among colleagues, and navigate institutional resistance. Using a game analogy, I had little control over the players, but I could, perhaps, influence the game's rules with the right strategies.

Resources and People

A national survey by Jimenez et al. (2019) supports that individuals engaged in diversity and inclusion activities often come from minoritized groups. In some cases, ADOs attain their positions due to their interest and not because they have the requisite support or resources to succeed. Coleman (2010) offered that exposure to people, resources, and opportunities is 60% of one's potential to achieve career success. Given that minoritized faculty arc often under-resourced, their overrepresentation in the role of ADO can contribute to a lack of success, despite their commitment and motivation.

For example, all of my degrees are in nursing, and my terminal degree is a Ph.D. in Nursing Science, which prepared me to conduct research. My postdoctoral fellowships were also in nursing research. Therefore, I arrived at the ADO role without formal diversity, equity, and inclusion training. I had my experiences as a first generation, minoritized faculty member and some limited experiences working with an ADO. I took on the ADO role, with more desire than resources to support my success. What did I do to improve my success and gain exposure to resources, people, and opportunities to develop a solid foundation for diversity, equity, and inclusion work? I provide examples in two exposure areas, resources and people, of things I did to build a more solid foundation to be an affective ADO.

Resources

One of the most important resources I obtained was a certificate in diversity and inclusion. The areas covered in this certificate included improving engagement, counteracting unconscious bias, diversity, and inclusion in the work environment, and fostering an inclusive climate. Completing the certificate improved my knowledge about essential issues related to diversity and inclusion and provided resources I could use, immediately, to positively influence my unit's climate. The course offered tools, such as checklists, to assess the environment and individuals. Exercises were well-suited to be implemented, such as developing an action plan to achieve a diversity and inclusion goal. Obtaining this resource was important, but it was not enough. I needed exposure to people.

People

As an ADO and a professor, I had a meaningful seat at the leadership table, to engage in critical conversations. I did not feel equipped to adequately exhibit the executive presence I knew I needed, to advocate for diversity, equity, and inclusion, especially as a minoritized ADO. Therefore, I sought out a leadership coach, and my coach has been very influential during my journey to improve my foundation. Coaching is a unique and distinct profession that borrows from consulting and therapy. My leadership coaching includes powerful questioning, leadership assessments, and reflection activities that guide the development of leadership agility, self-awareness, and emotional intelligence (Capstone Performance Solutions, 2019). My coach helps me solve problems, reach goals, design a plan of action, and make thoughtful decisions. She also provides psychological safety, so I can bring my authentic self to our sessions.

Because I desire to learn and grow in my position, coaching brings out the best in me and helps me create the best answers while attaining supporting. The leadership coach position is a resource that allows me to better use the certificate I obtained in diversity, equity, and inclusion. Because of my leadership training, I can communicate with peers more effectively and execute plans for inclusive excellence.

The other group of people who have been very important in my journey to build the foundation I need, to succeed as an ADO, are my fellow ADOs who comprise the Council of Academic Diversity Officers (CADO). Each ADO is responsible for developing and implementing unit-level strategic plans for diversity and inclusion. Still, we collectively work with the university's chief diversity officer, as CADO, to support and advance university inclusive excellence efforts. Moreover, CADO serves as an essential source of social support to lessen the stress and pressure of the ADO role.

Overcoming Collegial Pushback

Naturally, people are creatures of habit and want to maintain their comfort levels. When it comes to diversity, equity, and inclusion issues, individuals need to be "comfortable being uncomfortable," to enact change. Because individuals are resistant to being uncomfortable, they often push back and are reluctant to change, from the current state. There are several strategies that I have found helpful to overcome collegial pushback.

As I aforementioned, my training has been as a researcher, so I am accustomed to collecting data and using that data to support a case. Paraphrasing the words of rapper, Jay-Z, people may lie, but numbers don't. We know that not all data are in the form of numbers. We can use many forms of data to address collegial pushback. For example, colleagues may not believe that the climate is different from their perception. The data from a climate survey could be one way to dispel falsehoods about a unit's climate and illuminate a more accurate perspective. Once challenges and opportunities are identified with a climate survey, they can be addressed.

Another way to use data is to pull it from peer or aspirant institutions or the literature, to support a case around diversity, equity, and inclusion. When I arrived, principles of holistic admissions were not being used in some of the programs. Holistic admissions or using other criteria for admission decisions, beyond academic outcomes, can be challenging (Glazer et al., 2016). A decision was made to enact holistic admissions, but there was reluctance to give the holistic criteria much weight, compared to the student's grade point average (GPA). In other words, the faculty were comfortable basing admissions on GPA but were uncomfortable including criteria that would help diversify the profession and giving those criteria a significant weight. To help alleviate concerns, I collected and provided exemplars of other schools' holistic admissions criteria to support a more realistic first step in implementing holistic admissions criteria.

The last example of overcoming pushback lies in using the resources, access, and privileges to move toward inclusive excellence. Jana (2021) describes the differences between three groups of individuals that may be useful- allies, accomplices, and co-conspirators. Although each can be useful, Jana described them as a continuum, with allies being less engaged than accomplices and co-conspirators being the most active. Jana described an ally as supporting equal justice, in theory, but did little more than that. An accomplice does more than an ally in actively working to dismantle systems of oppression. Lastly, Jana described the co-conspirator as the most engaged individual who works alongside the communities and initiatives they support.

Regardless of the training and preparation of the ADO, the ADO may still need the support of allies, accomplices, and co-conspirators to elicit change. For this reason, it is essential to understand what role individuals can and are willing to play in supporting diversity and inclusion initiatives. For example, other unit leaders played essential roles in helping to establish holistic admissions in my unit. They helped make a case for the urgency, a critical step for change, to move to holistic admissions to support the unit's mission and the university. Despite where they may be, on the allyship continuum, ADOs must meet people where they are, acknowledge their value, and use their contributions to overcome pushback.

Navigating Institutional Resistance

Many of the challenges of diversity, equity, and inclusion lie in historical resistance to change. Institutions may have both written and unwritten policies, structures, and processes that negatively influence the pursuit of inclusive excellence. Some of the same strategies used to deal with pushback among colleagues can also help navigate institutional resistance. The first step is making sure you understand the institution and the context of the challenge. For example, if the goal is to change tenure and promotion, approaches could include becoming a tenure and promotion committee member. If that's not a possibility, one could seek out allyship among members of the tenure and promotion committee to make the committee member aware of the necessity for change.

Revisiting My Story

The role of an ADO is challenging and requires constant adaptation to the academic environment and self-awareness. I am now better positioned to be an effective ADO, because I have intentionally strengthened my foundation. Although I stand on solid ground, I know I may need to reinforce the foundation, as conditions change. I can be an ally, accomplice, or co-conspirator. I cannot change the players, but I will use my sphere of influence to change the game's rules, with inclusive excellence as the goal.

CHANNELING HEALTHY SELF-DOUBT INTO POSITIVE MOTIVATION: CHELLE'S REFLECTION

Friends, congratulations are in order! I recently began my new role as Associate Vice President of Diversity, Equity, and Inclusion. It is a huge step forward – the culmination of years of commitment to this work, no matter the role. Dare I say it's "the dream job," an opportunity to engage in strategic diversity leadership at the university level, while being mentored by a dynamic senior diversity officer who possesses deep knowledge and experience. And yet…this is not excitement on my face, not even close. In fact, it looks more like doubt and uncertainty. And what is perplexing is how familiar it feels.

Over the sixteen years, every time I have accepted a new role, I spent the weeks prior to assuming that role haunted by a peculiar fear that I would be "found out." I feared that I would have somehow duped folks into thinking I am more talented than I actually am. The fear feels like your good friend from high school to whom you only speak sporadically, but when you do, you pick up your conversation as if no time has passed! I suppose it does help, however, to know this form of anxiety has a name, or at least I thought it did: imposter syndrome.

Quit Pathologizing

Having stayed up far too late the night before the interview for my first academic position, preparing for a job talk, I fell asleep at the desk in my hotel room. I woke up at approximately 4am, completely out of sorts. My pulse was racing, my breathing was labored, and I felt nauseous. But most of all, I felt hot… I mean, seriously hot. As a migraineur, I spent my fair share of days laid out on the cool tiles of a dark bathroom floor, waiting for an episode to pass. So, out of sheer force of habit, that is where I sought refuge from whatever had a hold of me.

I knew it was not a migraine because they are not accompanied by a nagging sense of pending doom, nor do they make me emotional. Yet, fat tears rolled down my cheeks, as I struggled to come to terms with the fact that, having spent the last five years performing smartness in my doctoral program, the jig would finally be up tomorrow. Laying on the cool tiles, I fell back asleep thinking through a good response to offer my beloved doctoral advisor, when he asked why I had failed him.

Two hours later, I hopped in the shower, fixed my face, donned my "killing it!" suit, and prepared to fake it till I made it. And, I did! In fact, I knocked the entire interview out the park. Driving home, I entertained the thought that I might be good, academically, after all. But, that quickly gave to figuring out how to never experience another panic attack like that again. So, when I got home, I searched the internet, stringing together terms like "academic," "fear," "fraud," and "panic" and stumbled upon a concept I never heard before: impostor phenomenon. I spent three days at my computer, sliding down an impostor phenomenon rabbit-hole, until my attention was finally drawn away by the ringing of my cell phone. It was UofSC, the school with whom I interviewed – I had gotten the job.

Doubting your abilities and feeling like a fraud, or "imposter phenomenon," is attributed to research psychologists, Pauline Clance and Suzanne Imes, based on their 1978 study. Clance and Imes (1978) noted the phenomenon disproportionately affects "high achieving" women, who have trouble accepting their gifts and accomplishments, oftentimes attributing them to luck or circumstances, rather than their own intelligence and talent. Unfortunately, Clance and Imes' findings put the spotlight on women as *the* problem, which aided in its pathologizing into "imposter syndrome," spawning "decades of thought leadership, programs, and initiatives to address imposter syndrome in women" (Tulshyan & Burey, 2021, para. 7). Tulshyan & Burey's (2021) recent Harvard Business Review article considered the role workplace systems play in both fostering and exacerbating women's inclinations to distrust their successes. They argued:

The impact of systemic racism, classism, xenophobia, and other biases was categorically absent when the concept of imposter syndrome was developed. Many groups were excluded from the study, namely women of color and people of various income levels, genders, and professional backgrounds. Even as we know it today, imposter syndrome puts the blame on individuals, without accounting for the historical and cultural contexts that are foundational to how it manifests in both women of color and White women. (para. 8).

In other words, rather than assuming that feelings of insecurity, doubtfulness, or not belonging are self-generated, women of color should focus their interrogation on the organization. What about this place makes me feel unwelcomed? What we interpret as imposter syndrome might be a very real and legitimate response to exclusion and professional disrespect. Tulshyan and Burey (2021) re-framed feelings of uncertainty, discomfort, anxiety, and second guessing, particularly within the context of your workplace, as expected and normal aspects of a professional life. Moreover, they argued that women who experience these feelings don't need to be diagnosed or fixed. Rather, organizational leaders are responsible for cultivating inclusive environments, free from systemic bias, discrimination, and abuse of power. Tulshyan and Burey (2021) argued that, only by doing so, can we "reduce the experiences that culminate in so-called imposter syndrome among employees from marginalized communities – or at the very least, help those employees channel healthy self-doubt into positive motivation, which is best fostered within a supportive work culture" (para. 13).

So, as it turns out, I am not an imposter and, if you share this feeling, neither are you! So, rather than engaging in old behaviors (like letting my anxiety settle in), I have decided to sit down and draft a few suggestions towards helping us, collectively, manifest what it might look like to "channel healthy self-doubt into positive motivation."

As the number of topics encompassed under "diversity," "equity," and "inclusion" continues to grow, you may find yourself, as I did, feeling overwhelmed by all you need to learn. But, let me offer up some good news: it is my experience that roughly one-third of this work involves things you can learn "on the fly". Another third involves understanding your roles and responsibilities as a leader, and the final third is about *who* you know, rather than *what* you know. Below, I offer up a few points of wisdom, related to those last two-thirds.

Lesson One: Know Your Role

It is no surprise that those who take on a diversity officer position describe themselves as "doers," which often leads us to, mistakenly, believe diversity leadership is about *more* doing. While there is always work that needs doing, serving as a diversity officer is less about you *doing* and more about your capacity to set the conditions for others to engage in effective work. Indeed, no one can steward an organization's equity and inclusion efforts alone – you must have colleagues, collaborators, and partners who help carry out important projects and initiatives. Importantly, inviting others to join in this work comes with the responsibility of making it easy for them to participate. For example, the presence of diversity committees and councils on college campuses continues to grow; however, the individuals best suited for membership on these committees are already over-burdened because they are doers, too. Consequently, getting the right people to come to the table shifts your role from doer to facilitator, advocate, and champion.

In my second year as a college diversity officer, I was asked to create a taskforce on international education. Internationalization was not my area of expertise; however, because I had made meeting our faculty and learning their research interests an early agenda item, I immediately knew who was best positioned to lead this group. I also knew this individual, a highly respected International and Comparative Education scholar, was inundated with committee work. So, I decided to speak with their department chair first.

I informed the chair about the taskforce, its importance to the college's strategic plan, my desire to have one of their faculty members lead it, and I stressed the importance of not adding responsibilities to their plate without taking something else off. Together, we reviewed the department's committee assignments and were able to remove them from two obligations that were wasting their time and talents. As anticipated, when I informed the individual about the leadership opportunity, they were interested but reluctant (given their workload) and wanted to consult their chair, first. When I told them I had already spoken with the chair and explained what we had done, they enthusiastically agreed to serve.

As diversity leaders, our success depends on our capacity to differentiate between when something needs to be handled by us and when it is better served by a collective. Consequently, one of our primary responsibilities is identifying the right people to serve and ensuring the group's leader(s) has the necessary resources (in this case, time) to be successful. The good news, for the anxiety-ridden, is that most of what we do often requires a collective. Importantly, when the work is best approached, collaboratively, we must do all we can to set the conditions for others' success.

Lesson 2: When in Doubt, Tap Your Human Resources

I envisioned spending the first week of my new position, as Associate Dean of Diversity, Equity, and Inclusion, getting a handle on my surroundings and analyzing my job description, to better understand what was expected of me. But, three days before I started, the Unite the Right Rally occurred in Charlottesville, Virginia. I remember thinking I wasn't even close to being ready to lead a college-wide debriefing session, despite feeling like that is what the moment called for.

As a Foundations of Education scholar, who taught Critical Race Theory for several years, facilitating discussions on racism and White supremacy wasn't unfamiliar territory. But engaging a class of eager doctoral students is not the same thing as engaging an entire college in that conversation. Sticking to my personal mantra about "setting the conditions for others' success," which often includes providing others with opportunities to share their expertise, I realized the best way to rise to this occasion was to get the hell out of the way!

Later that week, as I sat in the back of the auditorium, learning from the five colleague-experts I invited to serve on a discussion panel to which the entire college had been invited, an important lesson settled in. As diversity leaders, we bring to our positions a set of experiences and understandings, as well as knowledge bases (both experiential and scholarly), that make us strong candidates for these positions. But, we often forget our single greatest asset is not what we know but who we know. It occurred to me that, while I still hold responsibility for growing my understanding, particularly around topics not yet in my wheelhouse, I would never need to know *everything about DEI* - it's simply not possible. Rather, those of us who assume a leadership role must continually grow our networks of colleagues, whose expertise can be called upon, in both good times and in crisis, by building meaningful relationships. As you grow your network, you will be able to make tapping your human resources a regular practice.

Lesson Three: Peer Mentoring Works

The literature I consumed in graduate school, on the experiences of women of color in the academy, made it clear I wasn't going to survive on my own. Given Black women represent 2.1% of tenure track professors (June & O'Leary, 2021), our strength is not our numbers but our relationships with one another. I have yet to meet a sister academic who claims sole responsibility for her professional accomplishments. Most often, they reel off a list of mentors, collaborators, and friends who kept them on their path, kept their feet to the fire, kept them out of trouble, and kept their sanity intact throughout their professional journey.

I was lucky to begin my academic journey alongside two Black women on the tenure-track. Together, we stumbled our way through the first three years of our careers, mentoring ourselves, given the lack of tenured Black women in our college. We reveled in our good fortune of walking down the hall or up the stairs to one another's offices to process, seek reassurance, and receive affirmation. That sisterhood saved me and my career, on occasions too numerous to count. Consequently, I continue to cultivate sisterhoods in every aspect of my professional life.

Currently, I have no fewer than four different professional sisterhoods that serve different purposes. The "Divas" are group of close friends with whom I gather for dinner and drinks, monthly. I also belong to two sisterhoods with Black women, committed to collectively accomplishing our professional goals. The first includes a group of associate professors and sistafriends, who aspire to write and publish ourselves into full professors. The second consists of myself, another associate professor, and our friend and mentor - a full professor who helps us strategize, theorize, and navigate around the obstacles on our paths. The final sisterhood consists of the women who co-authored this article. As the few Black female academic diversity officers at our university, our need for support, while engaging in this work, goes far beyond our formal, monthly meetings and spills over into monthly dinner groups.

Some sisterhoods are inherited, others are found, while still others are built. Regardless, being in relationship with colleagues who can help you navigate the trials and tribulations associated with being a diversity officer is vital. The diversity officer role is relatively new, so those of us called to it often have few colleagues who truly understand what we do. So, it is incumbent upon us to create our own support circles and networks. Not in one yet? Don't worry, we're out there, and we're only a Zoom call away!

MARKING THE PATH: SHIRLEY'S REFLECTION

This final section and story summarizes previous insights and discusses strategies that enable Black women in diversity, equity, and inclusion leadership roles to navigate the leadership path by (1) leaving evidence of their existence, (2) promoting and publicizing themselves (the DEI work), (3) creating archives for the future, and (4) mentoring other potential leaders. Black women in DEI leadership roles in the academy face several barriers, many of which are analogous to what may be described as the "crooked room" by Harris-Perry (2009):

When they confront race and gender stereotypes, Black women are standing in a crooked room, and they have to figure out which way is up. Bombarded with warped images of their humanity, some Black women tilt and bend themselves to fit the distortion. It can be hard to stand up in a crooked room (p.62).

My own lived experience in launching a career trajectory in higher education leadership began with this "crooked room." I had just been hired as chairperson of an academic department at a comprehensive university in the Southeast and became the first Black scholar to lead a department in my field, at a mainstream or predominantly White university. Armed with strong credentials that included a doctorate in my field from a prestigious Midwestern university, previous administrative experience at two other universities, including an R1(high research activity) designated university in the Southeast, and an HBCU, I was excited about beginning this new administrative career trajectory. Yet, I also felt mild trepidation. My dissertation advisor and mentor, a White male, had strongly urged me not to take the position, because he felt that I was being set up to fail, as a Black woman. I was one of three finalists for the position. The other finalists included another Black woman, who had been the first woman of color to receive the doctorate from the same university as I, and coincidentally, a White male, who was a professor at the very same university. Because the White male was not offered the position, he felt he had been a victim of reverse discrimination. My advisor and mentor's concerns gave me pause, and I pondered the consequences of my decision to take the position anyway. As I look back on my first academic leadership position, I relied on a survival technique that also worked for me in graduate school, where I was either the only one or one of three—assimilation. I didn't back down, but I assimilated, to be visible in the role. As leadership scholars explain, Black women often feel compelled to assimilate, to attain career advancement, success, and legitimacy and embody the feminine traits of leadership—empowering, networking, persuading, collaborating, contributing, and mentoring (Dean et al., 2000).

The assimilation leadership style marked my next role as department chair at another institution. Two ensuing directorships led me to my current position as an Associate Dean for DEI. I was appointed to the position after serving 15 years in the college. The first five years, I was the founding director of one of the college's two academic units, and I spent ten more years as a professor and chair of the diversity committee. Moving from academic to DEI leadership has contributed to my navigational capital and authenticity. The authentic leadership style is a choice that allows you to show up and be real. It is a style consistent with the age old wisdom, "to know thyself, and to thine own self be true" (Shakespeare, 1992). A proponent of authentic leadership theory (ALT), Johnson (2015) described authenticity as "the root construct or principle underlying all forms of positive leadership" (p.18). According to Gardner et al. (2011) the practice leads to sustainable (long term) and veritable (ethically sound) organizational performance. Authenticity has four components: self-awareness, balanced processing (remaining objective when receiving information), internalized moral perspective (regulating our behavior, according to our standards and values), and relational transparency, presenting the authentic self to others, openly expressing true thoughts and feelings appropriate for the situation.

Authenticity may be viewed as ethical leadership that guides our DEI work, as Johnson described as, "learning that ours is not the only act in town—learning the value of empowerment, sharing governance and that co-creation leaves us free to do only what we are called and able to do, and to trust the rest to others" (Johnson 2015, p. 242). The first step toward marking our path as Black women in the DEI space is to leave evidence of our existence. In doing so, my experience has been to be mindful of giving the best of me but saving the rest of me to be my true self. What we leave behind is important, but so is what we always keep within ourselves. When you give too much in a space where you aren't always visible, wanted, or expected to be, you can lose so much of yourself. Strive for leadership positions within your own groups, whether with a council such as CADO or committee. By doing so, we navigate our paths as authentic and transformational DEI leaders.

Evidence of our existence occurs when our voices are amplified, such as the establishment of a university-wide Council of Academic Diversity Officers, composed of Associate Deans of Diversity, Equity, and Inclusion, or similar titles, in every academic unit, plus admissions and athletics. This organizational structure develops a sustainable model for Black women DEI leaders in the academy to exist in an inviting yet inclusive environment. CADO becomes a powerful symbol of not only the existence of Black women leaders in DEI but of their power and impact, yielding power not out of privilege but out of purpose. Council leadership can also be used as a trajectory for higher-level visibility and leadership opportunities in central administration. Other markers of evidence that Black women DEI leaders have been seen and heard include collaborating with other university entities, such as a center for teaching excellence, to create a "Teaching Towards Inclusive Excellence," certificate of completion—a sustainable archetype of effective DEI practice within the academy. The CADO members report directly to their respective deans and have reporting relationships to the Vice President for Diversity, Equity and Inclusion and the University Provost, to advance the university's Diversity, Equity, and Inclusion goals and objectives.

The second step is to promote and publicize ourselves, but to do that, we must successfully promote and publicize DEI in our own units, the campus, and in community, national, and global organizations. The need to promote DEI relates to a larger concern that we, Black women, are usually unseen. Therefore, the work we do in this space would be unseen by most, thus the need to redouble promotional efforts. Shine your light in your unit by creating your web page on the unit's Web site, showcase all the DEI work in that venue, on social media, and annually publish and disseminate a DEI scorecard to publicize your goals, objectives, metrics and progress you are making towards those goals, such as The Strategic Diversity Leadership Scorecard (Williams, 2013). Collaborate with your DEI colleagues throughout the university, invite others to conduct training and workshops, and publicize those efforts. Don't shrink from the difficult work. A failed attempt to achieve a diverse faculty resulted in a successful promotion and publicity effort that yielded tangible results. The experience led to a push for more diversity hires within the unit, a faculty search committee for diversity workshop, and a new search for four new faculty of color under the auspices of a cluster hire that resulted in three new Black faculty and one Latina. Antagonists became allies, many of whom now serve on the DEI Inclusive Excellence Advisory Council within the college.

Other opportunities to promote and publicize DEI are by using faculty, staff, and student diversity awards, to promote contributions to DEI, a DEI certificate program, DEI newsletters, partnerships with organizations and institutions with diverse students, to create pipeline and pathway programs, seminars, symposia, and museums. Incentivizing DEI participation can effectively achieve faculty, staff, and student buy-in.

The third step toward marking the DEI path involves archiving for the future. Partner with university libraries to donate your DEI historical records, to archive your important initiatives, such as "Documenting Diversity at the University of Oregon," which collects pertinent records and raises awareness of the importance of preserving historic diversity records, especially of underrepresented groups. Other prominent examples on my campus are the Museum of Education and the Center for the Education and Equity of African American Students. The university libraries at the University of South Carolina maintain selected readings, films, and other materials about diversity, equity, and inclusion. Another example of diversity, equity, and inclusion archival programming is the biennial Media and Civil Rights History Symposium, co-sponsored by our University's Civil Rights Center.

Mentoring is the fourth step toward marking the DEI path. National organizations are dynamic resources for mentoring potential future leaders in the academy, in general, and DEI. One of the most prominent national organizations for chief diversity officers is the National Association of Diversity Officers in Higher Education, which offers the NADOHE Chief Diversity Officer Fellows Program (CDOFP), a professional leadership program of mentorship for new and early career chief diversity officers. According to NADOHE, the purpose of the one academic year mentorship is to provide each Fellow with mentoring, from a senior level CDO, for guided professional development opportunities and experiences.

Most universities sponsor their own leadership mentoring programs and national academic and professional associations. Informal mentoring among professional colleagues is another effective tool. Networking in your institution and professional association meetings and conventions can be fertile ground for mentoring, nurturing, sponsoring, and coaching the next generation of Black women, as authentic transformational leaders in DEI.

CONCLUSION: WALKING PARTNERS

The goal of this chapter was to critically reflect on our personal experiences as DEI professionals, to mine our memories for insights, strategies, and perspectives that might be useful to new Black women DEI officers. Many key concepts of critical race, such as authentic voice, story exchange, and naming one's reality, are essential to this work. As Delgado (1990) argued, people of color may speak from a very different experience. According to Banks-Wallace (2002), storytelling, the interactive process of sharing stories, is a vehicle of preserving culture and passing it on to future generations. Revisiting our Black Feminist Thought conceptual foundations for this chapter brings us back to the idea of African American women's shared experiences and ways of knowing that stem from navigating exclusionary and oppressive environments. By sharing our four stories, we understand, even more fully, Collins' (1989) assertion that these shared experience offer a powerful perspective to examine self, in relation to community or society. In this case, we examined our selves in relation to the challenges of doing activist work on predominantly white college campuses.

Just as from a broad, societal view, a BFT lens can help us to see "characteristic themes within an African American woman's standpoint" (Collins, 1989, p.20). BFT can also help us to identify such themes within smaller, more defined communities (e.g., Black women diversity officers in higher education). Core themes found in our shared stories include: (1) Work with purpose, (2) Work with confidence, (3) Work with friends, (4) Work with authenticity, and (5) Work with your resources. While each of our stories and our professional paths to the diversity officer position are very different, our experiences in the role parallel, intersect, and mirror each other. We have all found that a clear purpose for both why and how you work is essential to withstand the winds of resistance that you will face. Also, bringing your full, authentic self onto your campus is critical to helping you harness your power. This ties in with the importance of confidence to actually be the change agent, that is inherently the foundation of the job. Finally, through all of our stories, we share the value of resources—human resources, fiscal resources, and various other forms of support systems. As the poem "Footsteps" stressed, you can not walk alone.

Our stories in this chapter come from the field and offer an honest "in the trenches" dialogue often had when Black women gather. This is our effort to walk with our sisters in the struggle, mark the path, shine a light, clear the way, and lift you up. To use an old expression, let each one (of us) reach one of us.

ACKNOWLEDGMENT

This research received no specific grant from any funding agency in the public, commercial, or not-for-profit sectors.

REFERENCES

Ahmed, S. (2012). *On being included: Racism and diversity in institutional life*. Duke University Press. doi:10.2307/j.ctv1131d2g

Banks-Wallace, J. (2002). Talk that talk: Storytelling and analysis rooted in African-American oral tradition. *Qualitative Health Research, 12*(3), 410–426. doi:10.1177/104973202129119892 PMID:11918105

Bradley, S. W., Garven, J. R., Law, W. W., & West, J. E. (2018). The impact of chief diversity officers on diverse faculty hiring (No. w24969). *National Bureau of Economic Research.* https://papers.ssrn.com/sol3/papers.cfm?abstract_id=3244282

Buller, J. & Mary Baldwin College (2006). Coping with the Passive-Aggressive Faculty Member, *The Essential Department Chair: A Practical Guide to College Administration.* Anker Publishing Company https://tomprof.stanford.edu/posting/822

Capstone Performance Solutions, Inc. (2019). Excel coaching. *Capstone Performance Solutions, Inc.* https://www.capstonesolutionsinc.com/

Chun, E., & Evans, A. (2019). *Conducting an institutional diversity audit in higher education: A practitioners guide to systemic diversity transformation*. Stylus Publishing.

Chun, E. B., & Feagin, J. R. (2019). *Rethinking diversity frameworks in higher education,* (1st ed.). Routledge., doi:10.4324/9780429298929

Clance, P. R., & Imes, S. A. (1978). The imposter phenomenon in high achieving women: Dynamics and therapeutic intervention. *Psychotherapy (Chicago, Ill.), 15*(3), 241–247. doi:10.1037/h0086006

Coleman, H. J. (2010). *Empowering yourself: The organizational game revealed,* (2nd ed.). Author House.

Crookston, R.K. (2012). *Working with Problem Faculty: A 6-Step Guide for Department Chairs.* Jossey-Bass.

Dean, D., Bracken, S., & Allen, J. (2009). Academic leadership: Professional strategies, personal choices. *Stylus (Rio de Janeiro).*

Delgado, R. (1990). When a story is just a story: Does voice really matter? *Virginia Law Review, 76*(1), 95–111. doi:10.2307/1073104

Fenwick, T., & Edwards, R. (2014). Networks of knowledge, matters of learning, and criticality in higher education. *Higher Education, 67*(1), 35–50. doi:10.100710734-013-9639-3

Gardner, W. L., Cogliser, C. C., Davis, K. M., & Dickens, M. P. (2011). Authentic leadership. *The Leadership Quarterly*, 22.

Glazer, G., Clark, A., Bankston, K., Danek, J., Fair, M., & Michaels, J. (2016). Holistic admissions in nursing: We can do this. *Journal of Professional Nursing, 32*(4), 306–313. doi:10.1016/j.profnurs.2016.01.001 PMID:27424931

Guinier, L., & Torres, G. (2003). *The miner's canary: Enlisting race, resisting power, transforming democracy*. Harvard University Press.

Harper, S. (2015, December 10). Paying to ignore racism. *Inside Higher Education.* https://www.insidehighered.com/views/2015/12/10/colleges-should-stop-paying-money-ignore-racial-problems-essay#.YeRrgQtU v9A.link

Harris-Perry, M. (2011). *Sister citizen: Shame, stereotypes and Black women in America*. Yale University Press.

Hill-Collins, P. (1993). Toward a new vision: Race, class, and gender as categories of analysis and connection. *Race. Sex & Class, 1*(1), 25–45.

Hill-Collins, P. (2002). *Black feminist thought: Knowledge, consciousness, and the politics of empowerment*. Routledge. doi:10.4324/9780203900055

Jana, T. (2021, February 8). The differences between allies, accomplices & co-conspirators may surprise you. *An Injustice!* https://aninjusticemag.com/the-differences-between-allies-accomplices-co-conspirators-may-surprise-you-d3fc7fe29c

Jenkins, T. (2016, September 18). Committed to diversity? Show me the money. *The Chronicle of Higher Education.* https://www.chronicle.com/article/committed-to-diversity-show-me-the-money/

Jimenez, M. F., Laverty, T. M., Bombaci, S. P., Wilkins, K., Bennett, D. E., & Pejchar, L. (2019). Underrepresented faculty play a disproportionate role in advancing diversity and inclusion. *Nature Ecology & Evolution, 3*(7), 1030–1033. doi:10.103841559-019-0911-5 PMID:31160738

Johnson, C. E. (2015). Ethical challenges of leadership: Casting light or shadow. *Sage (Atlanta, Ga.).*

June, A. W., & O'Leary, B. (2021, May 27). How many Black women have tenure on your campus? *Chronicle of Higher Education.* https://www.chronicle.com/article/how-many-black-women-have-tenure-on-your-campus-search-here

Kohl, K. (2022). *Driving justice, equity, diversity, and inclusion,* (1st ed.). Auerbach Publications., doi:10.1201/9781003168072

Parker, E. (2020, August 20). Do colleges need a chief diversity officer? *Inside Higher Education*. https://www.insidehighered.com/views/2020/08/20/chief-diversity-officers-play-vital-role-if-appropriately-positioned-and-supported#.YeWhRKWj_eg.link

Patterson, A., Kinloch, V., Burkhard, T., Randall, R., & Howard, A. (2016). Black Feminist Thought as Methodology: Examining intergenerational lived experiences of Black women. *Departures in Critical Qualitative Research*, *5*(3), 55–76. doi:10.1525/dcqr.2016.5.3.55

Shakespeare, W. (1992). *Hamlet, prince of Denmark* (C. Watts & K. Carabine, Eds.). Wordsworth Editions.

Smith, D. G. (2020). *Diversity's promise for higher education: Making it work*. Johns Hopkins University Press.

Tulshyan, R., & Burey, J. (2021, February 11). Stop telling women they have imposter syndrome. *Harvard Business Review*. https://hbr.org/2021/02/stop-telling-women-they-have-imposter-syndrome

Williams, D. (2013). *Strategic diversity leadership: Activating change and transformation in higher education*. Stylus Publishing.

Williams, D., & Wade-Golden, K. C. (2006, April 18). What is a chief diversity officer? *Inside Higher Education*. https://drdamonawilliams.com/wp-content/uploads/DAW_KWG_CDO_What_IS.pdf

Yosso, T. (2005). Whose culture has capital? A critical race theory discussion of community cultural wealth. *Race, Ethnicity and Education*, *8*(1), 69–91. doi:10.1080/1361332052000341006

ADDITIONAL READING

Alexander, T. (2010). Roots of leadership: Analysis of the narratives from African American women leaders in higher education. *International Journal of Learning*, *17*(4), 193–204. doi:10.18848/1447-9494/CGP/v17i04/46973

Alston, J. A., & McClellan, P. A. (2011). *Herstories: Leading with lessons of the lives of Black women activists*. Peter Lang Publishing.

Beckwith, A. L., Carter, D. R., & Peters, T. (2016). The underrepresentation of African American women in executive leadership: What's getting in the way? *Journal of Business Studies Quarterly*, *7*(4), 115–134.

Durr, M., & Harvey Wingfield, A. M. (2011). Keep your 'N' in check: African American women and the interactive effects of etiquette and emotional labor. *Critical Sociology*, *37*(5), 557–571. doi:10.1177/0896920510380074

KEY TERMS AND DEFINITIONS

Assimilation: The pressure to conform as an acculturating option to overcome feelings of "otherness", in the presence of the dominant culture.

Authentic Leadership: The root construct or principle underlying all forms of positive leadership that leads to sustainable (long term) and veritable (ethically sound) organizational performance.

Black Feminism: Black feminism centers the social and political identities of Black women with an explicit understanding of their experiences in relation to racism, sexism, and classism.

Black Feminist Thought (BFT): BFT is an interpretative framework that explores the rich ideas and perspectives of Black women intellectuals (both within and outside of the academe). The framework seeks to make known the rich intellectual tradition of Black women that is often ignored.

Crooked Room: A phenomenon that describes what Black women confront, as race and gender stereotypes and warped images of their humanity.

DEI Scorecard: The diversity or inclusive excellence tool that is scalable, fluid, and contextual to help an organization determine what it is doing well and what needs to be improved.

Executive Presence: Demonstrating confidence, control, and a willingness to lead that inspires others to want to follow.

Intersectionality: Intesectionality concerns the inter-related nature of social categories such as race, class, and gender, and the ways in which they overlap to create interdependent systems of oppression and discrimination. The term was coined by Kimberle Crenshaw in 1989.

APPENDIX: RESOURCES TO EXPLORE

1. Certificate in Diversity and Inclusion https://online.cornell.edu/diversity-and-inclusion
2. Leadership Coaching https://www.capstonesolutionsinc.com/
3. American Council on Education https://www.acenet.edu/Pages/default.aspx
4. National Association of Diversity Officers in Higher Education Regional Chapters https://www.nadohe.org/current-chapters

Chapter 13
The DEI Industrial Complex: Undermining Black Woman Leadership

Aysa Gray
Queens College, USA

Norka Blackman-Richards
https://orcid.org/0000-0002-7431-7014
Queens College, USA

Selena T. Rodgers
https://orcid.org/0000-0002-3327-9517
York College, USA

ABSTRACT

The DEI initiative is a multi-year project to support campuses in shifting power to create an anti-racist and equity-based space through liberatory practices, grassroots organizing, and equity-centered education. In this paper, the authors reflect on their communal work to disrupt injustice through an intersectional framework. To frame this paper, the authors first outline the historical and present impact of DEI work within academia, highlighting anti-blackness and misogynoir. Next, the authors introduce the term DEI industrial complex and provide an overview of the framework. After providing this analytic framework, the authors further explore how incidents of undermining Black leadership manifest within the academy. Asserting agency over the DEI complex, the concluding section offers essential survival tools.

"I am, because we are" – The African Philosophy of Ubuntu

The work of transforming the state of racism and anti-Blackness does not happen in isolation but stands on the shoulders of foreparents in the work. The authors dedicate this writing to their mothers – Anita Torrence, Lucila Petrona Hines de Blackman, and Dorothy Louise McNeil Rodgers (1948-1986), who

DOI: 10.4018/978-1-6684-3564-9.ch013

limitlessly sacrificed, nurtured and prepared them for this work. This entry is also dedicated to DEI foremothers and pioneers upon whose shoulders we stand and contemporary comrades engaged in the daily fight for survival.

As Diversity Equity Inclusion (DEI) work continues to gain widespread funding within the academy, many Black and Indigenous DEI practitioners continue to see and experience the deep scars of racial harm within spaces of higher learning. Despite the proliferation of DEI initiatives post-summer 2020 uprisings, between writing drafts of this work, the authors faced new and daily additions of macroaggressions and racial undermining. Because there is deep love and dedication to the student-scholars, faculty, and staff the authors serve, the purpose of this writing aims to give voice to the perpetual dynamics and continued racialized harm faced within the era of DEI in higher education. In pushing back on the ways anti-Blackness in the traditional cannon can restrict Black voice, the authors chose to frame this work in ways that center their experience as Black changemakers. By employing essential tools, the practitioners can create new alternatives to address anti-Blackness in the academy at the root rather than the leaves.

INTRODUCTION

"Sometimes people try to destroy you, precisely because they recognize your power - not because they don't see it, but because they see it and they don't want it to exist." – Bell Hooks 1994a, p. 59.

Almost three decades later, hooks' quote resounds loudly for systemic oppression of Black practitioners engaging in Diversity, Equity, and Inclusion (DEI) work. DEI is the umbrella term used to describe work that forwards self and community actualization for all beings while creating interventions to shift the historical and present ways some groups have been unfairly marginalized. Since the racial justice protests of 2020, the demand for DEI practitioners, trainers, and administrators —who are often Black women or people of color —has taken off. However, as Black, lesbian, warrior mother poet Audre Lorde reminds us, the master's tools will never dismantle the master's house. Logan (2021) has shown that most of the DEI undertakings have offered the illusion of power to minoritized people and their comrades without providing the power needed to shift the structural systems. This dynamic leaves Black and minoritized people with little recourse against incessantly harmful environments, despite rhetoric claiming otherwise.

The objective of DEI work is to push the academy to redress oppressive harmful structures. However, it is unlikely that efforts funded by and accountable to an institution built on White, elitist, patriarchy, and ableist supremacy will be enough to overhaul inequities Black people and other minoritized groups confront. Claims of performative allyship that stand in solidarity against injustices often leave those who are both Black and women in double jeopardy and isolation (Beal, 2008). Performative allies observe harm but remain silent or identify as supporters and fail to use their voices in shared governance spaces and meetings to advocate radically against injustices experienced by all community members. Their actions, in turn, help sustain harm perpetrated against Black women and non-binary persons.

As DEI practitioners – a director of a multicultural center and co-director/co-founder of a university-wide DEI initiative, a director of a Percy Ellis Sutton SEEK (Search for Education, Elevation, and Knowledge) program, and the social work department chair-elect, founding director and program chief administrator of a Master of Social Work (MSW) program – the authors attempt to reconcile truths through a multi-prong approach. First, they provide a brief historical overview of DEI. Next, they outline its evolution into what they coin "the DEI Industrial Complex" historical overview (see the appendix for full description). Learnings from undermining leadership experience within the DEI Industrial Complex and the "Academic Anti-Racist Spaces" presentation at the CUNY 2021 Faculty Diversity & Inclusion Conference are discussed. The authors offer essential tools for surviving the DEI Industrial Complex to current and future research practitioners to close the discussion.

DEI has been increasingly recognized as a mechanism to encourage organizations to push systems, including institutions of higher education, to engage in critical conversations about inequity. Despite growing DEI leadership positions in academia, Black women and nonbinary persons remain marginalized in these spaces. From this perspective, the forthcoming section roots the backstory of the DEI narrative and affirms their vital leadership in the landscape of academia.

DEI INDUSTRIAL COMPLEX: HISTORICAL OVERVIEW AND FRAMEWORK

Before the 1964 Civil Rights Act, there was no formal work to address oppression within many institutions (Schantz, 2019). When the grassroots organizing efforts of many dedicated people led to legal shifts towards BIPOC enfranchisement and later the introduction of DEI work, there was hope, perhaps naively, that these DEI positions would create a shift in the culture of white elitist patriarchy supremacy. Purposely under-resourced, DEI initiatives lack capital, staff, and time and reinforce long-standing barriers to change. Unsupported, DEI practitioners are often accountable to administrations that continue to uphold the racism of the status quo.

When discussing the challenges and rewards of DEI work with practitioners from twelve campuses within the CUNY (City University of New York) system and with one-hundred and fifty (n=150) attendees at the CUNY 2021 Faculty Diversity & Inclusion Conference (Blackman-Richards et al., 2021), it became apparent that there are many DEI practitioners dedicated to shifting the higher education climate. However, most of the campus' DEI task forces widely ignored the recommendations of practitioners or produced sporadic workshops aimed at transforming the entire racial climate. Many practitioners felt that while the college emphasized DEI strategic plans, those most impacted by oppressive practices and policies continued to be disproportionately impacted (Ballard et al., 2020). These actions have converted DEI work into the DEI Industrial Complex.

While there are dedicated DEI practitioners creating shifts, currently, DEI work tends to experience short-lived gains that fail to lead to the systemic shifts necessary to change power dynamics that undergird systemic racism. After discussing white supremacy and DEI work in the academy with one-hundred and fifty staff and faculty from across the country, the authors landed on an expanded understanding of the DEI field, mainly as it shows up in Higher Education. The Appendix grounds in the ideologies, strategies, and actors associated with, what the authors have codified as, the DEI Industrial Complex.

Drawing from the Non-Profit Industrial Complex as popularized by INCITE (Smith, 2007), the DEI Industrial Complex (See the Appendix) is defined as the collusion of the state, non-profits, corporations, and higher education to use Diversity, Equity, and Inclusion work to restore social and financial gain to an institution, while consistently only addressing the lowest hanging fruit, and offering no shifts in the major and pervasive issues of systemic oppression, especially as they pertain to anti-Blackness. Within this model, this entry seeks to highlight the following concepts explored within the DEI industrial complex (a) Weaponization, (b) Tokenism, and (c) Commodified Emotional Labor.

Weaponization

"The most basic activism we can have in our lives is to live consciously in a nation living in fantasies. Living consciously is living with a core of healthy self-esteem. You will face reality; you will not delude yourself." – Bell Hooks, 2014

A prolific author and academic, but also a student and philosopher of American society, bell hooks (2014) reminds us of the need to center healthy self-worth to navigate the systems used to weaponize and erase Black women and nonbinary people. The challenges within DEI work continue to abound, mainly related to the weaponization of DEI within the complex. When Black women align with Black and other minoritized people towards the transformation that DEI aims to deliver, support, and advocate for marginalized student-scholars, faculty or staff, there is often a weaponization of Black motherhood (Buckingham, 2018). Black women's labor around support for student-scholars faculty and staff is often seen as an attack against the institution, and thus, DEI practitioners who choose to practice Black Motherhood in the institution can face erasure, ostracizing, and many other tools aimed to show contempt and impede the efficacy of Black women's work (Patton et al., 2019).

Whether unintentionally or otherwise, DEI can feel weaponized within the Black and Indigenous Truth concept outlined in the DEI industrial complex framework. Black faculty, staff, and student-scholars are often courted to share candidly in task forces and classrooms about racialized issues on campus. Once they share, they can be targeted as overly aggressive, overly sensitive, and combative (Mwangi et al., 2018). These individuals often face retaliation and bullying after sharing Black and Indigenous Truths of intentional or unintentional ongoing anti-Blackness within the academy (Pyke, 2018). In addition, when minoritized faculty and staff in the academy speak up against the status quo of harm and discrimination they are often met with lowered evaluations, micromanagement and microaggressions by department chairs/direct managers, resistance to the promotion, and social isolation by BIPOC and others (Jordan-Zachery, 2019; Pyke, 2018). The psychological and spiritual impact of fighting against personal incidents of racial harm has been linked to higher rates of depression and anxiety and even lower life expectancy (Williams, 2018).

Black female leaders who experience racialized trauma in academia are made to feel that their racialized experiences and pain do not matter (Cooper, 2018; Duncan, 2014; Rodgers, 2015). Many are often made to feel as though they should be thankful that they have a job at a prestigious institution of higher learning. Internal trauma is deepened when Black female leaders have to put their heads down and overwork to keep up with the status quo's racialized demands and disregard. In addition, institutions continue to perpetuate harm. Black women leaders who work in DEI can unlearn silence and should "hold institutions accountable for creating safe work environments for women of color; creating equitable work environments free from racialized aggression is 100 percent their problem to solve" (Harts, 2021, p.15).

In speaking racialized truths as outlined in the DEI Industrial Complex, there are additional ways practitioners face weaponization. There is a deep loneliness at times in DEI work; even the BIPOC– Black, Indigenous, and People of Color– in one's community may be complicit in upholding white, elitist, patriarchal supremacy by their silence. While we all share the fear of reprisal, the authors, as Black women and nonbinary people, have felt the profound loneliness of being the only one speaking up against intersectional harm at meetings with department chairs or administrators. It can be incredibly lonely when BIPOC and non-BIPOC colleagues text after the meeting to share their agreement privately after the moment has passed publicly. In the authors' experience, weaponization occurs not only when

Black women and nonbinary people face backlash within the institution from non-allied factions but also face increased social isolation from allied factions.

With the passing of intersectional feminist bell hooks, we are reminded that universities courted bell hooks for her brilliance and status for speaking out against anti-Blackness and misogynoir but often faced backlash from administrators when speaking against its manifestation in higher education. In DEI, practitioners must be mindful of how we performatively ask for candor on racialized issues on campus but offer retaliation when given, as the spiritual toll can be energy that cannot be returned.

For instance, after being asked to speak in a meeting with the college administration on diversity, author Aysa Gray spoke openly about how the high amounts of diversity within their university did not equate to specific higher rates of Black student-scholars, faculty, or staff. Gray was later excluded from sitting on a planning committee. There are views about Black women and nonbinary people as being unprofessional, too angry, and outspoken, which can lead to continued centering of whiteness or people who are White elite adjacent and the ostracization of Black women and nonbinary staff, faculty, and student-scholars even within DEI work (Cooper, 2018).

Tokenization

"In the end, anti-black, anti-female, and all forms of discrimination are equivalent to the same thing: anti-humanism." — Shirley Chisholm, Unbought and Unbossed, 1970, p. 176.

Shirley Chisholm, often tokenized for her role in American politics and largely uncredited for being the brainchild of opportunity programs (Winslow 2012), reminds us that any conscious or unconscious act undervalues any part of our humanity is an effort to erase it. Tokenization in higher education extends to student-scholars, administrators, and programs. Within this text, tokenization is defined as the management and control of dissent by elevating one individual or entity into a perceived role of limited power and support. Often the focus is mainly on hiring and admissions to demonstrate racial inclusivity, but administrative and financial support needed to sustain, keep safe and support are lacking.

SEEK (Search for Elevation Education and Knowledge) is a classic example of tokenism in the academy. Established in 1966, the SEEK Program provided access to the disenfranchised. It brought to the predominantly white "elitist" campuses of New York the pulsating energies of the Civil Rights and the Black Power Movements (Molloy, 2017). Initially, it was lauded as the tremendous multicultural (DEI) equalizer within CUNY for providing access to thousands of marginalized urban youths. To be admitted into the SEEK Program, student-scholars' family income must meet the federal poverty threshold. It remains one of the very few programs in CUNY with a holistic academic support component that has an attached income eligibility requirement. Yet, directors of these programs must endure the inequitable comparison of SEEK with newer programs.

According to Simien (2016), "Historic firsts cannot be assessed by traditional measures" (p. 129). As a historic first, SEEK student-scholars, faculty and staff paid heavy dues for forming part of a program that disrupted the status quo. In the '60s and '70s, they faced academic apartheid - they were physically isolated on some campuses, instructors faced unequal pay, student-scholars were racially targeted in the classroom and on campus. In the '90s, retrenchment brought University-wide layoffs and the demotion of SEEK from academic departments with SEEK-specific faculty lines to programs with quotas for student enrollment (Emerson, 2021). Programs have experienced significant downsizing, and most have since been unable to offer dedicated classes for SEEK student-scholars. SEEK and other opportunity programs designed to help minoritized student-scholars are crucial examples of tokenization. While institutionally lauding SEEK for its strong outcomes, the program continues to be financially divested even in the era of DEI advancement.

Furthermore, its leaders, mostly BIPOC females, with all their skill and success, have stunted careers because of this token status (Ghosh, 2017). In addition to the disproportionate amount of work, including "emotional labor" that they must invest (Misra et al., 2011) to usher BIPOC student-scholars to success, these leaders are rarely considered for promotions, nor is their expertise valued. When retention of BIPOC student-scholars remains an Achilles heel for many institutions (Banks et al., 2019), these BIPOC female leaders, who successfully work with the most vulnerable population of the entire University system, are not recognized, promoted, or their expertise sought after for innovative retention strategies.

Outside of opportunity programs like SEEK, tokenization continues to abound. Currently, there is a push for DEI administrators as a solution for addressing the cultural status quo of white supremacy on college campuses. Often the BIPOC DEI administrators who are hired are aligned with DEI initiatives but quickly can be used as chief antagonists to the systemic change becoming the Blackface/BIPOC face of white supremacy. In this position, these administrators are, at best, marginally supportive of advancing systemic shifts and, at worst, perpetually oppositional to advancing shifts they were hired to do (Cherry-Mcdaniel, 2019).

The push for a more diverse student body within DEI initiatives has been well documented. Often the push to diversify begins with the admissions process leading BIPOC student-scholars to feel courted by the institution to enroll (Collin, 2016). Upon enrollment, their numbers help create the optics of diversity. However, the necessary environment to foster support for BIPOC student-scholars' belonging, inclusion, and timely graduation is nonexistent. Dated pictures and marketing material on one author's university show a campus with a large community of joyful Black student-scholars; however, in actuality, the population of Black student-scholars is one of the smallest in the university system, under 6 percent in 2020. These actions translate as the tokenization of BIPOC student-scholars.

Lastly, along with gender marginalization, Black women faculty continue to face tokenization. While DEI initiatives often lead universities to court Black women faculty, there is documented sidelining of their tenure and promotion. Universities often view and treat Black women faculty as the proverbial "twofers" -they check both the gender and race boxes as faculty hires. However, these institutions tokenize Black women faculty by further dismissing their intellectual contributions and scholarly accomplishments. In addition, Black women faculty are often pressured to participate as tokenized uncompensated laborers or modern-day mammies to fulfill undervalued service requirements (Collins, 2004; Rodgers, 2015; et al., 2020).

Tokenization is of significant concern within the DEI industrial complex. When BIPOC programs, staff, faculty, or student-scholars are courted to address a persistent lack of diversity, the financial or systemic support needed to sustain their participation is lacking. Tokenization thus continues the trend of DEI initiatives being ineffective in ushering in changes in systemic racism and anti-Blackness in higher education. In the authors' experience, when BIPOC individuals are tokenized and elevated within the academy, it often comes with the price of commodified emotional labor.

Commodified Emotional Labor

"I was humbled and excited to be First Lady, but not for one second did I think I'd be sliding into a glamorous, easy role. Nobody who has the words "first" and "[B]lack" attached to them ever would." – Michelle Obama, Becoming, 2018, p 284.

Akin to Michelle Obama, the first African American First Lady of the United States, Black women and nonbinary people are expected to work twice as hard as their male and White counterparts. They are left to endure the intersectional weight of false tropes – "angry Black woman" "strong Black woman," and "superwoman" (Harris-Perry, 2011; Rodgers, 2021). Concomitantly, they call for action to address the DEI industrial complex encircling commodified emotional labor. The painstaking laborious journey of DEI practitioners in the academy is premised on hierarchical white supremacy. As Zora Neale Hurston (1990) reminds us, Black women are treated as the mules of the higher education system. Nevertheless, few studies have examined its impact on Black women in academia.

Emotional Labor

Black women continue to labor in the substrate of America's class hierarchy (Marable & Mullings, 2015). From the enforced wet-nursing that enslaved Black mothers performed, treated as mules for slave breeding by their White male enslavers, and raped for social and economic reasons, Black women's bodies have been exploited for their labor (Jones-Rogers, 2017; Rodgers, 2015; 2021).

Black Woman and Nonbinary Tax, like the Black Tax, the expected labor used to summarize the other duties that African American faculty and staff have to assume by skin color, is unique (Griffin et al., 2011). Black Woman and Nonbinary Tax is the intersection of the expected gendered and racial labor of Black Women and Nonbinary faculty and staff. It is the expectation of Black motherwork to advocate and support student-scholars, faculty, and staff who are Black women and beyond. However, the Black Woman and Nonbinary Tax cannot be explained by academic status alone. Even when they are highly sought after to share their expertise in the name of financial parity, they are prowess, and their mother work is invisible. The consequences for these Black women who carry hierarchical identities, such as those held by author Blackman-Richards, seem to reproduce white normative responses, even within DEI spaces.

After years of fighting the hard-earned attainment of academic accolades (which benefit the masses), Rodgers (2020; 2021) acknowledges the complicity of human hierarchy embedded within U.S. power culture (e.g., academic titles and positions), but warns against un-ranking and reduced compensation for DEI practitioners who are also Black women professors. Acknowledging their narratives provide the necessary grounding to honor mother work experiences that reinforce white supremacist practices embedded in the mythical mammy and the strong Black woman tropes (Harris-Perry, 2011, Rodgers, 2021), PhD shaming, and alienation, thus, ultimately obstructing collective workspaces and liberatory practices asserted by Perlow et al (2018).

Black women spend an insurmountable effort challenging White hegemony in academia. Simultaneously they perform "motherwork," a form of reproductive labor that involves Black women's efforts to promote the survival of Black children, families, and communities despite white supremacist practices (Collins, 1994). They fearlessly advocate for resources to support scholars to reach their academic milestones, provide critical academic mentorship and care, and carry the weight of oppressive univers[e]sity policies and practices meant to disrupt them from sustaining leadership positions (King, 2018, Rodgers, 2021; Rodgers et al., 2020).

Black motherwork is evident in programs like Black and Africana Studies and SEEK. Every generation of its early BIPOC leadership has experienced and can recount some Racial Battle Fatigue (RBF) level. The program's constant need to defend, protect, and react to racialized conditions, microaggressions, and threats (Smith, 2004) causes RBF. As a Black female leader standing at the intersections of race and gender, author Norka Blackman-Richards asserts that exhaustion from the subtle, targeted, layered, spoken. Unspoken policing, comparing, and criticizing SEEK, while the "White" academy continues to benefit from our labor (Smith et al., 2006), is great. According to Blackman-Richards, Black female leaders of opportunity programs, who hold administrative positionality as program directors, endure exhausting experiences of being "sandwiched" between two forces for which DEI is often performative.

At the same time as performing "othermothering" (Collins, 2000), how do Black DEI laborers deconstruct traditional quantitative methods while attempting to embody financial support parity values? How do Black women professors minimize harm to themselves as they support DEI movements? How do Black DEI practitioners build wealth to pay the Black tax to pass onto the next generation within an economically unjust system designed to disenfranchise financial stability?

This section acknowledged pioneering Black women and nonbinary persons and movements that have trailblazed DEI work. The below figure also frames autoethnographic reflections and learnings with overlapping learning from one-hundred and fifty attendees who attended (Blackman-Richards et al. 2021) Fighting Racism within Academic Anti-Racist Spaces presentation at the CUNY 2021 Faculty Diversity & Inclusion Conference, The Power of an Antiracist Academy: Reimagining Systems and Structures. Within their reflections on White supremacy within DEI spaces, there are recurring themes of tokenization, performative allyship, erasure, weaponizing, undervaluing, free (emotional) labor, etc., that are present.

Figure 1. Learnings for Fighting Racism within Academic Anti-Racist Spaces

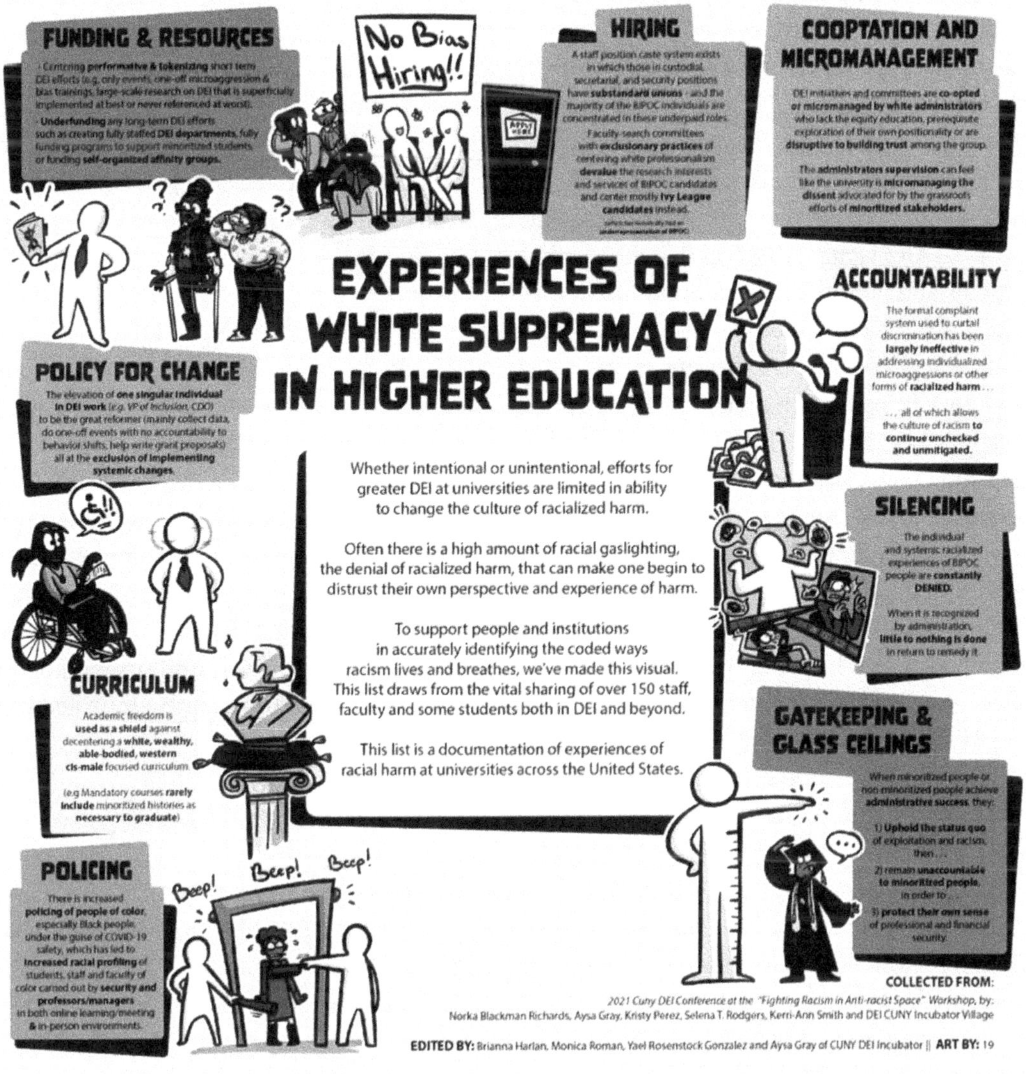

ESSENTIAL TOOLS FOR SURVIVING THE DEI INDUSTRIAL COMPLEX

Black and minoritized people continue to experience grave visceral harm within institutions with proposed DEI values. People committed to this work must do as bell hooks (2014) describes in *Sisters of the yam* as to not delude themselves or be deluded by those who create memos on Black lives mattering while closing their ears, eyes and hearts to the real harms and demands of Black people in their organizations.

DEI practitioners, particularly Black women and non-binary persons, must fully realize the temptations of the DEI Industrial Complex and go beyond traditional approaches to create tangible and sustainable change for themselves, the system at large, and those who are comrades in this work. Upon reflection on the critical themes outlined earlier, the authors have compiled a list of knowledge to navigate the inequality in presumably progressive waters.

If Black women and all co-conspirators in freedom and liberation are not careful, they will become complicit in that which seeks to oppress and destroy minoritized people. It is vital for our sista comrades in this work to use their third eyes and be evident in the ways DEI uses coded language to maintain the status quo of white elitist patriarchial ableist supremacy.

Within the DEI Industrial Complex, as DEI practitioners and academic leaders, the previously discussed racialized circumstances manifest as traumatic after-effects with lasting consequences that cause harm to Black women and non-binary lives in Higher Education. These after-effects present themselves as continuous experiences of dispossession and defunding from institutions and programs that are supposed to support BIPOC faculty, staff, and student-scholars.ongoing struggles for survival from historically Black studies and programs, the commodification of Black professionals used for their labor within unprotected spaces where there is a lack of environments to thrive professionally, and the undermining of Black female leadership and experiences. These named conditions place Black Female and Nonbinary lives in Higher Education in racialized circumstances that generate under-sourcing, underfunding, and understaffing. These after-effects create the conditions and atmosphere that further render Black Female Lives in Higher Education invisible and increases their labor.

In response to the "the masters tools will not dismantle the master's house" analogy (Lorde, 2003), the authors suggest the following essential tools for surviving the DEI Industrial Complex: knowledge and wisdom; village community care; and a call to action and unapologetic practices for survival. The authors developed these tools from their own experiences as Black women faculty, nonbinary persons, and DEI practitioners laboring in the university. After reviewing the tools, the authors are hopeful that other Black women and nonbinary DEI practitioners will add these tools to their toolbox and use them strategically as needed.

Knowledge and Wisdom

Drawing from the experiences of other Black women faculty and non-binary persons, we can create a foundation of awareness of our collective knowledge and wisdom. Establishing such a foundation is supported by: Awareness that Black History matters, understanding that initiatives and systems created by Black Power are not just historical occurrences, they are studies in Black survival. An awareness of why we are being hired is critical to understanding what we are up against and how we will need to strategize resistance. The possibility of Black persons being hired to keep white structures in place or forward harmful agendas is factual. Understanding the reason behind the power given to that position is critical to how work to elevate, re-imagine, build, or destroy structures will occur.

Wisdom and knowledge are necessary for decolonizing practices, policies, and curricula that center on white supremacy. Here are some ways to go about this: (a) Having an awareness of the academy's coded terms and strategies to avoid changing and continuing to uphold white elitist patriarchal supremacy, (b) Collecting information from various parties/allies to understand dynamics and using this information to work towards changing the culture of racial harm, (c) Becoming strategic in our movements and organizing to re-address the internal, purposeful dismantling that is taking place even with the availability of funding or new hires, (d) Becoming aware of institutional trends that impact BIPOC Student-Scholars, such as (1) Quota enrollments and lack of strategic recruitment to address low enrollment of Black/ BIPOC student-scholars, (2) attrition or lack of holistic academic models for BIPOC low-income and first-generation student-scholars success, (3) the reduction of crucial staffing roles, resulting in increasing labor, the commodification of Black professionals, and further deterioration of program services to BIPOC student-scholars.

Village Community Care

To move beyond the DEI industrial complex, Black women and nonbinary DEI practitioners must find ways to create a community or village in their institution. The village must be a space where cultural authenticity and accountability for harm are welcomed beyond performativity. The following are ways to embrace village community care: 1) Using Grounding activities (e.g., healing circles, music, dance) is critical for repairing unseen and unbandaged wounds sustained by remedial interventions. It also may be appropriate to consider starting or ending meetings using these practices to disrupt the normative white elitist professional culture of meetings. 2) Safeguarding one's energy. Black women and nonbinary DEI Practitioners must be clear that while fighting racism is the work, racism and white supremacy cannot consume all of one's life energy and identity. In other words, Black women are more than the mules of white supremacy. It is essential to have additional projects and passions that spiritually sustain DEI practitioners and can be poured into outside of paid work. 3) Create a working group with other staff, faculty, and student-scholars, who are values-aligned, to co-lead a racial justice initiative to both help stakeholders in the group obtain their needs and collectively disrupt the racially harmful status quo. Consider whose identity and positionality would be disruptive to the first iteration and if they should be included at the beginning. Village space is where practitioners receive familial support; however, to create structural shifts, village care and ways to call to action are necessary.

Call to Action for Survival and Beyond

Often practices for engaging with inequity within DEI industrial complex framework are individualized, which leads to burnout and limits the transformation aspirations of DEI to create structural change. Practitioners and the village that support them must go beyond individualized survival strategies and push for structural shifts. The following are ways calls to action that the authors have explored to push for structural shifts:

1) Interrogate the whiteness and classism within you as a practitioner and co-create an ongoing space that allows for staff, faculty, students, and administrators interrogation. Anti-blackness is deeply embedded in American institutions. Thus, racism pervasively impacts policies, funding, procedures, and practices and nurtures oppressive systems and structures. Unquestioning compliance or alliance with policies, systems, and structures that center the status quo are acquiescing to harmful anti-blackness and elitism. 2) Drawing from practices and strategies that are not always viewed as professional or traditional for academic space, like grassroots organizing (the collective creation of a counter-power led by those most impacted by harm) that is co-led by student-scholars, community members, staff, and faculty, as Angela Davis and Audre Lorde did. 3) Many practitioners, staff, faculty, and students are often unfamiliar with the skills necessary for grassroots organizing, identifying their own biases playing out on campus (beyond petitions), and maintaining organizational relationships within their workplace/campus. Therefore it is necessary to find money to skill up to gain the social capital necessary to shift the racially oppressive culture while staying gainfully employed. 4) DEI practitioners and villages must encourage and create pushes for accountability beyond the formal channels (human resources departments and complaint systems) as they are limited in efficacy as they are controlled by an institution willing to

allow-long standing Black harm. It is crucial to find values-centered ways to independently document the incidence and show the prevalence of racial harm in strategic and collective ways such as research, anonymous social media pages, and art installations. The work involved in moving beyond succumbing to the DEI industrial complex involves wisdom and knowledge, creating the village, and a call to action is necessary to begin shifting the culture of harm the DEI industrial continues to foster.

UNDOING THE UNDERMINING BLACK WOMEN'S LEADERSHIP: CONCLUSION

"When we drop fear, we can draw nearer to people, we can draw nearer to the earth, we can draw nearer to all the heavenly creatures that surround us." – Bell Hooks, 2012, p. 23.

bell hooks remind us of our birthright to own and possess all of the earth. It is our birthright to survive to transgress. The weaponization of Black women and non-binary persons has always existed. Since the inception of resistance movements in the academy, foremothers such as Audre Lorde, June Jordan, Toni Cade Bambara, Shirley Chisolm, and bell hooks have led efforts to transform oppression within higher education. The authors, endowed with their activist, educator, and leadership DNA, are organized under the CUNY DEI initiative and are organically positioned to lead radical efforts to dismantle the DEI Industrial Complex.

To deepen our understanding of the CUNY Diversity, Equity, and Inclusion (DEI) Incubator and lived experiences of diversity practitioners in academia, this chapter inextricably links equity and inclusion to existing diversity conversations. The introduction of the DEI industrial complex critiques performative measures of DEI that intentionally or unintentionally are superficial in approach. Motivated to relocate power and deconstruct racist and inequity-centered education, the authors provide examples describing ways Black woman leadership is undermined. The authors offer a window into the cascading effects of the DEI Industrial Complex. Together, they can forward DEI work to uplift Black people and humanity. Essential survival tools were provided to engage with the DEI Industrial Complex for solutions as envisioned by the "First Lady of the Struggle," Mary McLeod Bethune. While this discussion calls attention to a few experiences of Black women and nonbinary persons, concerns about present-day manifestations of the DEI Industrial Complex CUNY-wide and beyond are well-founded (Gray et al., 2021). Future study is needed to highlight different Black and POC narratives and to expand on skills essential for survival.

Anti-Blackness will try to deny and exclude Black humanity from the public sphere and position Blackness as a problem that requires solving instead of a people suffering from historical and systemic racism (Dumas, 2016). Within this pained history with continued challenging circumstances, Black women leaders are called to lead. It is critical to continue documenting Black women and non-binary persons' contributions, barriers, and complexities to organizing and leading movements – Black Lives Matter, CUNY DEI, 'MeToo' (Blackman-Richards et al., 2021; Burke, 2021; Garza, 2020). Thus, this entry is a critical analysis of Black womens' leadership undermining as they work to address intersectional racism in academia and transform the culture that reinforces it. Strategically, the authors use tools to organize social power to disrupt white, elitist, patriarchal supremacy, break glass ceilings to vertical leadership and gain access to human rights.

Yet, amid joint anti-racism efforts, statements to eliminate racism proposed implicit and explicit curricula changes (e.g., CSWE, 2021; NASW, 2021), the psychological harm, and the swell of recent massacres BIPOC folk continues. Some minoritized persons have voiced such in[actions] as disingenuous. Congress has yet to vote on H.R. 40 to study reparations for slavery. Furthering anti-Blackness, systemic inequities, and oppressions against DEI practitioners. Macro-level system policy responses are also warranted. Even under professed DEi leaders, performativity must be recognized as a deflection to working to uproot antiblackness.

ACKNOWLEDGMENT

This research received no specific grant from any funding agency in the public, commercial, or not-for-profit sectors.

REFERENCES

Bailey, M. (2018). On misogynoir: Citation, erasure, and plagiarism. *Feminist Media Studies*, *18*(4), 762–768. doi:10.1080/14680777.2018.1447395

Ballard, D., Allen, B., Ashcraft, K., Ganesh, S., McLeod, P., & Zoller, H. (2020). When words do not matter: Identifying actions to effect diversity, equity, and inclusion in the academy. *Management Communication Quarterly*, *34*(4), 590–616. doi:10.1177/0893318920951643

Banaji, M. R., & Greenwald, A. G. (2016). *Blindspot: Hidden biases of good people*. Bantam.

Banks, Tachelle, & Dohy, Jennifer (2019). Mitigating Barriers to Persistence: A Review of Efforts to Improve Retention and Graduation Rates for Students of Color in Higher Education. *Higher Education Studies*, p118-131

Beal, F. M. (2008). Double jeopardy: To be Black and female. *Meridians (Middletown, Conn.)*, *8*(2), 166–176. doi:10.2979/MER.2008.8.2.166

Bell, M. P. (2020). Anti-blackness, surface-level diversity continues to matter: What must we do? *Equality, Diversity and Inclusion*. https://doi-org.ezproxy.uta.edu/10.1108/EDI-06-2020-0160

Blackman-Richards, N., Gray, A., Perez, K. C., Rodgers, S. T., & Smith, K. A. M. (2021, April 15). Fighting Racism within Academic Anti-Racist Spaces. CUNY 2021 Faculty Diversity & Inclusion Conference. The Power of an Antiracist Academy: Reimagining Systems and Structures. *Virtual.*

Board of Education of Topeka. (1954). 347 U.S. 483

Boykin, C. M., Brown, N. D., Carter, J. T., Dukes, K., Green, D. J., Harrison, T., Hebl, M., McCleary-Gaddy, A., Membere, A., McJunkins, C. A., Simmons, C., Singletary Walker, S., Smith, A. N., & Williams, A. D. (2020). Anti-racist actions and accountability: Not more empty promises. *Equality, Diversity and Inclusion*, *39*(7), 775–786. doi:10.1108/EDI-06-2020-0158

Buckingham, D. (2018). Invisible labor: A mixed-method study of African American women and their emotional labor in the academy. *Electronic Theses and Dissertations*, 849. https://egrove.olemiss.edu/etd/849

Burke, T. (2021). *Unbound: My Story of Liberation and the Birth of the Me Too Movement*. Flatiron Books.

Cherry-McDaniel, M. (2019). Skinfolk ain't always kinfolk: The dangers of assuming and assigning inherent cultural responsiveness to teachers of color. *Educational Studies*, *55*(2), 241–251. doi:10.1080/00131946.2018.1500912

Chisholm, S. (1970). *Unbought & Unbossed*. Houghton Mifflin Harcourt.

Collins, D. E. (2016). The Token Commitment. *Diverse Issues in Higher Education*, *33*(9), 24.

Collins, P. (2000). *Black feminist thought: Knowledge, consciousness, and the politics of empowerment,* (2nd ed.). Routledge.

Collins, P. H. 1994. "Shifting the Center: Race, Class and Feminist Theorizing About Motherhood.," (Eds). Evelyn Nakano Glenn et al. Mothering: Ideology, Experience and Agency. New York: Routledge.

Collins, P. H. (2004). *Black sexual politics*. Routledge. doi:10.4324/9780203309506

Cooper, B. (2018). *Eloquent rage: A Black feminist discovers her superpower*. St. Martin's Press.

Council on Social Work Education (CSWE). (2021). *Commission on Accreditation 2022 Educational Policy and Accreditation Standards draft*. Author.

CUNY TV. (2016, April 7). The Percy Ellis Sutton SEEK Program: Opening Doors for 50 Years. YouTube. https://youtu.be/L-rugBBt4G4

Dobbin, F., & Kalev, A. (2020) Making Discrimination and Harassment Complaint Systems Better. *What Works?, 24*.

Dumas, M. J. (2016). Against the dark: Antiblackness in education policy and discourse. *Theory into Practice*, *55*(1), 11–19. doi:10.1080/00405841.2016.1116852

Duncan, P. (2014). Hot Commodities, Cheap Labor: Women of Color in the Academy. *Frontiers*, *35*(3), 39–63. doi:10.5250/fronjwomestud.35.3.0039

Garza, A. (2020). *The Purpose of Power : How We Come Together When We Fall Apart*. Random House Publishing Group.

Gates, Jr., H. L. (7 January 2013). The Truth Behind '40 Acres and a Mule. *The Root*.

Ghosh, D., & Barber, K. (2021). The Gender of Multiculturalism: Cultural Tokenism and the Institutional Isolation of Immigrant Women Faculty. *Sociological Perspectives*, *64*(6), 1063–1080. doi:10.1177/0731121420981098

Glennen, R. E., Baxley, D. M., & Farren, P. J. (1985). Impact of intrusive advising on minority student retention. *College Student Journal*.

Harris-Perry, M. V. (2011). *Sister citizen: Shame, stereotypes, and Black women in America*. Yale University Press.

Harts, M. (2021). Right Within: How To Heal From Racial Trauma. In *The Workplace*. Seal Press.

Hevesi, D. (1995, May 14) CUNY Campuses Prepare to Reduce Faculty and Classes. *The New York Times*.

Hill, M. (2020, October 12) Brittany Cooper Dissecting her New York Times Best Seller "An Eloquent Rage: A Black Feminist Discovers her Superpower". *Embassy Row*. https://podcasts.apple.com/us/podcast/brittney-cooper-dissecting-her-new-york-times-best/id1522592619?i=1000494456090

Hinrichs, P. (2016). An empirical analysis of racial segregation in higher education (No. w21831). National Bureau of Economic Research.

Holder, L. (2020). A Paradigm Shift in Race Consciousness Drives the Growing Demand for Diversity Equity and Inclusion Consultation. *California Labor and Employment Review*, *34*(5), 1–12.

Holder, M. (2020). *The Double Gap and the Bottom Line: African American Women's Wage Gap and Corporate Profits*. Report for The Roosevelt Institute. https://rooseveltinstitute.org/publications/the-double-gap-and-the-bottom-line-african-american-womens-wage-gap-and-corp
orate-profits/

Hooks, B. (1994a). *Outlaw Culture: Resisting Representations*. New York: Routledge.

Hooks, B. (1994b). Teaching to Transgress: Education as the Practice of Freedom. *Routledge*.

Hooks, B. (2012, July-August). Inner & outer worlds. *Spirituality & Health Magazine, 15*(4), p. 23.

hooks, b. (2014). Sisters of the yam: Black women and self-recovery. *Routledge*.

Hourston, Z. N. (1990). *Their eyes were watching God*. Harper & Row.

https://nces.ed.gov/ipeds/datacenter/institutionprofile.aspx
?unitId=190691

Johnsrud, L. K. (2003). Higher education support professionals: The fear of speaking out. *The NEA 2003 Almanac of Higher Education*, 109-118.

Jones-Rogers, S. (2017). '[S]he could…spare one ample breast for the profit of her owner': White mothers and enslaved wet nurses' invisible labor in American slave markets. *Slavery & Abolition*, *38*(2), 337–355. doi:10.1080/0144039X.2017.1317014

Jordan, B. (2021) Social Control and 'Black Lives Matter'. In: The Future of Social Work. Palgrave Macmillan, Cham. doi:10.1007/978-3-030-76371-8_5

Jordan-Zachery, J. S. (2019). Licking Salt: A Black Woman's Tale of Betrayal, Adversity, and Survival. *Feminist Formations*, *31*(1), 67–84. doi:10.1353/ff.2019.0009

King, T. C. (2018). Healing Circles as Black Feminist Pedagogical Interventions. In O. N. Perlow, D. I. Wheeler, S. L. Bethea, & B. Scott (Eds.), *Black Women's Laboratory Pedagogies: Resistance, transformation, and healing within and beyond the academy,* (pp. 21–44). Pelgrave Macmillan. doi:10.1007/978-3-319-65789-9_2

Logan, N. (2021). Breaking Down Barriers of the Past and Moving Toward Authentic DEI Adoption. In D. Pompper (Ed.). Public Relations for Social Responsibility: Affirming DEI Commitment with Action (Communicating Responsible Diversity, Equality, and Inclusion). (pp3-17). United Kingdom, Bingley: Emerald Publishing Limited. doi:10.1108/978-1-80043-167-620211001

Lorde, A. (2003). The master's tools will never dismantle the master's house. *Feminist postcolonial theory. REAd (Porto Alegre), 25*, 27.

Mahtani, M. (2004). Mapping race and gender in the academy: The experiences of women of colour faculty and graduate students in Britain, the US and Canada. *Journal of Geography in Higher Education, 28*(1), 91–99. doi:10.1080/0309826042000198666

Marable, M., & Mullings, L. (2015). *How Capitalism Underdeveloped Black America: Problems in Race, Political Economy, and Society*. Haymarket Books.

Mayorga-Gallo, S. (2019). The white-centering logic of diversity ideology. *The American Behavioral Scientist, 63*(13), 1789–1809. doi:10.1177/0002764219842619

Misra, J., Lundquist, J. H., Holmes, E., & Agiomavritis, S. (2011). The Ivory Ceiling of Service Work. *Academe, 97*(1), 22–26.

Molloy, S. (23 June 2017). SEEK's Fight for Racial and Social Justice (1965-1969). *CUNY Digital History Project*.

Montoya, M. C. (2020). *A Labor of Love: University Custodians Saliendo Adelante and Student Engagement Practices*. California State University.

Mwangi, C. A. G., Thelamour, B., Ezeofor, I., & Carpenter, A. (2018). Black elephant in the room": Black students contextualizing campus racial climate within US racial climate. *Journal of College Student Development, 59*(4), 456–474. doi:10.1353/csd.2018.0042

NASW apologizes for racist practices in American social work (2021, April 17). New Release. Alexandria, VA: Author. https://www.socialworkers.org/News/News-Releases/ID/2331/NASW-apologizes-for-racist-practices-in-American-social-work

National Center for Education Statistics (NCES) survey (2020).

Obama, M. (2018). *Becoming*. Crown.

Patton, L. D., & Njoku, N. R. (2019). Theorizing Black women's experiences with institution-sanctioned violence: A# BlackLivesMatter imperative toward Black liberation on campus. *International Journal of Qualitative Studies in Education: QSE, 32*(9), 1162–1182.

Perlow, O. N., Wheeler, D. I., Bethea, S. L., & Scott, B. (Eds.). (2018). *Black Women's Laboratory Pedagogies: Resistance, transformation, and healing within and beyond the academy*. Pelgrave Macmillan.

Pyke, K. D. (2018). Institutional betrayal: Inequity, discrimination, bullying, and retaliation in academia. *Sociological Perspectives, 61*(1), 5–13.

Robertson, R. (2021). A critical race theory analysis of transnational student activism, social media counter-stories, and the hegemonic logics of diversity work in higher education. *International Journal of Qualitative Studies in Education: QSE*, 1–18.

Rodgers, S. T. (2015). Being of Some Scholarly Service…: A New Take On The Scholarship of Engagement in Academe. In F.A. Bonner, II, C.W., R. M. Banda, P. A. Robinson, Lewis, F. A., & B. Lofton (Eds.). Priorities of the Professoriate: Engaging Multiple Forms of Scholarship Across Rural and Urban Institutions. (pp. 67-88). Charlotte, NC: Information Age Publishing.

Rodgers, S. T. (2015). Racism. In C. Franklin (Ed.), *Encyclopedia of Social Work Online (ESWO),* (21st ed.). Oxford University Press.

Rodgers, S. T. (2021). The Next Wave of Post Traumatic Slave Syndrome Survivors: Black Women Resisters in Academia. Advances in Social Work. *Special Issue: Dismantling White Supremacy in Social Work Education, 21*(2), 438–459. doi:10.18060/24159

Rodgers, S. T., & Lopez-Humphreys, M. (2020). Social Work Leadership: Grand Challenges for Black Women. *Social Work, 65*(4), 397–400.

Schantz, M. (2019). Affirming the Purpose of Affirmative Action: Understanding a Policy of the Past to Move Towards a More Informed Future.

Simien, E. M. (Ed.). (2016). *Historic Firsts: How Symbolic Empowerment Changes US Politics*. Oxford University Press.

Sleeter, C. E. (2011). The academic and social value of ethnic studies.

Smith, A. (2007). *The revolution will not be funded: Beyond the non-profit industrial complex*. INCITE.

Smith, A. (2009). Native studies beyond the academic-industrial complex. *I thought Pocahontas was a movie": Perspectives on race/culture binaries in education and service professions*, 79-89.

Smith, W. A. (2004). Black faculty coping with racial battle fatigue: The campus racial climate in a post-civil rights era. In D. Cleveland (Ed.), *A long way to go: Con- versations about race by African American faculty and graduate students* (pp. 171–190). Peter Lang Publishing.

Smith, W. A., Yosso, T. J., & Solórzano, D. G. (2006). Challenging racial battle fatigue on historically white campuses: A critical race examination of race-related stress. In C. A. Stanley (Ed.), *Faculty of color: Teaching in predominantly white colleges and universities* (pp. 299–327). Anker Publishing.

Squire, D., Williams, B. C., & Tuitt, F. (2018). Plantation politics and neoliberal racism in higher education: A framework for reconstructing anti-racist institutions. *Teachers College Record, 120*(14), 1–20.

Steinberg, S. (2018, April 9). Revisiting open admissions at CUNY. *PSC CUNY*. https://psc-cuny.org/clarion/february-2018/revisiting-open-admissions-cuny

Tevis, T., Hernandez, M., & Bryant, R. (2020). Reclaiming our time: An autoethnographic exploration of black women higher education administrators. *The Journal of Negro Education, 89*(3), 282–297, 381–382.

Thomas, J. M. (2020). *Diversity regimes: Why talk is not enough to fix racial inequality at universities*. Rutgers University Press.

Williams, D., & Wade-Golden, K. (2007). The chief diversity officer. *CUPA-HR Journal, 58*(1), 38.

Woodard, Q. (2014). *Understanding the implications of organizational culture and organizational structure for the role of the Chief Diversity Officer in higher education* [Doctoral dissertation]. University of Illinois at Urbana-Champaign, USA.

Zamani, E. M. (2003). African American women in higher education. *New Directions for Student Services, 104*, 5–18.

ADDITIONAL READING

Carruthers, C. A. (2018). *Unapologetic : a Black, queer, and feminist mandate for radical movements.* Beacon Press.

Ginwright, S. A. (2022). *The four pivots: Reimagining justice. Reimagining ourselves.* Penguin Random House.

Harris, A. P. (2020). Presumed incompetent II: Race, class, power, and resistance of women in academia. University Press of Colorado. hooks. b. (1981). Ain't I a woman : Black women and feminism. South End Press. hooks. b. (1989). Talking back : thinking feminist, thinking black. South End Press.

Menakem, R. (2017). *My grandmother's hands: racialized trauma and the pathway to mending our hearts and bodies.* Central Recovery Press.

Ransby, B. (2003). *Ella Baker and the Black freedom movement a radical democratic vision.* University of North Carolina Press.

Roberts, D. (1998). *Killing the Black body: Race, reproduction, and the meaning of liberty.* Vintage.

Taylor, K.-Y. (2017). How we get free : Black feminism and the Combahee River Collective (Taylor, Ed.). Haymarket Books.

White, D. G. (1999). Too Heavy a Load: Black Women in defense of themselves, 1894-1994 (p. NA–268).

Winters, M. F. (2020). *Black fatigue: How racism erodes the mind, body, and spirit.* Berrett-Koehler Publishers.

KEY TERMS AND DEFINITIONS

Anti-Blackness: Specific forms of racism that lead to the disenfranchisement of Black people.

BIPOC: Black Indigenous People of Color is a group of people of color that centers the experiences of Black and Indigenous people.

Black Tax: The expected labor used to summarize the other duties that African American faculty and staff have to assume by virtue of skin color (Griffin et al., 2011)

Black Woman and Nonbinary Tax: The gendered and racial labor expected of Black Women and Nonbinary faculty and staff. It's the expectation of black motherwork to advocate and support student-scholars faculty and staff who are black women and beyond.

Commodified Labor: The expectation of minoritized people (especially women and nonbinary people) to commit to DEI work with little to no compensation (committees/task-forces/councils/ affinity groups) (see the Appendix for further examples).

DEI: Diversity, Equity and Inclusion is the umbrella term used to describe work that forwards self and community actualization for all beings.

DEI Industrial Complex: The collusion of the state, non profits, corporations and higher education to use Diversity, Equity, and Inclusion work to restore social and financial gain to an institution, while consistently only addressing the lowest hanging fruit, and offering no shifts in the major and pervasive issues of systemic oppression, especially as they pertain to anti-Blackness.

Student-Scholars: Term used to describe students through a transformative lens as intellects, scholars, leaders, trailblazers, visionaries and the like.

Tokenization: The management and control dissent by elevating one individual into a perceived role of limited power (see the Appendix for further examples).

Weaponization: Using DEI rationale to undermine BIPOC leadership and contribution (see the Appendix for further examples).

White Supremacy: The explicit to subtle ways that the norms, preferences and fears of white European descended people overwhelmingly share how society organizes work and institutions, see individuals and makes decisions.

APPENDIX

Table 1. DEI Industrial Complex

DEI Industrial Complex Definition: The collusion of the state, non-profits, corporations, and higher education to use Diversity, Equity, and Inclusion (DEI) work to restore social and financial gain to an institution, while consistently only addressing the lowest hanging fruit, and offering no shifts in the major and pervasive issues of systemic oppression, especially as they pertain to antiBlackness. (institutions use DEI work to):
1. Weaponize and Erasure Using DEI rationale to undermine BIPOC leadership and contribution. Examples: Fear of Black and Indigenous Truth, Attack on Affinity A. Fear of Black and Indigenous Truth Opening up conversations/committees on DEI however when Black and Indigenous people speak up about serious racialized harm, they are punished with limitations on upward mobility or access to shared committee space in the future. B. Attack on affinity Using the need for equality to criticize and delegitimize the need/allowance of formal Black and Indigenous and other minoritized people-based affinity spaces.
2. Free/Undercompensated labor: (Lerma et al., 2019) Underfunding DEI works within an institution, while simultaneously finding funding for other more politically pressing concerns (Ahmed, 2012). Examples: Free Emotional Labor, Devaluing Black and Minoritized Programs A. Free Emotional Labor The expectation of DEI work with low or no compensation for minoritized people, especially women and nonbinary people. Ex. The explicit or implicit push to be on identity-related committees/task-forces/councils/ affinity groups. B. Devaluing of Black and Minoritized Programs The strategic underfunding of projects that support the survival of minoritized peoples. Such as: Hiring a DEI practitioner but not giving them a budget or team to support them in creating change.
3. Tokenization The management and control of dissent by elevating one individual or entity into a perceived role of limited power and support. (Mayorga-Gallo, 2019) Examples: Diversify the Status Quo and Cooptation A. Diversify the Status Quo Hiring a single minoritized person in a prominent position that will continue the status quo of exploitation and racism. These individuals frame themselves or are often framed as non-dangerous/sensible to the status-quo as compared to those BIPOC or allied people who are disruptive to the racist status-quo. AKA Becoming the Black/BIPOC Face of White Supremacy. B. Cooptation When stakeholders organize for meaningful and robust shifts in systemic racism and the response is to give the organizers a single administrator in DEI without addressing any of the other structural issues underpinning the harm and systemic discrimination experienced. Resulting in little shifts in the lived conditions of the BIPOC within the institution.
4. Performativity: Allowing institutions to use "good intent" to mask their continued exploitative and racist work practices through lip service, while often only addressing the lowest-hanging fruit, and continuing to avoid the major and systemic shifts necessary (Thomas, 2020, Ahmed, 2012, Mayorga-Gallo, 2019, Boykin et al., 2020). Examples: Lack of Accountability, Do As I Say A. Lack of Accountability Despite the longstanding institutionalization of complaint systems there is no effective accountability mechanism for holding the institution and its stakeholders accountable when oppression-related harm is committed. Therefore those within an institution feel as though they can uphold white supremacy by performing microaggressions, having racially exclusionary departments, performing racialized vandalism, and beyond with impunity. B. Do as I say DEI practitioners teach and facilitate work they are not doing individually or within their team that would be necessary for them to understand/ counter their own privilege and positionality.
5. The Master's Tools will never dismantle the master's house: Encourage DEI projects to model themselves after racialized, capitalist, patriarchal and ableist structures rather than challenge them (Mayorga-Gallo, 2019). Examples: The Overseer and Diversity ONLY A. The Overseer Having DEI practitioners report to executives/chairs who have limited/no experience in DEI work but can veto the necessary work to create shifts in the culture of white elitist patriarchal supremacy (Thomas, 2018). B. Diversity ONLY (but no Equity or Inclusion) Encouraging the focus of collecting data, having task forces/DEI committees, and/or creating more strategic plans to prove improvements in diversity rather than changing the underlying causes of the lack of diversity that relate to equity and inclusion (Ahmed, 2012).

Compilation of References

Abdel-Fattah. (2020). Emotional intelligence and emotional stability in crises. *Journal of Psychiatry and Psychiatric Disorders*, *4*(2), 56–52. doi:10.26502/jppd. 2572-519X0090

Adeniran, R. K. (2022). Black women and microaggression: The confirmation hearing of associate justice Ketanji Brown Jackson. *Holistic Nursing Practice*, *36*(4), 189–191. doi:10.1097/HNP.0000000000000533 PMID:35708554

ADL. (n.d.). Our mission. *.ADL.* https://www.adl.org/who-we-are/our-mission

Ahmed, S. (2012). *On being included.* Duke University Press.

Ahmed, S. (2012). *On being included: Racism and diversity in institutional life.* Duke University Press. doi:10.2307/j.ctv1131d2g

Ahmed, S. (2018). Rocking the boat: Women of colour as diversity workers. In J. Arday & H. S. Mirza (Eds.), *Dismantling race in higher education: Racism, whiteness and decolonising the academy,* (pp. 331–348). Palgrave Macmillan. doi:10.1007/978-3-319-60261-5_19

Allan, E. J. (2003). Constructing women's status: Policy discourses of university women's commission policy reports. *Harvard Educational Review*, *73*(1), 44–72. doi:10.17763/haer.73.1.f61t41j83025vwh7

Alonazi, W. B. (2020). The impact of emotional intelligence on job performance during covid-19 crisis: A cross-sectional analysis. *Psychology Research and Behavior Management*, *13*, 749–757. doi:10.2147/PRBM.S263656

American Association for Access, Equity, and Diversity. (2021). Affirmative action policies throughout history. *AAAED.* https://www.aaaed.org/aaaed/History_of_Affirmative_Action.asp

American Council on Education. (2017). Pipelines, pathways, and institutional leadership. *American Council on Education Higher Ed Spotlight.* https://www.acenet.edu/Documents/HES-Pipelines-Pathways-and-Institutional-Leadership-2017.pdf

AmeriCorps. (n.d.) Volunteering in America: Rankings. *Americorps/*https://americorps.gov/sites/default/files/document/Volunteering_in_America_Rankings_508.pdf

Amina, A., Hadi, N. U., Waheed, A., & Fayyaz, H. (2021). The effect of leader mindfulness on employee job performance: Investigating the mediating and moderating role of leader-member exchange and organization culture. *Journal of Behavioral Sciences*, *31*(2), 138–165.

Amott, T. J. M. (1996). *Race, Gender and Work: A Multi-cultural Economic History of Women in the United States.* South End Press.

Anderson, G. (2020). The emotional toll of racism. *Inside Higher Education.* https://www.insidehighered.com/booklet/leadership-pursuit-diversity-equity-and-inclusion

Anderson, T. (1988). Black encounter of racism and elitism in white academe: A critique of the system. *Journal of Black Studies*, *18*(3), 259–272. doi:10.1177/002193478801800301

Angelou, M. (1979). *I know why the caged bird sings*. Random House.

Anthias, F. (2013). Intersectional what? Social divisions, intersectionality and levels of analysis. *Ethnicities*, *13*(1), 3–19. doi:10.1177/1468796812463547

Anti-defamation League. (n.d.). Civil Rights Movement. *ADL*. https://www.adl.org/education/resources/backgrounders/civil-rights-movement

Arday, J., & Mirza, H. S. (Eds.). (2018). *Dismantling race in higher education: Racism, Whiteness and decolonising the academy*. Palgrave Macmillan. doi:10.1007/978-3-319-60261-5

Arie, I. (2006). I am not my hair. [Song]. On Testimony: Vol. 1, Life & Relationship [Album]. Motown Records.

Arminio, J. (2001). Exploring the nature of race-related guilt. *Journal of Multicultural Counseling and Development*, *29*(4), 239–252. doi:10.1002/j.2161-1912.2001.tb00467.x

Arnold, J., & Kowalski-Braun, M. (2011). The journey to an inaugural chief diversity officer: Preparation, implementation and beyond. *Innovative Higher Education*, *37*(1), 27–36. doi:10.100710755-011-9185-9

Asare, J. G. (2022, September 20). *5 Black Women Share What Equity Means To Them*. Forbes. https://www.forbes.com/sites/janicegassam/2022/09/20/5-black-women-share-what-equity-means-to-them/?sh=285e155f71db

Ashkanasy, N., & Daus, C. (2005). Rumors of the death of emotional intelligence in organizational behavior are vastly exaggerated. *Journal of Organizational Behavior*, *26*(4), 441–452. doi:10.1002/job.320

Ashley, W. (2014). The angry black woman: The impact of pejorative stereotypes on psychotherapy with black women. *Social Work in Public Health*, *29*(1), 27–34. doi:10.1080/19371918.2011.619449

Ayers, W., Hunt, J. A., & Quinn, T. (1998). Teaching for social justice. A Democracy and education reader. New Press, 450 West 41st Street, New York, NY 10036.

Baez, B. (2000). Race-related service and faculty of color: Conceptualizing critical agency in academe. *Higher Education*, *39*(3), 363–391. doi:10.1023/A:1003972214943

Bailey, M. (2018). On misogynoir: Citation, erasure, and plagiarism. *Feminist Media Studies*, *18*(4), 762–768. doi:10.1080/14680777.2018.1447395

Bailey, M. (2021). *Misogynoir transformed: Black women's digital resistance*. NYU Press. doi:10.18574/nyu/9781479803392.001.0001

Ballard, D., Allen, B., Ashcraft, K., Ganesh, S., McLeod, P., & Zoller, H. (2020). When words do not matter: Identifying actions to effect diversity, equity, and inclusion in the academy. *Management Communication Quarterly*, *34*(4), 590–616. doi:10.1177/0893318920951643

BallotPedia. (2022). Maxine Waters. *Ballotpedia*. https://ballotpedia.org/Maxine_Waters#Committee_assignments

Banai, A., Ronzoni, M., & Schemmel, C. (Eds.). (2011). *Social justice, global dynamics: Theoretical and empirical perspectives*. Routledge. doi:10.4324/9780203819296

Banaji, M. R., & Greenwald, A. G. (2016). *Blindspot: Hidden biases of good people*. Bantam.

Banks, N. (2019, February 19). *Black women's labor market history reveals deep-seated race and gender discrimination.* Economic policy institute. https://www.epi.org/blog/black-womens-labor-market-history-reveals-deep-seated-race-and-gender-discrimination/

Banks, Tachelle, & Dohy, Jennifer (2019). Mitigating Barriers to Persistence: A Review of Efforts to Improve Retention and Graduation Rates for Students of Color in Higher Education. *Higher Education Studies*, p118-131

Banks-Wallace, J. (2002). Talk that talk: Storytelling and analysis rooted in African-American oral tradition. *Qualitative Health Research*, *12*(3), 410–426. doi:10.1177/104973202129119892 PMID:11918105

Barkataki, S. (2019, July 26). *Why the heck are you white centering and what to do about it.* https://www.susannabarkataki.com/post/why-the-heck-are-you-white-centering-and-what-to-do-about-it

Barratt, B. (2020, June 19). The microaggressions towards black women you might be complicit in at work. *Forbes.* https://www.forbes.com/sites/biancabarratt/2020/06/19/themicroaggressions-towards-black-women-you-might-be-complicit-in-at-work/?sh=fe1cf542bda5-

Bass, B. M. (1985). *Leadership and performance*. Free Press.

Bass, B. M., & Avolio, B. J. (1993). Transforming leadership and organizational culture. *Public Administration Quarterly*, *17*, 112–121.

Bautista, T. G., Cash, T. A., Meyerhoefer, T., & Pipe, T. B. (2022). Equitable Mindfulness: The Practice of Mindfulness for All. *Journal of Community Psychology*. doi:10.1002/jcop.22821

BBC.com. (2020). Black lives matter founders: We fought to change history and we won. *BBC News.* https://www.bbc.com/news/world-us-canada-55106268

Beal, F. M. (2008). Double jeopardy: To be Black and female. *Meridians (Middletown, Conn.)*, *8*(2), 166–176. doi:10.2979/MER.2008.8.2.166

Beauboeuf-Lafontant, T. (2009). *Behind the mask of the strong black woman: Voice and the embodiment of a costly performance*. Temple University Press.

Becks-Moody, G. M. (2004). *African American women administrators in higher education: Exploring the challenges and experiences at Louisiana public colleges and universities* (Publication No. 2074) [Doctoral dissertation]. Louisiana State University, USA.

Belden, C. (2017, July 20). Equity vs. equality: An introduction. The Inclusion Solution. Retrieved from http://www.theinclusionsolution.me/equity-vs-equality-introduction

Bell, M. P. (2020). Anti-blackness, surface-level diversity continues to matter: What must we do? *Equality, Diversity and Inclusion.* https://doi-org.ezproxy.uta.edu/10.1108/EDI-06-2020-0160

Bell, D. (1992). *Faces at the bottom of the well.* Basic Books.

Bell, D. A. (2000). *Race, racism, and American law*. Palmer Press.

Bell, E., & Nkomo, S. M. (2001). *Our separate ways*. Harvard Business.

Bell, K. (2019). "This is not who we are": Progressive media and post-race in the new era of overt racism. *Communication, Culture & Critique*, *12*(1), 1–17. doi:10.1093/ccc/tcz005

Bell, L. A. (2007). Theoretical foundations for social justice education. In M. Adams, L. A. Bell, & P. Griffin (Eds.), *Teaching for diversity and social justice*. Routledge.

Berila, B. (2020, June 23). White urgency to end racism: Why now? *Open Democracy*. https://www.opendemocracy.net/en/transformation/white-urgency-end-racism-why-now/

Berila, B. (2015). *Integrating mindfulness into anti-oppression pedagogy: Social justice in higher education*. Routledge., doi:10.4324/9781315721033

Berkovich, I. (2014). A socio-ecological framework of social justice leadership in education. *Journal of Educational Administration*, *52*(3), 282–309. doi:10.1108/JEA-12-2012-0131

Berkup, S. B. (2014). Working with generations x and y in generation z period: Management Of different generations in business life. *Mediterranean Journal of Social Sciences, 5(19)*, p. 218. Blackhurst, A. E. (2000). Career satisfaction and perceptions of sex discrimination among women student affairs professionals. *NASAP Journal*, *37*(2), 7–78.

Betters-Reed, B. L., & Moore, L. L. (1995). Shifting the management development paradigm for women. *Journal of Management Development*, *14*(2), 24–38. doi:10.1108/02621719510078876

Bhattacharya, K. (2017). *Fundamentals of qualitative research: A practical guide*. Routledge. doi:10.4324/9781315231747

Biewen, J. (1997, August 19). Moving up: Part one. *Minnesota Public Radio*. http://news.minnesota.publicradio.org/features/199708/19_biewenj_migration/

Blackman-Richards, N., Gray, A., Perez, K. C., Rodgers, S. T., & Smith, K. A. M. (2021, April 15). Fighting Racism within Academic Anti-Racist Spaces. CUNY 2021 Faculty Diversity & Inclusion Conference. The Power of an Antiracist Academy: Reimagining Systems and Structures. *Virtual*.

Blackmore, J. (2013). A feminist critical perspective on educational leadership. *International Journal of Leadership in Education*, *16*(2), 139–154. doi:10.1080/13603124.2012.754057

Blanco, A. & Tan, S. (2022, March 20). How Ketanji Brown Jackson's path to the supreme court differs from the current justices. *The Washington Post*. https://www.washingtonpost.com/politics/interactive/2022/ketanji-brown-jackson-school-career/

Board of Education of Topeka. (1954). 347 U.S. 483

Bochner, A. P. (1997). It's about time: Narrative and the divided self. *Qualitative Inquiry*, *3*(4), 418–438. doi:10.1177/107780049700300404

Bogotch, I. E. (2000). Educational leadership and social justice: Theory into practice. *Journal of School Leadership*, *12*(2), 138–156. doi:10.1177/105268460201200203

Bolman, L., & Deal, T. (2003). *Reframing organizations: Artistry, choice and leadership*. Jossey-Bass and Sons, Inc.

Bonner, F. B. (2001). Addressing gender issues in historically Black college and university community: A challenge and call to action. *The Journal of Negro Education: Black Women in The Academy: Challenges and Opportunities*, *70*(3), 176–191. doi:10.2307/3211209

Booysen, L. (2014). The development of inclusive leadership practice and processes. In B. M. Ferdman & B. N. Deane (Eds.), *Diversity at work: The practice of inclusion,* (pp. 296–329). Jossey-Bass.

Boston Consulting Group (2021, May). The race for innovation. https://media-publications.bcg.com/BCG-Executive-Perspectives-Race-for-Innovation.pdf

Boyatzis, R., & Sala, F. (2004). Assessing emotional intelligence competencies. In Glenn Geher (Ed.), *The measurement of emotional intelligence*. https://www.eiconsortium.org/pdf/Assessing_Emotional_Intelligence_Competencies.pdf

Boyce-Davies, C. (2016). *Left of Karl Marx*. Duke University Press.

Boykin, C. M., Brown, N. D., Carter, J. T., Dukes, K., Green, D. J., Harrison, T., Hebl, M., McCleary-Gaddy, A., Membere, A., McJunkins, C. A., Simmons, C., Singletary Walker, S., Smith, A. N., & Williams, A. D. (2020). Anti-racist actions and accountability: Not more empty promises. *Equality, Diversity and Inclusion, 39*(7), 775–786. doi:10.1108/EDI-06-2020-0158

Boyle, M. (2021, October 6). Remote Work Has Vastly Improved the Black Worker Experience: A survey finds that Black employees in white collar jobs feel more valued and supported working from home. *Bloomberg*. https://www.bloomberg.com/news/articles/2021-10-05/return-to-office-black-workers-are-happier-more-valued-working-from-home

Bradberry, T., & Greaves, J. (2015). *Analysis & review of emotional intelligence 2.0*. Eureka Books.

Bradley Smith, S. (2021, March 5). How a lack of sponsorship keeps black women out of the c-suite. *Harvard Business Review*. https://hbr.org/2021/03/how-a-lack-of-sponsorship-keeps-black-women-out-of-the-c-suite

Bradley, S. W., Garven, J. R., Law, W. W., & West, J. E. (2018). The impact of chief diversity officers on diverse faculty hiring (No. w24969). *National Bureau of Economic Research*. https://papers.ssrn.com/sol3/papers.cfm?abstract_id=3244282

Branscombe, N. R., Schmitt, M. T., & Harvey, R. D. (1999). Perceiving pervasive discrimination among African Americans: Implications for group identification and well-being. *Journal of Personality and Social Psychology, 77*(1), 135–149. doi:10.1037/0022-3514.77.1.135

Breeden, R. (2021). Our presence is resistance: Stories of black women in senior-level student affairs positions at predominantly white institutions. *Journal of Women and Gender in Higher Education, 14*(2), 166–186. doi:10.1080/26379112.2021.1948860

British Broadcasting Corporation. (2020). George Floyd: What happened in the final moments of his life. *BBC*. https://www.bbc.com/news/world-us-canada-52861726

Brock, R., Pratt-Clarke, M., & Maes, J. B. (Eds.). (2019). *Journeys of social justice: Women of color presidents in the academy. Peter Lang Incorporated*. International Academic Publishers.

Brown, B. (2018, March 17). Dehumanizing always starts with language.https://brenebrown.com/articles/2018/05/17/dehumanizing-always-starts-with-language/

Brown, N. D. (2018). The impact of leader race and gender on perceptions of organizations in response to corporate error.

Brown, C. (2002). *Refusing racism: White allies and the struggle for civil rights*. Teachers College Press.

Brownlee, D. (2022, August 11). DEI tragically fails many black professionals. *Forbes*. https://www.forbes.com/sites/danabrownlee/2022/08/11/this-is-why-corporate-dei-tragically-fails-many-black-professionals/?sh=a3549e7efbcc

Brown, M. E., & Treviño, L. K. (2006). Ethical leadership: A review and future directions. *The Leadership Quarterly*, *17*(6), 595–616. doi:10.1016/j.leaqua.2006.10.004

Bruckmüller, S., & Branscombe, N. R. (2010). The glass cliff: When and why women are selected as leaders in crisis contexts. *British Journal of Social Psychology*, *49*(3), 433–451. doi:10.1348/014466609X466594 PMID:19691915

Buckingham, D. (2018). Invisible labor: A mixed-method study of African American women and their emotional labor in the academy. *Electronic Theses and Dissertations*, 849. https://egrove.olemiss.edu/etd/849

Bui, T. (2020, July 8). Minnesota racial-justice groups with sudden influx of money face new scrutiny. *MinnPost*. https://www.minnpost.com/community-sketchbook/2020/07/racial-justice-groups-with-sudden-influx-of-money-face-new-scrutiny/

Buller, J. & Mary Baldwin College (2006). Coping with the Passive-Aggressive Faculty Member, *The Essential Department Chair: A Practical Guide to College Administration.* Anker Publishing Company https://tomprof.stanford.edu/posting/822

Burke, S., & Collins, K. M. (2001). Gender differences in leadership styles and management skills. *Women in Management Review*, *16*(5), 244–257. doi:10.1108/09649420110395728

Burke, T. (2021). *Unbound: My Story of Liberation and the Birth of the Me Too Movement.* Flatiron Books.

Burns, T., Huang, J., Krivkovich, A., Yee, L., Rambachan, I. & Trkulja, T. (2021).Women in the workplace 2021. McKinsey & Company. https://www.mckinsey.com/featured-insights/diversity-and-inclusion/women-in-the-workplace

Burns, U. (n.d). Strategies for Influence coaching quotes and tips. https://strategiesforinfluence.com/ursula-burns-coaching-advice/

Burns, J. M. (1978). *Leadership*. Harper and Row.

Butler, J. (2006). *Precarious life: The powers of mourning and violence*. Verso.

Byrd, M. Y. (2012). Critical race theory: A framework for examining social identity

Cannon, J. (2016). Education as the practice of freedom: A social justice proposal for mindfulness educators. In R. Purser, D. Forbes, & A. Burke (Eds.), *Handbook of Mindfulness,* (pp. 397–409). Springer., doi:10.1007/978-3-319-44019-4_26

Capper, C. A. (2015). The 20th-year anniversary of critical race theory in education: Implications for leading to eliminate racism. *Educational Administration Quarterly*, *51*(5), 791–833. doi:10.1177/0013161X15607616

Capstone Performance Solutions, Inc. (2019). Excel coaching. *Capstone Performance Solutions, Inc*. https://www.capstonesolutionsinc.com/

Carr, E. W., Reece, A., Rosen Kellerman, G. & Robichaux, A. (2019, December 16). The value of belonging at work. *Harvard Business Review*. https://hbr.org/2019/12/the-value-of-belonging-at-work

Carrazana, C. (2020, August 10). When systemic racism meets the coronavirus, Black women suffer economically. *The 19th News(letter)*. https://19thnews.org/2020/08/black-women-economy-coronavirus-systemic-racism/

Carver, C. S. (2012). Self-awareness. In M. R. Leary, & J. P. Tangney (Eds.), *Handbook of self and identity* (pp. 50–68). The Guilford Press. Centers for Disease Control and Prevention. COVID Data Tracker. Atlanta, GA: US Department of Health and Human Services. https://covid.cdc.gov/covid-data-tracker

Cash, T. A., Gueci, N., & Pipe, T. (2021). Equitable Mindfulness: A framework for transformative conversations in higher education. *Building Healthy Academic Communities Journal*, *5*(1), 9–21. doi:10.18061/bhac.v5i1.7770

Caxaj, C. S. & Berman, H. (2010). Belonging among newcomer youths: Intersecting experiences of inclusion and exclusion. *Advances in Nursing Science, 33*(4), E17-E30. doi:10.1097/ANS.0b013e3181fb2f0f

CBS News. (2021, September 24). 'These officers have suffered': Ex-MPD officers, many citing PTSD, get six-figure settlements from city. *CBS.* https://www.cbsnews.com/minnesota/news/these-officers-have-suffered-ex-mpd-officers-many-citing-ptsd-get-six-figure-settlements-from-city/

Center for Disease Control. (2020). Disparities in death from COVID-19: Racial and ethnic health disparities. *CDC.* https://www.cdc.gov/coronavirus/2019-ncov/community/health-equity/racial-ethnic-disparities/disparities-deaths.html

Chang, A. (2020, May 28). Student actions prompt UMN to rethink its relationship with Minneapolis police. *National Public Radio.* https://www.npr.org/2020/05/28/864469597/student-actions-prompt-umn-to-rethink-its-relationship-with-minneapolis-police

Cheeks, M. (2018). How Black Women Describe Navigating Race and Gender in the Workplace. *Harvard Business Review*.

Cherry-McDaniel, M. (2019). Skinfolk ain't always kinfolk: The dangers of assuming and assigning inherent cultural responsiveness to teachers of color. *Educational Studies*, *55*(2), 241–251. doi:10.1080/00131946.2018.1500912

Chisholm, S. (1970). *Unbought & Unbossed.* Houghton Mifflin Harcourt.

Cho, C., Barrett, S. E., Solomon, R. P., Portelli, J. P., & Mujawamariya, D. (2009). Mentorship and induction: Negotiating a collaborative enterprise or apprenticing for status quo maintenance? *Brock Education*, *8*(2), 114–130.

Chun, E. B., & Feagin, J. R. (2019). *Rethinking diversity frameworks in higher education,* (1st ed.). Routledge., doi:10.4324/9780429298929

Chun, E., & Evans, A. (2019). *Conducting an institutional diversity audit in higher education: A practitioners guide to systemic diversity transformation*. Stylus Publishing.

Clance, P. R., & Imes, S. A. (1978). The imposter phenomenon in high achieving women: Dynamics and therapeutic intervention. *Psychotherapy (Chicago, Ill.)*, *15*(3), 241–247. doi:10.1037/h0086006

Clapp, J. R. Jr. (2010). Diversity leadership: The rush university medical center experience. *Hospital Topics*, *88*(2), 61–66. doi:10.1080/00185861003768993 PMID:20494886

Clarke, N. (2010). The impact of a training program designed to target the emotional intelligence abilities of project managers. *International Journal of Project Management*, *28*(5), 461–468. doi:10.1016/j.ijproman.2009.08.004

Clayborne, H. L., & Hamrick, F. (2007). Rearticulating the leadership experiences of African American women in midlevel student affairs administration. *Journal of Student Affairs Research and Practice*, *44*(1), 123–146.

Cleaver, K. (2007). Women, power, and revolution. *New Political Science*, *21*(2), 231–236. doi:10.1080/07393149908429865

Clement, R. E. (1966). The historical development of higher education for negro Americans. *The Journal o f Negro Education, 35*(4), 299-305.

CNN. (2020). Protests across the globe after George Floyd's death. *CNN*. https://www.cnn.com/2020/06/06/world/gallery/intl-george-floyd-protests/index.html

Cole, B. M. (2020). 8 reasons why diversity and inclusion are essential to business success. *Forbes*. https://www.forbes.com/sites/biancamillercole/2020/09/15/8-reasons-why-diversity-and-inclusion-are-essential-to-business-success/?sh=22d25fc21824

Coleman, H. J. (2010). *Empowering yourself: The organizational game revealed,* (2nd ed.). Author House.

Coles, S. M., & Pasek, J. (2020). Intersectional invisibility revisited: How group prototypes lead to the erasure and exclusion of Black women. *Translational Issues in Psychological Science, 6*(4), 314–324. doi:10.1037/tps0000256

Collier-Thomas, B. (1982). Guest editorial: The impact of Black women in education: An historical overview. *Journal of Education, 51*(3), 173–180.

Collins, P. H. (2001). Defining Black feminist thought. *Race Critical Theories,* 152-175.

Collins, P. H. (2002). *Black feminist thought: Knowledge, consciousness, and the politics of empowerment.* Routledge.

Collins, P. H. 1994. "Shifting the Center: Race, Class and Feminist Theorizing About Motherhood.," (Eds). Evelyn Nakano Glenn et al. Mothering: Ideology, Experience and Agency. New York: Routledge.

Collins, Y. R. (2022, October). *Home* [LinkedIn page]. LinkedIn. Retrieved October 19, 2022, from https://www.linkedin.com/in/contact-yolandarenee/

Collins, D. E. (2016). The Token Commitment. *Diverse Issues in Higher Education, 33*(9), 24.

Collins, P. (2000). *Black feminist thought: Knowledge, consciousness, and the politics of empowerment.* Routledge.

Collins, P. H. (1986). Learning from the outsider within: The sociological significance of Black feminist thought. *Social Problems, 33*(6), S14–S32. doi:10.2307/800672

Collins, P. H. (2000). *Black Feminist Thought.* Routledge.

Collins, P. H. (2000). *Black feminist thought: Knowledge, consciousness, and the politics of empowerment,* (2nd ed.). Unwin Hyman.

Collins, P. H. (2004). *Black sexual politics.* Routledge. doi:10.4324/9780203309506

Collins, P. H. (2019). *Intersectionality as critical social theory.* Duke University Press.

Collins, P. H., & Bilge, S. (2020). *Intersectionality.* John Wiley & Sons.

Collins, S. M. (1997). *Black corporate executives: The making and breaking of a Black middle class.* Temple University Press.

Columbus Chamber of Commerce (2021, August 18). Address the great resignation using psychological safety. https://columbus.org/address-the-great-resignation-using-psychological-safety/

Connley, C. (2021). Walgreens' new ceo roz brewer on bias in the c-suite: 'When you're a black woman, you get mistaken a lot'. CNBC. https://www.cnbc.com/2021/01/27/walgreens-new-ceo-roz-brewer-on-dealing-with-bias-in-the-c-suite.html

Cooper, A. (1988). *A voice from the South.* Oxford University Press.

Cooper, A. J. (1988). *A Voice from the South*. Oxford University Press.

Cooper, B. (2017). *Beyond respectability: The intellectual thought of race women*. University of Illinois Press. doi:10.5406/illinois/9780252040993.001.0001

Cooper, B. (2018). *Eloquent rage: A Black Feminist discovers her superpower*. Macmillan Publishing Group, LLC.

Cooper, B. (2018). *Eloquent rage: A Black feminist discovers her superpower*. St. Martin's Press.

Coqual, (2019). Being black in corporate America: an intersectional exploration. *Coqual*. https://coqual.org/reports/being-black-in-corporate-america-an-intersectional-exploration/

Corbett, H. (2022, February 22). *How To Be An Ally For Black Women In The Workplace*. Forbes. https://www.forbes.com/sites/hollycorbett/2022/02/22/how-to-be-an-ally-for-black-women-in-the-workplace/?sh=29dba0983123

Cortez, C. O. (2006). *Crusaders for social justice: Black female educator-activists in social welfare reform in Los Angeles during the golden age of the Black Power movement, 1966--1975*. [Doctoral Dissertation]. USC, USA.

Cote, S., & Miners, C. T. (2006). Emotional intelligence, cognitive intelligence, and job performance. *Administrative Science Quarterly*, *51*(1), 1–28. doi:10.2189/ asqu.51.1.1

Cotruș, A., Stanciu, C., & Bulborea, A. (2012). EQ vs. IQ which is most important in the success or failure of a student? *Social and Behavioral Sciences*, *46*, 5211–5213. doi:10.1016/j.sbspro.2012.06.411

Council on Social Work Education (CSWE). (2021). *Commission on Accreditation 2022 Educational Policy and Accreditation Standards draft*. Author.

Crenshaw, K. (1991). Mapping the margins: Intersectionality, identity politics, and violence against women of color. Stanford Law Review, 43(6), 1241–1299

Crenshaw, K. (1989). Demarginalizing the Intersection of Race and Sex: A Black Feminist Critique of Antidiscrimination Doctrine, Feminist Theory and Antiracist Politics. *University of Chicago Legal Forum*, *1*(8).

Crenshaw, K. (2013). Demarginalizing the intersection of race and sex: A Black feminist critique of antidiscrimination doctrine, feminist theory and antiracist politics. In *Feminist Legal Theories* (pp. 23–51). Routledge.

Crenshaw, K. W. (1991). Mapping the margins: Intersectionality, identity politics, and violence against women of color. *Stanford Law Review*, *43*(6), 1241–1299. doi:10.2307/1229039

Crenshaw, K. W. (2013). Mapping the margins: Intersectionality, identity politics, and violence against women of color. In *The Public Nature of Private Violence* (pp. 93–118). Routledge.

Creswell, J. W. (2007). *Qualitative inquiry and research design: Choosing among five approaches*, (2nd ed.). Sage.

Crichlow, W. (2015). Critical race theory: A strategy for framing discussions around social justice and democratic education. Higher Education in Transformation Conference, Dublin, Ireland, 2015, 187-201.

Crookston, R.K. (2012). *Working with Problem Faculty: A 6-Step Guide for Department Chairs*. Jossey-Bass.

Cross, T., Bazron, B., Dennis, K., & Isaacs, M. (1989). *Towards a culturally competent system of care: A monograph on effective services for minority children who are severely emotionally disturbed*. https://eric.ed.gov/?id=ED330171

CUNY TV. (2016, April 7). The Percy Ellis Sutton SEEK Program: Opening Doors for 50 Years. YouTube. https://youtu.be/L-rugBBt4G4

Cutter, C., & Webber, L. (2021, July 13). Demand for Chief Diversity Officers Is High. So Is Turnover. *Wall Street Journal*. https://www.wsj.com/articles/demand-for-chief-diversity-officers-is-high-so-is-turnover-11594638000?page=3

Dagbovie, P. G. (2004). Black women historians from the late 19th century to the dawning of the civil rights movement. *Journal of African American History*, *89*(3), 241–261. doi:10.2307/4134077

Danaher, K., & Branscombe, N. (2010). Maintaining the system with tokenism: Bolstering individual mobility beliefs and identification with a discriminatory organization. *British Journal of Social Psychology*, *49*(2), 343–362. doi:10.1348/014466609X457530 PMID:19646326

Daniels, J. P. (2022, May 25). She represents me: the black woman making political history in Colombia. *The Guardian*. https://www.theguardian.com/global-development/2022/may/25/francia-marquez-colombia-vice-president-black-candidate

Davidson, M. J., & Burke, R. J. (Eds.). (2000). *Women in management: Current research issues* (Vol. 2). Sage.

Davis, S. & Brown, K. (2017). Automatically discounted: Using Black feminist theory to critically analyze the experiences of Black female faculty. *NCPEA International Journal of Educational Leadership Preparation, 12*(1).

Davis, A. Y. (1981). *Women, race, and class*. Random House.

Davis, C. U. (2018). Laying new ground: Uprooting white privilege and planting seeds of equity and inclusivity. *Journal of Distance Education*, *18*(3), 120–125. doi:10.1080/15290824.2018.1481965

Davis, D. R., & Maldonado, C. (2015). Shattering the glass ceiling: The leadership development of African American women in higher education. *Advancing Women in Leadership Journal*, *35*, 48–64.

Day, D. V., & Antonakis, J. (2012). Leadership: Past, present, and future. *The Nature of Leadership*, 3-25.

Dean, D. R., Bracken, S. J., & Allen, J. K. (2009). *Women in academic leadership: Professional strategies, personal choices*. Stylus Publishing, LLC.

Dean, D., Bracken, S., & Allen, J. (2009). Academic leadership: Professional strategies, personal choices. *Stylus (Rio de Janeiro)*.

Dees, D. L. (2019). *"The help" & the unhelpful educator: An analysis of racial socialization, anti-Blackness, & prosocial behavior in post-secondary educators* [Doctoral dissertation]. California State University, USA.

Delgado, R. (1989). Storytelling for Oppositionists and Others: A Plea for Narrative. *Michigan Law Review*, *87*(8), 2411–2441. doi:10.2307/1289308

Delgado, R. (1990). When a story is just a story: Does voice really matter? *Virginia Law Review*, *76*(1), 95–111. doi:10.2307/1073104

Delgado, R., & Stefanic, J. (2017). *Critical race theory: An introduction*. NYU Press.

Deloite (2018). *Inclusive Mobility: How Mobilizing a Diverse Workforce Can Drive Business Performance*. https://www2.deloitte.com/us/en/pages/tax/articles/inclusive-mobility-diverse-workforce-drive-business-performance.html

Delpit, L. (1995). *Other people's children: Cultural conflict in the classroom*. The New Press.

DeWitt, P. M. (2016). *Collaborative leadership: Six influences that matter most*. Corwin Press.

Dezső, C. L., Ross, D. G., & Uribe, J. (2016). Is there an implicit quota on women in top management? A large-sample statistical analysis. *Strategic Management Journal*, *37*(1), 98–115. doi:10.1002mj.2461

Dhamoon, R. K. (2011). Considerations on mainstreaming intersectionality. *Political Research Quarterly*, *64*(1), 230–243. doi:10.1177/1065912910379227

DiAngelo, R. (2018). *White fragility: What it's so hard for White people to talk about racism*. Beacon Press.

DiAngelo, R., & Dyson, M. (2018). *White fragility: Why it's so hard for White people to talk about racism*. Beacon Press.

Dictionary.com. (2022). Guilt. *Dictionary.com LLC*. https://www.dictionary.com/browse/guilt#:~:text=the%20fact%20or%20state%20of.%2C%20whether%20real%20or%20imagined

Dinh, J. E., Lord, R. G., Gardner, W. L., Meuser, J. D., Liden, R. C., & Hu, J. (2014). Leadership theory and research in the new millennium: Current theoretical trends and changing perspectives. *The Leadership Quarterly*, *25*(1), 36–62. doi:10.1016/j.leaqua.2013.11.005

Diversity of Black Women in Positions of Leadership *Handbook of research on workforce diversity in a global society: Technologies and concepts*. IGI Global.

DiversityInc. (n.d.). Overview of the Top 50 companies for diversity. *Diversity Inc*. https://www.diversityinc.com/about-the-diversityinc-top-50-process/

Dixon, A. R. & Telles, E. E. (2017). Skin color and colorism: Global research, concepts and measurements. *Annual Review of Sociology, 43,* 405-424. doi:10.1146/annurev-soc-060116-053315

Dixon-Fyle, S., Dolan, K.,Hunt, D. V. & Prince, S. (2020). Diversity wins: How inclusion matters. https://www.mckinsey.com/featured-insights/diversity-and-inclusion/diversity-wins-how-inclusion-matters

Dobbin, F., & Kalev, A. (2020) Making Discrimination and Harassment Complaint Systems Better. *What Works?, 24*.

Dodd, B. (2018). 44 leadership quotes from Carla Harris – 2018 global leadership summit. https://briandoddonleadership.com/2018/08/10/44-leadership-quotes-from-carla-harris-2018-global-leadership-summit/

Domínguez, S. & Embrick, D. G. (2020). Racial microaggressions: Bridging psychology and sociology and future research considerations. *Sociology Compass, 14*(8), e12803. doi:10.1111/soc4.12803

Donahoo, S. (2021). Why we need a National CROWN Act. *Laws*, *10*(2), 26. https://www.mdpi.com/2075-471X/10/2/26. doi:10.3390/laws10020026

Donofrio, G. (2020, December 4). Racial dividing line. *Human Toll 35W*. https://humantoll35w.org/essays/racial-dividing-linc/

Donovan, R. A., & West, L. M. (2015). Stress and mental health: Moderating role of the strong black woman stereotype. *Journal of Black Psychology, 41*(4), 384–396. doi:10.1177/0095798414543014

Drake-Clark, D. (2009). *Discrimination happens without effort: How Balck Women Human Resources Managers Negotiate Diversity in a Corporation*. [Unpublished doctoral dissertation]. The University of Georgia, USA.

Dreachslin, J. L., & Hobby, F. (2008). Racial and ethnic disparities: Why diversity leadership matters. *Journal of Healthcare Management*, *53*(1), 8–13. doi:10.1097/00115514-200801000-00004 PMID:18283965

Drummond, M. E. (1995). Minorities in higher education leadership positions: A report of eight years of disappointment, 1986-1993. *Black Issues in Higher Education*, *23*, 43–47.

Duan, L., & Zhu, G. (2020). Psychological interventions for people affected by the COVID-19 epidemic. *The Lancet. Psychiatry*, *7*, 300–302. doi:10.1016/S2215-0366(20)30073-0

Dumas, M. J. (2016). Against the dark: Antiblackness in education policy and discourse. *Theory into Practice*, *55*(1), 11–19. doi:10.1080/00405841.2016.1116852

Duncan, P. (2014). Hot Commodities, Cheap Labor: Women of Color in the Academy. *Frontiers*, *35*(3), 39–63. doi:10.5250/fronjwomestud.35.3.0039

Eagly, A. H., Carli, L. L., & Carli, L. L. (2007). *Through the labyrinth: The truth about how women become leaders* (Vol. 11). Harvard Business School Press.

Eddy, P., VanDerLinden, K., & Hartman, C. (2022). Leadership for social justice in community colleges: A national survey.

Edes, A., & Taylor, J. (2017). #BlackWomenAtWork: Women speak out after criticism of journalist, congresswoman. *NPR*. https://www.npr.org/2017/03/29/521954040/-blackwomenatwork-women-speak-out-aftercriticism-of-journalist-congresswoman

Edgehill, V. E. (2007). Historical patterns of institutional diversity: Black women in race -specific positions on predominantly White college campuses (Order No. 3283238) [Doctoral Dissertation]. Howard University, USA.

Edghill, V. (2007). Black women in race-specific positions on predominantly white campuses: A historical materialist [Doctoral Dissertation]. Howard University, USA.

Egbuonu, O. (Director). (2021). *(In)Visible portraits* [Film]. OWN Spotlight.

El-Amin, A. (Ed.). (2022). *Implementing Diversity, Equity, Inclusion, and Belonging in Educational Management Practices*. IGI Global., doi:10.4018/978-1-6684-4803-8

Ellis, C. (1995). *Final negotiations: A story of love, loss, and chronic illness*. Temple University Press.

Ellis, C., Adams, T. E., & Bochner, A. P. (2000). Autoethnography, personal narrative, reflexivity. In N. K. Denzin & Y. S. Lincoln (Eds.), *Handbook of qualitative researchm* (2nd ed., pp. 733–768). Sage.

Ellis, C., Adams, T. E., & Bochner, A. P. (2010). Autoethnography: An overview. *Forum Qualitative Sozialforschung / Forum: Qualitative. Social Research*, *12*(1).

Equality and Human Rights Commission. (2010). How fair is Britain? Equality, human rights and good relations in 2010. *The First Triennial Review*, 664.

Erskine, S. E., & Bilimoria, D. (2019). White allyship of Afro-diasporic women in the workplace: A transformative strategy for organizational change. *Journal of Leadership & Organizational Studies*, *26*(3), 319–338. doi:10.1177/1548051819848993

Espino, M. M., Muñoz, S. M., & Kiyama, J. M. (2010). Transitioning from doctoral study to the academy: Theorizing trenzas of identity for Latina sister scholars. *Qualitative Inquiry*, *16*(10), 804–818. doi:10.1177/1077800410383123

Eubanks, D. L., Brown, A. D., & Ybema, S. (2012). Leadership, identity, and ethics. *Journal of Business Ethics*, *107*(1), 1–3. doi:10.100710551-012-1295-5

Evans, A., & Chun, E. B. (2007). Are the walls really down? Behavioral and organizational barriers to faculty and staff diversity. *ASHE Higher Education Report*, *33*(1), 1–139.

Evans, S. Y. (2008). *Black women in the ivory tower, 1850–1954: An intellectual history.* University Press of Florida. doi:10.5744/florida/9780813032689.001.0001

Evans-Winters, V. E. (2019). *Black feminism in qualitative inquiry: Mosaic for writing our daughter's body.* Routledge. doi:10.4324/9781351046077

Extremera, N. (2020). Coping with the stress caused by the COVID-19 pandemic: Future research agenda based on emotional intelligence. *International Journal of Social Psychology*, *35*(3), 631–638. doi:10.1080/02134748.2020. 1783857

Falagas, M. E., Kouranos, V. D., Arencibia-Jorge, R., & Karageorgopoulos, D. E. (2008). Comparison of SCImago journal rank indicator with journal impact factor. *The FASEB Journal*, *22*(8), 2623–2628. doi:10.1096/fj.08-107938 PMID:18408168

Falagas, M. E., Pitsouni, E. I., Malietzis, G. A., & Pappas, G. (2008). Comparison of PubMed, Scopus, web of science, and Google scholar: Strengths and weaknesses. *The FASEB Journal*, *22*(2), 338–342. doi:10.1096/fj.07-9492LSF PMID:17884971

Farah, S. (2020, June 11). George Floyd Was Killed in My Neighborhood. *Vanity Fair.* https://www.vanityfair.com/style/2020/06/growing-up-in-george-floyds-minneapolis-neighborhood

Federal Reserve Economic Data. (2021). Annual educational attainment: Bachelor's degree or higher by state. *Federal Reserve Bank of St. Louis.* https://fred.stlouisfed.org/release/tables?eid=391444&rid=330

Feiner, L. (2021). Tech companies made big pledges to fight racism last year – here's how they're doing so far. *CNBC.* https://www.cnbc.com/2021/06/06/tech-industry-2020-anti-racism-commitments-progress-check.html

Fenwick, T., & Edwards, R. (2014). Networks of knowledge, matters of learning, and criticality in higher education. *Higher Education*, *67*(1), 35–50. doi:10.100710734-013-9639-3

Ferdman, B. M. (2014). The practice of inclusion in diverse organizations: Toward a systemic and inclusive framework. In B. M. Ferdman & B. N. Deane (Eds.), *Diversity at work: The practice of inclusion,* (pp. 3–54). Jossey-Bass.

Ferdman, B. M., & Deane, B. R. (2014). *Diversity at work: The practice of inclusion.* Jossey-Bass.

Finnegan, A. C. (2022). Growing Up White Saviors. *Journal of Applied Social Science*, *16*(3), 617–636. doi:10.1177/19367244221082023

Flaherty, C. (2021, May 3). Multiple Black professors have resigned in recent years over racism. *Inside Higher Ed.* https://www.insidehighered.com/news/2021/05/03/multiple-black-professors-have-resigned-recent-years-over-racism

Flory, J. A., Leibbrandt, A., Rott, C., & Stoddard, O. (2021). Increasing workplace diversity: Evidence from a recruiting experiment at a Fortune 500 Company. *Journal of Human Resources, 56*(1), 73–N.PAG. https://doi-org.libproxy.lib.ilstu.edu/10.3368/jhr.56.1.0518-9489R1

Floyd-Thomas, S.M. (2019). Katie's Canon: Enfleshing womanism, mentoring, and the soul of the black community. *Journal of Feminist Studies in Religion, 35*(1), 101 104. doi:10.2979/jfemistudreli.35.1.12

Forbes Media, L. L. C. (2022). *Dr. Nika White.* Forbes. https://www.forbes.com/sites/forbesbooksauthors/people/drnikawhite/?sh=33272cf622a4

Forliti, A. (2022, October 22). Ex-cop Kueng cop pleads guilty in George Floyd killing. *Associated Press*. https://apnews.com/article/death-of-george-floyd-j-alexander-kueng-thomas-lane-tou-thao-e9d40eae8ac193e61f07004323a3193d

Frazier, D. (2021, May 25). *This is my truth. 1 Year Anniversary. Rest in peace to George Floyd* [Photograph]. Instagram. https://www.instagram.com/p/CPT5_oIBlie/?utm_medium=copy_link

Freire, P. (2005). *The pedagogy of the oppressed.* Continuum International Publishing Group.

Future Forum. (2022). Desire for flexibility intensifies among knowledge workers—and they're willing to walk to get it. *Future Forum by Slack*. https://futureforum.com/wp-content/uploads/2022/07/Future-Forum-Pulse-Report-Summer-2022.pdf

Gaines, K. K. (1996). *Uplifting the Race: Black Leadership, Politics, and Culture in the Twentieth Century*. University of North Carolina Press. doi:10.5149/uncp/9780807845431

Gamson, Z., & Carlos, A. H. (1978). Implications of the social context for higher education. In M. W. Peterson (Ed.), *Black Students on White Campuses: The Impact of Increased Black Enrollments,* (pp. 23–42). University of Michigan, Survey Research Center.

Gamson, Z., Peterson, M. W., & Blackburn, R. T. (1980). Stages in the response of white colleges and universities to Black students. *The Journal of Higher Education*, *51*(3), 255–267. doi:10.2307/1981008

García-Peñalvo, F. J., de Figuerola, C. G., Merlo, J. A., & Jacsó, P. (2010). Comparison of journal impact rankings in the SCImago Journal & Country Rank and the Journal Citation Reports databases. *Online Information Review*.

Gardner, W. L., Cogliser, C. C., Davis, K. M., & Dickens, M. P. (2011). Authentic leadership. *The Leadership Quarterly*, 22.

Garza, A. (2020). *The Purpose of Power : How We Come Together When We Fall Apart*. Random House Publishing Group.

Gates, Jr., H. L. (7 January 2013). The Truth Behind '40 Acres and a Mule. *The Root*.

Ghosh, D., & Barber, K. (2021). The Gender of Multiculturalism: Cultural Tokenism and the Institutional Isolation of Immigrant Women Faculty. *Sociological Perspectives*, *64*(6), 1063–1080. doi:10.1177/0731121420981098

Giddings, P. (1984). *When and where I enter: The impact of black women on race and sex in America*. Morrow.

Gipson, A. N., Pfaff, D. L., Mendelsohn, D. B., Catenacci, L. T., & Burke, W. W. (2017). Women and leadership: Selection, development, leadership style, and performance. *The Journal of Applied Behavioral Science*, *53*(1), 32–65. doi:10.1177/0021886316687247

Glazer, G., Clark, A., Bankston, K., Danek, J., Fair, M., & Michaels, J. (2016). Holistic admissions in nursing: We can do this. *Journal of Professional Nursing*, *32*(4), 306–313. doi:10.1016/j.profnurs.2016.01.001 PMID:27424931

Glennen, R. E., Baxley, D. M., & Farren, P. J. (1985). Impact of intrusive advising on minority student retention. *College Student Journal*.

Goethals, G. R., & Hoyt, C. L. (2017). *Women and leadership: History, theories, and case studies*. Berkshire Publishing Group LLC.

Goleman, D. (2005). *Emotional intelligence: Why it can matter more than IQ,* (3rd ed.). Bantam.

Goleman, D. (2013). The focused leader. *Harvard Business Review*, *91*(12), 50–60.

Gonzalez, T. (2017). Root to rise: Mindful lawyering for social justice. *NYU Rev. L. & Soc. Change*, *41*, 91.

Goodall, B. H. L. (2006). *A need to know: The clandestine history of a CIA family*. Left Coast Press.

Gould, E., & Kandra, J. (2021, June 2) Only one in five workers are working from home due to COVID, Black and Hispanic workers are less likely to be able to telework. *Economic Policy Institute Working Economics Blog*. https://www.epi.org/blog/only-one-in-five-workers-are-working-from-home-due-to-covid-black-and-hispanic-workers-are-less-likely-to-be-able-to-telework/

Gould, E., & Wilson, V. (2020, June 1). Black workers face two of the most lethal preexisting conditions for coronavirus—racism and economic inequality. *Economic policy institute*. https://www.epi.org/publication/black-workers-covid/

Goyette, J. (2022, September 15). New Minneapolis Public Safety Commissioner seeks $1M budget. *Fox 9 KMSP*. https://www.fox9.com/news/minneapolis-public-safety-commissioner-budget

Gravley-Stack, K., Ray, C. M., & Peterson, C. M. (2016). Understanding the subjective experiences of the Chief Diversity officer: A q method study. *Journal of Diversity in Higher Education*, *9*(2), 95–112. doi:10.1037/dhe0000012

Greene, J., & Paul, J. (2021). Diversity university: DEI bloat in the academy. *Heritage Foundation Backgrounder*, (3641).

Grim, J. K., Sánchez-Parkinson, L., Ting, M., & Chavous, T. (2019). The experiences of academic diversity officers at the University of Michigan. *NCID Currents, 1*(1).

Grogan, M., & Shakeshaft, C. (2010). *Women and educational leadership* (Vol. 10). John Wiley & Sons.

Gueci, N., & Cash, T. (2020, March 10). *The Expansive Model of Mindfulness*. LinkedIn. https://www.linkedin.com/pulse/expansive-model-mindfulness-nika-gueci-tiara-cash-nika-gueci/

Guinier, L., & Torres, G. (2003). *The miner's canary: Enlisting race, resisting power, transforming democracy*. Harvard University Press.

Gupton, S. L. (2009). Women in educational leadership in the US: Reflections of a 50-year veteran. In Forum on Public Policy Online (Vol. 2009, No. 2). Oxford Round Table. 406 West Florida Avenue, Urbana, IL 61801.

Guy-Sheftall, B. (2009). Black feminist studies: The case of anna julia cooper. *African American Review*, *43*(1), 11–15. doi:10.1353/afa.0.0019

Haas Institute. (2019). Whole Story, & Studio Pathways. The Circle of Human Concern. https://haasinstitute.berkeley.edu/sites/default/files/expanding_belonging_-_the_circle_of_human_concern.pdf

Hackmann, D. G. (2002). Using portraiture in educational leadership research. *International Journal of Leadership in Education*, *5*(1), 51 60. doi:10.1080/13603120110057109

Hammonds, E. (2021). A Moment or a Movement? The Pandemic, Political Upheaval, and Racial Reckoning. *Journal of Women in Culture and Society*, *47*(1).

Hancock, B., Williams, M., Manyika, J., Yee, L. & Wong, J. (2021, February 21). Race in the workplace: *The Black experience in the US private sector*. McKinsey & Company. https://www.mckinsey.com/featured-insights/diversity-and-inclusion/race-in-the-workplace-the-black-experience-in-the-us-private-sector

Han, K. T., & Leonard, J. (2017). Why diversity matters in rural America: Women faculty of color challenging Whiteness. *The Urban Review*, *49*(1), 112–139. doi:10.100711256-016-0384-7

Hanson, K., McLeod, C., & Ross, M. (2017). Mindfulness and Nature. A mindful teaching community: Possibilities for teacher professional learning, 89.

Harper, S. (2015, December 10). Paying to ignore racism. *Inside Higher Education*. https://www.insidehighered.com/views/2015/12/10/colleges-should-stop-paying-money-ignore-racial-problems-essay#.YeRrgQtU
v9A.link

Harper, J. (2018). (in review). Webinar recording [Why diversity and inclusion matter. Catalyst.]. *Year*.

Harris, D. (2020). No, I am not a proud latina. The future of latinidad. *Refinery 29*. https://www.refinery29.com/en-us/latinx-identity-black-history-personal-essay

Harris, C. H. (2020). Multiracial faculty members' experiences with teaching, research, and service. *Journal of Diversity in Higher Education*, *13*(3), 228–239. doi:10.1037/dhe0000123

Harris-Perry, M. (2011). *Sister citizen: Shame, stereotypes and Black women in America*. Yale University Press.

Harris-Perry, M. V. (2011). *Sister citizen: Shame, stereotypes, and Black women in America*. Yale University Press.

Harts, M. (2021). Right Within: How To Heal From Racial Trauma. In *The Workplace*. Seal Press.

Harvey, W. B. (2014). Chief diversity officers and the wonderful world of academe. *Journal of Diversity in Higher Education*, *7*(2), 92–100. doi:10.1037/a0036721

Hayles, V. R. (2014). Communicating about diversity and inclusion. In B. M. Ferdman & B. N. Deane (Eds.), *Diversity at work: The practice of inclusion*, (pp. 55–90). Jossey-Bass.

Heckemann, B., Schols, J., & Halfens, R. (2015). A reflective framework to foster emotionally intelligent leadership in nursing. *Journal of Nursing Management*, *23*(6), 744–753. doi:10.1111/jonm.12204

Helm, A. (2016, June 5). Black women now the most educated group in US. The Root. Retrieved from https://www.theroot.com/black-women-now-the-most-educated-group-in-us-1790855540

Helms, J. E. (1995). An update of Helms's White and people of color racial identity models. In J.G. Ponterotto, J.M. Casas, L.A., Suzuki, C.M. Alexander, eds. Handbook of multicultural counseling. Thousand Oaks, CA: Sage.

Helms, J. E. (Ed.). (1990). *Black and White racial identity: Theory, research and practice*. Greenwood Press.

Henley, W. E. (1888). *Invictus*. https://www.poetryfoundation.org/poems/51642/invictus

Henrich, J., Heine, S., & Norenzayan, A. (2010). The weirdest people in the world? *Behavioral and Brain Sciences*, *33*(2-3), 61–83. doi:10.1017/S0140525X0999152X

Henry, W. J., & Glenn, N. M. (2009). Black women employed in the ivory tower: Connecting for success. *Advancing Women in Leadership Journal, 29*.

Hernandez, K. A. C., Ngunjiri, F. W., & Chang, H. (2015). Exploiting the margins in higher education: A collaborative autoethnography of three foreign-born female faculty of color. *International Journal of Qualitative Studies in Education: QSE*, *28*(5), 533–551. doi:10.1080/09518398.2014.933910

Hernandez, M., Avery, D. R., Volpone, S. D., & Kaiser, C. R. (2019). Bargaining while Black: The role of race in salary negotiations. *The Journal of Applied Psychology*, *104*(4), 581–592. doi:10.1037/apl0000363

Hevesi, D. (1995, May 14) CUNY Campuses Prepare to Reduce Faculty and Classes. *The New York Times.*

Hewlin, P. F. (2009). Wearing the cloak. *The Journal of Applied Psychology*, *94*(3), 727–741. doi:10.1037/a0015228 PMID:19450009

Heyes, C. (2012, February 7). *Identity politics.* The Stanford Encyclopedia of Philosophy. https://plato.stanford.edu/archives/win2014/entries/identity-politics/

Higginbotham, E. (1993). Righteous discontent: The women's movement in the Black Baptist Church, 1880-1920. Cambridge.

Hill, M. (2020, October 12) Brittany Cooper Dissecting her New York Times Best Seller "An Eloquent Rage: A Black Feminist Discovers her Superpower". *Embassy Row.* https://podcasts.apple.com/us/podcast/brittney-cooper-dissecting-her-new-york-times-best/id1522592619?i=1000494456090

Hill, C., Miller, K., Benson, K., & Handley, G. (2016). *Barriers and bias: The status of women in leadership*. American Association of University Women.

Hill-Collins, P. (1993). Toward a new vision: Race, class, and gender as categories of analysis and connection. *Race. Sex & Class*, *1*(1), 25–45.

Hines, E., & Fitts, M. (2022). *Black Women Thriving. Every Level Leadership.* https://everylevelleads.com/bwt/

Hinrichs, P. (2016). An empirical analysis of racial segregation in higher education (No. w21831). National Bureau of Economic Research.

Hobson-Smith, C. (1984). Black female achievers in academe. *The Journal of Negro Education*, *51*(3), 318–341. doi:10.2307/2294699

Hodges, C. R., & Welch, O. M. (2018). *Truth without tears: African American women deans share lessons in leadership.* Harvard Education Press.

Hofstede, G. (2011). Dimensionalizing cultures: The Hofstede model in context. *Online Readings in Psychology and Culture*, *2*(1), 2307–0919. doi:10.9707/2307-0919.1014

Hogg, M. A., Fielding, K. S., Johnston, D., Masser, B., Russell, E., & Svensson, A. (2001). *On glass ceilings and demographic disadvantage: Social identity and leadership in small groups. Unpublished manuscript, University of Queensland, Centre for Research on Group Processes.*

Hogg, M. A., & van Knippenberg, D. (2003). Social identity and leadership processes in groups. *Advances in Experimental Social Psychology*, *35*, 1–52. doi:10.1016/S0065-2601(03)01001-3

Holder, M. (2020). *The Double Gap and the Bottom Line: African American Women's Wage Gap and Corporate Profits.* Report for The Roosevelt Institute. https://rooseveltinstitute.org/publications/the-double-gap-and-the-bottom-line-african-american-womens-wage-gap-and-corporate-profits/

Holder, L. (2020). A Paradigm Shift in Race Consciousness Drives the Growing Demand for Diversity Equity and Inclusion Consultation. *California Labor and Employment Review*, *34*(5), 1–12.

Holmes, S. L. (2003). Black female administrators speak out: Narratives on race and gender in higher education. *NASAP Journal*, *6*(1), 45–62.

Homeland Security Digital Library. (n.d.). Report on the National Advisory Commission on Civil Disorders: Summary of report. https://www.hsdl.org/?abstract&did=35837

Hooks, b. (1981). *Ain't I a woman? Black women and feminism.* South End Press.

Hooks, B. (1994). *Teaching to transgress: Education as the practice of freedom.* New York, NY, Routledge.

Hooks, B. (1994a). *Outlaw Culture: Resisting Representations.* New York: Routledge.

Hooks, B. (1994b). Teaching to Transgress: Education as the Practice of Freedom. *Routledge.*

Hooks, B. (2012, July-August). Inner & outer worlds. *Spirituality & Health Magazine, 15*(4), p. 23.

hooks, b. (2014). Sisters of the yam: Black women and self-recovery. *Routledge.*

Hooks, B., & West, C. (1991). *Breaking bread: Insurgent Black intellectual life.* South End Press.

Hooks, B. (2014). *Teaching to transgress.* Routledge. doi:10.4324/9780203700280

Hopfensperger, J. (2016, December 11). Minnesotans renew bond with Luther to revive faith. *Star Tribune.* https://infoweb-newsbank-com.ezp2.lib.umn.edu/apps/news/document-view?p=AWNB&docref=news/16147DA536F492B0

Horsford, S. D., James-Gallaway, A., & Smith, P. A. (2021). Leading While Black: The Paradox and Prospects of Black Education Leadership in Urban Schools. In Handbook of urban education (pp. 166-177). Routledge.

Hourston, Z. N. (1990). *Their eyes were watching God.* Harper & Row.

Houston, P. (2003). The truest eye. Toni Morrison on love, writing, the greater good. *Oprah Magazine.* https://www.oprah.com/omagazine/toni-morrison-talks-love/all

Howard-Hamilton, M. F. (2003). *Meeting the needs of African American women.* Jossey-Bass.

Howard-Hamilton, M. F. (2003). Theoretical frameworks for African American women. *New Directions for Student Services, 2003*(104), 19–27. doi:10.1002s.104

https://nces.ed.gov/ipeds/datacenter/institutionprofile.aspx
?unitId=190691

Hubain, B. S., Allen, E. L., Harris, J. C., & Linder, C. (2016). Counter-stories as representations of the racialized experiences of students of color in higher education and student affairs graduate preparation programs. *International Journal of Qualitative Studies in Education: QSE, 29*(7), 946–963. doi:10.1080/09518398.2016.1174894

Hu-DeHart, E. (2002). The diversity project: Institutionalizing multiculturalism or managing differences?" *Academe: Diversity on Campus. 86*(5), 38-42. American Association of University Professors .

Hughes, L. (1922). Mother to son. *Crisis Magazine., 25*(2), 48.

Hunter-Gadsden, L. (2020). Why People Of Color Feel The Loneliest At Work. *Forbes magazine.* https://www.forbes.com/sites/nextavenue/2020/05/19/why-people-of-color-feel-the-loneliest-at-work/?sh=632797281ad8

Hymowitz, C., & Schellhardt, T. D. (1986). The glass ceiling: Why women can't seem to break the invisible barrier that blocks them from the top jobs. *The Wall Street Journal, 24*(1), 1573-1592.

Hypolite, L. I. (2020). People, place, and connections: Black cultural center staff as facilitators of social capital. *Journal of Black Studies*, *51*(1), 37–59.

Ibrahim, M. (2022 September 15). A snapshot of Mayor Jacob Frey's proposed police budget. *MinnPost*. https://www.minnpost.com/public-safety/2022/09/a-snapshot-of-mayor-jacob-freys-proposed-police-budget/

In, L. (2022). *The state of black women in corporate America*. https://leanin.org/research/state-of-black-women-in-corporate-america/introduction#!

Institute for Women Policy Research (2017, November 21). Women's median earnings as a percent of men's, 1985-2016 (full-time, year-round workers) with projections for pay equity, by race/ethnicity. https://iwpr.org/iwpr-general/womens-median-earnings-as-a-percent-of-mens-1985-2016-full-time-year-round-workers-with-pr ojections-for-pay-equity-by-race-ethnicity/

Inzlicht, M., & Ben-Zeev, T. (2000). A threatening intellectual environment: Why females are susceptible to experiencing problem-solving deficits in the presence of males. Psychological Science, 11(5), 365–371.

Iverson, S. V. (2007). Camouflaging power and privilege: A critical race analysis of university diversity policies. *Educational Administration Quarterly*, *43*(5), 586–611. doi:10.1177/0013161X07307794

Jackson, A. (2022). *Black women are in 'survival mode' at work—and company diversity efforts' fall short'*. https://www.cnbc.com/2022/07/01/company-diversity-efforts-to-support-black-women-fall-short.html

Jackson, K. (2020, June 24). For Minnesotans of color, a new food desert underscored disparities. *TPT Originals*. https://www.tptoriginals.org/for-minnesotans-of-color-a-new-food-desert-underscores-disparities/

Jackson, R. G., Huskins, K., Skelton, S., & Thorius, K. (2020). Ally and accomplice: Two sides of the same coin. *Equity Dispatch, 4*(3). https://greatlakesequity.org/sites/default/files/202003022136_newsletter.pdf.

Jameel, M.& Yerardi, J. (2019, February 28).Workplace discrimination is Illegal. But our data shows it's still a problem. *Vox Magazine & Center for Public Integrity*. https://www.vox.com/policy-and-politics/2019/2/28/18241973/workplace-discrimination-cpi-investigation-eeoc

James, J. (1997). *Transcending the talented tenth*. Routledge.

Jan, T., McGregor, J. & Hoyer, M. (2021, August 23). Corporate america's $50 billion promise. *The Washington Post*. https://www.washingtonpost.com/business/interactive/2021/george-floyd-corporate-america-racial-justice/

Jana, T. (2021, February 8). The differences between allies, accomplices & co-conspirators may surprise you. *An Injustice!* https://aninjusticemag.com/the-differences-between-allies-accomplices-co-conspirators-may-surprise-you-d3fc7fe29c

Jenkins, N. (2022, October). *Home* [LinkedIn page]. LinkedIn. Retrieved October 20, 2022, from https://www.linkedin.com/in/nettajenkins/

Jenkins, T. (2016, September 18). Committed to diversity? Show me the money. *The Chronicle of Higher Education*. https://www.chronicle.com/article/committed-to-diversity-show-me-the-money/

Jimenez, M. F., Laverty, T. M., Bombaci, S. P., Wilkins, K., Bennett, D. E., & Pejchar, L. (2019). Underrepresented faculty play a disproportionate role in advancing diversity and inclusion. *Nature Ecology & Evolution*, *3*(7), 1030–1033. doi:10.103841559-019-0911-5 PMID:31160738

Johnson, T. B. (2021). The experiences of Black women in diversity roles at 4-Year predominantly White institutions. [Theses and Dissertations]. Illinois State University, USA. 1378. https://ir.library.illinoisstate.edu/etd/1378/

Johnson, T. B. (2021a). *The experiences of Black women in diversity roles at 4-year predominantly White institutions* (Order No. 28150595) [Doctoral Dissertation]. Illinois State University, USA.

Johnson, C. E. (2015). Ethical challenges of leadership: Casting light or shadow. *Sage (Atlanta, Ga.)*.

Johnson, N. N. (2021). Balancing race, gender, and responsibility: Conversations with four Black women in educational leadership in the United States of America. *Educational Management Administration & Leadership*, *49*(4), 624–643. doi:10.1177/1741143221991839

Johnson, N. N. (2022). Central Office Leadership: The Importance of Promoting Diversity, Equity, Inclusion, and Belonging in the Ivory Tower. In A. El-Amin (Ed.), *Implementing Diversity, Equity, Inclusion, and Belonging in Educational Management Practices* (pp. 14–32). IGI Global., doi:10.4018/978-1-6684-4803-8.ch002

Johnson, N. N., & Fournillier, J. B. (2021). Intersectionality and leadership in context: Examining the intricate paths of four Black women in educational leadership in the United States. *International Journal of Leadership in Education*, •••, 1–22. www.tandfonline.com/doi/abs/10.1080/13603124.2020.1818132. doi:10.1080/13603124.2020.1818132

Johnson, N. N., & Fournillier, J. B. (2022). Increasing diversity in leadership: Perspectives of four Black women educational leaders in the context of the United States. *Journal of Educational Administration and History*, *54*(2), 174–192. www.tandfonline.com/doi/full/10.1080/00220620.2021.1985976. doi:10.1080/00220620.2021.1985976

Johnson, T. B. (2021b). Perspectives from a multicultural affairs office professional: Diversity education during COVID-19. In L. Kyei-Blankson, J. Blankson, & E. Ntuli (Eds.), *Handbook of research on inequities in online education during global crisis,* (pp. 240–259). IGI Global. doi:10.4018/978-1-7998-6533-9.ch013

Johnson, T. B. (Ed.). (2023). *The Experiences of Black Women Diversity Practitioners in Historically White Institutions*. IGI Global., doi:10.4018/978-1-6684-3564-9

Johnsrud, L. K. (2003). Higher education support professionals: The fear of speaking out. *The NEA 2003 Almanac of Higher Education*, 109-118.

Jones, F. (2019, February 8). For CaShawn Thompson Black Girl Magic was always the truth. *Beacon Broadside*. https://www.beaconbroadside.com/broadside/2019/02/for-cashawn-thompson-black-girl-magic-was-always-the-truth.html

Jones, K., & Okun, T. (2000). White supremacy culture. *Dismantling racism: A workbook for social change groups*. Change Work. https://www.kbtheatre.org/uploads/4/6/5/8/46588037/white_supremacy_culture_1.pdf

Jones-Rogers, S. (2017). '[S]he could…spare one ample breast for the profit of her owner': White mothers and enslaved wet nurses' invisible labor in American slave markets. *Slavery & Abolition*, *38*(2), 337–355. doi:10.1080/0144039X.2017.1317014

Jordan, B. (2021) Social Control and 'Black Lives Matter'. In: The Future of Social Work. Palgrave Macmillan, Cham. doi:10.1007/978-3-030-76371-8_5

Jordan-Zachery, J. (2009). *Black women, cultural images, and social policy*. Routledge. doi:10.4324/9780203883167

Jordan-Zachery, J. S. (2019). Licking Salt: A Black Woman's Tale of Betrayal, Adversity, and Survival. *Feminist Formations, 31*(1), 67–84. doi:10.1353/ff.2019.0009

June, A. W., & O'Leary, B. (2021, May 27). How many Black women have tenure on your campus? *Chronicle of Higher Education*. https://www.chronicle.com/article/how-many-black-women-have-tenure-on-your-campus-search-here

Kanter, R. (1977). *Men and women of the corporation*. Basic Books.

Karp, T., & Helgø, T. I. (2009). Leadership as identity construction: The act of leading people in organisations: A perspective from the complexity sciences. *Journal of Management Development, 28*(10), 880–896. doi:10.1108/02621710911000659

Kaste, M. (2021, November 3). Minneapolis voters reject a measure to replace the city's police department. *National Public Radio*. https://www.npr.org/2021/11/02/1051617581/minneapolis-police-vote

Kayembe, B. (2021). Why are we still depicting black women as mammies? https://shado-mag.com/all/why-are-we-still-depicting-black-women-as-mammies/

Kellerman, B., Rhode, D. L., & O'Connor, S. D. (2007). *Women and leadership: The state of play and strategies for change* (Vol. 141). Jossey-Bass.

Kendi, I. X. (2019). *How to be an anti-racist*. One World.

Kernahan, C. (2019). *Teaching about race and racism in the college classroom: Notes from a White professor*. West Virginia University Press.

Kezar, A., & Eckel, P. (2000). *The effect of institutional culture on change strategies in higher education: Universal principles or culturally responsive concepts?* ERIC Clearinghouse on Higher Education.

King, T. C. (2018). Healing Circles as Black Feminist Pedagogical Interventions. In O. N. Perlow, D. I. Wheeler, S. L. Bethea, & B. Scott (Eds.), *Black Women's Laboratory Pedagogies: Resistance, transformation, and healing within and beyond the academy*, (pp. 21–44). Pelgrave Macmillan. doi:10.1007/978-3-319-65789-9_2

Kinouani, G.(2021). *Living while black: The essential guide to overcoming Racial trauma*. Penguin Random House.

Kohl, K. (2022). *Driving justice, equity, diversity, and inclusion*, (1st ed.). Auerbach Publications., doi:10.1201/9781003168072

Korejan, M. M., & Shahbazi, H. (2016). An analysis of the transformational leadership theory. *Journal of Fundamental and Applied Science, 8*(3), 452–461. doi:10.4314/jfas.v8i3s.192

Kotter, J. P. (1995). Leading change: Why transformation efforts fail. *Harvard Business Review, 73*, 59–67.

KPMG. (2021). Diversity, equity and inclusion: 2021 U.S. *DEI transparency report*. https://www.kpmg.us/content/dam/global/pdfs/2021/kpmg-us-2021-dei-report.pdf

Kraker, D. (2021, November 1). U of M to offer free tuition to many Native American students. *MPR News*. https://www.mprnews.org/story/2021/11/01/u-to-offer-free-tuition-to-many-native-american-students

KSTP. (2022, October 25). U of M Regent Sviggum resigns as vice chair after 'too diverse' question, will finish board term. *KSTP Eyewitness News*. https://kstp.com/kstp-news/top-news/u-of-m-regent-sviggum-resigns-as-vice-chair-after-too-diverse-question-will-finish-board-term/

Kulik, C. T., & Metz, I. (2015). Women at the top: Will more women in senior roles impact organizational effectiveness?
Lambert, L. (2002). A framework for shared leadership. *Educational Leadership*, *59*(8), 37–40.

Laloux, F. (2014). *Reinventing organizations: A guide to creating organizations inspired by the next stage of human consciousness*. Nelson Parker.

Lambert, L. (2003). Leadership redefined: An evocative context for teacher leadership. *School Leadership & Management*, *23*(4), 421–430. doi:10.1080/1363243032000150953

Lawrence-Lightfoot, S., & Davis, J. H. (2002). *The art and science of portraiture*. Jossey-Bass.

Lean In (2020). The state of black women in corporate america. https://media.sgff.io/sgff_r1eHetbDYb/2020-08-13/1597343917539/Lean_In_-_State_of_Black_Women_in_Corporate_America_Report_1.pdf

Lee, S. (Director). (1988). *School Daze* [Film]. Columbia Pictures.

Lencioni, P. (2020). *The motive*. John Wiley & Sons, Inc.

Le, T. N., & Shim, P. (2014). Mindfulness and the Aloha response. *Journal of Indigenous Social Development*, *3*(2).

Lewis, B. (2021). Diversity is no longer just a moral imperative, it's also critical for business. https://www.procore.com/jobsite/diversity-is-no-longer-just-a-moral-imperative-its-also-critical-for-business/#:~:text=If%20you%20need%20a%20lot%20of%20perspectives%2C%20you%20need%20a,experiences%20are%20born%20from%20people.%E2%80%9D

Liden, R. C., & Antonakis, J. (2009). Considering context in psychological leadership research. *Human Relations*, *62*(11), 1587–1605. doi:10.1177/0018726709346374

Linnabery, E., Stuhlmacher, A. F., & Towler, A. (2014). From whence cometh their strength: Social support, coping, and well-being of Black women professionals. *Cultural Diversity & Ethnic Minority Psychology*, *20*(4), 541–549. http://dx.doi.org.ezp1.lib.umn.edu/10.1037/a0037873. doi:10.1037/a0037873 PMID:25313433

Lloyd, J. B. (2009). Implications of race and gender in higher education administration: An African American women's perspective. *Advances in Developing Human Resources*, *11*(5), 606–618. doi:10.1177/1523422309351820

Logan, M. (2022, July 18). Linkedln post. *LinkedIn*. https://www.linkedin.com/posts/madialogan_womenintheworkplace-protips-50ways-activity-6953382501763452928-XSL5/?utm_source=linkedin_share&utm_medium=ios_app

Logan, N. (2021). Breaking Down Barriers of the Past and Moving Toward Authentic DEI Adoption. In D. Pompper (Ed.). Public Relations for Social Responsibility: Affirming DEI Commitment with Action (Communicating Responsible Diversity, Equality, and Inclusion). (pp3-17). United Kingdom, Bingley: Emerald Publishing Limited. doi:10.1108/978-1-80043-167-620211001

Lomax, T. (2021). DEI dreaming: Confusing inclusion and tokenism. *The Feministwire.* https://thefeministwire.com/2021/11/dei-dreaming-confusing-inclusion-and-tokenism/?fbclid=IwAR3JLd2_TP2pe-rxJwBXoW14FOCd5q7PHIcTLHqaGfcgBef5V4aecwaY7Yo

Lord, R., & Hall, R. (2003). Identity, leadership categorization, and leadership schema. *Leadership and power: Identity processes in groups and organizations*, 48-64.

Lorde, A. (1984). *Sister outsider*. Ten Speed Press.

Lorde, A. (1984). *Sister outsider: Speeches and essays*. Crossing Press.

Lorde, A. (1984). The master's tools will never dismantle the master's house. In A. Lorde (Ed.), *Sister outsider essays and speeches,* (pp. 110–114). Crossing Press Feminist Series.

Lorde, A. (2003). The master's tools will never dismantle the master's house. *Feminist postcolonial theory. REAd (Porto Alegre)*, *25*, 27.

Lutheran Social Service of Minnesota. (n.d.). Responding to Minnesota's changing needs. *LSSM*. https://www.lssmn.org/about-lss

MacDonald (2022). Diversity, equity and inclusion. https://corporate.mcdonalds.com/corpmcd/our-purpose-and-impact/jobs-inclusion-and-empowerment/diversity-and-inclusion.html

Machtig, A. (2020, October 16). University launches new equity training amid ongoing racial justice calls. *The Minnesota Daily*. https://mndaily.com/263065/news/university-launches-new-equity-training-amid-ongoing-racial-justice-calls/

Magee, R. V. (2016). Teaching mindfulness with mindfulness of race and other forms of diversity. In D. McCown, D. Reibel, & M. Micozzi (Eds.), *Resources for Teaching Mindfulness*. Springer., doi:10.1007/978-3-319-30100-6_12

Mahtani, M. (2004). Mapping race and gender in the academy: The experiences of women of colour faculty and graduate students in Britain, the US and Canada. *Journal of Geography in Higher Education*, *28*(1), 91–99. doi:10.1080/0309826042000198666

Mapping Prejudice. (n.d.). *Visualizing the hidden histories of race and privilege in the built environment*. https://mappingprejudice.umn.edu/

Mapping Prejudice. (n.d.). *What is a covenant?* https://mappingprejudice.umn.edu/racial-covenants/what-is-a-covenant

Marable, M., & Mullings, L. (2015). *How Capitalism Underdeveloped Black America: Problems in Race, Political Economy, and Society*. Haymarket Books.

Maraña, J. A. J. (2016). *The lived experiences of women of color chief diversity officers* (Order No. 10250697). ProQuest Dissertations & Theses Global. (1867777302).

Marana, J. A. J. (2016). *The lived experiences of women of color chief diversity officers* . [Doctoral dissertation]. The Claremont Graduate University, USA.

Marquis, J. P., Lim, N., Scott, L. M., Harrell, M. C., & Kavanagh, J. (2008). *Managing diversity in corporate America: An exploratory Analysis*. RAND Corporation. https://www.jstor.org/stable/10.7249/op206rc.6

Marshall, C., & Oliva, M. (Eds.). (2006). *Leadership for social justice: Making revolutions in education*. Allyn & Bacon.

Marshall, C., & Rossman, G. B. (1989). Designing qualitative research. *Sage (Atlanta, Ga.).*

Martin, J. (1993). The notion of difference for emerging womanist ethics: The writings of Audre Lorde and bell hooks. *Journal of Feminist Studies in Religion, 9*(1-2), 39–51.

Massey, M. (2014, June 27). [EnterpriseMediaVideo]. *What You Are Is Where You Were When... AGAIN!* [Video]. YouTube: https://www.youtube.com/watch?v=l6rPiehHQu8

Matthew, P. (2016). *Written/unwritten:Diversity and the hidden truths of tenure.* University of North Carolina Press. doi:10.5149/northcarolina/9781469627717.001.0001

Maurer, R. (2020). New DE&I roles spike after racial justice protests. *Society for Human Resource Management (SHRM).* https://www.shrm.org/resourcesandtools/hr-topics/talent-acquisition/pages/new-dei-roles-spike-after-racial-justice-protests.aspx

Mayer, J., Salovey, P., Caruso, D., & Cherkasskiy, L. (2011). Emotional intelligence. In R. Sternberg & S. Kaufman (Eds.), *The Cambridge handbook of intelligence, Cambridge handbooks in psychology* (pp. 528–549). Cambridge University Press. doi:10.1017/CBO9780511977244.027

Mayorga-Gallo, S. (2019). The white-centering logic of diversity ideology. *The American Behavioral Scientist, 63*(13), 1789–1809. doi:10.1177/0002764219842619

McCall, L. (2005). The complexity of intersectionality. *Signs (Chicago, Ill.), 30*(3), 1771–1800. doi:10.1086/426800

McCluney, C. L. & Rabelo, V. C. (2019). Conditions of visibility: An intersectional examination of black women's belongingness and distinctiveness at work. *Journal of Vocational Behavior, 113,* 143-152. doi:10.1016/j.jvb.2018.09.008

McCluney, C. L., Robotham, K., Lee, S., Smith, R. & Durkee, M. (2019). The costs of code-switching. *Harvard Business Review.* https://hbr.org/2019/11/the-costs-of-codeswitching

McCluney, C. L., Robotham, K., Lee, S., Smith, R., & Durkee, M. (2020). The costs of code-switching. *Harvard Business Review.* https://hbr.org/2019/11/the-costs-of-codeswitching

McClure, J. (2022). Rondo Neighborhood. *Saint Paul Historical.* https://saintpaulhistorical.com/items/show/160

McClusky, A. T. (1991). *Mary McLeod Bethune and the education of Black girls in the South, 1904-1923.* [Doctoral Dissertation]. Indiana University, USA.

McClusky, A. T. (1997). We specialize in the wholly impossible: Black women school founders and their mission. *Signs (Chicago, Ill.), 22*(2), 403–426.

Mcgirt, E. (2016). The subtle ways people of color feel excluded at work. *Fortune.* https://fortune.com/2016/10/06/inclusion-diversity-employers-race/

McGowan, B. L. (2022). Teaching diversity, equity, and inclusion outside of the classroom: An autoethnographic account of a Black male faculty in residence. *Journal of Diversity in Higher Education, 15*(3), 354–364. doi:10.1037/dhe0000289

McGrady, C. (2022, April 8). What Ketanji Brown Jackson's sisterlocks mean to black women. The Washington Post. https://www.washingtonpost.com/lifestyle/2022/04/08/ketanji-brown-jackson-hair-sisterlocks/

McIntosh, P. (1988). *White privilege and male privilege: A personal account of coming to see correspondences through work in women's studies.* (Working Paper No. #189). https://nationalseedproject.org/images/documents/White_Privilege_and_Male_Privilege_Personal_Account-Peggy_McIntosh.pdf

McIntosh, P. (2010). *Some notes for facilitators.* Wellesley Centers for Women. https://nationalseedproject.org/images/documents/White_Privilege_and_Male_Privilege_Personal_Account-Peggy_McIntosh.pdf

McKinsey & Company. (2021). *Women in the Workplace 2021*. https://www.mckinsey.com/featured-insights/diversity-and-inclusion/women-in-the-workplace?cid=eml-web

McLaughlin, M. B. (2022, October). *Home* [LinkedIn page]. LinkedIn. Retrieved October 20, 2022, from https://www.linkedin.com/in/mandybynum/

McLean, M. (2017). From Nanny of the maroons to Portia Simpson. In E. Brown & G. Gong (Eds.), *Global perspectives on gender and sexuality in education: Raising awareness, fostering equity, advancing justice*. Information Age Publishing.

McNair, T., Bensimon, E., & Malcom-Piquex, L. (2020). *From equity talk to equity walk.* Jossey-Bass. doi:10.1002/9781119428725

McNicholas, C., & Poydock, M. (2020). Who are Essential Workers: A Comprehensive Look at Their Wages, Demographics, and Unionization Rates. *Economic Policy Institute.* https://www.epi.org/blog/who-are-essential-workers-a-comprehensive-look-at-their-wages-demographics-and-unionization-rat
es/

Mehrabian, A. (1967). *Mehrabian's Communication Theory: Verbal, Non-Verbal, Body Language.* https://www.bl.uk/people/albert-mehrabian

Mena, J. A., & Vaccaro, A. (2017). I've struggled, I've battled. Invisibility microaggressions experienced by women of color at a predominantly white institution. NASPA Journal About Women in Higher Education, 10(3), 301-318. . doi:10.1080/19407882.2017.1347047

Merriam-Webster Dictionary. (n.d.). *Diversity.* https://www.merriam-webster.com/dictionary/diversity

Merriam-Webster Dictionary. (n.d.). *Inclusion.* https://www.merriam-webster.com/dictionary/inclusion

Mgadmi, M. (2009). Black women's identity: Stereotypes, respectability and passionlessness (1890-1930). *Revue LISA/LISA e-journal*, 7(1), 40-55.

Mgadmi, M. (2022). Black women's identity: Stereotypes, respectability and passionlessness (1890-1930*). Revue LISA/LISA e-journal, 7*(1), 40-55. doi:10.4000/lisa.806

Middaugh, D. (2021). Leading the Pack in Tough Times. *Medsurg Nursing*, *30*(3), 212–215.

Milem, J. F., Chang, M. J., & Antonio, A. L. (2005). *Making diversity work on campus: A research-bases perspective.* Association of American Colleges and Universities.

Miller, S. (2020). Black workers still earn less than their white counterparts. https://www.shrm.org/resourcesandtools/hr-topics/compensation/pages/racial-wage-gaps-persistence-poses-challenge.aspx

Minnesota Department of Corrections. (2020). *Adult prison population summary.* https://mn.gov/doc/assets/Adult%20Prison%20Population%20Summary%201-1-2020_tcm1089-418232.pdf

Minnesota Employment and Economic Development. (2022). Minnesota's Black Labor Force: An analysis of demographic, economic, and educational trends, and disparities. *DEED Labor Market Information Office.* https://mn.gov/deed/assets/black-african-american-data-report-acc_tcm1045-539222.pdf

Misra, J., Lundquist, J. H., Holmes, E., & Agiomavritis, S. (2011). The Ivory Ceiling of Service Work. *Academe, 97*(1), 22–26.

Mitchell, N. A., & Miller, J. J. (2011). The unwritten rules of the academy: A balancing act for women of color. In G. Jean-Marie & B. Lloyd-Jones (Eds.), *Women of color in higher education: Changing directors and new perspectives,* (pp. 193–218). Emerald Group. doi:10.1108/S1479-3644(2011)0000010013

Moen, M. (2019, November 21). Ask a 'sotan: Revisiting 'Minnesota Nice'. *MPRN News.* https://www.mprnews.org/story/2019/11/21/ask-a-sotan-revisiting-minnesota-nice

Mohamad, M., & Jais, J. (2016). Emotional intelligence and job performance: A study among Malaysian teachers. *Procedia Economics and Finance, 35,* 674–682. doi:10.1016/S2212-5671(16)00083-6

Molloy, S. (23 June 2017). SEEK's Fight for Racial and Social Justice (1965-1969). *CUNY Digital History Project.*

Montero-Marin, J., Tops, M., Manzanera, R., Piva Demarzo, M., Álvarez de Mon, M., & García Campayo, J. (2015). Mindfulness, resilience, and burnout subtypes in primary care physicians: The possible mediating role of positive and negative affect. *Frontiers in Psychology, 6,* 1895. doi:10.3389/fpsyg.2015.01895

Montoya, M. C. (2020). *A Labor of Love: University Custodians Saliendo Adelante and Student Engagement Practices.* California State University.

Montrie, C. (2022). *Whiteness in plain view: A history of racial exclusion in Minnesota.* Minnesota Historical Society Press.

Moody, J. (2015). *Rising above cognitive errors: Improving searches, evaluations, and decision-making.* CreateSpace Independent Publishing Platform.

Moore, W. Jr, & Wagstaff, L. H. (1974). *Black educators in white colleges.* Jossey-Bass Publishers.

Moorosi, P., Fuller, K., & Reilly, E. (2018). Leadership and intersectionality: Constructions of successful leadership among Black women school principals in three different contexts. *Management in Education, 32*(4), 152–159. doi:10.1177/0892020618791006

Morales, Isabel. Fighting for the visibility of the "nobodies": Francia Marquez. Panoramas A Wider Perspective. University of Pittsburgh.

Morrison, T. (1971, August 22). What the black woman thinks about Women's Lib. *The New York Times,* SM14.

Morrissette, M. (2021, January 27). How does Minnesota compare to other states in education? *Women's Press.* https://www.womenspress.com/how-does-minnesota-compare-to-other-states-in-education/

Motro, D., Evans, J. B., Ellis, A., & Benson, L. (2022). Race and reactions to women's expressions of anger at work: Examining the effects of the "angry Black woman" stereotype. *The Journal of applied psychology, 107*(1), 142–152. doi:10.1037/apl0000884

Motro, D., Evans, J., Ellis, A., & Beson, L. (2022). The "Angry Black Woman" Stereotype at Work. *Harvard Business Review.*

MPD150. (n.d.). About. *MPD150.* https://www.mpd150.com/about/

Mwangi, C. A. G., Thelamour, B., Ezeofor, I., & Carpenter, A. (2018). Black elephant in the room": Black students contextualizing campus racial climate within US racial climate. *Journal of College Student Development*, *59*(4), 456–474. doi:10.1353/csd.2018.0042

Myers, S., Jr. (n.d.). *The Minnesota Paradox*. University of Minnesota. https://www.hhh.umn.edu/research-centers/roy-wilkins-center-human-relations-and-social-justice/minnesota-paradox

NASPA. (2021). *Moving from words to action: The influence of racial justice statements on campus equity efforts.* https://naspa.org/report/moving-from-words-to-action-the-influence-of-racial-justice-statements-on-campus-equity-efforts

NASW apologizes for racist practices in American social work (2021, April 17). New Release. Alexandria, VA: Author. https://www.socialworkers.org/News/News-Releases/ID/2331/NASW-apologizes-for-racist-practices-in-American-social-work

Nathoo, Z. (2021). In homogeneous organisations, even the most talented hires can feel tokenised. It's a problem that hits everyone hard. *BBC.* https://www.bbc.com/worklife/article/20210902-why-diverse-hires-cant-always-escape-tokenism

National Center for Education Statistics (NCES) survey (2020).

National Institutes of Health [NIH]. (2021). Scientific workforce diversity seminar series (SWDSS). seminar proceedings. *National Institutes of Health.* https://diversity.nih.gov/sites/coswd/files/images/NIH_COSWD_SWDSS_Implicit_Bias_Proceedings_508.pdf

Naulty, K. (2016). Strategies for confronting unconscious bias. *Colorado Lawyer*, *45*, 45–52.

Newkirk, P. (2019). Diversity has become a booming business. So, where are the results? https://time.com/5696943/diversity-business/

Newkirk, P. (2019). *Diversity, Inc.* Boldtype Books.

Newkirk, P. (2020). *Diversity inc.: The fight for racial equality in the workplace*. Bold Type Books.

Newman, D., Joseph, D., & MacCann, C. (2010). Emotional intelligence and job performance: The importance of emotion regulation and emotional labor context. *Industrial and Organizational Psychology: Perspectives on Science and Practice*, *3*(2), 159–164. doi:10. 1111/j.1754-9434.2010.01218.x

Ngwainmbi, J. M. (2004). Feminism, feminist scholarship, and social integration of women: The struggle for African-American women. *Journal of International Women's Studies*, *5*(5), 93–104.

Ngyuen, J. (2021). A year later, how are corporations doing on promises they made to fight for racial justice? https://www.marketplace.org/2021/05/24/a-year-later-how-are-corporations-doing-on-promises-they-made-to-fight-for-racial
-justice/

Nicol, D. J., & Yee, J. A. (2017). "Reclaiming Our Time": Women of Color Faculty and Radical Self-Care in the Academy. *Feminist Teacher*, *27*(2–3), 133–156. doi:10.5406/femteacher.27.2-3.0133

Niemann, Y. F. (2012). Lessons from the experiences of women of color working in academia. In G. Gutiérrez y Muhs, Y. F. Niemann, C. G. González, & A. P. Harris (Eds.), *Presumed incompetent: The intersections of race and class for women in academia,* (pp. 446–499). University Press of Colorado. doi:10.2307/j.ctt4cgr3k.40

Nietzel, M. T. (2021 February 13). University of Minnesota will offer free tuition to lower income students. *Forbes*. https://www.forbes.com/sites/michaeltnietzel/2021/02/13/university-of-minnesota-will-offer-free-tuition-to-lower-income-students/?sh=526f83851611

Nixon, M. L. (2013). *Women of color chief diversity officers: Their positionality and agency in higher education institutions* (Publication No. 1428435516) [Doctoral dissertation]. University of Washington, USA.

Nixon, M. L. (2017). Experiences of women of color university chief diversity officers. *Journal of Diversity in Higher Education, 10*(4), 301–317. doi:10.1037/dhe0000043

Nussbaum, B. (2013). African culture and Ubuntu reflections of a South African in America. *World Business Academy, 17*(1), 1–12.

Nzinga, S. M. (2020). *Lean semesters: How higher education reproduces inequity*. Johns Hopkins University Press.

O'Meara, K., Campbell, C. M., & Martin, A. (2011). Women in academic leadership: Professional strategies, personal choices. *Journal of College Student Development, 52*(4), 507–509. doi:10.1353/csd.2011.0051

O'Neill, T. (2020). *Income and poverty in the Twin Cities metro area*. https://mn.gov/deed/newscenter/publications/review/december-2020/twincities-income-poverty.jsp

Obama, M. (2018). *Becoming*. Crown.

Obear, K. (2017). *But I'm not racist: Tools for well-meaning whites*. The Difference Press.

Oberholzer-Gee, F. (2021, May-June). Eliminate strategic overload: How to select fewer initiatives with greater impact. *Harvard Business Review*. https://hbr.org/2021/05/eliminate-strategic-overload

Okun, T. (2022). Sense of Urgency. *White Supremacy Culture*. https://www.whitesupremacyculture.info/urgency.html

Olayinka, J. T., Gohara, M. A., & Ruffin, Q. K. (2021). #BlackGirlMagic: Impact of the social media movement on Black women's self-esteem. *International Journal of Women's Dermatology, 7*(2), 171–173. doi:10.1016/j.ijwd.2021.01.006 PMID:33937485

Oliver, B. (2020). I went on 100 interviews in 8 months: This is what it's like to negotiate your salary as a Black woman. *CNBC*. https://www.cnbc.com/2020/03/31/what-its-like-to-negotiate-salary-as-a-black-woman-equal-pay-day.html

Oluo, I. (2020). *Mediocre:The dangerous legacy of white male America*. Seal Press.

Onile-Ere, B. (2021, November 15). Minnesota untold: I-35w freeway uprooted and divided African American business district. *Fox 9*. https://www.fox9.com/news/how-the-construction-of-i-35w-tore-apart-black-communities-in-minneapolis

Onwuamaegbu, N. (2021, July 24). Many Black women felt relieved to work from home, free from microaggressions. Now they're told to come back. *The Washington Post*. https://www.washingtonpost.com/lifestyle/2021/07/24/black-women-office-work-home/

Onyeador, I. N., Hudson, S. T. J., & Lewis, N. A. Jr. (2021). Moving beyond implicit bias training: Policy insights for increasing organizational diversity. *Policy Insights from the Behavioral and Brain Sciences, 8*(1), 19–26. doi:10.1177/2372732220983840

Ospina, S., & Foldy, E. (2009). A critical review of race and ethnicity in the leadership literature: Surfacing context, power and the collective dimensions of leadership. *The Leadership Quarterly, 20*(6), 876–896. doi:10.1016/j.leaqua.2009.09.005

Ospina, S., & Foldy, E. (2010). Building bridges from the margins: The work of leadership in social change organizations. *The Leadership Quarterly*, *21*(2), 292–307. doi:10.1016/j.leaqua.2010.01.008

Padilla, A. (1994). Ethnic minority scholars, research, and mentoring: Current and future issues. *Educational Researcher*, *23*(4), 24–27. doi:10.2307/1176259

Palmer, D. (2021). I Got a Lot to Be Mad About: Sista Circles as a Counterspace for Black Women Doctoral Students.

Parker, E. (2020, August 20). Do colleges need a chief diversity officer? *Inside Higher Education*. https://www.insidehighered.com/views/2020/08/20/chief-diversity-officers-play-vital-role-if-appropriately-positioned-and-supported#.YeWhRKWj_eg.link

Parker, M. (2022, June 8). Beyond employee well-being: Creating a sense of belonging in the workplace. *Harvard Business Review*. https://hbr.org/resources/pdfs/comm/google/BeyondEmployeeWell-Being.pdf

Parker, L., & Villalpando, O. (2007). A race(cialized) perspective on education leadership: Critical race theory in educational administration. *Educational Administration Quarterly*, *43*(5), 519–524. doi:10.1177/0013161X07307795

Pasque, P. A., & Nicholson, S. E. (2011). *Empowering women in higher education and student affairs*. Theory, Research, Narratives and Practice from Feminist Perspectives.

Patterson, A., Kinloch, V., Burkhard, T., Randall, R., & Howard, A. (2016). Black Feminist Thought as Methodology: Examining intergenerational lived experiences of Black women. *Departures in Critical Qualitative Research*, *5*(3), 55–76. doi:10.1525/dcqr.2016.5.3.55

Patton, L. D. (2010). Culture centers in higher education: Perspectives on identity, theory, and practice. Stylus Publishing, LLC. PO Box 605, Herndon, VA 20172-0605.

Patton, L. D., & Catching, C. (2009). 'Teaching while Black': Narratives of African American student affairs faculty. *International Journal of Qualitative Studies in Education: QSE*, *22*(6), 713–728. doi:10.1080/09518390903333897

Patton, L. D., & Njoku, N. R. (2019). Theorizing Black women's experiences with institution-sanctioned violence: A# BlackLivesMatter imperative toward Black liberation on campus. *International Journal of Qualitative Studies in Education: QSE*, *32*(9), 1162–1182.

Perkins, L. M. (1993). The role of education in the development of Black feminist thought, 1860-1920. History of Education, 22(2), 265–275.

Perkins, L. M. (1983). The impact of the "cult of true womanhood" on the education of Black women. *The Journal of Social Issues*, *39*(3), 17–28.

Perlow, O. N., Wheeler, D. I., Bethea, S. L., & Scott, B. (Eds.). (2018). *Black Women's Laboratory Pedagogies: Resistance, transformation, and healing within and beyond the academy*. Pelgrave Macmillan.

Pharm, J. (2022, October). *Home* [LinkedIn page]. LinkedIn. Retrieved October 19, 2022, from https://www.linkedin.com/in/jessica-pharm/

Phelps, P. M. (2016). *An examination of the effects of tokenism for female command officers in law enforcement* (Order No. 10239943) [Doctoral Dissertation]. Capella University, USA.

Phillips, F. B. (1990). NTU psychotherapy: An Afrocentric approach. *The Journal of Black Psychology*, *17*(1), 55–74. doi:10.1177/00957984900171005

Pierce, C. (1970). Offensive mechanisms. In F. B. Barbour (Ed.), The black seventies. Porter Sargent Publisher.

Pignatelli, F. (1993). Toward a postprogressive theory of education. *The Journal of Educational Foundations*, *7*(3), 7–26.

Pipe, T. B., & Bortz, J. J. (2009). Mindful leadership as healing practice: Nurturing self to serve others. *International Journal for Human Caring*, *13*(2), 34–38. doi:10.20467/1091-5710.13.2.34

Pope, R. L., Reynolds, A. L., & Mueller, J. A. (2019). *Multicultural competence in student affairs: Advancing social justice and inclusion*. John Wiley & Sons.

Poussaint, A. (1974). The Black administrator in the white university. *Black Scholar: The Journal of Black Studies and Research, 6*(1), 8-14.

Poussaint, A. (1974). The Black administrator in the white university. *Black Scholar: The Journal of Black Studies and Research*, *6*(1), 8–14.

Powell, J. S., & Kelly, A. (2017). Accomplices in the academy in the age of Black Lives Matter. *Journal of Critical Thought and Praxis*, *6*(2), 42–65. doi:10.31274/jctp-180810-73

Prather, S. (2016, September 25). Racial Chill Spurs Quiet Brain Drain // Professionals of color cite outsider status as reason to leave. *Star Tribune*. https://www.startribune.com/twin-cities-businesses-ask-why-professionals-of-color-leave/394688601/?refresh=true

Pratt-Clarke, M. (2010). *Critical race, feminism, and education: A social justice model*. Springer. doi:10.1057/9780230115378

Preer, J. L. (1982). *Lawyers v. educators: Black colleges and desegregation in public higher education*. Greenwood Press.

Prezerakos, P. E. (2018). Nurse managers' emotional intelligence and effective leadership: A review of the current evidence. *The Open Nursing Journal*, *12*, 86–92. doi:10.2174/1874434601812010086

Prime, J. L., Carter, N. M., & Welbourne, T. M. (2009). Women "take care," men "take charge": Managers' stereotypic perceptions of women and men leaders. *The Psychologist Manager Journal*, *12*(1), 25–49. doi:10.1080/10887150802371799

Prince, A. (2009). *The politics of black women's hair*. Insomniac Press.

Prutzman, P., & Johnson, J. (1997). Bias awareness and multiple perspectives: Essential aspects of conflict resolution. *Theory into Practice*, *36*(1), 26–31. https://eric.ed.gov/?id=EJ546687. doi:10.1080/00405849709543741

Pyke, K. D. (2018). Institutional betrayal: Inequity, discrimination, bullying, and retaliation in academia. *Sociological Perspectives*, *61*(1), 5–13.

Rabelo, V. C., Robotham, K. & McCluney, C. (2021). "Against a sharp white background": How Black women experience the white gaze at work. *Gender, Work & Organization,* 28(5), 1840-1858. doi:10.1111/gwao.12564

Rawls, J. (2009). *A theory of justice*. Harvard University Press.

Ray, V. (2019). A theory of racialized organizations. *American Sociological Review*. 84(1), 26–53. doi:10.1177/0003122418822335

Ray, V. (2022). *On critical race theory: Why it matters & why you should care* (1st ed.). Random House.

Reagle, J., & Rhue, L. (2011). Gender bias in Wikipedia and Britannica. *International Journal of Communication*, *5*, 21.

Reason, R. D. (2003). Gender-based salary differences in African-American senior student affairs officers. *NASAP Journal, 6*(1), 67-78.

Reclaim the Block. (2019). *About Reclaim the Block.* https://www.reclaimtheblock.org/home/#about

Reddick, R., & Sáenz, V. (2012). Coming home: Hermanos académicos reflect on past and present realities as professors at their alma mater. *Harvard Educational Review*, *82*(3), 353–380. doi:10.17763/haer.82.3.g311m72q432062uq

Reeves, R. V., & Guyot, K. (2017). *Black women are earning more college degrees, but that alone won't close race gaps.* Social Mobility Memos.

Reid, W. M., & Dold, C. J. (2018). Burns, Senge, and the study of leadership. *Tampa Library. Faculty and Staff Publications.* https://digitalcommons.usf.edu/cgi/viewcontent.cgi?article=1008&context=tlib_facpub

Reilly, K. (2017, January 6). *Read what Michelle Obama said in her final remarks as First Lady.* Time. https://time.com/4626283/michelle-obama-final-remarks transcript/

Rhode, D. L. (2014). *What women want: an agenda for the women's movement.* Oxford University Press. doi:10.1093/acprof:osobl/9780199348275.001.0001

Rhode, D. L. (2017). *Women and leadership.* Oxford University Press.

Richardson, A., & Loubier, C. (2008). Intersectionality and leadership. *International Journal of Leadership Studies*, *3*(2), 142–161.

Robertson, R. (2021). A critical race theory analysis of transnational student activism, social media counter-stories, and the hegemonic logics of diversity work in higher education. *International Journal of Qualitative Studies in Education: QSE*, •••, 1–18.

Rodgers, S. T. (2015). Being of Some Scholarly Service…: A New Take On The Scholarship of Engagement in Academe. In F.A. Bonner, II, C.W., R. M. Banda, P. A. Robinson, Lewis, F. A., & B. Lofton (Eds.). Priorities of the Professoriate: Engaging Multiple Forms of Scholarship Across Rural and Urban Institutions. (pp. 67-88). Charlotte, NC: Information Age Publishing.

Rodgers, S. T. (2015). Racism. In C. Franklin (Ed.), *Encyclopedia of Social Work Online (ESWO),* (21st ed.). Oxford University Press.

Rodgers, S. T. (2021). The Next Wave of Post Traumatic Slave Syndrome Survivors: Black Women Resisters in Academia. Advances in Social Work. *Special Issue: Dismantling White Supremacy in Social Work Education*, *21*(2), 438–459. doi:10.18060/24159

Rodgers, S. T., & Lopez-Humphreys, M. (2020). Social Work Leadership: Grand Challenges for Black Women. *Social Work*, *65*(4), 397–400.

Rogers, H. B. (2016). *The mindful twenty-something.* New Harbinger.

Rogers, I. H. (2009). *The Black campus movement: An Afrocentric narrative history of the struggle to diversify higher education, 1965–1972.* Temple University.

Rosette, A. S., Koval, C. Z., Ma, A., & Livingston, R. (2016). Race matters for women leaders: Intersectional effects on agentic deficiencies and penalties. *The Leadership Quarterly*, *27*(3), 429–445. doi:10.1016/j.leaqua.2016.01.008

Rosette, A. S., & Livingston, R. W. (2012). Failure is not an option for Black women: Effects of organizational performance on leaders with single versus dual-subordinate identities. *Journal of Experimental Social Psychology*, *48*(5), 1162–1167. doi:10.1016/j.jesp.2012.05.002

Rousseau, N. (2009). *Black woman's burden: Commodifying Black reproduction.* Palgrave and MacMillan.

Roux, M. (2021, August 3) Five facts about black women in the labor force. *The U.S. Department of Labor Blog.* https://blog.dol.gov/2021/08/03/5-facts-about-black-women-in-the-labor-force

Rusher, A. W. (1996). *African American women administrators.* University Press of America.

Ryan, M. K., Haslam, S. A., Morgenroth, T., Rink, F., Stoker, J., & Peters, K. (2016). Getting on top of the glass cliff: Reviewing a decade of evidence, explanations, and impact. *The Leadership Quarterly, 27*(3), 446–455. doi:10.1016/j.leaqua.2015.10.008

Sabharwal, M. (2013). From glass ceiling to glass cliff: Women in senior executive service. *Journal of Public Administration: Research and Theory, 25*(2), 399–426. doi:10.1093/jopart/mut030

Sadovyy, M., Sánchez-Gómez, M., & Bresó, E. (2021). COVID-19: How the stress generated by the pandemic may affect work performance through the moderating role of emotional intelligence: Corrigendum. *Personality and Individual Differences, 182*, 1–9. doi:10.1016/j.paid.2021.111092

Sala, F. (2002). *Do programs designed to increase emotional intelligence at work-work?* https://www.eiconsortium.org/reports/do_ei_programs_work.html

Sanchez-Hucles, J. V., & Davis, D. D. (2010). Women and women of color in leadership: Complexity, identity, and intersectionality. *The American Psychologist, 65*(3), 171–181. doi:10.1037/a0017459 PMID:20350016

Sawyer, K., Salter, N., & Thoroughgood, C. (2013). Studying individual identities is good, but examining intersectionality is better. *Industrial and Organizational Psychology: Perspectives on Science and Practice, 6*(1), 80–84. doi:10.1111/iops.12012

Sax, L. J. (2012). *Empowering Women in Higher Education and Student Affairs: Theory, Research, Narratives, and Practice From Feminist Perspectives.* Stylus Publishing, LLC.

Scazzero, P. (2015). *The emotionally healthy leader.* Zondervan.

Schantz, M. (2019). Affirming the Purpose of Affirmative Action: Understanding a Policy of the Past to Move Towards a More Informed Future.

Schubert, K. (2018, August 31). Entrepreneur works to curb Minnesota's POC retention problem. https://spokesman-recorder.com/2018/08/31/entrepreneur-works-to-curb-minnesotas-poc-brain-drain/

Schutte, N., Malouff, J., Hall, L., Haggerty, D., Cooper, J., Golden, C., & Dornheim, L. (1998). Development and validation of a measure of emotional intelligence. *Personality and Individual Differences, 25*(2), 67–177. doi:10.1016/S0191-8869(98)00001

SCImago Research Group. (2007). SJR-SCImago Journal & Country Rank.

Sellie-Dosunmu, M. (2016). Using emotional intelligence in the workplace. *Association For Talent Development, 33*, 1612. doi:10.1080/09669582.2020.1758708

Serrat, O. (2017). *Understanding and developing emotional intelligence. Knowledge solutions.* Springer. doi:10.1007/978-981-10-0983-9_37

Shah, H. (2021, June 3). Addressing the social determinants of health upstream. *Loma Linda University Health.* https://ihpl.llu.edu/blog/addressing-social-determinants-health-upstream

Shakespeare, W. (1992). *Hamlet, prince of Denmark* (C. Watts & K. Carabine, Eds.). Wordsworth Editions.

Shakur, A. (2001). *ASSATA: An autobiography.* Lawrence Hill.

Shear, M. D. & Savage, C. (2022, January 26). Biden expected to nominate a black woman to the supreme court. *The New York Times.* https://www.nytimes.com/2022/01/26/us/politics/supreme-court-nominee-black-woman.html

Shepherd, J. M. (2018). *Don't touch my crown: Texturism as an extension of colorism in the natural hair community.* Thesis. Master of Arts in Mass Communications. Texas State University.

Sherrill, A. (2010). Women in management: Female managers' representation, characteristics, and pay. *United States Government Accountability Office GAO-10-1064T.*

Shih, D. (2017). A theory to better understand diversity and who really benefits. *NPR,* https://www.npr.org/sections/codeswitch/2017/04/19/523563345/a-theory-to-better-understand-diversity-and-who-really-benefits

Showunmi, V. (2021, February). A Journey of Difference: The Voices of Women Leaders. [). Frontiers Media SA.]. *Frontiers in Education, 6,* 548870. doi:10.3389/feduc.2021.548870

Simien, E. M. (Ed.). (2016). *Historic Firsts: How Symbolic Empowerment Changes US Politics.* Oxford University Press.

Simon, A. (2022, April 28). Here's what the Department of Human Rights discovered while investigating the MPD. *Kare 11.* https://www.kare11.com/article/news/local/minneapolis-police-department-human-rights-investigation/89-82ed0eeb-ac93-4c8d-a55c-7f887eb63c9c

Slaughter, A. M. (2015). *Why women still can't have it all.* OneWorld.

Sleeter, C. E. (2011). The academic and social value of ethnic studies.

Smith, A. (2009). Native studies beyond the academic-industrial complex. *I thought Pocahontas was a movie": Perspectives on race/culture binaries in education and service professions,* 79-89.

Smith, D. E. (2020). *Black while leading: Unmasking the anti-Black lived experiences of senior-level black men administrators at historically White institutions* (Order No. 28150659) [Doctoral Dissertation]. Illinois State University, USA.

Smith, A. (2007). *The revolution will not be funded: Beyond the non-profit industrial complex.* INCITE.

Smith, D. G. (2020). *Diversity's promise for higher education: Making it work.* Johns Hopkins University Press.

Smith, K. M., Alves, K., Weathersby, I., & Yi, J. (2020). Invictus: Race and emotional labor of faculty of color at the urban community college. *Journal of the Assembly for Expanded Perspectives on Learning, 25,* 119–135.

Smith, W. A. (2004). Black faculty coping with racial battle fatigue: The campus racial climate in a post-civil rights era. In D. Cleveland (Ed.), *A long way to go: Con- versations about race by African American faculty and graduate students* (pp. 171–190). Peter Lang Publishing.

Smith, W. A. (2008). Higher education: Racial battle fatigue. In R. T. Schaefer (Ed.), *Encyclopedia of race, ethnicity, and society,* (pp. 615–618). SAGE Publications.

Smith, W. A., Yosso, T. J., & Solórzano, D. G. (2006). Challenging racial battle fatigue on historically white campuses: A critical race examination of race-related stress. In C. A. Stanley (Ed.), *Faculty of color: Teaching in predominantly white colleges and universities* (pp. 299–327). Anker Publishing.

Sobers, S. T. (2014). *Can I get a witness?: The resilience of four Black women senior student affairs administrators at predominantly White institutions* (Order No. 3625189) [Doctoral Dissertation]. Illinois State University, USA.

Sparks, E. (1998). *Against all odds: Resistance and resilience in African American welfare mothers*. Wellesley College.

Spillers, H. (2000). Mama's baby, Papa's maybe: An American grammar book. In J. James & T. D. Sharpley-Whiting (Eds.), *The black feminist reader,* (pp. 257–279). Blackwell Publishers.

Squire, D., Williams, B. C., & Tuitt, F. (2018). Plantation politics and neoliberal racism in higher education: A framework for reconstructing anti-racist institutions. *Teachers College Record, 120*(14), 1–20.

St. Catherine University (2021, April 16). Overcome barriers to female leadership. https://www.stkate.edu/academics/women-in-leadership-degrees/barriers-to-female-leadership

Staggers-Hakim, R. (2009). *The moderating effect of discrimination and the intersection of race, class, and gender on obesity.* [Doctoral Dissertation]. Howard University, USA.

Stanley, C. A. (2016). Reflections on changing a university's diversity culture. *Insight Into Diversity.* www.insightintodiversity.com.

Stanley, W., Watson, K. L., Reyes, J. M., & Varela, K. S. (2019). Organizational change and the chief diversity officer: A case study of institutionalizing a diversity plan. *Journal of Diversity in Higher Education, 12*(3), 255–265. doi:10.1037/dhe0000099

Statistica (2022). Percentage of people without health insurance in the United States from 2010 to 2021 by ethnicity. https://www.statista.com/statistics/200970/percentage-of-americans-without-health-insurance-by-race-ethnicity/

Steele, C.M., & Aronson, J. (1995). Stereotype threat and the intellectual test performance of African Americans. Journal of Personality and Social Psychology, 69, 797–811.

Steinberg, S. (2018, April 9). Revisiting open admissions at CUNY. *PSC CUNY*. https://psc-cuny.org/clarion/february-2018/revisiting-open-admissions-cuny

Stein, S. (2018). Confronting the racial-colonial foundations of US higher education. *Journal for the Study of Postsecondary and Tertiary Education, 3*, 77–98. doi:10.28945/4105

Sternlicht, A. (2020, June 2). Over 4,400 Arrests, 62,000 National Guard Troops Deployed: George Floyd Protests By The Numbers. *Forbes.* https://www.forbes.com/sites/alexandrasternlicht/2020/06/02/over-4400-arrests-62000-national-guard-troops-deployed-george-floyd-protests-by-the-numbers/?sh=67e5b954d4fe

Stewart, J. (2006). Transformational Leadership: An evolving concept examined through the works of Burns, Bass, Avolio, and Leithwood. *Canadian Journal of Educational Administration and Policy, 54*, 1–29. https://eric.ed.gov/?id=EJ843441

Streeter, C. (2020). Breathing Power and Poise. *Australasian Journal of American Studies, 39*(1), 5–46. https://www.jstor.org/stable/10.2307/26972999

Stuart, R. (2010). Diversity to the next level. *Diverse Issues in Higher Education, 27*(8), 12–14. http://diverseeducation.com/

Subramanian, S. & Gilbert, T (2021, March 11). A new era of workplace inclusion: Moving from retrofit to redesign. *Future Forum.* https://futureforum.com/2021/03/11/dismantling-the-office-moving-from-retrofit-to-redesign/

Sue, D. W. (2010). *Microaggressions in everyday life: Race, gender & sexual orientation.* John Wiley & Sons, Inc.

Sue, D. W., Capodilupo, C. M., & Holder, A. M. B. (2008). Racial microaggressions in the life experience of Black Americans. *Professional Psychology: Research and Practice, 39*(3), 329–336. doi:10.1037/0735-7028.39.3.329

Sue, D. W., Capodilupo, C. M., Torino, G. C., Bucceri, J. M., Holder, A. M., Nadal, K. L., & Esquilin, M. E. (2007). Racial microaggressions in everyday life: Implications for clinical practice. *The American Psychologist, 62*(4), 271–286. doi:10.1037/0003-066X.62.4.271 PMID:17516773

Sun, H., Wang, S., Wang, W., Han, G., Liu, Z., Wu, Q., & Pang, X. (2021). Correlation between emotional intelligence and negative emotions of front-line nurses during the COVID-19 epidemic: A cross-sectional study. *Journal of Clinical Nursing, 30*(3-4), 385–396. doi:10.1111/jocn.15548

Suyemoto, K., Hochman, A., Donovan, R., & Roemar, L. (2021). Becoming and fostering allies and accomplices through authentic relationships: Choosing justice over comfort. *Research in Human Development, 18*(1), 1–28. doi:10.1080/15427609.2020.1825905

Sykes, T. A. (2021). The elite 100: A tribute to black women executives: The change is here. *Diversity Woman Media.* https://www.diversitywoman.com/the-elite-100-a-tribute-to-black-women-executives-2/

Tàlàbí, A. (3 April, 2022). Kpoem: soft life. [Video]. Instagram. https://www.instagram.com/p/Cb5VV53Im2i/

Talan, T. (2022, August 9). *Diversity, Equity, and Inclusion: When values become actions.* McCormick Center For Early Childhood Leadership, At National Louis University. https://mccormickcenter.nl.edu/library/dei-iposter-080922/

Tate, W. F. IV. (1997). Chapter 4: Critical race theory and education: History, theory, and implications. *Review of Research in Education, 22*(1), 195–247. doi:10.3102/0091732X022001195

Taylor, K. (2017). *How we get free: Black Feminism and the Combahee Collective.* Haymarket Books.

Taylor, K. Y. (2017). *How we get free: Black feminism and the Combahee River Collective.* Haymarket Books.

Terhune, C. P. (2008). Coping in Isolation: The Experiences of Black Women in White Communities. *Journal of Black Studies, 38*(4), 547–564. doi:10.1177/0021934706288144

Terrill, W., & Reisig, M. (2003). Neighborhood Context and Police Use of Force. *Journal of Research in Crime and Delinquency, 40*(3), 291–321. doi:10.1177/0022427803253800

Tevis, T., Hernandez, M., & Bryant, R. (2020). Reclaiming our time: An autoethnographic exploration of black women higher education administrators. *The Journal of Negro Education, 89*(3), 282–297, 381–382.

Thomas, R., Cooper, M., McShane Urban, K., Cardazone, G., Bohrer, A., Mahajan, S., Yee, L., Krivkovich, A., Haung, J., Rambachan, I., Burns, T., & Trkulja, T. (2021). Women in the workplace. *McKinsey & Company.* https://wiw-report.s3.amazonaws.com/Women_in_the_Workplace_2021.pdf

Thomas, J. M. (2020). *Diversity regimes: Why talk is not enough to fix racial inequality at universities.* Rutgers University Press.

Thomas, V. G., & Jackson, J. A. (2007). The education of African American girls and women: Past to present. *The Journal of Negro Education*, *76*(3), 357–372.

Thompson, S. (2019). Despite being the most educated, black women earn less money at work, in entrepreneurship and venture capital: here are three ways to fix it: when black women win, we all win. https://www.inc.com/sonia-thompson/black-women-equal-pay-equity-how-to-make-progress.html

Tierney, W. G. (1997). Organizational socialization in higher education. *The Journal of Higher Education*, *68*(1), 1–16. doi:10.2307/2959934

Titcomb, C., & JBHE (2022). *Key Events in Black Higher Education.* Journal of Blacks in Higher Education. https://www.jbhe.com/chronology/

Tuelon, A. (1973). Nanny, maroon chieftainess. *Caribbean Quarterly*, *19*(4), 20–27. doi:10.1080/00086495.1973.11829168

Tulshyan, R., & Burey, J. (2021, February 11). Stop telling women they have imposter syndrome. *Harvard Business Review.* https://hbr.org/2021/02/stop-telling-women-they-have-imposter-syndrome

Turner, C. S. V. (2002). Women of color in academe: Living with multiple marginality. *The Journal of Higher Education*, *73*(1), 74–93. doi:10.1080/00221546.2002.11777131

Turner, C. S. V., González, J. C., & Wong, K. (2011). Faculty women of color: The critical nexus of race and gender. *Journal of Diversity in Higher Education*, *4*(4), 199–211. doi:10.1037/a0024630

Turner, C., & Grauerholz, L. (2017). Introducing the invisible man: Black male professionals in higher education. *Humboldt Journal of Social Relations*, *39*(39), 212–227. doi:10.55671/0160-4341.1013

U.S. Bureau of Labor Statistics. (2022). Unemployment rates for states. *USBLS.* https://www.bls.gov/web/laus/laumstrk.htm

U.S. Census Bureau. (2020). Reported voting and registration for states: November 2020. *U.S. Department of Commerce.* https://www.census.gov/data/tables/time-series/demo/voting-and-registration/p20-585.html

U.S. Census Bureau. (2021). Quick facts: Minneapolis city, Minnesota. *U.S. Department of Commerce.* https://www.census.gov/quickfacts/minneapoliscityminnesota

U.S. Census Bureau. (2021). Quick facts: Saint Paul city, Minnesota. *U.S. Department of Commerce.* https://www.census.gov/quickfacts/stpaulcityminnesota

U.S. News and World Report (2022) Best Places to live in the U.S. in 2022-2023. *US News.* https://realestate.usnews.com/places/rankings/best-places-to-live

United States Census Bureau. (2020). Annual estimates of the resident population by sex, race, and hispanic origin [Dataset]. 2019 Population Estimates by Age, Sex, Race, and Hispanic Origin. https://www.census.gov/newsroom/press-kits/2020/population-estimates-detailed.html

United States Census Bureau. (2021). QuickFacts. USCB. https://www.census.gov/quickfacts/fact/table/US/LFE046220

University of Minnesota. (n.d.). *About us.* https://twin-cities.umn.edu/about-us

University of North Carolina Pembroke. (2021). Why diversity and inclusion are good for business. https://online.uncp.edu/articles/mba/diversity-and-inclusion-good-for-business.aspx

US Government Accountability Office. (2010). Women in management: Analysis of female managers' representation, characteristics, and pay.

Vaught, S. E. (2008). Writing against racism: Telling white lies and reclaiming culture. *Qualitative Inquiry*, *14*(4), 566–589.

Verma, S., Aggarwal, A., & Bansal, H. (2017). The Relationship between Emotional Intelligence (EQ) and adversity quotient (AQ). *Journal of Business and Management*, *19*, 49–53. doi:10.9790/487X-1901024953

Wallace, S. L., Moore, S. E., Wilson, L. L., & Hart, B. G. (2012). African American women in the academy: Quelling the myth of presumed incompetence. In G. Gutierrez y Muhs, Y. Niemann, C. González, & A. Harris (Eds.), *Presumed incompetent: The intersections of race and class for women in academia,* (pp. 421–438). University Press of Colorado. doi:10.2307/j.ctt4cgr3k.38

Walton, G. M., & Cohen, G. L. (2011). A brief social-belonging intervention improvesacademic and health outcomes of minority students. Science, 331(6023), 1447–1451.

Warner, J., Ellmann, N., & Boesch, D. (2018, November 20). Women's leadership by the numbers. Center for American Progress. Retrieved from https://www.americanprogress.org/issues/women/reports/2018/11/20/461273/womens-leadership-gap-2/

Warren, K., & Hadden, J. (2020, June 4). How all 50 states are responding to the George Floyd protests, from imposing curfews to calling in the National Guard. *Business Insider*. https://www.businessinsider.com/us-states-response-george-floyd-protests-curfews-national-guard-2020-6

Webb, K. S. (2009). Why emotional intelligence should matter to management: A survey of the literature. *Advanced Management Journal*, *74*(2), 32–41.

West, N. M. (2019). In the company of my sister-colleagues: Professional counterspaces for African American women student affairs administrators. *Gender and Education*, *31*(4), 543–559. doi:10.1080/09540253.2018.1533926

West, N. M. (2021). Embodying Black feminist epistemology to make green grass grow: The transition from administrator to academic for a Black woman in student affairs. *Journal of Diversity in Higher Education.*

Whang, N. Y. (2018). School leadership for social justice and its linkage with perilous politics. *Asia Pacific Education Review*, 1–17.

Whitaker, M. C., & Grollman, E. A. (Eds.). (2018). *Counternarratives from women of color academics: Bravery, vulnerability, and resistance,* (1st ed.). Routledge., doi:10.4324/9780429465505

White, E. (1890). *Patriarchs and Prophets*. Review and Herald Publishing Association.

Wiley, Z., Kubes, J., Cobb, J., Jacob, J., Franks, N., Plantinga, L., & Lea, J. (2022). Age, Comorbid Conditions, and Racial Disparities in COVID-19 Outcomes. *Journal of Racial and Ethnic Health Disparities*, (9), 117–123.

Williams, D. A., & Wade-Golden, K. C. (2013). The chief diversity officer. Sterling, VA. Stylus Publishing, LLC.

Williams, D., & Wade-Golden, K. C. (2006, April 18). What is a chief diversity officer? *Inside Higher Education*. https://drdamonawilliams.com/wp-content/uploads/DAW_KWG_CDO_What_IS.pdf

Williams, J. C., Andrews, O. & Boginsky, M. (2022). Why many women of color don't want to return to the office. https://hbr.org/2022/05/why-many-women-of-color-dont-want-to-return-to-the-office

Williams, M. T., Skinta, M. D., & Martin-Willett, R. (2021). After pierce and sue: A revised racial microaggressions taxonomy. *Perspectives on Psychological Science, 16*(5), 991–1007. doi:10.1177/1745691621994247

Williams, D. (2013). *Strategic diversity leadership: Activating change and transformation in higher education.* Stylus Publishing.

Williams, D. A., Berger, J. B., & McClendon, S. A. (2005). *Toward a model of inclusive excellence and change in post-secondary institutions.* Association of American Colleges and Universities.

Williams, D. A., & Wade-Golden, K. C. (2007). *The chief diversity officer: A primer for college and university presidents.* American Council on Education.

Williams, D., & Wade-Golden, K. (2007). The chief diversity officer. *CUPA-HR Journal, 58*(1), 38.

Willis, J. M. (2019). *Pushing through despite the bullshit: Black women graduate students in higher education at historically White institutions* (Publication No. 13862212) [Doctoral dissertation]. California State University, USA.

Wing, A. K. (Ed.). (1997). *Critical race feminism: A reader.* NYU Press.

Wing, A. K. (Ed.). (2003). *Critical race feminism: A reader,* (2nd ed.). NYU Press.

Winters, M. F. (2014). From diversity to inclusion: An inclusion equation. In B. M. Ferdman & B. N. Deane (Eds.), *Diversity at work: The practice of inclusion,* (pp. 205–228). Jossey-Bass.

Winters, M. F. (2020a). *Inclusive conversations.* Berrett-Koehler Publishers, Inc.

Winters, M. F. (2020b). *Black fatigue: How racism erodes the mind, body, and spirit.* Berrett-Koehler Publishers, Inc.

Witynski, M. (2021). 100 years ago Georgiana Simpson made history as the first black woman to graduate with a PhD. *UchicagoNews.* https://news.uchicago.edu/story/100-years-ago-georgiana-simpson-made-history-first-black-woman-graduate-phd

Wolfman, B. R. (1997). Light as from a beacon: African American women administrators in the academy L. Benjamin (Ed.), Black Women in the Academy: Promises and Perils (pp. 158–167). University of Florida Press.

Wong, Y. L. R. (2004). Knowing through discomfort: A mindfulness-based critical social work pedagogy. *Critical Social Work, 5*(1), 1–19.

Woodard, Q. (2014). *Understanding the implications of organizational culture and organizational structure for the role of the Chief Diversity Officer in higher education* [Doctoral dissertation]. University of Illinois at Urbana-Champaign, USA.

Workneh, L. (2016, June 26). *Jesse Williams: 'Just because we're magic, does not mean we're not real'.* HuffPost. https://www.huffpost.com/entry/jesse-williams-bet-awards-humanitarian-award_n_57708cebe4b017b379f65077

Worthington, R. (2020). Antiracism as an institutional imperative: A primer and review. file:///C:/Users/Gigi%20Secuban/Downloads/Antiracism%20and%20Self-Study%20Slides.pdf.

Worthington, R. L., Stanley, C. A., & Lewis, W. T. Sr. (2014). National Association of Diversity Officers in Higher Education standards of professional practice for chief diversity officers. *Journal of Diversity in Higher Education, 7*(4), 227–234. doi:10.1037/a0038391

Worthington, R. L., Stanley, C. A., & Smith, D. G. (2020). Advancing the professionalization of diversity officers in higher education: Report of the presidential task force on the revision of the NADOHE standards of professional practice. *Journal of Diversity in Higher Education, 13*(1), 1–22. doi:10.1037/dhe0000175

Yakaboski, T., & Donahoo, S. (2011). In (re) search of women in student affairs administration. *Empowering women in higher education and student affairs: Theory, research, narratives, and practice from feminist perspectives*, 270-286.

Yancy, G. (2008). *Black bodies, white gazes: The continuing significance of race*. Rowman & Littlefield Pub.

Yorth Group. (2020). Restorative Rondo: Building equity for all. https://reconnectrondo.com/wp-content/uploads/2021/01/Rondo-Past-Prosperity-Study.pdf

Yosso, T.J. (2005). Whose culture has capital? A critical race theory discussion of community cultural wealth. Race, Ethnicity and Education, 8(1), 69–91.

Yosso, T. J. (2005). Whose culture has capital? A critical race theory discussion of community cultural wealth. *Race, Ethnicity and Education*, *8*(1), 69–91. doi:10.1080/1361332052000341006

Yukl, G. (2009). Leading organizational learning: Reflections on theory and research. *The Leadership Quarterly*, *20*(1), 49–53. doi:10.1016/j.leaqua.2008.11.006

Zamani, E. M. (2003). African American women in higher education. *New Directions for Student Services*, *104*, 5–18.

Zelevansky, N. (2019). The big business of unconscious bias. *The New York Times*.

Zippia (2022). Chief diversity officer demographics and statistics in the US. *Zippa.* https://www.zippia.com/chief-diversity-officer-jobs/demographics/

About the Contributors

lTristen Johnson (she, her, hers) is a TEDx Speaker and currently works as a Diversity Education Specialist for a top-ranking cancer center in Florida. She is a former higher education professional. She holds a master's degree from Southern Illinois University-Carbondale and a bachelor's degree from Western Illinois University. She recently defended her dissertation for her Ph.D. at Illinois State University. Her research focused on Black women professionals who work in diversity roles at predominantly white institutions. She is the founder and owner of The Tristen Johnson, LLC, a business dedicated to consulting, trainings, and workshops surrounding diversity and inclusion initiatives.

Norka Blackman-Richards is a curator of anti-racist equity-needing spaces. With over twenty years supporting the academic success of high-need student populations at Queens College of the City University of New York (CUNY), she is a skilled advocate, strategist, and negotiator. In 2019, she was the recipient of the Presidential Award for Excellence in Service for the Queens College Division of Enrollment and Student Retention. Blackman-Richards is the director of the Percy E Sutton SEEK Program, lectures in English literature and composition, serves on academic, enrollment, retention, and student affairs committees, and is a member of the CUNY DEI Incubator. The daughter of missionaries she was educated under the British, Dutch and Latin American educational systems, an experience that afforded her a unique appreciation and understanding for justice, equity, diversity and inclusion. A direct descendant of the builders of the Panama Canal, Norka acknowledges that the intersections of her lived experiences and identities are ever-present in her many roles in and outside of the academy.

Michelle Bryan earned a Doctor of Philosophy, Education (Culture, Curriculum & Change) from The University of North Carolina at Chapel Hill; Master of Arts in Teaching, Secondary Social Sciences - The University of North Carolina at Chapel Hill; and a Bachelor of Arts, African American Studies/ American History - The University of North Carolina at Chapel Hill. She currently serves as the Assistant Vice President of Diversity, Equity & Inclusion at the University of South Carolina.

Shirley Carter earned a B.S., English/Secondary Education fromTuskegee University (AL), M.A., Journalism from The Ohio State University, and Ph.D., Journalism from the University of Missouri-Columbia. She serves as Professor and Associate Dean for Diversity, Equity, and Inclusion in the College of Information and Communications at the University of South Carolina.

Tiara Cash, MS, MCMA (she/they), is founder and owner of Crowned Vitta LLC - a multi-disciplinary company serving communities through the concepts of mindfulness, meta-awareness, and meaningful self-relationships and relationships with others. Featured on NPR (National Public Radio) as an expert, Tiara is creator of the Equitable Mindfulness Framework - which includes a model that she utilizes for contentious conversations across social differences. She currently uses these concepts to curate conferences, create presentations and workshops, and conduct trainings on mindfulness and equity through her business. Academically, Tiara has published papers, and been granted scholarships, grants, and awards for her work with mindfulness in the student-athlete population, mindfulness and equity/social justice, and creating transformative art with a foundation of mindful practice. During her career, Tiara has been invited internationally to the Netherlands, Canada, and the UK to present on her research involving mindfulness and overlooked populations. Her research and career focus include: delving into the intersections of mindfulness in marginalized and unrepresented populations, and how prosocialiality buffers wellbeing during life transitions.

Vernese Edghill-Walden joined Northern Illinois University in 2015 as the first chief diversity officer. In June 2020, she was promoted to vice president for diversity, equity and inclusion. In the same year she was asked to lead efforts to transform NIU's Human Resources division as interim Chief Human Resources Officer from 2020-2021. As a creative implementer, she is leading the university's strategic initiatives to advance access, academic equity, inclusion, and belonging. As a senior executive, she has led transformative strategies to improve student success, transform policies and procedures, advance employee professional development & training on DEI, belonging and social justice. Vernese has the uncanny ability to bring groups together to collaborate for a common goal. With over 30 years of professional experience in pre-K-12th and higher education, Vernese continues to build bridges and to cultivate important relationships with many different industries, non-profits and community organizations with the goal of creating environments where all people feel welcomed, valued, respected and seen. Prior to NIU, Dr. Edghill-Walden held several roles at Richard J Daley College and the system office of the City Colleges of Chicago including Director of Institutional Research, Associate Vice Chancellor for Academic Affairs and Provost for the City Colleges' system. Prior to her tenure at City Colleges of Chicago, she served as the first Director of Diversity at Georgetown Day School, in Washington, D.C. and the Director of the Center for Black Culture at the University of Delaware. She holds a Ph.D. in Sociology from Howard University, Master of Science in Counseling and Higher Education Administration from the University of Delaware, and a Bachelor of Arts in Sociology from Bucknell University. Her research and publications focus on Black women's career mobility, specifically in cultural centers within higher education, Black women and social movements and closing academic equity gaps. Her love for higher education leadership has always been balanced with a desire to be a role model in the classroom by teaching undergraduate and graduate level online and face to face courses. She has had the privilege of teaching courses like: Black women and Social Movements, Diversity and Inclusion in the Workplace, Social Problems and Intro to Sociology.

Anne M. Edwards served as the director of the Center for Black Studies at Northern Illinois University from 2018-2022. Currently, she is the director of the Black Cultural Center at Purdue University. Prior to this role, she has held various roles in higher education, working in career services and admissions. She received a B.S. and M.S. in Hospitality and Tourism Management from Purdue University and worked in the hospitality industry for several years until returning to school to obtain an M.B.A. from Valparaiso University. She earned a doctorate in educational psychology in August of 2021 where her emphasis centers Black women and identity development in the higher education environment. Her other research interests include topics around race, motivation, leadership, and career development. Dr. Edwards is interested in ways of making research accessible to the public. Dr. Edwards is an active member of the Association of Black Culture Centers (ABCC), National Council for Black Studies (NCBS), and NASPA. She has presented at ABCC, NCBS, MWERA, NASPA, ACPA, Association for the Study of African American Life and History (ASALAH) and at the International Self-Determination theory conference. Dr. Edwards is one of the co-hosts of the podcast Blkwomynvoices, a show about Black womyn and higher education. In her free time Anne Marie enjoys traveling, cooking, reading, community service and spending time with family, friends, and her beloved mini schnauzer Buffy.)

Alana Dionne Fields, PhD A Black Queer Feminist, graduate of the University of Pittsburgh, with a PhD in Sociology. My dissertation title, "Coaching Boys Into Men": Exploring Implementation, Evaluation and Content of a Gender-Transformative Violence Prevention Program. My research and teaching interest lie at the intersections of Gender, Race, Violence Prevention/Intervention and Community based participatory research and Sports, Feminist Thought, Critical Race Theory, Black Queer Theory and Ethnomethodology. I earned a BS in African American Studies with a Minor in Graphic Design from Washington University (St. Louis, MO), Masters in American Culture Studies from Washington University (St. Louis, MO), PhD in Sociology with a certificate in Gender, Sexuality and Women's Studies from the University of Pittsburgh (Pittsburgh, PA), completed two year postdoctoral appointment with the University of Pittsburgh School of Medicine Center for Adolescent and Young Adult Health (CAYAH). Currently serving as staff scientist in CAYAH, directing youth violence intervention programing.

Aysa Gray, MA, is a change-maker grounded in a racial justice praxis that allows Black and POC people, at the margins, to be existentially and spiritually well in the future. Aysa is a member of the Black and Latinx Faculty and Staff group, a founding member of the QC Mutual Aid Group, a founding member of the DEI Incubator, and the first Black Nonbinary Interim Director of the Center for Ethnic, Racial and Religious Understanding. Aysa is a thought-leader in Antiracist DEI work for their work on the bias of professionalism. They come to this work with the framing that freedom from the racialized, capitalist, gendered and ableist oppression of overworking is possible in this lifetime.

Coretta Jenerette received a Ph.D. and MSN from the University of South Carolina and her BSN from Clemson University. She completed a certificate in nursing education at The University of North Carolina at Chapel Hill and is a certified nurse educator. She also completed post-doctoral fellowships at both Yale University and The University of North Carolina at Chapel Hill. Recently, she completed a certificate in Diversity and Inclusion from Cornell University.

Toby Jenkins is an Associate Professor of Higher Education and Director of the Museum of Education. She also serves as Interim Associate Dean of Diversity, Equity & Inclusion in the Graduate School. She completed her B.A. in Public Relations from the University of South Carolina; Masters of Arts in Higher Education from the University of Maryland College Park; and PhD in Educational Theory & Policy from Penn State University.

Adela E. Jiménez is a former COO and CFO with 30+ years of experience in multiple non-profit and for-profit organizations, including multiple fortune 500 companies. An avid traveler, who has also lived and worked in several countries, Dr. Jiménez leverages her global knowledge and the intersectionality of her identities – Black, Hispanic, Woman and Immigrant to educate and offer solutions to organizations in search of improved bottom-line results that come from diversity. Her work within DEI has also centered on coaching women of color who have experienced challenges in meeting their organization's goals while keeping themselves truthfully whole. In addition to a Ph.D. in business with focus on emotional intelligence, Dr. Jiménez also holds undergraduate degrees in Computer Science and Accounting and a master's degree in Business Administration. She is also a licensed Certified Public Accountant and Chartered Global Management Accountant.

Jilma Jiménez is a visionary, engaging, and inspirational leader with more than 30 years of experience in the the engineering consulting space. Her work within DEI, was born from her experiences as typically being the "only" Black, Hispanic, Woman, or Immigrant within the room. She leverages her unique viewpoints to seek outlier perspectives, create platforms for thought diversity, and to design effective DEI initiatives. Jiménez is the recipient of the 2022 Woman of Color in STEM award for Managerial Leadership. Jiménez holds a bachelor's degree in Mechanical Engineering, a master's degree in Biomedical Engineering, and professional licenses in both Civil and Mechanical engineering. She also has advanced executive and business training and certification from the Wharton School of Business. Jiménez is a native of the Republic of Panama.

Natasha N. Johnson is a Clinical Instructor and director of the M.I.S. program in Criminal Justice Administration at Georgia State University. A career educator since 2001, her research focuses on critical theory, equity, and social justice leadership, particularly within the K-20 sector. Her other research areas include intersectionality, educational law, policy, and governance, and curriculum development. Dr. Johnson holds multi-state reciprocity and has previously worked as a teacher, guidance counselor, assistant dean, instructional leader, and curriculum developer domestically and abroad. She is a David L. Clark scholar, a CETLOE Faculty Teaching Fellow, and her work is published in SAGE, the Oxford Research Encyclopedia of Criminology and Criminal Justice, Taylor & Francis, the Routledge Focus series, Psychology of Violence, the popular press, and several highly acclaimed educational leadership journals.

Lauren Jones is a director of diversity, equity and inclusion at the University of Minnesota. She believes in speaking truth to power and centering the marginalized. Lauren provides leadership and oversight for the DEI activities across the school, including strategic planning and implementation, training, and programming. She helps the school to operationalize its values by working with administrators, faculty, staff, students, and alumni. She has a bachelor's degree from Western Illinois University, a master's degree from Old Dominion University, and is working on a PhD at the University of Minnesota (CEHD). She has over 15 years of experience working in higher education institutions and owns Maroon Consulting LLC, a small DEI consulting firm. Lauren is a native Chicagoan and currently lives in North Minneapolis with her partner and their 2 dogs.

Tracie Jones is the Assistant Dean for Diversity, Equity, & Inclusion in the School of Humanities, Arts, and Social Sciences at MIT (SHASS). She serves as a strategic partner to the dean and leaders in the school's departments, labs and centers (DLCs). She works with members of the SHASS community to develop and collaboratively implement programs and activities that advance the school's commitment to a diverse, respectful, and caring community for staff, students, and faculty.

Andriette Jordan-Fields, PhD A Womanist Ethicist, graduate of the University of Denver and Iliff School of Theology joint PhD program, with a PhD in Religion and Theological Studies concentrating in Social Ethics. Her research and teaching interest lie at the intersection of ethics, womanist/feminist studies, Black Church, critical race theory and postcolonial studies with an overall approach to the study of social ethics that engages wide-ranging issues of moral agency, cultural memory, ethical accountability and social justice. She earned a BS in Political Science from Tuskegee University (Tuskegee, Ala.), MPA–Master of Public Administration from Northeastern University (Boston, MA) and a MASC–Master of Arts in Social Change from Iliff School of Theology (Denver, CO). In addition, she is a Denver 2019 HERS Institute graduate (Higher Education Resource Services for women in Higher Education), a transformational, leadership development program for women in higher education, founded to fill leadership pipelines across the United States with dynamic women, each capable of ushering their respective institutions into a more inclusive and equitable future.

Timothy Lynch is a distinguished historian and seasoned administrator who has held a range of leadership roles in higher education. He served as interim president of Queensborough Community College (2018-2020) and Provost and Senior Vice President (2017-2018 and 2020-2021). A first-generation college student, he earned a B.A. in history from Brooklyn College (CUNY) and his Ph.D. in history at the CUNY Graduate Center. Dr. Lynch is now the Interim President at the College of Staten Island (CSI).

Charnise Virgil Moore is a healthcare compliance officer with more than 10 years experience in various hospital settings. She earned an undergraduate degree from Tougaloo College, a Masters degree in Public Health from Brown University, and a Doctorate degree in Public Health from the University of Arkansas for Medical Sciences. In addition to her professional career, Dr. Moore is an advocate of women and girls, especially Black women and girls. She has dedicated research and advocacy work to teen pregnancy prevention among Black girls, ensuring women and girls have access to reproductive healthcare services, advancement of women and girls in science, technology, engineering, and math (STEM) fields, mentoring minority undergraduate students, and creating scholarship opportunities for youth to seek higher education.

Eleonor Pusey-Reid is an Associate Professor at the MGH Institute of Health Professions (MGH IHP) in the School of Nursing (SON). She is passionate about teaching Evidence-Based and Leadership in Nursing to prelicensure students. Her primary scholarly work interest is in the area of dark skin tone representation in the teaching-learning literature. She co-chairs the SON Justice, Equity, Diversity, and Inclusion (JEDI) Collaborative Committee and is the inaugural JEDI award-winning recipient at IHP 2022.

Stephanie Reed, Executive Director and Founder of the Aspire2Higher movement, is a mother of three and a higher education professional with over 15 years experience. Stephanie began her higher education journey earning a Masters degree, specializing in Higher Education Administration from Indiana University of Pennsylvania. From there, her higher education journey took her to The University of Georgia, serving as a career counselor for the Terry College of Business. Stephanie's career in higher education has since been in several small private universities as well as a public midsize research institution. As Stephanie garnered the respect and engagement of students of a variety of backgrounds and experiences, she began to serve as advisor to organizations such as the Black student union, PRIDE student organizations and multicultural student associations. This led to a pivot in her career from career counseling to becoming Director of Student Diversity Initiatives in her hometown of Philadelphia, Pennsylvania. Serving in this role for 6 years equipped Stephanie with subject matter expertise in diversity, equity & inclusion. Stephanie also has experience working for a Fortune 500 company where she spent time as a corporate sales manager for Philip Morris, International, the largest manufacturer of cigarettes, smoke-free products and associated electronic devices. Stephanie's passions though, are making colleges/universities and other organizations more equity-minded and inclusive; creating programs & curricula centered around intersectional race conscious engaged scholarship. Stephanie also cares deeply about youth empowerment and does work focusing on building high "career esteem " and "career resiliency". As Stephanie worked with more and more students in the north and southeastern regions, she began to more specifically, help young people recognize their inherent abilities to be leaders and scholars. Over the course of her career in higher education, students and young professionals often asked if it was possible to have a career that was both personally and professionally fulfilling. This led Stephanie to begin her entrepreneurial pursuits and through the work of Aspire2Higher, Stephanie demonstrates that YES YOU CAN! Stephanie created Aspire2Higher Personal & Professional Development Services, Inc.; which is an educational consulting company with a variety of programs and services. Currently, Stephanie serves as Executive Director of Aspire2Higher, based in Raleigh NC and serves as a DEI Consultant for a NC municipality. Stephanie's current work taps into her experience in sales, her career counseling abilities as well as her knowledge and expertise in diversity, equity and inclusion. The A2H company and movement were established to help people manifest their dreams into professional realities with the Elements A2H. She enjoys working for herself, with her family, encouraging excellence, inclusive leadership and engaged scholarship in communities all over the country.

Selena T. Rodgers is an Arthur O. Eve HEOP Alumna and first-generation PhD graduate who has worked at the City University of New York for more than nineteen years as a member of the instructional staff. She is the Chairperson of the Social Work Department and holds affiliated faculty and union leadership appointments. Her funded research examines the well-being and experiences of Black women through an intersectional and a structural lens with special attention to various forms of violence, antiBlackness, and historical trauma. She is recognized nationally and internationally for developing ADEI programs and curricula aimed to decolonize social and economic injustice created by interlocking stratified systems of oppression. Dr. Rodgers earned the rank of full professor in social work and is the first person to lead Queens, New York's accredited graduate social work program (launched in 2018). She is also the first Black person to serve in this role in CUNY's nearly 65-year-old history of social work education.

Kerri-Ann M. Smith is the Inaugural Faculty Fellow for Diversity, Equity, and Inclusivity at Queensborough Community College (CUNY). An Associate Professor of English, her work centers culturally responsive pedagogy and diversity, equity, and inclusivity in education. She earned her Ed.D. and B.A. at Binghamton University (SUNY), and her M.A. in teaching at Brooklyn College (CUNY). She has conducted multiple professional development conferences for educators in Ghana and Nigeria and has worked to support educational efforts in Jamaica, as an education liaison to various Jamaican diaspora organizations.

Raja Staggers-Hakim is a social researcher and skilled facilitator in the areas of health inequities, social inequality, and race & racism. Raja Staggers-Hakim received a doctorate in medical sociology and race, class, and gender studies (social inequality) from Howard University and a Master of Public

Health (MPH) in Community Health Education from New York University. Dr. Staggers-Hakim has over 10-years teaching experience in higher education and has presented her research nationally. Additionally, she has worked in an accelerated leadership capacity with community health centers and non-profit organizations. Dr. Staggers-Hakim has facilitated national conversations on discrimination and the impact on health and led trainings on diversity, cultural competency, advocacy, and equity. She has worked with national non-profits and provided technical assistance in strategic planning, program development, program evaluation, and board development. In 2012 Dr. Staggers-Hakim founded CHEER Institute, a non-profit organization dedicated to eliminating health inequities through community building and engagement, and diversity, equity, and inclusion training. She currently serves as Executive Director.

Atiya Kai Stokes-Brown is Professor of Political Science at Coastal Carolina University (CCU). A dynamic leader with more than 15 years of experience working in higher education, Dr. Stokes-Brown has worked collaboratively in numerous capacities across college communities, demonstrating strong academic and administrative leadership, and a deep passion for liberal arts education. Most recently, she provided campus-wide leadership regarding the importance of diversity, equity, inclusion and belonging to the educational mission of the university serving as Vice President for Diversity, Equity and Inclusion. In this role, she was responsible for advancing strategies and policies that advance diversity, equity, inclusion and belonging as key parts of the institution's strategic plan. Her many responsibilities included developing and conducting CCU's first All Campus Climate Survey; developing and implementing CCU's first diversity, equity and inclusion strategic plan; developing bias response policy; advancing DEI professional development opportunities; and enhancing efforts to recruit and retain a diverse faculty and staff. She led the Division of Diversity, Equity and Inclusion and ran the division's administrative and faculty/staff facing office, the Office of Diversity and Inclusion (ODI). She also provided administrative supervision for the office of Intercultural and Inclusion Student Services and the office of Accessibility and Disability Services. Prior to serving as Vice President for Diversity, Equity and Inclusion at CCU, Dr. Stokes-Brown served as a tenured faculty member in the Department of Political Science at Bucknell University and held several administrative positions at the university including Interim Associate Provost for Diversity, Faculty Fellow in the Office of the Associate Provost for Diversity, and Assistant Dean of the College of Arts & Sciences. Dr. Stokes-Brown has presented and/or participated in a number of diversity and multicultural workshops and organizations such as the Association of American Colleges and Universities (AAC&U), the Consortium for Faculty Diversity, and the Liberal Arts Diversity Officers (LADO), as well as at various colleges and universities. Drawn to academia by the desire to give back and help build inclusive communities, Dr. Stokes-Brown received her Ph.D. in Political Science from the University of Maryland, College Park and her master's in Political Science from Temple University. She graduated Phi Beta Kappa with bachelor degrees in Politics and Dance from Randolph-Macon Woman's College (currently known as Randolph College). She is also a graduate of several competitive leadership programs including the Penn State Center for the Study of Higher Education Academic Leadership Academy; the National Association of Diversity Officers in Higher Education (NADOHE) Standards of Professional Practice Institute, and Higher Education Resource Services (HERS) Bryn Mawr Summer Institute. Dr. Stokes-Brown's teaching interests include American Politics, Racial/Ethnic Minority Political Behavior, Latino Politics, Women and Politics, Campaigns and Elections, and Congressional/State Politics. She has more than 15 publications broadly centered on the political incorporation of women and racial/ethnic groups into the American political system, and issues of representation. She is the author of The Politics of Race in Latino Communities:

Walking the Color Line (Routledge, 2012, 2014) and her work has appeared in several peer-reviewed journals including the Journal of Politics, American Politics Research, Politics and Policy, the Journal of Elections, Public Opinion, and Parties, Social Science Quarterly, National Political Science Review, and Political Research Quarterly. She is also the author of several peer-reviewed book chapters. A native of Philadelphia, PA and a graduate of the Baldwin School in Bryn Mawr, PA, Dr. Stokes-Brown resides in Myrtle Beach with her family.

Index

A

Accomplice 57, 59, 66, 73, 248-249
Active Listening 158, 165
Activism 7, 25, 194, 207, 220, 242, 264, 276
Allyship 57-60, 66, 71-72, 75, 221, 226, 248, 262, 268
Anti-Blackness 101-102, 173, 193, 196, 210, 237, 261-266, 271-273, 278-279
Anti-Blackness in higher education 266
Antiracism 55, 69, 99, 106, 109, 170, 261
Antiracism in Higher Education 261
Assimilation 206, 253, 259
Authentic Leadership 253, 257, 259
Authenticity 14, 97, 253, 255, 271

B

Belonging 12, 34, 67, 69, 125-126, 140, 154, 172, 177-178, 180, 186, 189, 206, 218, 222, 225, 229, 232-233, 238, 250, 266
Bias 7, 15, 47, 54, 66, 73-74, 113, 128, 131, 136, 171, 178, 181, 183-184, 186, 189-190, 192, 194-197, 203-206, 208, 212, 218, 228, 233, 235, 247, 250
BIPOC 14, 63, 136-137, 175, 193, 196-198, 201-202, 204-209, 212, 242, 263-264, 266, 268, 270-272, 278-279
Black Cultural Centers 21-22, 24, 28, 30-32, 38
Black Fatigue 133, 142-143, 278
Black Feminism 19, 122-123, 129, 133, 140, 142-143, 240-241, 259, 278
Black Feminist Theory 57, 72
Black Feminist Thought (BFT) 11, 17, 21, 24, 36-37, 39, 52, 55, 72, 79-80, 96, 139, 186, 240-241, 255, 257-259, 274
Black Liberation 24, 58-59, 75, 276
Black Tax 261, 267-268, 278
Black Woman and Nonbinary Tax 267, 278
Black Women (BW) 1-27, 29-34, 36-42, 44, 49-51, 53, 55, 58-60, 64, 66, 71, 75, 79-80, 84-87, 89, 93-97, 99, 107, 111-113, 116, 118, 121-123, 127-130, 133-143, 145-148, 150-151, 154, 161-163, 165-170, 172-175, 178, 180, 185-186, 188-191, 193, 195-198, 200, 202-203, 207, 210-211, 213-235, 237, 239-241, 243, 252-259, 261-263, 265-272, 274-278
Black Women Academic Leaders 213, 218-219
Black Women Higher Education Leaders 40, 213
Black Women in Educational Leadership 213, 217, 233-234
Black Women Leaders 21, 27, 29-31, 33-35, 168, 211, 213, 215-222, 225, 227-228, 254, 264, 272
Black Women's Power 16, 191
Brave Container 128, 143
Bridging 128, 143, 152, 187

C

Centered Praxis 57
Chief Diversity Officer 40-41, 43-46, 51-56, 61, 66, 165, 172, 195, 247, 255, 258, 277-278
Code Switching 179, 191
Coded Language 203, 212, 270
Code-Switching 113, 117, 158, 166, 188
Commodified Labor 279
Community Colleges 57, 72, 211
Conflict Resolution 74, 166
Critical Race Theory 40-42, 51-52, 54-55, 57, 64, 71, 74-75, 102, 109, 118, 186, 215, 230-231, 235, 251, 258, 276
Crooked Room 252-253, 259
Cultural Capital 64, 240
Cultural Taxation 58

D

DEI 6-7, 9, 15, 40, 43, 48-50, 56-58, 60-68, 70-71, 73, 78, 99, 103, 105-113, 121-123, 128, 130-138, 143, 145-146, 148, 153-155, 157-161, 167-169,

171-173, 176-179, 183-185, 188, 191-201, 204-210, 213, 215, 222-227, 239, 241-244, 252-255, 259, 261-273, 275, 279-280
DEI in Higher Education 198, 262
DEI Industrial Complex 261-264, 266-267, 269-272, 279-280
DEI Practitioner 60, 67-68, 103, 108, 111, 137-138, 153, 171, 192, 194, 197, 199, 204, 222, 224
DEI Scorecard 254, 259
Diversity Officers 38, 40, 53-55, 64, 71, 73, 86, 112, 115, 155, 195, 206, 210-211, 239-241, 244, 247, 252, 254-256, 260
Diversity Practices 239
Dog Whistle 1

E

Emotional Intelligence 145-146, 148, 150-151, 161-166, 247
Empathy 62, 132, 145, 148-152, 154, 157-158, 160-161, 165, 204
Equitable Mindfulness 121-123, 126-128, 130-131, 134-135, 137-139, 144
Essential Workers 147, 163, 166
Executive Presence 247, 259

F

Facilitation 106, 121-122, 133, 135, 137
Faculty Fellow 57, 63-64, 75
Faith 35, 86, 98, 112, 116, 204
Femininity 1-2, 4-6, 8, 20
Feminist 1-2, 8-9, 11, 17-21, 24, 36-39, 52, 54-55, 57-58, 72-73, 79-80, 96-97, 128-129, 139, 143, 162, 174, 186, 211, 215, 218, 230-231, 234-237, 240-241, 255, 257-259, 265, 273-276, 278

G

Generational Leadership 29, 39
George Floyd 34, 61-62, 72, 81-83, 89, 99-102, 104-105, 107-108, 110-111, 113-115, 118-119, 122-123, 133, 139, 146-147, 157-158, 168, 173, 177, 222
Global Majority 127, 144

H

Hair Politics 1-2, 5-6, 8, 20
Hatch Act 26, 39
HBCU 7, 192-193, 196-197, 207, 253
Herstories 1, 10, 20, 258
Higher Education 11, 13, 16-17, 21-28, 30, 33-38, 40-43, 51-55, 58, 64, 67, 71-75, 79, 84, 95-97, 99, 108-110, 112, 122-124, 128, 134, 139, 142-143, 169, 171, 188, 192-198, 208-211, 213, 216, 218-219, 221-222, 227-231, 233, 235-237, 239, 241-242, 253, 255-258, 260-263, 265-267, 270, 272-279
Historically White Academic Institutions 213, 215, 217, 219, 221-222, 225, 227-228
Holding Space 122, 128, 144
Humanizing 79, 83

I

Identity Politics 1-2, 5-8, 14, 18, 20, 52, 186, 231
Inclusivity 57-58, 63, 65, 67, 72, 121-122, 127, 133, 144, 168, 174, 191, 229, 238, 245, 265
Intersectionality 1, 20-21, 24, 39, 42, 52, 146, 167, 173-174, 186, 212-213, 215-219, 228-229, 231, 234, 236, 259
Intersectionality Theory 21, 39, 217
Ivy League Schools 79

J

Job Performance 145, 147-148, 158, 161-162, 164

L

Leadership 5-6, 8-9, 11, 13, 16, 27, 29-31, 33-35, 37, 39, 42, 44-47, 49-50, 52, 55, 57-60, 62, 64-68, 70-75, 96-97, 105-106, 110-111, 113, 123-125, 139, 142-143, 146, 148, 150, 153, 163-165, 168, 178-179, 185-187, 189, 194-195, 199, 205-207, 209-211, 213-225, 227-237, 246-247, 249-261, 263, 268, 270, 272, 277, 279
Liberation 9, 21, 24-26, 34-35, 58-59, 71, 75, 80, 85, 98, 105, 113, 218, 270, 273, 276
Lived Experience 160, 226, 238-240, 253

M

Marginalization 22, 42, 47, 49, 64, 75, 125, 196-197, 220, 222-223, 266
Matrix of Domination 24, 39, 241
Microaggressions 2, 8-9, 14-15, 19-20, 75, 90, 97, 111, 113, 118, 127, 152, 160, 167, 173, 175-176, 178, 181, 184-185, 187-188, 190, 196-197, 200, 204, 223-224, 243, 264, 268
Microdevaluations 176, 191
Microinsults 2, 8-9, 15, 20, 175-176, 191

Microinvalidations 8, 20, 175-176, 191, 197
Millennials 10, 29-30, 39
Minnesota Paradox 99-100, 104, 117, 120
Mircroassaults 2, 8-9, 15, 20

N

Navigational Capital 238-240, 253

O

Organizational Culture 43, 47, 52, 146, 152, 159, 166, 278

P

Pandemic 14, 16, 62, 68, 79-82, 84, 87, 91-92, 94, 100, 107, 111, 113, 123, 126, 133, 145-146, 148, 150, 162-164, 166, 177, 179, 181
Personal Narrative 52, 200, 202-203, 207, 212
Protest 60, 82, 89-90, 99-100, 122, 207, 243
Public University 22
PWI 1-3, 7-8, 11, 13-15, 40, 192-199, 206-207, 240

R

Race-Gender Dyad 213, 215, 228
Race-Specific Positions 21, 28, 30-31, 33-34, 37, 39
Racial Equity 102, 104, 123, 212, 222
Racial Identity 42, 115-116, 134, 212
Racial Uplift 21-22, 24-35, 39
Racism 1, 6-8, 11-13, 19, 21, 23, 25, 27-28, 30, 32-33, 35-36, 39, 42, 52, 54, 58, 61-62, 64-66, 68-69, 72, 75, 81-85, 96, 100-112, 114-115, 119-120, 124, 128-130, 133-134, 140, 142-144, 147-148, 157, 162-163, 169-170, 173-174, 192-194, 197, 204-205, 208-210, 214, 219-220, 223, 225-226, 229-230, 241, 250-251, 256-257, 259, 261, 263, 266, 268-269, 271-273, 277-278

S

Safe Spaces 15, 64, 155, 166, 220-221, 224, 227
Second Morrill Act 26, 39
Self-awareness 43, 145, 148-149, 153-154, 161-162, 247-248, 253
Self-Care 13-14, 17, 23, 96, 98, 137, 221, 235
Self-Motivation 148-149, 155-156, 161
Self-Preservation 79, 198, 207
Self-Regulation 148-149, 154-155, 161
Social Skills 148-150, 152, 158-159
Spirituality 9, 35, 86, 98, 215, 275
Strategic Planning 30, 40-41, 46-51, 56, 105, 107, 110, 195
Student-Scholars 262, 264-267, 270-271, 278-279
Survival 3, 11, 20, 38, 80, 121, 123, 127, 137, 163, 168, 171, 240, 253, 261-262, 267, 270-272, 275

T

Tokenism 42, 65, 73, 115, 124-125, 142, 144, 263, 265, 274
Transformational Leadership theory 60, 66, 73

V

Voice 10, 17, 36, 42-43, 50, 61, 79-82, 128-129, 135, 166-168, 172, 174, 181, 183, 223-224, 243, 255-256, 262
Vulnerability 66, 79, 83, 95, 97, 179

W

Weaponization 263-264, 272, 279
White Fragility 6, 23, 104, 111, 115, 131, 133-135, 140, 144
White Guilt 99, 103-104, 107-108, 111-112, 120
White Privilege 59, 62, 72-73, 76
White Savior Complex 104, 120
White Standard 167, 169, 191
White Supremacy 6, 9, 11, 59, 67, 105, 109, 118, 169, 172, 195-196, 200, 202, 208, 210, 251, 263, 266-268, 270-271, 277, 279
White Urgency 103-105, 114, 120
Whiteness 4, 13, 16, 47, 59, 75, 99, 117, 167, 169, 171-172, 175-176, 198, 206, 209, 220, 226, 232, 265, 271
Womanist 1-2, 5, 9-10, 18, 20
Work Environment 145, 150, 160, 240, 247

www.ingramcontent.com/pod-product-compliance
Lightning Source LLC
LaVergne TN
LVHW062140300926
849161LV00010B/2579